KT-403-504

International Judicial Assistance

International Judicial Assistance

DAVID McCLEAN

DCL (Oxon.)
of Gray's Inn, Barrister
Pro-Vice-Chancellor and Professor of Law
University of Sheffield

CLARENDON PRESS · OXFORD
1992

Oxford University Press, Walton Street, Oxford OX2 6DP
Oxford New York Toronto
Delhi Bombay Calcutta Madras Karachi
Petaling Jaya Singapore Hong Kong Tokyo
Nairobi Dar es Salaam Cape Town
Melbourne Auckland
and associated companies in
Berlin Ibadan

Oxford is a trade mark of Oxford University Press

Published in the United States
by Oxford University Press, New York

© David McClean 1992

All rights reserved. No part of this publication may be reproduced,
stored in a retrieval system, or transmitted, in any form or by any means,
electronic, mechanical, photocopying, recording, or otherwise, without
the prior permission of Oxford University Press

This book is sold subject to the condition that it shall not, by way of
trade or otherwise, be lent, re-sold, hired out or otherwise circulated ·
without the publisher's prior consent in any form of binding or cover
other than that in which it is published and without a similar condition
including this condition being imposed on the subsequent purchaser

British Library Cataloguing in Publication Data
data available

Library of Congress Cataloging in Publication Data
McClean, David.
International judicial assistance/David McClean.
Includes index.
1. Judicial assistance.   I. Title.
K7624.M35   1992   341.7'8–dc20   92–5648
ISBN 0–19–825224–2

Typeset by Joshua Associates Ltd, Oxford
Printed in Great Britain by
Biddles Ltd, Guildford & King's Lynn

Preface

WRITERS of law books often bemoan the pace of legal change, but it has made the writing of this book an exhilarating, if sometimes a tantalizing, experience.

It was first planned in 1987, after I had acted as principal draftsman of the Commonwealth Scheme for Mutual Assistance in Criminal Matters and had been involved for a decade as the Commonwealth Secretariat's regular Observer of the work of The Hague Conference on Private International Law in the field of civil procedure. It seemed that the time was ripe for a study of the way in which the techniques of international judicial assistance in civil and commercial matters could usefully be extended to co-operation in criminal investigation and prosecutions.

The time was riper than I had realised. Governments were becoming uncomfortably aware of the need to respond urgently to drug trafficking and the international criminal enterprises so often financed by it. The traditional caution over co-operation between States in criminal law matters gave way to an eagerness for improved arrangements; international organizations, regional groupings of States, national legislatures, and specialist investigative and regulatory agencies gave a high priority to their development. As a result, pieces of legislation, agreements, and memoranda of understanding have been produced in quantity.

The first part of the book deals with assistance in civil and commercial matters, where there is a century and more of experience. The Hague Conference has been in the lead, and its work has been the subject of commentary and judicial analysis in many countries. I approach the material from an English perspective, but I have tried to give full weight to developments elsewhere; in this context decisions of the United States courts have been of particular significance.

The latter part of the book, dealing with assistance in criminal matters, has a rather different texture. The international instruments are almost all recent, breaking new ground, and there is limited experience of their actual operation. I have sought to explain the nature of the problems being addressed and to give an account of developing practice. The United Kingdom focus remains, but I have drawn fully on experience elsewhere, for example the valiant efforts of Australian draftsmen in tackling the confiscation of the proceeds of crime and the pioneering initiatives of the United States in the context of insider dealing and related issues.

Taken as a whole, international judicial assistance is a subject of rapidly growing importance. Lawyers and policy-makers are increasingly aware of that, but tend to see only a part, perhaps one specialist area, of the whole. The very urgency of recent international initiatives has produced a rather untidy and fragmented scene. My hope is that the present study, bringing together the different strands, will not only prove of practical value to those working in or interested in this area, but will contribute to its greater coherence.

I want to record my debt to many individuals and groups of friends and colleagues with whom I have discussed these matters in recent years. They come from many countries, but there are notable concentrations in Marlborough House and on Scheveningseweg. My university department was able to fund a research assistantship for one year; I was very fortunate to have the skill and enthusiasm of Anne Dickson, who made a major contribution to the chapters dealing with mutual assistance in criminal matters.

The text reflects material available to me in October 1991.

DAVID MCCLEAN
Sheffield, All Saints' Day 1991

Contents

Table of United Kingdom Statutory Instruments ix
Table of Statutory Material xii
Table of Conventions xxv
Table of Cases xxxvii

1 INTRODUCTION 1

2 SERVICE OF PROCESS 6

3 TAKING OF EVIDENCE: NATIONAL PRACTICES 56

4 TAKING OF EVIDENCE: INTERNATIONAL
CO-OPERATION 82

5 MUTUAL ASSISTANCE IN CRIMINAL MATTERS 119

6 INTERNATIONAL ACTION IN CRIMINAL MATTERS 130

7 DRUG-TRAFFICKING 172

8 MONEY-LAUNDERING 184

9 THE PROCEEDS OF CRIME 199

10 UNITED KINGDOM LEGISLATION AND TREATIES 239

11 TWO SPECIAL PROBLEMS: BANK SECRECY AND
INSIDER TRADING 271

Appendix of Selected Documents 305

INDEX 361

Table of United Kingdom Statutory Instruments

County Court Rules 1981
Ord. 7 r.10(1), (2) 7
Ord. 7 r.10(4) 7
Ord. 8 rr.8–10 54
Ord. 13 r.7 60
Ord. 14 59
Ord. 14 r.11 61
Criminal Justice (International Co-operation) Act 1990
(Designation of Prosecuting Authorities) Order 1991
(SI 1991/1224) 242
Criminal Justice (International Co-operation) Act 1990
(Enforcement of Overseas Forfeiture Orders) Order 1991
(SI 1991/1463) 247
Criminal Justice (International Co-operation) Act 1990
(Exercise of Powers) Order 1991 (SI 1991/1297)
art. 2 245
art. 3 245
Criminal Justice Act 1988 (Designated Countries and Territories)
Order 1991 (SI 1991/2873) 247
Crown Court (Amendment) Rules 1982 (No 2157) 73
Crown Court Rules 1982 (No 1109)
r.23B 73

Drug Trafficking Offences Act 1986 (Designated Countries and
Territories) (Amendment) Order 1991 (SI 1991/1465) 247
Drug Trafficking Offences Act 1986 (Designated Countries and
Territories) Order 1990 (SI 1990/1199) 247
arts. 4–7 247
art. 7(1) 247
art. 8 247
Sched. 3 247

Evidence (European Court) Order 1976 (SI No 428) 105

Financial Services Act 1986 (Delegation) Order 1987 (SI No 942) 68

Magistrates' Courts (Criminal Justice (International Co-operation))
Rules 1991 (SI 1991/1074)
r.3 241
r.4 241
rr.5–7 242

Rules of the Supreme Court (Amendment No 2) 1989 208
Rules of the Supreme Court 1965
Ord. 2 r.1 53
Ord. 6 r.7 8
Ord. 10 r.1(1) 52
　　　　(2) 53
　　　　(4) 52
　　　　(5) 52
Ord. 10 r.2 37
Ord. 11 66
Ord. 11 r.1 8
　　　　(1)(i) 66
Ord. 11 r.10 54
Ord. 11 r.2 8
Ord. 11 r.5–11 52
　　　r.5(1) 20, 52, 53
　　　　(2) 26, 53
　　　　(3)(*a*) 52, 53
　　　　　(*b*) 53
　　　　(5) 54
　　　r.6 . . . . 52, 53
　　　　(1) 54
　　　　(2) 54
　　　　(2A) 54
　　　　(3) 54
　　　　(4)–(7) 54
　　　r.7 52
　　　r.9 54
Ord. 12 r.7 52
Ord. 24 rr.1–3 58
　　　r.1(1) 60
　　　r.7A 59, 61
　　　r.11 99
Ord. 26 61
Ord. 29 r.2 62
　　　　(5) 62
　　　r.3 62
Ord. 38 r.1 . . . . 73, 75

r.2 73
r.2A 58
r.9 . . . . 73, 74
rr.14–19 73
Ord. 39 r.1 74
r.2(1)(*a*), (*b*) 74
(2)(*a*), (*b*) 74
r.3 75
r.9 80
r.11 73
r.13 78
rr.16–18 73
Ord. 65 r.2 7
r.4 . . . . 20, 53
Ord. 69 r.1 55
r.2 55
r.3(1) 55
(2)–(5) 55
r.4 55
r.5(6)(ii) 55
Ord. 70 105
Ord. 73 r.7 54
Ord. 75 r.8 7
Ord. 81 r.3 37
r.9 37
Ord. 115 r.3 208
(2)(*b*) 208
r.4 209
App. A Form 35 75

Table of United States Rules

Federal Rules of Civil Procedure 288
r.4(c) 7
(i)(1) 26
r.15 121
r.26 98

Federal Rules of Evidence
r.804(a) 121

Table of Statutory Material

Australia

Cash Transactions Reports Act 1988 (Cwlth) 194
  s.3(1) 195
  s.7 195
Confiscation of Proceeds of Crime Act 1989 (NSW) 194
  s.4(1) 231
  s.18(1), (2) 231
  s.19(1)(*b*) 233
  s.20 233
  s.23 229
  s.24 228
  s.25 229
     (5) 230
  ss.28–44 230
Crimes (Confiscation of Profits) Act (SA)
  s.3 230
  s.4 230
  s.4(2) 231
  s.5(2) 233
Crimes (Confiscation of Profits) Act 1985 (NSW) 194
  Pt. 4 195
Crimes (Confiscation of Profits) Act 1986 (Vic) 194
  s.7(1), (2) 231
  s.8 233
  s.9(4) 233
  s.12 228
  s.12(1)(*b*) 229
  s.13 229
Crimes (Confiscation of Profits) Act 1988 (WA) 194
  Pt. 6 195
  s.10(1), (2) 231
  s.11 233
  s.12(4) 233
  s.15 228
  s.16(4) 230
  s.17 228
Crimes (Confiscation of Profits) Act 1989 (Qd) 194
  Pt. V 195

s.3(1) 231
(7), (8) 229
s.8(2) 231
s.9 233
s.10(4) 233
s.13 228
s.14 229
(3) 230
s.14(6) 230
s.14(8) 230
Crimes (Forfeiture of Proceeds) Act 1988 (NT) 194
Pt. VII 195
s.3(1) 231
s.5(1) 231
s.6(1)(*b*) 233
s.7 233
s.10 228
s.11(5) 230
s.12 229
Crimes Legislation Amendment Act 1987 (Cwlth)
s.37 234

Mutual Assistance in Criminal Matters Act 1987 (Cwlth) 250
s.8 156
Mutual Assistance in Criminal Matters Act 1988 (Cwlth) 194

Proceeds of Crime Act 1987 (Cwlth) 194
s.4(1) 194, 231
s.19(1) 231
(4) 231
s.21 233
s.24 229
s.26 228
(4) 230
s.27 229
(6) 230
(8) 230
s.28 229
s.30 234
s.31(6)(*a*), (*b*) 234
s.66 194
s.73 194
s.75 194
ss.76–80 195

Bahamas

Mutual Legal Assistance (Criminal Matters) Act 1988
s.3(1) 285
s.7 286

Tracing and Forfeiture of Proceeds of Drug Trafficking Act 1986
s.22(8)(*b*) 186

Canada

Criminal Code
s.420.1 231
s.420.13(3)(*a*) 214
　　　　(5) 214
s.420.14 214
s.420.15 214
s.420.17(1)–(3) 232
s.420.19 232
s.420.21 234
s.420.22 234

Foods and Drugs Act 232

Mutual Legal Assistance in Criminal Matters Act
s.6(3), (4) 163
s.8 163

Narcotics Control Act 232

Cayman Islands

Banks and Trust Companies Regulation (Amendment) Act 1980 284
Banks and Trust Companies Regulation Act 1965
s.1 284
s.2 284
s.10 283–4
Banks and Trust Companies Regulation Law 1966 280

Confidential Relationships (Preservation) (Amendment) Law;
Law 26 of 1979 282
Confidential Relationships (Preservation) Law;
Law 16 of 1976 . . . . 280, 282

European Community

Council Decision No. 90/611/EEC 181
Council Regulation 1468/81/EEC 181
Council Regulation 945/87/EEC 181
Council Regulation 3677/90/EEC 181
  art. 1 182
    (2) 183
  art. 2 182
  art. 3 182
  art. 4 . . . . 182, 183
  art. 5 183
  art. 6 183
Directive. 77/280 on Credit Institutions
  art. 12(1) 273
Directive. 89/592/EEC on Insider Trading
  art. 1 296
  art. 2 296
    (1) 298
  art. 4 298
  art. 6 297
  art. 8 296
    (1) 297
  art. 9 297
  art. 10 296
    (1) 297
    (3) 297
  art. 11 297
  art. 14(1) 296
Directive. 91/308/EEC on Money Laundering 181
  Preamble 191
  art. 1 . . . . 190, 191
  art. 2 189
  art. 3(1)–(4) 190
  art. 4 190
  art. 5 190
  art. 7 190
  art. 8 190
  art. 9 191
  art. 10 191
  art. 11 191
  art. 13 191
  art. 14 191
  art. 16(1) 190

France

Decret No 67–636, 23 July 1967 131

Nouveau Code de Procedure Civil
art. 686 9
arts. 739–40 95
art. 740 116

Guyana

Narcotic Drugs and Psychotropic Substances (Control) Act 1988 215

Malaysia

Dangerous Drugs (Forfeiture of Property) Act 1988
s.3(2) 232, 233
ss.7–11 233

Netherlands

Civil Code
art. 1946 273
Code of Civil Procedure
art. 407(5) 35

Law of 3 July 1985 (Stb 384) 35

New Zealand

Misuse of Drugs (Amendment) Act 1978
s.39 215

Switzerland

Law on Banks and Savings Associations of 8 November 1934 279
art. 47 278
(*b*) 277

Penal Code
art. 273 279
Sect. II para. 3 288
Sect. III para. 1 288

Schweizerische Strafgesetzbuch
art. 161 286

United Kingdom

Arbitration Act 1950 54
s.12(6) 67
Arbitration Act 1979 54

Bankers Books Evidence Act 1879 . . . . 6, 207, 244, 272, 275
s.7 273
s.10 273
Banking Act 1987 . . . . 301, 302
s.84(1) 301
Building Societies Act 1986 301
s.53(7)(*b*)(iii) 301

Carriage of Goods by Sea Act 1924
s.8 67
Cinemas Act 1985 225
Civil Jurisdiction and Judgments Act 1982
s.25 . . . . 65, 68
(1)(*b*) 68
(3)–(7) 68
(3) 65
s.26 68
Companies Act 1980 286
Companies Act 1985 302
ss.431–53 301
s.447 301
s.449(1)(*c*) 301
(*m*) 301
s.691(1)(*b*)(ii) 36
s.695(1), (2) 36
Companies Act 1989
Pt. III 301
s.65(2)(*d*) 301
(*i*) 301
(*f*) 301
s.80 301
s.81(2) 301
ss.82–91 301
s.82(2) 301
(*c*) 302

s.82(3)–(6) 302
s.83 . . . . 302, 304
   (1)–(6) 303
   (8) 303
s.84 304
   (1), (2) 303
s.84(5) 303
s.85(1), (2) 304
s.86(1)–(4) 304
s.87 304
   (4) 304
s.88(5) 304
s.89 304
s.90 304
s.91 304
Company Directors Disqualification Act 1986 301
Company Securities (Insider Dealing) Act 1985 . . . . 286, 301, 302
s.1(3)(*a*) 298
s.9 296
Consular Relations Act 1968
s.10 102
County Courts Act 1984
s.52(2) 61
s.53 61
Criminal Justice (International Co-operation) Act
1990 . . . . 105, 141, 160, 163
s.1 157
   (1) 239
     (*a*), (*b*) 241
   (2)–(5) 241
   (3) 159
s.2(1) 241
   (3), (4) 241
s.3(1)–(7) 242
   (8) 243
s.4 . . . . 123, 275
   (2) 244, 275
   (2)–(4) 243
   (6) 275
s.5 275
   (1)–(9) 244
s.6 244
s.7(1), (2) 245
   (4), (5) 245

s.9(1) 247
  (2) 247
  (6) 247
s.14 . . . . 176, 197
s.16 224
s.25 197
  (2), (3) 198
s.26 198
s.27 198
s.28 198
s.19(1)–(3) 197
Sched. 1 para. 1 244
Sched. 1 para. 4–6 244
Criminal Justice (Scotland) Act 1987 . . . . 218, 222
Pt. I 246
s.1 247
s.2 220
s.31 246
Criminal Justice Act 1967
s.2 122
s.9 122
Criminal Justice Act 1972
s.46 122
Criminal Justice Act 1987
s.1(7) 242
Criminal Justice Act 1988 . . . . 204, 207, 218
Pt. VI 224–6, 246, 247
s.23 123
s.24 123
s.25 243
s.29 123
s.32(1) 73
s.69 . . . . 200, 202
s.70 200
s.71(1) 224
  (2), (3) 225
  (4)–(6) 225, 226
  (9)(*c*) 225
s.72 226
s.73 227
s.74(1)–(3) 226
s.74(12) 226
s.74(7)–(10) 226
ss.76–9 212

s.77 212
s.89 212
s.94 246
s.96(2) 246
s.97 246
s.98 . . . . 196, 246
s.102 225
s.103 246
    (1) 209, 222
s.170(2) 223
Sched. 4 225
Sched. 5 para. 1 . . . . 208, 209, 211, 222
        para. 2 208
        para. 3 209
        para. 4 222
        para. 12 211
        para. 15 246
Sched. 16 223
Customs and Excise Management Act 1979
s.14(1) 201
s.49 201

Drug Trafficking Offences Act 1986 . . . . 186, 192, 204, 207
s.1(1), (2) 216
    (3) 216, 225
    (4) 221
    (5) 220
s.2 . . . . 218, 221
    (2) 221
    (3)(*a*), (*b*) 217
s.3 218
    (6) 220
s.4 217
    (3) 218, 219
s.5 217
    (1) 208, 219
    (3) 210, 218, 219
    (4) 209, 210
        (*b*) 219
    (5A) 209
    (7) 210, 218
    (9) 209, 218
s.6 223
s.7(4) 208

s.8(1) 207, 209
   (2)(*a*), (*b*) 208
   (5) 209
s.9 222
s.11(4) 222
   (6) 222
   (8) 222
s.14 223
s.19(1)–(2A) 211
s.24 . . . . 175, 197, 272
   (1) 196
   (3)(*a*), (*b*) 196
s.24A 246
s.25 246
s.26 . . . . 246, 247
   (1), (2) 246
s.26A 246, 247
s.27 . . . . 192, 193
s.19(1), (2) 193
s.38(1) 200, 216, 247

Evidence (Proceedings in Other Jurisdictions) Act 1975 74
  s.1 . . . . 87, 105
  s.2 . . . . 106, 160
    (1), (2) 105
    (3) 99, 105, 106
    (4) 99
  s.3 107
    (2), (3) 107
  s.5 . . . . 123, 154
  s.9(1) 87, 105
Evidence by Commission Act 1859 74
Extradition Act 1870
  s.24 123
Extradition Act 1873
  s.5 . . . . 123, 124, 154, 275

Financial Services Act 1986 . . . . 302, 304
  s.6 68
  s.114(3) 301
  s.177 301
  s.180(1)(*qq*) 301
  s.207(1) 301
  Sched. 11 para. 28(4) 301

Sched. 13 para. 9(1)(*c*) 301
Firearms Act 1968
s.52 200
Foreign Tribunals Evidence Act 1856 . . . . 89, 98, 106, 123

Insurance Companies Act 1982 301–2

Magistrates' Courts Act 1980
s.102 122
    (7) 122
Merchant Shipping Act 1894
s.691 122
Misuse of Drugs Act 1971 247
s.4 201
s.27 201
    (1) 200, 201
s.36(1) 193

Oaths and Evidence (Overseas Authorities and Countries) Act
    1963 102
Obscene Publications Act 1964
s.1(4) 200

Police and Criminal Evidence Act 1984 204
Pt. II 245
s.8 245
s.9 192
s.10 193
s.11 193
s.22 193
s.24(1) 245
Sched. 1 192
Powers of Criminal Courts Act 1973
s.43 . . . . 202, 203, 216
    (1) 200
    (1A) 202
Prevention of Crime Act 1953
s.1 200
Prevention of Terrorism (Temporary Provisions) Act 1989 204
Pt. III 225, 227
s.9(3), (4) 227
s.10 227
s.12 228
s.13(5) 227

s.13(6), (7) 228
Sched. 4 227
　　　para. 1 228
　　　para. 3 228
　　　paras. 8–10 228
　　　para. 27 228
Sched. 7 228
Sched. 8 para. 10 . . . . 225, 226
Protection of Children Act 1978
s.5 200
Protection of Trading Interests Act 1980
s.4 107

Supreme Court Act 1981
s.33(1) 59
　　(2) 59, 61
s.34 61
s.36 73
s.37 67
　　(1) 69, 206
　　(3) 69
s.72 64

Theft Act 1968
s.22 187

Video Recordings Act 1984 225

United States

18 USC 3506 381
19 USC 1595a 201
28 USC 1782 . . . . 72, 80, 90
28 USC 1783 81

Bank Secrecy Act 1982 195

Foreign Corrupt Practices Act 1977 283
Freedom of Information Act 295

Insider Trading and Securities Fraud Enforcement Act 1988 . . . 294
International Securities Enforcement Co-operation Act 1990
s.202 295
　　(a) 295

Money Laundering Control Act 1986 195

Right to Financial Privacy Act 1978
   12 USC 3401 295
   12 USC 3401 et seq 277
   12 USC 3403(a) 277
   12 USC 3405(1), (2) 277

Securities Exchange Act 1934
   15 USC s.78(a) 287
   15 USC s.78(d) 287

Table of Conventions

1889 Montevideo Convention on Civil Procedure (11 January)
art. 9 41
1896 Hague Convention on Civil Procedure
art. 1 . . . . 12, 13
art. 6 13
  (1) 26
art. 8 82
art. 9(1) 83
1905 Hague Convention on Civil Procedure
art. 1 . . . . 12, 13
art. 2 16
art. 3 16
art. 6 13
art. 8 82
art. 9 83
art. 10 83
art. 11 83
art. 14 83
art. 15 83
1912 Hague Convention Relating to the Suppression of the Abuse of
Opium and Other Drugs 173
1922 UK–France Bilateral Civil Procedure Convention
art. 4 14
1924 Central American Treaty of Confraternity (12 April)
art. 13 125
1925 Second International Opium Convention (Geneva) 173
1928 Bustamente Code
arts. 388–93 42
1931 Geneva Convention for Limiting the Manufacture and Regulating
the Distribution of Narcotic Drugs 173
1939 Harvard Draft Convention on Judicial Assistance
Pt. II 43
art. 1(d) 43
art. 2(1) 43
  (1)(3) 43
  (2) 44
  (4) 43
  (6) 43
art. 3 43

art. 6 125
art. 7 . . . . 43, 125
art. 8 125
art. 9 125
art. 13 43
1940 Montevideo Convention on International Procedural Law
(19 March)
art. 11 41
1950 European Convention on Human Rights
art. 8 64
art. 24 65
1953 Protocol Limiting and Regulating the Cultivation of the Poppy
Plant, the Production of, International and Wholesale Trade in,
and Use of Opium (New York) 173
1954 Hague Convention on Civil Procedure of 1st March 15, 82
art. 1(4) 29
art. 2 14
art. 7 32
art. 10 83
art. 11 83
art. 14 83
arts. 22–5 29
1955 Convention on Mutual Judicial Assistance between France and
Italy
art. 4 14
1959 European Convention on Mutual Assistance in Criminal
Matters 130, 239
art. 1(1) 131, 133, 165
(2) 165
art. 2 . . . . 132, 165
(a) 132
(b) 132, 133, 143
arts. 3–5 140
arts. 3–6 133
art. 3 . . . . 142, 145
(1), (2) 134
art. 4 135
art. 5 . . . . 133, 135
(1) 135
(a) 143
(2) 135
art. 6 135
art. 7 135
art. 7(2), (3) 136

art. 8 . . . . 136, 137, 159
arts. 8–12 136
art. 9 . . . . 137, 168
art. 10(1) 137
    (3) 140
arts. 10–12 161
art. 11 . . . . 137, 139, 140, 167
    (2) 137, 142, 245
    (3) 138
art. 12 . . . . 138, 142, 245
    (1)–(3) 138
art. 13 138
    (1), (2) 138
art. 14 . . . . 139, 146
art. 15 139
    (1) 139
    (2) 139, 165
    (3) 132, 133
    (4) 133
    (5) 133, 140
    (6) 139, 141
    (7) 140
art. 16 . . . . 140, 141
art. 16(2), (3) 140
art. 17 . . . . 140, 168
art. 18 140
art. 19 140
art. 20 . . . . 140, 168
art. 21 . . . . 142, 146
art. 21(1)–(3) 141
art. 22 . . . . 139, 144
art. 24 132
art. 26(1), (2) 141
1961 Hague Convention Abolishing the Requirement of Legalisation
    for Foreign Public Documents of 5 October 2
1961 Single Convention on Narcotic Drugs
    (New York) 173, 193, 251, 252, 283
art. 12 174
art. 19 173
art. 20 173
arts. 21–9 173
arts. 30–2 173
art. 36 . . . . 173, 252, 282

1965 Hague Convention on Service Abroad of
 15 November 8, 16, 85, 115, 157
 Title III (arts. 25–49) 33
 art. 1 17
  (1) 34
  (2) 31
 art. 2(1) 20
 art. 3 22
  (1) 21
  (2) 23
 art. 4 . . . . 18, 24
 art. 5 23
 art. 5(3) 23
  (4) 22
 art. 6 22
 art. 7 23
 art. 7(2) 22
 art. 9 25
 art. 10 52
  (*a*) 18, 26–28
  (*b*) 28
  (*c*) 27, 28
 art. 11 29
 art. 12 32
 art. 13 . . . . 19, 24, 48
 art. 15 . . . . 20, 29, 34, 39, 48, 52
  (1) 29
   (*b*) 30
  (2) 30, 34
  (3) 31
 art. 16 . . . . 29, 39, 48, 52
  (1)–(4) 31
 art. 18 20
  (1) 21
  (2) 20
  (3) 21
 art. 20(*a*) 23
  (*b*) 22, 23
 art. 21(1)(*c*) 25
 art. 21(2)(*a*) 26, 28
 art. 22 33
 art. 24 33
 art. 25 33
 Annex 22

1967 Naples Convention on Customs Co-operation 128
1968 Brussels Convention on Jurisdiction and the Enforcement of
     Judgments in Civil and Commercial Matters 18, 28
     art. 20(2) 33
     art. 27(2) 33, 34
1970 Hague Convention on the Taking of Evidence Abroad in Civil
     or Commercial Matters 85–86, 160
     Ch. II 102, 104
     art. 1 . . . . 86, 98
         (1) 82
         (2) 90, 97, 10
         (3) 90
     art. 2 . . . . 91, 93
     art. 3 91
         (*e*)–(*g*) 90
     art. 4 92
     art. 5 93
     art. 6 93
     art. 7 94
     art. 8 94
     art. 9 . . . . 92–94, 106
     art. 9(3) 95
     art. 10 . . . . 95, 129
     art. 11 . . . . 92, 104
         (1)(*b*) 96
     art. 11(2) 96
     art. 12 93
     art. 13 96
     art. 14(1), (2) 96
         (3) 97
     arts. 15–17 103
     art. 15(1), (2) 102
     art. 16 103
         (2) 102
     art. 17 103
     art. 18 . . . . 103, 104
         (2) 103
     art. 19 104
     art. 20 104
     art. 21 104
     art. 23 . . . . 97–101, 106, 112, 113, 115
     art. 26 97
     art. 27 116
         (*a*) 91

art. 27(*c*) 112
(*d*) 115
art. 28(*a*) 91
art. 32 91
art. 33 . . . . 92, 102
1971 Montreal Convention for the Suppression of Unlawful Acts
against the Safety of Civil Aviation
art. 11 129
1971 Psychotropic Substances Convention (Vienna) 173
1972 European Convention on the Transfer of Proceedings in
Criminal Matters 146, 169
Preamble 147
art. 2 . . . . 147, 149
art. 3 147
art. 6 147
art. 7(1) 147
art. 8 147
(2) 149
art. 9 147
art. 10 147
art. 11 147
art. 13 147
art. 17 147
art. 20 147
art. 21 149
art. 22 149
art. 23 149
art. 25 149
art. 26(2) 149
art. 27 149
art. 28 149
art. 29 149
art. 30 147
art. 31 147
art. 32 147
art. 33 147
art. 35 147
art. 35(3) 149
art. 37 149
1972 Protocol amending the 1961 Single Convention on Narcotic Drugs
(New York) 173
1973 US–Swiss Mutual Assistance Treaty 278, 287
art. 1(1) 288
art. 3(1)(*a*) 279

art. 4(2) 287
art. 10(2) 279
art. 15 279
1975 Inter-American Convention on Letters Rogatory
(Panama) 45, 104
art. 2 . . . . 18, 45, 46
    (*a*) 49
art. 3 46
art. 4 46
art. 5(*a*), (*b*) 47
art. 6 . . . . 47, 50
art. 7 46
art. 8 47
art. 9 . . . . 48, 52
art. 10 47
art. 11 47
art. 12 47
art. 13 49
art. 16 46
art. 17 48
art. 18 47
1977 Nairobi Convention on Mutual Administration for the Prevention,
Investigation and Repression of Customs Offences (June 1977) . 127
1978 Additional Protocol to the European Convention on Mutual
Assistance in Criminal Matters of 1959 . . . . 132, 139
art. 1 . . . . 142, 143
art. 2(1), (2) 143
art. 3 143
art. 4 144
art. 8(2)(*a*) 143
art. 10 142
1979 Protocol to the Inter-American Convention on Letters Rogatory . . 48
art. 1 . . . . 48, 49
art. 2 49
art. 2(a) 48
art. 3 49
art. 4 49
art. 5 50
art. 6 50
art. 7 51
1980 Hague Convention on International Access to Justice of
25 October 2
1984 Additional Protocol to the Inter-American Convention on the
Taking of Evidence Abroad 104
art. 16 100

1985 US–Canada Mutual Assistance Treaty (18 March) 293
1986 UK–Cayman Islands Treaty on Mutual Assistance in Criminal
      Matters
      art. 1(1) 254
         (2) 283
         (3) 255, 262
      art. 2 . . . . 255, 283
         (2) 285
      art. 3(2)–(4) 257
         (2) 253
      art. 4 . . . . 255, 283
      art. 5(1) 257
         (3) 257
         (4) 256
      art. 6 262
      art. 7 283
         (1) 257
         (2)–(4) 258
      art. 8(1)–(3) 258
         (4) 259
      art. 9 285
         (3) 259
      art. 10 260
      art. 11(1), (2) 260
      art. 12 260
      art. 13 258
      art. 14(1) 259
         (3) 259
      art. 15 260
      art. 16(1) 261
      art. 17(3) 262, 282–3
      art. 19(3) 255
1988 UK–Australian Treaty on Mutual Assistance in Criminal Matters
      art. 1(1) 254
         (2) 262
      art. 2(*a*), (*b*) 254
         (*e*) 254
      art. 3 255
      art. 4 255
      art. 5(1) 257
         (2) 256
      art. 6 256
         (3) 257
      art. 7(2) 259

(*b*) 258
(*c*) 259
(3) 260
art. 9(4), (5) 261
art. 10(1), (2) 258
(3) 257
art. 12 262
art. 14 254

1988 UK–Canada Treaty on Mutual Assistance in Criminal Matters
Art. II(2) 254
(3)(*g*) 254
(4) 255
Art. III 254
Art. IV 262
Art. V 255
Art. VI 255
Art. VII 255
Art. VIII 256
(1) 253
(4) 257
Art. IX(1), (2) 257
(4) 260
Art. X(1) 258
(3) 258
(4) 257
(5) 258
Art. XI 258
Art. XII 260
Art. XIII 259
Art. XIV 258
Art. XV 259
Art. XVII(1)–(5) 261
Art. XVIII(2), (3) 262
Art. XX(1) 262

1988 United Nations Convention against Illicit Traffic in Narcotic
Drugs and Psychotropic Substances (Vienna) . . . 164, 174, 224, 239
art. 2 175
art. 2(1), (2) 175
art. 3 . . . . 175, 176, 187, 197
(1) 176, 188
(*a*)(iv), (v) 175
(*b*) 189, 190
(i), (ii) 175
(*c*)(i) 175

art. 3(4) . . . . art. 176
art. 4 . . . . art. 176
art. 5 . . . . art. 179
   (1) 178
   (3) 186
art. 6 . . . . art. 176
   (1)–(3) 176
art. 7 . . . . 175, 177, 178
   (4) 159
   (18) 245
art. 8 . . . . art. 177
art. 12 181
   (8) 182
   (9) 182
     (*b*) 183
art. 17 176
   (4), (5) 180
   (10), (11) 180
art. 27 181
art. 29(1) 175

1989 Council of Europe Convention on Insider Trading
art. 1 . . . . 297, 299
   (*c*) 298
art. 2 . . . . 297, 299
art. 3 . . . . art. 297
art. 6(1)–(3) 298
art. 6(5) 299
art. 7(2) 298, 299
   (4) 300
   (5) 299
art. 8 . . . . art. 299
art. 12 300
art. 14 297
art. 16bis 300

1990 Council of Europe Convention on Laundering, Search, Seizure
and Confiscation of the Proceeds from Crime
art. 1 . . . . art. 189
art. 2 . . . . 235, 236
art. 3 . . . . 235, 236
art. 4(1) 236
art. 4(2) 236
art. 6(1) 188
arts. 7–35 236
art. 8 . . . . art. 192

art. 13 236
art. 14(1), (2) 236
art. 16(2) 236
art. 17 236
art. 18(1)–(6) 237
art. 22 238
art. 35 238
1990 United Nations Model Treaty on Mutual Assistance in Criminal
Matters 164
art. 1 165
(1) 165
(2)(*g*) 165
(3) 165
art. 3 165
art. 4(1)(*a*) 166
(*c*) 166
art. 4(2) 165
art. 6 166
art. 7 166
art. 8 166
art. 9 166
art. 10 166
art. 11 166
art. 12 166
art. 13 167
art. 14 168
art. 15(1) 167
art. 17 167
art. 18 167
art. 19 168
Optional Protocol, para. 1 169
paras. 2–6 168
1990 United Nations Model Treaty on the Transfer of Proceedings in
Criminal Matters 169
art. 1 169
(3) 171
art. 2 169
art. 3 169
art. 4 169
art. 5 169
art. 6 170
art. 7 170
art. 8 170
art. 9 170

art. 10 170
art. 11(1), (2) 171
art. 12 170
art. 13 169
art. 14 169

Table of Cases

Australia

Asean Resources Ltd v. Ka Wah International Merchant Finance
Ltd [1987] LRC (Comm) 835 70

Ballabil Holdings Pty Ltd v. Hospital Products Ltd. (1985) 1 NSWLR
155 70
Bangkok Bank Ltd v. Swatow Lace Co Ltd [1963] NSWLR 488 79
Brereton v. Milstein [1988] VR 508 70

Coombs & Barrei Construction Pty Ltd v. Dynasty Pty Ltd (1986)
42 SASR 413 70

Hardie Rubber Co Pty Ltd v. General Tire and Rubber Co
(1973) 129 CLR 521 . . . . 76, 77, 79, 80

La Baloise Compagnie d'Assurances Contre L'Incendie v. Western
Australia Insurance Co Ltd [1939] VLR 363 79
Lucas Industries Ltd v. Chloride Batteries Australia Ltd (1978) 45 FLR
160 (Fed Ct) 76, 77

Mason v. Delargy (1884) 1 WN (NSW) 68 76
Merry v. R (1884) 10 VLR(E) 135 75

National Australia Bank v. Dessau [1988] VR 521 70

R v. Fagher (1989) 16 NSWLR 67 218

Willis v. Trequair (1906) 3 CLR 912 76

Canada

Coristine Ltd v. Haddad (1915) 21 DLR 350 (Sask) 75
Corr, Re (1912) 5 DLR 367 (Ont) 77

Fidelity Trust Co v. Schneoder (1913) 14 DLR 224 (Alta) 78

Hawes, Gibson & Co v. Hawes (1912) 3 DLR 396 (Ont) 77
Haynes v. Haynes (1962) 35 DLR (2d) 602 (BC) 76

Kaye v. Burnsland Addition Ltd (1915) 24 DLR 232 (Alta) 78

Mills v. Mills (1888) 12 PR (Ont) 473 77
Murray v. Plummer (1913) 11 DLR 764 . . . . 77, 78

Niewiadomski v. Langdon (1956) 6 DLR (2d) 361 (Ont) 77

Park v. Schneider (1912) 6 DLR 451 (Alta) 76–78

Richard Beliveau Co v. Tyerman (1911) 16 WLR 492 (Sask) 78
Romano v. Maggiora [1936] 2 DLR 329 (BC CA) 77

Stewart v. Sovereign Bank of Canada (1912) 2 DLR 913 79

Weingarden v. Noss (1953) 9 WWR (NS) 335 (Man) 76

Cayman Islands

Interconex Case 280–1

Maynard and Double A Consultants Ltd's Application;
Re, 11 Apr. 1984, Georges CJ 284, 285

Royal Bank of Canada v. Appollo Development Ltd,
30 Apr. 1985, Georges CJ 284

United States v. Carver (No 5)
Cayman Islands Civil Appeals 1982 (Unpublished) 280

European Court of Human Rights

Chappell Case Judgment of 30 Mar. 1989, Series A, no. 152–A 64, 65

European Court of Justice

Denihauler v. SNC Couchet Frères [1980] ECR 1553 65

Klomps v. Michel (Case 166/80) [1982] 2 CMLR 773 33

LTU GmbH & Co KG v. Eurocontrol (Case 29/76) [1976] ECR 1541;
[1977] 1 CMLR 88 18

Municipality of Hillegom v. Hillenius (Case 110/84) [1985] ECR 3947 . 273

Pendy Plastic Products BV v. Pluspunkt Handelsgesellschaft mbH
[1983] 1 CMLR 665 33

France

Tristany v. Astruc, Cour de Cassation, 29 Nov. 1973; Rev Cit DIP
1974, 690 82

Israel

Frankel v. Kaufman (1976) 30 PD 449 (Sup Ct of Israel) 26

Netherlands

Officier van Justie in het Arrondissement Middleburg v. S [1988] NJ
2458 (Hoge raad, 15 Dec. 1987) 136

Segers and Rufa BV v. Mabanaft GmbH (27 June 1986) NJ 1986, 764
(Netherlands Sup Ct) 35

New Zealand

New Zealand Towel Supply and Laundry Ltd v. New Zealand
Tri-cleaning Co Ltd [1935] NZLR 204, CA 75, 77, 80

Wong Doo v. Kana Bhana [1973] NZLR 1455, CA 76, 80

Switzerland

Justizkomission Zug, 4 Apr. 1985 [1986] SJZ 301 133

Mercedes Zunder v. Chambre d'Accusation du Canton de Genève
[1986] 1 BGE (110/1) 385 132

S v. Camera dei Ricorsi Penali del Tribunale di Appello del Cantone
Ticino [1987] 1 BGE (112/6) 576 . . . . 131, 134
Sante Fe Litigation 288
Schweizerisches Bundesgericht [1982] I BGE 261 132

X v. Appellationsgericht des Kantons Baselstadt [1985] I BGE (111)
52 135

United Kingdom

Abdul Raman Bin Turki Al Sudairy (Prince) v. Abu Taha [1980]
  1 WLR 1268, CA 69
Adolf Leonhardt, The [1973] 2 Lloyd's Rep. 318 79
Altertext Inc v. Advanced Data Communications Ltd [1985]
  1 WLR 457 . . . . 64, 66
American Express Warehousing Co v. Doe [1967] 1 Lloyd's Rep.
  222, CA 99
Ammar v. Ammar [1954] P 468 76
Amplaudio v. Snell (1938) 55 RPC 237 64
Armour v. Walker (1883) 25 Ch D 673, CA 76, 80
Arnott v. Hayes (1887) 36 Ch D 731, CA 272
Asbestos Insurance Coverage Case [1985] 1 WLR 331, HL . . 100, 105, 106
Ashtiani v. Kashi [1987] QB 888, CA 69, 70

Babanaft International Co SA v. Bassatne [1990] Ch 13, CA;
  [1990] QB 202 69–71
Bank of Crete SA v. Koskotas [1991] 2 Lloyd's Rep. 587, CA 71
Bankers Trust Co v. Shapiro [1980] 1 WLR 1274, CA 61, 273, 274
Barber (J) & Sons v. Lloyds Underwriters [1987] QB 103 106
Barclay-Johnson v. Yuill [1980] 1 WLR 1259 69
Bekhor (J A) & Co v. Bilton [1981] QB 923; [1981] 2 All ER 565,
  CA 69, 212
Berdan v. Greenwood (1880) 20 Ch D 764, CA 76, 78
Boeing Co v. PPG Industries Inc [1988] 3 All ER 839, CA 106
Bonalumi v. Secretary of State for the Home Dept [1985] QB 675,
  CA 274, 275
Boyse, Re (1882) 20 Ch D 760
78, 79

Chaplin v. Burnett (1912) 28 TLR 256, CA 62
Chaplin v. Puttick [1898] 2 QB 160 62
Chic Fashions (West Wales) Ltd v. Jones [1968] 1 All ER 229 . . . . 205, 206
Chief Constable of Hampshire v. A [1985] QB 132, CA 206
Chief Constable of Kent v. V [1983] QB 34, CA 205
Chief Constable of Leicestershire v. M [1989] 1 WLR 20; [1988] 3 All ER
  1014 . . . . 68, 206
Chief Constable of Surrey v. Abbott, Unreported, 24 Oct 1988 207
Coch v. Allcock & Co (1888) 21 QBD 178, CA 78
Columbia Picture Industries Inc v. Robinson [1987] Ch 38 64
Commissioners of Customs and Excise v. Norris [1991] 2 All ER 395,
  CA 211

Compagnie Générale Trans-Atlantique v. Thomas Law & Co; La
Bourgogne [1899] P 1, CA; aff'd [1899] Ac 431 36
Conway v. Rimmer [1968] AC 910 272
Cook Industries Inc v. Galliher [1979] Ch 439 . . . . 63, 64

D v. National Society for the Prevention of Cruelty to Children
[1978] AC 171 272
Derby & Co v. Weldon (No 1) [1990] Ch 48, CA 70
Derby & Co v. Weldon (No 3 & 4) [1990] Ch 65, CA 71
Derby & Co v. Weldon (No 6) [1990] 1 WLR 1139, CA 70
Dillon v. O'Brien and Davis (1887) 16 Cox CC 245 205
DPP v. P and W, *The Times*, 11 Apr. 1990 210
Drug Trafficking Offences Act 1986, Re, Unreported, March
1987 . . . . 208, 212
Dunlop Pneumatic Tyre Co Ltd v. A G Cudell & Co [1902] 1 KB 342,
CA 36

Ehrmann v. Ehrmann (1896) 2 Ch D 611, CA 77
Eisenberg v. Malone, PC, 1991; noted at 17 CLB 1028 255
Elder v. Carter (1890) 25 Ch D 194 60
Emanuel v. Soltykoff (1892) 8 TLR 331, CA 76, 78
Emmott v. Star Newspaper Co Ltd (1892) 67 LT 829 272

Farquarson v. Balfour (1823) Turn & R 184 61
Ferrarini SpA v. Magnol Shipping Co Inc; The Sky One [1988]
1 Lloyd's Rep. 238 . . . . 6, 63, 54
Folliott v. Ogden (1789) 1 Hy Bl 123 119
Freeman v. Fairlie (1812) 3 Mer 29 61

Hosein, Re, Unreported, 20 Mar. 1991 212
House of Spring Gardens Ltd v. Waite [1984] FSR 277 . . . . 66, 67
Huntington v. Attrill [1893] AC 150 119

I, Re, Unreported, July 1988 . . . . 208, 210
International Power Industries Inc, Re, *The Times*, 25 July 1984 105

K, Re [1990] 2 QB 298, DC 210, 212
Konstandinidis v. World Tankers Corpn Inc; World Harmony, The
[1967] P 341 36

Langen v. Tate (1883) 24 Ch D 522, CA 77
Lawson v. Vacuum Brake Co (1884) 27 Ch D 137, CA 78
Liangsikriprasert v. United States Government [1990] 2 All ER 866 . . 120

Lisboa, The. See Mike Trading and Transport Ltd v. R Pagnan
& Fratelli; Lisboa, The
London and County Securities v. Caplan, Unreported, 26 May 1978 . . 274

MacKinnon v. Donaldson, Lufkin and Jenrette Securities Corpn
[1986] Ch 482 . . . . 62, 273, 274
Malone v. Commissioner of Police of the Metropolis [1980] QB 49,
CA 207
Mantovani v. Carapelli SpA [1980] 1 Lloyd's Rep. 375, CA 67
Mareva Compania Naviera SA v. International Bulk Carriers SA
[1975] 2 Lloyd's Rep. 509, CA 65
Maynard v. Maynard [1947] OWN 493 77
Mike Trading and Transport Ltd v. R Pagnan & Fratelli; Lisboa, The
[1980] 2 Lloyd's Rep. 546, CA 67
Mostyn v. Fobrigas (1774) 1 Cwp 161 123

Nadin v. Bassett (1883) 25 Ch D 21, CA 79, 80
Norwich Pharmacal Co v. Customs and Excise Commissioners
[1974] AC 133 . . . . 60, 62

O, Re [1991] 1 All Er 330, CA 212, 224, 225
Okura & Co Ltd v. Forsbacka Jernverks A/B [1914] 1 KB 715, CA 36
Owen v. Sambrook [1981] Crim LR 329, DC 273

Parnell v. Wood [1892] P 137 273
Penn v. Baltimore (1750) 1 Ves Sen 444 59
Penn-Texas Corpn v. Murat Anstalt [1964] 1 QB 40, CA 106
Penn-Texas Corpn v. Murat Anstalt (No 2) [1964] 2 QB 647, CA 106
Peters, Re [1988] QB 871, CA 208, 210
Piller (Anton) KG v. Manufacturing Processes Ltd [1976] Ch 55,
CA 63
Plummer v. May (1750) 1 Ves Sen 426 60
Portarlington (Lord) v. Soulby (1843) 3 My & K 104 63
Protector Alarms Ltd v. Maxim Alarms Ltd [1978] FSR 442 . . . . . . 63, 64

Queen of Portugal v. Glyn (1840) 7 Cl & Finn 466 60

R, Re [1990] 2 WLR 1232 . . . . 208, 211
R v. Blackford (1989) 89 Cr App R 239, CA 216
R v. Boothe (1987) 9 Cr App R (S) 8, CA 200, 202
R v. Bragason (1988) 10 Cr App R (S) 258 . . . . 218, 220
R v. Bucholz, Current Sentencing Practice J4.4(b) (10 May 1974) 202
R v. Carroll [1991] Crim LR 720, CA 219

R v. Central Criminal Court, ex parte Francis & Francis [1989]
AC 346, HL 193
R v. Chrastney [1991] Crim LR 721, CA 218
R v. Chrastney (No 1) *The Times*, 14 Mar. 1991 218
R v. Comiskey (1991) 93 Cr App R 227 . . . . 217, 219
R v. Cox (1986) 8 Cr Ap R (S) 384 200
R v. Crown Court at Snaresbrook, ex parte DPP [1988] QB 532 193
R v. Crown Court at Southwark, ex parte Customs and Excise
[1990] QB 650, DC 193
R v. Cuthbertson [1981] AC 470, HL 199–201, 203
R v. Dickens [1990] 2 All ER 626, CA 217–219, 222
R v. Dickson [1990] 2 All Er 626, CA 218
R v. Enwezor [1991] Crim LR 483, CA 217, 222
R v. Grossman (1981) 73 Cr App R 302, CA 274
R v. Harper (1989) 11 Cr App R (S) 240 220
R v. Harrow Justices, ex parte DPP [1991] 1 WLR 395; [1991]
3 All Er 873 223
R v. Hedley (1990) 90 Cr App R 70 220
R v. Highbury Corner Stipendiary Magistrates' Court, ex parte
Di Matteo [1991] Crim LR 307 202
R v. Hopes (1989) 11 Cr App R (S) 38 218
R v. Isemann (1990) 12 Cr App R (S) 398 219
R v. Jenkins [1991] Crim LR 481, CA 217
R v. Johnson [1991] 2 QB 249 220
R v. Joyce and Others (1989) 11 Cr App R (S) 253 202
R v. Lemmon [1991] Crim LR 791, CA 218
R v. Llewellyn (1985) 7 Cr App R (S) 225 200
R v. Lucas [1976] Crim LR 79, CA 202
R v. Morgan [1977] Crim LR 488, CA 200
R v. Neville (1987) 9 Cr App R (S) 222, CA 202
R v. O'Farrell [1988] Crim LR 387, CA 202
R v. Osei (1988) 10 Cr App R (S) 289, CA 217
R v. Preston [1990] Crim LR 528, CA 219
R v. Rathbone, ex parte Dikko [1985] QB 630 107
R v. Robson [1991] Crim LR 222, CA 207
R v. Robson (1991) 92 Cr App R 1, CA 219
R v. Saunders (1991) 92 Cr App R 6 220
R v. Scully (1985) 7 Cr App R (S) 119 202
R v. Slater [1986] 1 WLR 1340, CA 202
R v. Small (1989) 88 Cr App R 184 218
R v. Smith (Ian) [1989] 1 WLR 765, CA 217
R v. Taverner, Current Sentencing Practice J4.4(b) (5 Apr. 1974) 202
Radio Corporation of America v. Rauland Corpn [1956] 1 QB 618,
DC 98

Randle and Pottle, Re, *The Independent*, 26 Mar 1991 225
Rank Film Distributors v. Video Information Centre [1982] AC 380 . . . 64
Rena K, The [1979] QB 377 67
Republic of Haiti v. Duvalier; An Application by Mr Turner and
   Mr Matlin [1990] QB 202; CAT No 490, 7th June 1988 69–71
Rio Tinto Zinc Corporation v. Westinghouse Electric Corporation
   [1978] AC 547, HL 89, 93–95, 100, 105, 106, 107
Rose, Re, Unreported, 6 Dec 1989 217
Roseel NV v. Oriental Commercial and Shipping (UK) Ltd [1990]
   1 WLR 1387, CA 70
Ross v. Woodford [1894] 1 Ch 38 78

S v. E [1967] 1 QB 367 89
Saccharin Corporation Ltd v. Chemische Fabrik von Heyden AG
   [1911] 2 KB 516, CA 36
Securities and Exchange Commission v. Certain Unknown
   Purchasers of the Common Stock and Call Options for the
   Common Stock of Santa Fe International Corpn, Unreported, QBD
   23 Feb 1984 89
Securities and Investment Board v. Pantell SA [1990] Ch 426 67
Siskina v. Distos Compania Naviera SA [1979] AC 210 66
Sociedade Nacional de Combustiveis de Angola UEE v. Lundqvist
   [1990] 3 All Er 283, CA 72
South Carolina Insurance Co v. Assurantie Maatschappij 'De Zeven
   Provincien' NV [1987] AC 24 . . . . 57, 60, 66, 72
South India Shipping Corpn Ltd v. Export–Import Bank of Korea
   [1985] 1 WLR 585, CA 36
South Staffordshire Tramways Co v. Ebbsmith [1895] 2 QB 669,
   CA 273
State of Norway's Application (No 1), Re [1987] QB 433,
   CA 87, 273, 275
State of Norway's Application (No 2), Re [1990] Ac 723; [1989]
   1 All Er 701, CA 88, 121, 273, 275
Strauss v. Goldschmidt (1892) 8 TLR 239, DC 73

Tate Access Floors Inc v. Boswell [1990] 3 All Er 303 . . . . 64, 71
Thames and Mersey Marine Insurance Co v. Società di Navigazione
   a Vapore del Lloyd Austriaco (1914) 111 LT 97, CA 36
Tournier v. National Provincial and Union Bank of England [1924]
   1 KB 461, CA 271, 272, 284
Tucker (A Bankrupt), Re [1990] Ch 148, CA 79, 87

Waterhouse v. Barker [1924] 2 KB 759, CA 273
Watson, Re, Unreported, 13 Feb 1990 . . . . 209, 210

West Mercia Constabulary v. Wagener [1981] 3 All ER 378 . . . . . 205, 206

Westinghouse Case. See Rio Tinto Zinc Corporation v. Westinghouse
   Electric Corporation

Williams v. Summerfield [1972] 2 QB 512, DC 273

Wipperman, Re [1955] P 59 78

X AG v. A Bank [1983] 2 All Er 464 . . . . 275, 276

United States

Acapalon Corpn v. Ralston Purima Co, Unreported (Mo App 1991) . . . 41

Ackermann v. Levine 788 F 2d 830 (2nd Cir 1986) 27

Adidas (Canada) Ltd v. SS Seatrain Bennington, Unreported (SDNY
   1984) sub nom Navi Fonds KG v. Les Toles Inoxydables 110, 114

All Terrain Vehicles Litigation, Re, Unreported (EED Pa 1989) 27

Androux v. Geldermann Inc, Unreported (ND Ill 1990) 75

Anscheutz & Co GmbH, Re, 754 F 2d 602 (5th Cir 1985); 107 S Ct
   3223 (1988) 108, 112, 114–117

Antelope, The (1825) 10 Wheat 123 (US Sup Ct) 119

Arthur v. Nissei ASB Co, Unreported (DC Kan 1988) 27

Aérospatiale. See Société Nationale Industrielle Aérospatiale v. US
   District Court for Iowa

Bankston v. Toyota Motor Corpn 889 F 2d 172 (8th Cir 1989) 27

Barclays Bank SA v. Tsakos 543 A 2d 802 (DC App 1988) 66

Benton Graphics v. Uddeholm Corpn 118 FRD 386 (DC NJ 1987) 118

Bourjaily v. United States 107 S Ct 2775 (1987) 122

Brown v. Bellaplast Maschinenbau 104 FRD 585 (ED Pa 1985) 24

California Bankers Assn v. Schultz 416 US 21 (1974) 277

California Power and Light Co v. Uranex 451 F Supp 1044 (ND Cal
   1977) 66

Chowaniec v. Heyl Truck Lines, Unreported (ND Ill 1991) 27

Chrysler Corpn v. General Motors Corpn 589 F Supp 1182 (DC
   Col 1984) 27

Cie. Française d'Assurance pour le Commerce Extérieur v. Phillips
   Petroleum Co 105 FRD 16 (SDNY 1984) 109

Cintron v. W & D Machinery Co Inc 440 A 2d 76 (NJ Super 1981) 26

Cipolla v. Picard Porsche Audi Inc 496 A 2d 130 (RI 1985) 24, 34

Club Mediterranée SA v. Dorin 469 US 913 (1984) 112

Cooper v. Makita USA Inc 117 FRD 16 (DC Maine 1987) 27

De James v. Magnificence Carriers Inc 654 F 2d 280 (3rd Cir 1981) 34

Derso v. Volkswagen of America Inc 552 NYS 2d 1001 (AD 1990) 41

Eickhoff (Gebr) Maschinenfabrik und Eisengieberei mbH v. Starcher
    328 SE 2d 492 (2 Va 1985) 109, 112
Euramco Case June 1989 292

Fill v. Fill 68 Bankr 923 (Bankr Ct SDNY 1987) 114
Fleming v. Yamaha Motor Corpn, Unreported (WD Va 1991) 27, 41
Fonseca v. Blumenthal 620 F 2d 322 (2nd Cir 1980) 90
Fox v. Régie Nationale des Usines Renault 103 FRD 453 (W E Tenn
    1984) 22

General Electric Co v. North Star International Inc Unreported
    (ND Ill 1984) 109, 111
Goldschmidt (Th) Ag v. Smith 676 SW 2d 443 (Tex App 1984) . . . 109, 118
Gould Entertainment Corpn v. Bodo 107 FRD 308 (SDNY 1985) . . . 22, 30
Graco Inc v. Kremlin Inc 101 FRD 503 (ND Ill 1984) 110–13

Hantover Inc v. Omet SNC 688 F Supp 1377 (WD Mo 1988) 27
Harris v. Browning-Ferris Industries Chemical Services Inc
    100 FRD 775 (MD La 1984) 24, 26
Hartley v. Wheatherford Crane Co, Unreported (ED Pa 1986) 34
Hastings v. Graphics Systems Division, Unreported (DC Kan 1987) . . . 24
Hayes v. Evergo Telephone Co Ltd 397 SE 2d 325 (NC App 1990) 27
Hudson v. Pfauter (Hermann) GmbH & Co 117 FRD 33 (NDNY 1987) . 118

ITEL Container International Corpn v. Atlanttrafik Express Service
    Ltd 686 F Supp 438 (SDNY 1988) 25
Ing (Dr) HCF Porsche AG v. Superior Court for the County of
    Sacremento 177 Cal Rptr 155 (Cal App 1981) 25, 26
Interhandel Case. See Société Internationale pour Participations
    Industrielles et Commerciales SA v. Rogers
International Society for Krishna Consciousness Inc v. Lee
    105 FRD 435 (SDNY 1984) 110–12

Jenckes, In the matter of, 6 RI 18 (1859) 124
Jenco v. Martech International, Unreported (ED La 1987) 26
Julen v. Larsen 25 Cal App 3d 325 (1972) 24

Kaduta v. Hosofai 608 P 2d 68 (Ariz App 1980) 34

Lamb v. Volkswagenwerk AG 104 FRD 95 (SD Fla 1985) 38
Lasky v. Continental Products Corpn 569 F Supp 1227 (ED Pa
    1983) 111, 112
Lemme v. Wine of Japan Import Inc 631 F Supp 456 (EDNY 1986) 27

Letter of Request from the United Kingdom Crown Prosecution
Service, Re [1990] 1 L Pr 29 (DC Cir 1989) 81
Letter Rogatory from the Justice Court, District of Montreal,
Canada 523 F 2d 562 (6th Cir 1975) 124
Letters Rogatory from Examining Magistrate of Tribunal of
Versailles, Re, 26 F Supp 852 (DC Md 1939) 124
Letters Rogatory Issued by the Director of Inspection of
Government of India, Re, 385 F 2d 1017 (2nd Cir 1967) 90
Letters Rogatory out of the First Civil Court of City of Mexico,
Re, 261 F 652 (SDNY 1919) 42, 44
Lyman Steel Corpn v. Ferrostaal Metals Corpn 747 F Supp 389
(ND Ohio 1990) 26

McLaughlin v. The Fellows Gear Shaper Co 102 FRD 956 (ED Pa
1984) 110
McNulty (A J) & Co Inc v. Rocamat 506 NYS 2d 393 (1986) 38
Marc Rich Case 279
Messerschmidt Bolkow Blohm GmbH, Re, 757 F 2d 729 (5th Cir
1985) 114
Mexico City Case. See Letters Rogatory out of the First Civil Court
of City of Mexico, Re
Mommsen v. The Toro Co 108 FRD 444 (SD Iowa 1985) 27
Morton-Norwich Products Inc v. Rhone-Poulenc SA, Unreported
(Ct of Chancery Del 1981) 108
Murphy v. Reifenhauser KG Maschinenfabrik 101 FRD 360 (DC
Vermont 1984) 109, 112

Newport Components Inc v. NEC Home Electronics (USA) Inc
671 F Supp 1525 (CD Cal 1987) 27

O'Brien v. Bayer AG, Unreported (DC Kan 1986) 24
Ormqandy v. Lynn 472 NYS 2d 275 (NY Sup Ct 1984) 27

Pain v. United Technologies Corpn 637 F 2d 775 (DC Cir 1980) 107
Painter v. Texas 380 US 400 (1965) 121
Parsons v. Bank Leumi Le-Israel BM 565 So 2d 20 (Ala 1990) 28
Peterson v. Idaho First National Bank 367 P 2d 284 (1961) 277
Philadelphia Gear Corpn v. American Pfauter Corpn 1001 FRD 58
(ED Pa 1983) 109, 112
Pierburg GmbH & Co KG v. Superior Court of Los Angeles
County 186 Cal Rptr 876 (Cal App 1982) 109
Pochop v. Toyota Motor Corpn 111 FRD 464 (SD Miss 1986) 27

Quaranta v. Merlini 237 Cal Rptr 19 (Cal App 1987) 25

Rachis v. Maschinenfabrik Hehl & Soehne, Unreported (ED Pa
1986)... 114
Re v. Breezy Point Lumber Co 460 NYS 2d 264 (NY Sup Ct 1983) 34
Reinsurance of America v. Administratia Asigurarilor de Stat
902 F 2d 1275 (7th Cir 1990) 118
Renfield Corpn v. E Remy Martin & Co SA 98 FRD 442 (DC Del
1982)... 111
Request for Judicial Assistance from the Seoul Criminal Court,
Seoul, Korea 555 F 2d 720 (9th Cir 1977) 81
Reynolds v. Koh 490 NYS 2d 295 (App Div 1985) 27
Richardson v. Volkswagenwerk AG 552 F Supp 73 (WD Mo 1982) 38
Rissew v. Yamaha Motor Co Ltd 515 NYS 2d 252 (App Div 1987) 27
Rivers v. Stihl Inc 434 So 2d 766 (Ala 1983) 22, 23
Roberts v. Heim 130 FRD 430 (ND Cal 1990) 118
Romero, in the matter of 107 NYS 621 (NY Sup Ct 1907) 42

S & S Screw Machine Co v. Cosa Corpn 647 F Supp 600 (MD Tenn
1986)... 114
Sandoval v. Honda Motor Co Ltd 527 A 2d 564 Pa 1987) 27, 28
Sandsend Financial Consultants Ltd v. Wood 743 SW 2d 364
(Tex App 1988) 118
Scarminach v. Goldwell GmbH 531 NYS 2d 188 (NY Sup Ct 1988) ... 118
Schaffer v. Heitner 433 US 186 (1977) 66
Schroeder v. Lufthansa German Airlines 118 Av Cas (CCH) 17,222
(ND Ill 1983) 109
SEC v. Collier, EC Litigation Release 11817, 26 July 1988 292
Shoei Kako Co Ltd v. Superior Court for the City and County of
San Francisco 109 Cal Rptr 402 (Cal App 1973) 24, 27
Slauenwhite v. Bekum Maschinenfabrik GmbH 104 FRD 616
(DC Mass 1985)... 110, 111
Smith v. Daninichi Kinzoku Kogyu Co Ltd 680 F Supp 847 (WD Tex
1988)... 27
Société Internationale pour Participations Industrielles et
Commerciales SA v. Rogers 357 US 197 (1958) 62, 278
Société Nationale Industrielle Aérospatiale v. US District Court
for Iowa 482 US 522 (1987) 108, 110, 112, 115–118
Spanish Consul, In the Matter of 1 Ben 225 (SDNY 1867) 124
Suzuki Motor Co Ltd v. Superior Court of San Bernardino County
249 Cal Rptr 376 (Cal App 1988) 27

Tamari v. Bache & Co (Lebanon) SAL 431 F Supp 1226 (ND Ill
1977); aff'd on other points 565 F 2d 1194 (7th Cir 1977) 28
Tax Lease Underwriters Inc v. Blackwall Green Ltd 106 FRD 595
(ED Mo 1985) 28

Taylor v. Uniden Corpn of America 622 F Supp 1011 (DC Mo
1985) 23
Teknekron Management Inc v. Quante Fernmeldetechnik GmbH
115 FRD 175 (DC Nev 1987) 23
Turner v. State of Louisiana 379 US 466 (1964) 121

United States v. Bank of Nova Scotia; Grand Jury Proceedings,
In re 691 F 2d 1384 (11th Cir 1982); cert den 462 US 1119
(1983) 281, 282, 285
United States v. Field; Grand Jury Proceedings, In re 532 F 2d 404
(5th Cir 1976) 281
United States v. First National City Bank 396 F 2d 897 (2nd Cir
1968) 276
United States v. Mann 829 F 2d 849 (P9th Cir 1987) 283
United States v. Miller 425 US 435 (1976) 277
United States v. Salim 855 F 2d 944 (2nd Cir 1988) 121

Vincent v. Ateliers de la Motobecane SA 475 A 2d 686 (NJ Super
AD 1984) 109
Volkswagenwerk AG, ex parte 443 So 2d 880 (Ala 1983) 38
Volkswagenwerk AG v. Falzon 461 US 1303 (1983) 112
Volkswagenwerk AG v. Schlunk 486 US 694 (1988); 503 NE 2d
1045 (Ill App 1986) 37–40, 115
Volkswagenwerk AG v. Superior Court of Alameda County 176
176 Cal Rptr 874 (Cal App 1981) 108
Volkswagenwerk AG v. Superior Court of Sacremento County
109 Cal Rptr 219 (Cal App 1973) 108
Vorhees v. Fischer & Krecke GmbH 697 F 2d 574 (4th Cir
1983) 24, 26, 34

Wasden v. Yamaha Motor Co Ltd 131 FRD 206 (MD Fla 1990) 27
Weight v. Kawasaki Heavy Industries Ltd 597 F Supp 1082
(ED Va 1984) 27, 28, 34
Wilson v. Lufthansa German Airlines 108 AD 2d 393 (NY 1985) 114

Zisman v. Sieger 106 FRD 194 (ND Ill 1985) 27

1

Introduction

THE subject-matter of this book is international co-operation in civil and criminal proceedings. The scale of that activity has grown quite dramatically in very recent years; it increasingly engages the attention of lawyers in private practice, in the offices of corporate legal counsel, and in government service.

The reasons are not difficult to find. They lie in part in technological developments: the growth of ever faster air services for both passengers and freight; the possibilities opened up by electronic fund transfer and by more and more sophisticated telecommunications. Others are in the political sphere: regional trade groupings such as the European Community remove barriers to movement of people, goods, and services, and themselves develop extensive legislative or quasi-legislative powers. Others again reflect the sad realities of drug abuse, political violence, and terrorism, and the growth of highly organized international criminal syndicates with resources greater than those of the governments of smaller States.

There has always been an international dimension to civil litigation, and States have found it desirable to devote some efforts to easing the difficulties experienced by their citizens and business enterprises in pursuing or defending claims involving persons or entities in other countries. The State interest is much more direct in the criminal area. A growing realization of the threat posed to the economies and stability of States and the well-being of their citizens by drug-trafficking and international crime has prompted governments in recent years to give very high priority to the development of effective international mechanisms to meet that threat.

The result is that 'international judicial assistance' now comprises well-established techniques and procedures for co-operation in civil and commercial proceedings, together with a very much more recent growth of international agreements, bilateral, regional, and multilateral, in which those techniques and procedures are extended and developed for use in the field of criminal investigations, prosecutions, and to trace and seize the proceeds of crimes. The latter area is developing so rapidly, and sees so many new initiatives, that its shape is still relatively unclear and the techniques are still being refined; but they are firmly based on the much longer experience gained through co-operation in the civil area.

As a legal category, 'international judicial assistance' is perhaps better known in countries of the civil law tradition than those of the common law.

The treaty practice of some common law States seeks to avoid the term because of its suggestion that all types of co-operation require judicial authorization or involvement; they prefer 'international *legal* assistance'. Perhaps the latter term suggests too wide a subject-matter; it would seem, for example, to include extradition (which has a long and separate history, and is not examined in this book) as well as the provision of technical assistance in, for example, legislative drafting. The traditional term will serve, even if it is one the scope of which requires further explanation.

INTERNATIONAL JUDICIAL ASSISTANCE IN CIVIL PROCEEDINGS

In the context of civil proceedings, international judicial assistance is primarily concerned with the service of documents, 'process' of one sort or another but also extrajudicial documents of significance, and the taking of evidence; post-trial assistance, in the form of the enforcement of judgments and orders, is traditionally treated as a (major) topic in its own right.

As will become clearer, each State may have its own mechanisms enabling its courts to authorize the service of process or the taking of evidence outside its territorial jurisdiction; there may also be measures of compulsion available against persons within the jurisdiction which enable the court effectively to secure evidence or information even though the primary sources of information are abroad. More typically, however, the active involvement of the authorities of the relevant foreign State will be required (especially if the attitudes of those authorities derives from the civil law tradition) or at least desirable.

The following three chapters focus, therefore, on arrangements for the service of process and the taking of evidence abroad, setting international arrangements in the context of national practices. In each context, the major international instrument is a Convention elaborated under the aegis of the Hague Conference on Private International Law; these conventions have attracted the support of many of the States most involved in international trade, and other regional agreements have been heavily influenced by the Hague models.

There are two other Hague Conventions relevant to international civil practice which are not examined here. The first is the Convention Abolishing the Requirement of Legalisation for Foreign Public Documents of 5 October 1961, a convention which has been ratified by the United Kingdom and implemented without the need for any legislation. It provides for the use of a simple and standard certificate or *apostille* in place of what can in some parts of the world be an elaborate and tortuous process of legalization, a concept little known in the common law world. The second is the more recent Convention on International Access to Justice of 25 October 1980, which is concerned with the extension of legal aid and advice schemes to parties from other States; this convention is in force, but has no ratifications from common law countries.

THE HAGUE CONFERENCE

The work of the Hague Conference on Private International Law is of the first importance in this area.[1] Its title conceals the fact that it is an inter-governmental organization as significant in its field as, for example, the World Intellectual Property Organization. It first met in 1893 under the leadership of T. C. M. Asser, a notable Dutch scholar, though it was the work of the Italian Mancini which first promoted the idea of such a meeting. Civil procedure was high on its agenda.

The Conference was originally very much a European, and a civil law, club. After an interruption in its activities from 1928 to 1951, it was revived. Its present Statute entered into force on 15 July 1955, and declares it to have a permanent character, with the object of 'the progressive unification of the rules of private international law'.[2] Despite its international character, the conference continues to function under the supervision of a Commission of State of the Netherlands established by Royal Decree in 1897, and the Netherlands Government bears the costs of the Sessions of the Conference held generally every four years;[3] however, the budget of its Permanent Bureau[4] is approved by the diplomatic representatives in The Hague of Member States.[5]

The membership of the Conference is now much more representative of the various legal traditions, with a number of Eastern European countries and China representing the socialist tradition, and Australia, Canada, Ireland, the United Kingdom, and the United States playing an active role from the common law perspective.[6] There are some Latin American members, whose participation has been handicapped by the lack of official (or even agreed unofficial) Spanish texts of the conventions, and the absence until 1991 of simultaneous translation into Spanish at Conference meetings.[7] Most of the conventions are open to non-Member States, and countries in all parts of the world are signatories of one or more conventions; a notable addition was New Zealand which signed the Child Abduction Convention in 1991.

The Conference has a regular pattern of work. A preliminary study prepared within the Permanent Bureau is considered by a Special Commission of experts appointed by, but at that stage not usually under detailed instructions from, governments. This group prepares a Draft Convention, a

---

[1] See J. Offerhaus '*La Conférence de la Haye de droit international privé*' (1959) 16 Annuaire Suisse de droit international 27; M. van Hoogstraten, 'The United Kingdom Joins an Uncommon Market: the Hague Conference on Private International Law' (1963) 12 I.C.L.Q. 148; P. M. North 'Hague Conventions and the Reform of English Conflict of Laws' (1981) 6 Dalhousie LJ 417.

[2] Statute, Art. 1. The Statute has a single French-language text.

[3] Ibid., Arts. 3(6) and 10.

[4] Ibid., Art. 4, which provides for a Secretary-General and two Secretaries; in practice there is a third member of Secretary rank.

[5] Statute, Art. 9.

[6] The Commonwealth Secretariat has had Observer status since 1978.

[7] French alone was used for many years; the first official English text was adopted in 1961.

process usually taking several meetings each of some weeks duration, for consideration at the next Session of the Conference. The major documents of Special Commissions and the full papers, including minutes, of the Sessions of the Conference are published in the invaluable *Actes et Documents* series.[8] Each convention is accompanied by a very full Explanatory Report.

INTERNATIONAL JUDICIAL ASSISTANCE IN CRIMINAL MATTERS

The Hague Conference has never worked in the field of criminal law. Continental legal doctrine, and common law practice, treats criminal law as falling outside the domain of private international law. And, apart from extradition, States were unwilling for the most part to contemplate co-operation in criminal prosecutions. Criminal law was almost wholly 'territorial', concerned with acts or omissions on the territory of the forum State, and that was that. The mobility of criminals, the international effects of their activity, and the easy transfer of illicit profits to overseas havens have transformed attitudes.

Perhaps because different agencies have been involved, the term 'international judicial assistance' tends to be replaced in this new context by 'mutual assistance in criminal matters' or simply 'mutual legal assistance'. The concepts are, however, very similar and address many of the same problems. In the criminal area, however, one aspect of post-judgment assistance is of growing importance: the enforcement of orders for the confiscation of the proceeds of crime. This is seen as a shade different from the enforcement of a sentence as such; and there can be a practical difference where, as is often the case, the enforcing State keeps the confiscated property rather than than transmitting it to the State in which the order was made.

In the criminal field, the political will to act springs largely from the reaction of Governments to drug-trafficking; the large profits generated by the drugs trade lead to elaborate money-laundering schemes, often with an international dimension; that in turn raises issues such as the (diminishing) effect of bank secrecy and the need for mutual assistance in the financial services area generally. As a result the later chapters of this book explore some of these areas; they cannot be as focused on the specifically procedural aspects of prosecution and trial.

Political interest in these areas has led to a large number of initiatives. Arguably too many separate agencies have found themselves involved in working for international co-operation.[9] Not only may the meetings of the relevant bodies absorb time and energy, but there is a danger that the number of approaches and instruments may lead to incoherence in international and domestic law. As it is, some aspects of the field, notably that of dealing with

---

[8] Cited in this book as *AetD* followed by the number of the Session; e.g. *AetD* (14) refers to the *Actes et Documents* of the Fourteenth Session held in 1980.

[9] See pp. 125–9.

the proceeds of crime, have proved to be technically difficult for the legislator and the courts alike.

The hope must be that the available conventions and agreements in the criminal area will prove as successful as the established conventions on civil procedure, and will indeed escape some of the divergences in interpretation which have afflicted the Hague Conventions in recent years.[10]

---

[10] See pp. 37 and 107.

2

Service of Process

(A) Introduction

PRIMUS, a resident of State A, believes that he has a good claim against Secundus, who lives in State B. Secundus does not acknowledge the rightness of the claim, so Primus must go to court. He will prefer to go to his own courts in State A, assuming they have jurisdiction. Justice requires that Secundus be given proper notice of the fact that litigation is pending against him, of the nature of the case, and of the date by which action on his part is required; and that this notice be given promptly and in time for the defence to be adequately prepared. How these requirements of justice are given practical effect is the subject of this chapter.

It might be thought that this was essentially a matter for the internal law of State A, the forum State. As a matter of doctrine, procedural matters are governed by the *lex fori*. The court will look to its own law to determine whether there has been good service, sufficient in a common law system to found jurisdiction; the same law will identify the steps required to set running the time which must elapse before a default judgment can be entered; and the same law will, in some countries, apply to determine whether service was so defective that a default judgment must be set aside. This, however, is to ignore the legal and practical interests of State B, the country in which the defendant is to be found.

Whatever method of service is used, the object is the giving of information to the defendant. It must involve some acts being done in State B, over which the law of that State may properly exercise a measure of control. That control might be exercised on the basis of considerations of sovereignty; some countries in the civil law tradition see service of process as an act of State, an exercise of its judicial power, and are reluctant to permit within their borders an expression of the sovereignty of another State; in Switzerland service on behalf of the plaintiff of foreign process without the permission of the Swiss authorities appears to be an offence punishable by imprisonment (and even, theoretically, solitary confinement and hard labour).[1] Or control might be exercised in the interests of defendants, seeking to ensure that if they are to be proceeded against abroad information reaches them with the speed and

---

[1] Art. 271, the scope of which was examined, with a review of relevant authorities, in the English High Court in *Ferrarini S.p.A.* v. *Magnol Shipping Co. Inc., The Sky One* [1988] 1 Lloyd's Rep 238 (affd. C.A., ibid.).

security which the use of official channels is supposed (probably quite unrealistically) to guarantee. Ultimately it may well fall to the authorities of State B to enforce the judgment against Secundus and his assets. Compliance with the procedural rules of the *lex fori* will not ensure that enforcement, for State B may impose its own requirements and is likely to scrutinize default judgments with particular care. So international agreement and co-operation is in this field not merely an ideal but a practical necessity for effective justice.

Differing Approaches

Each country has its own law and practice as to the service of process and other documents issued for use in ordinary, non-international, cases. International discussion of service of process is influenced—and often confused— by the differing assumptions of the participants, each of whom tends to project on to the international plane the familiar features of his own national system. So, in many common law jurisdictions, and in countries such as those in Scandinavia with a similar approach, the responsibility for service rests with the plaintiff himself or the agents (solicitors, process-servers) whom he employs. There are in fact quite a number of exceptions to this proposition, so that in England a county court summons will normally be served by an officer of the court sending it by post[2] and some writs in admiralty may be served by the Admiralty Marshal;[3] in the United States federal courts, summonses in civil actions are served by a United States Marshal;[4] but service by the plaintiff or his agent is none the less seen as the common law norm. In English practice 'personal service of a document is effected by leaving a copy of the document with the person to be served';[5] it is not sufficient to leave the document with a member of his family or an obliging neighbour. Under this practice it is not possible to draw any meaningful distinction between 'formal' or 'informal' service, or between service 'accepted voluntarily' and 'enforced' service.

Normal practice in civil law countries is very different. Originating summonses and equivalent documents will be served by an officer of the court, who may be the clerk to the court (as in Switzerland), or an officer with specific functions including the service of process (such as the *ufficiale giudiziario* in Italy), or in some countries such as France a *huissier de justice*, a process-server appointed by the State authorities but engaged in a professional capacity by the plaintiff. Whatever the precise position of the person effecting service, his activities will typically be closely regulated by legislation and service by him will be regarded as 'formal'. In some contexts, and particularly where the document to be served originated abroad, an informal mode of service is used; typically the document is passed to a local police

---

[2] C.C.R. 1981, Ord. 7, r. 10(1)(2). For service by bailiff, see r. 10(4).
[3] R.S.C. Ord. 75, r. 8.
[4] Federal Rules of Civil Procedure, r. 4(c).
[5] R.S.C. Ord. 65, r. 2.

station, and is either taken round to the defendant's address or the defendant is invited to call in to collect it. This 'simple delivery' (*remise simple* in French) is referred to in the text of the Hague Convention on Service Abroad of 15 November 1965 as 'delivery to an addressee who accepts it voluntarily'. A reader from a common law background is often puzzled by this, because it looks like the single concept of 'service' with which he is familiar; he has to keep in mind the civil law distinction between more and less solemn modes.

FACTORS TO BE CONSIDERED

The form which is taken by international assistance in the service of process depends upon a number of, necessarily interrelated, factors. International discussion is eased if they are distinguished as far as possible.

The first issue concerns the *initiation of international action within the state of origin*.[6] The law of that state, as *lex fori*, will prescribe any special procedures to be followed where service is to be effected abroad. Where the common law approach of treating service as a matter for the plaintiff prevails, there are usually few special requirements. The leave of the court or of some other official agency may be required[7] and official assistance may be available to those who choose to avail themselves of it; but no special steps to initiate the actual business of service abroad will be mandatory. The *lex fori* will be satisfied by proof that the plaintiff has secured the service of the documents on the defendant abroad, either by taking them personally or (much more usually) by employing an agent.

The more formal civil law tradition requires international service to be initiated by specified officials.[8] Action may be required by the court itself, the court issuing a Letter of Request asking either a foreign court or another competent authority in the state of destination to assist in having the documents served; this practice is particularly entrenched in Latin America. In many other countries the initiating steps will be taken by an officer attached to the court. Taking the French system as an example, the *huissier de justice* engaged by the plaintiff will deliver the documents to the *ministère public*; this is a body of officers attached to the court and primarily responsible for the public prosecution function in the criminal jurisdiction, and customarily and conveniently referred to as the *parquet* (which literally means 'the well of the court' where these officers used to be placed). The *parquet* is responsible for the onward transmission of the documents via central government agencies. The law may allow the *huissier* himself, given his semi-official position, to initiate contact with the competent authorities (or a brother *huissier*) in the

---

[6] In this Chapter, except where a direct quotation is made from a legal text, the countries concerned will be referred to as 'the state of origin' and 'the state of destination'.

[7] See the English procedure: R.S.C. Ord. 6, r. 7; Ord. 11, rr. 1–2.

[8] See the detailed country-by-country survey of then-current practice in H. Smit (ed.), *International Co-operation in Litigation: Europe* (Nijhoff, 1965). Useful information can also be found in the *Practical Handbook* on the Hague Service Convention, published by the Permanent Bureau of the Hague Conference.

state of destination, or may (as has French law since 1966)[9] require the *huissier* to take informal steps such as the use of the postal channel to supplement the official service initiated by the *parquet*.

The second issue is in a sense the counterpart of the first, for it concerns the *proper addressee in the state of destination*. The law of that state as to the service of documents originating abroad may permit documents to be sent directly to the defendant without the use of any local official acting as intermediary, or it may insist on the documents passing through, for example, the court having jurisdiction at the defendant's place of residence, the *parquet* attached to that court, or a *huissier* practising in the relevant area.

The third issue is the precise *mode of service on the defendant*, and in particular whether it is service in solemn form or 'simple delivery'.

The interaction of these issues affects the final point, the actual *mode of transmission of documents from country to country*. Official modes, such as the diplomatic channel, are more likely to be associated with communications which must pass between officials in the two countries, whilst the postal channel may be more appropriate for communications between *huissiers* or directly to the defendant.

(B) International Procedures

Taking these factors into account, it is possible to list a range of forms of procedure which are, or have in the past been, found in national legislation and in practice under international conventions.

(a) The diplomatic channel

The most venerable and most formal mode of communication is the diplomatic channel. It may lend a certain dignity to the whole transaction but is notoriously slow. This is due to the number of distinct administrative hierarchies whose active co-operation is required, and whose officers frankly have other tasks of much greater priority and interest. Under this procedure, documents emanating from, say, a court or *parquet* in the state of origin are transmitted (perhaps via the Ministry of Justice of that state) to its Ministry for External Affairs. They are then sent to the Embassy maintained in the state of destination which conveys them to the External Affairs Ministry of that state, which will pass them over to its Ministry of Justice to be sent down to the appropriate local agency for delivery to the addressee. If some acknowledgement of due service is required, it may have to retrace the path of the original documents.

---

[9] See P. Amran, 'The Revolutionary Change in Service of Process Abroad in French Civil Procedure', (1968) 2 International Lawyer 650. For current French law, see N.C.P.C., Art. 686 as substituted by Decret 85–1330.

(b) The (direct) consular channel

The service of judicial documents is a well-recognized consular function. Its exercise depends very much on the conventions governing consular relations between the states concerned. It may be that the consul for the state of origin can serve documents only on nationals of his state, or he may be allowed to effect service on anyone in the area of his responsibility. In some cases, notably where consuls are not in post, these consular functions may actually be performed by diplomatic officers.

(c) The indirect consular channel

Many writers treat the diplomatic and (direct) consular channels as part of the customary practice of states. Arguably the indirect consular channel, like the modes of transmission still to be noted, is solely a creature of conventions. The 'indirectness' lies in the fact that the consul does not approach the defendant directly, but the appropriate authority in the state of destination; this will usually be some central government agency, within the Ministry of Justice for example, but local officers can be specified.

(d) Ministry of Justice (or central authority) to Ministry of Justice (or central authority)

A considerable simplification can be effected by excluding the relevant Ministries for External Affairs and their diplomatic or consular staffs from the process. The administration of justice is a central concern of a Ministry of Justice, and direct communication between the two Justice Ministries is likely to produce greater understanding and a speedier response. What is essential to this mode is that each country should communicate via some agency of central government located in that part of the state's apparatus which is concerned with the administration of justice. This agency can have a style other than that of Ministry of Justice (for example, Attorney General's Department) or may be located in the courts service or form a specialist bureau. In every case, the agency will communicate with its counterpart in the other country.

(e) Competent official to ministry of justice (or central authority)

Most of the modes considered so far require the involvement in each state of an agency of central government as well as the competent official (*parquet* etc.) at the local level. There is a readily identified 'central government interest' within the state of destination where considerations of sovereignty may be seen to be involved and where some knowledge of the nature of the documents is necessary if the state of destination is to be sure that its public policy (e.g. as to bank secrecy) is not offended. The interest of central government in the outward transmission of documents intended for service abroad is less pressing. There may be real practical advantages in having a central source of expertise; such a source is more likely to send documents in a form, and with accompanying material, required by the state of destination or specified in the applicable bilateral or multilateral convention. If however the local officials in the state of origin have access to appropriate procedural guidance, there is no strong reason of principle why they should not be allowed to communicate directly with the Justice Ministry or other central authority of the state of destination. This mode comprises just that procedure.

One theoretical possibility which is thought not to be found in actual practice would be for the plaintiff, in a state of origin which regarded service as a matter for the parties to handle, to be allowed to make a direct approach to the Justice Ministry or other central authority of the state of destination. Ministries of Justice are, however, quite properly unwilling to enter into dialogues with private citizens of other states in this context, or to operate an advisory service for foreign lawyers.

(f) *Competent official to competent official*

The argument supporting mode (*e*) can be taken a stage further. Provided the competent local officials in the state of destination have adequate administrative guidance, their Justice Ministry may be content, or even happy, to withdraw from active involvement. This opens the way for direct communication between the appropriate officer (*parquet* etc.) in the state of origin and his counterpart in the state of destination.

(g) Huissier de justice *to* huissier de justice

Where both concerned states have the institution of *huissier de justice*, a variant of the last mode is possible. The facts that *huissiers* are appointed or licensed by the state and have a defined role in Codes of Civil Procedure in respect of service enable them to be treated as in a similar position to the competent state officials, and direct communication from *huissier* to *huissier* (who will then act in the state of destination to involve the local *parquet*) can be authorized.

(h) *Plaintiff to competent official*

This mode represents the ultimate 'deregulation', always supposing that service by some official of the state of destination is required. It allows a direct approach by the plaintiff or his agent to the competent local official in that state. No official of the state of origin is involved.

(i) *Service by post*

The final mode eliminates all official involvement and permits the plaintiff or his agent to send the documents, with some appropriate means of obtaining confirmation of their delivery, by post. It may be that 'post' will need progressive reinterpretation to include telex, facsimile transmission, and other forms of 'electronic mail' but international conventions appear not to have explored these possibilities thus far.

(C) The Development of International Assistance in Europe

EARLY WORK AT THE HAGUE

Until the end of the nineteenth century, practice amongst the states of Europe as to service of process has been described as being in *un état anarchique*.[10] The diplomatic channel was generally used, and few bilateral treaties dealt with the subject.[11] The second session of the Hague Conference on Private International Law held in 1894 agreed a draft Convention on Civil Procedure which was signed on 14 November 1896, the first of four Hague Conventions to deal with service of process.

The 1896 Convention, like each of its successors, selected one mode of assistance as the primary or preferred mode while recognizing others as permissible. Article 1 of the 1896 Convention provided for service at the request of officers of the *ministère public* or of the courts of a Contracting State addressed to the competent authority in the state of destination; the diplomatic channel was to be used for communication from country to country unless direct communication between the relevant authorities of the two states was allowed by bilateral agreement.[12] Article 6 of the Convention also declared that its provisions did not preclude any of the following so far as the laws of the concerned states or conventions entered into between them allowed:

 (i) service by post;
 (ii) direct approach by the plaintiff to the competent official in the state of destination;
 (iii) direct service on the defendant by diplomatic or consular agents of the state of origin.

The 1896 Convention was revised and replaced by a Convention on Civil Procedure of 17 July 1905. The text of the 1905 Convention is much fuller when compared with the terse formulation of its predecessor, and it contains a number of changes of principle.

The first is the selection as the primary or preferred mode of transmission of the indirect consular channel. Article 1 provides that service will be effected in Contracting States on the request of a consul of the state of origin addressed to an authority designated for the purpose by the state of destina-

---

[10] G. A. L. Droz, 'Mémoire sur la Notification des Actes Judiciares et Extrajudiciares à l'Etranger', *AetD (10)*, vol. 3, p. 15.

[11] See 33 Am. Jo.I.L. (Supp.) (hereafter *Harvard Research*), pp. 26–7, where the text of a treaty between France and Baden of 16 Apr. 1846 creating in very general terms an obligation to effect service of process is set out.

[12] For the text of the 1896 and 1905 Hague Conventions, see *Harvard Research*, App. VI, pp. 148 ff.

tion. Nothing is prescribed as to those entitled to initiate this process; this is left to the law of the state of origin. The authority initiating the request had, however, to be identified in the written request delivered by the consul, which was also to contain information about the parties and the nature of the document to be served and was to be prepared in the language of the state of destination.

The 1905 text gives some flexibility as to the precise method of communication. The use of the diplomatic channel, normal under the 1896 Convention, is not prescribed but an individual Contracting State might insist upon it. The possibility of pairs of states allowing direct communication between their respective authorities, bypassing the consul, is also recognized, as it was in the earlier text.[13]

Another change of principle made in the 1905 text affects Article 6, which in 1896 permitted three other modes of service (service by post; direct approach by plaintiff to competent authority; the direct consular mode) only to the extent that the relevant laws or bilateral conventions expressly permitted. In the 1905 text these other modes enjoy a rather higher status. The text provides that they are available if they are permitted under a bilateral convention, or, in the absence of a convention, if the state of destination does not object; and provides further that the direct consular channel shall always be available where service is to be effected without any compulsion on a national of the state of origin.[14]

The 1905 Convention was considered at the Sixth Session of the Conference in 1924 when a Protocol was agreed permitting accession by States not represented in 1905[15] and some further work was set in hand which led to the publication in 1929 of a proposed revised Convention.[16] No changes were envisaged in Chapter I dealing with service, and the long intermission in the activities of the Conference until its revival in 1951 prevented any action.

A Phase of Bilateralism

No common law country took part in this work at The Hague, but the 1905 Convention was examined by the Committee on British and Foreign Legal Procedure (the Sumner Committee) in 1918–19. It advised against accession by the United Kingdom. One reason was political: the fact that some parties to the Convention were recent enemies. The two legal reasons were that full adherence would require greater changes in English law than could be recommended, and that the Convention was concerned with service via official channels, whereas 'the great need is to obtain facilities for the use of less official channels'.[17] The Committee did stress that there was 'a real desire

---

[13] See Art. 1 of each Convention. For the bilateral agreements entered into under each Convention see *Harvard Research*, pp. 49–50; J. Kosters and F. Bellemans, *Les conventions de la Haye de 1902 et 1905*, pp. 922–72. [14] 1905 Convention, Art. 6.

[15] *AetD* (6), 515–16. [16] Reproduced in *AetD* (7), vol. 2, pp. 60ff.

[17] Report, Cmd. 251, para. 44.

for improvement'[18] and prepared a draft Convention which provided for service via the consular channel, or by an agent appointed either by a party or by the Court whose process was involved.[19] The Committee's advice was that bilateral Conventions should be concluded with Allied countries.

This advice was accepted and the first such Convention was concluded with France on 2 February 1922. This provides for service, directly upon the addressee and without the use of any form of compulsion, by consular agents[20] and also for the use of the indirect consular channel, service being effected in France through the *procureur de la République* within whose area the addressee was to be found, and in England through the Senior Master of the Supreme Court.[21] This was followed by twenty-two other conventions, including three with the Baltic Republics which lapsed on the incorporation of those States in the USSR;[22] now that those Republics have regained their independence, and have entered into diplomatic relations with the United Kingdom, the position of the Conventions will fall to be re-examined. Details of the Conventions other than those three are given in Table 1.

Although originally solely bilateral, the UK Conventions have some wider significance. Many of them were extended to territories for the foreign relations of which either the United Kingdom or the other party was responsible. In 1976 Australia, Canada, Fiji, New Zealand, Sri Lanka, and Trinidad and Tobago expressed themselves, in response to a questionnaire circulated by the Commonwealth Secretariat, as parties to the Conventions listed in the Table 1 except that with Israel.[23]

Of the twenty States listed in the Table 1, thirteen are parties to the more recent Hague Convention of 1965 which does not involve the abrogation of the earlier bilateral Conventions but has in practice superseded them so far as the United Kingdom is concerned.

Between the parties to the 1905 Convention,[24] a further set of bilateral agreements grew up, taking advantage in particular of the option to allow direct communication between designated authorities. So, for example, France entered into a bilateral Convention with Austria on 11 July 1966 providing for direct communication between the Ministries of Justice of the two countries,[25] and with Italy on 12 January 1955 allowing documents to be sent by the competent authority to the *parquet* in France and the corresponding officers in Italy.[26]

---

[18] Sumner Report, para. 43.

[19] Ibid., Appendix B. The text is reproduced in the *Harvard Research*, App. V, pp. 140–3.

[20] Convention, Art. 4.   [21] Ibid., Art. 3(*a*).

[22] The Conventions were those with Estonia, 132 LNTS 231 (23 Dec. 1931); Latvia, 201 LNTS 37 (23 Aug. 1939); and Lithuania, 169 LNTS 373 (24 Apr. 1934).

[23] There were minor variations in the listings; Fiji excluded Hungary; New Zealand listed Iceland, *semble* within the scope of the UK–Denmark Convention.

[24] And to the 1954 revision; see below.

[25] Convention supplemental to the Hague Convention of 1954, Art. 2.

[26] Convention on Mutual Judicial Assistance, Art. 4 (which applies equally to service of documents in criminal cases).

RESUMED WORK AT THE HAGUE

The activities of the Conference at its Seventh Session in 1951 led to the signature of a new Convention on Civil Procedure of 1 March 1954, but its substantive provisions are almost identical with those of 1905. There is a certain irony about the events leading up to the 1954 Convention. The British

TABLE 1: *United Kingdom Bilateral Conventions*

Reference	Other party	Date signed	Service modes							
			1	2	3	4	5	6	7	8
127 LNTS 167	Austria	31 Mar. 1931	1	2	3	4		6		
24 LNTS 91	Belgium	21 June 1922	1	2	3			6	7	
48 LNTS 425	Czechoslovakia	11 Nov. 1924	1	2			5	6		
139 LNTS 9	Denmark	29 Nov. 1932	1	2*	3*	4*		6	7	8
149 LNTS 131	Finland	11 Aug. 1933	1	2	3	4		6		
10 LNTS 448	France	2 Feb. 1922	1	2						
90 LNTS 287	Germany	20 Mar. 1928	1	2*	3*	4*		6	7	
185 LNTS 113	Greece	27 Feb. 1936	1	2	3	4		6		8
170 LNTS 51	Hungary	25 Sept. 1935	1	2*				6*		
176 LNTS 229	Iraq	25 July 1935	1	2						
630 UNTS 189	Israel	5 July 1966	1	2				6		8
131 LNTS 79	Italy	17 Dec. 1930	1	2	3‡	4‡			7	8
140 LNTS 287	Netherlands	31 May 1932	1	2	3	4		6	7	
123 LNTS 343	Norway	30 Jan. 1931	1	2	3	4		6		
131 LNTS 19	Poland	26 Aug. 1931	1	2	3	4		6		8
129 LNTS 417	Portugal	9 July 1931	1	2*	3*	4*		6		8
101 LNTS 375	Spain	27 June 1929	1	2	3	4		6	7	8
114 LNTS 9	Sweden	28 Aug. 1930	1	2	3	4		6		
141 LNTS 225	Turkey	28 Nov. 1931	1	2*				6*		
181 LNTS 241	Yugoslavia	27 Feb. 1936	1	2				6		

Key to service modes:
* = not permitted on nationals of the foreign country (or in the case of the Turkish Convention, permitted only on subjects of the country of origin)
‡ = the agent in Italy must be a Notary Public or an Advocate.
1 = by the judicial authority.
2 = by a diplomatic agent or consular officer.
3 = by agent appointed by the tribunal of the requesting State.
4 = by agent appointed by party.
5 = by solicitor or notary of the country where service effected appointed by the requesting authority or a party.
6 = by post
7 = by persons concerned, directly through competent officials of the country in which the document is to be served.
8 = by any other mode not illegal in the country where service is to be effected.

Government had proposed to the Council of Europe that it should examine a range of questions including that of service of process abroad, which the United Kingdom had hitherto included in its bilateral civil procedure conventions. At this the Netherlands government drew attention to the past work and impending revival of the Hague Conference. The Council of Europe stayed its hand, and the Seventh Session of the Conference found that by making two small amendments to the service provisions of the 1905 text (the definition of *'autorité compétente'* in Article 2, so as to include solicitors; an addition to Article 3 providing for the supply of *two* copies of the document to be served) the Hague text could be made entirely acceptable to the British Government. In the event, the United Kingdom never acceded to the Convention.[27]

A more radical review of the system for service abroad had to await the Tenth Session of the Conference in 1964. It was prompted by a memorandum from the *Union Internationale des Huissiers de Justice et Officiers Judiciaires* which reviewed current practice and suggested the introduction of a new mode of service involving direct communication between a *huissier de justice* in the country of origin and a similar officer in the country of service. That particular proposal was of interest only to the limited number of countries which have *huissiers de justice*, which prompted Professor Graveson when the issue was discussed in 1960 to express the traditional preference of the British Government for bilateral conventions,[28] but the topic attracted more general interest and it was decided to re-examine the whole range of possibilities.

(D) The Hague Convention of 15 November 1965

A draft Convention was prepared by a Special Commission of the Hague Conference in February 1964[29] and by the Tenth Session of the Conference in the following October.[30]

The starting points for the revision of the existing Conventions of 1905 and 1954 were a dissatisfaction with the indirect consular channel, as being inappropriate in current conditions, and a concern that the non-obligatory nature of the channels provided for in the existing text enabled some countries to make use of the system of *notification au parquet* to which increasing exception was taken. This latter system, which was then available in at least some cases in Belgium, France, Greece, Italy, and The Netherlands,[31]

---

[27] These events can be traced in *AetD* (7), vol. 1, pp. 274–84 and 293–310. Ireland had also raised the issue in the Council of Europe but was not represented at The Hague.

[28] *AetD* (9), vol. 1, p. 171.

[29] See *AetD* (10), vol. 3, pp. 65–73 (preliminary draft, with English translation at pp. 112–19) and 74–111 (explanatory report).

[30] See *AetD* (10), vol. 3, pp. 141–331 (minutes and working documents of the Third Commission), 335–81 (plenary session, final text, and explanatory report). The text of the Convention is reproduced below in the Appendix of Selected Documents.

[31] *AetD* (10), vol. 3, p. 75.

allows legally effective service on a defendant resident abroad to be made by leaving the relevant document at the office of the *parquet* in the forum state. Although the *parquet* was then expected to take steps to bring the document to the attention of the defendant, service was already complete and time began to run for various purposes regardless of the date upon which the defendant received actual notice of the proceedings. The principal changes introduced in response to these points were:

(a) the introduction of a new preferred mode, service through a designated Central Authority in each Contracting State, using prescribed forms and procedures;
(b) the giving of some obligatory quality to the new Convention;
(c) the addition of 'guarantees' to safeguard the position of defendants who remained in ignorance of the proceedings being taken against them.

SCOPE OF THE CONVENTION

The Convention applies 'in all cases, in civil and commercial matters, where there is occasion to transmit a judicial or extra-judicial document for service abroad'.[32] This provision was the product of long debate, focusing on its obligatory character ('in all cases') and on the meaning of 'civil and commercial'.

Obligatory character

The authors of the Convention were never quite of one mind as to the obligatory quality they wished to give their text. It is clear that *if* there is occasion to serve documents abroad, the modes of transmission and the 'guarantees' of the Convention apply universally. Unfortunately, this does not address the question in which cases such service is required; it does not, read strictly, touch those provisions of the law of the state of origin which allow valid service by *notification au parquet* or, for that matter, affixing the document to the courthouse door. This whole matter was destined to create much controversy and is addressed further below,[33] but it is necessary here to note that the problem was of concern to the Rapporteur, Mr Taborda Ferreira of Portugal, who expressed his anxieties in his commentary on the preliminary draft.[34] The issue received no profound discussion at the Tenth Session of the Conference, but the Rapporteur felt able to declare, in a passage set in capital letters, that the 'authentic interpretation of the Commission' favoured its obligatory application.[35]

---

[32] Convention, Art. 1. 'Service' is used in the English text to translate two terms, *signification* and *notification* in the French. In a number of continental systems, and in Scotland, the former implies service by an officer of the court or *huissier*, the latter having a wider meaning; see the discussion in *AetD* (*10*), vol. 3, pp. 165–7 and R. H. Graveson, 'The Tenth Session of the Hague Conference on Private International Law', (1965) 14 I.C.L.Q. 528, 539.

[33] See pp. 34–41.   [34] *AetD* (*10*), vol. 3, p. 81.

[35] Ibid., p. 367.

Civil and commercial matters

The Convention applies to 'civil and commercial matters'. This phrase has appeared in Hague Conventions since 1896, in many bilateral civil procedure conventions including those entered into by the United Kingdom, in other multilateral conventions[36] and, outside the area of civil procedure in the Brussels Convention on jurisdiction and the enforcement of judgments in civil and commercial matters 1968.[37] Discussion of the phrase at The Hague is something of a hardy perennial, because of the evident fascination of different methods of categorizing legal rules, and the issue arises in the context of the taking of evidence abroad as well as in the present context.[38] A common law country will usually interpret the phrase to include almost anything which is not a criminal matter,[39] but civil lawyers use a larger number of categories and take differing views on the relationship of administrative or public law matters, fiscal cases, or those including questions of personal status, to the categories of 'civil' and 'commercial'. All are agreed, however, that it is the nature of the 'matter' which is important, and it was recognized early in the history of the Hague Conventions on Civil Procedure that some civil or commercial matters could arise in the context of an administrative jurisdiction.[40]

It is well recognized that these differences in styles of legal thinking do exist, and the Convention is interpreted in practice in such a way that its objectives will be secured despite those differences. If a document is regarded as within the 'civil and commercial' field in its country of origin, it will be served by the authorities in other Contracting States.[41] In many cases, the state of destination will either accept the classification of the state of origin, or waive any right it may have to reject the document under Article 4, or simply serve the document as an act of goodwill even if the Convention is regarded as not strictly applicable. One exception to this statement was the attitude taken by the Bavarian Central Authority in the late 1980s in connection with products liability cases in the courts of the United States. Where the plaintiff

[36] e.g. the Inter-American Convention on Letters Rogatory 1975, Art. 2; A-ALCC Model for Bilateral Agreement for the Service of Process and Taking of Evidence Abroad in Civil or Commercial Matters 1986.

[37] On the phrase in this context, where it is given an 'independent' meaning, not necessarily following that of any national law, see Case 29/76 *L.T.U. G.m.b.H. & Co. K.G.* v. *Eurocontrol* [1976] E.C.R. 1541, [1977] 1 C.M.L.R. 88; L. Collins, *The Civil Jurisdiction and Judgments Act 1982*, pp. 17–23; Dicey and Morris, *The Conflict of Laws* (11th edn., 1987), pp. 267–9.

[38] See pp. 87–9.

[39] Cf. the Draft Convention on Judicial Assistance prepared as part of the *Harvard Research*, Art. 1(*f*) of which defines 'civil proceeding' (not 'matter') as 'any contentious or non-contentious proceeding before a tribunal of a State, not directed to the investigation of crime or to conviction or punishment for crime': *Harvard Research*, p. 40.

[40] See an official French statement to this effect (Foreign Ministry, 20 Jan. 1910) and the views of French and German writers collected at *Harvard Research*, p. 37.

[41] Where service is effected by a means not involving the authorities of the state of destination (e.g. by post under Art. 10(*a*)) the characterization of the lex fori will inevitably prevail.

claimed punitive damages as well as compensation, the request for service was refused apparently on the basis that this was a claim for a penalty and not a civil claim. The Bavarian position appears untenable, as the *matter* is surely a civil one and Article 13 expressly prohibits a refusal based on the ground that the internal law of the state of destination would not permit the action on which the application was based.[42]

A generous interpretation aids both plaintiffs (who may need to have service effected before proceeding to judgment) and defendants (who can benefit from knowledge of pending proceedings); and the state of destination does not commit itself to recognize any judgment the plaintiff may ultimately obtain, for service facilitates proceedings and does not authenticate them. For these reasons, the uncertainty about the scope of 'civil and commercial matters' does not have the serious implications it has in the context of the taking of evidence for use abroad. It was, therefore, a little surprising that a Special Commission of the Hague Conference in April 1989 took a rather conservative position on the matter. Largely at the prompting of the Swiss representative, Professor Volken, who raised the issue as one of principle (Switzerland, not being a party to the Convention, had no actual practical experience), the Commission considered it desirable that the words 'civil or commercial matters' should be interpreted in an 'autonomous' manner, without reference exclusively either to the law of the state of origin or to that of the state of destination, or to both laws cumulatively. This interpretation should be common both to the Service and to the Evidence Convention.[43] The Commission did, however, recognize a diversity of practice, a freedom to adopt a broad reading of the phrase, and a 'historical evolution' which treated the Convention as applicable to at least some of the topics in the grey area between public and private law: bankruptcy, insurance and employment but not tax matters. It may be that growing co-operation between States in respect of tax, and indeed criminal, matters will reduce the importance of this whole issue.

The case of the unknown address

During the meeting of the Special Commission which prepared the preliminary draft of the Convention there was considerable, but inconclusive, discussion of the position which should obtain when service was required on someone strongly suspected of being in a particular country but whose address within the country was unknown. The discussion centred on the extent to which the authorities of the state of destination should be placed under an obligation to trace the person concerned.[44] The United Kingdom, in its observations on the preliminary draft, expressed the hope that the

---

[42] The German Federal Government does not share the views of the Bavarian *Land* authorities; the issue has not been tested in the German courts.

[43] See pp. 87–9.

[44] See the report of M. Taborda Ferreira, *AetD (10)*, vol. 3, pp. 108–11.

Convention would not apply at all in cases in which the address of the person on whom documents were to be served was unknown; it was unhappy about the possible effect of what was to become Article 15 in such cases[45] and more generally felt that the provisions of the Convention were not apt where the address was unknown.[46] Although there was only fragmentary discussion of the matter at the Tenth Session, the United Kingdom view prevailed; an example perhaps of the effect of shortage of time on the content of international conventions.[47] The express exclusion of this case from the scope of the Convention leaves the Contracting States free to make whatever provision they judge appropriate, for example the use of substituted service in English law.[48]

THE SYSTEM OF CENTRAL AUTHORITIES

The main innovation in the 1965 Convention was the creation of the system of Central Authorities. Each Contracting State must designate such a Central Authority to receive requests for service coming from other Contracting States;[49] the expectation, borne out in practice, was that this would involve not the creation of some new agency but the designation as Central Authority for the purposes of this Convention of some existing office or ministry.[50] The greatest number of Contracting States have designated their Ministries of Justice (or some organ of the Ministry, for example, the French Ministry's specialist *bureau de l'entraide judiciaire internationale*); a substantial group of countries have placed the Central Authority within the courts service (for example The Netherlands' designation of the *Officier van Justitie* or public prosecutor attached to the District Court of The Hague); and relatively few have retained the Foreign Ministry. The United Kingdom is in this last category, the Secretary of State for Foreign and Commonwealth Affairs being the designated Central Authority.[51]

Article 18 of the Convention, introduced at the suggestion of the United Kingdom, allows a Contracting State to designate 'other authorities' in addition to the Central Authority. The purpose of this provision for what were referred to in discussion as 'subsidiary authorities' was to cater for the needs of composite States such as the United Kingdom, where different systems of law are to be found within the same State. An applicant in another state may be unaware of the nature and significance of the divisions within the country of destination, so it is expressly provided that he always has the right to address a request directly to the Central Authority itself.[52] The system was complicated by the introduction at a late stage of a further provision

---

[45] See pp. 29–31. [46] *AetD* (*10*), vol. 3, pp. 130, 133.
[47] See ibid., pp. 259 and 293, and Convention, Art. 1(2).
[48] R.S.C. Ord. 11, r. 5(1), Ord. 65(4). [49] Convention, Art. 2(1).
[50] See *AetD* (*10*), vol. 3, p. 174 (M. Taborda Ferreira, the Rapporteur).
[51] The designations and objections made by Contracting States are usefully collected in the *Practical Handbook* on the Convention published by the Permanent Bureau of the Hague Conference. [52] Convention, Art. 18(2).

enabling federal states to designate more than one *Central* Authority;[53] this was done on the suggestion of the German Federal Republic (which had previously resisted the British proposal as tending to multiply Central Authorities) to enable expression to be given to the sovereignty of the German *Länder* in the field of justice, and does require the applicant to identify the *Land* in question.[54] Advantage has also been taken of this facility by Czechoslovakia. The United Kingdom and The Netherlands have designated 'other authorities' under Article 18(1); in the case of the United Kingdom, the Senior Master of the Supreme Court for England and Wales, the Crown Agent for Scotland, and the Master (Queen's Bench and Appeals) for Northern Ireland.[55]

Initiation of the Request

During the discussions of the draft Convention it was argued by some delegates that the Central Authority should have a double task, acting as a transmitting or forwarding agency as well as receiving requests from abroad, but their opinion did not prevail.[56] The case for using a Central Authority as a transmitting agency rests on the argument that the familiarity of its officers with the system of the Convention and with the practice of other countries would ensure that requests which it prepared or approved for transmission were in order and so would be handled expeditiously and without any need to refer a request back for clarification. The strength of this argument is increasingly recognized, as the expertise of Central Authorities has grown; some countries have chosen to use their Central Authorities as transmitting agents, although not required to do so by the Convention, and have discovered that the advantages outweigh any risk of slight delays caused by the extra agency involved within the state of origin. However, a significant number of countries are wedded to a principle which requires all outgoing requests to emanate directly from a court; for such countries the superimposition of an administrative agency in the context of a judicial function is impossible.

In the result, the Convention provides that the request is initiated by an 'authority or judicial officer competent under the law of the State in which the documents originate'.[57] Some countries, including the United Kingdom, have chosen to provide that outgoing requests must be forwarded through the Central Authority;[58] others allow local court officials or *huissiers* to act. Private parties may not themselves originate requests, but a party's lawyer

---

[53] Ibid., Art. 18(3). [54] See *AetD* (*10*), vol. 3, pp. 172–83 and 315.
[55] The Netherlands has designated the public prosecutors of all its District Courts other than that of The Hague as 'other authorities'.
[56] *AetD* (*10*), vol. 3, pp. 170–2. [57] Convention, Art. 3(1).
[58] For requests originating in Scotland, the forwarding authority is the Foreign Secretary (i.e. the Central Authority); for requests originating in England and Wales or in Northern Ireland the appropriate 'other authority' under Art. 18(1) is the forwarding authority.

may do so if the law of the state of origin so allows, as is the case with attorneys in several States of the USA.

Practice appears to be fairly relaxed on this matter. The Special Commission of the Hague Conference held in 1977 to review the working of the Convention found that there was no systematic monitoring of the competence of forwarding authorities:

It appeared to the Commission that, aside from certain cases involving fantasy or malice, a request for service forwarded abroad met a precise need, and it could be presumed that such a request was in compliance with the procedural law of the forum, since this step would otherwise make no sense.[59]

PROCEDURES FOR SERVICE

The Convention prescribes in some detail the documentation to be used, the extent to which translations may be required, and the actual mode of service to be employed in the state of destination; these various issues are interconnected.

An Annex to the Convention prescribes a form of 'Request for Service' which is to be used. It is in three parts. The actual request is set out in the first part, which gives the relevant addresses and which may specify a particular mode of service. The second, printed on the reverse of the first, is a Certificate either that service was effected on a stated date or that service has proved impossible for stated reasons; the Certificate will be tendered in proof of service in any proceedings in the state of origin, and the law of that state will determine whether its contents can be challenged[60] or whether the absence or incomplete nature of the Certificate is fatal.[61] The third is a Summary of the document to be served, which is served with the document itself.[62] Unless the Contracting States concerned have agreed to dispense, in dealings between their two countries, with this requirement,[63] all three parts of the Request must be completed either in the language of the state of destination or in French or English.[64]

There must be sent to the Central Authority of the state of destination *two* copies of the Request and of the document to be served (either the original or a copy);[65] so far as the Request is concerned this requirement for duplicates is always applicable, but pairs or groups of States may agree to dispense, as between themselves, with the need for duplicate copies of the document to be

---

[59] *AetD (14)*, vol. 4, p. 386.

[60] See *Gould Entertainment Corpn.* v. *Bodo* 107 F.R.D. 308 (S.D.N.Y., 1985) (challenge to accuracy of Italian certificate failed on facts).

[61] See *Fox* v. *Régie Nationale des Usines Renault* 103 F.R.D. 453 (W. E. Tenn., 1984) (absence of French certificate not fatal: 'The Hague Convention should not be construed so as to foreclose judicial discretion when such discretion needs to be exercised' (at p. 455)).

[62] See Convention, Arts. 3, 5(4), and 6.

[63] Ibid., Art. 20(*b*). [64] Ibid., Art 7(2).

[65] See *Rivers* v. *Stihl Inc.* 434 So. 2d 766 (Ala., 1983) (German Central Authority refused request because document not in duplicate).

served.[66] The practice is for the second copy of the Request to be retained in the files of the Central Authority as a record of its action in the matter, and for the second copy of the document itself to be returned with the completed Certificate of service so as to eliminate any doubt as to which document is covered by the Certificate.

If the applicant requests a particular method of service (which in practice is seldom done)[67] that request will be complied with unless to do so would be incompatible with the law of the country of destination. The text of the Convention suggests that in all other cases the Central Authority may choose to serve the document *either* by the method prescribed by its internal law for the service of documents in actions brought against defendants within the jurisdiction *or* by 'delivery to an addressee who accepts it voluntarily', i.e. *remise simple*.[68] However, the Request as set out in the Annex suggests that the applicant may delete either of these possibilities, and so limit the Central Authority's options. The matter is further complicated by the rules as to translations: if the document[69] is to be served under Article 5 by any method other than that of simple delivery, the Central Authority may require the document to be written in, or translated into, an official language of the state of destination.[70] Unless the applicant for service has good reason to believe that service by simple delivery will be accepted, he should supply a translation, for there is otherwise a risk of delay while the Central Authority reports that that mode of delivery has failed and requests a translation of the document.[71] If a translation is required, the whole document must be translated including any appended material treated by the law of the state of origin as an essential part of the document.[72]

In practice, each Central Authority has a preferred method of dealing with requests for service. For example, in the United States where the Central Authority is an agency of the Federal Government, service is effected by the use of US Marshals attached to the (Federal) District Courts. In France and Germany, on the other hand, the informal method of 'simple

---

[66] Convention, Arts. 3(2), 20(*a*).

[67] At the 1989 Special Commission to review the Convention, the US Delegation reported that applicants familiar with US practice sometimes asked for a variation in it, e.g. that the Marshal attempt personal service at once rather than use that only after the failure of postal service.

[68] Ibid., Art. 5; for *remise simple*, see pp. 7–8, above.

[69] As opposed to the Request for Service, the language of which is governed by Art. 7: *Taylor v. Uniden Corpn. of America* 622 F. Supp. 1011 (D.C. Mo., 1985).

[70] Convention, Art. 5(3). Pairs or groups of contracting States may agree to waive this provision in dealings between themselves: Art. 20(*b*).

[71] e.g. Arrondissementsrechtbank Amsterdam, 2 May 1979 (Asser 2/168). (References in the form 'Asser 2/168)' are to the collections of material published by the T. M. C. Asser Instituut under the title *Les Nouvelles Conventions de la Haye: leur application par les juge nationaux* (ed. M. Sumampouw), identified by volume and page number.)

[72] *Teknekron Management Inc.* v. *Quante Fernmeldetechnik G.m.b.H.* 115 F.R.D. 175 (D.C. Nev., 1987). There seems no merit in the point reportedly taken by a German Central Authority that the translations should be set out on separate pages from the original text: *Rivers* v. *Stihl Inc.* 434 So. 2d 766 (Ala., 1983).

delivery' is preferred.[73] Practice as to translation requirements varies greatly; although the relevant information is set out in the *Practical Handbook* published by the Permanent Bureau of the Hague conference, which is held by all Central Authorities, other applicants often fall foul of the rules. Some countries always require the document to be translated (Botswana, France, Germany,[74] Japan, Luxembourg, and the United Kingdom). Others have some flexibility, being prepared to serve documents in any language which the addressee is likely to understand; a short document addressed to a commercial firm in English or a language similar to that of the state of destination (e.g. a document in Norwegian for service in Sweden) will be accepted, but a long document addressed to a private individual in a relatively obscure language will not.[75]

Even if there is no formal translation requirement, the provision of a translation may be advisable. There is some United States authority for the proposition that service on a person who does not understand the language of the document in question is not good service on want of due process grounds. Although developed in a case to which the Hague Convention was inapplicable,[76] the point has been recognized, though held unjustified on the facts, in a Convention case.[77] The relevance in this context of the Summary of the document to be served under the Convention system appears not to have been addressed.

If a Central Authority considers that a request for service does not fall within the Convention it may reject it.[78] Otherwise, rejection may only be on the ground of infringement of 'sovereignty or security'; neither a claim to exclusive jurisdiction by the state of destination over the subject-matter with which the document deals, nor the fact that no cause of action would exist under the law of that state is a proper ground for rejection.[79] In practice rejection of requests is very rare; examples reported to the 1977 Special Commission of the Hague Conference included attempts to serve documents on the monarch of the state of destination and to bring proceedings against judges or police chiefs.[80]

A more frequent cause for the return of documents unserved is the expiry

---

[73] *AetD* (14), vol. 4, p. 384.

[74] For cases in which service was held bad for failure to observe the German requirement, see *Vorhees* v. *Fischer & Krecke G.m.b.H.* 697 F. 2d 574 (4th Circ., 1983); *Harris* v. *Browning-Ferris Industries Chemical Services Inc.* 100 F.R.D. 775 (M.D.La., 1984); *Cipolla* v. *Picard Porsche Audi Inc.* 496 A. 2d 130 (R.I., 1985); *Brown* v. *Bellaplast Maschinenbau* 104 R.F.D. 585 (E.D.Pa., 1985); *O'Brien* v. *Bayer A. G.* (D. C.Kan., 1986) (unreported); *Hastings* v. *Graphics Systems Division* (D. C.Kan., 1987) (unreported). In many of these cases service was also bad because it was effected by mail rather than via the Central Authority system.

[75] See also Arrondissementsrechtbank Breda, 21 Apr. 1981 (Asser 3/136) (no translation requirements for service in Turkey).

[76] *Julen* v. *Larsen* 25 Cal. App. 3d 325 (1972).

[77] *Shoei Kako Co. Ltd.* v. *Superior Court for the City and County of San Fransisco* 109 Cal. Rptr. 402 (Cal. App., 1973) (where the Japanese defendant familiar with English).

[78] Convention, Art. 4.   [79] Ibid., Art. 13.

[80] *AetD* (14), vol. 4, p. 383.

of the time-limit, to which attention is specifically drawn by an entry in the Summary of the Document to be Served. This may be given by reference to time elapsing after the date of issue of the document, and it is quite possible for the time-limit to be passed before the document can be served or even before it is received by the Central Authority. The better practice in such cases is to attempt service even after the stated time-limit: a trial or other procedural step is unlikely to follow immediately after the expiry of the time-limit, so belated service may still give the defendant a useful opportunity to intervene; and under Article 15[81] a six-month waiting period is often imposed before proceedings can be taken to the stage of a default judgment.

The Central Authority system has many advantages, but it cannot of course ensure effective or speedy service. In the Californian case of *Quaranta v. Merlini*,[82] three attempts were made to serve documents on a defendant in Italy, trying three different addresses and two different names; on each occasion the defendant could not be located or had already moved on. Even between New York and England, with no possible language problems to cause difficulty, it took in one case more than 180 days to effect service in London through the English subsidiary authority.[83]

OTHER PERMITTED MODES OF SERVICE

Although the system of Central Authorities is the primary mode under the Convention, other modes of service are permitted, subject to a number of provisos. These are as follows:

(i) *Service by diplomatic or consular agents* directly on the addressee, without the use of any compulsion. Any Contracting State may declare its opposition in this mode of service unless the document is to be served upon a national of the state of origin.[84] Many countries, mainly those in the civil law tradition, have made this declaration, including Belgium, Czechoslovakia, Egypt, France, Germany, Luxembourg, Norway, Portugal, Seychelles, and Turkey (but not Italy); accordingly an attempt to serve process via a United States Vice-Consul in the German Federal Republic has been held to be ineffective[85] and the Netherlands Ministry of External Affairs was held to have acted properly when it refused to accept a document intended for service via the diplomatic channel on a defendant in France.[86]

(ii) *The indirect consular channel*. This mode is carried forward from the 1954 Convention, and it is expressly provided that 'if exceptional circumstances so require' diplomatic channels may be used for the same purpose.[87] Contracting States are to designate the authorities which consuls may approach.[88] Not

---

[81] See below, pp. 29–31.   [82] 237 Cal. Rptr. 19 (Cal. App., 1987).
[83] *I.T.E.L. Container International Corpn.* v. *Atlanttrafik Express Service Ltd.* 686 F. Supp. 438 (S.D.N.Y., 1988).   [84] Convention, Arts. 8, 21(2)(*a*).
[85] *Dr Ing. H.C.F. Porsche A.G.* v. *Superior Court for the County of Sacramento* 177 Cal. Rptr. 155 (App., 1981).
[86] Gerechtshof Den Bosch, 19 Nov. 1980, N.J. 1982, 416 (Asser 3/138).
[87] Convention, Art. 9.   [88] Ibid., Art. 21(1)(*c*).

all have done so; most have designated the Central Authority (including in the case of the United Kingdom the subsidiary authorities in each part of the UK), but others have specified the president or registrar of or public prosecutor attached to a local court within whose area the addressee is to be found.

(iii) *The postal channel*. The convention speaks of 'the freedom to send judicial documents, by postal channels, directly to persons abroad',[89] but makes it clear that this is subject to any objection by the state of destination.[90] A few Contracting States have indicated their objection (Czechoslovakia, Egypt, Germany,[91] Norway,[92] and Turkey; Luxembourg has withdrawn its original objection). It is of course difficult to 'police' this objection, and there is a certain ambivalence in the attitude of some countries; recognizing the usefulness of postal service, they welcome it as a supplementary method designed to back up the 'official' service effected in other ways, but are unhappy to see the postal channel treated as appropriate or sufficient in itself.[93] It is unfortunate that the United States Federal Rules of Civil Procedure, while expressly authorizing service in a manner prescribed by the law of the foreign country,[94] contains no provision corresponding to that in the English Rules of the Supreme Court that nothing in the Rules authorizes or requires the doing in a foreign country of anything contrary to the law of that country;[95] the issue is referred to merely in the official commentary of the Advisory Committee and then only as affecting the chances of the recognition and enforcement in the foreign country of a judgment obtained in the United States.

The language of Article 10(*a*), which authorizes the use of the postal channel, has been closely examined in United States courts. It seems to have been assumed throughout the discussions leading up to the signature of the Convention that the use of the postal channel was indeed a mode of service, of *notification*. The text has remained substantially unchanged since the original 1896 Convention which spoke of '*la faculté d'addresser directement, par la voie de la poste, des actes aux intéressés se trouvant à l'étranger*'.[96] Such conduct would clearly be a form of 'delivery' rather than the formal service effected by the authorities of the state of destination, but there seems to be nothing in the various Hague Conventions to suggest that the postal channel was any less valid than any other permitted mode.

---

[89] Convention, Art. 10(*a*).   [90] Ibid., Arts. 10, 21(2)(*a*).
[91] A fact which is overlooked by practitioners with some frequency. See, e.g., *Cintron* v. *W. & D. Machinery Co. Inc.* 440 A. 2d 76 (N.J. Super., 1981); *Dr Ing. H.C.F. Porsche A.G.* v. *Superior Court for County of Sacramento* 177 Cal. Rptr. 155 (Cal. App., 1981); *Vorhees* v. *Fischer & Krecke G.m.b.H.* 697 F. 2d 574 (4th Cir, 1983); *Harris* v. *Browning-Ferris Industries Chemical Services Inc.* 100 F.R.D. 775 (M.D.La., 1984); *Lyman Steel Corpn.* v. *Ferrostaal Metals Corpn.* 747 F. Supp. 389 (N.D.Ohio, 1990).   [92] See *Jenco* v. *Martech International* (E.D.La., 1987) (unreported).
[93] Cf. *AetD* (14), vol. 4, p. 387. See also *Frankel* v. *Kaufman* (1976) 30 P.D. 449 (Sup. Ct. of Israel) (Asser 3/137) (service by post valid in Israel).
[94] F.R.C.P., r. 4(i)(1)(A).   [95] R.S.C. Ord. 11, r. 5(2); see p. 53.
[96] 1896 Convention, Art. 6(1).

However, a number of United States courts have considered cases in which service has been effected by registered mail upon defendants in Japan, a state which has objected to the other modes of service listed in Article 10 but *not* to the use of the postal channel. Some of those courts have seized upon the use of the word 'send' in Article 10(*a*), as opposed to 'serve'; although this distinction could be explained by reference to civil law ideas of formal service as opposed to informal delivery, these courts have concluded that Article 10(*a*) does *not* allow effective 'service' in Japan.[97] This reasoning has also been applied to service in Italy (which has objected to none of the methods listed in Article 10), with the assertion that Article 10(*c*) does not authorize a separate method of service.[98] It is submitted that these conclusions are wholly unjustified; they have been rejected by other United States courts[99] and it is difficult to see what purpose would be served by the inclusion of Article 10(*a*) in a convention on service of process if that was not its subject-matter. The fact, much relied on in some more recent cases in the *Ormandy* line, that service by mail is not allowed in domestic Japanese cases cannot be relevant; Japan could have objected to Article 10(*a*) but chose not to do so.[100]

Although the contrary has been argued, it is clear that there are no

---

[97] *Ormandy* v. *Lynn* 472 N.Y.S. 2d 275 (N.Y. Sup. Ct., 1984); *Reynolds* v. *Koh* 490 N.Y.S. 2d 295 (App. Div., 1985); *Mommsen* v. *The Toro Co.* 108 F.R.D. 444 (S.D. Iowa, 1985); *Pochop* v. *Toyota Motor Corpn.* 111 F.R.D. 464 (S.D. Miss., 1986); *Cooper* v. *Makita USA Inc.* 117 F.R.D. 16 (D.C. Maine, 1987); *Suzuki Motor Co. Ltd.* v. *Superior Court of San Bernardino County* 249 Cal. Rptr. 376 (Cal. App., 1988); *Arthur* v. *Nissei A.S.B. Co.* (D.C. Kan., 1988); Bankston v. *Toyota Motor Corpn.* 889 F. 2d. 172 (8th Cir., 1989); *Wasden* v. *Yamaha Motor Co. Ltd.* 131 F.R.D. 206 (M.D.Fla., 1990); *Fleming* v. *Yamaha Motor Corpn. USA* (W.D.Va, 1991). See E. C. Routh, 'Litigation between Japanese and American Parties' in J. Hailey (ed.), *Current Legal Aspects of Doing Business in Japan* at pp. 190–1: 'if this particular provision allowed one to circumvent the [Central Authority] procedure [which the author describes as cumbersome and involved] by simply sending something through the mail, the vast bulk of the Convention would be useless'.

[98] *Hantover Inc.* v. *Omet S.N.C.* 688 F. Supp. 1377 (W.D.Mo., 1988).

[99] *Shoei Kako Co. Ltd.* v. *Superior Court for City and County of San Francisco* 109 Cal. Rptr. 402 (Cal. App., 1973); *Weight* v. *Kawasaki Heavy Industries Ltd.* 597 F. Supp. 1082 (E.D.Va., 1984); *Chrysler Corpn.* v. *General Motors Corpn.* 589 F. Supp. 1182 (D.C. Dist. Col., 1984); *Zisman* v. *Sieger* 106 F.R.D. 194 (N.D.Ill., 1985); *Lemme* v. *Wine of Japan Import Inc.* 631 F. Supp. 456 (E.D.N.Y., 1986); *Sandoval* v. *Honda Motor Co. Ltd.* 527 A. 2d 564 (Pa., 1987); *Rissew* v. *Yamaha Motor Co. Ltd.* 515 N.Y.S. 2d 252 (App. Div., 1987); *Newport Components Inc.* v. *N.E.C. Home Electronics (USA) Inc.* 671 F. Supp. 1525 (C.D. Cal., 1987); *Smith* v. *Daninichi Kinzoku Kogyu Co. Ltd.* 680 F. Supp. 847 (W.D. Tex., 1988); *Re All Terrain Vehicles Litigation* (E.D.Pa., 1989); *Hayes* v. *Evergo Telephone Co. Ltd.* 397 S.E.2d 325 (N.C. App., 1990); *Chowaniec* v. *Heyl Truck Lines* (N.D.Ill., 1991). See also *Ackermann* v. *Levine* 788 F 2d 830 (2nd Cir., 1986) supporting this line of cases in the context of service by mail in the United States by a German consul; and also Ristau, *International Judicial Assistance*, vol. 1, para. 4–28, supporting this line of cases but on the ground that 'send' in Art. 10(*a*) represents 'careless drafting'.

[100] This was emphasized in a formal statement made by the Japanese delegation to the 1989 Special Commission to the Hague Conference: 'Japan has not declared that it objects to the sending of judicial documents, by postal channels, directly to persons abroad. . . . Japan . . . has made it clear that no objection to the use of postal channels . . . does not necessarily imply that sending by such a method is considered valid service in Japan; it merely indicates that Japan does not consider it an infringement of its sovereign power.'

translation requirements when Article 10(*a*) (or, indeed, any part of Article 10) is relied upon.[101]

(iv) Subject again to any objection by the state of destination, the Convention recognizes a mode of service *from official to official*. The text speaks of:

the freedom of judicial officers [*officiers ministériels* in the French text], officials or other competent persons of the State of origin to effect service of judicial documents directly through the judicial officers, officials or other competent persons of the State of destination.[102]

At first sight, the inclusion of this mode is puzzling; it seems so clearly inferior to the system of Central Authorities. In practice, however, it enables those countries which have the institution of *huissier* to allow direct communication from *huissier* to *huissier*.[103] It has little relevance in other countries, though a few (e.g. Denmark and Norway) have recorded a formal objection, and it appears to have been used in one case for communication from a US attorney to a French *huissier*.[104] The United Kingdom's objection limits the scope of this mode, in effect, to direct communication from a foreign judicial officer to one of the designated central or subsidiary authorities in the United Kingdom.

(v) Subject to the same rights of objection, '*any person interested in a judicial proceeding*' may effect service directly through the judicial officers, officials or other competent persons of the State of destination.[105] Little practical use seems to be made of this mode of service in the sense in which it was drafted, which envisaged an approach by a party directly to a competent local court official, for example, in the state of destination. Because English solicitors have always been regarded as 'competent persons' in this and similar contexts, the familiar common law practice of effecting service via a solicitor in the state of destination is in fact covered by this provision, but it is very doubtful if this strikes the consciousness of anyone concerned in the operation.[106]

BILATERAL ARRANGEMENTS

The preliminary draft of the Convention contained a provision which would enable two Contracting States to permit 'direct communication between their respective authorities'. This picked up language used in earlier Hague

---

[101] Paris C.A., 6 Apr. 1979, J.T. 1980, 156 (Asser 3/5); Oberlandesgericht Hamm, 16 Mar. 1981 (2 U 182/80) (Asser 3/136); *Weight* v. *Kawasaki Heavy Industries Ltd.* 597 F. Supp. 1082 (E.D.Va., 1984); *Sandoval* v. *Honda Motor Co. Ltd.* 527 A. 2d 564 (Pa., 1987).

[102] Convention, Art. 10(*b*). Cf. the Annexed Protocol to the Brussels convention on jurisdiction and the enforcement of judgments in civil and commercial matters, 1968, Art. IV, which speaks of service via 'appropriate public officers' in the two states concerned.

[103] See, e.g., Ghent C.A., 5 Oct. 1978 (Asser 2/169) (Belgium and Netherlands).

[104] *Tamari* v. *Bache & Co. (Lebanon) S.A.L.* 431 F. Supp. 1226 (N.D.Ill, 1977) (affd. on other points, 565 F. 2d 1194 (7th Cir., 1977)).   [105] Convention, Arts. 10(*c*), 21(2)(*a*).

[106] Cf. *Tax Lease Underwriters Inc.* v. *Blackwall Green Ltd.* 106 F.R.D. 595 (E.D.Mo., 1985); *Parsons* v. *Banl Leumi Le-Israel B.M.* 565 So. 2d 20 (Ala., 1990).

Conventions;[107] given the establishment of the Central Authority system, this provision seemed to have little point, as the Rapporteur himself admitted.[108] It was none the less retained in the final text, as Article 11, and extended to include any other channel of transmission not included in the earlier Articles. The Rapporteur was notably unenthusiastic about this text *'que nous n'estimons pas très heureux'*;[109] its effect appears to be that a Contracting State can enter an objection to the modes of service provided for in Article 10 (which would otherwise be available in respect of all Contracting States) but allow their use in respect of particular, and perhaps especially neighbouring, states. For example, although France objects to the use of the postal channel, an exception exists in favour of documents emanating from Luxembourg[110] but it has to be admitted that as this arrangement is the subject of a bilateral convention it is actually saved by provisions in the General Clauses of the 1965 Convention, and does not attract Article 11.[111]

Safeguards

In the broadest sense, the Convention is about the passing of information, something which can be of value both to the giver and to the receiver of the information. However, it is more realistic to regard the Convention as primarily about the service of process which is in turn an essential step in the conduct of proceedings designed to secure the interests of the plaintiff. So the Convention's main provisions operate to further the interests of plaintiffs rather than those of defendants. The authors of the Convention perceived the need for some balancing provision, some safeguards for defendants, and Articles 15 and 16 contain carefully constructed guarantees which have been described as the keystone of the text.[112]

Article 15 contains in effect two alternative sets of rules. The first reads as follows:

Where a writ of summons or an equivalent document[113] had to be transmitted abroad for the purpose of service, under the provisions of the present Convention, and the defendant has not appeared, judgment shall not be given until it is established that:

(a) the document[114] was served by a method prescribed by the internal law of the State addressed for the service of documents in domestic actions upon persons who are within its territory, or

(b) the document was actually delivered to the defendant or to his residence by another method provided for by this Convention,

and that in either of these cases the service or the delivery was effected in sufficient time to enable the defendant to defend.[115]

---

[107] See 1954 Convention, Art. 1(4).   [108] *AetD (10)*, vol. 3, p. 114.
[109] Ibid., p. 374.   [110] Déclaration of 14 Mar. 1884, Art. 2.
[111] See Convention, Arts. 22–5; Art. 25 catches the example in the text.
[112] *AetD (10)*, vol. 3, p. 92 (the Rapporteur, writing of the equivalent text in the preliminary draft).   [113] e.g., notice of an appeal.
[114] i.e., in its original language, not merely a translation: Arrondissementsrechtbank Amsterdam, 11 May 1983, NIPR 1984, 131.   [115] Convention, Art. 15(1).

Commenting on these provisions in a case in which, through no fault of the plaintiff, process had failed to reach a defendant in France until some two months after the leaving date, a Dutch court said that 'the Convention subordinates the interests of plaintiffs in enforcing their rights as quickly as possible against foreign defendants to the latter's interest in having an opportunity of defending themselves'.[116]

It will be noted that Article 15(1)(*b*) is satisfied if the document is actually delivered to the defendant *or to his residence*. It is sufficient if the document is, for example, handed to a part-time cleaner employed by the defendant in his home.[117]

If the matters set out in Article 15(1) are not established, the court will normally adjourn to allow either the gathering of further evidence or the making of fresh attempts to effect service.[118] In some countries, however, that is not the end of the matter. The Convention, largely as a result of the efforts of the French delegation which sought some *quid pro quo* for surrendering the system of *notification au parquet*, allows individual Contracting States to opt for rules which create, in effect, a presumption in favour of a diligent plaintiff:

Each contracting State shall be free to declare that the judge, notwithstanding the provisions of the first paragraph of this article, may give judgment even if no certificate of service or delivery has been received, if all the following conditions are fulfilled:

    (*a*) the document was transmitted by one of the methods provided for in this Convention,

    (*b*) a period of time of not less than six months, considered adequate by the judge in the particular case, has elapsed since the date of the transmission of the documents,

    (*c*) no certificate of any kind has been received, even though every reasonable effort has been made to obtain it through the competent authorities of the State addressed.[119]

In the event, this second option was not chosen by the French Government, but has been taken by a majority of Contracting States.[120] Practice under this option can be seen in a number of Netherlands decisions. In a divorce case, a Dutchwoman was unable to prove actual service of process on her husband in Great Britain, so by virtue of Article 15(1) judgment could not be given in the matter; the court, however, was prepared to give judgment in default under Article 15(2), the Netherlands having made the necessary declaration, once the petitioner could satisfy it as to the items listed in that

---

[116] Arrondissementsrechtbank Breda, 16 May 1978 (Asser 2/172).

[117] *Gould Entertainment Corpn.* v. *Bodo* 107 F.R.D. 308 (S.D.N.Y., 1985).

[118] See the cases collected at Asser 2/171–2 and the decision of the Hoge Raad, 1 July 1982, N.J. 1983, 781 (Asser 3/140).   [119] Ibid., Art. 15(2).

[120] Belgium, Botswana, Czechoslovakia, Denmark, Japan, Luxembourg, Malawi, Netherlands, Norway, Portugal, Seychelles, United Kingdom (including overseas territories to which the Convention has been extended), and the United States.

provision.[121] In a later case in which service had been attempted in Belgium, the Belgian Central Authority certified that service had proved impossible, the defendant not having been found at the address given. The Hoge Raad, treating this as a case within the Convention and not one in which the defendant's address was unknown,[122] ordered that the plaintiff might publish a notice in a Belgian daily paper with a view to obtaining judgment under Article 15(2).[123]

Whichever set of rules has been adopted, nothing in Article 15 prevents a court in the state of origin from taking, in case of urgency, any provisional or protective measures.[124]

A further protection for defendants is contained in Article 16 which contains provisions safeguarding the position of a defendant against whom judgment in default has been entered:

When a writ of summons or an equivalent document had to be transmitted abroad for the purpose of service, under the provisions of the present Convention, and a judgment has been entered against a defendant who has not appeared, the judge shall have the power to relieve the defendant from the effects of the expiration of the time for appeal from the judgment if the following conditions are fulfilled -

(*a*) the defendant, without any fault on his part, did not have knowledge of the document in sufficient time to defend, or knowledge of the judgment in sufficient time to appeal, and

(*b*) the defendant has disclosed a *prima facie* defence to the action on the merits.

An application for relief may be filed only within a reasonable time after the defendant has knowledge of the judgment.[125]

However, a Contracting State is entitled to declare that an application must be filed within a stated period from the date of entry of the judgment, a period which must not be less than one year.[126] Most Contracting States have made such a declaration, and all but one[127] of declarant States have specified a one-year time limit.[128] Article 16 is expressly declared not to apply to judgments concerning status or capacity of persons, fields in which certainty is essential.[129]

EXTRA-JUDICIAL DOCUMENTS

Chapter II of the Convention, consisting solely of the brief Article 17, applies the provisions of the Convention to extra-judicial documents 'emanating

---

[121] Arrondissementsrechtbank Alkmaar, 3 Feb. 1977 (Asser 2/171).

[122] Excluded by Art. 1(2).

[123] Hoge Raad, 25 Nov. 1977, 1978 NJ 313 (Asser 2/172). See also Hoge Raad, 1 May 1981, RvdW 1981, 71 (Asser 3/136); Cour de cassation, 16 Dec. 1980 (Asser 3/141) (see Droz (1981) Rev.crit.d.i.p. 714) (six month delay not observed).

[124] Convention, Art. 15(3).   [125] Ibid., Art. 16(1)(2).

[126] Ibid., Art. 16(3).   [127] Norway, which specifies three years.

[128] Belgium, Denmark, France, Israel, Luxembourg, Netherlands, Portugal, Seychelles, Turkey, the United Kingdom (in respect of Scotland only), and the United States.

[129] Art. 16(4).

from authorities and judicial officers of a Contracting State'. The cited words are important. Without them the phrase 'extra-judicial documents' would appear almost unlimited in scope, while its French equivalent *'actes extra-judiciares'* has been given, at some times and in some jurisdictions, a narrow and technical meaning.[130] The Convention text emphasizes the source of the document, and the capacity in which the person concerned is acting; a notary may be acting as a public officer or as the agent of a private party, and only in the former case will the Convention apply to documents issued by him.[131]

The discussions at the Special Commission held in 1977 to review the working of the Convention revealed that 'a great number' of extra-judicial documents were in fact sent under the Convention.[132] Examples included demands for payment, notices to quit, protests in connection with bills of exchange, and written consents to adoption or to marriage. In a civil law context these documents would have an 'official' quality, but many would in a common law system emanate from private persons. The Special Commission 'encouraged the Central Authorities to serve extrajudicial documents not emanating from an authority or from a judicial officer if these documents were of a type which normally would call for the intervention of an authority in their countries',[133] a striking example of the generous approach taken in operating this Convention.

Costs

The general principle as to the cost of effecting service is that the authorities of the state of destination seek no reimbursement of any costs they incur. This is expressed in Article 12 of the Convention which is an adaptation to meet the new range of modes of service of corresponding provisions in the 1954 Convention.[134] However, the applicant must pay or reimburse costs occasioned by the use of the services of a judicial officer (*officier ministériel*) or of a person competent under the law of the state of destination or by the use of a particular method of service.

These provisions are rather awkwardly drafted as a result of the need to accommodate both the use of the system of Central Authorities and the other permitted modes of transmission. No attempt is made in the Convention to prescribe details of procedure for the payment or reimbursement of costs. Some countries impose a fixed fee (e.g. the United States, where actual costs incurred by US Marshals can vary enormously depending on travel distances involved), others seek to recover actual charges levied by, e.g. a *huissier*, and others will in practice make no charge, especially where the state of origin is known to operate a similar policy. 'Simple delivery' (*remise simple*) is always free of charge.[135]

---

[130] See *Harvard Research*, p. 47, for usage in different branches of French law.
[131] *AetD (10)*, vol. 3, p. 108.   [132] *AetD (14)*, vol. 4, p. 388.
[133] Ibid.   [134] Convention on Civil Procedure 1954, Art. 7.
[135] See *AetD (14)*, vol. 4, p. 385.

RELATIONSHIP WITH OTHER CONVENTIONS

Although the 1965 Convention was designed to replace the relevant Articles of the 1954 text,[136] supplementary agreements between parties to the earlier Convention are continued in respect of the new Convention unless the parties otherwise determine.[137] The Hague Convention does not derogate from other relevant Conventions to which Contracting States are, or become, parties[138] a provision of particular importance in a European context. Many Contracting States to the Hague Convention are also parties to the Brussels Convention on jurisdiction and the enforcement of judgments in civil and commercial matters of 1968, and the latter contains provisions dealing with the interrelationship of the two instruments.

Article 20 of the Brussels Convention provides that where a defendant domiciled in one Contracting State is sued in a court of another Contracting State the court shall stay the proceedings so long as it is not shown that the defendant has been able to receive the document instituting the proceedings or an equivalent document in sufficient time to enable him to arrange for his defence, or that all necessary steps have been taken to this end.[139] But these provisions are declared to be replaced by those of Article 15 of the Hague Convention[140] if the document instituting the proceedings or notice thereof was transmitted abroad in accordance with that Convention.[141]

Under the scheme of the Brussels Convention, a judgment given in one Contracting State is entitled, subject to certain conditions, to recognition and enforcement in the other Contracting States.[142] A default judgment must, however, not be recognized if the defendant was not duly served with the document which instituted the proceedings or with an equivalent document in sufficient time to enable him to arrange for his defence.[143] This plainly parallels the text dealing with the staying of proceedings, save that there is no reference to the alternative 'taking of all necessary steps'. The European Court of Justice has held that the court in the state in which enforcement is sought must examine for itself the requirements of Article 27(2) even if the court granting the judgment had considered similar issues in relation to Article 20.[144]

The effect of this in a Hague Convention case was examined in a later European Court case, *Pendy Plastic Products B.V.* v. *Pluspunkt Handelsgesellschaft m.b.H.*[145] Proceedings in a Dutch court were begun by a document transmitted under the Hague Convention to a local court in Germany which certified under Article 6 that it had not been possible to serve the document.

---

[136] Convention, Art. 22. [137] Ibid., Art. 24.
[138] Ibid., Art. 25. [139] Brussels Convention, Art. 20(2).
[140] See above, pp. 29–31. [141] Ibid., Art. 20(3).
[142] See Title III (Arts 25–49) of the Convention.
[143] Brussels Convention, Art. 27(2).
[144] Case 166/80 *Klomps* v. *Michel* [1982] 2 C.M.L.R. 773.
[145] Case 228/81, [1983] 1 C.M.L.R. 665.

The defendant had moved a few weeks before to another address in the same town, but this fact was not discovered at the time. The Dutch court, acting under Article 15(2) of the Hague Convention which the Netherlands Government had declared applicable,[146] issued a default judgment. It was satisfied that every reasonable effect had been made to obtain a certificate of service. When enforcement was sought in Germany, the Oberlandesgericht Düsseldorf, holding itself required to examine the matter for itself under Article 27(2) of the Brussels Convention, held that service had not been effected in sufficient time to allow the defendant to make a defence. After an appeal to the Bundesgerichtshof, the European Court of Justice affirmed that a fresh examination had to be made under Article 27(2), and the court in the state where enforcement was sought was not bound by the determination made under Article 15 of the Hague Convention.

The Relationship between the Convention and National Law

It is clear that where service is required to be effected in a Contracting State, the provisions of the convention, as given effect in national law or as a self-executing Treaty, will prevail over the general law as to service of process. So United States courts have declared invalid service which met the requirements of state law or of the Federal Rules of Civil Procedure but which did not meet the terms of the convention[147] and a Netherlands court has refused to grant *exequatur* to a Belgian judgment granted after service which complied with Belgian law but not the convention's requirements.[148] On the other hand, the Hague Convention deals with a limited issue, that of service abroad; it does not affect the rules as to the extent of the jurisdiction of the courts of a particular state,[149] the rules of the forum court as to which documents are required to be served,[150] nor the time-limits set for procedural steps under that law.[151]

Between these areas of relative clarity lies one of difficulty and controversy. It will be recalled that the convention's text is less than clear on the question of its obligatory nature;[152] it applies 'where there is occasion to transmit a . . . document for service abroad'.[153] On a strict reading, this leaves untouched those cases in which the procedural law of the forum recognizes some action within the jurisdiction as legally sufficient to constitute service on a

---

[146] See above, p. 30.
[147] See, e.g. *Vorhees* v. *Fischer & Krecke G.m.b.H.* 697 F. 2d 574 (4th Cir., 1983); *Kaduta* v. *Hosofai* 608 P. 2d 68 (Ariz. App., 1980); *Weight* v. *Kawasaki Heavy Industries Ltd.* 597 F. Supp. 1082 (E.D.Va., 1984); *Cipolla* v. *Picard Porsche Audi Inc.* 496 A. 2d 130 (R.I., 1985); *Hartley* v. *Wheatherford Crane Co.* (E.D.Pa., 1986) (unreported).
[148] Arrondissementsrechtbank Breda, 15 Oct. 1979 (Asser 2/173).
[149] *DeJames* v. *Magnificence Carriers Inc.* 654 F 2d 280 (3rd Cir., 1981).
[150] *Re* v. *Breezy Point Lumber Co.* 460 N.Y.S. 2d 264 (N.Y. Sup. Ct. 1983).
[151] Cour supérieure de justice, Luxembourg, 21 Jan. 1981 (Asser 3/134); see Droz, Rev. crit. d.i.p., 1981, 708.
[152] See above, p. 17.   [153] Art. 1(1).

defendant who is actually resident abroad. This would leave intact the procedure of *notification au parquet* to which the authors of the Convention took such exception, or even a device such as that once recognized in the English ecclesiastical courts of affixing citation of a foreign resident 'upon one of the columns of the Royal Exchange, or in front of some other well-known building, in a place of public resort, which merchants are in the daily habit of frequenting or passing by'.[154] Luxembourg and United States courts have addressed the matter, and the judgments reveal the reality of these fears.

The Luxembourg case concerned a notice of appeal from the decision of a lower court, required by the *lex fori* to be given within 15 days of the date of the judgment. Notice was given within that time-limit by '*exploit*' of a *huissier* acting for the appellant and a copy posted at the door of the courthouse. Another copy was sent to a Belgian *huissier* who delivered it to the Belgian respondent 20 days after the date of the judgment. The Court held that this amounted to good service in accordance with the Convention (read with a Belgium-Luxembourg agreement made under the 1954 Hague Convention) but also that service of the notice of appeal was validly completed by the posting of the notice as required by internal Luxembourg law.[155]

The Netherlands *Hoge Raad* (Supreme Court) considered a not dissimilar case in 1986, that of *Segers and Rufa B.V.* v. *Mabanaft G.m.b.H.*[156] For the purposes of proceedings before the appeal court in The Hague, the respondent had 'elected domicile' at the office of its attorney in that city. A summons relating to the further appeal to the *Hoge Raad* was served at that office in accordance with an amendment to the Netherlands Code of Civil Procedure introduced in 1985.[157] The *Hoge Raad* held that the point as to the cases in which there was 'occasion to transmit a . . . document for service abroad' was entirely left to the domestic law of the state of origin of the documents. On the other hand, given the importance The Netherlands attached to the Convention, the 1985 amendment was interpreted as not displacing the application of the Convention, and so the requirements of Article 15 had to be complied with.

The United States cases are in one sense less threatening to the policy of the Convention, in that typically they do involve the actual delivery of the relevant document rather than some notional equivalent such as publication at the courthouse door. But in another sense they raise a much more serious issue, one likely to arise in many jurisdictions whenever the defendant is not an individual but a corporation or some other form of association; and it will be recognized that a very great proportion of international litigation does involve corporate defendants. In this type of case, the nearest equivalent to

---

[154] Oughton's *Ordo Judiciorum* (1728); see the translation in Law, *Forms of Ecclesiastical Law*, 2nd ed., 1844, p. 93.

[155] Cour supérieure de justice, Luxembourg, 21 Jan. 1981 (Asser 3/134).

[156] (27 June 1986), N.J. 1986, 764.

[157] Code of Civil Procedure, Art. 407(5), introduced by a Law of 3 July 1985 (Stb 384).

direct personal service on an individual defendant would be service at the registered office or 'seat' of a company, or at the principal place of business of some other type of business association, on a senior executive of the company or association. Many jurisdictions have taken the view that to insist on such service would unfairly disadvantage potential plaintiffs, and have provided that where an enterprise based abroad does business within the jurisdiction service may be effected at some business address there, without the need to serve any document abroad. If there is *no* 'occasion to transmit a . . . document for service abroad', then the Convention does not apply.

This can be illustrated by reference to the provisions of English law. Where a company incorporated outside Great Britain establishes a place of business in Great Britain it must deliver to the Registrar of Companies a list of names and addresses of one or more persons resident in Great Britain and authorized to accept on the company's behalf service of process and any notices required to be served on it.[158] Service is sufficient if the document is addressed to a person named in that list and left at or sent by post to his listed address.[159] If no list has been registered, or the persons named have died, or ceased to reside in Great Britain, or refuse to accept service on the company's behalf or for any reason cannot be served, a document may be served on the company by leaving it at, or sending it by post to, any place of business established by the company in Great Britain.[160] For these purposes, a 'place of business' means some fixed place at which, for some period of time,[161] some part of the company's business has been carried out.[162] Those who act at the place of business must be doing so on the business of the company and not their own account; the crucial question has been said to be, 'Does the agent in carrying out the foreign corporation's business make a contract for the corporation, or does the agent in carrying out his own business, sell a contract for the foreign corporation?'.[163] The establishment of a locally-based subsidiary company will commonly be regarded by a foreign or multinational holding company as a sensible and effective way of carrying out the business of the latter company; but the English courts will see it differently. In law, the

---

[158] Companies Act 1985, s. 691(1)(*b*)(ii).

[159] Ibid., s. 695(1).

[160] Ibid., s. 695(2).

[161] See *Dunlop Pneumatic Tyre Co. Ltd.* v. *A.G. Cudell & Co.* [1902] 1 K.B. 342 (C.A.) (nine days at stand in exhibition hall sufficed).

[162] *South India Shipping Corpn. Ltd.* v. *Export-Import Bank of Korea* [1985] 1 W.L.R. 585 (C.A.) (representative office in London carrying out preliminary work in respect of decisions made abroad held a place of business).

[163] *Thames and Mersey Marine Insurance Co.* v. *Società di Navigazione a Vapore del Lloyd Austriaco* (1914) 111 L.T. 97 (C.A.) per Lord Wrenbury. See also *Compagnie Générale Trans-Atlantique* v. *Thomas Law & Co., La Bourgogne* [1899] P. 1 (C.A.), affd. [1899] A.C. 431; *Saccharin Corporation Ltd.* v. *Chemische Fabrik von Heyden A.G.* [1911] 2 K.B. 516 (C.A.); *Okura & Co. Ltd.* v. *Forsbacka Jernverks A/B* [1914] 1 K.B. 715 (C.A.); *Konstantinidis* v. *World Tankers Corpn. Inc., The World Harmony* [1967] P. 341; Dicey and Morris, *The Conflict of Laws* (11th edn., 1987), pp. 294–8.

subsidiary company is a distinct entity, regardless of the control exercised over it, and it will be doing its *own* business not that of its parent.[164]

Where the business association takes the form of a partnership, a writ or originating summons can be served on any one or more of the partners; at the principal place of business of the partnership within the jurisdiction on any person having at the time of service the control or management of the partnership business there; or by sending a copy of the document by post to the firm at that principal place of business.[165] It is irrelevant that the partners are foreign nationals and resident at the time of service outside the jurisdiction.

Even an individual carrying on business in England under a business name which is not his own name is within similar provisions. Service may be effected at his principal place of business in the jurisdiction, regardless of his current residence.[166] In respect of a particular contract, service may, with leave of the court, be effected on an agent residing or doing business within the jurisdiction on behalf of an oversea principal;[167] the style under which the agent does business is then immaterial, and the agent may be an individual or a body corporate (including in this context a subsidiary company of the oversea principal). A copy of the writ must be sent by post to the principal, but the effective service is that within the jurisdiction.

Many legal systems have procedures of this general type. It may be that a distinction can be drawn between two different groups of provisions. In one there is something which can almost be regarded as 'submission to service': the registration of an address for service, the express appointment of an agent, the 'election of domicile' at a lawyer's office. This element is lacking in another group of cases, where nothing turns on any prior act of the potential defendant but rather on the delivery of the document to the official of the forum state or its publication at some prescribed place. The practical significance of this distinction is that in the first group of cases there is a greater likelihood of the necessary information being passed rapidly to the defendant, and that will in turn meet the objective of the Convention's authors and also the standards set by 'due process' tests. But these distinctions and considerations were not expressly addressed in the Convention's negotiating process and so do not feature explicitly in its text.

THE *SCHLUNK* CASE

Against this background, there can be considered the case of *Volksvagenwerk A.G.* v. *Schlunk*,[168] something of a *cause célèbre*. The case arose out of a fatal road accident in Illinois, the plaintiff's parents having been killed as a result

---

[164] See on this aspect, J. J. Fawcett, 'Jurisdiction and Subsidiaries' [1985] J.B.L. 16 and 'A New Approach to Jurisdiction over Companies in Private International Law' (1988) 37 I.C.L.Q. 645.
[165] R.S.C. Ord. 81, r. 3.
[166] R.S.C., Ord. 81, r. 9.
[167] R.S.C. Ord. 10, r. 2.
[168] 486 US 694 (1988).

of a head-on collision between their Volkswagen Rabbit and another vehicle. Proceedings were commenced against Volkswagen of America (VWoA), a New Jersey corporation which did business in Illinois and had a registered address for service there. Subsequently the plaintiff sought to join the German parent company, Volkswagen AG (VWAG) as co-defendant, alleging design defects in the car. Service was effected in Illinois on VWoA 'as Agent for' VWAG. VWAG moved that service be quashed, arguing that VWoA was not its agent for service, and that an attempt to serve process on an agent in Illinois violated the Hague Convention. The Appellate Court of Illinois, affirming the decision at first instance, rejected both arguments,[169] holding that VWoA was agent by operation of law as an 'involuntary agent' under a well-established doctrine in the law of Illinois, and that the Convention was inapplicable to service effected within the borders of the United States.

Although this was not the first case in which this view had been taken,[170] it was the first in which an appellate court had squarely addressed the point.[171] It provoked a remarkably hostile response from foreign governments, and those of four Contracting States to the Convention addressed notes of protest to the United States Government. The German Government declared that the decision ignored the 'mandatory character' of the Convention, producing effects similar to those of *notification au parquet*. Similar protests were made by Japan, France, and the United Kingdom, the last-named making the additional point that the uniformity which was the hope of the authors of the Convention would be frustrated if it were subject to the inconsistencies between the service rules of fifty different States.[172]

The United States Supreme Court granted *certiorari*. In the various briefs prepared for the Supreme Court, the major argument surrounded the notion of 'service abroad'. VWAG argued that the case was one in which there *was* 'occasion to transmit a judicial document for service abroad', because VWAG, which was not present in Illinois, would need, and was expected, to answer the allegations made against it. Although 'service' was in one sense effected in Illinois the purpose of, and assumption behind, it was that the documents would be transmitted by VWoA to Germany for the attention of VWAG. This, it was argued, amounted to 'service abroad'; any other view would infringe the right of other Contracting States to object to certain modes of service, such as Germany's objection to the use of registered mail; would circumvent

---

[169] 503 N.E. 2d 1045 (Ill. App., 1986).

[170] See *Richardson* v. *Volkswagenwerk A.G.* 552 F. Supp. 73 (W.D. Mo., 1982); *Lamb* v. *Volks-wagenwerk A.G.* 104 F.R.D. 95 (S.D. Fla., 1985): 'There is nowhere among the provisions of the Hague Convention any indication that it is to control attempts to serve process on foreign corporations or agents of foreign corporations within the State of origin.' See also *A. J. McNulty & Co., Inc.* v. *Rocamat* 506 N.Y.S. 2d 393 (1986) decided a few weeks after *Schlunk*.

[171] The point was raised but not reached in *Ex p. Volkswagenwerk A.G.* 443 So. 2d 880 (Ala., 1983).

[172] See the *amicus curiae* brief filed by the United States in the Supreme Court proceedings.

the translation requirements existing under the Convention;[173] and would deprive defendants of the guarantees in Articles 15 and 16.[174]

The Illinois decision about 'involuntary agency' illustrated only one possible basis for an assertion of proper service; each of the States could develop its own alternatives to the Convention. The petitioner took the view that involuntary agency could not properly be distinguished either from *notification au parquet*, to which the authors of the Convention were clearly opposed, or from such devices as service upon a State official, typically the Secretary of State, permitted in various United States jurisdictions. In all these cases, the relevant legal provisions required there to be onward transmission of the documents to the defendant.

The respondents, supported by an *amicus* brief by the United States Solicitor General, rested on the argument that service was accomplished wholly within the United States. This was plainly the position under the procedural rules of the forum, Illinois. On this point, the Supreme Court fully accepted the respondents' position:

Service of process refers to a formal delivery of documents that is legally sufficient to charge the defendant with notice of a pending action. . . . The legal sufficiency of a formal delivery of documents must be measured against some standard. The Convention does not prescribe a standard, so we almost necessarily must refer to the internal law of the forum state.[175]

What are the implications of that for practices such as *notification au parquet* and service upon a Secretary of State? The respondents tried to distinguish the former on what it is submitted is the irrelevant ground that it operated in legal systems, such as the French, in which the criteria for establishing jurisdictional competence did not always guarantee a close connection between the defendant and the forum. The United States' *amicus* brief tried, unconvincingly, to demonstrate that both these forms of procedure should be regarded, and had been by the drafters of the Convention, as forms of 'service abroad'. If this argument has any substance, it lies in the fact that service on an involuntary agent attracts no legal as opposed to practical requirement that there be any supplemental transmission of information to the defendant abroad, whereas supplemental transmission of the actual documents served is required to be effected by the *huissier* initiating *notification au parquet* and by a Secretary of State on whom documents are served under the similar United States practice. The Supreme Court expressly declined to address the issue of *notification au parquet*, merely observing that whatever the negotiating history had to teach about that, it was silent on involuntary agency.[176] In so doing the Court gave evidence of an approach

---

[173] A point emphasized in the German Federal Republic's *amicus curiae* brief; the widespread use of English, the language of the documents in the *Schlunk* case, does not detract from the general force of this point.   [174] See above, pp. 29–31.

[175] 486 US 694 (1988), at p. 700.   [176] Ibid., at p. 704.

which views the Convention in the light of its treatment by American commentators and legislators, putting it in a United States, rather than an international, context.

Three members of the Supreme Court, Justices Brennan, Marshall and Blackmun, joined in a concurring opinion, rejecting the view of the majority that each forum had, in effect, complete freedom to decide when the Convention should control; it was 'implausible' that that represented the intention of the drafters of the Convention. The three Justices found that the Convention embodied a substantive standard, directed at the purpose of the Convention which was seen as being to ensure timely notice to the defendant. There was, in other words, an unarticulated 'due process' requirement in the Convention, against which the law of a forum state could be measured. On the particular facts of the case, service on a wholly owned, closely controlled subsidiary was reasonably calculated to secure timely notice to the parent company, and so to meet the United States version of due process.

Various factors have to be borne in mind in assessing the effects of the *Schlunk* decision. In terms of the effect on potential parties, an argument advanced by the petitioners was that the notion of 'involuntary agency' was an established part of the *lex fori*, and to disapply it in the case of foreign defendants would be to give such defendants an advantage denied to their domestic counterparts. There is clearly force in this 'equal treatment' argument, which was later deployed in defence of the *Schlunk* decision by the United States delegation at a Special Commission of the Hague Conference held in April 1989; but as between the United States and the German Federal Republic it is German plaintiffs who emerge at a disadvantage, for German law has no doctrine similar to that of involuntary agency of which they could make use.[177] The impact of the *Schlunk* decision on actual practice may well turn out to be quite limited, for the Court went out of its way to spell out the advantages of using the machinery of the Convention:

The Convention provides simple and certain means by which to serve process on a foreign national. Those who eschew its procedures risk discovering that the forum's internal law required transmittal of documents for service abroad, and that the Convention therefore provided the exclusive means of valid service. In addition, parties that comply with the Convention ultimately mey find it easier to enforce their judgments abroad.

The limitations on the *Schlunk* doctrine need to be borne in mind. It certainly did not establish that service on a subsidiary company was the equivalent of service on its parent; there has to be 'agency for the purpose of service' as that concept is understood in the *lex fori*. So in New York, the subsidiary company must be so dominated by its parent corporation that it acts

---

[177] Bundesgerichtshof, 24 Feb. 1972, 58 BGHZ 177. See the GFR Government's amicus brief to the Supreme Court in *Schlunk*.

as a 'mere department' of the parent.[178] In Virginia, however, it seems that the very fact that parent and subsidiary maintain separate, even if wholly formal, corporate identities prevents service on the subsidiary amounting to good service on the parent.[179] In appropriate cases, service on a United States parent may be held under the doctrine to be service on the foreign subsidiary.[180]

ASSESSMENT OF THE CONVENTION.

There is litle doubt that the Convention has not only produced an orderly framework within which the various forms of procedure can operate but has also, in the Central Authority system, produced a very successful and increasingly well-used mechanism. In the fiscal year 1987, the United States Central Authority received 5,433 requests for service,[181] and the German Federal Republic's Central Authorities reported increasing numbers of requests from United States plaintiffs, reaching 661 in the year 1986.[182] Reviews of the operation of the Convention held in 1977 and 1989 produced no demand for its revision. The hints in the *Schlunk* opinions that 'due process' requirements are implicit in the Convention show, perhaps, a hankering for a 'model law' approach, familiar enough to those whose legal experience is of a federal system, but not yet realisable between the diverse legal systems represented at The Hague. The Convention's strength is that it copes with their diversity and provides an effective mechanism acceptable to all.

(E) INTER-AMERICAN ARRANGEMENTS

Latin American lawyers are conscious of a strong regional tradition in private international law. One of its earliest expressions was the great *Congreso Sudamericano de Derecho Internacional Privado* held in Montevideo in 1888–9. One result of that Congress was the Convention on Civil Procedure of 11 January 1889, Article 9 of which read as follows:

Letters rogatory which have as their object the service of legal notices, the taking of testimony of witnesses, or the performance of any other judicial act, shall be complied with in any Contracting State provided such Letters meet the requirements of this Convention.[183]

Just over fifty years later a second Montevideo Congress produced a revised Convention, that on International Procedural Law of 19 March 1940.[184] To the existing text of what became Article 11 were added two further

---

[178] *Derso* v. *Volkswagen of America Inc.* 552 N.Y.S. 2d 1001 (A.D., 1990).
[179] *Fleming* v. *Yamaha Motor Corpn, USA* (W.D. Va., 1991).
[180] *Acapalon Corpn* v. *Ralston Purima Co.* (Mo. App., 1991).
[181] See US *amicus* brief in the *Schlunk* case, p. 4.
[182] For table, see the German Federal Republic's *amicus* brief, pp. 7–8.
[183] See *Harvard Research*, p. 147 (a different translation).
[184] See J. Irizarry y Puente, 'Treaties on Private International Law' (1943) 37 Am.J.Int.L. (Supp.) 95, 119.

sentences, one requiring that letters rogatory be translated into the language of the state of destination and the other dispensing with the requirement of legalization provided transmission was through the diplomatic (or, in their absence, consular) agents of the state of origin. Meanwhile the Bustamente Code of 1928 contained similar provisions, dealing additionally with the power of the judges issuing and receiving letters rogatory to determine questions as to the jurisdiction they were asked to exercise.[185]

It has been commented, not unfairly, that a reader from the common law tradition finds the sparse language of these texts almost unintelligible.[186] They take for granted that the service of process requires the involvement of State officials, the usual civil law approach; that international co-operation between officials of different states in matters of civil procedure is initiated by letters rogatory transmitted by the diplomatic channel; and that in these respects the service of documents is in exactly the same category as the taking of evidence abroad. For many years, courts in the United States failed to understand the Latin American approach; the failure was so fundamental that a plaintiff in a Latin American republic had no means of serving process on a defendant in the United States.

In 1919 a United States District Court held that foreign letters rogatory seeking the service of process could not be executed. The judgment in the case, *Re Letters Rogatory out of the First Civil Court of City of Mexico*,[187] is badly flawed but was followed almost without exception for half a century.[188] Judge Hand's refusal to comply with the request addressed to him in the *Mexico City* case rested on two grounds. The first was the narrow perception of letters rogatory as 'exclusively limited by understanding and in practice' to requests for the taking of evidence; their use in the context of service of process he described as 'novel', one requiring express statutory authority. The second was that, on theories of jurisdiction then prevailing in the United States, Mexico's claim to assert personal jurisdiction against a non-resident defendant was regarded as exorbitant; Judge Hand thought that he should not 'aid a foreign tribunal to acquire jurisdiction' in these circumstances, a phrase really quite inappropriate, for a civil law system would not regard the service of process as a basis for jurisdiction.

Practitioners gradually became aware of the extent of the problems created not only by this approach but also by the inability of any Latin American country to recognize a United States judgment given after service had been effected by post on a defendant resident in such a country. The pressure grew for some international action.

---

[185] See Code, Arts. 388–93; *Harvard Research*, p. 152.

[186] H. L. Jones, '*International Judicial Assistance*', (1953) 2 Am.J.Comp.L. 365, 367.

[187] 261 F. 652 (S.D.N.Y., 1919), See, to similar effect, *Matter of Romero* 107 N.Y.S. 621 (N.Y.Sup.Ct., 1907).

[188] For some variations in judicial practice see the (unreported) cases discussed in G. Everett, 'Letters Rogatory—Service of Summons in Foreign Action', (1944) 44 Col.L.R. 72.

THE HARVARD DRAFT CONVENTION

A Harvard University research project produced in 1939 a Draft Convention on Judicial Assistance, Part II of which dealt with service of documents abroad. The draft Articles draw on the earlier Hague Conventions and on the bilateral Conventions negotiated by the United Kingdom, but also incorporate provisions reflecting, somewhat naïvely, United States perceptions.

The Draft provides for the service of documents required for the purpose of a civil proceeding at the request of a tribunal (defined to include courts, and administrative agencies engaged in the exercise of judicial or quasi-judicial functions)[189] of the state of origin.[190] The request, addressed to a named tribunal or generally to 'any competent tribunal' in the state of destination, together with its accompanying documents, was to be translated into the language of that state.[191] A variety of modes of transmission are provided for: the diplomatic channel; communication to the ministry of justice or other relevant authority of the state of destination, or to a particular tribunal in that state, directly by the tribunal in the state of origin; such communication via a diplomatic or consular agent;[192] by a diplomatic or consular agent of the state of origin directly to a national of that state; by an agent appointed by the tribunal in the state of origin; by an agent appointed by a party to the proceedings.[193] Finally, Article 13 provided that nothing in the Convention was to be construed as preventing service 'by any method provided for by the law of the state of origin and not forbidden by the law of the other state, or by any method provided for in any agreement between the States concerned'.

Many of these provisions would be quite unacceptable to a civil law country. The explanatory commentary to Article 3, dealing with service by agents of the court or of the parties, observes that 'there is no cogent reason why States should be free to oppose service by such regularly established means as agents of a tribunal or a party where no compulsion is exercised, and where no political problem, such as is involved in the exercise of diplomatic or consular functions, is raised'.[194] This wholly fails to take into account the sensitivities of those in the civil law tradition who see service of process as implying on judicial sovereignty. Similarly, Article 13 is expressly[195] designed to allow service by post unless the law of the state of destination contains what the commentary describes as a 'positive prohibition' of such service, a requirement which is quite unrealistic in the context of the legal tradition of many countries which would actually take grave exception to such service.

So far as methods of service are concerned, Article 7 of the Draft Convention begins with the clear statement that 'in the execution of a request service

---

[189] Art. 1(*d*).
[190] Art. 2(1).
[191] Art 2(1)(3).
[192] These three modes are all contained in Art. 2(4).
[193] These modes are allowed by Art. 3.
[194] *Harvard Research*, p. 65.
[195] Ibid., pp. 64–5, 116.

shall be effected as nearly as practicable in the manner prescribed by the law
of the [state of destination] for analogous documents of local origin'. This is
however accompanied by a proviso, referring to the 'suggestions' as to the
time, place, and manner of service which may be included in the request.[196]
Despite the term 'suggestions', their observance is mandatory unless a particular manner of service suggested is 'forbidden' by a positive prohibition in
the law of the state of destination. Here again it is unrealistic to expect the
law of any state to list modes of service which are *not* allowed; the policy of
the authors of the draft that only a positive prohibition should 'stand in the
way of granting a request for service'[197] gives inadequate weight to the
interests of the state of destination.

Reference may be made to one other feature of the draft. Article 2(6) lists
grounds for refusal to comply with a request for service. The first ground is
that:

the service requested is intended to confer on the tribunal making the request jurisdiction over a person who by the law of the State of execution cannot be subjected to
such jurisdiction.

The commentary to this provision is remarkable.[198] Having stressed the
importance of reducing as far as possible the number of permissible reasons
for refusal, the authors refer to the cited ground, which they admit has no
precedent in international agreements on judicial assistance. It is 'intended to
permit the operation of the American rule' in the *Mexico City* case.[199] No
attempt is made to explore the practical effects of the rule.

Although based on research of lasting value, the draft Articles on service of
documents rest overmuch on United States perceptions and would not have
survived the sort of examination to which they would have been exposed at
an international diplomatic conference.

Further Inter-American discussion

Eventually, the Inter-American Council of Jurists, meeting at Rio de Janeiro in
1950, asked the Inter-American Juridical Committee to examine the matter.
Its report[200] suggested some principles which might provide a basis for
action. These principles[201] would accept both the formal approach of letters
rogatory and the informal approach of direct (and usually postal) service, but
would also note that no such service would be sufficient of itself to extend the
jurisdiction of the state of origin. The Hague Convention of 1965 reflects this
general approach and in later inter-American discussions the United States
pressed for the acceptance of that Convention as the basis for regional co-

---

[196] Art. 2(2).

[197] *Harvard Research*, p. 60.   [198] Ibid., p. 56.

[199] *Re Letters Rogatory out of the First Civil Court of City of Mexico* 261 F. 652 (S.D.N.Y. 1919), discussed above.

[200] Report on Uniformity of Legislation in International Co-operation in Judicial Procedures,
Sept. 1952.   [201] Reproduced at (1953) 2 Am.J.Comp.L. 368–70.

operation, but unavailingly. The absence of any authentic Spanish or Portuguese text of any of the Hague Conventions militates against their acceptance in Latin America (and is responsible in part for the limited number of South American states which are members of the Hague Conference), and the Latin American attachment to the Letters Rogatory procedure proved too strong to allow a more broadly based solution in that region. What was there seen as more desirable was clear international agreement on the operation of the letters rogatory procedure.

After a good deal of further debate in the various Inter-American bodies, the General Assembly of the Organization of American States resolved in 1971 to convene an Inter-American Specialized Conference on Private International Law (CIDIP from its Spanish title, *Conferencia Especializada Inter-Americana sobre Derecho Internacional Privado*). This produced six conventions, including the Inter-American Convention on Letters Rogatory signed in Panama on 30 January 1975.[202] This convention retained something of the laconic style of drafting of its Latin American predecessors, and like them applied in principle to both the service of documents and the taking of evidence. It found little favour in the United States, where there was however considerable interest in securing some workable arrangement. As a result, the United States delegation at the Second Inter-American Specialized Conference on Private International Law (CIDIP 2), held in Montevideo in 1979, secured the adoption of an Additional Protocol, limited to service of documents but containing a fuller treatment of that topic drawing inspiration from some aspects of the Hague Convention. Of the total of fourteen states now party to the Convention, half have ratified the Protocol.[203]

THE INTER-AMERICAN CONVENTION OF 1975.

The Convention was drafted by Committee II of CIDIP on the basis of a preliminary draft prepared by the Inter-American Judicial Committee in 1973.

Scope

The scope of the convention is indicated by Article 2: the convention applies to:

letters rogatory, issued in conjunction with proceedings in civil and commercial matters held before a judicial or other adjudicatory authority[204] of one of the States Parties to this Convention, that have as their purpose:

(a) The performance of procedural acts of a merely formal nature, such as service of process, summonses or subpoenas abroad;

---

[202] For text, see (1975) 14 I.L.M. 339.

[203] Parties to the Protocol are Argentina, Ecuador, Mexico, Paraguay, Peru, the United States, and Uruguay; parties only to the Convention are Chile, Costa Rica, El Salvador, Guatemala, Honduras, Panama and Venezuela.

[204] The original version of the English text spoke merely of 'the appropriate authority'; the language cited in the text was later substituted under the OAS 'slip' rule.

(*b*) The taking of evidence and the obtaining of information abroad, unless a reservation is made in this respect.

The drafting of this key Article leaves some questions unresolved. The limitation to 'civil and commercial matters' accords with the approach taken at The Hague,[205] and the phrase is not formally defined. However, Article 16 allows 'the States Parties' (and the use of the plural is puzzling, as the action contemplated seems to be by individual states, and will be effective in this context only insofar as the declarant state is the state of destination) to declare that the convention's provisions cover the execution of letters rogatory in criminal, labour, and 'contentious-administrative' cases. It is clear from the *travaux préparatoires*[206] that this declaration operates to 'extend' the assumed meaning of 'civil and commercial' which therefore must be taken to exclude all such cases. Only one state, Chile, has actually made a declaration under Article 16.

The reference in Article 2 to the judicial or other adjudicatory authority before which proceedings are held would seem, by a similar process of reasoning, not to cover all the courts and official tribunals of the state of origin. Article 16 allows extension to arbitrations and 'other matters within the jurisdiction of special courts'; it is not at all clear how this latter phrase is to be picked up in a declaration, as different states (of origin and of destination) may establish specialist courts for a variety of purposes, including adjudication on matters plainly civil or commercial in nature.

The limitation to procedural acts 'of a merely formal nature' seems to be explained, albeit indirectly, by the provision in Article 3 that the convention is not to apply to acts involving measures of compulsion.

Modes of transmission

The actual transmission of letters rogatory to the authority to which they are addressed is governed by Article 4 which allows six possible modes of transmission. These involve action by diplomatic or consular agents (presumably of the state of origin, though this is not made clear in the text), by the Central Authority designated for the purposes of the convention in either the state of origin or that of destination, by 'the interested parties', or 'through judicial channels'. This last phrase presumably means that action to transmit a letter rogatory is to be taken by the staff of the court of origin. The clarity of the phrase is not advanced by the inclusion in Article 7 of the statement that 'courts in border areas of States Parties' (meaning, presumably, areas close to a common frontier between states of origin and destination) 'may directly execute the letters rogatory contemplated in this Convention'. It appears from the context that this is not intended as a limitation on the use of 'judicial channels' but rather as a preliminary observation before a specific provision

---

[205] See pp. 18–19.
[206] See Report of Committee II, 25 Jan. 1975, CDIP/35, p. 5.

that in such border cases legalization is not required. Legalization is required in other cases unless the letters rogatory are transmitted through consular or diplomatic channels or through 'the' Central Authority (*semble* of the state of origin);[207] a letter rogatory legalized by a competent consular or diplomatic agent is 'presumed to be duly legalized in the State of origin'.[208] The drafting of these provisions, at least as they appear in the English text, is of very poor quality.

Documentation required

When transmitted, the letter must be accompanied by certain other documents, intended for delivery to the person on whom the process, summons or subpoena is to be served, and all must be translated into the official language of the state of destination.[209] The other required documents are:

(*a*) An authenticated copy of the complaint with its supporting documents, and of other exhibits or rulings that serve as the basis for the measure requested;

(*b*) Written information identifying the authority issuing the letter, indicating the time-limits allowed the person affected to act upon the request, and warning of the consequences of failure to do so;

(*c*) Where appropriate, information on the existence and address of the court-appointed defense counsel or of competent legal aid societies in the State of origin.[210]

Procedure for execution

The execution of letters rogatory is governed by the law of the state of destination, though special procedures or formalities requested by the issuing authority may be observed if to do so would not be contrary to that law.[211] An authority in the state of destination which finds that it lacks jurisdiction to execute the letter of request, for example because the defendant is not resident in its area, must forward 'the documents and antecedents of the case to the authority of the State [i.e. within the same state[212]] which has jurisdiction'.[213]

Costs and expenses

Article 12 of the Convention specifies that costs and other expenses must be borne by the interested parties. The state of destination is given a discretion (though the convention does not specify by which organ of the state the discretion is to be exercised) to execute a letter rogatory which does not indicate the person to be held responsible for the costs and expenses; the point here is that there is a discretion to *refuse* to execute letters in such

---

[207] Art. 6.

[208] Art. 5(*a*). See also Art. 18 which obliges States Parties to inform the General Secretariat of OAS as to their legal requirements as to the legalization and translation of letters rogatory.

[209] Arts. 5(*b*), 8, 18.   [210] Art. 8

[211] Art. 10.   [212] Cf. Report of Committee II, CIDIP/35, p. 9.

[213] Art. 11.

circumstances. In addition, the convention contains an express provision allowing a state of destination to refuse to execute a letter rogatory that is manifestly contrary to public policy (*ordre public*).[214]

Protection for defendants

The Inter-American Convention contains no material comparable to that on safeguards for defendants in Articles 15 and 16 of the Hague Convention. It does however provide expressly[215] that execution of letters rogatory does not imply ultimate recognition of the jurisdiction of the authority issuing the letter rogatory or a commitment to recognize or enforce any judgment.

Relationship to other instruments

Finally, three Articles of the Convention deal with other international arrangements which may be used. Article 13 allows the service of documents and the taking of evidence by consular and diplomatic agents in the state in which they are accredited, provided their acts are not contrary to the law of that state and involve no means of compulsion. Article 14 allows states which belong to 'economic integration systems', by which was meant groupings such as the Latin American Free Trade Association or the Andean Common Market, to agree upon 'special methods and procedures more expeditious than those provided for' in the convention. These could presumably include methods not involving the use of letters rogatory at all,[216] though given the legal traditions of the region such radicalism seems unlikely. Article 15 preserves the liberty of States Parties to apply existing or future bilateral or multilateral agreements as to letters rogatory, including of course the earlier Latin American instruments.

THE INTER-AMERICAN PROTOCOL OF 1979

The Protocol was prepared by Committee I of the Second Inter-American Specialized Conference on Private International Law, almost entirely on the basis of successive proposals from the United States' delegation. Although in form supplementary to the 1975 Convention, it is in truth a substantial revision of it, creating an alternative treaty régime.

Scope and Modes of Transmission

This is best illustrated by reference to Article 1 of the Protocol. This declares that the Protocol applies only to those procedural acts set forth in Article 2(*a*) of the Convention. This immediately excludes from the scope of the Protocol the whole area of taking evidence and obtaining information abroad; this area could be excluded by Reservation from the scope of the Convention, and is

---

[214] Art. 17.
[215] Art. 9.
[216] Cf. to the contrary, but without giving reasons, B.M. Carl, 'Service of Judicial Documents in Latin America' (1976) 53 Denver LJ 455, 462.

also the object of a distinct Inter-American Convention.[217] Remaining within the scope of the present instrument were only 'the performance of procedural acts of a merely formal nature, such as service of process, summonses or subpoenas abroad'.[218] These are redefined for the purposes of the Protocol as

procedural acts (pleadings, motions, orders and subpoenas) that are served and requests for information that are made by a judicial or administrative authority of a State Party to a judicial or administrative authority of another State Party and are transmitted by a letter rogatory from the Central Authority of the State of origin to the Central Authority of the State of destination.[219]

Not only does this clarify the nature of the authorities competent to issue and execute letters rogatory but it makes mandatory as between parties to the Protocol the use of Central Authorities both for the outward transmission and inward receipt of letters rogatory; that there is an obligation to designate a Central Authority, a matter not wholly clear in the text of the Convention, is specifically provided in Article 2 of the Protocol. The duties of the receiving Central Authority are set out in detail in Article 4. The understanding of the United States in drafting the Protocol was that while the United States would ratify the Convention as well as the Protocol, ratification of the latter alone not being permitted, this would create treaty obligations binding upon the United States only with other states which had ratified the Protocol and in accordance with its terms. It is submitted that this leaves in place the binding character of Articles 4 and 13 of the original Convention as to service of documents by accredited consular or diplomatic agents.[220]

Documentation

There are elaborate provisions in Articles 3 and 4 of the Protocol as to the appropriate documentation, and these provisions are very obviously inspired by provisions of the Hague Convention. In particular three forms are prescribed, which to minimize translation problems are required to be printed either in all four official languages of the Organization of American States (English, French, Portuguese, and Spanish) or at least in the languages of the states of origin and destination. The forms are of the Letter Rogatory itself, which follows the functional layout of the Hague 'Request' rather than the formal, almost supplicatory, style of a traditional letter rogatory; a statement of Essential Information for the Addressee, corresponding to the Hague 'Summary of the Document to be Served'; and a Certificate of execution or non-execution again on the model of the corresponding Hague document. Two copies, in addition to the originals, are to be supplied; one is for service, one for retention by the state of destination; one for return with the relevant Certificate to the Central Authority of the state of origin.

---

[217] i.e., the Inter-American Convention on the Taking of Evidence Abroad.
[218] Convention, Art. 2(*a*).　　　　　　　　[219] Protocol, Art. 1.
[220] See p. 46.

The translation requirements are considerably lightened. As the Report of Committee I observed,[221] 'One of the greatest obstacles to international judicial co-operation is the necessity of translating innumerable documents into the official language of the country of destination for each international procedural act, given the high cost of translation services.' Under the Protocol the only document which need be translated is the complaint or pleading that initiated the action in which the letter rogatory was issued. Attached documents and the actual rulings ordering that a letter rogatory be issued are to be supplied, but need not be translated. The precise scope of the translation requirements is not completely clear, especially in cases in which the letter rogatory is issued at some interlocutory stage; the specific motion there relevant surely should be translated, but the Protocol speaks only of the document which 'initiated the *action*'. The interpretation of this would appear to be within the competence of the state of origin, and it is to be hoped that an interpretation reflecting the realities of the position would always be adopted; what is important to the defendant is prompt access to the information he needs in order to judge how to respond to the current move by the other party.

Legalization is not required, as the Convention already provided for the exclusion of this requirement when transmission was through a Central Authority.[222]

Costs and expenses

The other area which is given detailed attention in the Protocol is that of responsibility for costs and expenses; the text comes close to adopting the principles used in the Hague Convention, but practice is rather different.

The relevant Article, Article 5, begins by declaring a new principle, that 'the processing of letters rogatory by the Central Authority of the State Party of destination and its judicial or administrative authorities shall be free of charge'. However, as the *travaux préparatoires* indicate, many countries in the Americas require the costs of judicial acts to be borne by the interested parties,[223] and the Protocol reflects this by allowing a state of destination to seek payment from the party seeking execution of the letter rogatory of charges payable under its local law. The Protocol makes detailed provision to cover the practicalities: each State Party must provide the OAS General Secretariat with a schedule of costs and expenses payable under its law, together with a statement of a fixed amount which it estimates will cover the sums due in a typical case.[224] The applicant party must either pay this latter amount by cheque in advance, or indicate in the letter rogatory form the person who is responsible in the state of destination for the payment of sums due. If the actual charges exceed the sum paid in advance, the letter rogatory is still to be executed and the balance claimed after the event.

[221] CIDIP-II/64.   [222] Convention, Art. 6.
[223] Report of Committee I, CIDIP-II/64, p. 6.   [224] Art. 6.

There would be obvious advantages for the parties, and probably a saving in administrative costs, were reciprocal waiver of charges between states to be adopted. This is not possible in some of the legal systems of the region, but Article 7 of the Protocol encourages moves in this direction wherever possible. A state may declare that, provided there is reciprocity, it will make no charge for the services necessary for executing letters rogatory or will accept in complete satisfaction of the cost of such services either the fixed amount mentioned above or some other amount.

(F) Asian–African Model Arrangements

The Asian–African Legal Consultative Committee adopted at its Seventh Session in 1965 a set of Model Rules for the Service of Judicial Process and the Recording of Evidence in Civil and Commercial Cases. This is a remarkably brief document, providing so far as service of documents is concerned for letters of request to be addressed by a diplomatic or consular officer of the requesting state to the competent authority of the requested state, and for the execution of any request the authenticity of which was not in doubt unless the requested state considered that this would be contrary to its public policy. The Model Rules did not prove influential in practice, but they did serve to establish a commitment on the part of the Committee to a comprehensive approach covering criminal as well as civil matters.

The question of a regional convention in this whole field was put on the agenda of the Committee in 1975 and detailed reports were considered at its Twentieth Session in 1979 and its Twenty-Second Session in 1981. The Committee's Secretariat reviewed the existing models, particularly the Hague and Inter-American instruments and an Agreement relating to Writs and Letters of Request adopted in 1952 by the Council of the League of Arab States,[225] but recommended a 'common integrated and comprehensive approach' which would cover civil and criminal matters, and both service and the taking of evidence. This proved too ambitious; the Twenty-Second Session favoured separate texts for civil and for criminal matters, and a subsequent Expert Group, meeting in New Delhi in 1982, decided that a model bilateral agreement in each of these areas was more appropriate than a draft convention.

After a further Expert Group had met, unusually for an Asian-African body, in The Hague with participation from the Permanent Bureau of the Hague Conference, the Arab League and the Commonwealth Secretariat,[226] a Model for Bilateral Agreement for the Service of Process and Taking of Evidence Abroad in Civil or Commercial Matters was adopted at the Twenty-Fifth Session of the Committee in 1986. Its text is clearly influenced by both the Hague Convention and the Inter-American instruments.

---

[225] This was signed in 1953 by Egypt, Lebanon, Jordan, Saudi Arabia, Syria, and Yemen.
[226] Represented *inter alios* by the present author.

Chapter I of the Model contains general provisions applying to both service of documents and the taking of evidence and adopting the system of transmission through central authorities (called 'Central Agencies' in this text) in both the state of origin and that of destination. The provisions as to service of process in Chapter II are in other respects very close to the Hague Convention's provisions, especially in relation to the prescribed forms of Request, Summary, and Certificate, and in the range of other modes of transmission, such as service by post or by direct communication between judicial or other personnel in the two states, which may be allowed in addition to the Central Agency channel.[227] There are no provisions corresponding to the 'guarantees' of Articles 15 and 16 of the Hague Convention, but there is a provision as to non-commitment to recognition of a judgment based on the Inter-American Convention.[228]

No information is available as to the extent to which this Model has been relied upon in international negotiations.

(G) English Practice

SERVICE OF ENGLISH PROCESS ABROAD

Service of English process abroad is governed by Order 11, rules 5 to 10, of the Rules of the Supreme Court. These rules deal with the requirements of English law as to the actual method of service and also set out the procedure for securing official assistance in the transmission of documents for service overseas.

A writ for service out of the jurisdiction is regarded as duly served in each of the following sets of circumstances:

(*a*) it is served personally on the defendant by the plaintiff or his agent;[229]

(*b*) where the defendant's solicitor indorses on the writ a statement that he accepts service of the writ on behalf of the defendant;[230]

(*c*) where, despite the fact that the writ has not been duly served on the defendant, he acknowledges service of it;[231]

(*d*) the writ, though not served personally on the defendant, is served on him in accordance with the law of the country in which service is effected;[232]

(*e*) it is served through the authorities of the foreign country or through British consular authorities in accordance with Order 11, rule 6, which is examined in more detail below, or (in the case of service on a foreign State itself) under Order 11, rule 7;[233]

---

[227] Art. 15 of the Model is virtually identical to Art. 10 of the Hague text.
[228] Model, Art. 3, following Inter-American Convention, Art. 9.
[229] R.S.C. Ord. 10, r. 1(1) applied by Ord. 11, r. 5(1).
[230] R.S.C. Ord. 10, r. 1(4) applied by Ord. 11, r. 5(1).
[231] R.S.C. Ord. 10, r. 1(5) applied by Ord., 11, r. 5(1); this is subject to proof to the contrary, and to Ord. 12, r. 7 (acknowledgement not to constitute waiver of certain irregularities).
[232] R.S.C. Ord. 11, r. 5(3)(*a*).   [233] R.S.C. Ord. 11, r. 5(3)(*b*).

(*f*) it is served in accordance with an order for substituted service made under Order 65, rule 4.[234]

This is subject to an overriding provision that nothing in the relevant Rule or in any order or direction of the court made by virtue of it authorizes or requires the doing of anything in a country in which service is to be effected which is contrary to the law of that country.[235]

The effect of this last provision fell to be considered in *Ferrarini S.p.A.* v. *Magnol Shipping Co. Inc., The Sky One.*[236] The English court had given leave for the service of a writ upon the president of a Panamanian shipping operation at a stated address in Lugano or elsewhere in Switzerland. It was personally served on the president at the Lugano address by an agent of the plaintiffs. The defendants successfully applied to the English court for this service to be set aside on the grounds that personal service by the agent of a foreign litigant without the approval of the Swiss authorities was a criminal offence under the Swiss Penal Code and could not be regarded as valid service, as no English court could authorize service which was contrary to the internal law of the country in which service was to be effected. The court recognized that it did have a discretion under the Rules of the Supreme Court to allow service to stand despite the failure to comply with the relevant Rules,[237] but declined to do so on the facts; it would take 'a very strong case', for example express representation by the defendant that the method of service adopted was lawful, before the discretion would be exercised. The court did, however, renew the validity of the writ for a period of four months, notwithstanding the expiry both of the writ and the limitation period, to allow alternative means of service to be used.

Methods of service other than those listed above may not be used. It will be noted that no reference has been made to service by post; the provisions in the Rules of the Supreme Court permitting the use of 'ordinary first-class post' or service by inserting the writ through the letter-box at the defendant's address[238] are not applied to service out of the jurisdiction. Service by post can be permitted in an order for substituted service. It may also be that such service would be regarded as valid on the ground that it amounted to service on the defendant in accordance with the law of the country in which service is effected.[239] The editors of the *Supreme Court Practice*[240] formerly suggested that postal service 'in pursuance of a convention' will also be valid, but it is difficult to identify any provision of the Rules of the Supreme Court which would support this proposition.

Official assistance is available in cases specified in Order 11, rule 6. Where the writ is to be served in a Hague Convention country the writ may be served under this rule through the Central Authority of that country or, if the

---

[234] As applied by R.S.C. Ord. 11, r. 5(1).
[235] R.S.C. Ord. 11, r. 5(2). [236] [1988] 1 Lloyd's Rep 238 (C.A.).
[237] R.S.C. Ord. 2, r. 1. [238] R.S.C. Ord. 10, r. 1(2).
[239] i.e. under R.S.C. Ord. 11, r. 5(3)(*a*). [240] 1988 edn., p. 92.

law of that country permits, through the judicial authorities of that country or through a British consular authority there.[241] Cases not falling within the Hague Convention fall into one of three categories.

(a) If service is to be effected in another part of the United Kingdom, the Isle of Man, the Channel Islands, the Republic of Ireland, a colony, or an independent Commonwealth country, official assistance is not available and service must be effected by the plaintiff or his agent;[242]

(b) If service is to be effected in a country with which the United Kingdom has a bilateral Civil Procedure Convention, the writ may be served through the judicial authorities of that country or through a British consular authority there (subject to any provision in the relevant Convention as to the nationality of persons who may be served, for example a restriction to persons of British nationality);[243]

(c) If service is to be effected in any other country, the writ may be served through the government of that country, if that government is willing to effect service, or through a British consular authority there (except where service through such an authority is contrary to the law of that country).[244]

In all cases, official assistance is optional; service by private means will always satisfy the English rules, provided nothing is done which is contrary to· the law of the state in which service is to be effected.[245] Where official assistance is sought, a translation of the writ into the official language of the state of destination is required (even in those cases where the Hague Convention imposes no such requirement), unless the writ is to be served by a British consular authority on a British subject and no relevant bilateral Convention imposes an express translation requirement.[246]

The relevant Rules of the Supreme Court governing the procedure for service of process abroad are drafted by reference to writs. They apply equally to originating summonses, notices of originating motions, and petitions, including originating summonses and notices of originating motions under the Arbitration Acts 1950 and 1979.[247] Equivalent provision is made in the County Court Rules.[248]

---

[241] R.S.C. Ord. 11, r. 6(2A).

[242] R.S.C. Ord. 11, r. 6(1).

[243] R.S.C. Ord. 11, r. 6(2).

[244] R.S.C. Ord. 11, r. 6(3). For some information about the attitude of different countries to service by British consular authorities, see *Supreme Court Practice* (1991 edn.), para. 11/6/3.

[245] *Ferrarini S.p.A.* v. *Magnol Shipping Co. Inc., The Sky One* [1988] 1 Lloyd's Rep. 238.

[246] For translations, their certification and procedure generally, see R.S.C. Ord. 11, r. 6(4)–(7). For the acceptability of certificates of service issued by British consuls, government and judicial authorities of foreign countries, or by a Hague Convention Central Authority as evidence of the facts stated, see Ord. 11, r. 5(5).

[247] R.S.C. Ord. 11, r. 9; Ord. 73, r. 7.

[248] C.C.R. 1981, Ord. 8, r. 8–10; and see R.S.C. Ord. 11, r. 10 for the role of the Senior Master in some cases.

Service of Foreign Process in England

Order 69 of the Rules of the Supreme Court contains a single set of provisions applying as to the service of foreign process in England. For Order 69 to apply the process must be in connection with 'civil or commercial proceedings[249] in a foreign court or tribunal'[250] and must have been received by the Senior Master with a written request for service from a consular or other authority in a convention country (which term includes countries with which the United Kingdom has a relevant bilateral Convention and countries party to the Hague Convention[251]) or from the Foreign Secretary (who would have been approached via diplomatic channels by the authorities of another state).[252] The request must be accompanied by an English translation, two copies of the process and, unless the foreign court or tribunal certifies that the person to be served understands the language of the process, two copies of an English translation of it.[253]

Actual service is effected on a corporation by using the usual English procedures; on an individual by a process server (in practice a county court bailiff appointed for this purpose[254]) leaving a copy of the process and a copy of the translation or the certificate, as the case may be, with the person to be served, or by inserting the documents through the letter-box at his address; or in accordance with an order for substituted service.[255]

In a straightforward case, no fees will be charged, but a provision is retained enabling the costs of effecting or attempting to effect service to be certified by a taxing master of the Supreme Court.[256] The United Kingdom's policy is to make charges only in difficult cases or where the foreign country concerned makes a disproportionate number of requests or itself imposes charges.

---

[249] *Not* 'matter', cf. pp. 18–19.

[250] R.S.C. Ord. 69, r. 2.

[251] R.S.C. Ord. 69, r. 1.

[252] R.S.C. Ord. 69, r. 2.

[253] R.S.C. Ord. 69, r. 3(1). In Hague Convention cases, the process is likely to come with a translation in any event.

[254] See R.S.C. Ord. 69, r. 4.

[255] R.S.C. Ord. 69, r. 3(2)–(5).

[256] R.S.C. Ord. 69, r. 5(6)(ii).

3

Taking of Evidence: National Practices

(A) Introduction

THE last chapter noted the differing approaches taken by legal systems in the common law and civil law traditions to the service of process. Those differences were important despite the fact that the actual concept of service of process is relatively straightforward. Legal systems may vary enormously in the types of civil claim they will entertain and in the conduct of the proceedings by which claims are adjudicated, but all but the most primitive of legal systems will know the idea of giving notice to the other party of the making of a claim or of the initiation of a significant step in the resulting proceedings.

Conceptual differences loom much larger in any discussion of international co-operation in the taking of evidence. The subject-matter is much more closely related to the actual business of judicial decision-making and so to the ideology and practice of particular systems of civil procedure. Those systems are almost infinitely variable, and merely to categorize a system as within the common law or civil law tradition would conceal important differences. All that can be done here is to identify some of the relevant variables, using what must inevitably be a broad brush in their description[1].

Some of the crucial variables are best identified by posing a single question, in some such form as, 'What happens at the eventual hearing of the case by the trial court?' One possible answer, which might be given where the relevant legal system remains close to the classical approach of the civil law tradition, would be along these lines: 'The court, having reviewed the written minutes containing the evidence as to the facts of the case, hears submissions on behalf of the parties as to the conclusions to be drawn in the light of the applicable law.' Another answer, characteristic of a system within the common law tradition, might be, 'The court hears oral evidence as to the facts from the parties or their witness or both, and then hears submissions on behalf of the parties as to the conclusions to be drawn in the light of the applicable law.'

The first answer describes a procedure in which the trial court deals, so far as the facts of the case are concerned, with *written* material, which will have been assembled and put into a particular form by one or more members of the court's personnel. The preparation of the material may be undertaken by the

---

[1] For a detailed analysis of different systems of civil procedure, see 16 Int. Ency. Comp. L., chaps. 1 and 6.

trial judge, or one of the trial judges, or by another judge or court officer whose primary work consists of such preparation. The material itself may include some original documents and written reports of experts, but will also contain a record, in the form of a deposition or summary, of *oral* testimony given by witnesses and, in some systems, by the parties. The second answer describes a procedure which relies, in principle, upon *oral* evidence received at the actual trial, a good deal of importance being attached to the impression the court forms of the parties and the witnesses as they give their evidence.

This contrast between written and oral procedures is seldom absolute. Many civil law systems find room for oral evidence at the eventual hearing. A common law court will receive some evidence in writing, whether in the form of reports, exhibits or 'agreed bundles of documents'; but in principle the evidence is 'heard' at the actual trial, the form of which is influenced by the needs of the jury even in those systems, such as the English, where the actual presence of a jury in a civil trial is now quite exceptional. It will be seen that the taking of evidence abroad, which must necessarily be done before the eventual trial and (unless modern techniques such as video recordings are brought into use) be reduced to writing, fits more naturally into the written than the oral tradition.

The two hypothetical answers point to another contrast. The common lawyer was able to speak of 'the parties or *their* witnesses'. In that tradition, with very limited exceptions, the witnesses are selected and called by the parties, and examined and cross-examined by the parties or their counsel.

Under the civil procedure of the High Court the court does not, in general, exercise any control over the manner in which a party obtains the evidence which he needs to support his case. The court may give him help, certainly; for instance by discovery of documents inter partes . . .; by allowing evidence to be obtained or presented at the trial in various ways . . .; and by the issue of subpoenas . . . . Subject, however, to the help of the court in these various ways, the basic principle underlying the preparation and presentation of a party's case in the High Court in England is that it is for that party to obtain and present the evidence which he needs by his own means, provided always that such means are lawful in the country in which they are used.[2]

Civil law systems see these aspects of evidence-gathering as a judicial function. While the parties may proffer the names of witnesses, and may have considerable scope for suggesting questions to be put to the witnesses, the civil law judge typically decides which witnesses to summon, conducts the questioning, and settles the deposition or minute which records the evidence. This means that the taking of evidence, even more emphatically than the service of process, is an exercise of the judicial sovereignty of the State. The taking of evidence within the territory of one State by the authorities of another, or on behalf of the parties to litigation in another State,

---

[2] *South Carolina Insurance Co.* v. *Assurantie Maatschappij 'De Zeven Provincien' N.V.* [1987] A.C. 24, 41–2.

will be seen as a serious affront to that sovereignty, unless of course official permission is sought and given. This has obvious implications for the mode of obtaining evidence for use abroad.

The differing roles of the parties and the judge in the process of taking evidence have practical implications when it comes to evidence being taken for use in a country with a different procedural tradition. The end-product of such an exercise in a common law jurisdiction would normally be a verbatim transcript of examination, cross-examination and re-examination, which will sit somewhat awkwardly with the depositions and minutes of evidence accumulated in the civil law procedure. The reverse case, of evidence taken in a civil law country for use in common law proceedings, presents greater difficulties; a deposition or minute taken by a judicial officer, with no cross-examination and perhaps without the parties being represented at all, may have limited probative value or be actually inadmissible in the common law country. If the process of taking evidence abroad is to serve its purpose, the evidence must be in a form which makes it admissible and gives it proper weight in the proceedings for which it was prepared, and this requires the authorities of the country in which the evidence is to be taken to show considerable flexibility in allowing, and it may be operating, modes of procedure which are quite unfamiliar.

One further distinction needs to be drawn. The hypothetical question posed above spoke of 'the eventual hearing of the case by the trial court'. A common lawyer would almost certainly refer, much more simply, to 'the trial', taking as granted the distinction between the trial itself and 'pre-trial proceedings', between the 'day in court' and the preparatory work done on behalf of the parties. Such language would be quite inappropriate if applied to the typical civil law system. The trial process there must include the various hearings at which evidence is received. Instead of a concentrated 'day in court' which provides a focus for the whole operation, there is a sequence of 'audiences' at which progress is made. It has been said that in the civil law tradition proof-taking 'often resembles a series of isolated pre-trial conferences rather than a concentrated trial'[3], which is helpful but must not be read as suggesting that these earlier stages are merely interlocutory; they are an integral part of the judicial process.

This means in turn that lawyers trained in the civil law tradition find it difficult to characterize certain features of common law pre-trial procedures. This applies in particular to such features of English High Court procedure as mutual discovery of documents by the parties with or without a court order;[4] orders for the service on other parties of proofs of oral evidence intended to be led at the trial;[5] and certain orders which may be made even before the commencement of proceedings (disclosure of documents by potential parties

---

[3] Cappelleti and Garth, 16 Int. Ency. Comp. L., chap. 1, para. 5.
[4] R.S.C. Ord. 24, rr. 1–3.   [5] R.S.C. Ord. 38, r. 2A.

to an action in respect of personal injuries or death,[6] and orders for the inspection, preservation or testing of property which may become the subject-matter of proceedings).[7] Even greater difficulty is found with the extensive facilities for discovery provided for in many United States jurisdictions, the intrusive nature of which presents another ground for serious concern.

(B) English Practice: Discovery, Disclosure, Preservation of Property

Quite apart from the courts' power to order the taking of evidence out of the jurisdiction, which is considered below,[8] there are a number of procedures available during the pre-trial phase which lead to the exposure of information or material relevant to the matter in hand. Where the information concerns, or the material consists of, property outside the jurisdiction, the effect of the procedures is akin to the taking of evidence abroad.

There has been no profound analysis of the precise basis for the English court making orders which have, in this sense, an extra-territorial effect. It has, however, long been recognized that the court can exercise jurisdiction *in personam* against an individual present in England or capable of being made a party to English proceedings in cases in which Equity so requires, even where the subject-matter is foreign immovable property.[9] A court must be able to exercise some measure of control over the cases which are brought before it, to prevent injustice to either party and to ensure that the various issues can be fully and effectively dealt with. These objectives could not be attained were the court's powers to be strictly limited to its territorial jurisdiction. In recent years, the English courts have been making greater and more assertive use of their powers; they retain, however, a proper sensitivity to the position of foreign countries, and exercise their discretion with that in mind. The result is a much more restrained use of orders with extra-territorial effects than is the practice in the United States.[10]

DISCOVERY

Nature of English practice

In England, discovery is dealt with under Order 24 of the Rules of the Supreme Court.[11] After the close of pleadings in an action begun by writ there must be discovery by the parties to the action of the documents which are or have been in their possession, custody or power relating to matters in

---

[6] Supreme Court Act 1981, s. 33(2); R.S.C. Ord. 24, r. 7A.

[7] Supreme Court Act 1981, s. 33(1); R.S.C. Ord. 29, r. 7A.

[8] See pp. 73–80.

[9] See *Penn* v. *Baltimore* (1750) 1 Ves. Sen. 444; Dicey and Morris, *The Conflict of Laws* (11th edn., 1987), rule 117.

[10] Aspects of US practice are considered below; see pp. 80–1 and 96–7.

[11] See also C.C.R. 1981, Ord. 14.

question in the action.[12] The parties exchange lists of the relevant documents; if there is a failure to comply with this requirement, the court may make an order for discovery.[13] A number of features of this system of discovery are noteworthy because of the contrast between discovery in England and the very much broader concept, known by the same name, in United States practice.[14]

The first is that the obligation to make discovery does not arise until the close of pleadings. The nature of the plaintiff's claims, and the questions in issue, will have been identified. Discovery is not available at the earlier stages in which the plaintiff may still be deciding how to formulate his claim, or whom to sue; that would be to countenance 'fishing expeditions'.

The second is that the obligation to make discovery is limited to those who are parties to the action. Discovery cannot, save in exceptional and anomalous cases, be ordered against third parties. As long ago as 1750, Lord Hardwicke LC declared that it would be 'very mischievous' to seek to make one who was 'merely a witness' a party in order to obtain discovery; even if he were properly examinable as a witness, his evidence could not be gathered in advance in this way.[15] In 1840 the House of Lords accepted the proposition that bills for discovery, the procedure in the Courts of Equity in aid of actions at law, could not be maintained except by and against parties to the record at law.[16] After the fusion of the courts of Law and Equity, Lindley LJ declared, 'It has long been a rule well established (the origin of it I do not recollect) that you cannot get discovery except from a party to your action. There is another rule, equally old and equally well-established—that you cannot make a mere witness a party in order to get discovery from him.'[17] The position was again stated in the House of Lords in 1986: 'there is no way in which a party to an action in the High Court in England can compel pre-trial discovery as against a person who is not a party to such action, either by way of the disclosure and inspection of documents in his possession or power, or by way of giving oral or written testimony.'[18]

In *Norwich Pharmacal Co.* v. *Customs and Excise Commissioners*,[19] Lord Denning MR expressed the view that it would be 'intolerable if an innocent person—without any interest in a case—were to be subjected to an action . . . simply to get papers or information out of him. The only permissible course is to issue a subpoena for him to come as a witness or to produce the documents

---

[12] R.S.C., Ord. 24, r. 1(1).

[13] Ibid., r. 3.

[14] See pp. 96–7. *South Carolina Insurance Co.* v. *Assurantie Maatschappij 'De Zeven Provincien' N.V.* [1987] A.C. 24, 35–6; and L. A. Collins, 'The Hague Evidence Convention and Discovery: A Serious Misunderstanding?' (1986) 35 I.C.L.Q. 765, 768–70.

[15] *Plummer* v. *May* (1750) 1 Ves. Sen. 426.

[16] *Queen of Portugal* v. *Glyn* (1840) 7 Cl. & Finn. 466. For the view of Lord Kilbrandon that this case is not authoritative, see *Norwich Pharmacal Co.* v. *Customs and Excise Commissioners* [1974] A.C. 133, 202. [17] *Elder* v. *Carter* (1890) 25 Ch.D. 194, 198.

[18] *South Carolina Insurance Co.* v. *Assurantie Maatschappij 'De Zeven Provincien' N.V.* [1987] A.C. 24, 35 per Lord Brandon of Oakbrook. [19] [1974] A.C. 133.

to the court.'[20] However, in the House of Lords Lord Kilbrandon expressed grave doubts about the wisdom of the 'mere witness' rule: 'Why should A be bound to disclose to B the information which he must have before he can sue C if, and only if, B could, if he wishes, also have sued A, although he has no intention of so doing? There is no rational distinction observable here.'[21] The House of Lords did not disturb the basic rule, but affirmed an exception. Discovery to find the identity of a wrongdoer was held to be available against anyone against whom the plaintiff has a cause of action in relation to the same wrong; someone who has become 'mixed up in the affair' and incurred any liability to the person wronged must make full disclosure on that point even though the person wronged has no intention of proceeding against him.[22]

There are further exceptions dating from 1970 and applying only in actions in respect of personal injuries or death. Discovery can be ordered before the commencement of such proceedings against a person likely to be a party to the proceedings,[23] and after the commencement of such proceedings against third parties,[24] but not where compliance would be likely to be injurious to the public interest.[25]

The third feature of English discovery to be noted is that it is limited to the discovery of documents. Although there are procedures for putting 'interrogatories' to another party at the pre-trial stage,[26] they are little used in practice and bear little or no resemblance to the United States practice of 'oral depositions' before trial.

Territorial reach

Is it in any way relevant that the person required to make discovery, or a document, is outside the jurisdiction? It seems that such facts are wholly irrelevant, at least in the standard case of discovery by a party to the action. It has long been established that a defendant may be required to discover documents under his control but situated abroad; in the early cases, the fact that relevant documents were in Calcutta[27] or in Tobago[28] led merely to an extension in the time allowed for their production. In 1985, Hoffman J., in dealing with a case concerning an order under the Bankers' Books Evidence Act 1879

---

[20] At p. 139.

[21] At p. 203.

[22] Per Lord Reid, at pp. 174, 175. See also *Bankers Trust Co.* v. *Shapiro* [1980] 1 W.L.R. 1274 (C.A.).

[23] Supreme Court Act 1981, s. 33(2); R.S.C. Ord. 24, r. 7A; County Courts Act 1984, s. 52(2); C.C.R. 1961, Ord. 13, r. 7.

[24] Supreme Court Act 1981, s. 34; R.S.C. Ord. 24, r. 7A; County Courts Act 1984, s. 53; C.C.R. Ord. 13, r. 7.

[25] Supreme Court Act 1981, s. 35(1); County Courts Act 1984, s. 54(1).

[26] See R.S.C. Ord. 26; C.C.R. Ord. 14, r. 11.

[27] See *Freeman* v. *Fairlie* (1812) 3 Mer. 29, 44–5 (Lord Eldon, LC).

[28] See *Farquharson* v. *Balfour* (1823) Turn. & R. 184, 190–1 (Lord Eldon, LC).

and a *subpoena duces tecum*, distinguished cases of discovery by 'ordinary parties to English litigation who happen to be foreigners'.[29] As he put it,

If you join the game you must play according to the local rules. This applies not only to plaintiffs but also to defendants who give notice of intention to defend . . . Of course, a party may be excused from having to produce a document on the grounds that this would violate the law of the place where the document is kept.[30] But in principle, there is no reason why he should not have to produce all discoverable documents wherever they are.[31]

It would seem that different considerations apply in the exceptional cases in which discovery may be obtained from a third party. Hoffman J. expressed the view that discovery under the principle in *Norwich Pharmacal Co.* v. *Customs and Excise Commissioners*[32] was more akin to the subpoena directed to a witness than the discovery required of an ordinary defendant.[33] It followed that the proper jurisdictional limits were the same as those applying to subpoenas, which cannot be addressed to persons outside the United Kingdom.[34]

DETENTION, CUSTODY AND PRESERVATION OF PROPERTY

Under the English Rules of the Supreme Court (and comparable rules of court in other Commonwealth jurisdictions), the court may make an order for the 'detention, custody or preservation' of any property which is the subject-matter of a cause or matter before the court or as to which any question may arise in the case; and may order the inspection of any such property in the possession of a party.[35] Related powers deal with orders for the taking of samples of the property, and observations of and experiments upon it.[36] All these orders are made after an application by summons or notice,[37] giving the defendant an opportunity to be heard.

The court seems to give a broad interpretation to these powers. The power to make orders for the 'preservation' of property has been used in the context of the transfer of the mortgage of land by a mentally disordered person, even though the land was in Monte Carlo.[38] References in the text of the rules to 'custody' and 'observation' support a decision that the court could properly order the sending of an item of property out of the jurisdiction, in the instant case to South Africa, so that it could be identified by a witness whose evidence was being taken on commission there.[39]

---

[29] *MacKinnon* v. *Donaldson, Lufkin and Jenrette Securities Corpn*. [1986] Ch. 482.

[30] Hoffman J. cites *Société Internationale pour Participations Industrielles et Commerciales S.A.* v. *Rogers* 357 US 197 (1958); see p. 278.

[31] [1986] Ch. 482, 494–5.   [32] [1974] A.C. 133. See above, pp. 60–1.

[33] *MacKinnon* v. *Donaldson, Lufkin and Jenrette Corpn*. [1986] Ch. 482, 498–9.

[34] See p. 73.   [35] R.S.C. Ord. 29, r. 2.

[36] Ibid., Ord. 29, r. 3.   [37] Ibid., Ord. 29, r. 2(5).

[38] *Chaplin* v. *Burnett* (1912) 28 T.L.R. 256 (C.A.).

[39] *Chaplin* v. *Puttick* [1898] 2 Q.B. 160.

ANTON PILLER ORDERS

Of much greater significance in recent practice are the so-called '*Anton Piller* orders, made under the inherent jurisdiction of the court.[40] This type of order is made *ex parte*, the court sitting in camera, for the object of the exercise is to enable the plaintiff to enter premises and obtain access to documents or objects without the defendant having an opportunity to remove, hide or destroy them. The order is that the defendant should consent to such steps being taken and the existence of personal jurisdiction over him is therefore essential. Although Ormrod LJ observed in the *Anton Piller* case that orders should 'rarely' be made,[41] within a few years Goulding J. remarked that 'such is the proven efficiency of that type of order and such is the extent of dishonest trading in this country at the present time, that it is a matter of weekly occurrence and sometimes of daily occurrence for the Chancery Division' to make such orders,[42] which are also regularly made in the Queen's Bench Division.

The territorial reach of *Anton Piller* orders has been considered in a number of cases. In *Cook Industries Inc.* v. *Galliher*[43] the court ordered the defendant to disclose full particulars of a flat in Paris (which was thought to contain valuable pictures and *objets d'art* allegedly transferred to the defendant in fraud of the creditors of another), to verify the information on affidavit, and to permit a named French *avocat* to inspect the contents of the flat. This was coupled with an injunction preventing the removal of any of the contents. The defendant moved for the discharge of both injunctions, and a hearing *inter partes* followed in which the injunctions were upheld. Counsel on both sides seem to have accepted that an *Anton Piller* order could have extra-territorial reach; the challenge made for the defendant rested partly on an argument that an English court could not deal with title to or possession of foreign immovables (rejected as there was an equity between the parties) and partly on a plea of *forum non conveniens* (rejected on the facts, and because reliance on an application in an alternative forum would cause a delay during which assets could be disposed of).

A few months later, apparently before *Cook Industries Inc.* v. *Galliher* had been reported, another judge of the Chancery Division declined to include Scottish premises in an *Anton Piller* order.[44] Goulding J. made it clear that he was not expressing, on an *ex parte* application, any decided view of the jurisdictional issue, though he accepted that where orders *in personam* were concerned it was enough that the court should have the party who must obey its order within its power.[45] On the other hand, the order was 'highly localized'

---

[40] *Anton Piller K.G.* v. *Manufacturing Processes Ltd.* [1976] Ch. 55 (C.A.).
[41] [1976] Ch. 55, 61.
[42] *Protector Alarms Ltd.* v. *Maxim Alarms Ltd.* [1978] F.S.R. 442 (Ch.D.).
[43] [1979] Ch. 439.
[44] *Protector Alarms Ltd.* v. *Maxim Alarms Ltd.* [1978] F.S.R. 442.
[45] Citing *Portarlington (Lord)* v. *Soulby* (1843) 3 My. & K. 104.

(and so unlike a negative injunction or even a mandatory order to commence proceedings abroad)[46] and was normally to be executed under the supervision of the plaintiff's solicitor, who was an officer of the court. If the Court of Session could make an order of the same nature, it was better to resort to its jurisdiction; if it would not make such an order, the English court would hesitate the more before seeking to make an order to be effective in Scotland. As a matter of discretion, Scottish premises were excluded from the proposed order.

In *Cook Industries Inc.* v. *Galliher*, the defendant had been served with the writ in England. The defendant in the *Protector Alarms* case was a Scottish company but it had a place of business in England at which service could be effected. In *Altertext Inc.* v. *Advanced Data Communications Ltd.*,[47] a similar point arose where it proposed to serve the writ and an *Anton Piller* order out of the jurisdiction on a Belgian company. Although leave was given for the service of the writ, Scott J. was unwilling to allow the *Anton Piller* order to be served (and immediately executed) at the same time. Although service of a writ out of the jurisdiction with leave placed the defendant within the power of the court, the assumption of jurisdiction was in a sense only provisional, as the defendant could apply to set it aside. It was undesirable to make an order which would in practice be executed before the defendant could avail himself of that opportunity.

It seems, therefore, that *Anton Piller* orders should not be made for service and execution outside the jurisdiction. It has to be noted that the courts and commentators have shown growing concern about the potential, and actual, abuse of the power to make such orders[48] and their effect on the privilege against self-incrimination[49] even in purely English contexts. That scarcely encourages attempts to justify extra-territorial application of the principle. Perhaps more significant in this context was the stance taken by the United Kingdom and the European Court of Human Rights when a case was brought before the Court alleging that the service and execution of a particular *Anton Piller* order amounted to an unjustified interference with the applicants 'right to respect for his private and family life, his home and his correspondence' under Article 8 of the European Convention on Human Rights.[50] The Court emphasized the importance of that element of the English practice that entrusts the execution of an order to the plaintiff's solicitors and requires

---

[46] As in *Amplaudio* v. *Snell* (1938) 55 R.P.C. 237.

[47] [1985] 1 W.L.R. 457.

[48] See the notable judgment of Scott J. in *Columbia Picture Industries Inc.* v. *Robinson* [1987] Ch. 38; M. Dockray and H. Laddie, 'Piller Problems' (1990) 106 L.Q.R. 601.

[49] *Rank Film Distributors Ltd.* v. *Video Information Centre* [1982] A.C. 380 (but see Supreme Court Act 1981, s. 72 for the current position in intellectual property contexts); *Tate Access Floors Inc.* v. *Boswell* [1990] 3 All E.R. 303, where Sir N. Browne-Wilkinson V.-C. recognized that the effect of his judgment might render the *Anton Piller* jurisdiction to a large extent incapable of exercise and called for Parliamentary consideration.

[50] *Chappell case*, judgment of 30 Mar. 1989, Series A, no. 152–A. See Collins (1990) 106 L.Q.R. 173.

them to give a series of undertakings as to the manner of execution and the use made of the information or documents obtained.[51] An English solicitor might find it impossible to exercise the appropriate degree of supervision and control were the order to be executed abroad; and a local agent acting on his behalf might not be subject to the disciplinary jurisdiction of the English court to which the Court also attached weight.

It may, however, be possible for a plaintiff to achieve the desired result by making a concurrent application for a similar order in the courts of the relevant foreign country, though the availability of such orders will obviously depend upon the local law. Under section 25 of the Civil Jurisdiction and Judgments Act 1982, the High Court has power to grant interim relief where proceedings have been or are to be commenced in another Contracting State to the Brussels Convention or in another part of the United Kingdom, or where there are or will be any other proceedings within the scope of the 1968 Convention even if that Convention does not directly apply.[52]

Mareva Injunctions

A *Mareva* injunction is one granted, either after judgment to the successful plaintiff or before trial to a plaintiff who has a good arguable case on the merits, restraining a defendant 'from dealing with or disposing of or removing from the jurisdiction' any or all of his assets.[53] Its purpose is to prevent the enforcement of a judgment being rendered impossible, and so justice defeated, by the dissipation of assets which would be available to satisfy the judgment. It takes its name from one of the first cases in which such an injunction was granted, *Mareva Compania Naviera S.A.* v. *International Bulkcarriers S.A.*[54] The scope of *Mareva* injunctions has expanded at a remarkable speed, and on many points (and especially the territorial reach of injunctions) events have overtaken cases decided only a few years ago.

Closely associated with *Mareva* injunctions, and of direct relevance to the subject-matter of the present work, are orders requiring a defendant to disclose the whereabouts of his assets.

The requirement of personal jurisdiction

Subject to one very important exception,[55] the English courts will not grant a *Mareva* injunction unless the plaintiff's cause of action against the defendant

---

[51] Judgment, paras. 17 and 61.

[52] See also the power to enlarge the scope of this power still more widely: Civil Jurisdiction and Judgment Act 1982, s. 25(3). For the Convention provision, see Art. 24 and Case 125/79 *Denilauler* v. *SNC Couchet Frères* [1980] E.C.R. 1553.

[53] For precedents, see S. Gee, *Mareva Injunctions and Anton Piller Relief* (2nd edn., 1990), App. 3.

[54] [1975] 2 Lloyd's Rep. 509 (C.A.).

[55] Where proceedings have been or will be commenced in another part of the United Kingdom or in another Contracting State to the Brussels Convention 1968: Civil Jurisdiction and Judgments Act 1982, s. 25. see pp. 68–9, post.

is one which may properly be adjudicated upon in England. In other words, the defendant must be subject to the jurisdiction of the English courts.[56]

That principle was established by the House of Lords in _Siskina_ v. _Distos Compania Naviera S.A._[57] The only possible basis for jurisdiction in that case was the service of the writ out of the territorial jurisdiction under Order 11 of the Rules of the Supreme Court. The only provision of Order 11 under which leave might be given was that dealing with the case where 'in the action begun by the writ an injunction is sought ordering the defendant to do or refrain from doing anything within the jurisdiction . . .'.[58] The House of Lords held that 'the action' must be founded on a pre-existing cause of action against the defendant arising out of an invasion, actual or threatened, by him of a legal or equitable right of the plaintiff[59] for the enforcement of which the defendant is amenable to the jurisdiction of the court. An interlocutory injunction could not stand on its own. In _Siskina_, the plaintiff's major claim for compensation was not itself justiciable in England; Lord Diplock pointed out that to argue in effect that it could be treated as justiciable because, if it were, an interlocutory injunction might be granted was a logical fallacy, _petitio principii_ (pulling oneself up by one's own bootstraps).

It seems plain from the speeches in _Siskina_ that where leave can be given for service out of the jurisdiction under one of the other paragraphs of Order 11 (for example those dealing with breach of contract), a _Mareva_ injunction can be granted. On this point a _Mareva_ injunction can be distinguished from an _Anton Piller_ order; it was the fact that the latter is immediately and irreversibly executed as soon as it is served which led the court in _Altertext Inc._ v. _Advanced Data Communications Ltd._[60] to hold that an _Anton Piller_ order could not be made in an Order 11 case.

If there is a cause of action in England, it is immaterial that the plaintiff decides to limit active pursuit of his claim to foreign proceedings. So, in _House of Spring Gardens Ltd._ v. _Waite_[61] actions were begun both in the English and the Irish courts in respect of breach of a licensing agreement providing for the manufacture in Ireland of bullet-proof vests for the Libyan authorities. A _Mareva_ injunction was granted by the English court, but the Irish action was

---

[56] For the position of foreign States, see State Immunity Act 1978, s. 13(2).

[57] [1979] A.C. 210. See C. McLachlan, 'Transnational Applications of _Mareva_ and _Anton Piller_ Orders', (1987) 36 I.C.L.Q. 669. In the United States, where the issue only became a live one with the effective abolition of _quasi in rem_ jurisdiction in the Supreme Court's decision in _Shaffer_ v. _Heitner_ 433 US 186 (1977), a number of courts have been prepared to order prejudgment attachment of assets which are in the forum State otherwise than fortuitously even though no _in personam_ jurisdiction exists: _California Power and Light Co._ v. _Uranex_ 451 F.Supp. 1044 (N.D.Cal., 1977); _Barclays Bank S.A._ v. _Tsakos_ 543 A. 2d 802 (D.C.App., 1988).

[58] R.S.C. Ord. 11, r. 1(1)(i). Note that the last three words quoted in the text would in any event exclude some forms of 'worldwide' _Mareva_ under the practice later developed.

[59] Cf. observations by Lord Goff in _South Carolina Insurance Co._ v. _Assurantie Maatschappij 'de Zeven Provincien' N.V._ [1987] A.C. 24 (considered below, pp. 72–3) which cast some doubt on this way of expressing the scope of the power to grant injunctions; but the major point in _Siskina_ is not affected.

[60] [1985] 1 W.L.R. 457.   [61] [1984] F.S.R. 277.

the one which went to trial, judgment being given for the plaintiff in the sum of some £3.4 million. In later proceedings for the continuation of the *Mareva* injunction, it was held to be regular and proper practice for a plaintiff to commence proceedings on the same cause of action in several jurisdictions in order to obtain *Mareva* or corresponding relief. He could then press his claim in one jurisdiction and the effect of the English injunction could be continued until he obtained enforcement in England of the resulting foreign judgment.

In the *House of Spring Gardens* case, the English proceedings simply lay dormant; no order was made staying those proceedings on the ground of *lis alibi pendens*. It would be entirely consistent with the practice described in the case for a *Mareva* injunction to be continued in force despite an order staying proceedings on that ground. Similar arguments would seem applicable were proceedings in the English courts to be stayed on the basis of *forum non conveniens*, the injunction continuing subject to proceedings in the alternative forum being commenced within a prescribed period of time.

Similar considerations apply in the case in which English proceedings are stayed to give effect to an arbitration agreement. In *The Rena K.*,[62] Brandon J. noted that *Mareva* injunctions had been made to provide security for the payment of any award which the plaintiff might obtain in the arbitration, and he saw 'no good reason' against this practice. It would seem, however, that appropriate language in the relevant arbitration clause may prevent a party seeking a *Mareva* injunction (or corresponding orders in other jurisdictions). This was held to be the case in *Mantovani* v. *Carapelli S.p.A.*[63] where the clause prevented either party from bringing 'any action or other legal proceedings' until an award had been made in the arbitration. A similar result was avoided in *The Lisboa*[64] where the clause was so widely drawn as to suggest that even proceedings for execution of the award were prohibited; as such an interpretation would lead to the clause being null and void by virtue of section 8 of the Carriage of Goods by Sea Act 1924, the Court of Appeal adopted a more limited interpretation under which proceeds for execution or to obtain security, including security by means of a *Mareva* injunction, were allowed. Both these cases involved applications for orders to the Italian courts; it may be that an English court would resist a contractual fetter on the power to grant injunctions under section 37 of the Supreme Court Act 1981.

A *Mareva* injunction will be available whatever the cause of action, provided that it is one which may ultimately lead to enforcement against the defendant's assets; it would not be available where the relief sought was purely declaratory. There seem to be no other restrictions on the nature of the cause of action. So, in *Securities and Investment Board* v. *Pantell S.A.*,[65] the plaintiff Board sought a *Mareva* injunction against a Swiss and an English

---

[62] [1979] Q.B. 377 at 407. See Arbitration Act 1950, s. 12(6) applying where there is to be arbitration in England.   [63] [1980] 1 Lloyd's Rep. 375 (C.A.).
[64] *Mike Trading and Transport Ltd.* v. *R. Pagnan & Fratelli, The Lisboa* [1980] 2 Lloyd's Rep. 546 (C.A.).   [65] [1990] Ch. 426.

company associated with it. Criminal proceedings had been commenced against the managers of the Swiss company in Lugano, but the application to the English court was not in aid of those proceedings.[66] The Board had no beneficial interest in the assets it was seeking to freeze, nor any common law right of action. Sir Nicolas Browne-Wilkinson V.-C. held, however, that the statutory right of the Board, acting as delegate of the Secretary of State for Trade and Industry, to seek an order against persons carrying on investment business in the United Kingdom without authority to make good losses suffered by others[67] was a sufficient basis for a *Mareva* injunction.

The exception: Mareva *injunctions in aid of certain foreign proceedings*

Section 25 of the Civil Jurisdiction and Judgments Act 1982 creates a significant exception to the *Siskina* rule that a *Mareva* injunction can only be granted when the plaintiff has a cause of action justiciable in England. It contains these provisions.

(1) The High Court in England and Wales or Northern Ireland shall have power to grant interim relief where:
   (*a*) proceedings have been or are to be commenced in a Contracting State other than the United Kingdom or in a part of the United Kingdom other than that in which the High Court in question exercises jurisdiction; and
   (*b*) there are or will be proceedings whose subject-matter is within the scope of the 1968 Convention as determined by Article 1 (whether or not the Convention has effect in relation to the proceedings).
(2) On an application for any interim relief under subsection (1) the court may refuse to grant that relief if, in the opinion of the court, the fact that the court has no jurisdiction apart from this section in relation to the subject-matter of the proceedings in question makes it inexpedient for the court to grant it.

There is power, not yet exercised, to apply similar provisions in relation to proceedings in non-Contracting States,[68] and equivalent provisions are made as to provisional and protective measures in Scotland.[69]

The effect is to reverse the decision in the *Siskina* case in respect of civil or commercial cases brought, or to be brought, in the courts of any other Contracting State. This applies, for example, to an action brought by a French plaintiff in the Paris court against a company incorporated in the United States and having no place of business in France; the proceedings do not have to be based on any of the grounds for jurisdiction elaborated in the Convention.[70]

Section 25(7) excludes from the category of available interim relief a 'provision for obtaining evidence'. This will not, however, preclude the granting

---

[66] It seems that such aid would be impossible: cf. *Chief Constable of Leicestershire* v. *M.* [1989] 1 W.L.R. 20.

[67] Financial Services Act 1986, s. 6; Financial Services Act 1986 (Delegation) Order 1987, S.I. 1987 No. 942.　　　　　[68] Civil Jurisdiction and Judgments Act 1982, s. 25(3)–(6).

[69] Ibid., s. 26.　　　　　[70] Ibid., s. 25(1)(*b*), (the words in parentheses).

of an injunction, or an associated disclosure order, if needed for the purpose of freezing assets; it is immaterial that the information gained may also have value in the substantive dispute between the parties.[71]

Territorial reach

It was thought at one time that a *Mareva* injunction was a remedy only available against foreign defendants, perhaps because the risk of assets being removed was usually greater and more obvious in such cases.[72] It was however accepted by the Court of Appeal in 1980 that an injunction could properly be granted even if the defendant was based in England if in the circumstances there was a danger of the assets being removed,[73] and this was put beyond doubt by section 37(3) of the Supreme Court Act 1981 which provides:

The power of the High Court under [section 37(1)] to grant an interlocutory injunction restraining a party to any proceedings from removing from the jurisdiction of the High Court, or otherwise dealing with, assets located within that jurisdiction shall be exercisable in cases where that party is, as well as in cases where he is not, domiciled, resident or present within that jurisdiction.

It will be noted that section 37(3) refers to 'assets located within that jurisdiction', a reference which reflects, but does not directly confirm, the understanding of the position which prevailed in 1981, that an injunction could only attach to assets within England and Wales. Indeed, in *Ashtiani* v. *Kashi*[74] the Court of Appeal held that an injunction should be limited to the assets of the defendant within the jurisdiction of the court, and Dillon LJ advanced a series of policy arguments in support of this conclusion.[75] At the time *Ashtiani* v. *Kashi* was interpreted as holding that 'there is no basis for the injunction if the defendant's assets are situate abroad'.[76] Another reading of the case was later to prevail and its supposed principle was decisively rejected in a remarkable series of Court of Appeal decisions in June and July 1989.

The first of these, *Babanaft International Co. S. A.* v. *Bassatne*,[77] involved an injunction (coupled with other orders) made after the plaintiff had obtained judgment. Neill and Nicholls LJJ, both of whom had been members of the court sitting in *Ashtiani* v. *Kashi*, distinguished that case as being concerned

---

[71] See S. Gee, *Mareva Injunctions and Anton Piller Relief* (2nd edn., 1990), pp. 46–7, discussing *Republic of Haiti* v. *Duvalier: re an application by Mr Turner and Mr Matlin* (C.A., 7 June 1988, C.A. Transcript No. 490.)

[72] This was the explanation offered by Megarry V.-C. in *Barclay-Johnson* v. *Yuill* [1980] 1 W.L.R. 1259.

[73] *Prince Abdul Rahman Bin Turki Al Sudairy* v. *Abu Taha* [1980] 1 W.L.R. 1268 (C.A.). See also *A. J. Bekhor & Co.* v. *Bilton* [1981] Q.B. 923 (C.A.).

[74] [1987] Q.B. 888 (C.A.).

[75] The arguments are cogently criticized by Collins at (1989) 105 L.Q.R. 268–70.

[76] Dicey and Morris, *The Conflict of Laws* (11th edn, 1987), p. 193.

[77] [1990] Ch. 13 (C.A.).

with a pre-judgment injunction, though Neill LJ did recognize that the developing state of the law might require a reconsideration of the position even in that context. Kerr LJ, after an extended consideration of Commonwealth and European developments, expressly held that, in appropriate cases, there was nothing to prevent the grant of injunctions extending to assets outside the jurisdiction.

A week after the judgment in the *Babanaft* case, the Court of Appeal began hearing argument in *Republic of Haiti* v. *Duvalier*,[78] in which a prejudgment *Mareva* injunction was sought in aid of proceedings in the French courts. *Ashtiani* v. *Kashi* was directly in point, but the judgments in that case were treated as statements of the then settled practice and not as declaring any restriction upon the powers of the court. The Court of Appeal adopted the reasoning of Kerr LJ in *Babanaft*.

In *Derby & Co. Ltd.* v. *Weldon (No. 1)*,[79] which was before another division of the Court of Appeal as judgment was being given in *Republic of Haiti* v. *Duvalier*, the power to grant a *Mareva* injunction in respect of assets outside England and Wales, both before and after judgment, was declared to be established law. The position thus reached brought English practice into line with the majority of decisions in other Commonwealth jurisdictions.[80] In a later phase in the same litigation, the Court of Appeal held that it had jurisdiction in appropriate cases to order the transfer of assets subject to a *Mareva* injunction from one foreign country to another, enforcement considerations being especially relevant.[81] The Court of Appeal has, however, subsequently held that in the exceptional cases in which a *Mareva* injunction might be granted in support of a foreign judgment or arbitration award (enforcement of which is being sought in England) the injunction will normally be limited to assets in England.[82]

A world-wide *Mareva* injunction now always contains a proviso designed to afford some protection for third parties from what would otherwise be 'an altogether exorbitant, extra-territorial jurisdiction'.[83] This provides that

in so far as this order purports to have any extraterritorial effect, no person shall be affected thereby or concerned with the terms thereof until it shall be declared enforceable or be enforced by a foreign court and then it shall only affect them to the extent of such declaration or enforcement unless they are:

(a) a person to whom this order is addressed or an officer or an agent appointed by a power of attorney of such a person or

---

[78] [1990] Q.B. 202 (C.A.).　　　　　　　　　　　　　　　　[79] [1990] Ch. 48 (C.A.).

[80] See *Ballabil Holdings Pty. Ltd.* v. *Hospital Products Ltd.* (1985) 1 N.S.W.L.R. 155; *Coombs & Barrei Construction Pty. Ltd.* v. *Dynasty Pty. Ltd.* (1986) 42 S.A.S.R. 413; *National Australia Bank* v. *Dessau* [1988] V.R. 521 (but cf. *Brereton* v. *Milstein* [1988] V.R. 508, where the contrary held in an earlier phase of the same litigation); *Asean Resources Ltd.* v. *Ka Wah International Merchant Finance Ltd.* [1987] L.R.C.(Comm.) 835.

[81] *Derby & Co.Ltd.* v. *Weldon (No. 6)* [1990] 1 W.L.R. 1139 (C.A.).

[82] *Rosseel N.V.* v. *Oriental Commercial and Shipping (UK) Ltd.* [1990] 1 W.L.R. 1387 (C.A.).

[83] See *Babanaft International Co. S.A.* v. *Bassatne* [1990] Ch. 13, per Nicholls LJ.

(*b*) persons who are subject to the jurisdiction of this court and
  (i) have been given written notice of this order at their residence or place of business within the jurisdiction, and
  (ii) are able to prevent acts or omissions outside the jurisdiction of this court which assist in the breach of the terms of this order.

Disclosure orders

In the present context, the importance of the *Mareva* injunction lies in the associated order that there be disclosure of the nature and location of the assets covered by the injunction (and possibly of other assets, though the courts do not seem to have gone this far)[84] and of documents relating to those assets. Disclosure orders may be made in respect of assets outside the jurisdiction, for example documents relating to a Swiss bank account.[85] In some circumstances, the information thus gained may itself be relevant to issues in pending proceedings, in which case the order is a means of obtaining evidence abroad. In many more cases, once a plaintiff discovers that there are assets in a State he will wish (and sometimes be enabled by the very presence of the assets) to commence proceedings in the courts of that State; there is what might be described as a 'jurisdiction-fishing expedition'.

Some protection is afforded by the practice of requiring the plaintiff to give an express undertaking not to use the information obtained without first seeking the leave of the court,[86] and it was held in *Tate Access Floors Inc.* v. *Boswell*[87] that even in the absence of an express undertaking the implied undertaking against using information for an improper or collateral purpose could be relied upon to the same effect.

However, there are serious difficulties in the way of 'policing' such an undertaking by the plaintiff. Although any breach would be contempt of court, and could lead to the lifting of the *Mareva* injunction, the information will have been obtained and can still be put to use in another State; and the sanctions available are much reduced where, as may often be the case, the plaintiff is not resident in the jurisdiction of the English court. The use of substantial bank guarantees in support of the plaintiff's undertakings would not necessarily be either practicable or, certainly where a foreign State was plaintiff, appropriate.[88]

A related issue concerns the extent to which claims of privilege can be made in resisting the making or enforcement of a disclosure order. It has been held by the Court of Appeal that the privilege against self-incrimination can

---

[84] See *Derby & Co.Ltd.* v. *Weldon (Nos. 3 and 4)* [1990] Ch. 65 (C.A.), at 86, 94. The main practical importance of this question is that there might be circumstances in which it was inappropriate to grant an injunction in respect of assets abroad, but disclosure would enable proceedings to be taken for similar relief in the foreign jurisdiction.
[85] *Bank of Crete S.A.* v. *Koskotas* [1991] 2 Lloyd's Rep. 587 (C.A.)
[86] See *Babanaft International Co. S.A.* v. *Bassatne* [1990] Ch. 13 (C.A.)
[87] [1990] 3 All E.R. 303.
[88] *Republic of Haiti* v. *Duvalier* [1990] Q.B. 202 (C.A.).

be invoked in this context where, accepting the facts as alleged by the plaintiff, there is a reasonable apprehension on the part of the defendant that he might be prosecuted in the United Kingdom.[89]

USE OF PRE-TRIAL PROCEDURES OF OTHER JURISDICTIONS

By comparison with some other jurisdictions, and especially those in the United States, the scope of discovery and related procedures available in England is quite limited. Is there any reason why a party to litigation in England, either as plaintiff or defendant, should not take advantage of any procedures which might be open to him to obtain discovery or other access to relevant material in some such foreign jurisdiction?

This point arose for decision in _South Carolina Insurance Co._ v. _Assurantie Maatschappij 'de Zeven Provincien' N.V._[90] The defendants in an English action wished to inspect documents of admitted relevance to the subject-matter of the case (which involved a series of reinsurance contracts) in the possession of a company not itself a party to the litigation and having no place of business in England; the documents were situated in the State of Washington. As the company was not a party, discovery as understood in England was not available; as it was not within the United Kingdom no _subpoena duces tecum_ could be issued (and that would only secure the production of documents at the trial, not for pre-trial inspection). The defendants sought an order under a United States statutory provision[91] dealing specifically with assistance to litigants in foreign courts. Under it, 'any interested person' could seek an order of US District Court that any person within its district should produce documents for use in the foreign proceedings.

Before Hobhouse J. and in the Court of Appeal, the plaintiffs were successful in arguing that the defendants should be restrained by injunction from seeking or enforcing such a District Court order. The defendants had not contested the jurisdiction of the English court and must be taken to have accepted that the dispute would be settled in accordance with English procedure; the English court must be in full control of its own procedures and not allow procedural battles to develop in other countries which would add to the expense and dislocate the timetable of English litigation.

The House of Lords unanimously allowed the defendants' appeal. Given the freedom which the parties enjoy in a common law system in the matter of gathering evidence, their resort to foreign procedures could not be said to interfere with English procedures or the control over those procedures which the English court would exercise. The defendants' conduct was not unconscionable, nor an interference with any legal or equitable right of the plaintiffs. Any possibility of excessive delay could be met by the English court fixing a date for trial; and it could control the allocation of costs.

In the result, therefore, there may be foreign pre-trial procedures available

---

[89] _Sociedade Nacional de Combustiveis de Angola U.E.E._ v. _Lundqvist_ [1990] 3 All E.R. 283 (C.A.).
[90] [1987] A.C.24.   [91] 28 USC. 1782. See further below, p. 80.

to the parties which will enable them to overcome the limitations on the territorial scope of the procedures normally available in England.

(C) English Practice: Orders for the Taking of Evidence Abroad

The characteristic mode of proof in common law jurisdictions is reflected in the general rule stated in the English Rules of the Supreme Court:

> any fact required to be proved at the trial of any action begun by writ by the evidence of witnesses shall be proved by the examination of witnesses orally and in open court.[92]

This obviously requires the attendance of the witnesses at the trial, and a subpoena may be issued to compel the attendance of those who are within the jurisdiction or in some other part of the United Kingdom.[93] A subpoena may not be issued where the proposed witness is out of the United Kingdom. Even in the case of a willing witness, considerations of cost and convenience may make it very desirable to avoid the requirement of attendance.

In some cases this can be achieved by obtaining an order that an affidavit by the witness be read at the trial in place of oral evidence.[94] Such an order will not be made where the evidence is strongly contested or in cases where the trial judge will need to form an impression of the demeanour of the witness in order to assess his credibility. In some circumstances, the course of the trial will be such that a witness whose affidavit has been received will after all be required to attend for cross-examination; this applies no less to witnesses abroad as to those within the jurisdiction.[95]

The alternative is to receive a deposition prepared on the basis of an examination of the witness (including his cross-examination) before a person appointed by the court.[96] If the deposition is to be taken in England (and there may be cases in which a foreign witness can be available in England but not at the date of the trial), the examination will be before a judge, officer or (usually) an examiner of the court;[97] if the deposition is to be taken abroad, alternative ways of proceeding are available. The distinction between them is of considerable importance.

Perhaps the neatest way of expressing the distinction is to contrast *unilateral* and *co-operative* procedures. The former is an exercise of the authority

---

[92] R.S.C. Ord. 38, r. 1, which is subject to numerous statutory exceptions. A striking one, applicable only in a criminal context, is Criminal Justice Act 1988, s. 32(1) allowing evidence to be given through a live television link when the witness is abroad; see, for procedure, Crown Court Rules, r. 23B (added by S.I. 1990 No. 2157).

[93] R.S.C. Ord. 38, rr. 14–19; Supreme Court Act 1961, s. 36 (subpoena to run throughout United Kingdom).   [94] R.S.C. Ord. 38, r. 2.

[95] *Strauss* v. *Goldschmidt* (1892) 8 T.L.R. 239 (D.C.) (though on the facts foreign witness not required to attend).

[96] See, for the content of depositions, R.S.C. Ord. 39, r. 11; for their admissibility, Ord. 38, r. 9.

[97] Ibid., Ord 38, r. 1; for the appointment of barristers of not less than 3 years' standing to a panel of examiners, see Ord. 39, rr. 16–18.

of the forum State; in the language of an old Chancery writ, *dedimus potestatem* (we have given power). The latter invokes international judicial assistance in that it requires the active involvement of the judicial authorities of the State in which the evidence is to be taken.

Unilateral procedures

In current English practice, the High Court can appoint a 'special examiner' to take evidence at any place, including a place outside the jurisdiction. The order for the appointment of such an examiner is the modern equivalent of the long-obsolete practice of issuing a commission for the taking of evidence out of the jurisdiction.[98] Because of the need to respect the sensitivities of foreign States, careful limits are set to the power to make orders:

(*a*) the general power to appoint a special examiner may be exercised only 'if the government of [the relevant] country allows a person in that country to be examined before a person appointed by the Court';[99]

(*b*) a more specific power to appoint a British consul or his deputy as a special examiner may be exercised where a Civil Procedure Convention subsists between the United Kingdom and the relevant foreign country providing for the taking of the evidence of any person in that country for the assistance of proceedings in the High Court (the unspoken assumption being that any such Convention will permit consuls to act);[100] and

(*c*) the same power may be exercised, despite the absence of a Civil Procedure Convention, with the consent of the Secretary of State (who would presumably have regard to the known attitude of the foreign government and the terms of any relevant Convention as to consular relations).[101]

Co-operative procedures

The alternative mode of procedure is for the court to make an order under Order 39, rule 1 of the Rules of the Supreme Court for the issue of a letter of request to the judicial authorities of the country in which the proposed witness is, asking that they take, or cause to be taken, the evidence of that person.[102] The prescribed form of letter of request describes the nature of the proceedings, with a summary of the facts, and asserts the necessity for the purposes of justice of the examination of the witnesses whose names and addresses are given. As to the mode of their examination, the letter contains this paragraph:

The witnesses should be examined on oath or if that is not possible within your laws or is impossible of performance by reason of the internal practice and procedure of

---

[98] See Evidence by Commission Act 1859 for the operation of the old procedure between different parts of HM's dominions; it was repealed by the Evidence (Proceedings in Other Jurisdictions) Act 1975.

[99] R.S.C. Ord. 39, r. 2(1)(*b*). Note that the order is always technically made under ibid., Ord. 39, r. 1, so securing the application of Ord. 38, r. 9 and so the admissibility of the resulting deposition. [100] Ibid., Ord. 39, r. 2(2)(*a*).

[101] Ibid., Ord. 39, r. 2(2)(*b*). [102] R.S.C. Ord. 39, r. 2(1)(*a*).

your court or by reason of practical difficulties, they should be examined in accordance with whatever procedure your laws provide for in these matters.

It is then asked that the witnesses be examined either in accordance with a given list of questions, which will have been drafted by the applicant party, or regarding certain matters summarized in the letter of request itself; an example might be 'a road traffic accident believed to have taken place in the sight of the witness at such-and-such a place and time'. The former might appear a more powerful technique from the point of view of the applicant; but, comparing it with a 'live' examination, in which the questioner can frame follow-up questions in terms of the way in which the facts evolve from earlier answers, a United States court has described the framing of questions in advance as 'a supreme test of the questioning lawyer's powers of pre-science'.[103] The foreign court is asked to notify the English court or any appointed agents of the parties of the date and place of the examination, and to reduce the evidence into writing.[104]

What is notable about all this is that certain things are *not* included in the letter of request. Nothing is said about cross-examination, not even a request for the facility to be afforded if it would be compatible with foreign pro-cedures; no detail is given as to the manner in which the evidence is to be 'reduced into writing', so that, for example, no preference is expressed for a verbatim transcript rather than a summary minute prepared by the foreign judge.

There is little doubt that where the appointment of an examiner is per-mitted under the law of the relevant foreign country, it offers the English practitioner a much better chance of securing a procedure with which he is familiar than does use of a letter of request to a foreign court. This is reflected in the relative use made of the two methods; though use of The Hague Evidence Convention is increasing and may ultimately change this pattern.

The practice of the courts

Rules of court in many Commonwealth jurisdictions follow the relevant English text, so there is quite a voluminous body of case-law in which the practice of taking evidence out of the jurisdiction is examined.

An order for such examination will be made 'where it appears necessary for the purposes of justice'.[105] The courts have repeatedly stressed that the making of an order is discretionary; it is not a matter of right, something to which a litigant is entitled *ex debito justitiae*.[106] 'The purposes of justice' does

---

[103] *Androux* v. *Geldermann, Inc.* (N.D.Ill, 1990).
[104] See ibid., Ord. 39, r. 3 and Form No.35 in Appendix A to the Rules.
[105] R.S.C. Ord. 38, r. 1.
[106] *Merry* v. *R.* (1884) 10 V.L.R.(E.) 135; *Coristine Ltd.* v. *Haddad* (1915) 21 D.L.R. 350 (Sask.); *New Zealand Towel Supply and Laundry Ltd.* v. *N.Z. Tri-cleaning Co. Ltd.* [1935] N.Z.L.R. 204 (C.A.).

not mean 'in the interest of either party to the litigation'; the interests of all parties need to be considered.[107]

Courts in various jurisdictions have developed lists of factors which should regularly be taken into account in exercising the discretion. For example, Canadian courts have approved a statement in the Canadian *Annual Practice*[108] listing as criteria:

(1) that the application is made bona fide; (2) that the issue in respect of which the evidence is required is one that the Court ought to try; (3) that the witnesses to be examined may give evidence material to the issue; (4) that there is good reason why they cannot be examined here; and (5) that the examination abroad will be effectual.

A slightly less elaborate statement is much cited in Australia: the applicant must satisfy the court 'that the witness is out of the jurisdiction of the court, that his evidence is material and that his attendance within the jurisdiction cannot be procured';[109] it seems to have been derived from a similar observation of Lindley LJ in an early English case.[110] These tests provide reliable guidance in straightforward cases, but often there are additional factors varying with the circumstances which must be considered before the court will authorize a departure from the normal method of trial.[111] It is possible to identify rather more closely some of the relevant considerations:

(a) *Non-availability of the witness at the trial.*   The witness must be outside the jurisdiction[112] and there must be some good reason why he cannot attend for examination in the usual way. The serious ill-health of the witness is a strong reason,[113] but it needs to be clearly proved; the courts have shown themselves suspicious of mere assertions of unfitness to travel.[114] The cost of travel to the place of trial will also be relevant; in an extreme case, the expense of the plaintiff's own journey to the only available forum might exceed the value of the claim,[115] though in other cases legal aid may be available to cover those costs.[116] Given the non-availability of subpoenas, a mere refusal by a poten-

---

[107] *Berdan* v. *Greenwood* (1880) 20 Ch.D. 764 n. (C.A.), per Bagallay LJ at p. 765n. In some circumstances, greater weight will be given to the convenience of the defendant: *Emanuel* v. *Soltykoff* (1892) 8 T.L.R. 331 (C.A.) (see further below on this point).

[108] See *Haynes* v. *Haynes* (1962) 35 D.L.R. (2d) 602 (B.C.).

[109] Per Gibbs J. in *Hardie Rubber Co. Pty. Ltd.* v. *General Tire and Rubber Co.* (1973) 129 C.L.R. 521 at 528. See also *Willis* v. *Trequair* (1906) 3 C.L.R. 912.

[110] *Armour* v. *Walker* (1883) 25 Ch.D. 673 at 677.

[111] See *Lucas Industries Ltd.* v. *Chloride Batteries Australia Ltd.* (1978) 45 F.L.R. 160 (Fed.Ct.).

[112] His presence within the jurisdiction at some earlier date (with the possibility of taking his evidence in some form then) does not preclude the making of an order: *Mason* v. *Delargy* (1884) 1 W.N.(N.S.W.) 68.

[113] *Haynes* v. *Haynes* (1962) 35 D.L.R. (2d) 602 (evidence by elderly plaintiff, resident in England, with serious heart complaint); *Weingarden* v. *Noss* (1953) 9 W.W.R. (N.S.) 335 (Man.) (advanced age and serious ill-health of plaintiff).

[114] *Berndan* v. *Greenwood* (1880) 20 Ch.D. 764 n. (C.A.) (heart condition said to make crossing of English Channel dangerous to life); *Park* v. *Schneider* (1912) 6 D.L.R. 451.

[115] e.g., *Wong Doo* v. *Kana Bhana* [1973] N.Z.L.R. 1455 (C.A.) (travel from China).

[116] *Ammar* v. *Ammar* [1954] P. 468.

tial witness to attend in England may be sufficient, as may evidence that his employer would not grant the necessary leave of absence.[117]

Where the witness is also a party to the proceedings, the courts will be less eager to dispense with attendance. The fact that bigamy charges were pending against the defendant in the forum Province was accepted as a valid reason in one case;[118] not surprisingly, a Saskatchewan judge was markedly unimpressed by a defendant's assertion that he could not travel from Oregon because the trial would occur at 'a very busy period in the building industry'.[119]

(b) *Materiality of the evidence.* Taking evidence abroad can involve both delay and added expense. The courts will not make an order with these consequences unless they are satisfied that the evidence proposed to be taken is genuinely material to the issues in the case. While the court will avoid going into the merits of the case at the interlocutory stage, the applicant for an order must establish materiality on the balance of probabilities.[120] In marginal cases, courts have sometimes allowed the applicant an opportunity to provide more details pointing to materiality[121] or agreed to an order subject to the applicant giving security for costs.[122] An order will not be made to secure evidence which merely serves to 'bolster up' other evidence.[123]

Some Canadian courts fell into the practice of declaring that 'controversial' evidence should not be taken by an examiner out of the jurisdiction; it was better that such evidence be fully tested in the trial court. It is now recognized that this approach, seldom if ever actually applied in practice, is based on a confusion of thought. Questions of the witness's *credibility* may be relevant, and will be considered below; that his evidence is *controversial*, taken alone, merely establishes that it is material to the issues in the case; it is a reason for making an order, not for refusing to do so.[124]

Even if the evidence sought is material, a court will not order the taking of evidence abroad if equally satisfactory evidence on the same point can be obtained from another source within the jurisdiction.[125]

---

[117] *Hardie Rubber Co. Pty. Ltd.* v. *General Tire and Rubber Co.* (1973) 129 C.L.R. 521; *Lucas Industries Ltd.* v. *Chloride Batteries Australia Ltd.* (1978) 45 F.L.R. 160 (Fed. Ct.) (Swedish employer would allow witness to travel to London but not to Australia). Cf. *Romano* v. *Maggiora* [1936] 2 D.L.R. 329 (B.C. C.A.) where very precise evidence of unwillingness and expense demanded.
[118] *Mills* v. *Mills* (1888) 12 P.R. (Ont.) 473.
[119] *Murray* v. *Plummer* (1913) 11 D.L.R. 764.
[120] *Hardie Rubber Co. Pty. Ltd.* v. *General Tire and Rubber Co.* (1973) 129 C.L.R. 521; *Lucas Industries Ltd.* v. *Chloride Batteries Australia Ltd.* (1978) 45 F.L.R. 160 (Fed. Ct.); *New Zealand Towel Supply and Laundry Ltd.* v. *N.Z. Tri-cleaning Co. Ltd.* [1935] N.Z.L.R. 204 (C.A.).
[121] *Langen* v. *Tate* (1883) 24 Ch.D. 522 (C.A.).
[122] *Hawes, Gibson and Co* v. *Hawes* (1912) 3 D.L.R. 396 (Ont.); *Re Corr* (1912) 5 D.L.R. 367 (Ont.).
[123] *Ehrmann* v. *Ehrmann* (1896) 2 Ch.D. 611 (C.A.); *Maynard* v. *Maynard* [1947] O.W.N. 493.
[124] See *Niewiadomski* v. *Langdon* (1956) 6 D.L.R. (2d) 361 (Ont.).
[125] See, e.g., *Park* v. *Scheider* (1912) 6 D.L.R. 451 (Alta.).

(c) *Credibility; and issues of identity.*   By making an order, the trial court denies itself the chance to observe the demeanour of the witness and especially his reaction to cross-examination. Although the examiner appointed by the court may submit a report which accompanies the deposition,[126] this is merely intended to give him the opportunity of recording facts, including incidents during the examination (for example, that the witnesses fainted or rose up and tried to assault cross-examining counsel); the examiner cannot indicate his opinion as to the credibility of the witness or his own impressions of the witness's demeanour.[127] In some cases, and especially where the witness has no interest in the outcome of the case, the lost opportunity to assess demeanour is of no great significance; in others it is too great a price to pay.

A leading illustration is *Berdan* v. *Greenwood.*[128] The Russian Government had purchased firearms, and the plaintiff claimed that this was a result of influence he had exerted; if this were true, he would be entitled to commission on the sale value. The defendants contested the claim, and the relevant Russian officials were to give evidence on their behalf. The plaintiff's case rested solely on his own evidence, and he asked that it be taken on commission in Bucharest pleading ill-health. Reversing the courts below, the Court of Appeal refused his application; his credibility was the key issue, and in such a case it was of 'extreme importance' that his evidence be tested by cross-examination in open court. There is an even stronger case for such cross-examination where the evidence the plaintiff wishes to give (for example, as to the state of his knowledge at a particular date) is very difficult to challenge by calling other witnesses; if he is believed, his point is established.[129]

A similar result is likely where the witness is suspected of complicity in a fraudulent scheme, especially where he can be regarded as the 'real' plaintiff.[130] An element in a number of such cases is a tendency to apply the tests more strictly when the application is made by the plaintiff, after he had selected the forum, especially where the application concerns his own evidence.[131] However, the 'credibility' factor can be relevant where the evidence is that of the defendant (for example, in a contested divorce case)[132] or of some other key witness.[133]

---

[126] R.S.C. Ord. 39, r. 13.

[127] *Re Wipperman* [1955] P. 59 (where Pearce J. gives the examples used in the text).

[128] (1880) 20 Ch.D. 764 n. (C.A.).

[129] See *Park* v. *Schneider* (1912) 6 D.L.R. 451 (Alta.), distinguished on this point in *Kaye* v. *Burnsland Addition Ltd.* (1915) 24 D.L.R. 232 (Alta.).

[130] e.g. *Fidelity Trust Co.* v. *Schneider* (1913) 14 D.L.R. 224 (Alta.); *Lawson* v. *Vacuum Brake Co.* (1884) 27 Ch.D. 137 (C.A.) (suspected accomplice; application of a 'shadowy, frivolous and vexatious' character); *Murray* v. *Plummer* (1913) 11 D.L.R. 764 (Sask.) (witness a co-defendant, allegedly implicated in fraud).

[131] *Coch* v. *Allcock & Co.* (1888) 21 Q.B.D. 178 (C.A.); *Emanuel* v. *Soltykoff* (1892) 8 T.L.R. 331 (C.A.); *Ross* v. *Woodford* [1894] 1 Ch. 38; *Richard Beliveau Co.* v. *Tyerman* (1911) 16 W.L.R. 492 (Sask.).   [132] *Ammar* v. *Ammar* [1954] P. 468.

[133] e.g. *Re Boyse* (1882) 20 Ch.D. 760 (where witness had interest in outcome, and his behaviour judged suspicious).

Questions of the witness's identity are an especially strong illustration of the principle. In *Nadin* v. *Bassett*,[134] the plaintiff, who had lived in New Zealand for over twenty years, claimed to be the heir-at-law of an intestate who had died some ten years before the claim. The issue was whether he was the person he claimed to be, and the Court of Appeal held that this must be tested by his appearance in court where cross-examination could be fully informed by the recollections of several people in England who knew the missing heir before his emigration. The court allowed a deposition to be taken in New Zealand, which might convince the other parties of the genuineness of the claim, but it was only to be admitted in evidence with their consent.[135]

(d) Likely outcome and adequacy of foreign procedure. No court will make an order, especially one likely to cause delay, unless it is clear that some useful purpose will be served. In the absence of powers of compulsion, the evident determination of the proposed witness not to co-operate in any way may well dissuade the court from making an order.[136] Even if the witness is willing, the law of the place in which he is to be examined may be such as to render the examination inadequate. There might, for example, be some legal reason why the examiner could not administer the oath. Where a letter of request is addressed to a foreign court, that court may be unaccustomed to the process of cross-examination. A century ago, an English judge could say:

the habits and practice of the French courts are different from our own, and . . . when the cross-examination of [the] witness is most material, and will alone enable me to judge of the effect of his examination-in-chief, I decline to delegate my discretion to any other tribunal.[137]

In modern conditions, courts are increasingly willing to operate modes of procedure, including cross-examination, with which they are unfamiliar.[138] There are inevitable difficulties in giving instructions as to cross-examination when those instructions must be settled before the examination-in-chief, and before other witnesses have been heard.[139] The courts recognize these limitations, which are inherent in any system of taking evidence abroad ahead of the trial, but cannot regard them as a sufficient objection to the making of the order.[140] In some circumstances, a locally-resident examiner

---

[134] (1883) 25 Ch.D. 21 (C.A.).

[135] See *Bangkok Bank Ltd.* v. *Swatow Lace Co. Ltd.* [1963] N.S.W.R. 488; *La Baloise Compagnie d'Assurances Contre L'Incendie* v. *Western Australian Insurance Co. Ltd.* [1939] V.L.R. 363.

[136] *Re Tucker (A Bankrupt)* [1990] Ch. 148 (C.A.).

[137] *Re Boyse* (1882) 20 Ch.D. 760 at 772 per Fry J.

[138] For practice under The Hague Evidence Convention, see pp. 94–5.

[139] Cf. *Stewart* v. *Sovereign Bank of Canada* (1912) 2 D.L.R. 913, where it was made a condition of the order that the evidence should be taken only after certain other evidence had been received, and *The Adolf Leonhardt* [1973] 2 Lloyd's Rep. 318 where Brandon J. appointed himself a special examiner and sat to hear evidence in Rotterdam for two days in the middle of the trial.

[140] See *Hardie Rubber Co. Pty. Ltd.* v. *General Tire and Rubber Co.* (1973) 129 C.L.R. 521 (difficulties of cross-examination in Japan surmountable).

may have special expertise, as where evidence as to a marriage in China was ordered to be taken in Hong Kong.[141]

(*e*) *Other considerations.*   As with any other interlocutory application, the applicant must act promptly[142] and with frankness.[143] The courts will not allow the taking of evidence abroad to develop into a 'roving enquiry', but in many jurisdictions it is not essential to name in advance all the witnesses to be examined.[144] However, under the English Rules of the Supreme Court an examiner may take the evidence of persons other than those named in the order only with the written consent of all parties to the cause or matter.[145]

(D) A Note on United States Practice

An account of United States practice in this field is well beyond the scope of this work. It may however be useful to mention two important federal statutory provisions.

The first[146] provides a means whereby a United States court may provide material for use in foreign proceedings. This provides, in relevant part:

The district court of the district in which a person resides or is found may order him to give his testimony or statement or to produce a document or other thing for use in a proceeding in a foreign or international tribunal. The order may be made pursuant to a letter rogatory issued, or request made, by a foreign or international tribunal or upon the application of any interested person and may direct that the testimony or statement be given, or the document or other thing be produced, before a person appointed by the court.

The power of United States federal courts to take evidence in aid of foreign proceedings was first introduced in 1855 but as a result of a series of what are now seen as misunderstandings[147] fell into disuse. It was revived in 1948 and the present law emerged in 1964 after a report from a Congressional Commission and Advisory Committee on International Rules of Judicial Procedure.

It will be seen from the text of the section that it does not require a Letter of Request to be issued; an application may be made directly by any interested person, a litigant, a foreign government official, or a prosecutor such as the

---

[141] *Wong Doo* v. *Kana Bhana* [1933] N.Z.L.R. 1455 (C.A.).

[142] *New Zealand Towel Supply and Laundry Ltd.* v. *N.Z. Tri-cleaning Co. Ltd.* [1935] N.Z.L.R. 204 (C.A.) (lack of promptness a factor in decision to refuse order).

[143] *Hardie Rubber Co. Pty. Ltd* v. *General Tire and Rubber Co.* (1973) 129 C.L.R. 521.

[144] Ibid., where relevant officers or employees of two named companies were to be examined. The court cited *Nadin* v. *Bassett* (1883) 25 Ch.D. 21 (C.A.) and *Armour* v. *Walker* (1883) 25 Ch.D. 673 (C.A.) as showing a similarly liberal practice in England.

[145] R.S.C. Ord. 39, r. 9.   [146] 28 USC. s. 1782.

[147] See W. B. Stahr, 'Discovery under 28 USC. 1782 for Foreign and International Proceedings' (1990) 30 Va. Jo. Int. L. 597 at 600–5. For another study see 'Much Ado about 1782: A Look at Recent Problems with Discovery in the United States for Use in Foreign Litigation under 28 USC. 1782' (1989) 20 Inter-Am. L. Rev. 429.

English Director of Public Prosecutions.[148] There is no requirement that foreign proceedings should have been instituted, or even be pending,[149] and the United States court's ability to act does not depend upon any issue as to reciprocity. It is available in criminal as well as civil cases.[150]

In addition, the United States courts have a wide subpoena power applying to persons in foreign countries:

A court of the United States may order the issuance of a subpoena requiring the appearance as a witness before it, or before a person or body designated by it, of a national or resident of the United States who is in a foreign country, or requiring the production of a specified document or other thing by him, if the court finds that particular testimony or the production of the document or other thing by him is necessary in the interests of justice, and, in other than a criminal action or proceeding,[151] if the court finds, in addition, that it is not possible to obtain his testimony in admissible form without his personal appearance or to obtain the production of the document or other thing in any other manner.[152]

[148] *Re a Letter of Request from the United Kingdom Crown Prosecution Service* [1990] I.L.Pr. 29 (D.C.Cir, 1989).

[149] Ibid.

[150] e.g. *Re Request for Judicial Assistance from the Seoul Criminal Court, Seoul, Korea* 555 F. 2d 720 (9th Cir., 1977).

[151] For the international implications of this subpoena power in the criminal context, see pp. 157–70.

[152] 28 USC. s. 1783.

4

Taking of Evidence: International Co-operation

(A) The Development of International Assistance in Europe

EARLY WORK AT THE HAGUE

REFERENCE has already been made, in the context of service of process,[1] to the early work of the Hague Conference in the field of civil procedure. Provisions as to the taking of evidence abroad were included in the Civil Procedure Conventions of 1896 and 1905, and in that of 1954 which reproduced the evidence provisions of the 1905 Convention. They are primarily concerned with the use of letters rogatory, the device which had over the centuries become well established in the practice of States, and not only those of the civil law tradition,[2] and which remains central to the procedures for obtaining evidence from another jurisdiction.

Article 8 of each Convention had the same text which survives, with only minor drafting changes, in the text of the most recent Hague Convention on the topic, that on the Taking of Evidence Abroad of 1970.[3] It provided that in civil or commercial matters a judicial authority of a Contracting State might, in conformity with the provisions of its legislation, communicate by letter rogatory with the competent authority of another Contracting State in order to request that the latter should, within its jurisdiction, effect either an examination (*un acte d'instruction*) or other judicial acts (*actes judiciaires*).[4] These terms are not further defined; they include taking the evidence of witnesses and of experts, viewing a place, and examining commercial books and records;[5] they do not include any *acte d'execution* such as ordering the return of an abducted child.[6]

The 1896 Convention provided for the use of the diplomatic channel unless

---

[1] See pp. 12–13.
[2] See (1295) 1 Rolle's Abr. 530 (letters of request from the English court to the authorities in Holland for evidence in a trespass action).
[3] The text forms Art. 8 of the 1954 Convention, and Art. 1(1) of the 1970 Convention.
[4] The text of the 1896 and 1905 Conventions is reproduced in the *Harvard Research*, App. VI, pp. 149–52; that of chapter II of the 1954 Convention, with an unofficial English translation, at *AetD (11)*, vol. 4, pp. 76–7.
[5] See the exchanges recorded in *AetD (4)*, p. 92.
[6] *Tristany* v. *Astruc*, Cour de cassation, 29 Nov. 1973, Rev. Crit. D.I.P. 1974, 690 (noted Couchez) (Asser 2/14).

the authorities of the States concerned had allowed direct communication between their competent authorities.[7] In the 1905 text, changes were introduced which closely parallel those made in the context of service of process.[8] So, the primary or preferred mode of transmission was the indirect consular channel, from the consul of the requesting State to an authority designated for the purpose by the State addressed; a Contracting State could, however, still insist on the use of the diplomatic channel, and the new Convention did not preclude more direct communication between competent authorities by agreement between the States concerned.[9]

Nothing was said in the early conventions about the contents of the letters rogatory, although from 1905 there was a requirement that letters should be drawn up in, or accompanied by a certified translation into, the language of the requested authority[10] (or another language agreed between the States concerned).[11] The execution of the letters rogatory might be refused only if the authenticity of the document was not established; or if in the requested State its execution was not included within 'the attributes of judicial power';[12] or if the request infringed the sovereignty or security of the requested State.[13] The forms to be followed in executing the request[14] were those of the requested State, but a request that a special form be followed would be complied with provided the form specified were not contrary to the legislation of that State.[15] So, for example, a request that evidence be taken on oath would be complied with in Switzerland despite the fact that the oath was not used under local procedure.[16]

Finally, Article 15 of the 1905 Convention expressly preserved the right of States to take evidence through their diplomatic and consular agents, in so far as consular conventions between the two States permitted, or if the State in which the evidence was to be taken did not object.

[7] 1896 Convention, Art. 9(1).   [8] See pp. 12–13.

[9] 1905 Convention, Art. 9. See Oberlandesgericht Koln, 16 June 1975 (13 W 40/75), NJW 1975, 2349 (Asser 2/14): German courts encouraged to make use of the direct communication available under Dutch–German agreement of 1962.

[10] This usage, identifying the relevant language as that of the requested *authority* rather than of the requested *State* is to be found in each of The Hague Conventions on this subject.

[11] See Art. 10 in each of the 1905 and 1954 texts.

[12] e.g. the ordering of a blood sample in a paternity case held not to be within the attributes of Italian judicial power: Cagliari C.A., 29 Feb. 1968, R.D.I.P.P., 1968, 461 (Asser 1/17) (applying, *per incuriam*, the 1905 text, which is, however, to the same effect as that of 1954).

[13] Ibid., Art. 11. There were provisions to the same effect in the 1896 text. A request for evidence as to the relationship between the parties to a paternity case was held by the Milan C.A not to threaten the sovereignty or security of Italy: 5 Apr. 1968 (Asser 1/17).

[14] This will apply to matters of procedure (e.g. the administration of the oath) but not to questions of the competence of the witness (e.g. a spouse): Brussels C.A., 18 May 1966, Pas. 1967, 87 (Asser 1/16).

[15] 1905 and 1954 Conventions, Art. 14; again, similar provisions were in the 1896 text.

[16] Bezirksgerichtsprasidium Appenzell, 25 Oct. 1976, [1977] SJZ 141. Cf. Roermond, 16 Mar. 1972 (Asser 1/18), where a Dutch court had omitted to ask the German court to administer the oath. See also Oberlandesgericht Stuttgart, 13 Feb. 1968 (1 V A 3/67) (Asser 1/15) (Art. 14 should be given a liberal interpretation; evidence provided for Austrian application for the maintenance of a child despite possible inadmissibility of evidence sought under German law).

TABLE 2: *United Kingdom Bilateral Conventions*

Reference	Other party	Date signed	Procedures		
127 LNTS 167	Austria	31 Mar. 1931	1	2*	3*
24 LNTS 91	Belgium	21 June 1922	1	2*	3*
48 LNTS 425	Czechoslovakia	11 Nov. 1924	1	2	
139 LNTS 9	Denmark	29 Nov. 1932	1	2*	3*
149 LNTS 131	Finland	11 Aug. 1933	1	2*	3*
10 LNTS 448	France	2 Feb. 1922	1	2*	
90 LNTS 287	Germany	20 Mar. 1928	1	2n	
185 LNTS 113	Greece	27 Feb. 1936	1	2*	3*
170 LNTS 51	Hungary	25 Sept. 1935	1	2*n	
176 LNTS 229	Iraq	25 July 1935	1	2*	
630 UNTS 189	Israel	5 July 1966	1	2	3
131 LNTS 79	Italy	17 Dec. 1930	1	2	3
140 LNTS 287	Netherlands	31 May 1932	1	2*	3*
123 LNTS 343	Norway	30 Jan. 1931	1	2*	3*
131 LNTS 19	Poland	26 Aug. 1931	1		3
129 LNTS 417	Portugal	9 July 1931	1	2*	3*
101 LNTS 375	Spain	27 June 1929	1	2*	3*
114 LNTS 9	Sweden	28 Aug. 1930	1	2*	3*
141 LNTS 225	Turkey	28 Nov. 1931	1	2*n	
181 LNTS 241	Yugoslavia	27 Feb. 1936	1	2*	

Key to permitted procedures:
  1 = Letters of request
  2 = Consular agent
  3 = Other special examiner

Note: The procedures indicated are those available in the case of requests originating from England; the Conventions sometimes make more generous provision in respect of the taking of evidence in England.

Limitations
  * = Measures of compulsion not to be used
  n = Only to take evidence of British nationals

ENGLISH BILATERALISM

Reference has already been made to the examination by the Sumner Committee of the 1905 Hague Convention, and the reasoning which led to the Committee's recommendation that the United Kingdom should not accede to that Convention but proceed rather by way of bilateral treaties.[17] The Com-

[17] See pp. 13–14.

mittee produced a draft text, which on this subject contained three quite different formulations each permitting a different range of procedures. [18]

A number of Civil Procedure Conventions were duly negotiated; details, ignoring those with the three Baltic Republics later incorporated into the USSR but now enjoying renewed independence, are given in the Table 2.

In addition to these United Kingdom bilateral conventions, there was a very large number of bilateral arrangements between States, many of whom were parties to the 1905 Hague Convention, regulating procedures and providing for other modes of communication; the Hague Conference Permanent Bureau listed over fifty such arrangements known to it in 1967. [19]

RESUMED WORK AT THE HAGUE

The revived Hague Conference on Private International Law renewed the Civil Procedure Convention in 1954, but a full revision was not undertaken until 1964. In that year chapter I, dealing with Service of Process, was revised to become The Hague Service Convention of 1965.[20] The revision of chapter II on Evidence followed and was completed at the Eleventh Session of the Conference in October 1968.

The United States, whose law on the subject had recently been overhauled,[21] played a prominent part in the process of revision. In its Memorandum, circulated at the start of the revision process,[22] the United States Government argued that 'Letters rogatory are a useful but scarcely perfect technique for securing evidence from persons abroad' and listed a number of limitations of the technique, limitations which were especially important where the two legal systems involved differed in their practice. It suggested a number of objectives for the revision:

1. A relaxation of barriers against voluntary testimony by 'willing' parties or witnesses.
2. A willingness to permit, under court supervision, use of the techniques of examination of the foreign forum.
3. A resort to a more efficient and less expensive method of transmitting documents of international judicial assistance; and
4. An expansion of the categories of officers before whom testimony may be taken to include, for example, commissioners and consuls.

The ensuing revision successfully attained these objectives.

(B) The Hague Convention on the Taking of Evidence Abroad

The Convention on the Taking of Evidence Abroad in Civil or Commercial Matters, drafted at the Eleventh Session of the Conference in 1968, was

---

[18] See the Report (Cmd. 251), and the *Harvard Research*, App. V, pp. 140–3.
[19] *AetD (11)*, Vol. 4, pp. 19–20.   [20] See p. 16 *et seq.*
[21] See pp. 80—1.   [22] *AetD (11)*, pp. 15–18.

signed on 18 March 1970.[23] It has proved to be one of the most successful of The Hague conventions.[24] The Convention provides for the taking of evidence or the performing of other judicial acts abroad, by means of Letters of Request or by the use of diplomats and consuls, and of commissioners. Chapter I deals with the contents of Letters of Request, the establishment of Central Authorities, and related matters. Chapter II regulates the taking of evidence by diplomats, consuls, and commissioners. Chapter III contains general clauses and preserves existing State laws which permit evidence to be taken by other equally liberal procedures.

Contributing to the success of the Convention has been the continuing review of its operation. So, Special Commissions of the Conference were called for this purpose in 1978 and 1985.[25] The two meetings examined in detail the practical workings of the Convention and were able to make suggestions to facilitate its operation, but no major difficulties were discovered. As a related exercise, the Permanent Bureau of the Hague Conference published a Practical Handbook on the Operation of the Convention, in English and French editions. In loose-leaf format, it contains the text of the Convention in both languages, lists of parties, the explanatory report of Mr P. W. Amram, the rapporteur of the Third Commission of the 1968 Session which prepared the Convention, the text of reservations and declarations made under the various articles of the Convention, a note of the 1978 Special Commission meeting, a digest of case-law on the Convention, and detailed practical information, including addresses and telephone numbers of the Central Authorities, for each member State.

LETTERS OF REQUEST

Scope

Chapter I of the Convention contains fresh provisions for the operation of the system of Letters of Request. Article 1 provides that a judicial authority of a contracting State may, in civil or commercial matters, request the competent authority of another contracting State, by means of a Letter of Request, to obtain evidence or to perform some other judicial act.

---

[23] The text is reproduced below in the Appendix of Selected Documents.

[24] It is currently in force in the following States and territories. All have ratified it, or acceded [A] or had it extended to them by a member State responsible for their foreign relations [E]: Akrotiri and Dhekelia [E]; Barbados [A]; Cayman Islands [E]; Cyprus [A]; Czechoslovakia; Denmark; Falkland Islands and Dependencies [E]; Finland; France; Germany; Gibraltar [E]; Guam [E]; Hong Kong [E]; Israel; Italy; Luxembourg; Man, Isle of [E]; Netherlands; Norway; Portugal; Puerto Rico [E]; Singapore [A]; Sweden; United Kingdom; United States; Virgin Islands of the US. In addition Spain and Switzerland have signed but not yet ratified. The Irish Law Reform Commission is preparing a report with a view to legislation.

[25] The report of the 1978 Special Commission is to be found at *AetD* (*14*), Vol. 4, pp. 418–28. The Report of the 1985 Special Commission is published as a separate document and has yet to appear in the AetD series.

Civil and commercial

The text, and indeed the full title, of the Convention limits its field of application to 'civil or commercial matters'. The difficulties inherent in the use of this phrase, and the view taken by a Special Commission of the Conference examining the Service Convention, but hoping to give guidance in this context also, have already been noticed.[26]

The meaning of this troublesome phrase was a central issue in the English case of *The State of Norway's Application* which was twice considered by the Court of Appeal and once by the House of Lords. A request under the Convention was received in England from the Sandefjord City Court, Norway, asking that a director and a senior employee of a London merchant bank be examined as to the ownership and control of certain assets and of a charitable trust said to control those assets. The context was an action in the Norwegian court to set aside a retrospective tax assessment which had been raised by the Norwegian tax authorities against the estate of a deceased taxpayer who, it was alleged, was the beneficial owner of the assets which he had not declared for tax purposes.

The English courts had to consider the meaning of the phrase 'civil or commercial matter' as used in section 9(1) of the Evidence (Proceedings in Other Jurisdictions) Act 1975, passed mainly to give effect to the Convention; the precise question was whether the evidence sought was 'for the purposes of *civil proceedings* . . . before the requesting court' within section 1 of the Act, the italicized phrase being interpreted in section 9 to mean proceedings in any civil or commercial matter.

When the case first came before the Court of Appeal,[27] the court, finding no assistance in the text of the Convention itself, held in effect that the proceedings had to be regarded as in a 'civil or commercial matter' both under the law of the requesting country, which must necessarily be the starting-point, and that of England, the courts of which had to be satisfied that the request did fall within the terms of the Act. As Glidewell LJ pointed out, the latter requirement might be wholly theoretical, given the breadth of the English concept of 'civil proceedings' as anything which is not criminal in nature.[28] Kerr LJ said that that there was no generally accepted international meaning of the phrase; he recognized that in some jurisdictions, public law matters were regarded as outside the categories of civil and commercial, but that this was not universally the case; he, but not the other members of the court, felt that there was insufficient evidence as to the approach of Norwegian law, but was prepared to give the request the benefit of the doubt.

[26] See pp. 18–19. The 1985 Special Commission on the Evidence Convention noted that many bankruptcy cases, other than those with a penal aspect, would properly be regarded as 'civil or commercial': Report, p. 8. See *Re Tucker (a bankrupt)* [1987] 1 W.L.R. 928 (on the Service Convention).   [27] *Re State of Norway's Application (No. 1)* [1987] Q.B. 433 (C.A.).

[28] Note that, as was pointed out by Balcombe LJ in the second Court of Appeal decision, criminal 'proceeding' may not be the same as criminal 'matter'.

The first Letters of Request were, however, rejected as too widely drawn, under principles as to 'fishing expeditions' to be considered below.[29] The Norwegian court issued a second Letter of Request and the 'civil or commercial' point was taken again, and argued before a differently constituted Court of Appeal.[30] A majority (May and Balcombe L JJ.), considering substantial additional material[31] and encouraged by academic criticism of the first decision,[32] held that 'civil or commercial matter' not only could but should be given an 'international' interpretation. May LJ recognized that the phrase had no intelligible meaning in a wholly common law context, which suggested that attention had to be given to the civil law origins of the phrase. Viewed in this light, the Norwegian proceedings would be categorized as being concerned with fiscal, and therefore public law, matters and not with matters civil or commercial. Woolf LJ reached a similar result by a different route; he could not identify an 'international' meaning of the phrase, but interpreting it by reference to English law (but not adopting 'any parochial classification of a procedural nature') he held that fiscal matters were a special category, outwith that of 'civil or commercial'.

In the House of Lords, the argument went off on a rather different tack. The 1975 Act had been accepted in the Court of Appeal as having been passed mainly to give effect to the Hague Convention, but that purpose nowhere appears in the text of the Act which was also designed to replace earlier United Kingdom legislation, notably the Foreign Tribunals Evidence Act 1856 in which the phrase 'civil or commercial matter' was used in a context wholly divorced from any international convention and which formed part of the law of many Commonwealth (and common law) countries. This, and the deliberate decision of those who drafted the Hague Convention to include no definition of the phrase in that context,[33] led Lord Goff, with whom the other members of the House agreed, to reject any 'international' meaning. Instead he applied, as had the first Court of Appeal, a combination of the laws of the requesting and requested countries. It was found that the matter was viewed as 'civil' in Norwegian law, and it was held that (contrary to the view of Woolf LJ) there was nothing to take fiscal matters outside the civil category in English law, which embraced everything which was not a criminal matter. The House rejected, it is submitted quite correctly, an argument that the refusal of the English courts to *enforce* foreign penal or revenue law[34] precluded the English court from giving the assistance requested; to

---

[29] See pp. 106—7.

[30] *Re State of Norway's Application (No.2)* [1989] 1 All E.R. 701 (C.A.).

[31] Including C. Szladits' chapter on 'The Civil Law System' in 2 Ency. Comp. L.

[32] F. A. Mann (1986) 102 L.Q.R. 505; though in some respects the Court of Appeal rejected Dr Mann's reasoning.

[33] See *AetD (11)*, Vol. 4, pp. 56–7 (explanatory report of Mr Amram on the preliminary draft of the Convention).

[34] See Dicey and Morris, *The Conflict of Laws* (11th edn., 1987), p. 100.

provide evidence which is to be used in foreign proceedings, even enforcement proceedings, is not to 'enforce' the foreign law in England.

In the end result, therefore, the *State of Norway* litigation provides no real guidance as to the meaning of the phrase in the Hague context. As Dr Mann has argued,[35] it does allow the English courts to provide assistance, in practice under the Hague Convention, in certain fiscal and administrative contexts which would be judged by some other countries to fall outside its scope; Dr Mann's unease at this needs to be balanced against the enormous and considered growth, recounted elsewhere in this book, in international co-operation in such fields.[36]

One closely related question has also been the subject of much recent discussion. If a request is made to obtain evidence abroad for use in what are clearly civil proceedings, is it a sufficient ground for rejecting the request that there is a possibility that the evidence might subsequently be used in the requesting country in a *criminal* matter?

The general opinion amongst Central Authorities is that a request should not be rejected on this ground;[37] and this appears to accord with the views expressed in the House of Lords in the *Westinghouse* case.[38] As Lord Wilberforce pointed out,[39] once evidence is brought out in court it is in the public domain; unless the terms of relevant legislation or international agreements provide otherwise, there is nothing to prevent other interested persons or authorities acting upon the information thus made available. However it is quite proper to reject a request if the evidence is really being sought with a view to its use in criminal procedings. This was emphasized in the *Westinghouse* case by Viscount Dilhorne who said:

I hope that the courts of this country will always be vigilant to prevent a misuse of the convention and will not make an order requiring evidence to be given . . . unless it is clearly established that, even if required for civil proceedings, it is not also sought for criminal [proceedings].[40]

Judicial authorities

The request must emanate from a 'judicial authority', but there is no definition of this expression. The Commission responsible for preparing the Convention decided not to include courts of arbitration,[41] but there is no clarity on the position of administrative tribunals, many of which closely resemble

---

[35] (1989) 105 L.Q.R. 341.

[36] See also *Securities and Exchange Commission* v. *Certain Unknown Purchasers of the Common Stock of and Call Options for the Common Stock of Santa Fe International Corpn.* (Q.B.D., 23 Feb. 1984, unreported) where S.E.C. proceedings were treated as a civil matter. In *S.* v. *E.* [1967] 1 Q.B. 367 affiliation proceedings were held to be civil proceedings within the Foreign Tribunals Evidence Act 1856.

[37] See the conclusions of the 1978 Special Commission, at *AetD* (14), Vol. 4, pp. 419–20.

[38] *Rio Tinto Zinc Corporation* v. *Westinghouse Electric Corporation* [1978] A.C. 547 (H.L.).

[39] At p. 611.

[40] At p. 631.

[41] *AetD* (11), Vol. 4, pp. 97–9.

ordinary courts, whilst others do not. Each case must be examined on its own facts, examining the function rather than just the formal categorization of the requesting authority.[42] An illustration, from a not dissimilar field, of this approach in practice is *Re Letters Rogatory Issued by the Director of Inspection of Government of India*,[43] where a United States Court of Appeals decided, after an analysis of the powers and duties of a tax assessment agency in India, that it was not a 'tribunal' entitled to the execution in New York of a Letter of Request seeking action under 28 USC. 1782.[44]

'Evidence'

No definition of this term is given, but some guide to the meaning of 'obtain evidence' is given in Article 3(*e*), (*f*) and (*g*) which refer to witnesses, questions to be asked, and documents or property to be inspected. The pre-liminary draft of Article 1 did in fact contain, in the English text only, an explanatory gloss to the word 'evidence' as 'including the taking of state-ments of witnesses, parties or experts and the production or examination of documents or other objects or property'; its eventual omission was for reasons of style rather than of substance.

Article 1(2), excluding attempts to obtain evidence which is not intended for use in judicial proceedings, commenced or contemplated, is considered below in the context of pre-trial discovery.[45]

'Other judicial act'

This is a phrase retained from the earlier Hague Conventions. In order to minimize doubts as to its scope, Article 1(3) makes it clear that certain matters which are either dealt with in other Conventions, or which might involve the exercise of the Court's discretion, such as the service of process, the enforcement of judgments and orders, and orders for provisional or pro-tective measures, are excluded.[46] The act must be 'judicial'; if it is not within the functions of the judiciary in the State of execution, e.g. conducting con-ciliation in matrimonial proceedings or valuing property, the Request may be refused (even if it is a judicial act in the requesting State).[47]

In practice, many States seem willing to adopt a generous view of the scope of the Convention, responding to requests to obtain the results of blood-grouping tests (at least where the subject is willing) and to provide copies of public documents or of entries in registers of civil status.[48] In England,

---

[42] See the Report of the 1985 Special Commission, p. 8.

[43] 385 F (2d) 1017 (2nd Cir. 1967).

[44] For this provision, see p. 80. See also *Fonseca* v. *Blumenthal* 620 F.2d 322 (2nd Circ., 1980) (similar decision re the Superintendent of Exchange Control of the Republic of Colombia).

[45] See pp. 97–100.

[46] e.g. many types of injunctions, forced sales, and receiverships: se the Explanatory Report of Mr Amram, *AetD* (*11*), Vol. 4, p. 203.   [47] Article 12(*a*).

[48] See the 1978 Special Commission report, *AetD* (*14*), Vol. 4, p. 420.

obtaining extracts of public records would not be seen as a judicial act, and the phrase 'other judicial acts' seems to remain a source of puzzlement.[49]

Central Authorities

Each Contracting State must establish a Central Authority,[50] and there is freedom to designate additional 'other authorities' or, in the case of federal States, more than one Central Authority.[51] It is customary for the same body to be designated as the Central Authority for other Hague Conventions dealing with civil procedure, notably that on Service of Process.[52]

In the United Kingdom, the Foreign and Commonwealth Office is the Central Authority but 'other authorities' designated for England, Scotland and Northern Ireland discharge the practical functions, and all are more closely court-related officers (e.g. in England, the Senior Master of the Supreme Court). In Commonwealth jurisdictions, the designated Central Authority is frequently the Registrar of the Supreme Court or its equivalent (so in Barbados, Singapore, Hong Kong) but sometimes the Ministry of Justice (as in Cyprus) or the Governor (as in the Cayman Islands).

To ensure the simplicity of the system, it is expressly provided in Article 2 that no intervening agency in the requested State is to deal with the Letter of Request on its way to the Central Authority. However, Article 27(*a*) permits a State to declare that it will accept transmission of Letters of Request to its judicial authorities by other channels (no State has done so); Article 28(*a*) enables two or more Contracting States to make other arrangements inter se; and Article 32 protects existing bilateral Conventions.

The Convention does not prescribe how a Letter of Request should be dispatched from within the requesting State. In the United States the courts transmit Letters directly to the Central Authority abroad. In the United Kingdom and France Letters are transmitted through their own Central Authorities, a procedure which has the advantage of making it more likely that the formal requirements of the Convention will be fully complied with.

Contents of Letters of Request

The detailed information which the Letter of Request must contain is set out in Article 3. It includes the name of the requesting authority, and the name of the requested authority if known; otherwise the Letter could simply refer to 'the appropriate authority'. Details of the parties, the proceedings, the evidence to be obtained, or other judicial act to be performed and questions to be put must be included. If, under the law of the requesting authority, the evidence is to be given on oath or any special form is to be used, this should

---

[49] See ibid., p. 411, where the United Kingdom's response to the Hague Conference questionnaire assumes that 'other judicial acts' form a middle category between 'judicial' and 'nonjudicial' acts, which was never the intention.

[50] Art. 2.

[51] Art. 24.

[52] See what is said in the context of that Convention, pp. 20–1.

be included, along with any special procedure to be followed under Article 9.[53] No legalization of the Letter or other like formality may be required.

The Special Commissions of 1978 and 1985 considered that there was a need for a model or standard form of Letter of Request to overcome the problem of inadequate information, for example, as to the precise nature of the evidence to be obtained, or the authority to whom the Letter should be returned, as well as difficulties of interpretation over legal terminology used in different systems. Accordingly a model form was devised and revised in 1985. It is designed to operate as a 'check list' of all information which is considered to be desirable or necessary for the successful execution of the Request and its prompt return to the requesting authority. The model form is not obligatory but is recommended in the interest of both requesting and requested States. What is most needed is a clear explanation of the particular point on which evidence is sought; the model form includes requests for summaries of the parties' positions and suggests that relevant documentation (court orders, pleadings) might be attached; but these should be restricted to matters illuminating the particular request for evidence and should not seek to rehearse the whole case.

Language of the Request

Letters of Request must be in the language of the authority requested to execute it (or be accompanied by a translation into that language); or in English or French, unless a party has made a reservation under Article 33 excluding the use of English or French; or in another language which a Contracting State has declared its readiness to accept.[54] A State with more than one official language may, if necessary under internal law, declare the language of Letters to be used in specified parts of its territory. Failure to comply with this declaration, 'without justifiable excuse', renders the State of origin liable to pay the cost of translation.[55]

The Convention does not prescribe the language to be used in responding to the Letter; the normal expectation is that the language to be used will be that in which the Letter was sent, but documents and evidence taken orally will be sent in the original language, whatever that may be.

Rejection of Letter of Request

The Convention creates an obligation to execute Letters of Request falling within its terms; and the Letter is to be executed 'expeditiously'.[56] The exceptional circumstances in which execution may be refused are very narrowly defined.

A Central Authority may object to a Letter on the ground that it does not comply with the Convention, for example because the contents are insuf-

---

[53] See pp. 94–5. The Letter may also contain information about the privileges and duties of witnesses required under Article 11.   [54] Art. 4.
[55] Ibid.   [56] Art. 9.

ficiently full, whereupon it must promptly inform the sending authority.[57] If the Letter of Request complies with the Convention, its execution may be refused only on the grounds set out in Article 12, and only to the extent that it is objectionable on those grounds. They are that in the State of execution the execution of the Letter does not fall within the province of the judiciary; and that the State addressed considers that its sovereignty or security would be prejudiced thereby.

The *Westinghouse* case[58] illustrates the reference to prejudice to the sovereignty of a State, the Attorney-General appearing to represent that HM Government regarded as an unacceptable invasion of its own sovereignty the use of proceedings in the United States courts as a means by which the United States government sought to investigate activities outside the United States of British companies and individuals which might infringe American anti-trust laws As has already been noted, a request for extracts from a public record is an example of a Request falling outside the judicial function in some States.

The meeting of Experts in June 1978 discussed a difficult question, raised by the United States, as to whether or not a Central Authority was obliged to prosecute or to defend an appeal against a decision of the judicial authority granting or refusing execution of a Letter. In the United States, the Central Authority has, on several occasions, responded to appeals made to higher courts by one of the parties. The discussion was not conclusive but views were expressed that, while there was no such obligation on the Central Authority, if it felt that good grounds existed for an appeal, it could properly act.[59]

Execution of Letters of Request

Letters of Request are to be executed by an 'authority competent to execute them',[60] later referred to as a 'judicial authority'.[61] If a Request is sent to an authority which is not competent to execute it, it must be sent forthwith to the correct authority,[62] either by the former authority direct, or by the Central Authority.

A question was raised in the 1978 Special Commission as to whether a 'judicial authority' meant a judge. The practice of States was more liberal: the United States, for example, is prepared to appoint as commissioners any persons who are entitled to administer oaths. In England, the competent authorities are the Masters of the Queen's Bench Division, who make orders appointing examiners, almost always barristers, to take the testimony. In other countries, such as Austria, Sweden, Norway, and Denmark, the local court where the witness resides is the authority. In France, the authorities include not only the judiciary but also other persons designated as commissioners by the French Government. The Commission felt that, to save time and expense,

---

[57] Art. 5.
[58] *Westinghouse* [1978] A.C. 547. See further. pp. 100–1.
[59] *AetD* (14), Vol. 4, p.423.
[60] Art. 2.
[61] Art. 9.
[62] Art. 6.

authorities able to execute requests should include not only courts, but commissioners, notaries public, lawyers, and others, in so far as they could be given 'certain attributes of a judicial authority'.[63]

Attendance at the execution of the Letter of Request

Notice of the time and place of the proceedings must, on request, be sent to the requesting authority, or direct to the parties, to enable them and their representatives to be present.[64] The notice can be given either by the Central Authority or, to save time, directly by the competent authority.[65]

Contracting States may declare that 'judicial personnel of the requesting authority' may be present at the execution of the letter.[66] The declaration may also require prior authorization by the competent authority to be obtained in each particular case. Although the text was carefully drafted to limit the rights of the visiting judge, in that he could be present at, but play no active part in, the proceedings, more active participation is in practice allowed in some countries.[67] In some, for example, the United Kingdom and France, judges are permitted to attend (pursuant either to a declaration under the Convention or other procedures) but it has been rare for them to do so and they could normally only ask questions with the leave of the court. The United States adopts a liberal approach and some foreign judges have actually been sworn in as commissioners by American courts, for example, German and Italian judges have been allowed to execute the Letters themselves in the United States by examining witnesses in their own language and according to their own procedures. United States judges also have gone abroad on rare occasions, for example, to England in the *Westinghouse* case, but it is understood that the United States now discourages this practice.

Special procedures and methods

The judicial authority executing the request applies its own laws and procedures, save where a request is made to follow a special method or procedure, which is not incompatible with the law of the State of execution or impossible of performance by reason of its internal practice and procedure or by reason of other practical difficulties.[68]

Some requesting States may only accept evidence taken in a particular way and the Convention tries to ensure that a request for a special procedure (for example, for verbatim transcripts or, on the other hand, for a summary of the evidence in deposition form; or for video-taped evidence) will not be refused merely because it is inconvenient to the requested State. 'Incompatible' with internal law does not mean simply 'different' from such law, but that there must be some constitutional or statutory prohibition. It is, of course, for the

---

[63] *AetD (14)*, Vol. 4, p. 422.   [64] Art. 7.

[65] In England, the information is sent to the requesting authority by the Queen's Bench Masters' Secretary on behalf of the Senior Master.   [66] Art. 8.

[67] See *AetD (14)*, Vol 4., p. 422.   [68] Art. 9.

requested State to determine whether the special method is impractical or impossible of performance.

In appropriate cases a commissioner from the Requesting State might be appointed to carry out the special method or procedure requested, for example, to overcome the difficulty which a civil law State may have in satisfying a Request from a common law State to take evidence under cross examination, because no judge or local lawyer in the requested State had any experience in that field. There are indications, however, that the operation of the Convention leads to a greater willingness on the part of requested countries to adapt their procedures so that the needs of countries with different traditions are more readily met. The German courts, for example, have developed a procedure for taking depositions in response to requests from foreign countries, with provision for cross-examination, which appears entirely to meet the needs of common law countries; the French Code of Civil Procedure now allows verbatim recording and a limited form of cross-examination to meet the needs of parties using the Convention.[69]

Letters of Request are to be executed expeditiously.[70] At the 1985 Special Commission, various estimates were given as to the length of time taken to comply with a Letter of Request. A fair number of countries indicated that a response could be given within three months. Those with a slower response time indicated that special treatment would be given to Requests which indicated genuine urgency. The recommended model form of Letter of Request as revised in 1985 includes questions as to the date by which a response is needed, and the reasons for the choice of that date.

Measures of compulsion against a witness

The requested authority is required by Article 10 to apply the same measures of compulsion against an unwilling witness as it would do under its internal law in local proceedings. Although no serious problems have arisen under this Article, there is a divergence of practice in applying compulsion for blood tests in paternity cases, where the Convention is often used. Some countries, including England but not Scotland, will use compulsory powers, but this is not the case in many countries, including France, The Netherlands, Portugal, Scotland and the United States, where it may be unconstitutional to force a person to give body samples.

Privileges and duties of witnesses

A witness may refuse to give evidence if he has a privilege or duty to do so either under the law of the State where the Letter of Request is to be executed or under the law of the requesting State.[71] So in the *Westinghouse* case, one

---

[69] See Arts. 739–40 of the Code. For Germany, see D. R. Shemanski, 'Obtaining Evidence in the Federal Republic of Germany: The Impact of The Hague Evidence Convention on German-American Judicial Co-operation' (1983) 17 Int. L. 465.

[70] Art. 9(3).

[71] Art. 11.

group of witnesses successfully claimed a privilege existing in English law, while another group of witnesses successfully relied upon a privilege existing in the law of the United States, the requesting State. Where the privilege arises under the law of the requesting State and the privilege has not been stated in the Letter, the requested authority may ask the requesting authority to confirm whether such privilege or duty exists,[72] in order to safeguard the witness's interests. It is obviously more convenient if the requesting authority anticipates any possible claim of privilege under its own law, preferably by supplying a copy of the relevant legal provisions with the Letter of Request.

These provisions have no counterpart in the earlier Hague texts. There was no great difficulty as to privileges existing under the law of the two States principally concerned, but the question of privileges under the law of third States proved much more difficult.[73] There was seen to be a need to protect such witnesses as a Swiss banker who is prevented by Swiss law from disclosing bank details, or a French physician whose duty of professional secrecy is enforced under severe professional sanctions. In place of a draft provision which gave protection in all cases where criminal or disciplinary proceedings were possible in a third State, the final Convention text allows States to declare that they will respect privileges and duties under the law of third States to the extent specified in the declaration.[74] The United Kingdom has made no such declaration.

Return of executed Letter of Request

The documents establishing the execution of the Letter are to be sent by the requested authority to the requesting authority by the same channel as was used for transmission of the Request. If the Letter is not executed in whole or in part, the requesting authority must be informed immediately.[75] In practice, some States (including the United Kingdom and the United States) always return the documents through their Central Authorities because it enables them to monitor the implementation of the Convention. Other States, in the interests of speed, leave it to the competent authority to return the documents, or to inform the requesting authority that the Letter of Request has not been executed.

Taxes and costs

A State may not claim reimbursement of taxes and costs of any nature for executing a Letter, but it may recover from the requesting State any fees paid to experts and interpreters, as well as the cost of any special procedure requested under Article 9.[76] Furthermore, a requested authority, whose law obliges the parties themselves to secure the evidence, and which is not able

---

[72] See Art. 11(1)(*b*).
[73] See *AetD* (*11*), Vol. 4, pp. 60–1, 116–18, 136, and 166–7.   [74] Art. 11(2).
[75] Art. 13.   [76] Art. 14(1)(2).

itself to execute the Letter may, with the consent of the requesting authority, appoint a suitable person to do so and recover the appropriate costs.[77] The requesting State and not the moving party is liable for these costs, and it is of interest that this provision enables a judge of the requesting State to impose an international fiscal obligation on his Government.

Under Article 26 a State may, if required to do so because of constitutional limitations (and on the basis of reciprocity), request reimbursement by the requesting State of fees and costs for the service of process on an unwilling witness and for his attendance, and for transcripts or evidence. This provision does not appear to have been formally invoked but it may prove of particular assistance in some federal systems where there can be constitutional problems in appropriating funds for these expenses.

Certain States in fact claim reimbursement of high fees and daily allowances and travel costs of witnesses who have to travel long distances, although these costs should normally be borne by the requested State, unless Article 26 can be invoked.

Pre-trial discovery of documents

Article 1(2) of the Convention provides that:

A Letter shall not be used to obtain evidence which is not intended for use in judicial proceedings, commenced or contemplated.

Article 23 further provides:

A Contracting State may at the time of signature, ratification or accession, declare that it will not execute Letters of request issued for the purpose of obtaining pre-trial discovery of documents as known in Common Law countries.

Neither provision featured in the draft text prepared before the Eleventh Session of the Hague Conference. Both had their origin in a Working Document presented by the United Kingdom delegation[78] and designed to apply the Convention only to evidence 'for use in proceedings pending in the State of origin'. As the text emerged from the drafting committee, the English text, but not the French text, of Article 1 made express reference to 'discovery'; a request was not to be used for the purpose of obtaining discovery *between the parties* before the trial.[79] After some unhelpful discussion, which did at least confirm that the main concern of the United Kingdom delegation was that of discovery, that was dealt with in Article 23, Article 1 retaining some residual signs of the drafting history. What nobody seemed to notice was that the text of Article 23, by referring to 'pre-trial discovery of documents as known in Common Law countries', and especially in omitting the earlier reference to discovery *between the parties*, covered some types of the form of discovery

---

[77] Art. 14(3). This provision enables a common law jurisdiction such as England to recover the fees of private examiners appointed by the Court.
[78] Working Document 10, *AetD (11)*, Vol. 4, p. 94.   [79] Ibid., p. 137.

known in the United States, which is far wider in its scope than that known in other Common Law countries.

It is appropriate to set out the opening words of Rule 26 of the United States Federal Rules of Civil Procedure:

> (a) *Discovery Methods.* Parties may obtain discovery by one or more of the following methods: depositions upon oral examination or written questions; written interrogatories; production of documents or things or permission to enter upon land or other property, for inspection and other purposes; physical and mental examinations; and requests for admission.
>
> (b) *Discovery Scope and Limits.* Unless otherwise limited by order of the court in accordance with these rules, the scope of discovery is as follows:
>
>> (1) *In General.* Parties may obtain discovery regarding any matter, not privileged, which is relevant to the subject matter involved in the pending action, whether it relates to the claim or defense of the party seeking discovery or to the claim or defense of any other party, including the existence, description, nature, custody, condition and location of any books, documents, or other tangible things and the identity and location of persons having knowledge of any discoverable matter. It is not ground for objection that the information sought will be inadmissible at the trial if the information sought appears reasonably calculated to lead to the discovery of admissible evidence.

It will be noted that not only does this permit the discovery, which may be enforced by court order, of information which is not admissible in evidence, but no reference is made to the status of the person obliged to make discovery; that is, the Rule applies in respect of non-parties as well as parties.

The limitation of Article 23 to discovery *of documents* leaves other forms of pre-trial discovery such as oral depositions under United States practice outside its scope. As Collins has convincingly argued,[80] the exclusion permitted by Article 23 is in one sense very surprising, as very few of the countries present would have regarded discovery, especially when ordered against third parties, as within the concepts of evidence or other judicial acts. What must be clear is that no reservation under Article 23, however worded, can operate to extend the scope of the Convention beyond that established in Article 1.

So far as English law is concerned, a crucial distinction was drawn in *Radio Corporation of America* v. *Rauland Corpn.*,[81] decided under the Foreign Tribunals Evidence Act 1856. The Divisional Court in that case distinguished between the obtaining of evidence for use in a trial, 'direct' material, which constituted 'testimony' under that Act and which would be gathered in response to a Letter of Request, and the obtaining of 'indirect' material, which might lead to a line of enquiry pointing to actual evidence; the English

---

[80] Lawrence Collins, 'The Hague Evidence Convention and Discovery: A Serious Misunderstanding?' (1986) 35 I.C.L.Q. 765.
[81] [1956] 1 Q.B. 618 (D.C.).

courts would not assist a foreign court to otain such 'indirect' material.[82] It would seem that this distinction was in the mind of the United Kingdom delegation in formulating their Working Document No. 10, and that the subsequent references to 'discovery' served only to confuse the issues.

A number of States made the declaration, commonly called 'the Article 23 reservation' that they would not act on requests for the pre-trial discovery of documents. But the United Kingdom, the proponent of Article 23, made a declaration in particular terms. It declared that it understood the scope of the Letters of Request which it would not execute as including[83] Letters of Request which require a person:

(a) to state what documents relevant to the proceedings to which the Letter of Request relates are, or have been, in his possession, custody or power; or
(b) to produce any documents other than particular documents specified in the Letter of Request as being documents appearing to the requested court to be, or to be likely to be, in his possession, custody or power.

It is possible to read paragraph (b) of this declaration as implying that the United Kingdom will execute Letters of Request seeking the production of particular documents specified in the Letter and required by way of 'discovery', even if they do not (in the words of the corresponding Rule of the Supreme Court)[84] 'relate to a matter in question in the cause or matter'. In the *Westinghouse* case, the House of Lords, in interpreting the Evidence (Proceedings in Other Jurisdictions) Act 1975, which gives effect to the Convention in the United Kingdom, did not share this view. Both Lord Wilberforce and Viscount Dilhorne referred to the distinction drawn in the earlier cases between 'direct' evidence and other 'indirect' material. Lord Wilberforce, noting that the United Kingdom declaration corresponded to section 2(4) of the Act, held that the distinction was preserved in section 2. If anything, the 1975 Act took 'a stricter line' on pre-trial discovery than its predecessor. Viscount Dilhorne similarly held that if the requested court was not satisfied that evidence was required, direct evidence for use at a trial as contrasted with information which might lead to the discovery of evidence, it had no power to assist. Without relying on pre-1975 cases, Lord Diplock interpreted section 2(3)(4) as excluding the obtaining, by oral deposition or the disclosure of documents, of anything other than evidence which would be admissible at the trial of the action. Lord Keith held that the distinction between evidence and discovery was recognized both in the Act and in Article 23 of the Convention; it was not disputed by counsel that effect could not be given to a request merely seeking discovery.

The matter has been further discussed in the two Special Commissions which have reviewed the operation of The Hague Convention. In 1978, the

---

[82] See also *American Express Warehousing Co.* v. *Doe* [1967] 1 Lloyd's Rep. 222 (C.A.).
[83] So the words which follow do not necessarily exhaust the category.
[84] R.S.C. Ord. 24, r. 11.

Special Commission heard explanations from both the United States and United Kingdom experts.[85] The United States expert sought to re-assure the Commission that pre-trial discovery procedures in his country were all after the commencement of proceedings (the relevance of this being, presumably, that it picks up the requirement of Article 1(2) of the Convention) and were under the control of a judge. It will be seen that this explanation does not touch the question of whether what is sought is in any sense 'evidence'. The United Kingdom expert, very surprisingly, was equally silent on this matter; he explained the purpose of Article 23 as being to enable Contracting States to refuse to execute Letters of Request which lacked specificity in that they did not describe precisely enough the documents to be obtained or examined. This appears to rest on the view of the United Kingdom position which was expressly rejected in the *Westinghouse* case. The Commission responded by urging Contracting States which had made the Reservation under Article 23 to withdraw it, or at least adopt the language of the United Kingdom Reservation.

In 1985 the United States delegation made similar remarks to those at the earlier Special Commission, but the United Kingdom expert offered a much fuller statement of the position as it had emerged in the *Westinghouse* and *Asbestos Insurance Coverage* cases; but he still identified the Article 23 Reservation in the United Kingdom version as meeting the case. The Commission again urged adoption of that language or language based on Article 16 of the additional Protocol 1984 to the Inter-American Convention on the Taking of Evidence Abroad. It reads as follows:

The States Parties to this Protocol shall process a letter rogatory that requests the exhibition and copying of documents if it meets the following requirements:

(*a*) The proceeding has been initiated;
(*b*) The documents are reasonably identified by date, contents, or other appropriate information;
(*c*) The letter rogatory specifies those facts and circumstances causing the requesting party reasonably to believe that the requested documents are or were in the possession, control, or custody of, or are known to the person from whom the documents are requested.

The person from whom documents are requested may, where appropriate, deny that he has possession, control or custody of the requested documents, or may object to the exhibition and copying of the documents, in accordance with the rules of the Convention.

At the time of signing, ratifying or acceding to this Protocol a State may declare that it will process the Letters rogatory to which this article applies only if they identify the relationship between the evidence or information requested and the pending proceeding.

---

[85] See *AetD* (14), Vol 4, p. 420.

As discussion at the 1985 meeting of Experts made clear, the sensitivity of the issues surrounding Article 23 is increased by the use of United States discovery processes in anti-trust actions and other contexts in which the United States courts claim to have jurisdiction more extensive than other countries are willing to approve, to combat which a series of 'blocking statutes' have been enacted to deal with some features of this problem. In this context, two agreed conclusions of the 1985 meeting of experts can usefully be quoted:

Statutes which prohibit the production of evidence abroad, commonly known as 'blocking statutes', many of which have been adopted since the 1978 meeting . . ., are in part a response to what are perceived in some countries as exorbitant assertions of jurisdiction by the courts of other countries. Such statutes however constitute a complicating factor and emphasize the need for long-term solutions through international understanding.

The combined effect of a blocking statute and an unqualified reservation under article 23, when both are adopted by a State, may be to discourage use by other States of the Hague Convention.

TAKING OF EVIDENCE BY DIPLOMATIC OFFICERS, CONSULAR AGENTS AND COMMISSIONERS

The drafting of the Convention brought out interesting differences between the common law and civil law countries as to the degree of acceptability of consuls and commissioners. In a common law country, the preparation of a case for trial is the private responsibility of the parties, and so the taking of evidence, without compulsion, by a consul or a commissioner does not necessarily offend such a country's concept of judicial sovereignty; but the position may be very different where, as in many civil law countries, the obtaining of evidence is part of the judicial function, and official permission is be required before the evidence can be taken privately. The Convention, partly drawing on United Kingdom bilateral conventions, sought to harmonize these different concepts by providing a procedural device acceptable to all systems. In so doing, it achieved a successful bridge between the two systems.

It is convenient to reproduce the summary of the English legal position concerning the taking of evidence by consuls and similar officers, a summary prepared as part of the preliminary work leading up to the Convention:

There is no legal objection to the taking of evidence in England for use outside the jurisdiction without the intervention of the English court. Evidence can be freely taken by agents acting on behalf of foreign litigants; but no compulsory processes may be used, nor may the evidence be taken on oath. A foreign court is at liberty to appoint a consul in England of its own country, or any other person it desires as an examiner to take evidence. So long as the witnesses are willing to attend to give evidence the examination may be completed and the result returned to the foreign court without the intervention of the court in England. The administration of an oath in England without lawful authority is an offence, but a person appointed by order of a foreign court or other judicial authority has the necessary authority by virtue of section 1 of the Oaths and Evidence (Overseas Authorities and Countries) Act 1963, for use in civil proceedings carried on under the law of that country, and a consul may administer an oath under certain other statutory provisions.[86]

Civil law countries take a much stricter line on the permissibility of such actions in their jurisdiction by the agents of foreign courts. For this reason the whole of chapter II of The Hague Convention, while providing much fuller and clearer guidance than the earlier 1954 text, is subject to optional clauses and rights of reservation. Indeed the whole chapter may be excluded by a reservation under Article 33 and Germany has taken this course.

In chapter II, the reference is only to the taking of 'evidence', which is a well recognized function of consuls, as reflected, for example, in United Kingdom bilateral conventions and in the 1954 Convention, and not the performance of 'other judicial acts' (regarded as exclusively judicial functions). Moreover, the proceedings for which the evidence is required must be actually 'commenced', and not merely 'contemplated'.

Taking of evidence by diplomats and consuls

(a) *from nationals of the state the consul represents.* The Convention provides first that a diplomatic officer and consular agent may take evidence without compulsion in civil or commercial matters from nationals of the State he represents in aid of procedings commenced in the courts of the State represented.[87] However, even the exercise of this right may, by the declaration of the Contracting State in which the evidence is to be taken, be made subject to the permission of the appropriate authority designated by that State.[88] Although several countries have made the declaration requiring permission, many encourage the use of consuls as saving the expense of employing personnel of the receiving State.

(b) *from nationals of the host state and of third states.* In contrast, Article 16 provides that a diplomatic officer or consular agent may only take evidence, without compulsion, of nationals of the State in which he exercises his functions, or of third States, if a competent authority in the requested State has given its permission, either generally or in the particular case, and subject to any conditions imposed. A State may, however, by declaration dispense with the need for such permission.[89] Many States have made such declarations, subject, however, to a variety of conditions, mainly requiring the requested State to be informed about, or to be present at, the taking of the evidence. The United Kingdom does not require prior permission, if reciprocity is accorded. The United States does not require advance permission. France has indicated the terms upon which permission will be given, and these include an

---

[86] *AetD* (*11*), Vol. 4, pp. 41–2. For the 'other statutory provisions', see now the Consular Relations Act 1968, s.10.   [87] Art. 15(1).
[88] Art. 15(2).   [89] Art. 16(2).

insistence that the evidence be taken exclusively within the premises of the foreign Embassy or Consulate.

Taking of evidence by commissioners

Commissioners may, without compulsion, take evidence in one State in aid of court proceedings commenced in another State, on the same conditions as apply under Article 16.[90] Declarations similar to those referred to in the last paragraph have also been made in this context.

Commissioners may be appointed by a judicial authority of either the requesting or the requested State, and the Convention enables courts to appoint foreign judges as 'commissioners' to examine witnesses directly (under compulsion if necessary) in their own language and under their own procedures and without the intervention of the local courts.

Some indication of practice under these provisons can be gleaned from the discussions in the Special Commissions on the Convention. So, commissioners have mainly been used by the United States in its relations with France and the United Kingdom. The American authorities appoint as commissioners persons from the United States itself, or American consuls, or judicial authorities or other persons residing in the requested State. This procedure can minimize costs, for example, where the alternative would be to transport witnesses to the United States, but, as the French authorities have pointed out, where the request is a straightforward one, it is sometimes cheaper to use a Letter of Request, rather than appoint a commissioner.

Measures of compulsion

A State may declare that a diplomatic officer, consular agent or commissioner may apply to the designated competent authority for 'appropriate' assistance to obtain evidence by compulsion.[91] The declaration may impose conditions. The measures of compulsion will be those prescribed by law for use in internal proceedings.[92] Czechoslovakia, Italy, the United Kingdom, and the United States have made the declaration under this Article.

States vary in their practice. The United Kingdom and United States can be expected to employ their ordinary procedures for issuing subpoenas or other measures. In contrast, France which has made no declaration under Article 18, will only make compulsion available to a commissioner if he is a French judicial authority, appointed as commissioner.

Conditions on grant of permission

In giving permission for diplomats, consuls, or commissioners to take evidence under Articles 15–17, or in granting measures of compulsion, the competent authority of the State in which the evidence is to be taken may prescribe such conditions as it deems fit, including the time and place of the

---

[90] Art. 17.   [91] Art. 18.   [92] Art. 18(2).

taking of evidence and the giving of reasonable advance notice of the hearing.[93] So, a representative of the authority is entitled to be present at the taking of evidence; for example, the authority may wish to ensure that there is no infringement of his State's sovereignty or security, or to uphold privileges of the witness. Examples of other conditions might be to limit the scope and subject-matter of the examination, to specify the persons who may be present at the taking of the evidence other than the parties and the witnesses, and to limit the right to enter and inspect real property. These conditions may not affect the following provisions as to legal representation and certain other matters.

Legal representation

Persons concerned in the taking of evidence under Chapter II may be legally represented.[94] They would, no doubt, include the parties and witnesses, but whether others such as the employer of a witness, or an insurance company, would be so entitled, is not clear.

Administrative rules

The diplomatic officer or consular agent or commissioner may take all kinds of evidence which are not incompatible with local law or contrary to any permission granted and, within such limits, they may administer oaths. (The power to administer oaths may thus be limited, where local law provides that only judges and notaries may administer oaths.) A request to a person to appear or to give evidence must be in the language of the place where the evidence is to be taken, unless the witness is a national of the requesting State. The person must be told that he may be legally represented. If the requested State has not filed a declaration under Article 18, and measures of compulsion are not available by other means under internal law, the request must state that he is not compelled to appear or to give evidence. The evidence may be taken in the manner provided by the law of the requesting State if this is not forbidden in the requested State. The privileges and duties to refuse to give evidence contained in Article 11[95] are also available under chapter II.[96] As any privilege to refuse to give evidence can be invoked by witnesses, the 'commission' or other document appointing the diplomatic officer or consular agent or commissioner should contain the necessary details about such privilege.

RELATED INTERNATIONAL INSTRUMENTS

Similar work has been undertaken by regional organizations working in the legal field. There is an Inter-American Convention on the Taking of Evidence Abroad 1975 (with a supplementary Protocol of 1984) and the Asian-African Legal Consultative Committee has drafted model bilateral conventions

---

[93] Art. 19.   [94] Art. 20.
[95] See pp. 95–6.   [96] Art. 21.

including provisions on the same topic. Close co-operation between the relevant bodies and the Hague Conference have ensured compatibility between these various documents.

(C) United Kingdom Implementation of the Hague Convention

Although its text nowhere mentions the Hague Convention, the Evidence (Proceedings in Other Jurisdictions) Act 1975 was enacted to enable the United Kingdom to ratify the Convention. The Act is drafted so as to apply to any foreign State, a practice followed in the criminal context by the Criminal Justice (International Co-operation) Act 1990.

The Act gives certain powers to the High Court where an application is made for an order for evidence to be obtained in England, and the court is satisfied that the application is made in pursuance of a request[97] issued by or on behalf of a court or tribunal[98] exercising jurisdiction in another part of the United Kingdom or some other country,[99] and that the evidence sought is to be obtained for the purposes of civil proceedings[100] which have either been instituted before the requesting court or whose institution is contemplated.[101] The English court will not investigate the likely relevance of the evidence sought to issues raised in the foreign proceedings, regarding that as a matter for the foreign court (which will not have made its request without due consideration).[102]

The court, in practice a Master of the Queen's Bench Division, can make an appropriate order to give effect to the request underlying the application.[103] Such orders may make provision for the examination of witnesses, either orally or in writing; for the production of documents; for the inspection, photographing, preservation, custody, or detention of any property; for the taking of samples of any property and the carrying out of any experiments on or with any property; for the medical examination of any person; and for the taking and testing of samples of blood from any person.[104]

Under the Convention, a requested State is to apply the same measures of compulsion as would be available in purely domestic cases;[105] this is reflected in the provision in section 2(3) of the Act that an order under that section may

---

[97] Including any commission, order, or other process (Evidence (Proceedings in Other Jurisdictions) Act 1975, s. 9(1)) as well as a Letter of Request.

[98] Cf. the Convention term 'judicial authority'; p. 93.

[99] Or by the Court of Justice of the European Communities: Evidence (European Court) Order 1976, S.I. 1976 No. 428.

[100] Defined to mean proceedings in any civil or commercial matter: Evidence (Proceedings in Other Jurisdictions) Act 1975, 9(1) and see pp. 87—9.

[101] Evidence (Proceedings in Other Jurisdictions) Act 1975, s. 1. Cf. *Re International Power Industries Inc., The Times*, 25 July 1984.

[102] *Rio Tinto Zinc Corporation* v. *Westinghouse Electric Corporation* [1978] A.C. 547 (H.L.); *Re Asbestos Insurance Coverage Cases* [1985] 1 W.L.R. 331 (H.L.).

[103] Evidence (Proceedings in Other Jurisdictions) Act 1975, s. 2(1). See R.S.C. Ord. 70.

[104] Evidence (Proceedings in Other Jurisdictions) Act 1975, s. 2(2).

[105] See p. 95.

not require any particular steps to be taken unless they are steps which can be required to be taken by way of obtaining evidence for the purposes of civil proceedings in the court making the order, i.e. the High Court.[106] To this there is one exception, to comply with Article 9 of the Convention;[107] an order may be made that a person should give evidence otherwise than on oath where this is asked for by the requesting court.[108] Section 2(3) was not referred to in the judgment in *J. Barber & Sons* v. *Lloyd's Underwriters*,[109] where despite the opposition of the defendants it was ordered that the taking of depositions before an examiner of the court should, as had been requested by the foreign court, be videotaped. Evans J. held that a request by the foreign court for a particular mode of examination to be followed should be complied with, in the exercise of discretion, unless what was asked for was so contrary to English established procedures that it should not be permitted; although in the spirit of the Convention, this ruling is not altogether easy to reconcile with the language of the Act.

An order may not be made under section 2 requiring a person to state what documents relevant to the proceedings to which the application relates are, or have been, in his possession, custody or power; or to produce any documents other than particular documents specified in the order as being documents appearing to the High Court court to be, or to be likely to be, in his possession, custody or power.[110] This provision reflects the language of the reservation made by the United Kingdom under Article 23 of the Convention, the origins and effect of which have already been discussed.[111] So far as the production of documents is concerned much attention has focused on the words 'particular documents specified in the order'. This phrase is to be given a strict construction;[112] to avoid countenancing 'fishing expeditions', the documents must be either individual documents separately described or documents falling within a compendious description which none the less indicates the exact documents required.[113] A request too widely drawn can sometimes be acted upon in part, the court striking out the parts which are unacceptable; but the court will not undertake the task of redrafting the request.[114]

An order under section 2 may also not be made if it is shown that the request infringes the jurisdiction of the United Kingdom or is otherwise pre-

---

[106] For the implications of this for requests that corporations should give evidence see *Penn-Texas Corpn* v. *Murat Anstalt* [1964] 1 Q.B. 40 (C.A.) and *Penn-Texas Corpn* v. *Murat Anstalt (No. 2)* [1964] 2 Q.B. 647 (C.A.), both decided under the Foreign Tribunals Evidence Act 1856.

[107] See p. 94.   [108] Evidence (Proceedings in Other Jurisdictions) Act 1975, s. 2(3).

[109] [1987] Q.B. 103.   [110] Ibid., s. 2(4).

[111] See pp. 97–101.

[112] *Rio Tinto Zinc Corporation* v. *Westinghouse Electric Corporation* [1978] A.C. 547 (H.L.) per Lord Wilberforce at 609 and Lord Diplock at 635; *Re Asbestos Insurance Coverage Cases* [1985] 1 W.L.R. 331 (H.L.) per Lord Fraser at 337–8.

[113] e.g. 'monthly bank statements for the year 1984 relating to [a specified] account'; but *not* 'all X's bank statements for 1984': *Re Asbestos Insurance Coverage Cases* [1985] 1 W.L.R. 331 (H.L.) per Lord Fraser at 337–8.

[114] See *Boeing Co.* v. *P.P.G. Industries Inc.* [1988] 3 All E.R. 839 (C.A.).

judicial to the United Kingdom; on these matters a certificate of the Secretary of State is conclusive.[115] This last provision, part of the United Kingdom's 'blocking statute', builds upon the opinions in the House of Lords in the *Westinghouse* case,[116] where the Attorney-General intervened to express the policy of the Government against the recognition of investigatory orders made in the United States against United Kingdom companies. If an order is made, a person is not to be compelled to give evidence where this would be prejudicial to the security of the United Kingdom; here again, a certificate of the Secretary of State is conclusive.[117]

Provision is made as to claims of privilege in section 3 of the Act. Where the claim arises under the law of the requesting State, and is neither supported by material in the request or conceded by the applicant for the order, the court may order that the evidence be taken, but the evidence is not transmitted to the requesting court if that court, on the matter being referred to it, upholds the claim.[118]

(D) American Approaches to the Convention

The relationship between the Hague Convention and the other methods of obtaining evidence abroad provided for in the United States Federal Rules of Civil Procedure and comparable State rules has occupied much judicial time. Predictably the case-law has been almost wholly in the context of pre-trial discovery which is both of great importance in United States practice and most open to objection or misunderstanding in other countries. It is perhaps significant that the first reported comment by a United States court on the Convention concerned this very area. Citing academic analysis,[119] the Court of Appeals for the District of Columbia Circuit took into account in considering a plea of *forum non conveniens* the perceived cost and difficulty of proceeding under the Convention, and noted that the breadth of material ordinarily expected from a full-fledged American-style discovery deposition might be constricted under its rules.[120]

The essential issue was the extent to which the procedural rules of the forum court could be used notwithstanding the Convention. In the reported cases there can be found a wide range of different approaches, from that which treats the Convention as exclusively regulating the procedures to be

---

[115] Protection of Trading Interests Act 1980, s. 4.

[116] *Rio Tinto Zinc Corporation* v. *Westinghouse Electric Corporation* [1978] A.C. 547 (H.L.).

[117] Evidence (Proceedings in Other Jurisdictions) Act 1975, s. 3(3).

[118] Ibid., s. 3(2). See on the procedure to be followed where other objections are raised in the course of the examination, R. v. *Rathbone, ex parte Dikko* [1985] Q.B. 630.

[119] Borel and S. M. Boyd, 'Opportunities for and Obstacles to Obtaining Evidence in France for Use in Litigation in the United States' (1979) 13 Int.L. 35; J. H. Carter, 'Obtaining Foreign Discovery and Evidence for Use in Litigation in the United States: Existing Rules and Procedures', ibid., 5.

[120] *Pain* v. *United Technologies Corpn.* 637 F. 2d. 775 (D.C.Circ., 1980).

followed to that which recognizes the availability of the Convention but asserts that the powers and practice of United States courts are essentially unaffected. Early cases, especially in State courts[121] tended to give some priority to the Convention. The plaintiff's bar responded vigorously, developing a series of arguments many of which were accepted in a leading case in the Fifth Circuit, *Re Anschuetz & Co. G.m.b.H.*, in 1985.[122] Finally, the Supreme Court addressed the matter in *Societé Nationale Industrielle Aérospatiale* v. *US District Court for the Southern District of Iowa*[123] (*'Aérospatiale'*); while rejecting many of the arguments previously deployed, the Supreme Court gave a limited, and somewhat uncertain, place to the Convention.

Priority to the Convention

Even before the Convention procedures became available, there had been some discussion of the relationship between the procedural rules of the forum and hostile attitudes encountered in foreign practice. So a markedly internationalist stance was taken by a Californian court in 1973 in the much-cited case of *Volkswagenwerk A.G.* v. *Superior Court of Sacramento County.*[124] A discovery order appointing a commissioner to take depositions from witnesses in Germany was quashed. The court took the view, which was to be expressly repudiated in later cases,[125] that although there was jurisdiction to entertain the action against the German corporation, this did not give the Californian court jurisdiction over persons or property in Germany. It also adopted 'a policy of avoiding international discovery methods productive of friction with the procedures of host nations'. Those procedures, resting on the civil law understanding of judicial sovereignty, required the use of letters rogatory, and 'whatever the generous provisions of the California discovery statutes, courts ordering discovery abroad must conform to the channels and procedures established by the host nation'.

Eight years later, another California Court of Appeals reconsidered the position in the light of the Hague Convention.[126] While asserting that procedure was wholly within the control of the forum court even when persons abroad were affected, the court adopted a similar stance in terms of policy. Considerations of comity dictated a practice of judicial self-restraint, which meant in effect that a party seeking to obtain evidence abroad in a Hague Convention county must resort first to the procedures provided by the Convention. The Convention was a treaty entered into by the United States and so a part of federal law pre-empting State rules.

---

[121] But see *Morton-Norwich Products Inc.* v. *Rhone-Poulenc S.A.* (Ct. of Chancery, Del., 1981) (unreported) for an exception. [122] 754 F. 2d. 602 (5th Cir, 1985).
[123] 482 U.S. 522 (1987). See generally, S. F. Black 'United States Transnational Discovery: the Rise and Fall of The Hague Evidence Convention' (1991) 40 I.C.L.Q. 901.
[124] 109 Cal. Rptr. 219 (Cal. App., 1973).
[125] See *Volkswagenwerk A.G.* v. *Superior Court, Alameda County* 176 Cal. Reptr. 874 (Cal. App. 1981).
[126] *Volkswagenwerk A.G.* v. *Superior Court, Alameda County* 176 Cal. Rptr. 874 (Cal. App., 1981).

The Californian position was developed in a fully reasoned judgment in *Pierburg G.m.b.H. & Co. K.G.* v. *Superior Court of Los Angeles County*[127] in 1982, in which a number of fundamental issues were addressed. The Californian plaintiffs had sought to obtain answers from the defendant West German corporation to 315 written interrogatories. A lower court had ordered that the procedures of the Hague Convention were to be followed by both parties. Pierburg then sought to obtain photographs of a car which was situated in California, and it was held (plainly correctly) that this was not a case of evidence being obtained 'abroad' and so the Convention was inapplicable. The plaintiffs then argued that they were entitled to equal treatment by the law; it was unjust that they should be compelled to use the Convention, the translation requirements of which they found insurmountably expensive, whilst the foreign defendant was under no such burden.

The court followed the earlier Californian cases in holding that the Convention should be followed. The 'equal protection' argument was misconceived, for the types of discovery sought by plaintiff and defendant were quite different; the principle of equal protection was offended only if parties similarly placed received disparate treatment. The court also rejected an argument which was to be advanced, in varying forms, in many later cases: that the evidence sought could be provided within the territorial jurisdiction of the Californian courts either by the defendant's officials travelling to California, or by the answers being provided by counsel in Los Angeles. As the court observed, these arguments 'would automatically destroy the Convention in all discovery matters other than those involving physical inspection of the foreign national's property in its state of citizenship' and that could not have been the intention.

The majority of reported decisions over the next few years in other State courts took the Californian position, that first resort was to be had to the Convention procedures. There were decisions to that effect in Texas,[128] New Jersey,[129] and West Virginia.[130] United States District courts, exercising the federal jurisdiction, were divided; the argument that State law was preempted was irrelevant in that context[131] and the issue was whether there was a conflict between the Federal Rules of Civil Procedure and the requirements of the Hague Convention. A number of District Courts took the position on that issue that first resort should still be had to the Convention.[132]

---

[127] 186 Cal. Rptr. 876 (Cal. App., 1982).

[128] *Th. Goldschmidt A.G.* v. *Smith* 676 S.W. 2d. 443 (Tex. App., 1984).

[129] *Vincent* v. *Ateliers de la Motobecane S.A.* 475 A. 2d. 686 (N.J. Super. A.D., 1984).

[130] *Gebr. Eickhoff Maschinenfabrik und Eisengieberei m.b.H.* v. *Starcher* 328 S.E. 2d. 492 (W.Va., 1985).

[131] See *Murphy* v. *Reifenhauser K.G. Maschinenfabrik* 101 F.D.R. 360 (D.C. Vermont, 1984).

[132] *Philadelphia Gear Corpn.* v. *American Pfauter Corpn.* 100 F.R.D. 58 (E.D.Pa., 1983), Asser 3/170; *Schroeder* v. *Lufthansa German Airlines* 18 Av. Cas. (C.C.H.) 17,222 (N.D.Ill., 1983); *Cie. Française d'Assurance pour le Commerce Extérieur* v. *Phillips Petroleum Co.* 105 F.R.D. 16 (S.D.N.Y., 1984); *General Electric Co.* v. *North Star International, Inc.* (N.D.Ill., 1984) (unreported).

Reaction against first resort

The first resort position was, however, rejected by many federal courts. In part their stance depended on pre-Convention United States practice and upon observations, notably by one of the United States delegation at the Hague,[133] that the Convention required no significant change in that practice. The maintenance of United States practice was regarded as crucial for, as the plaintiffs in *Aérospatiale* shrilly asserted,

Without just, speedy and inexpensive discovery, the courthouse is effectively barred to those who so desperately need it—United States citizens injured by defective foreign products.[134]

Another major element in the argument rested on a particular view of where the 'evidence-taking' took place. This view was clearly articulated in *Graco Inc.* v. *Kremlin, Inc.*:[135]

This court believes that discovery does not take place within [a state's] borders merely because documents to be produced somewhere else are located there. Similarly, discovery should be considered as taking place here, and not in another country, when interrogatories are served here, even if the necessary information is located in another country. The court's view is the same with respect to people residing in another country. If they are subject to the court's jurisdiction, or if the court can compel a party to produce them . . ., violation of the other country's judicial sovereignty is avoided by ordering that the deposition take place outside the country.

Similarly in a case involving a French corporation,[136] an order for depositions and document production at the offices of New York attorneys was not regarded as in conflict with the Convention; all that was to happen on French soil was 'certain acts preparatory to the giving of evidence', the selection of appropriate employees to travel to New York and of relevant documents to be disclosed in New York.

It scarcely needs to be observed that from the viewpoint of the defendant's country these arguments are unacceptable. Witnesses and documents located there are required to be taken out of that country for production before the authorities of the United States or before persons acting with the backing of the courts of that country; it must appear to be an attempt to give world-wide application to the procedural rules of the United States. There is, of course, no such difficulty if the evidence sought, though owned by a foreign corpora-

---

[133] P. W. Amram, 'The Proposed Convention on the Taking of Evidence Abroad' (1969) 55 A.B.A.J. 651. See also the Report of the US Delegation, reprinted at (1969) 8 I.L.M. 785, 807–15.

[134] Brief for Respondents and Real Parties in Interest.

[135] 101 F.R.D. 503 (N.D.Ill., 1984), Asser 3/171. See also *International Society for Krishna Consciousness, Inc.* v. *Lee* 105 F.R.D. 435 (S.D.N.Y., 1984); *McLaughlin* v. *The Fellows Gear Shaper Co.* 102 F.R.D. 956 (E.D.Pa., 1984); *Slauenwhite* v. *Bekum Maschinenfabriken G.m.b.H.* 104 F.R.D. 616 (D.C.Mass., 1985).

[136] *Adidas (Canada) Ltd.* v. *S.S. Seatrain Bennington* (S.D.N.Y., 1984, unreported) (noted Asser 3/173 sub nom. *Navi Fonds K.G.* v. *Les Toles Inoxydables*).

tion, is physically located within the territorial jurisdiction of the United States.[137]

The truth of this matter seems to be that the authors of the Convention never really took into account the mobile quality of people and documents. Testimony and documentary evidence would, they envisaged, be presented either to the forum court or obtained by Letter of Request in the foreign country in which they were to be found. The Convention simply does not address the movement of persons or documents from that country to the forum State or a third State; nor, of course, the extensive nature of such movement required to comply with some American discovery orders.

Another strand in the arguments explored in these cases was that of 'unfairness'. As one court put it,

if the Convention were deemed to supplant the Federal Rules as the governing law on discovery from a litigant, in this case it would entirely deprive plaintiffs of a major tool of discovery against [the defendant]. The unfairness of such a result is compounded by the fact that, as a litigant, [the defendant] would be able to avail itself of the . . . procedures against plaintiffs.[138]

This argument is distinctly unappealing to lawyers outside the United States system. Part of the alleged unfairness is that some plaintiffs in the United States courts will be denied the extensive discovery available to plaintiffs generally; but that is to give absolutely no weight to the specifically international aspects present in particular cases. It is not at all clear why a plaintiff seeking material located in, say, France or Germany, but able to invoke United States jurisdiction (available, perhaps, as a result of the long-arm claims to extensive jurisdiction made by Federal or State courts) should be able to claim that American practices should apply as exclusively as in a purely domestic case. And the supposed unfairness, or disparity of treatment, between plaintiff and defendant is more apparent than real; at least in the present context, discovery is a device beloved of plaintiffs as they seek relevant material on which to rest their claims. One could, not unfairly, argue that it is an inherently biased device, that its limitation actually improves the balance of abstract fairness between the parties.

Related considerations led a number of courts to distinguish between party and non-party witnesses. Although this distinction has no basis in the text of the Convention, it was argued that if the person required to produce material or provide a deposition were a party subject to the in personam jurisdiction of the United States courts then the Convention did not offer any protection.[139]

---

[137] *Renfield Corpn. v. E. Remy Martin & Co. S.A.* 98 F.R.D. 442 (D.C.Del., 1982); *Lasky v. Continental Products Corpn.* 569 F. Supp. 1227 (E.D.Pa., 1983); *General Electric Co. v. North Star International Inc.* (N.D.Ill, 1984) (unreported); *International Society for Krishna Consciousness, Inc. v. Lee* 105 F.R.D. 435 (S.D.N.Y., 1984).

[138] *International Society for Krishna Consciousness, Inc. v. Lee* 105 F.R.D. 435 (S.D.N.Y., 1984).

[139] *Graco, Inc. v. Kremlin, Inc.* 101 F.R.D. 503 (N.D.Ill., 1984), Asser 3/171; *Slauenwhite v. Bekum Maschinenfabriken G.m.b.H.* 104 F.R.D. 616 (D.C. Mass., 1985).

The courts did, of course, have regard to the particular circumstances of each case. The range and scale of discovery sought is not perhaps strictly relevant, but in practice courts were more ready to allow the use of discovery under the Federal Rules of Civil Procedure when relatively modest demands were made. An example is *Murphy* v. *Reifenhauser K.G. Maschinenfabrik*[140] where discovery procedures were in their third year, the defendant having already answered two sets of interrogatories without taking any point about the applicability of the Convention. After referring to the possibility of delay when the Convention was used, and the impact of Article 23 reservations, the court held that the interest of the German Federal Republic in the integrity of its judicial rights was 'less compelling in this instance than, for example, where a non-party witness is sought for deposition or where the scope of discovery sought involves more intrusive methods'.

More fundamentally, many courts failed to find a basis for the first resort approach. The issue was presented in more sharply polarised terms. Was the Convention 'exclusive' (or 'mandatory') or not? At one stage the United States government supported the position that the Convention dealt comprehensively, and so exclusively, with the procedures to govern the taking of evidence abroad,[141] but it later resiled from this.[142] No District Court accepted the exclusivity argument, many relying on a superficial reading of Article 27(c) of the Convention, which allows Contracting States to permit 'by internal law or practice, methods of taking evidence other than those provided for in this Convention';[143] the better view is that this freedom is given only to the requested country and does not refer to the country from which the discovery request originates.[144] Whichever view was taken, the compromise first resort position could well be disregarded as unnecessary, and—until comity analysis was emphasized in later cases—to lack any jurisprudential basis.

Re Anschuetz

In March 1985 the US Court of Appeals for the 5th Circuit addressed these issues in *Re Anschuetz & Co. G.m.b.H*.[145] The briefs and opinions in the case were immediately circulated by the Permanent Bureau of the Hague Conference to the experts who were shortly to attend a Special Commission of the Conference

---

[140] 101 F.R.D. 360 (D.C. Vermont, 1984).

[141] See Solicitor-General's *amicus* brief in *Volkswagenwerk A.G.* v. *Falzon* 461 US 1303 (1983).

[142] See Solicitor-General's *amicus* brief in *Club Méditeranée S.A.* v. *Dorin* 469 US 913 (1984).

[143] *Lasky* v. *Continental Products Corpn.* 569 F. Supp. 1227 (E.D.Pa., 1983); *Graco, Inc.* v. *Kremlin, Inc.* 101 F.R.D. 503 (N.D.Ill., 1984), Asser 3/171; *International Society for Krishna Consciousness, Inc.* v. *Lee* 105 F.R.D. 435 (S.D.N.Y., 1984).

[144] See to this effect *Philadelphia Gear Corpn.* v. *American Pfauter Corpn.* 100 F.R.D. 58 (E.D.Pa., 1983), Asser 3/170; *Gebr. Eickhoff Maschinenfabrik und Eisengieberei m.b.H.* v. *Starcher* 328 S.E. 2d. 492 (W.Va., 1985).

[145] 754 F. 2d. 602 (5th Cir., 1985). The judgment was ultimately vacated and remanded for further consideration in the light of the *Aérospatiale* case (considered below): 107 S.Ct. 3223 (1988).

to review the workings of the Convention, and this gave the case a prominence (and in some quarters a notoriety) which it might otherwise have escaped. The court held that the Convention did not 'supplant the application of the discovery provisions of the Federal Rules over foreign, Hague Convention State nationals, subject to *in personam* jurisdiction in a United States court', and adopted most of the arguments deployed by earlier courts which had taken this view. The case concerned discovery sought from a German third-party defendant in proceedings pending in Louisiana. This involved the production of large numbers of documents, many, if not all, of which were located in Germany; the taking of depositions from representatives of the corporation, to be carried out in a designated office in Germany; and interrogatories seeking information as the corporation's organization at the relevant time and the identity of employees engaged in work relevant to the (products liability) issue in the litigation.

The Federal Republic of Germany filed an *amicus* brief arguing that the Convention was exclusive and that it was contrary to its spirit for the United States to circumvent the Convention. The brief rejected the relevance of United States *in personam* jurisdiction over the person required to produce evidence, and asserted the co-operative attitude of German courts and authorities to requests made under the Convention. It expressly stated that

compliance in Germany with the order of the U.S. District Court mandating the taking of oral depositions in Kiel, Germany, and the production of documents located in Kiel, Germany, would be a violation of German Sovereignty unless the order is transmitted and executed by the method of Letter of Request under the Evidence Convention.[146]

The United States filed a brief denying the supposedly exclusive character of the Convention, but urging that principles of comity should be applied to determine whether an order should be made under the Federal Rules when the foreign country had unequivocally stated that it regarded such an order as a violation of its sovereignty; and argued that a District Court could in any event not order the taking of depositions in Germany without compliance with the procedures prescribed by the German authorities (in this case, those of the Convention). It will be seen that this falls somewhat short of the first resort approach, which the brief does not directly address.

The Court of Appeals expressly rejected the first resort cases as not well reasoned, and as giving an advantage to foreign litigants. It held that the Convention was permissive, not mandatory, and noted that the provisions of the Convention did not guarantee the full range of discovery available in a United States court.[147] Compliance in the United States with discovery orders requiring 'preparatory acts' abroad was regarded as not constituting 'discovery in a

[146] F.R.G. *amicus* brief, p. 8.
[147] The court cites at length from *Graco, Inc.* v. *Kremlin, Inc.* 101 F.R.D. 503 (N.D.Ill., 1984), Asser 3/171, discussed above, p.110.

foreign nation as addressed by the Hague Convention'.[148] The 'impressive and general' wording of Article 23 was seen as demonstrating that the Convention would not have been a proper vehicle for a treaty which would have done the barely conceivable by giving other countries control over American litigation. First resort to the Convention, subject to the eventual overriding of foreign objections under the Federal Rules, was characterized as 'the greatest insult to a civil law country's sovereignty'.

Having said all this, the court accepted the need to pay healthy respect to the principles of comity. Applying those principles, the court held:

that the Hague Convention is to be employed with the involuntary deposition of a party conducted in a foreign country, and with the production of documents or other evidence gathered from persons or entities in the foreign country who are not subject to the court's *in personam* jurisdiction. The Hague Convention has no application at all to the production of evidence in [the United States] by a party subject to the jurisdiction of a district court pursuant to the Federal Rules.

The orders in the particular case were to be reconsidered by the District Court, and there was a broad hint from the Court of Appeals that the production of documents and the examination of witnesses should be ordered to take place not in Germany but in the United States. But by failing to develop its comity analysis, the Court of Appeals left room for many of the old arguments to re-appear in a new guise.

In most subsequent cases, it became clear that considerations of comity would not prevail against the usual procedures of the Federal Rules so long as deponents or documents were to be produced within the United States, from whatever source. That would not result in 'alien procedures' on foreign soil, so the interests of the foreign country did not prevail over those of the United States litigant.[149]

The first resort notion was not, however, quite extinguished by *Re Anschuetz*. It was stoutly maintained by a District Court in *S & S Screw Machine Co.* v. *Cosa Corpn*.[150] The court declined to adopt what it described as 'the geographic fiction' that discovery required mere acts of preparation abroad, and found the distinction between parties and non-parties equally lacking in merit as a basis for decision. Comity considerations were viewed with much more favour, and reference was made to the Second Restatement of Foreign Relations Law of the United States which, in a recent revision, had identified factors to be weighed in cases of discovery abroad:

---

[148] Citing *Adidas (Canada) Ltd.* v. *S.S. Seatrain Bennington* (S.D.N.Y., 1984) (unreported) (noted Asser 3/173 sub nom. *Navi Fonds K.G.* v. *Les Toles Inoxydables*).

[149] *Re Messerschmidt Bolkow Blohm G.m.b.H.* 757 F. 2d. 729 (5th Circ, 1985); *Rachis* v. *Maschinenfabrik Hehl & Soehne* (E.D.Pa., 1986) (unreported); *Wilson* v. *Lufthansa German Airlines* 108 A.D. 2d. 393 (N.Y., 1985) (though on facts evidence more likely to be in New York than in Germany). See also *Fill* v. *Fill* 68 Bankr. 923 (Bankr. Ct. S.D.N.Y., 1987).

[150] 647 F. Supp. 600 (M.D.Tenn., 1986).

(1) the importance to . . . the litigation of the documents or other information requested;
(2) the degree of specificity of the request;
(3) whether the information originated in the United States;
(4) the availability of alternative means of securing the information; and
(5) the extent to which non-compliance with the request would undermine important interests of the United States, or compliance with the request would undermine important interests of the state where the information is located.[151]

Weighing these factors and the circumstances of the case, including the pending change in the legislation of the Federal Republic of Germany on the matter of discovery requests from abroad,[152] the court held that the balance favoured first resort to the Convention. But the court went on to urge the adoption, perhaps by the United States Supreme Court which was about to consider the matter in the *Aérospatiale* case, of a principle that resort should first be had to the Convention procedures in every foreign discovery case unless their use appeared futile from the outset. This would give greater predictability to litigants and presumably effect a reduction in the amount of judicial time devoted to these matters.

AÉROSPATIALE

The comity debate was central to the Supreme Court's consideration of the *Aérospatiale* litigation in 1987. The majority of the court, while dismissing many of the arguments that had found favour in *Re Anschuetz* and earlier cases, did little to advance the position from that reached by the Court of Appeals in *Re Anschuetz*.

The Supreme Court rejected what it characterized as the 'extreme position' that the Convention was exclusive and mandatory. That position had been urged in *amicus* briefs filed by the French Republic and (less emphatically) by the Federal Republic of Germany, although the petitioners who had taken this position in the lower courts did not maintain it in the Supreme Court. The Court saw no mandatory language in the text of the Convention, and contrasted it with the language of the Hague Service of Process Convention—a contrast which was to prove a source of embarrassment when the court later held that the Service Convention was not mandatory either.[153] The very existence of Article 23 was regarded as indicating that the Convention was not mandatory, on the rather tortuous argument that if the Convention had been intended to replace the broad discovery powers previously exercised by the United States, acceptance of Article 23 (which enables other States to refuse to operate the Convention in this area) 'would have been most anomalous'. The Court also favoured the interpretation of Article 27(*d*) which would enable requesting as well as requested States to use domestic law procedures, but even on a

---

[151] Restatement (Revised) of Foreign Relations Law of the United States, s.437(1)(*c*) (Tentative Draft No. 7, 1986).
[152] As to which, see p. 95.
[153] i.e. in the *Schlunk* case, 108 S.Ct. 2104 (1988), see p. 37.

narrower reading saw nothing in Article 27 to limit the power of a requesting State.

On the other hand, the Supreme Court rejected the argument, successful in the Court of Appeals,[154] that the Convention 'did not apply' where discovery was sought from a foreign litigant who was subject to the jurisdiction of an American court. The text of the Convention drew no distinction between evidence obtained from third parties and that obtained from litigants themselves. Nor did it support the 'geographic fiction' that evidence to be produced in the United States was not 'abroad' even though it was in fact located in a foreign country or must be gathered or otherwise prepared abroad.[155] In rejecting these arguments, the Supreme Court destroyed the authority of many of the previous decisions on the matter.

The majority's own starting point is perhaps best identified in this passage:

An interpretation of the Hague Convention as the exclusive means for obtaining evidence located abroad would effectively subject every American court hearing a case involving a national of a contracting state to the internal laws of that State. Interrogatories and document requests are staples of international commercial litigation, no less than of other suits, yet a rule of exclusivity would subordinate the court's supervision of even the most routine of these pre-trial proceedings to the actions or, equally, to the inactions of foreign judicial authorities.

The first sentence in that passage is, of course, a gross exaggeration. The second accepts as normative American practice, with which foreign judicial authorities must not be allowed to interfere.

However, the Supreme Court in *Aérospatiale*, like the Court of Appeals in *Re Anschuetz*, saw a place for comity analysis, as was urged upon it by several of the briefs including that of the United Kingdom Government. Its position was that considerations of comity should be fully addressed before discovery should be allowed to proceed by means not fully recognized by the foreign sovereign State concerned. In practical terms this meant that a court should not lightly disregard foreign blocking statutes or 'defensive laws'; that perceived national interests should be carefully defined and weighed, so that some delay might well be accepted in the interest of promoting respect for the sovereign equality of States under international law; and that evidence of the willingness of the foreign state to assist United States courts (e.g. by a civil law country enacting legislation to enable cross-examination to take place)[156] should be taken into account.

There is quite a marked contrast between this view of comity analysis and that developed in the *amicus* brief of the United States. In commenting critically on the proposed text of the Restatement, cited above,[157] the Solicitor General stressed the strong policy of the United States procedural rules to secure

---

[154] 782 F. 2d. 120 (8th Cir., 1986).
[155] See the *amicus* brief of Switzerland on these points.
[156] As France had done: Nouveau Code de Procedure Civil, Art. 740.
[157] p. 115.

efficient and effective discovery in all cases; declared foreign reliance on judicial sovereignty to have an abstract quality, which did not elucidate substantive foreign interests, and which needed to be evaluated in the light of the established American principle that its courts could require foreign nationals to produce evidence located abroad; and urged that objections based on a blocking statute should be greeted with caution and scepticism in any proper comity analysis.

The judgment of the Supreme Court does little to resolve this evident difference of opinion as to the nature and likely outcome of comity analysis. It does, however, clearly reject any approach requiring first resort to the Convention, whether based upon an interpretation of the Convention text or on comity, as a blanket rule. There had to be prior scrutiny in each case of the particular facts, sovereign interests, and the likelihood that the Convention procedures would prove effective.[158] American courts were to exercise a special vigilance to protect foreign litigants from abusive discovery, for example demands for excessive numbers of depositions or documents involving high transportation costs and capable of being used as a device to secure a settlement of the case. But the court declined to articulate specific rules to guide the 'delicate task of adjudication'.

Four of the court's nine justices joined in a separate opinion by Blackmun J. This opinion favoured a presumption of first resort to the Convention's procedures, and feared that the majority's preference for case-by-case comity analysis, unaccompanied by any guidance as to its conduct, would lead to the Convention's procedures being invoked infrequently.[159] Blackmun J. proposed a tripartite analysis that would consider the foreign interests, the interests of the United States, and the mutual interests of all nations in a smoothly functioning international legal régime.

AFTER *AÉROSPATIALE*

The Supreme Court having removed quite a few familiar landmarks without issuing much in the way of fresh navigational guidance, the courts faced some difficulties in addressing the issue of the Convention's applicability. The Court of Appeals for the 5th Circuit, reconsidering *Re Anschuetz* on remand from the Supreme Court in the light of *Aérospatiale*, declined to re-interpret the *Aérospatiale* decision as requiring first resort to the Convention or as sanctioning the use of Blackmun J.'s tripartite analysis.[160] The discretion was for the District

---

[158] The Court dismissed an argument advanced both in *Re Anschuetz* and in the Court of Appeals in *Aérospatiale* itself that to resort first to the Convention but reserving the possibility of subsequent reliance on domestic rules would be a great insult to foreign states; in effect, the Court says they know the score.

[159] The separate opinion supports the majority's rejection of the 'geographic fiction' and of the supposed distinction between litigants and non-party witnesses, but rejects the majority's favoured interpretation of Art. 27, and its references to the 'unfairness' of depriving plaintiffs of access to domestic discovery rules.

[160] 838 F. 2d. 1362 (5th Cir., 1988).

Courts to exercise, but they were urged to be sensitive to the interests expressed in the Convention.

Courts under pressure tend to rely on devices which take attention away from the underlying issues. Appeal courts emphasize that the discretion is vested in the court of first instance and are reluctant to interfere;[161] first instance judges fall back on issues such as that of the burden of proof. So, in *Hudson* v. *Hermann Pfauter G.m.b.H. & Co.*[162] a District Court held that the party opposing the use of the Convention's procedures had the burden of proof, had that is to show good reasons for departing from its prima facie applicability. The 'foreign interests' of the Federal Republic of Germany, in terms of Blackmun J.'s tripartite analysis, were seen as particularly compelling and no good cause had been shown for doing other than resort to the Convention's procedures. Later cases took a different approach: starting from the assumption that the Convention was or could be time-consuming and expensive, a number of courts held that the party wanting to 'impose' the use of those procedures must show good cause.[163] Relatively little weight seems to have been given in practice to comity considerations.[164]

Attention later shifted to the possibility of revising the Federal Rules of Civil Procedure to reverse or qualify the *Aérospatiale* decision. The Advisory Committee on the Rules proposed in 1989 an amendment to Rule 26 which would add a provision that 'discovery within a country having a treaty with the United States applicable to such discovery shall be conducted by methods authorized by the treaty unless the court determines that those methods are inadequate or inequitable and authorizes other discovery methods not prohibited by the treaty'.[165] This text would leave a number of unresolved questions, notably the position of persons subject to the jurisdiction of the United States whose discovery could be ordered there and not within the foreign country, and the precise meaning and scope of the final clause as to the supposed inadequacy or inequitable nature of foreign rules.

---

[161] See *Sandsend Financial Consultants Ltd.* v. *Wood* 743 S.W. 2d. 364 (Tex. App., 1988) noting the overruling of the first resort approach of *Th. Goldschmidt A.G.* v. *Smith* 676 S.W. 2d. 443 (Tex. App., 1984), but emphasizing the importance of judicial discretion.

[162] 117 F.R.D. 33 (N.D.N.Y., 1987).

[163] *Benton Graphics* v. *Uddeholm Corpn.* 118 F.R.D. 386 (D.C.N.J., 1987); *Haynes* v. *Kleinwefers* 119 F.R.D. 335 (E.D.N.Y., 1988) (where the court is sharply critical of *Hudson* v. *Hermann Pfauter G.m.b.H.*, *supra*); *Scarminach* v. *Goldwell G.m.b.H.* 531 N.Y.S. 2d. 188 (N.Y. Sup. Ct., 1988).

[164] See e.g. *Roberts* v. *Heim* 130 F.R.D. 430 (N.D.Cal., 1990) but *cf. Reinsurance Company of America* v. *Administratia Asigurarilor de Stat* 902 F.2d 1275 (7th Circ., 1990). For reviews of the case-law see G. B. Born, 'Comity and the Lower Courts: Post *Aérospatiale* application of the Hague Evidence Convention' (1990) 24 Int.L. 393; J. P. Griffin and M. N. Bravin, 'Beyond *Aérospatiale*: A Commentary on Foreign Discovery provisions of the Restatement (Third) and the Proposed Amendments to the Federal Rules of Civil Procedure' (1991) 25 Int.L. 331.

[165] See Griffin and Bravin, *loc. cit.*, at 340–349.

5

Mutual Assistance in Criminal Matters

THE practice of international judicial assistance in civil and commercial matters is well established and relatively well known. But, at least in countries of the common law tradition, similar co-operation in criminal matters has been, until recent years, strangely neglected. Why is this so?

As a topic, mutual assistance in criminal matters has no obvious place in the legal categories familiar to common lawyers. It lies rather forlornly in a no man's land between private international law on the one hand and criminal procedure on the other. For understandable, but on examination insufficient, reasons it is shunned by specialists in both those areas.

(A) Grounds for Hesitations

FOREIGN PENAL LAWS

Private international lawyers ('conflicts' specialists) feel that their subject has little or nothing to do with criminal matters of any sort. This attitude is largely derived from the principle expressed in Rule 3 of Dicey and Morris' treatise: 'English courts have no jurisdiction to entertain an action . . . for the enforcement, either directly or indirectly, of a penal . . . law of a foreign State'.[1] The Rule expresses a principle found in judicial pronouncements and the writings of commentators in many jurisdictions:

'Penal laws of foreign countries are strictly local, and affect nothing more than they can reach, and can be seized by virtue of their authority';[2]

'[C]rimes, including in that term all breaches of public law punishable by pecuniary mulct or otherwise, at the instance of the state government, or of someone representing the public, are local in this sense, that they are only cognizable and punishable in the country where they are committed';[3]

'The courts of no country execute the penal laws of another';[4]

'No society takes concern in any crime, but what is hurtful to itself'.[5]

---

[1] *Dicey and Morris, The Conflict of Laws* (11th edn, 1987), pp. 101–4.
[2] *Folliott* v. *Ogden* (1789) 1 Hy. Bl. 123, per Lord Loughborough at 135.
[3] *Huntington* v. *Attrill* [1893] A.C. 150, per Lord Watson at 156.
[4] *The Antelope* (1825) 10 Wheat 123 (U.S. Sup. Ct.), per Marshall CJ.
[5] Lord Kames, *Equity*, Book 3, chap. 8, s. 1 (cited by Story as representing the Scottish position: *Conflict of Laws*, s. 622).

These statements of principle, most clearly the last-cited, were made in a time in which virtually all criminal activity was local in its effects. Even the most serious crimes would be 'hurtful' only to one society, and other States could afford to stand aloof. The position is now very different, as the following extract from a United Nations report published in August 1990 makes very clear:

In a world which is becoming increasingly interdependent, corrupt activities, often interlinked with organized crime and drug traffic, are increasingly transcending national borders.

The enormous sums (hundreds of billions of dollars) generated by the illicit drugs traffic trade have concentrated tremendous economic power in the hands of drugs lords who can corrupt whole governments. The drug lords subvert the criminal justice system, and their nefarious influence corrodes the basic values of society. These criminals are ready to intimidate prosecutors, judges, politicians and their families to get their way. If bribery does not work against certain honest officials, they use violence against individuals who stand in their way. The targeted killing of law enforcement officers, journalists and witnesses, in addition to the indiscriminate violence associated with drug trafficking, has created climates where basic law and order are threatened and public trust in government has been lost.

In some countries, the central government is under siege by the 'drug barons'; in others, whole regions or parts of cities have become the traffickers' inviolable 'turf' where law enforcement personnel dare not enter.

However, the economic subversion of financial institutions and legitimate economic enterprises is even more insidious. The financial systems of many countries, even those far away from the sources of production of illicit drugs, are now completely dependent on narco-dollars. This money is reinvested in associated criminal enterprises (gambling, prostitution, slave trade, illegal arms), or in important businesses (tourism, hotels, banks) so that crime syndicates can exercise a decisive influence in key economic sectors. Because of the transnational linkages with international banks and companies, investigation and prosecution of the narcocrats are extremely difficult. They can move themselves and their assets into friendly jurisdictions, and in many countries their activities are protected by bank secrecy laws. In the absence of effective transnational investigation and law enforcement agreements, the leaders of the drug cartels remain beyond the law.[6]

As Lord Griffiths put it, much more concisely, in the Privy Council case of *Liangsiriprasert* v. *United States Government*,[7] 'international crime has to be fought by international co-operation between law enforcement agencies'.

In these changed circumstances, the principle that one State will not take cognisance of the penal law of another State, to which the practice of extradition has always been an exception, requires re-examination. It is now recognized, so far as English law is concerned in the House of Lords' decision in *Re*

---

[6] *Corruption in Government*, the report of an Interregional Seminar, The Hague, Dec. 1989 (UN Doc. TCD/SEM 90/2), p. 8.

[7] [1990] 2 All E.R. 866, 871–2.

State of Norway's Application,[8] that the provision of assistance to the prosecution authorities of another State may not amount to even 'indirect' enforcement of the penal law of that State. In that case, the Letters of Request sought evidence for use in proceedings in a Norwegian court concerning allegedly unpaid tax, and it was argued that this contravened the principle (which applies to revenue law no less than to penal law), but it was held that the execution of the Letters of Request, even though the result might assist in the enforcement of the foreign law in the foreign proceedings, did not constitute enforcement, direct or indirect, of that law in England. It is believed that this judgment is of general application, and that it removes any doubts as to the legitimacy at common law of the provision of assistance in criminal matters.

CONFRONTATION

From the point of view of criminal procedure, an important principle of the common law tradition has had the effect of rendering mutual assistance in criminal matters appear of limited value. This applies to the taking of evidence abroad, which seems to conflict with the principle that, in the words of the Sixth Amendment to the United States Constitution, 'in all criminal prosecutions, the accused shall enjoy the right . . . to be confronted with the witnesses against him'. As the Supreme Court observed, this necessarily implies that the evidence against a defendant

shall come from a witness stand in a public courtroom where there is full judicial protection of the defendant's right of confrontation, of cross-examination, and of counsel.[9]

United States practice

However, so far as United States practice is concerned, the authors of the 1939 *Harvard Research* felt able to assert that 'the principle that no evidence taken out of the presence of the accused may be admitted has been substantially modified'.[10] This is evident from the practice under the Federal Rules of Criminal Procedure, rule 15 of which renders admissible the depositions of witnesses who are 'unavailable'[11] whenever 'due to exceptional circumstances of the case it is in the interests of justice' that a court orders the deposition to be taken.

The effect of this rule in the present context was fully explored in *United States v. Salim*.[12] In a drug-trafficking case, the prosecution in United States proceedings sought the trial court's permission to take a deposition in France; the witness whose evidence was required was in custody in France awaiting trial on drug-smuggling charges and it was not possible for her to be brought

[8] [1900] 1 A.C. 723.
[9] *Turner* v. *State of Louisiana* 379 U.S. 466, 472–3 (1964); *Pointer* v. *Texas* 380 U.S. 400 (1965) (applicability to State courts).   [10] (1939) 33 Am. Jo. Int. L. (Supp.), p. 99.
[11] Defined by reference to the Federal Rules of Evidence, r. 804(*a*).
[12] 855 F.2d. 944 (2nd Circ., 1988).

across the Atlantic to give evidence. Nor was it possible to transport the defendant to France. It was therefore proposed to arrange for two open telephone lines to be available between the courthouse in New York, where the defendant would be, and the court in France where the witness and the attorneys for both sides would be present. The defendant would be able to hear the proceedings on one telephone line and consult privately with his attorney on the other. It was proposed further to record the deposition on either audio or video tape. In the event, the French court held that French law did not allow the use of these procedures, but the defendant's attorney was allowed to be present and to cross-examine (albeit only by submitting questions in writing to the *juge d'instruction*); and a verbatim (or almost verbatim) record was made by a New York court reporter. Noting that physical confrontation of opposing witnesses is not always constitutionally required,[13] and that there was sufficient opportunity for cross-examination to satisfy the confrontation clause of the Sixth Amendment, the Court of Appeals for the Second Circuit held the deposition admissible. The Court recognized that in some cases the use of 'unconventional foreign methods of examination[14] may exceed the limits of accepted American standards of fairness and reliability, such as underlie the confrontation clause and the rule against hearsay'; but case-by-case analysis was required.

English practice

In England, the principle behind the confrontation clause proved equally influential. It was plainly recognized in the Merchant Shipping Act 1894, section 691 of which is of much wider application than the Short Title of the Act suggests. In relevant part, the section provides that whenever the testimony of any witness is required in any legal proceedings in the United Kingdom and the witness cannot be found in the Kingdom, any deposition made on oath by such witness before a British consular officer should be admissible in evidence, subject to certain conditions. One of these is that

if the proceeding is criminal, [the deposition] shall not be admissible unless it was made in the presence of the person accused.

Later legislation allowed certain types of written statement to be admitted, both in committal proceedings[15] and in criminal proceedings generally.[16] Written statements made outside the United Kingdom were at one time admissible in committal proceedings but not at trial,[17] but a more liberal

---

[13] Citing *Bourjaily* v. *U.S.* 107 S.Ct. 2775, 2782 (1987).
[14] Meaning, of course, 'unconventional' to American eyes.
[15] Criminal Justice Act 1967, s. 2, later re-enacted as Magistrates' Courts Act 1980, s. 102.
[16] Criminal Justice Act 1967, s. 9.
[17] See Criminal Justice Act 1972, s. 46; but note also Magistrates' Courts Act 1980, s. 102(7) (admissibility at trial of certain written statements received at committal proceedings even not made in presence of accused).

approach is now established by provisions in the Criminal Justice Act 1988,[18] and in the Criminal Justice (International Co-operation) Act 1990.[19]

It would seem a fair statement that in common law jurisdictions the practice of admitting in criminal proceedings written statements made before some foreign authority was slow to develop, remains exceptional, and is probably relatively little known to practitioners.

Evidence for the defence

Where foreign evidence is required not for the prosecution but for the defence, the difficulties of principle are very much reduced.[20] The practice of admitting such evidence seems to have been established at a relatively early date. In the eighteenth century, a woman accused of obtaining a pension by the false pretence that she was the widow of a deceased officer, to whom it was alleged she had never been married, wished to produce evidence of a marriage in Scotland. As the witnesses were in Scotland and could not be compelled to appear at the trial in England, the court adjourned the proceedings pending the taking of evidence before a judge of the Court of Session in Scotland.[21]

Assistance to foreign courts

Few of the difficulties outlined above stand in the way of the provision of assistance to a foreign court, including the taking of evidence in England for use in foreign proceedings where such evidence would be admissible. Section 24 of the Extradition Act 1870 recognized this, providing:

The testimony of any witness may be obtained in relation to any criminal matter pending in any court or tribunal in a foreign state in like manner as it may be obtained in relation to any civil matter under [the Foreign Tribunals Evidence Act 1856] . . . and all the provisions of that Act shall be construed as if the term civil matter included a criminal matter . . .[22]

Offences of a political nature were, however, excluded.

This section remained in force until 1975 and is now replaced by more modern provisions.[23] Again, however, there are signs that the procedure was little used and that requests for action caused some uncertainties. Something of this comes through these extracts from a 1913 Home Office Memorandum on *Practice in Extradition Cases*:[24]

In February 1900, two door-plates bearing inscriptions in French and Dutch 'Chancellerie de la Légation de la République Sud-Africaine' were taken from Dr Leyds's

---

[18] Ss. 23, 24 and 25.   [19] See pp. 242–3.
[20] In the United States until 1975 F.R.Crim.P. r. 15 was only available to the defence.
[21] See Lord Mansfield's account of the case in *Mostyn* v. *Fobrigas* (1774) 1 Cwp. 161, 174; *Harvard Research*, p. 98.   [22] See also Extradition Act 1873, s. 5.
[23] See successively the Evidence (Proceedings in Other Jurisdictions) Act 1975, s. 5 (repealed) and the Criminal Justice (International Co-operation) Act 1990, s. 4, considered below, pp. 243–4.
[24] Pp. 135, 143–4, cited in *British Digest of International Law*, vol. 6, p. 549.

door at Brussels. Later a London newspaper published a statement that both plates were exhibited in the window of the office of *Black and White* in Fleet Street. Thereupon a Commission Rogatoire in due form was issued by the judicial authorities at Brussels stating that criminal proceedings were pending with regard to the theft, and asking that the door-plates might be seized and the proprietors of *Black and White* examined as to how they became possessed of them. After consulting the Foreign Office it was decided to ignore the request, it being considered that Dr Leyds 'had no doubt obtained the Commission as a piece of impertinence'[25] . . . But the Chief Magistrate (Sir F. Lushington) advised that the holders might be summoned to give evidence and at the same time served with a Crown *subpoena duces tecum* to produce the plates, . . . which had an inscription and were, therefore, referable to the class of documents on examination.

In 1904, the French Government sent a Commission Rogatoire in the case of a certain Madame Gayet against whom some criminal proceedings not defined were in progress. The evidence of a French lady living in London was required *inter alia* as to certain premises at Nantes in which Madame Gayet kept a school, and the relationship of Madame Gayet and the school to the Congrégation D'Alençon. In view of this, and as the Commission referred to an article of the Penal Code which dealt both with commercial frauds by companies and associations and with associations detrimental to the public interest, it was considered possible that the Commission might be connected with proceedings against a religious society on religious and political grounds. Sir M. Chalmers discussed the question informally with the Chief Magistrate, and it was decided that as the Commission was perfectly regular on the face of it, the Secretary of State must issue his Order;[26] but if any political complexion should appear in the course of the evidence, the Chief Magistrate would deal with it.

In the United States, a similar development can be traced. Early refusals to countenance requests that evidence be taken for use in foreign proceedings[27] have given way to a more co-operative attitude, now clearly reflected in legislation.[28]

(B) Movement to the Modern Position

EARLY EFFORTS TO SECURE INTERNATIONAL CO-OPERATION

The spread of multilateral and bilateral agreements for international judicial assistance in civil and commercial matters was not accompanied by similar developments in the criminal context; progress in mutual assistance in criminal matters can fairly be said to be half a century behind.

Some work was done on the subject by the League of Nations Committee of Experts for the Progressive Codification of International Law. A Draft Con-

---

[25] [The point being that the Boer War was in progress.]

[26] i.e. under Extradition Act 1873, s. 5.

[27] e.g. *In the Matter of Jenckes* 6 R.I. 18 (1859); *In the Matter of the Spanish Consul* 1 Ben. 225 (S.D.N.Y., 1867); *Re Letters Rogatory from Examining Magistrate of Tribunal of Versailles* 26 F. Supp. 852 (D.C.Md, 1939); and see *Re Letter Rogatory from the Justice Court, District of Montreal, Canada* 523 F. 2d 562 (6th Circ., 1975).

[28] 28 USC 1782, see p. 80, applies to criminal as well as civil cases.

vention was prepared by a sub-committee, whose rapporteur was Professor Schücking, in 1928.[29] This provided for requests to be sent, in the normal case, through diplomatic channels.[30] In the original draft there was a strong link with extradition practice in that assistance could be refused if the relevant offence were not extraditable. There is no such link in modern mutual assistance agreements, but it reflected the earlier position in which it was only in extradition treaties that some limited provision for related mutual assistance could be found. The Committee of Experts itself removed the references to extraditable offences; it substituted provisions allowing assistance to be refused in the case of political offences.

The Draft Convention covered 'measures of enquiry',[31] the summoning of witnesses and experts to attend in the requesting State (with immunity from prosecution in respect of earlier conduct),[32] the transfer of persons in custody to appear as witnesses (available only on the basis of reciprocity),[33] and the surrender of exhibits.[34] The striking omission from the text is any reference to the actual taking of evidence in the requested State; presumably it was thought that this was, or could be, covered by international practice as to letters rogatory.

The Harvard Draft Convention published in 1939 followed a few earlier models[35] in assimilating mutual assistance in criminal matters to the procedures available or proposed in the civil and commercial field. It dealt with service of process,[36] obtaining evidence abroad,[37] and the supply of certain records relating to convictions and to convicted offenders.[38]

It was some years after the Second World War before the first modern multilateral mutual assistance treaty was signed. This was the European Convention on Mutual Assistance in Criminal Matters of 1959,[39] which antedated by a decade or more the recent wave of activity in the field.

THE CURRENT SCENE

If mutual assistance in criminal matters developed relatively slowly, the current scene is one of almost frenetic activity. Concern about the drugs trade, international terrorism, and commercial crime generally, have led to the creation of a considerable number of *ad hoc* international groups supplementing the work of longer-established organizations. In Europe, the development of the European Community, especially since the adoption of the Single European Act, has fuelled this process. Generally, it seems that the impetus has come in recent years from bodies which are essentially political

---

[29] League of Nations Doc A.15.1928.V, reproduced in the *Harvard Research*, (1939) 33 Am. Jo. I. L. (Supp.) 143.

[30] Draft Convention, Art. 5.

[31] Ibid., Art. 1.

[32] Ibid., Art. 2.

[33] Ibid.

[34] Ibid., Art. 3.

[35] e.g. the Central American Treaty of Confraternity of 12 Apr. 1924, Art. 13; 6 Int. Leg. 829.

[36] Harvard Draft Convention, Art. 6 and (immunity of those responding to witness summonses) 7.

[37] Ibid., Art. 8.

[38] Ibid., Art. 9.

[39] See pp. 130–142.

in nature rather than, as one might expect, primarily from the specialist bodies in the law enforcement community. The material which follows is intended to sketch the nature of some of this activity, which has either produced or forms an important background to the particular legal measures which constitute international judical assistance.

Interpol

The best-known of all the specialist organizations is the International Criminal Police Organization or Interpol. First established in 1923, it was revived after the Second World War in 1946 and has grown to an organization with 150 member countries. It has an annual General Assembly and headquarters in Lyon, and works through a network of National Central Bureaux in each member country.[40] Interpol spokesmen tend to be defensive about its work, anxious to dispel the popular perception of the organization as an international investigative agency but equally concerned that it should not be seen as a mere communications centre.[41]

Its communications role is none the less a very important one. It operates a system of international notices, for example red notices for wanted persons and green notices about professional offenders believed to be operating in several countries, and circulates *modus operandi* reports. Over 100,000 files are held at Lyons on international offenders, and some 350,000 messages are received there each year; much work is being done to enhance the technical sophistication of the operation, to create a high quality and secure database. The Interpol member countries within Europe have their own regional Bureau servicing an annual Regional Conference and specialist meetings of Heads of National Drugs Departments and of Fraud officers, and a system of European Contact Officers.

The ethos of Interpol, with its strong emphasis on practical police work, reflected in the fact that police officers make up a high proportion of its international staff, has prevented it taking major initiatives in the strictly legal field. It has tended to follow rather than lead the development of legal provision for international judicial assistance.

Customs Co-operation Council

As its name indicates this is an international organization for co-operation between customs administrations, work made more complex by the different allocation of functions in member States as between customs, police forces, border militia or coastguards, and revenue authorities. The Council has headquarters in Brussels; its Enforcement Committee is important in the present context.

---

[40] See M. Anderson, *Policing the World: Interpol and the Politics of International Police Co-operation* (Oxford, 1989).

[41] See also the professional criticisms of Interpol's work, at least in previous years, recorded in the report of the House of Commons Home Affairs Committee on *Practical Police Co-operation in the European Community* (H.C 363, Session 1989–90).

A central legal instrument in its work is the International Convention on Mutual Administrative for the Prevention, Investigation and Repression of Customs Offences adopted in Nairobi in June 1977; an amending Protocol of 1985, enabling administrations which were not members of the Council to be parties to the Nairobi Convention, came into force in July 1989. The Convention has a number of Annexes and its structure allows Contracting Parties[42] to accept each Annex separately. For example, Annex IV deals with assistance, on request, in surveillance operations, Annex V the appearance of customs officials before a court or tribunal abroad, and Annex X with assistance in the drugs field. The Convention is supplemented by Recommendations of the Council, for example that of 13 June 1985 on the development of co-ordinated enforcement and intelligence operations aimed at identifying and intercepting concealed illicit drugs.

The Council works closely with Interpol, both in practical matters such as *modus operandi* reports and in arranging joint studies of such topics as money-laundering techniques and draft legislation.

United Nations

The United Nations organizes every five years a Congress on the Prevention of Crime and the Treatment of Offenders. The nature of these gatherings has varied over the years, that held in Habana in 1990 being unusually well prepared, with an elaborate series of Regional and Interregional Preparatory Meetings, and productive. In particular, it adopted Model Treaties on a number of matters, including Mutual Assistance in Criminal Matters,[43] the Transfer of Proceedings in Criminal Matters,[44] and Extradition. The United Nations has also been very active in the drugs field, notably in sponsoring the negotiation, which led to the 1988 Vienna Convention against Illicit Traffic in Narcotic Drugs and Psychotropic Substances.[45] In 1991 it reorganized its continuing work in the field, establishing the United Nations International Drug Control Programme based in Vienna.

Group of Seven

The Group of Seven leading industrial nations has taken an interest in this field, having established in 1989 an influential Financial Action Task Force. This concentrated on money-laundering, and its work is considered more fully in that context.[46]

The Commonwealth Secretariat

The Commonwealth Secretariat, based in London, provides a range of services to Commonwealth governments; it is answerable ultimately to Commonwealth Heads of Government Meetings. Its Legal Division contains

---

[42] There were twenty-seven Parties as at Jan. 1990.
[43] See pp. 164–9.   [44] See pp. 169–71.
[45] See pp. 174–80.   [46] See pp. 185–6.

the Commonwealth Commercial Crime Unit,[47] which has operated a co-operative network of specialist officers in member countries since 1981, and has responded to requests by Law Ministers by developing a series of Schemes for mutual assistance in the administration of justice including the Harare Scheme of 1986 for Mutual Assistance in Criminal Matters, examined in detail below.[48] These Schemes are kept under review at Senior Official level, and work is being undertaken to develop a Scheme for co-operation between securities regulatory agencies.

European regional arrangements

(a) *The Council of Europe.* The Council of Europe, a regional organization established in 1949, predates and has a wider membership than the European Community. It has always taken a keen interest in crime problems, and was early in the international assistance field with the European Convention on Mutual Assistance in Criminal Matters being signed in 1959. Its provisions and subsequent development are examined in detail below.[49] More recently, the Council has developed a Convention dealing with money-laundering and the confiscation of the proceeds of crime;[50] one notable feature of this Convention is that non-European countries were involved in the process of negotiation and can be parties to it.

(b) *TREVI.* In 1976, the United Kingdom suggested a new European inter-governmental forum for co-operation at a practical and operational level in combating terrorism, drugs trafficking, and serious crime and public order generally. Its name, TREVI, is a reference to the fountain in Rome, where the inital meeting was held, and to M. Fontaine a leading participant; such whimsical humour is a rare commodity in international organizations. Membership is limited to European Community member States, but the grouping is technically outside the Community framework as the Community institutions have no standing on police questions.

Working Groups of TREVI, which report through Senior Officials to twice-yearly ministerial meetings, deal with terrorism (Group I), a range of public order (including football crowd control) and equipment issues (Group II) and drugs and organized crime (Group III). A 1992 Group, corresponding to the customs MAG '92 Group, looks to greater co-operation in the Single Market. A full Programme of Action was agreed in Dublin in June 1990 as a 'reference text' for the work of the Groups.

(c) *Customs co-operation in Europe.* The Naples Convention of 1967 regulates co-operation and assistance between the customs administrations of European Community member States; the United Kingdom acceded in 1974.

---

[47] Originally the Commonwealth Fraud Liaison Office.
[48] See pp. 149–62.   [49] See pp. 130–42.
[50] See pp. 188–9 and 235–8.

A Mutual Assistance Group (MAG) meets regularly to oversee the practical workings of the Convention. A special group, MAG '92, was established to examine customs co-operation in the new conditions which will prevail in Europe after 1992.

(d) Schengen agreements. The first Schengen Agreement, the Agreement between the Governments of the States of the Benelux Union, the Federal Republic of Germany and the French Republic on the gradual abolition of controls at frontiers, was signed in 1985. The context is the desire of the European Commission and many member States of the Community to abolish border controls as part of the Single European Market. The necessity and desirability of such a development are alike controversial, and there are important implications for law enforcement.[51] The removal of internal barriers to the free movement of criminals places more weight on security at the external border of the Community, and creates new requirements for co-operation between law enforcement agencies within each member State.

Schengen I drew on the experience of the Benelux countries in removing border controls, and was followed by a much more sensitive agreement, Schengen II, in June 1990. This contemplates 'hot pursuit' by national police forces across frontiers. It is far from clear that 'Schengen principles' will be capable of generalization to the rest of the Community.[52]

Mutual assistance in specialized fields

In a number of other contexts, international instruments provide, usually in the most general terms, for States to afford one another measures of assistance in connection with criminal proceedings. Examples are to be found in the various conventions seeking to protect civil aviation from terrorism and hijacking.[53]

---

[51] See a report of the House of Lords Select Committee on the European Communities, 1992: Border Control of People (H.L. 90, Session 1988–9).

[52] The implications for the Northern Ireland land frontier are examined in the report of the House of Commons Home Affairs Committee on *Practical Police Co-operation in the European Community* (H.C 363, Session 1989–90), para. 31 *et seq.*

[53] See Hague Convention 1970, Art. 10; Montreal Convention 1971, Art. 11; *Shawcross and Beaumont on Air Law*, Division VIII.

6

International Action in Criminal Matters

THERE is now a large number of international instruments providing a vehicle for States to join in providing mutual assistance in criminal matters. This chapter reviews the major multilateral instruments, produced under the aegis of the Council of Europe, the Commonwealth or the United Nations.

(A) The Work of the Council of Europe

EUROPEAN CONVENTION ON MUTUAL ASSISTANCE IN CRIMINAL MATTERS

It was inevitable that the traditional reluctance of States to co-operate in criminal law matters would ultimately break down. The greatest shift in attitudes dates from the 1970s and 1980s, and that makes all the more remarkable the pioneering work of the Council of Europe which led to the European Convention on Mutual Assistance in Criminal Matters 1959.[1]

In 1953 a Committee of Governmental Experts was convened under the auspices of the Council of Europe to discuss the possibility of a European Convention in relation to extradition. In the report of the Committee the question of mutual assistance in criminal matters was raised as being of great importance. It was felt that extradition was only one aspect of this co-operation and in view of the development of international relations in general and European relations in particular, it was becoming essential to apply common standards to other matters. It was noted that although some States did already have rules in this area these tended to regulate on the municipal rather than the international level. The Committee of Ministers therefore agreed to the widening of the experts' terms of reference to allow preparation of a Draft Convention in this area, and after deliberation this was opened for signature on 20 April 1959.[2]

As this was the first multilateral agreement in this area it was decided that

---

[1] European Treaty Series No. 30.

[2] *Explanatory Report on the European Convention on Mutual Assistance in Criminal Matters*, at p. 5. Further information is contained in *Problems Arising from the Practical Application of the European Convention on Mutual Assistance in Criminal Matters*, Council of Europe 1971. This document is cited hereafter as *PPA*. For its origins, in the discussions which led up to the Additional Protocol of 1978, see p. 142.

the main objectives were to produce a Convention which was sufficiently flexible to allow it to be adapted to the diversity of legal systems in Europe, with recognition of a general obligation to render assistance in criminal matters and minimum rules laying down the limits on the provision of that assistance. It was felt to be easier to draw up rules in relation to mutual assistance as in this field, unlike that of extradition, there was no question of affecting the liberty of the individual. Therefore, if assistance were granted independently of extradition there was no necessity for a requirement of dual criminality and more minor offences could also be included.[3] It was, however, still felt to be advisable to exclude military offences, and to allow discretion in relation to the more contentious areas of political and fiscal offences.[4] It was also felt that the Convention need not deal with detailed matters of police co-operation as this was better handled through the work of ICPO–Interpol.

The resulting Convention has achieved these aims in that it is sufficiently simple to allow it to be applied without the need for elaborate implementing legislation[5] but it is not a uniform and comprehensive European law on criminal procedure as it often leaves execution of the request to be governed by the law of the requested State. The Convention was opened for signature on 20 April 1959 and after obtaining the three ratifications necessary entered into force on 12 July 1962. In 1990 the United Kingdom belatedly became a party to what is undoubtedly one of the Council of Europe's most successful agreements to date.[6]

Scope of the Convention

The Convention is divided into eight chapters which each deal with a different area of the provision of mutual assistance; the first of these chapters lays down the foundation on which the rest of the Convention rests. Article 1(1) provides that the Parties are to afford each other the 'widest measure of mutual assistance in proceedings in respect of offences, the punishment of which, at the time of the request for assistance, falls within the jurisdiction of the judicial authorities of the requesting Party'. It appears to be immaterial on what date the offence was committed and the Swiss courts have held the Convention applicable in respect of crimes committed before it came into force.[7] Article 1(1) is intended to be interpreted in a broad sense as extending not only to the sorts of mutual assistance specifically covered by the Convention, but also every other kind of mutual legal assistance which might be sought.[8]

It is clearly necessary that 'proceedings' have been commenced, though

---

[3] *Explanatory Report*, at p. 7.

[4] Ibid. The Convention was later extended in relation to fiscal offences; see pp. 142–3.

[5] For example, the Convention was brought into force for France by a law which simply gave effect to the actual text: Decret No. 67–636, 23 July 1967.

[6] See pp. 141–2.

[7] *S.* v. *Camera dei Ricorsi Penali del Tribunale di Appello del Cantone Ticino* [1987] I B.G.E. (112/6) 576.

[8] *Explanatory Report*, at p. 11.

this will cover formal investigatory proceedings,[9] and these proceedings must be judicial proceedings.[10] The provision is so drafted as to apply to proceedings which 'at the time of the request' are within the jurisdiction of the judicial authorities; this is to enable the Convention to extend to certain offences in Germany which are initially dealt with by an administrative body but which may be transferred to a judicial authority.[11]

It has been held by the Swiss courts that the discontinuance of penal proceedings for reasons of expediency does not prevent the provision of mutual assistance as no decision on the culpability of the accused has been made, and the maxim *ne bis in idem* is not in jeopardy.[12] The Parties are entitled to make a declaration in which they define what they deem to be judicial authorities.[13] Mutual assistance is not to be provided in respect of arrests or the enforcement of verdicts or offences under military law which are not offences under ordinary criminal law.[14]

Refusal of assistance

The cases in which there is a discretion to refuse to provide assistance are set out in Article 2. First, assistance may be refused if the request concerns an offence which the requested Party considers to be a political offence, an offence connected with a political offence or a fiscal offence.[15] Even the Swiss, with their reputation for protecting all information in matters fiscal, have decided that the information provided by Swiss authorities may be used by a foreign State in the investigation of political and associated offences and tax offences unless a condition expressly prohibiting this has been made by the relevant Swiss authority.[16] The discretionary nature of Article 2 is important as co-operation in these areas is not automatically precluded. However, the categorization of the crime within the requesting State is irrelevant as refusal depends on the subjective opinion of the authorities of the requested State.

Secondly, assistance may be refused if the requested Party considers that execution is 'likely to prejudice the sovereignty, security, *ordre public* or other essential interests of its country'.[17] The essential interests referred to are those of the State and not any individual,[18] and extend to the protection of economic interests.[19]

The authors of the Convention admitted only these grounds for refusing assistance; it was considered that accepting obligations in relation to mutual assistance implies some surrender of sovereignty to the extent which the

[9] See Art. 15(3) and p. 133.
[10] Ibid.   [11] *PPA*, at p. 14.
[12] *Mercedes Zunder* v. *Chambre d'Accusation du Canton de Genève* [1986] I B.G.E. (110/1) 385.
[13] Art. 24.   [14] Art. 1(2).
[15] Art. 2(*a*). Although the Additional Protocol of 1978 amends this exception in relation to fiscal offences, the adoption of the Protocol is not obligatory and therefore for those States which have not become Party to it the original form of Article 2(*a*) is still valid. See below, pp. 142–3.
[16] Schweizerisches Bundesgericht, [1982] I B.G.E. 261.   [17] Art. 2(*b*).
[18] *Explanatory Report*, at p. 13.   [19] Ibid.

requested State considers compatible with its fundamental concepts and its essential political or economic interests.[20] The adoption of a provision precluding assistance where the requested State felt that it might facilitate persecution on the grounds of race, religion, nationality or political opinions was not felt to be necessary both because of the narrow territorial application of the Convention and the width of Article 2(*b*).[21] A provision preventing assistance when either the case in question was pending or had already been decided within the requested State was also felt to be undesirable as it would have unduly restricted the scope of the Convention.[22]

The limitations implied by Article 1(1) are of great importance. The Convention is about assistance 'in proceedings . . . within the jurisdiction of the judicial authorities' and all types of request are to originate from 'judicial authorities' (even if Interpol channels are used).[23] While this pattern is a reflection of civil law practice, under which even the investigatory stage of a criminal matter may fall within the competence of a *juge d'instruction* or similar judicial officer, it is also a mark of the early date of the Convention. Later international agreements have dealt more fully with assistance to prosecution and investigatory agencies at times before any proceedings have been commenced, and even in some cases before any crime has been committed. In the text of the European Convention, the stage in the criminal matter at which assistance may first be requested is addressed only obliquely; it is only in Article 15(3), in the context of the procedure for sending requests, that the text refers clearly to 'requests for investigation preliminary to prosecution'.

Letters Rogatory

Chapter II of the Convention (Articles 3–6) deals essentially with the taking of evidence for use in criminal proceedings. It specifies that the request shall in this context take the form of Letters Rogatory defined in the official *Explanatory Report* as 'a mandate by a judicial authority of one country to a foreign judicial authority to perform in its place one or more specified actions'.[24] On the basis of this understanding, it has been held by a Swiss court that where a foreign court has made an application to question a witness through a Swiss court the foreign court has legal standing to appeal against questioning which it feels has not been properly carried out, as the requested judge acts in place of the requesting judge in discharging his investigatory duty.[25]

This type of procedure was familiar to the member States from its use in international civil procedure, especially as a means for taking of evidence. It had not previously been much used in the criminal context, and in subsequent

---

[20] *PPA*, at p. 15. See, however, Art. 5, considered below.
[21] *Explanatory Report*, at p. 13.   [22] Ibid.
[23] See Art. 15(4)(5).   [24] At p. 14.
[25] Justizkommission Zug, 4 Apr. 1985 [1986] S.J.Z. 301.

international agreements where the emphasis on co-operation between *judicial* authorities has been less marked, a more neutral term (such as 'request' *simpliciter*) has commonly been substituted.

Article 3(1) provides that 'the requested Party shall execute in the manner provided for by its law any Letters Rogatory relating to a criminal matter and addressed to it by the judicial authorities of the requesting Party for the purpose of procuring evidence or transmitting articles to be produced in evidence, records or documents'. 'Evidence' is to be construed as referring *inter alia* to hearing witnesses, experts and accused persons and providing for transport and search and seizure.[26] It has been suggested that it should be construed in its widest sense as meaning anything which may be evidence for the prosecution or the defence and liable to lead to the establishing of the true facts,[27] and also that the requested authority must judge whether the objects in question are connected with the alleged offence and truly required as evidence rather than as, for example, security for civil claims.[28] The Swiss courts have decided that the proceeds of crime can be handed over under the Swiss legislation giving effect to the Convention (which does not specifically refer to proceeds at any point); but they have also indicated that this will not normally be the case where the proceeds of tax fraud are concerned.[29]

The examination of witnesses and experts is to be carried out in accordance with the law of the requested State. The requesting Party may, however, ask that the witnesses and experts be examined on oath and this is to be complied with if not prohibited by the law of the requested State.[30] No provision is made to enable the record of the evidence to be taken in a particular form, or for procedures such as cross-examination to be allowed; the law of the court executing the request governs, but in practice some procedural codes will be flexible enough to accommodate the needs of requesting States. The Convention does provide that where sight of documents and records is requested, certified copies or certified photostat copies are to be sufficient unless originals are expressly requested, in which case every effort is to be made to comply.[31] The Swiss authorities have indicated that although it is accepted that information about the relatives of criminals may also be sought, this may not be used in evidence against them without the consent of the Swiss authorities.[32]

It is also to be noted that while the Letters Rogatory must be addressed to the requested Party by the judicial authorities of the other State, the Convention does not prohibit third parties making requests to those authorities for transmission. Officials and interested persons may also expressly request permission to attend the execution of the Letters Rogatory, but this is subject

---

[26] *Explanatory Report*, at p. 14.
[27] *PPA*, at p. 42.   [28] Ibid.
[29] S. v. *Camera dei Ricorsi Penali del Tribunale di Appelo del Cantone Ticino* [1987] I B.G.E. (112/6) 576.
[30] Art. 3(2).   [31] Art. 3(3).
[32] S. v. *Camera dei Ricorsi Penali del Tribunale di Appello del Cantone Ticino*, above.

to the consent of the requested Party.[33] The consent may only be given where not prohibited by the law of the requested Party, as it was considered to be unacceptable that the authorities of the requesting State and the parties in criminal proceedings have better rights than equivalent parties in domestic proceedings in the requested State.[34]

Limitations on compliance with requests for the seizure of property are to be found in Articles 5 and 6. First, the Contracting Parties may reserve the right to make execution of Letters Rogatory for the search and seizure of property dependent on one or more of the following conditions:[35]

(*a*) That the offence concerned is punishable under both the law of the requesting and requested States;

(*b*) That the offence is an extraditable offence in the requested country;

(*c*) That the execution of Letters Rogatory is consistent with the law of the requested State.

Where such a reservation is made reciprocity may be applied against that State by any other contracting Party.[36]

Where property is to be handed over pursuant to a request, compliance may be delayed if the property, records or documents are required in connection with pending criminal proceedings in the requested State; any property handed over in execution of a request is to be returned as soon as possible unless the requested Party waives the right to demand its return.[37] It has been held that no breach of the Convention takes place until the requested State, which had not waived the right to reclaim the property, has made a request for its return and that request has been ignored.[38] In this case the Italian authorities had requested the transfer of valuable grave stones from Switzerland for use in criminal proceedings in Italy. Italy subsequently refused to hand back the stones claiming that they were historic treasures under public international law, but it was held that the claim could not succeed as the refusal to return the stones or to execute the Swiss court order for their seizure amounted to a breach of good faith. It was agreed by the Committee of Experts when drafting the Convention that the requesting Party would not be permitted to dispose of the property even when it was obliged to determine the question of ownership under its own domestic law,[39] but this has been criticized as doing nothing to protect third party rights and as failing to meet the many and varied legal problems which can arise.[40]

Service of Writs and Records of Judicial Verdicts

Article 7 provides that the requested Party shall effect service of writs and records of judicial verdicts transmitted to it for that purpose. Service may

[33] Art. 4.
[34] *PPA*, at p. 16.
[35] Art. 5(1).
[36] Art. 5(2).
[37] Art. 6.
[38] *X. v. Appellationsgericht des Kantons Baselstadt* [1985] I B.G.E. (111) 52.
[39] *Explanatory Report*, at p. 16.
[40] *PPA*, at p. 44.

either be by simple transmission or, where expressly requested, in the manner provided for the service of analogous documents under the domestic law of the requested State or in a special manner consistent with that law. This is intended to allow the requested Party to make use of whichever mode of service is easiest for it to provide,[41] and although no definition of 'writs and records of judicial verdicts' is provided, it is intended to extend to notification of all matters relating solely to criminal proceedings.[42] Where service is requested in a particular form, or where provisions as to modes of service are contained in a supplementary bilateral agreement between the two States, service in some other form will be at risk of being declared invalid for the purpose of the proceedings in the requesting State.[43]

As proof of service may be required in certain jurisdictions to show that due notice has been given of the proceedings, Article 7(2) provides that the requested Party must provide either a receipt bearing the date and the signature of the person on whom the documents were served, or a declaration made by the requested Party stating that service was effected giving details of the form and date of service. Criticisms have been made, however, that it is a serious flaw in the Convention that there is no attempt to deal with the effects of service or whether service may be refused. Finally, because of strict requirements in the law of some Scandinavian countries that no accused can be convicted without being given specified periods of notice of the charge against him, Article 7(3) allows any contracting Party to enter a reservation that service of a summons on an accused person within its territory must be transmitted to its authorities by a certain time before the date set for appearance.

Appearance of witnesses, experts and prosecuted persons

The sub-heading appears in the Convention as part of the title to Chapter III. This makes clear, what might otherwise be obscure to an English reader of the text, that the 'service of writs' includes the service of witness summonses. 'Prosecuted persons' is a term which is not used in the text of the Articles of the Convention; it means persons in custody (for whatever reason) whose appearance as a witness in the requesting State is required. It is also clear, though only implied in the text, that Articles 8–12 are concerned with the appearance of persons to give evidence in the requesting State; appearance in the requested State is covered by the Letters Rogatory provisions of Chapter II.

Article 8 prevents a witness or expert summoned to appear in the requesting State from being punished for failing to answer a summons unless they subsequently enter the territory of the requesting Party and are again summoned.[44] This is to be the case even where the summons contains a notice of

---

[41] Explanatory Report, at p. 16.   [42] PPA, at p. 45.
[43] *Officier van Justitie in het Arrondissement Middelburg* v. *S.* [1988] N.J. 2458 (Hoge Raad, 15 Dec. 1987).   [44] *Explanatory Report*, at p. 18.

penalty,[45] and 'penalty' is to be construed as including all forms of restraint on personal liberty, including fines.[46] From the point of view of the prosecution, there are some cases in which progress cannot be made unless the witness attends in the requesting State; this is more likely to be the case if the officials of that State are not permitted to be present at the examination of a witness, perhaps after the use of compulsory powers, in the requested State in response to a Letter Rogatory. However, these considerations are outweighed by considerations of individual liberty and the unacceptability of the extra-territorial effect of subpoenas.[47]

The payment of an allowance and travelling expenses is guaranteed for witnesses and experts by Article 9 which provides that they are to be paid by the requesting Party at rates at least equal to those applicable in the country where the hearing is to take place. Where the appearance of a witness is especially necessary this is to be expressly mentioned in the request and the requested Party is required to invite that person to appear.[48] Where this is the case the summons should indicate the approximate allowances and expenses refundable, and when requested by the witness or expert, an advance should be made to him by the requested Party which will then be refunded by the requesting Party. These advances are considered necessary to encourage attendance,[49] but it has been suggested that they should be available to all witnesses and experts as every person whose presence is requested must be considered to be especially necessary for mutual assistance to have been invoked.

Where the person summoned is being held in custody in the requested State the provisions of Article 11 apply. The Convention permits temporary transfer for the purposes of personal appearance with return to be within a period stipulated by the requesting Party provided that certain conditions are met. Transfer may be refused if the person in custody does not consent; if his presence is necessary at criminal proceedings pending in the requested State; if transfer would be liable to prolong his detention; or if there are 'other overriding grounds' for refusing transfer. If a transfer takes place, the person transferred is not to be required to do anything other than give evidence or take part in a confrontation.[50]

Where the transfer involves transit through a third State which is also a Party to the Convention an application requesting permission should be made to the Ministry of Justice of that State, the only ground for refusing such permission being that a contracting Party may refuse to permit transit of its own nationals.[51] The person is to remain in custody during transit and while within the territory of the requesting State unless the requested Party

---

[45] Art. 8.   [46] *Explanatory Report*, at p. 18.
[47] See *PPA*, at p. 18, and pp. 157–60 for a fuller account of the issue as it arose in the context of the Commonwealth Scheme for Mutual Assistance in Criminal Matters.
[48] Art. 10(1).
[49] PPA, at p. 18.
[50] PPA, at p. 48.
[51] Art. 11(2).

applies for his release.[52] There is no mention within the Convention itself of whether the time spent in custody in the requesting State should count towards the person's sentence, but the general view of the group of experts which reviewed the practical application of the Convention was that this should be the case.[53]

An important provision is Article 12 which grants witnesses, experts and persons in custody a certain immunity from prosecution when responding to a summons; a distinction necessarily being made between witnesses and experts on the one hand and persons being summoned to answer charges on the other.

Witnesses and experts are granted immunity from prosecution, detention or other restraints on their personal liberty in respect of acts or convictions dating from prior to their departure from the requested State.[54] In the case of persons being summoned to face criminal proceedings it is obviously impracticable to provide such a blanket immunity from prosecution; a person summoned to answer for acts forming the subject of proceedings against him is entitled to be free from prosecution, detention or other restraints on his personal liberty in respect of acts or convictions dating from prior to their departure from the requested State and which are not specified in the summons.[55]

It was decided that it was equitable for the immunity to cease when the person had had an opportunity of leaving the territory of the requested State for a period of fifteen consecutive days from the date when his presence was no longer required by the judicial authorities but has nevertheless remained in the requesting State or was returned to it (e.g. under normal extradition procedures).[56]

Judicial records

Article 13, the sole Article of Chapter IV, requires that a Party shall communicate on request extracts from and information relating to judicial records to the judicial authorities in a contracting Party when needed in a criminal matter. This is subject to the limitation that information may only be disclosed to the same extent that it would be made available to domestic judicial authorities in a similar case.[57] Where the request does not fall within the terms of Article 13(1) it is still to be complied with, but in such cases compliance will be governed by the domestic law, regulations or practice of the requested State which will tend to be more restrictive.[58] This impliedly enables requests by non-judicial authorities, or by judicial authorities with no jurisdiction over criminal matters.[59] Article 13 lacks any limits on the extent of the assistance which may be requested or on the nature of the offences to

---

[52] Art. 11(3).
[53] *PPA*, at p. 95.
[54] Art. 12(1).
[55] Art. 12(2).
[56] Art. 12(3).
[57] Art. 13(1).
[58] Art. 13(2).
[59] *Explanatory Report*, at p. 19.

which the request relates, but similarly there is no requirement as to a minimum content for the information provided.[60] This lack of specificity may prove to be a hindrance in some cases, but in others the discretion afforded may encourage co-operation.

Exchange of information on judicial records

As part of the general obligation to provide mutual assistance each contracting Party is also obliged to inform any other Party of all criminal convictions and subsequent measures taken in respect of nationals of that other Party which are entered in the judicial records.[61] This information is to be communicated at least once a year and where a person is a national of two or more contracting Parties, each of these shall be informed unless the person is a national of the State where he was convicted.[62] The term 'criminal convictions' is to be given a wide construction and 'subsequent measures' is to be taken as including, in particular, rehabilitation.[63] This obligation is potentially onerous, and is only appropriate in a regional treaty such as the European Convention, where the Parties are geographically close and often contiguous. Article 22 was further developed in the 1978 Additional Protocol.[64]

Procedure

The requirements for contents of requests are briefly set out in Article 14, but more importantly the manner in which these requests are to be transmitted is dealt with in Article 15. The normal channel for Letters Rogatory and for applications for transfers of persons in custody under Article 11 is to be from Ministry of Justice to Ministry of Justice.[65] This cuts through some of the delays and complexities associated with the diplomatic channel which was the normal route prior to the Convention, but still permits for a measure of governmental supervision. Contracting Parties are, however, entitled to make a reservation under Article 15(6) that some or all requests are to go through channels other than those provided for in this Article, allowing States to require that the diplomatic channel be used.

Despite the right thus to retain the use of the diplomatic channel the Convention also makes it possible to use even more direct communication than that between Ministries of Justice. In cases of 'urgency' the Convention permits the Letters Rogatory to be sent directly between the judicial authorities of each State,[66] although the States are entitled to demand, through a reservation under Article 15(6), that a copy of a request sent in this way be forwarded to the Ministry of Justice. The information provided in response to an urgent request must still be returned through the normal channel established by Article 15(1).

---

[60] *PPA*, at p. 50.
[61] Art. 22.
[62] Ibid.
[63] *Explanatory Report*, at p. 23.
[64] See p. 144.
[65] Art. 15(1).
[66] Art. 15(2).

The direct route between judicial authorities may always be used where the request is not in the form of Letters Rogatory under Articles 3 to 5 nor a request for the transfer of a person in custody under Article 11. Whenever direct transmission is permitted it may take place via ICPO–Interpol.[67] It should also be noted that the Convention does not take precedence over any bilateral agreements or arrangements between the contracting Parties which provide for direct transmission of requests.[68]

When reviewing the practical application of the Convention it was acknowledged that the scheme could never achieve its full potential unless its operation were both quick and easy.[69] The direct route from one judicial authority to another appears to be both the quickest and the simplest method of transferring requests, and the opinion of the review committee would suggest that the aim of future co-operation should be to make the use of this channel the norm rather than the exception.

The remaining significant procedural provision is Article 16 which deals with translation of requests. Unless a reservation is made under Article 16(2), translations of requests and annexed documents are not to be required; where the reservation is made the other contracting Parties are entitled to apply reciprocity.[70] This is without prejudice to the provisions on this topic in any agreement or arrangement in force or to be made between two or more contracting Parties.[71] In keeping with the notion that the process should be kept as simple as possible, evidence or documents transmitted under the Convention are not to require any form of authentication.[72] Where an authority receives a request which it has no jurisdiction to comply with, it is to pass that request on to the competent authority of its own country and notify the requesting Party of this through the direct channels, if that was how the request was made.[73] Reasons are to be given for any refusal of assistance.[74]

The question of the expense of complying with requests for assistance is dealt with by Article 20 which provides that subject to Article 10(3) the expenses incurred in executing requests are not to be refunded unless caused by the attendance of experts within the requested State or by the transfer of a person in custody under Article 11. This has led to complaints as in some cases the execution of Letters Rogatory may prove to be very costly.[75] This was also the subject of much debate when drafting the Commonwealth Scheme for Mutual Assistance in Criminal Matters,[76] as when authorities are required to operate on a small budget expensive assistance to other States may significantly curtail their own activities. The compromise reached in relation to the Commonwealth Scheme was that expenses would be refunded when of an extraordinary nature.

---

[67] Art. 15(5).
[68] Art. 15(7).
[69] *PPA*, at p. 51.
[70] Art. 16(2).
[71] Art 16(3).
[72] Art. 17.
[73] Art 18.
[74] Art. 19.
[75] *PPA*, at p. 53.
[76] See pp. 161–2.

Information in connection with proceedings

When information is laid by a contracting Party with a view to proceedings in the courts of another Party, this information is to be transmitted between the Ministers of Justice concerned unless a reservation in terms of Article 15(6) has been made which permits States to require that information be transmitted other than via this channel.[77] When action is taken on such information the requesting Party is to be informed and a copy of the record of any verdict pronounced must be provided.[78] The provisions of Article 16 which deals with translation of requests and accompanying documents apply equally in this context.[79] This Article is intended to allow any Party to request another to institute proceedings in its own territory against an individual, and is of particular relevance where extradition is for some reason not possible.[80]

Reservations and other Conventions

Reservations may be made in respect of any provision or provisions of the Convention, although where a reservation has been made a contracting Party may not claim application of that provision except in so far as it has itself accepted it.[81] This provision is unfortunately very wide, as is often the case with agreements produced within the Council of Europe, as the large number of Member States can prevent full agreement being reached. It does, however, provide the benefit of achieving a full scheme to which exceptions are allowed, rather than a minimal approach which would allow no scope for improvement. As will be seen, the Commonwealth Scheme is based on a similar philosophy, although one expressed in a different form.

The Convention is to supersede any existing arrangements concerning mutual assistance in criminal matters, but is not to affect obligations under any international convention which contains or may contain clauses governing specific aspects of mutual assistance in a given field.[82] Further agreements may only be concluded to supplement the provisions of the Convention or to facilitate their application.

Implementation and reservations by the United Kingdom

The United Kingdom enacted legislation, the Criminal Justice (International Co-operation) Act 1990, enabling it to ratify the Convention; the Act is considered in detail elsewhere.[83] It was however found necessary for the United Kingdom to make a number of Reservations and Declarations in respect of the Convention.

[77] Art. 21(1).
[78] Art. 21(2).
[79] Art. 21(3).
[80] *Explanatory Report*, at p. 23.
[81] Art. 23.
[82] Art. 26(1), (2).
[83] See pp. 239–45.

The Reservations are:

(*a*) a reservation of the right to refuse assistance if the person concerned has been convicted or acquitted of an offence based on the relevant conduct in the United Kingdom or in a third State;

(*b*) in respect of Article 3, a reservation of a right not to take evidence or gather other material in the face of a privilege, absence of compellability, or other applicable exemption;

(*c*) in respect of search and seizure, a reservation of a right to make action dependent on double criminality and consistency of the execution of the letters rogatory with the law of the United Kingdom;

(*d*) a refusal of requests under Article 11(2) for the transit across its territory of persons in custody;

(*e*) a statement that the United Kingdom will consider the grant of immunity under Article 12 only where it is specifically requested, and will refuse to grant it if it would be against the public interest;

(*f*) a reservation of the right not to apply Article 21, dealing with information in respect of proceedings.

Amongst the Declarations, which mainly deal with the offices and courts to be designated under the Convention, is one reserving the right to stipulate that requests and annexed documents be accompanied by translations into English.

THE ADDITIONAL PROTOCOL OF 1978

As part of the process of monitoring the working of the European Convention and of encouraging more ratifications, a meeting was held in June 1970 of the persons responsible at national level for its implementation, and certain proposals aimed at facilitating its practical application were made.[84] These proposals were examined by the European Committee on Crime Problems and as a result of its deliberations and the work of a sub-committee an Additional Protocol to the Convention was produced.[85]

The Protocol entered into force on 12 April 1982 and is to be kept under review by the European Committee on Crime Problems.[86] It makes three main changes to the Convention.

Fiscal Matters

The Protocol expands the role of the Convention in relation to fiscal matters by providing that the right to refuse assistance under Article 2(*a*) of the Convention solely on the ground that the request concerns an offence which is considered to be a fiscal matter is removed.[87] This does not, however, affect

---

[84] *Problems Arising from the Practical Application of the European Convention on Mutual Assistance in Criminal Matters (PPA)*, Council of Europe, 1971.

[85] Additional Protocol to the European Convention on Mutual Assistance in Criminal Matters, 17 Mar. 1978, European Treaty Series No. 99.   [86] See Protocol, Art. 10.

[87] Protocol, Art. 1.

the right to refuse assistance in fiscal cases under Article 2(*b*) of the Convention on the grounds of prejudice to the sovereignty, security, *orde public*, or other essential interests of the country.[88]

In order to clarify the position in cases where a reservation has been made under Article 5(1)(*a*) of the Convention making execution of requests conditional on the offence in question being punishable in both States, Article 2(1) of the Protocol states that this condition shall be fulfilled in relation to fiscal offences where the offence is punishable under the law of the requesting Party and corresponds to an offence of the same nature under the law of the requested Party. Assistance is not to be refused because the law of the requested Party does not impose the same tax or duty or does not contain a tax, duty, customs, and exchange regulation of the same kind.[89]

The extension of the application of the Convention to fiscal matters is important as often these may be the only offences which will have been committed by certain members of a criminal organization. For example, the more senior members of an organized crime ring will probably never take part in the actual smuggling or trafficking of narcotic drugs, but may have committed other offences in relation to the proceeds of the crime including in particular those of a fiscal nature.

The Protocol contains generous provisions as to Reservations, of particular importance in connection with fiscal offences. A Party may decline to accept Chapter I of the Protocol, dealing with this subject; or accept it only in respect of certain offences or certain categories of the offences referred to in Article 1; or decline to comply with Letters Rogatory for search and seizure of property in respect of fiscal offences.[90]

Enforcement of penalties

The second change extends the provision of mutual assistance into areas concerned with the enforcement of penalties. So, the Convention is extended to cover

(*a*) the service of documents concerning the enforcement of a sentence, the recovery of a fine or the payment of costs of proceedings; and

(*b*) measures relating to the suspension of pronouncement of sentence or its enforcement, conditional release, deferment of the commencement of the enforcement of a sentence or the interruption of such enforcement.[91]

The measures only fall within the scope of the Convention if they are taken by judicial authorities; there was no intention to expand the concept of mutual assistance to cover general co-operation between penal authorities.

---

[88] *Explanatory Report on the Additional Protocol to the European Convention on Mutual Assistance in Criminal Matters* at p. 7.
[89] Art. 2(2).
[90] Protocol, Art. 8(2)(*a*). The United Kingdom has accepted Chapter I, but has reserved the right not to accept the other Chapters of the Protocol.
[91] Art. 3.

Information on criminal records

The Protocol requires that where a contracting Party has supplied information to another Party on convictions and related measures under Article 22 of the Convention, a copy of the convictions and measures in question as well as any relevant information is to be provided on request in order to enable that Party to consider whether any measures at national level are necessary.[92]

Letters Rogatory for the Interception of Telecommunications

In 1981 the Committee of Ministers of the Council of Europe established the Select Committee of Experts on the Operation of European Conventions in the Penal Field (PC-R-OC) to review the practical application of these Conventions and to suggest measures to facilitate their smooth functioning.[93] When the European Convention on Mutual Assistance in Criminal Matters was subjected to this scrutiny there were perceived to be problems within the specific area of Letters Rogatory for the interception of telecommunications; although the Parties presumed that the Convention did in fact apply to such Letters Rogatory, there was some confusion over which provisions governed their execution and to what extent domestic law requirements could be taken into consideration.[94] As a result of the Select Committee's deliberations a Recommendation of the Committee of Ministers was produced[95] with three main aims:

(*a*) to facilitate mutual assistance in this area;
(*b*) to protect the individual against unjustified interceptions; and
(*c*) to provide guidance with regard to the adoption of domestic law requirements.

This particular form of action was chosen as it merely provides guidance for the Member States without creating any positive duty to act and it leaves the method of implementation of the recommendations to the discretion of the Member States.

The Recommendation lays down rules governing Letters Rogatory for the 'interception of telecommunications'; this being defined as 'the interception of messages conveyed through telephones, teleprinters, telecopiers and similar means of communication, and the transmission of records relating thereto'. It was decided that an exhaustive definition of 'telecommunications' should not be provided so that the Recommendation could apply to future developments.[96] The Recommendation only applies to Letters Rogatory

---

[92] Art. 4.
[93] *Explanatory Memorandum of Recommendation No. R(85)10 on Letters Rogatory for the Interception of Telecommunications*, at p. 9.   [94] *Explanatory Memorandum*, at p. 10.
[95] 28 June 1985, Recommendation No. R(85)10.
[96] *Explanatory Memorandum*, at p. 11.

within the scope of Article 3 of the European Convention and therefore only to requests from 'the judicial authorities of the requesting Party for the purpose of procuring evidence or transmitting articles to be produced in evidence, records or documents'.

In order to promote co-operation only two grounds for refusal of a request are suggested:[97]

(*a*) If, according to the law of the requested Party, the nature or gravity of the offence or the status of the person whose telecommunications are to be intercepted do not permit the use of this measure; or
(*b*) If, in view of the circumstances of the case, the interception would not be justified according to the law of the requested Party governing the interception of telecommunications in that State.

The first exception allows the States to ensure that limitations in their domestic law may be applied; for example, some States do not permit the interception of telecommunications of certain categories of persons such as lawyers and clergymen, and most do not permit interception in relation to minor offences. The second exception is relevant where the power of interception is a discretionary one in the law of the requested Party; it allows the authorities of the requested State to exercise the discretion in the usual way, the intention of the Recommendation being that equal treatment should be given to an application for interception whether it was made by an external or an internal authority.[98]

The Recommendation also allows the requested Party to make execution of Letters Rogatory in this area dependent on one or more of a number of specific conditions.[99] These conditions cover destruction of the irrelevant parts of the intercepted communications, either by the requesting or the requested Party; informing the persons concerned of the interception; and using the evidence obtained only for the purposes specified in the Letter Rogatory. It goes without saying that the requested Party may require the keeping of records on any copies of the information that might be made and the use that is made of them.[100]

The *Explanatory Memorandum* suggests that destruction of the irrelevant parts of a communication by the requested Party is not something which is to be lightly undertaken as without full understanding of the case in question it would be difficult to know what was truly irrelevant.[101] The condition that information may be required to be used only for the purposes specified in the Letter Rogatory is not one which is found in the Convention, but was felt to be necessary in this particular area because of the violation of the right to privacy which is necessarily involved in the interception of telecommunications.

---

[97] Recommendation, Appendix, para. 1.
[98] *Explanatory Memorandum*, at p. 12.
[100] *Explanatory Memorandum*, at p. 15.
[99] Recommendation, Appendix, para. 4.
[101] Art. p. 14.

Without this safeguard the Parties might have felt it necessary to impose more stringent requirements through their own domestic law.[102]

In addition to guidelines on the execution of requests and the conditions that may be attached, the Recommendation also deals with the content of requests.[103] The requirements are similar to those applying to requests by virtue of Article 14 of the Convention; there is, however, a further requirement that the request should contain an indication why its purpose cannot be achieved by other means, a requirement designed to ensure that this method of obtaining information is only used where absolutely necessary.

The permissible duration of interceptions is dealt with in the Recommendation.[104] The inclusion of this provision was felt to be necessary as the time periods for which warrants may be granted vary greatly from State to State. The Recommendation provides that if the period for which interception is requested exceeds what may be permitted under the law of the requested Party, that Party is to indicate this without delay 'and indicate possibilities, if any, for extending the period'. It may be, for example, that the usual maximum may be extended if some special application is made; or it may be that a request can be made at a later date for the extension of the period initially available. In all cases, the period requested should be the minimum 'absolutely necessary.'[105]

The final suggestion made by the Recommendation is that if it appears from the intercepted communication that an offence was committed wholly or mainly in the territory of the requested Party, the requesting Party should consider laying information in accordance with Article 21 of the Convention.

Recommendations issued by the Council of Ministers have no formal status and do not purport to bind the governments of the Member States to whom they are addressed, but they none the less perform a useful role in the harmonization of laws as is evidenced by the frequent use made of them.[106] In this particular case, the Recommendation is distinctly cautious in tone, effectively leaving the whole matter in the control of the requested State. If this seems to place little emphasis on positive co-operation, it needs to be borne in mind that the subject-matter is politically highly sensitive and also that by clarifying the legal position the Recommendation provides a firmer basis on which States can take decisions.

EUROPEAN CONVENTION ON THE TRANSFER OF PROCEEDINGS IN CRIMINAL MATTERS

This Convention[107] was signed on 15 May 1972 and entered into force on 30 March 1978; its aim was to supplement the work which the Member States of the Council of Europe had already done in the field of criminal law by

---

[102] *Explanatory Memorandum*, at p. 15.   [103] Appendix, para. 2.
[104] Appendix, para. 3.   [105] *Explanatory Memorandum*, at p. 15.
[106] F. Dowrick, 'Council of Europe: Juristic Activity 1974–86', (1987) 36 I.C.L.Q. 633 at p. 641.
[107] European Treaty Series No. 73.

addressing the disadvantages resulting from conflicts of jurisdiction.[108] Ten States are parties to the Convention, but they do not include the United Kingdom, France, or Germany.

The Convention operates by permitting the transfer of proceedings between Contracting States when the requested State appears to be in a better position to bring those proceedings to a successful conclusion. It offers, therefore, an interesting alternative to the more conventional types of mutual assistance in criminal matters, which contemplate trial in the requesting State.

The various grounds permitting transfer are set out in Article 8, which is broadly drawn. A request may be made in any of these cases:

(*a*) if the suspected person is ordinarily resident in the requested State;

(*b*) if the suspected person is a national of the requested State or if that State is his State of origin;

(*c*) if the suspected person is undergoing or is to undergo a sentence involving deprivation of liberty in the requested State;

(*d*) if proceedings for the same or other offences are being taken against the suspected person in the requested State;

(*e*) if it [i.e., the requesting State] considers that transfer of the proceedings is warranted in the interests of arriving at the truth and in particular that the most important items of evidence are located in the requested State;

(*f*) if it considers that the enforcement in the requested State of a sentence if one were passed is likely to improve the prospects for the social rehabilitation of the person sentenced;

(*g*) if it considers that the presence of the suspected person cannot be ensured at the hearing of proceedings in the requesting State and that his presence in person at the hearing of proceedings in the requested State can be ensured;

(*h*) if it considers that it could not itself enforce a sentence if one were passed, even by having recourse to extradition, and that the requested State could do so.

The transfer of proceedings is made competent by Article 2 which simply states that any Contracting State shall have competence to prosecute under its own criminal law any offence to which the law of another Contracting State is applicable. This competence is to be exercised solely pursuant to a request for proceedings presented by another Contracting State.

The transfer of proceedings is also to be considered where a State is aware of proceedings in another Contracting State for the same offence.[109] The two States are to evaluate the circumstances found in Article 8 and determine which of them should alone continue the proceedings[110] as Article 3 gives States the power to waive or desist from proceedings against a suspect who is being or will be prosecuted for the same offence by another Contracting State. Proceedings should also be continued in a single State when two or

---

[108] Convention, preamble.

[109] Art. 30 (in Part IV of the Convention dealing with 'Plurality of Criminal Proceedings').

[110] Art. 31.

more Contracting States have jurisdiction over several offences which are materially distinct but ascribed either to a single person or several persons acting in unison; or where a single offence is ascribed to several persons so acting.[111] Where a State waives its proceedings in favour of another State, it is to be deemed to have transferred its proceedings.[112]

While the Convention itself is a detailed document, the procedure for transferring proceedings is relatively simple. When a person is suspected of having committed an offence under the law of a Contracting State that State may request another Contracting State to take action on its behalf in accordance with the Convention.[113] Requests are to be transmitted between the Ministries of Justice and in cases of urgency through Interpol, although States may also reserve the right to use other channels.[114] There are various other procedural requirements, most notably that if the competence of the requested State is grounded solely on Article 2 then the suspect must be informed of the request with a view to allowing him to present his views on the matter before a decision on the request is taken.[115] It should also be noted that Parties may not claim the refund of any expenses resulting from the application of the Convention.[116]

The Convention does not permit the requested State to take any action unless dual criminality is present and sanctions could have been imposed on the suspect in the requested State in those particular circumstances.[117] Once this has been established, the requested State decides in accordance with its own law what action should be taken on a request for assistance,[118] although the grounds on which a request may be refused are limited by Article 11. The grounds given in Article 11 are numerous, ranging from procedural requirements to permitting refusal where the offence was purely military or fiscal or of a political nature. Assistance may also be refused where proceedings would be contrary to the fundamental principles of the legal system of the requested State. A request may not be granted under the Convention if the case is time-barred in the requesting State, or when action is prevented by the application of the double jeopardy principle (*ne bis in idem*) as stated in article 35.[119] Article 35 provides that a person in respect of whom a final and enforceable criminal judgment has been rendered may neither be prosecuted nor sentenced nor subjected to enforcement of a sanction in another Contracting State for the same act, where he was acquitted; or the sanction imposed has been completely enforced or is being enforced, or has been wholly or partly the subject of a pardon or amnesty, or can no longer be enforced through lapse of time; or if the court did not impose a sanction on conviction. This is not to prevent the application of wider domestic provisions relating to the effect of *ne bis in idem* attached to foreign criminal judg-

---

[111] Art. 32.   [112] Art. 33.   [113] Art. 6.
[114] Art. 13.   [115] Art. 17.   [116] Art. 20,
[117] Art. 7(1).   [118] Art. 9.   [119] Art. 10.

ments.[120] Where the act in question was committed in a Contracting State or was considered by the law of that State to have been committed there, that State is not bound to accept the effect of *ne bis in idem* unless it has itself requested the proceedings.[121]

Where the suspect has been finally sentenced in a Contracting State the transfer of proceedings may only be requested where the State cannot itself enforce the sentence even by having recourse to extradition and the other State does not accept enforcement of a foreign judgment as a matter of principle or refuses to enforce such sentence.[122]

Once a State has made a request for assistance it can no longer prosecute the suspect in respect of the requested offence or enforce a judgment which has previously been pronounced against him. However, until the requested State makes a decision on the request, the requesting State may continue to take all the steps in a prosecution up to bringing the case to trial. The right to prosecute may revive in certain circumstances.[123]

Provisional powers are granted to the requested State where an intention to transmit a request has been announced and the requested State's jurisdiction is based solely on Article 2. If the law of the requested State authorizes remand in custody for the offence in question and there are reasons to fear that the suspect will abscond or cause evidence to be suppressed the requested State may provisionally arrest the suspect on the application of the requesting State.[124] Detention must in no circumstances be for longer than 40 days.[125] In addition, the requested State has jurisdiction to apply all such provisional measures, including remand in custody and seizure of property, as would have been available had the offence been committed in its territory.[126]

Making a request for assistance also has the important effect of delaying the time limit for proceedings in the requesting and requested States for six months; in the case of the requested State this is subject to the requirement that jurisdiction be founded solely on article 2.[127] Where something has been done in the requesting State which validly interrupts the limitation period this has the same effect in the requested State and vice versa.[128] Punishment for the offence cannot be any more severe than that which could have been imposed by the Requesting State unless jurisdiction is not founded on article 2. Where it is not so founded, the sanction is to be that prescribed by the law of the requested State unless that law provides otherwise.[129]

(B) The Commonwealth Scheme

The Commonwealth Scheme for Mutual Assistance in Criminal Matters was a product of the triennial meetings of Commonwealth Law Ministers. The

---

[120] Art. 37.
[121] Art. 35(3).   [122] Art. 8(2).   [123] Art. 21.
[124] Art. 27.   [125] Art. 29.   [126] Art. 28.
[127] Arts 22 and 23.   [128] Art. 26(2).   [129] Art. 25.

possibility of co-operation in this field was referred to in general terms in the Communiques of the meetings held in 1975 and 1977 and various reports were prepared for the consideration of Ministers. Eventually in 1983, the Law Ministers asked the Commonwealth Secretariat to prepare proposals. They

> expressed the hope that consultation might lead to the formulation of a scheme in which their countries would unite in the determination to respond effectively to the challenge presented by increasing levels of criminal activity. This might in the first instance take the form of a Commonwealth Scheme for Mutual Assistance in Criminal Matters which would respect the characteristics of shared Commonwealth criminal procedures. [130]

A possible Scheme was prepared by the present writer, drawing on the experience under earlier regional conventions, and an outline of its provisions was circulated for Government observations in June 1984.[131] A Draft Scheme was published in October 1985; it took into account the observations submitted by 14 Commonwealth Governments and by Interpol,[132] and was influenced by Canada's draft treaty with the United States and by the current version of a model negotiating text being prepared within the Australian Attorney-General's Department.

The negotiation of bilateral mutual assistance treaties is commonly a protracted business; it is something of an art-form in its own right, with its own critical literature.[133] By contrast, the Commonwealth Scheme was settled with almost disconcerting speed. A meeting of Senior Officials from twenty-nine countries held in London in January 1986 devoted some four days of plenary sessions to the negotiations on this topic, with the equivalent of one extra day's work by a small drafting committee. This process settled a text which, after further consideration by Governments, was endorsed at the Law Ministers' meeting at Harare the following July with only one small drafting amendment[134] and the incorporation of additional material on the seizure of the proceeds of crime which had been prepared in the interim.[135]

NATURE OF A COMMONWEALTH SCHEME

The negotiating process was made much easier by the initial decision to use the device of a 'Commonwealth Scheme'. It is Commonwealth practice, previously exemplified by the London Scheme for the Rendition of Fugitive

---

[130] Communiqué of the Law Ministers' Meeting, Colombo, 1983, para. 18.

[131] Commonwealth Secretariat Circular letter 50/84. The text of the proposed Scheme was not published at that stage, but appeared in the Working Papers for the Senior Officials' Meeting, Jan. 1986.

[132] The draft and the full text of the Government observations formed Criminal Working Paper 2 for the Jan. 1986 meeting.

[133] See E. Nadelmann, 'Negotiations in Criminal Law Assistance Treaties' (1985) 33 Am. Jo. Comp. L. 465.

[134] The use of the term 'country' for the more cumbrous 'part of the Commonwealth' used in the earlier drafts following the model of the Commonwealth Scheme for the Rendition of Fugitive Offenders.   [135] See further, pp. 234–5.

Offenders (i.e. the Commonwealth Extradition Scheme), to embody certain types of multilateral agreement in the form of Schemes rather than in treaties or conventions. A Scheme does not create binding international obligations, and is not registered under Article 102 of the UN Charter; it represents more an agreed set of recommendations for legislative implementation by each Government. The Scheme device is not without its critics and its use in this context was consistently opposed by the representatives of Jamaica. It is significant that the fullest critique of the Scheme device in the literature was written by the Director of the Division of International Law of the Jamaican Attorney-General's Department, albeit in a personal capacity.[136] His primary concern is the absence of any guaranteed reciprocity. If the pace, the precise mode, and even the extent of legislative implementation is left to individual Commonwealth Governments, one country may accept obligations, for example to provide a certain type of assistance at the request of a prosecution authority in any other Commonwealth member country, which are not accepted elsewhere. In the extradition context, in which this criticism was first made, the point has obvious force:

[I]t may be . . . that two Commonwealth countries would never, because of radical differences in foreign policy, enter into an extradition arrangement. But, if they cannot agree on a treaty regime for extradition, an expectation that they would none the less extradite to each other pursuant to a non-binding, non-reciprocal, non-conventional Scheme, by reason merely of a similarity in legal background, is idle, unwarranted, quaint and naïve.[137]

It was on these grounds that the Jamaican representatives argued for the elaboration of a multilateral treaty; and the Jamaican Government ultimately entered a Reservation to the Scheme,[138] reserving 'the right not to grant requests from countries which would not be competent under their laws to accede to similar requests from Jamaica'.

The great majority of Governments did, however, support the continued use of the Scheme technique. The features identified by the critics as weaknesses were seen by the majority as affording real advantages. It was recognized that there would have to be considerable flexibility in handling what was for most countries a wholly new area. Some countries might have real difficulties in implementing the whole Scheme, for constitutional reasons (for example, the complexity facing a federal state in legislating for immunity from prosecution for certain types of witness) or because of paucity of resources. There is none the less real value in all Commonwealth countries being able to take some part in determining the shape of the whole Scheme, and in using a device which permits of relatively easy amendment and

---

[136] P. L. Robinson, 'The Commonwealth Scheme relating to the Rendition of Fugitive Offenders: A Critical Appraisal of some Essential Elements' (1984) 33 I.C.L.Q. 614, especially at 617–24.　　　　　　　　　　　　　　　　　　　　　　　　　　　　　　　　[137] At 619.

[138] Given that the Scheme is non-binding, the precise status of such a Reservation is a matter of considerable obscurity.

development of the procedures in the light of experience. It was agreed that the Scheme would be reviewed periodically by Senior Officials meeting in the interval between the triennial meetings of Law Ministers, and such a meeting in 1989 recommended amendments which were agreed by Law Ministers at Christchurch in 1990; such amendments would have been virtually impossible had the treaty procedure been followed.

CONTENTS OF THE SCHEME

Scope

A striking feature of the Scheme, when compared with earlier multilateral conventions, is the wide range of types of assistance which it covers. Paragraph 1(3) provides:

Assistance in criminal matters under this Scheme includes assistance in

(*a*) identifying and locating persons;
(*b*) serving documents;
(*c*) examining witnesses;
(*d*) search and seizure;
(*e*) obtaining evidence;
(*f*) facilitating the personal appearance of witnesses;
(*g*) effecting a temporary transfer of persons in custody to appear as a witness;
(*h*) obtaining production of judicial or official records; and
(*i*) tracing, seizing and confiscating the proceeds or instrumentalities of crime.[139]

In 1983 Law Ministers considered a paper on the principles of mutual assistance[140] which examined at length the question of jurisdiction in criminal matters, examining a number of alternative principles upon which a claim to exercise jurisdiction could be based. However, the view taken in preparing the Scheme was that in intra-Commonwealth relations it should be sufficient that a Commonwealth country requesting assistance was in fact able to take jurisdiction under its own legal principles. That is, there should be no provision seeking to identify the 'proper' jurisdiction for trial, nor any provision that a requested country should in any way test or examine the claim to jurisdiction. Similarly, no provision was included to the effect that the provision of assistance should not imply recognition of the ultimate judgment.[141]

In order to obtain assistance, a law enforcement agency or public prosecution or judicial authority competent under the law of the requesting

---

[139] The last entry was amended in 1990, notably by adding the reference to 'instrumentalities'.
[140] By Dr D. Chaikin (paper LMM(83)29).
[141] Such a provision is found in the Asian–African Legal Consultative Committee's model bilateral agreement. This may be appropriate in the context of civil and commercial matters, but was judged unnecessary in the penal area.

country[142] initiates a 'request for assistance' which is transmitted, and received in the requested country, by a designated 'Central Authority' following the practice adopted first in the Hague Service and Evidence Conventions[143] and later in bilateral mutual assistance treaties. There was no provision for the use of a Central Authority in the original draft of the Scheme, which in this respect followed the pattern of the Commonwealth Extradition Scheme, but many Governments advocated the adoption of the Central Authority system. It was argued that this system was essential if Governments were to be in a position to monitor the use made of the Scheme, evaluate its strengths and weaknesses, assess the contribution of the Scheme to effective law enforcement, ensure compliance with its provisions in their own jurisdiction (especially in matters relating to authentication of evidence to be transmitted to other jurisdictions), and adequately to contribute to any future evaluation and review of the Scheme. In a Commonwealth context, its acceptance was eased by the proven usefulness of a network of experienced officers, able to enter into direct communication with their opposite numbers, centred on the Commonwealth Commercial Crime Unit with headquarters in London.

The authors of the Scheme rejected a suggestion that there should be a prescribed form of Request, along the lines of the forms prescribed or recommended for use with the Hague Service and Evidence Conventions, believing that requests under the Scheme were likely to be so diverse in character that a prescribed form would be of limited value. Instead the Scheme contains provisions specifying the information to be included.[144]

As with other arrangements for mutual assistance, the effective limits of the Scheme are largely set by the two key decisions which had to be taken by its authors: when may a request for assistance be made, and on what grounds can assistance be refused?

When may assistance be sought?

The Scheme requires the giving of assistance in response to a request made in respect of a criminal matter 'arising in' the requesting country. At what stage does a criminal matter arise? A number of positions were taken on this point in the observations made on the draft Scheme.

It was argued, notably by New Zealand, that no request for assistance should be made until criminal proceedings had actually been instituted. The main anxieties underlying this position were a fear of 'fishing expeditions' (a fear which has great force in the case of civil and commercial matters, but may appear in a different light in the case of police investigations); and a fear that the Scheme might be abused by the use of information or evidence for purposes unrelated to the criminal matter originally relied upon; and a fear

---

[142] Scheme, para. 5(1). The full text of the Scheme is reproduced below in the Appendix of Selected Documents.
[143] See pp. 20–1.   [144] Scheme, para. 13.

that a premature request could alert a prospective defendant. To a considerable extent these fears were met by the inclusion of a requirement of confidentiality[145] and of a provision prohibiting the use of information or evidence in connection with any matter other than the criminal matter specified in the request without the prior consent of the Central Authority of the requested country.[146]

A quite different view, taken by Australia, stressed that Commonwealth co-operation should extend to mutual assistance in investigating serious crime, as it does in the practice of the Commonwealth Commercial Crime Unit, and that this should include preventive action:

[A]s the Scheme is one to advance world public order by rendering the rule of law more effective, assistance should be available to prevent the commission of offences where there are reasonable grounds to suspect that such offences may be committed—for example, offences of a terrorist nature against persons, premises or vehicles such as ships or aircraft of the requesting state.

The United Kingdom inclined to support the Australian position, despite the fact that English law as it then stood[147] allowed assistance to be given only where proceedings had been instituted; changes in this position were required in any event if the United Kingdom was to ratify the European Convention on Mutual Legal Assistance.

What might be seen as a compromise position was taken in the eventual text of the Scheme, which provides that

a criminal matter arises in a country if the Central Authority of that country certifies that criminal proceedings have been instituted in a court exercising jurisdiction in that country or that there is reasonable cause to believe that an offence in respect of which such proceedings could be instituted has been committed.[148]

The exact stage which has been reached will be specified in the request; where 'reasonable cause' is relied upon a summary of the known facts will be provided.

It must be kept in mind that the Scheme 'augments, and in no way derogates from, existing forms of co-operation, both formal and informal'.[149] Much co-operation at the investigative stage already takes place between police forces and other law enforcement agencies, either through Interpol or by direct bilateral contacts; the fact that the Scheme can be relied upon from a particular time does not preclude earlier co-operation.

Refusal of assistance

Paragraph 7 of the Scheme, which sets out the grounds upon which the requested country may refuse to grant assistance as asked, was the result of much discussion. It will be convenient to set it out in full:

---

[145] Para. 10.   [146] Para. 11.
[147] i.e. Extradition Act 1873, s. 5; Evidence (Proceedings in Other Jurisdictions) Act 1975, s. 5.
[148] Para. 3(1).   [149] Para. 1(1).

(1) The requested country may refuse to comply in whole or in part with a request for assistance under this Scheme if the criminal matter appears to the Central Authority of that country to concern

   (*a*) conduct which would not constitute an offence under the law of that country; or

   (*b*) an offence or proceedings of a political character; or

   (*c*) conduct which in the requesting country is an offence only under military law or a law relating to military obligations; or

   (*d*) conduct in relation to which the person accused or suspected of having committed an offence has been acquitted or convicted by a court in the requested country.

(2) The requested country may refuse to comply in whole or in part with a request for assistance under this Scheme

   (*a*) to the extent that it appears to the Central Authority of that country that compliance would be contrary to the Constitution of that country, or would prejudice the security, international relations or other essential public interests of that country; or

   (*b*) where there are substantial grounds leading the Central Authority of that country to believe that compliance would facilitate the prosecution or punishment of any person on account of his race, religion, nationality or political opinions or would cause prejudice for any of these reasons to any person affected by the request.

(3) The requested country may refuse to comply in whole or in part with a request for assistance to the extent that the steps required to be taken in order to comply with the request cannot under the law of that country be taken in respect of criminal matters arising in that country.

(4) An offence shall not be an offence of a political character for the purposes of this paragraph if it is an offence within the scope of any international convention to which both the requesting and requested countries are parties and which imposes on the parties thereto an obligation either to extradite or prosecute a person accused of the commission of the offence.

A major issue was that of 'double criminality'. The early drafts of the Scheme made no provision for a double criminality requirement, which was felt to be inappropriate in the context of mutual assistance. The requirement (that the facts must constitute an offence under the law of the requested as well as the requesting country) features in extradition practice, but there the liberty of an individual present in the requested country is at stake. Most bilateral mutual assistance treaties contain no such requirement.[150] However, strong support emerged in the discussions for a *discretionary* double criminality rule. This would ease the constitutional difficulties anticipated in some countries, and it also reflected a particular concern expressed within the Asian–African Legal Consultative Committee. The revival of Islamic law is

---

[150] The only US bilateral with such a provision appears to be the first, that with Switzerland, but even there the rule is waived in the case of organized crime; see Treaty, Art. 7 and generally, pp. 248–9.

producing a situation in which certain acts are heavily punished (perhaps even with death) in some Islamic law jurisdictions but not seen as appropriate for any penal sanctions in neighbouring States; the latter might not wish to assist in the enforcement of the harsher criminal regime. Paragraph 7(1)(*a*) accordingly includes a discretionary double criminality rule.

Paragraph 7(1)(*d*) is a double jeopardy provision, which was originally drafted to cover cases in which there had been an acquittal or conviction in any State, not just the requested country. The final text was given a more restricted scope, mainly on the very pragmatic basis that the authorities of the requested country would be unlikely to learn of proceedings elsewhere.

Paragraph 7(2)(*a*) is drawn in broad terms, the phrase 'other essential public interests' (based on a similar phrase in the US-Canada Treaty) being susceptible to a generous interpretation. By way of example, the Australian Mutual Assistance in Criminal Matters Act 1987, which generally reflects the provisions of the Scheme, is very much fuller at this point. It provides for the refusal of a request if, in the opinion of the Attorney-General, the request relates to the assertion of extra-territorial jurisdiction in circumstances in which Australia would not make a corresponding claim to jurisdiction; if the request relates to the prosecution of a person entitled to plead a statute of limitations or some similar bar to prosecution under Australian law; and if the provision of assistance could prejudice an investigation or proceeding in relation to a criminal matter in Australia, or the safety of any person, or impose an excessive burden on the resources of Australia or one of its States or Territories.[151]

Paragraph 7(3) is of considerable significance. The general philosophy of the Scheme is that procedures and facilities available in support of criminal investigations and prosecutions initiated in one country should also be made available to assist similar endeavours undertaken in another Commonwealth country. A requested country is not, however, required to do more than it would do in a purely domestic case. For example, if the taking of body samples is not provided for under the law of the requested country it will refuse a request for assistance in obtaining such samples; the availability of such procedures under the law of the requesting country is immaterial.

This principle applies where 'measures of compulsion' are needed.[152] A search warrant, for example, may be obtained in order to provide the assistance desired by the requesting country; but only in circumstances corresponding to those in which a warrant would be issued in a purely domestic case. Where an individual is willing to provide evidence or samples, without any recourse to measures of compulsion, the requested country will make available any necessary facilities.

---

[151] Mutual Assistance in Criminal Matters Act 1987, s. 8. For the general question of costs, see pp. 161–2.

[152] Scheme, para. 8(1).

PARTICULAR TYPES OF ASSISTANCE

Location of individuals; service of process

Assistance in 'identifying or locating persons believed to be within the requested country'[153] can be provided in most countries administratively, without legislative action, and the same is likely to be true of the service of documents.[154] In fact both the model legislation prepared by the Commonwealth Secretariat to assist Governments and the United Kingdom Criminal Justice (International Co-operation) Act 1990[155] do make express provision for the service of foreign process.

Provisions on the latter topic were drafted with an eye on the Hague Service Convention of 1965, but contain two additional safeguards. Both apply where the documents relate to attendance in the requesting country (typically a witness summons). The requesting country's Central Authority must provide information as to outstanding warrants or other judicial orders in criminal matters against the person to be served.[156] This is to ensure that if the person served decides to attend in the requesting country, his decision is a fully informed one.

The second safeguard was added to the text of the Scheme in 1990, after extensive discussion which began at a Commonwealth Regional Workshop held in Bermuda in December 1988. That Workshop had before it the text of the Treaty between the United States of America and the Commonwealth of the Bahamas on Mutual Assistance in Criminal Matters.[157] Article 17(1) of that Treaty reads as follows:

The Requested State shall effect service of any document relating to or forming part of any request for assistance properly made under the provisions of this Treaty transmitted to it for this purpose by the Requesting State; *provided that the Requested State shall not be obliged to serve any subpoena or other process requiring the attendance of any person before any authority or tribunal in the Requesting State.*

The proviso (emphasized above) was added in the course of negotiating the Treaty;[158] it was the absence of any corresponding provision in paragraph 15 of the Commonwealth Scheme which attracted comment in Bermuda. The basic question concerns the attitude which should be taken to a request from a foreign Government for assistance in serving a document in the nature of a

---

[153] Para. 14.　　　　　　　　　　　　　　　　　　　[154] Para. 15.
[155] s. 1.　　　　　　　　　　　　　　　　　　　　　[156] Para. 15(2).

[157] For the full text of the Treaty, see volume 3 of the Commonwealth Secretariat's *Materials* on the Scheme, p. 181 *et seq.* The issue is of considerable importance to those countries close to the United States (which applies sanctions readily) and especially those whose air routes are almost wholly via the US mainland.

[158] An identical text appears as Art. 13(1) in the UK–US Treaty concerning mutual assistance between the United States and the Cayman Islands (*Materials*, volume 3, p. 263).

summons or subpoena in any of four circumstances (of which the first two are the more important in the present context) These are where:

(a) the foreign Government wishes measures of compulsion to be available in and under the law of the requested country; or

(b) failure to obey the summons will expose the person on whom it is served to penalties under the law of the requesting country; or

(c) to obey the summons will expose that person to prosecution for a crime in connection with which the summons was issued;[159] or

(d) to obey the summons will expose that person to prosecution for other crimes or to other penalties or legal proceedings.[160]

The first issue identified above is generally referred to as the question of the 'international subpoena'. The introduction of any provision in the Scheme along the lines of the international subpoena was decisively rejected in 1986, despite the arguments that in a number of cases evidence crucial to the success of a prosecution might be inadmissible if taken abroad on commission, perhaps because of the absence of an opportunity for cross-examination by the defendant, and that reliance could not be placed on the willing co-operation of the witness. It was argued that service of an enforceable subpoena might be an advantage even to willing witnesses, who could more easily obtain leave of absence from an employer and might be released from some obligations of confidentiality which would otherwise apply.

Although there do exist useful regional arrangements for 'backing' witness summonses, giving them the status of international subpoenas;[161] human rights and constitutional considerations ensure that international treaty practice reveals little support for the 'international subpoena' notion. There is, exceptionally, provision in the United States–Italian Mutual Assistance Treaty for the compulsory appearance of a witness in the requesting State;[162] persons compelled to appear are given immunity from prosecution based on truthful testimony given pursuant to a request under the Treaty.[163] In general, however, international practice is that 'witnesses and experts are completely free not to go to the requesting country'.[164] It is significant that even in the UN Convention

---

[159] The Commonwealth Scheme does not provide for this type of assistance, the provisions in paras. 23–5 referring expressly to a request relating to appearance 'as witness'. The European Convention does provide for the service of summonses addressed to defendants; the provision is designed to assist the issuing of default judgments (i.e. in the absence of any appearance by the defendant) which are common in civil law jurisdictions.

[160] Immunity of witnesses from prosecution is fully dealt with in para. 25 of the Commonwealth Scheme. Some countries are prepared to give more extensive immunities, e.g. s. 19 of the Mutual Assistance in Criminal Matters Act 1987 of Australia protects the person concerned from civil actions and from having to give evidence in any proceedings other than the proceeding to which the request related.

[161] e.g. Australia has such arrangements with New Zealand and Fiji; Malaysia with Singapore and Brunei.

[162] Applying both to witnesses in custody for other reasons in the requested State (Treaty, Art. 16(1)) and those at liberty there (Art. 15(1)).　　　　　　　　[163] Art. 17(1).

[164] *Explanatory Report to the European Convention on Mutual Assistance*, Art. 8.

against Illicit Traffic in Narcotic Drugs and Psychotropic Substances 1988, the obligation to provide assistance in this context is merely to 'facilitate or encourage, to the extent consistent with . . . domestic law and practice, the presence' of witnesses 'who consent to assist in investigations or participate in proceedings'.[165] Similarly, the Criminal Justice (International Cooperation) Act 1990 of the United Kingdom provides in section 1(3) that 'Service by virtue of this section of any [witness summons] shall not impose any obligation under the law of any part of the United Kingdom to comply with it.'

Where failure to obey the summons will expose the person on whom it is served to penalties under the law of the requesting country, international treaty practice seeks to exclude (or at least severely limit) the possibility of such penalties being applied. Amongst treaties which exclude that possibility entirely is the European Convention on Mutual Assistance, Article 8 of which reads:

A witness or expert who has failed to answer a summons to appear, service of which has been requested [under the Convention] shall not, even if the summons contains a notice of penalty, be subjected to any punishment or measure of restraint, unless subsequently he voluntarily enters the territory of the requesting Party and is there again duly summoned.

Similarly, treaties entered into by Australia contain a provision on the following lines:

A person who does not answer a summons to appear [in the Requesting State] as a witness or expert shall not by reason thereof be liable to any penalty or be subjected to any coercive measures notwithstanding any contrary statement in the summons.[166]

Some treaties apply a similar rule only where the person served is not a national of the requesting country.[167] This position was also taken by the Government of Jamaica in its 1986 Reservation in respect of paragraph 15 of the Commonwealth Scheme. Jamaica reserved the right to protect from legal sanction for failure to appear in proceedings in obedience to a document served pursuant to the Scheme any person who was not a national of the requesting country.

The position taken by the Bahamas in its treaty negotiations with the United States goes further. It involves the reservation of a right to refuse to serve any subpoena or other process requiring the attendance of a person before a court in the Requesting State. Presumably 'subpoena' is used in its literal sense, of a document to which penalties or sanctions are attached; the reservation of the right to refuse to serve 'other process', including witness summonses carrying no (overt) sanctions, takes the position still further.

[165] Vienna Convention, Art. 7(4).
[166] Australia-Austria Treaty, Art. 10(4). See to the same effect the Treaties with Italy, Art. 14(5); Luxembourg, Art. 13(5); Netherlands, Art. 14(4).
[167] e.g. the United States–Switzerland Treaty, Art. 24(1).

In the event, Law Ministers at their meeting in 1990 accepted a recommendation to add paragraph 15(5) of the Scheme, which addresses the possibility of penalties in either of the relevant countries, providing:

A person served in compliance with a request with a summons to appear as a witness in the requesting country and who fails to comply with the summons shall not by reason thereof be liable to any penalty or measure of compulsion in either the requesting or the requested country notwithstanding any contrary statement in the summons.

Obtaining evidence

Paragraph 16 of the Scheme deals with the examination of witnesses in the requested country, its provisions again influenced by the work of the Hague Conference, in its Evidence Convention of 1970. Following the Hague model, a witness may claim any privilege open to him in criminal proceedings in either the requested or the requesting country.[168] This was not uncontroversial: an alternative view was that the law of the requesting country alone should govern, so that, for example, an Australian request for the evidence of a witness who could otherwise plead the privilege against self incrimination in the requested country could be acted upon if he were compellable under Australian law having been given an indemnity against prosecution by the Director of Public Prosecutions. Practice under bilateral treaties varies greatly. To deal with practical issues concerning the operation of the 'double privilege' rule adopted in the Scheme, the request for assistance must contain an indication of any provisions of the law of the requesting country as to privilege or exemption from giving evidence which appear especially relevant to the request.[169] This last provision might appear a little odd in that it invites a prosecution agency to indicate reasons why it should be denied the evidence it seeks, but it accords with the general approach of fair and open dealing between the Central Authorities, whose trust and goodwill are essential if the Scheme is to operate effectively.

Paragraphs 17 and 18 deal with search and seizure of evidence, where the Central Authority of the requested country acts, in effect, as an agent for that of the requesting country in applying for any necessary warrant, and with other procedures such as inspecting or photographing evidence, or taking and analysing samples. The list of such procedures is broadly similar to that found in English law at the time the Scheme was drafted, in section 2 of the Evidence (Proceedings in Other Jurisdictions) Act 1975.[170]

Further provisions govern the disclosure of judicial and official records, broadly on the same terms as they would be disclosed to the appropriate agencies in a purely domestic context,[171] and regulate the actual transmission, return and authentication of material.[172]

---

[168] Para. 19. [169] Para. 16(2)(*c*).

[170] Since repealed by the Criminal Justice (International Co-operation) Act 1990.

[171] Para. 22.

[172] Paras. 21 and 22. The text of para. 22 was amended in 1990, making it clear that the specification of procedures such as the use of the seal or stamp of a Ministry did not preclude the more traditional verification by the oath of a witness or competent official.

Appearance of witnesses in the requesting country

The Scheme contains quite elaborate provisions[173] designed to enable evidence to be taken in the courts of the requesting country itself, either by facilitating the travel of a witness from the requested country or by arranging for the transfer in custody of a prisoner detained in that country but who is willing to give evidence in the requesting country. The provisions are similar to those in the European Convention on Mutual Assistance in Criminal Matters[174] and in bilateral treaties negotiated by the United States. These provisions apply only where the potential witness is willing to appear; there is no question of measures of compulsion, or of any penalty for failure to appear,[175] and the provisions grant a carefully limited immunity from prosecution while the witness is in the requesting country.

So far as the transfer of persons in custody is concerned, the United Kingdom insisted on the inclusion of what became paragraph 24(2):

The requested country may refuse to comply with a request for the transfer of persons in custody and shall be under no obligation to inform the requesting country of the reasons for such refusal.

It is not entirely clear why the United Kingdom's representatives were so insistent on this point. They prayed in aid practice in respect of the repatriation of prisoners, which is of course a much more long-term measure, and argued that the reasons for refusing a request might be so sensitive that it would be undesirable for them to be discussed with the requesting country or with the person concerned.

In contrast, Australia was anxious to include in the Scheme provision for 'trial transfer', that is the transfer of someone already detained in State A to stand trial in State B (while evidence was available and fresh) on the understanding that he would be returned to State A to complete his sentence there. It was felt, however, that this was a form of (temporary) extradition, with which the present Scheme did not deal, and the Law Ministers eventually agreed (despite some hesitations on the part of a few countries) to deal with the matter by way of an amendment to the Commonwealth Scheme on the Rendition of Fugitive Offenders.

Expenses of compliance

It was recognized by the authors of the Scheme that, no matter how much goodwill might exist in the Commonwealth for the success of the proposals for enhanced co-operation, that goodwill would be tested by the expenses of providing assistance. The proposal in the preliminary draft that expenses should fall to be carried by the requested country in each case, its contribution in one

---

[173] Paras. 23–5. [174] Convention, Arts. 10–12.
[175] See paras. 23(4) and 24(5), both added in 1990 for the reasons discussed above in the context of the service of witness summonses.

case being rewarded by free assistance when it acted as the requesting country in another case, proved unacceptable.

The discussions were much influenced by the course of Canada's treaty negotiations with the United States, in which considerable time was spent in deciding how this topic could be best handled. Neither country wanted to be burdened with administrative accounting tasks, but it was recognized that a requested state could incur significant costs in providing some forms of assistance. For example, a requested state might be asked to conduct surveillance of suspected criminals which could involve assigning extra police officers to this task at great expense, i.e. overtime pay, and commercial fraud cases might involve extensive examination of records. A competent authority in the requested state might not be able to afford this extraordinary expense, with the result that the request would not be proceeded with or be carried out in an unsatisfactory manner. Article VIII(3) of the Canada–US Treaty enables the requested state to notify the requesting state of unusual expenses; if the assistance was important to the requesting state, it would bear those costs.

In the end, paragraph 12 of the Scheme adopts a similar approach. Some types of expenses, the travel and incidental expenses of witnesses, the fees of experts, and the costs of any translation work required by the requesting country, will always be borne by that country;[176] where there are other expenses 'of an extraordinary nature', discussions take place and in the absence of agreement the requested country may decline to comply further with the request.[177]

Proceeds of crime

At the time the Scheme was being drafted, the question of the seizure and forfeiture of the proceeds of crime was just coming to the fore. No provisions on this subject were in the text settled in January 1986, but additional paragraphs were incorporated at the Law Ministers' Meeting in Harare in the following August. They were revised at Christchurch in 1990. This complex topic is considered in detail below,[178] and the relevant provisions of the Scheme are there noted.

IMPLEMENTATION

A Model Bill to assist countries in preparing legislation implementing the Scheme was developed at a series of regional Workshops in the period following the Scheme's adoption at Harare.[179] This has proved a useful tool, and has been used as the model for legislation in a number of countries from Grenada to Vanuatu. The larger Commonwealth member countries, possessing both more highly developed mutual assistance policies and larger numbers of legislative draftsmen, have tended to produce their own models.

---

[176] Para. 12(2).
[177] Para. 12(3).   [178] See pp. 199–238.
[179] Its evolution can be traced in successive volumes of the *Materials* on the Scheme.

Australia is one example. The Mutual Assistance in Criminal Matters Act 1987 bears many resemblances to the Commonwealth model, not surprisingly in view of the large contribution made by Australian officials in the negotiation of the Scheme and its subsequent discussion. There are some notable differences, one of which is that in section 8 of the Act refusal of assistance is mandatory on certain grounds which under the Scheme give only a discretionary power of refusal. In treaty negotiations, Australia has found that many foreign States prefer discretionary language; in the words of a senior negotiator, 'Australia has agreed to this on the clear understanding that in respect of [those grounds] Australia could only exercise that discretion one way—namely by refusing assistance'.[180]

Canada's approach was very different. As a matter of policy, and also because of federal constitutional issues, Canada decided to insist on a treaty based approach. Its Mutual Legal Assistance in Criminal Matters Act 1988 limits the powers of the responsible Minister to cases in which 'the relevant treaty provides for mutual legal assistance with respect to the subject-matter of the request'.[181] However, the Act contains other provisions which mean that the actual position in practice is less restrictive than that might suggest. Section 6 of the Act provides that:

Where there is no treaty between Canada and another state, the Secretary of State for External Affairs may, with the agreement of the Minister [of Justice], enter into an administrative arrangement with that other state providing for legal assistance with respect to an investigation specified therein relating to an act that, if committed in Canada, would be an indictable offence.

Such an arrangement can be implemented as if it were a treaty,[182] and attracts all the types of assistance covered by the Act (which does not deal with the confiscation of proceeds) for a period not exceeding six months.[183]

The practical implications are that Canada will negotiate bilateral treaties with countries, such as the United States and the United Kingdom, with which it can expect a considerable volume of mutual assistance business. For other countries within the Commonwealth Scheme, a request under the Scheme will be translated for the purposes of Canadian law into an administrative arrangement and assistance given on that basis.

The United Kingdom gave effect to the principles of the Scheme in the Criminal Justice (International Co-operation) Act 1990. This also implements other international agreements and is considered more fully below.[184] The United Kingdom has notified the Secretary-General of the Commonwealth that it will apply the Scheme with certain exceptions and adaptations:

(*a*) Paragraph 7(1)(*d*) of the Scheme gives a right of refusal of assistance when the person concerned has ben acquitted or convicted by a court in the requested

---

[180] See *Materials*, vol. 4, at p. 105.   [181] Act, s. 8.
[182] Ibid., s. 6(3).   [183] Ibid., s. 6(4).
[184] See pp. 239–47 and (for the Vienna Convention aspects) 175–6.

country.[185] The United Kingdom will apply the same right to cases of conduct in respect of which the person has been acquitted or convicted in any other country.

(b) The provisions of paragraph 11 of the Scheme as to the limitations on the use of information or evidence need to be understood in the light of the legal position in the United Kingdom, that information disclosed in the course of proceedings is thereby made public and is thereafter available for use in matters not directly related to the original request.

(c) The United Kingdom will not routinely authenticate material as required by paragraphs 21 and 22, except by citation in a covering letter from the Central Authority; full authentication needs to be requested specifically.

(d) Similarly a grant of immunity under paragraph 25 will need to be specifically requested and will be considered on a case-by-case basis; immunity will not be given if the United Kingdom considers it not in the public interest.

(e) The United Kingdom will only use measures of compulsion of search and seizure in the context of drug trafficking or where the material is likely to be of 'substantial value' to the investigation of a criminal offence.

(f) Assistance in respect of the seizure of the proceeds or instrumentalities of crime will be afforded only to countries designated under the relevant United Kingdom legislation.[186]

(3) United Nations Action

The United Nations has taken a number of steps to promote international action in the field of mutual assistance. The most influential is the negotiation of the Vienna Convention against Illicit Traffic in Narcotic Drugs and Psychotropic Substances, considered in detail below.[187] Here two model treaties in more general aspects are to be considered.

MODEL TREATY ON MUTUAL ASSISTANCE IN CRIMINAL MATTERS

In order to encourage the further development of mutual assistance in criminal matters, the United Nations agreed on the recommendation of its Eighth Congress on the Prevention of Crime and the Treatment of Offenders[188] to adopt the text of a model treaty to be used as a basis in future negotiations between its Member States. As a model treaty the text is simple, providing a mere framework and containing none of the more complex procedural provisions found in existing agreements. As the negotiation of mutual legal assistance treaties (MLATs) has now become a common activity, new treaties tend not to contain any innovative material. The United Nations Model Treaty is no exception to this rule, with many of its provisions bearing a close resemblance to earlier texts.

---

[185] See above, pp. 155–6.   [186] See pp. 245–7.
[187] See pp. 174–80.   [188] Havana, 27 Aug.–7 Sept. 1990.

Scope

The general practice in the negotiation of MLATs is for the parties to agree to provide each other with mutual assistance with particular reference to certain types of assistance, such as the taking of evidence from witnesses, the execution of searches and seizures, the service of documents and the provision of copies of documents and records.[189] The United Nations Model Treaty contains no surprises in this area, with the statement of the scope of the Treaty being taken directly from the European Convention as a tried and tested definition.[190]

One unusual feature is that while the Treaty adopts the usual practice of permitting the provision of originals or certified copies of relevant documents and records, it also specifically permits provision of copies of bank, financial, corporate, or business records;[191] the secrecy of banks and similar financial institutions is not to be used as a sole ground for refusing assistance.[192]

The making and processing of requests has now also become a matter of convention, with the accepted procedure being to require each Party to such a treaty to establish a central authority through which all assistance is sought. The Model Treaty follows this practice.[193] Unlike some other texts, there is no provision for oral requests to be dealt with by the central authority in cases of urgency.[194]

Certain requests for assistance will always be refused as falling outside the scope of the Treaty[195]: the Model Treaty does not apply to extradition, enforcement of criminal judgments,[196] the transfer of persons in custody to serve sentences, or to the transfer of proceedings in criminal matters which is dealt with in a separate Model Treaty.[197] The number of exclusions reflects in part difficulties in reaching agreement. While the number of exclusions from the Model Treaty is larger than, for example, that in the European Convention,[198] there is no exclusion applying to fiscal cases; this presumably reflects the attitude taken to the related issue of bank secrecy.

When a request falls within the scope of the Treaty there are a number of discretionary grounds on which assistance may be refused. What is not apparent from the text is exactly who may exercise this discretion: under the Commonwealth Scheme it is clearly stated that the requested country may refuse to comply with a request *when it appears to the Central Authority* that certain conditions are satisfied.[199] The text of the Model Treaty permits the

---

[189] See, e.g. United Nations Model Treaty, Art. 1; Commonwealth Scheme, para. 1.

[190] United Nations Model Treaty, Art. 1(1); European Convention, Art. 1(1).

[191] United Nations Model Treaty, Art. 1(2)(*g*).

[192] Ibid., Art. 4(2). For bank secrecy generally, see pp. 271–86.

[193] United Nations Model Treaty, Art. 3 (using the expression 'competent authority').

[194] Art. 5. Cf., e.g. the Commonwealth Scheme, para. 13(2), or the European Convention, Art. 15(2).   [195] United Nations Model Treaty, Art. 1(3).

[196] Except those within the scope of the Optional Protocol.

[197] See pp. 169–71.   [198] European Convention, Arts. 1(2) and 2.

[199] Commonwealth Scheme, para. 7.

refusal of assistance where the 'Requested State is of the opinion' that certain conditions are fulfilled,[200] or 'there are substantial grounds for believing' that the request has been made for a certain purpose.[201] This raises a question over whether the discretion should be exercised by the central authority, or whether government in the form of a Secretary of State or Minister for Justice should make the decision. Different practices could conceivably produce different types of decision as to the grant and level of assistance. The grounds for the refusal of a request are not extensive, but the notes to the Treaty state that the list is merely illustrative and is therefore liable to be expanded by individual States. In particular, it should be noted that dual criminality is not included as one of the grounds for refusal.

Once the decision as to whether or not assistance should be granted has been taken by the relevant body, execution is to be carried out in the manner requested to the extent permitted by the law of the Requested State.[202] As is also now customary, the use of the information or evidence provided to the Requesting State in pursuance of the request is limited to the purposes stated in the request, unless the Requested State gives its consent, and the material must be returned to the Requested State as soon as possible unless the right to claim its return is waived.[203] The confidentiality of the request and the information provided is also guarantied.[204]

There is a provision in the Commonwealth Scheme that allows the requested country to use measures of compulsion in connection with a request to the extent that those measures are available under its domestic law.[205] There is no equivalent provision in the United Nations Model Treaty.

The Treaty then moves on to give particular instructions for those heads of assistance that are specifically provided for; in keeping with the status of the text as a model for future agreements, these provisions are not detailed. For example, the service of documents is permitted under the Treaty,[206] but there is no guidance as to the method of service that should be used or as to how proof of service might be provided.

Similarly, Requested States are to obtain evidence on request by taking testimony or requiring production of items from the witnesses;[207] the text merely provides that this is to be done in conformity with its own law, with no special instructions about cases where compliance with the law of the Requesting State might be necessary to ensure that the evidence obtained is admissible in proceedings there. Provision is made for witnesses to decline to give evidence in reliance on a privilege so to decline existing under the law of either the Requested State or that of the Requesting State.[208] This is no less favourable than comparable provisions in other texts.[209]

---

[200] United Nations Model Treaty, Art. 4(1)(*a*).   [201] Ibid., Art. 4(1)(*c*).
[202] Ibid., Art. 6.   [203] Ibid., Arts. 7 and 8.
[204] Ibid., Art. 9.   [205] Commonwealth Scheme, para. 8.
[206] United Nations Model Treaty, Art. 10.   [207] Ibid., Art. 11.
[208] Ibid., Art. 12.   [209] e.g. Commonwealth Scheme, para. 19.

Among the categories of assistance commonly found in MLATs is provision for the invitation of witnesses to attend for questioning in the Requesting State and for the transfer of persons in custody to be examined. The Model Treaty follows this practice, and provision is made for inviting both persons at liberty and those in custody to appear in the Requesting State. The transfer of persons in custody may only be made where permitted by the law of the Requested State and agreement is given for that particular prisoner to be handed over. The prisoner himself must also consent to the transfer.[210] As it is intended purely as an outline, the text does not deal with such problems as whether the time spent in the other country is to count towards the sentence imposed in the Requested State, or whether special considerations apply where the person who is requested to attend is a national of the Requesting State. The Model Treaty differs from the Commonwealth Scheme and the European Convention in this area, as they each contain special grounds for refusing a request of this type, but there are no such special grounds here.[211]

As a necessary corollary to the attendance of witnesses in the Requesting State MLATs normally seek to afford some kind of immunity from prosecution. The protection given by the Model Treaty is that which is normally provided—the witness is not to be subjected to restriction of his personal liberty in respect of any acts or omissions, or convictions, that preceded his departure from the Requested State; he may not be required to give evidence other than as specified in the request; and the summons may not impose any compulsion to appear or penalty for failing to comply with it, whether it purports to do so or not.[212] The immunity also ceases as is normal: where the person does not leave the requesting country within fifteen days of being told that he is no longer required for the investigations, or where he leaves the country within that period but return to it of his own free will.

The Model Treaty also follows the common practice of permitting the provision of copies of documents and records available to the public and of such other documents and records as would be made available to domestic law enforcement agencies in similar circumstances.[213] The text dealing with search and seizure contains no more than the absolute minimum: 'the Requested State shall, in so far as its law permits, carry out requests for search and seizure and delivery of any material to the Requesting State for evidentiary purposes, provided that the rights of *bona fide* third parties are protected'.[214]

A noteworthy feature of the Model Treaty is that under Article 18 it is expressly provided that a request for assistance and its supporting documents,

---

[210] United Nations Model Treaty, Art. 13.
[211] Commonwealth Scheme, para. 24; European Convention, Art. 11.
[212] United Nations Model Treaty, Art. 15(1).
[213] Ibid., Art. 16. Cf. Commonwealth Scheme, para. 20(1).
[214] United Nations Model Treaty, Art. 17.

and any documents or other material supplied in response to that request are not to require certification or authentication; this is also the case under Article 17 of the European Convention which states that authentication is not necessary. Under the Commonwealth Scheme authentication is required of both of materials submitted to the Requested State as part of a request, and material transmitted by the Requested State in response to a request.[215]

On the sensitive matter of costs, sensitive because small states in particular are aware that the expense of complying with a request for assistance can prove to be prohibitive, the United Nations text again follows standard international practice, with the ordinary costs of complying with a request to be borne by the Requested State, unless otherwise agreed but with provision for consultation in cases where expenses of an extraordinary nature are likely to be incurred.[216] The Requesting State is responsible for the travel and incidental expenses of witnesses travelling to the requesting country, and for any cash advances made to a witness prior to arrival in the Requesting State.[217]

Optional Protocol on the Proceeds of Crime

While the concept of States providing one another with mutual assistance in the investigation and prosecution of crime is still a relatively new concept, even more recent is the provision of assistance in taking measures against the proceeds of crime.[218] The Model Treaty contains, but only in an Optional Protocol, provision as to the search for, freezing and seizing of the proceeds of crime.

In response to a request for assistance the Requested State is to attempt to discover if any proceeds of the alleged crime are located within its jurisdiction and to endeavour to trace assets, investigate financial dealings and obtain other information or evidence that may help to secure the recovery of proceeds of crime. Where such proceeds are found, such measures are to be taken as are permitted under the law of the Requested State to freeze the assets until a final decision has been made by a court of the Requesting State. The Requested State must then to the extent permitted by its law, enforce a forfeiture or confiscation order of the Requesting State, or take other appropriate action to secure the proceeds. The rights of *bona fide* third parties are to be respected.[219]

The term 'proceeds of crime' is defined as any property suspected, or found by a court, to be property directly or indirectly derived or realised as a

---

[215] For the United Kingdom's reservation on this point, see p. 164.

[216] United Nations Model Treaty, Art. 19.

[217] Ibid., Art. 14. These are the same provisions as are made in the Commonwealth Scheme (para. 12) and the European Convention (Arts. 9 and 20).

[218] See generally, pp. 234–8.

[219] United Nations Model Treaty, Optional Protocol, paras. 2–6.

result of the commission of an offence or to represent the value of property and other benefits derived from the commission of an offence.[220]

The notes to the Optional Protocol recognize that further details will often need to be provided, and suggest as matters needing examination the issue of bank secrecy and that of the destination of confiscated assets.

MODEL TREATY ON THE TRANSFER OF PROCEEDINGS IN CRIMINAL MATTERS

The United Nations has also prepared a Model Treaty dealing with the transfer of proceedings in criminal matters. The transfer of proceedings can be of use where extradition is not a viable alternative, or where an offender is already on trial in one state for certain crimes and another state also wishes to prosecute that person. A Convention on this topic has also been prepared by the Council of Europe[221] but as it is intended to provide comprehensive regulation of requests for assistance between its Contracting Parties it is much more detailed than the United Nations Model which is designed only to provide a guide in negotiations.

The provisions of the Model Treaty are simple. Where a person is suspected of having committed an offence, the state whose laws were violated may, if the proper interests of justice so require, request that another state take proceedings in respect of that offence and all Contracting Parties are to make legislative provision extending their criminal jurisdiction to enable proceedings to be taken, despite their necessarily extra-territorial nature.[222]

Requests for such transfers of proceedings are to be made in writing and transmitted either through diplomatic channels, between the respective Ministries of Justice, or via any other authorities that the parties may designate.[223] The costs of executing a request are not to be refunded unless otherwise agreed between the two states.[224]

Where proceedings are pending in two or more states against the same person for the same offence the states are to decide which one of them is to continue with the prosecution. Such a decision is to have the same consequences as follow under the Model Treaty from a request for the transfer of proceedings.[225]

On receipt of a request the competent authorities of the Requested State are to determine what action they can take under their own law in order to comply as fully as possible with the request.[226] However, the request may only be complied with if there is dual criminality, that is that the relevant

---

[220] Ibid., para. 1.

[221] European Convention on the Transfer of Proceedings in Criminal Matters, Strasbourg, ETS No. 73; see pp. 146–9.   [222] United Nations Model Treaty, Art. 1.

[223] Ibid., Art. 2. For the documentation required, see Arts. 3 and 4.

[224] Ibid., Art. 14.   [225] Ibid., Art. 13.   [226] Ibid., Art. 5.

conduct is also an offence under the law of the Requested State.[227] Assistance may be refused on four grounds:

(a) If the suspect is not a national of or ordinarily resident in the Requested State:
(b) If the act is an offence under military law but not also under the ordinary criminal law;
(c) If the offence is connected with taxes, duties, customs or exchange matters; or
(d) If the offence is regarded by the Requested State as being of a political nature. [228]

When the Requesting State announces its intention to transmit a request, it may seek the application of such provisional measures including detention and seizure as would be applied under the law of the Requested State if the offence had been committed in its own territory.[229]

The Model Treaty makes provision for the rights both of the suspect and the victim of the crime. An 'interest' may be expressed in the transfer by the suspect, or by his close relatives or his legal representatives. Before the request is made, the Requesting State is, if practicable, to allow the suspect to express his views on the alleged offence and the transfer, unless the suspect has absconded or otherwise obstructed the course of justice;[230] the text is silent as to what is to be done with these views, there being no obligation to communicate them to the Requested State. The rights of the victim of the crime, in particular those relating to restitution or compensation, are not to be affected by the transfer of proceedings. If there has been no settlement prior to the transfer the Requested State is to permit the representation of the claim in the transferred proceedings if this is permitted by its law; this is a reference to procedures akin to the intervention of a *partie civile* in French criminal cases. If the victim of the crime has died, this right is to be extended to his dependants.[231]

While the Model Treaty does not attempt to deal with the finer points of procedure, it has to cover those procedural matters which are of especial importance. These include the effects of the transfer on the Requesting State. When the request is accepted the Requesting State must provisionally discontinue the prosecution, to avoid double jeopardy, except to the extent that it is necessary to continue investigation and provide judicial assistance for the benefit of the Requested State, The discontinuance becomes final when the Requesting State is informed that the case has been finally disposed of in the Requested State.[232]

The Treaty also deals with the effects of the transfer of proceedings on the Requested State. The proceedings are to be governed by the law of the

---

[227] United Nations Model Treaty, Art. 6.
[229] Ibid., Art. 12.
[231] Ibid., Art. 9.

[228] Ibid., Art. 7.
[230] Ibid., Art. 8.
[232] Ibid., Art. 10.

Requested State, but where that State only has jurisdiction by virtue of the extended jurisdiction created by the Model Treaty,[233] the sentence imposed must not more severe than that which might be imposed in the Requesting State.[234] This could, of course, raise difficult questions: is a suspended sentence of imprisonment, with no immediate penalty, more severe than a very heavy fine? As far as possible any acts which were performed in the Requesting State with a view to proceedings or procedural requirements and in accordance with its law, are to have the same validity in the Requested State as if they had been performed by its authorities.[235]

---

[233] i.e. jurisdiction is based on Art. 1(2).
[234] United Nations Model Treaty, Art. 11(1).
[235] Ibid., Art. 11(2).

7

Drug-Trafficking

IF there is one field in which in recent years States have moved decisively to a new level of co-operation in the detection and prosecution of crimes it is that of drug-trafficking. The distribution and use of drugs threatens the health not only of individuals but of societies and political systems, and there is considerable political will in most countries to undertake legislative action in response.

After a short review of the relevant features of the problem, an account will be given of the major response to it in terms of law enforcement, the Vienna Convention, and of action in the European Community. Drugs issues are central to the questions of money-laundering and the confiscation of the proceeds of crime, examined subsequently.

(A) The Drug-trafficking Problem

Traffic in drugs has a long and complex history, and there are features of that history which explain the nature of the legal responses to it.

The nature of drug-trafficking has changed over the years in a number of ways. Perhaps the most obvious set of changes concerns the *substances* which are used. There has been a shift from opium to cannabis, and on to LSD, heroin and cocaine. The trend is towards more powerful drugs, which mount a more ferocious assault on the human mind and body, can be sold (and so usefully transported) in smaller amounts, and yet generate a greater profit for their distributors. Although the misuse of 'licit' drugs, those with a legitimate medical or scientific use, remains a problem, the production and use of wholly illicit drugs has called for close and urgent attention.

The *geographical spread* of the problem has also changed over time. There are now, to give one example, many more addicts in the countries which have traditionally been countries of production rather than major use. The trafficking process has also become more complex, and many countries hitherto uninvolved have found themselves used as staging posts in the transit of drugs around the world. This may be because they lie directly between areas of production and use, for example, the island States of the Caribbean between producer countries in South America and the profitable market in the United States. But other countries, for example a number in Africa, are used as seemingly 'innocent' countries of origin of consignments of goods within which drugs are concealed. The development of new routes of this sort may reflect contacts first established by the presence of migrant workers (for example Pakistani workers in the Nigerian oil industry) or of the Chinese and Indian diaspora in many parts of the world.

The *corrupting effect* of drug-trafficking on the economic and political life of drug-producing States such as Colombia, and of States along the trade routes, is becoming increasingly obvious and of growing international concern.[1]

LEGAL RESPONSES

Attempts at co-ordinated international action against drug-trafficking began in 1909 with a conference in Shanghai on the trade in opium. This produced the International Opium Convention of 1912.[2] Several other Conventions and Protocols followed, dealing both with opium[3] and narcotics generally.[4] These were all consolidated in the Single Convention on Narcotic Drugs of 1961[5] and extended to man-made hallucinogenic and other substances in the Psychotropic Substances Convention 1971.[6]

These instruments have attracted much international support[7] but, as some of their titles indicate, their emphasis is on the administrative regulation of the production and movement of the drugs themselves; they were not law enforcement conventions dealing with the conduct of those trafficking in drugs or with their profits. So, for example, the Single Convention of 1961 (as amended) assigns functions to the Commission on Narcotic Drugs of the Economic and Social Council of the United Nations and to an International Narcotics Control Board;[8] it requires States to provide annual estimates of the quantities of drugs to be used for various purposes and of stocks held, of the area of land devoted to the cultivation of the opium poppy, and of the number of establishments manufacturing synthetic drugs and of their output.[9] There are then detailed provisions as to limits upon the manufacture, production and importation of drugs, and as to controls on poppy straw, the coca bush and its leaves, and cannabis,[10] and the regulation of international trade.[11] The only 'penal provisions' are those in Article 36, requiring State

---

[1] See the passage from the UN report *Corruption in Government* (1990) cited on p. 120.

[2] Convention relating to the Suppression of the Abuse of Opium and other Drugs, The Hague, 23 Jan. 1912, 8 L.T.N.S. 187.

[3] See the Second International Opium Convention, Geneva, 19 Feb. 1925, 81 L.T.N.S. 317; the Protocol Limiting and Regulating the Cultivation of the Poppy Plant, the Production of, International and Wholesale Trade in, and Use of Opium, New York, 23 June 1953, 456 U.N.T.S. 3.

[4] e.g. the Convention for Limiting the Manufacture and Regulating the Distribution of Narcotic Drugs, Geneva, 16 July 1931, 139 L.N.T.S. 301, with a number of amending Protocols.

[5] New York, 30 Mar. 1961, 520 U.N.T.S. 204, amended by a Protocol of 25 Mar. 1972, 976 U.N.T.S. 3. [6] Vienna, 21 Feb. 1971, 1019 U.N.T.S. 175.

[7] As at 20 March 1992, 134 States were party to the 1961 Convention, of which 107 had ratified the 1972 amending Protocol; there were 107 States Parties to the 1971 Convention.

[8] Convention, Arts. 5–11. [9] Art. 19. See Art. 20 for statistical returns to be made.

[10] Arts. 21–9. [11] Arts. 30–2.

Parties to create criminal offences relating to the possession, supply, and transport of drugs, and making such offences extraditable.[12]

Many of the recognized types of mutual assistance are of value in the drugs context as in other criminal matters; for example, summonses may need to be served, and evidence obtained. The drugs context does, however, have its own special requirements.

The evidence needed for a successful drugs prosecution will usually include scientific evidence based on an analysis of the substances with which the accused was dealing. With the development of increasingly sophisticated man-made drugs, the forensic testing of samples requires more elaborate resources which may well be beyond the capacity of a Third World country. With United Nations assistance, a network of specialist laboratories, each serving a region comprising a number of countries, is being developed; reports provided by the staff of these laboratories will commonly be received in evidence under rules applying to evidence obtained abroad.

Another special feature of drugs cases is the extent of joint operations between enforcement agencies in different countries. A good example is that of 'controlled delivery' under which a consignment of drugs, the existence of which has become known to the authorities, is allowed to complete the journey planned for it by the traffickers, either to discover their *modus operandi* or to identify the ultimate consignees and their agents along the route. It sometimes happens that some or all of the drugs are removed, an innocent substance of similar weight and appearance being substituted. Wherever any resulting prosecution is mounted, evidence will be needed from the countries along the route, especially where this type of substitution has taken place.

Finally, there is no area in which the location of assets and the forfeiture of the proceeds of crime is more important than that of drug-trafficking; the amounts of money involved can be enormous, and the movement across international boundaries is inherent in the whole business.

During the 1980s there was a major effort on the part of many Governments and international agencies to put in place adequate legal responses, both in domestic law and through international legal co-operation. The most significant achievement was the Vienna Convention 1988, to which States and regional organizations (such as the European Community) are actively responding.

(B) The Vienna Convention

In response to a United Nations General Assembly resolution of 4 December 1984,[13] a new convention designed to cover topics, such as those in the law enforcement area not adequately dealt with in the existing instruments, was

---

[12] See Art. 36(2)(*b*).   [13] Resolution 39/141.

prepared and adopted as the United Nations Convention against Illicit Traffic in Narcotic Drugs and Psychotropic Substances 1988.[14] The Convention rapidly obtained the twenty ratifications required to bring it into force[15] and duly entered into force on 11 November 1990. The United Kingdom ratified the Convention in June 1991; by March 1992 there were 59 Parties.

The purpose of the Convention is stated as being the promotion of co-operation among the Parties to address more effectively those aspects of drug-trafficking having an international dimension.[16] Although only one Article specifically addresses mutual assistance as such,[17] the whole thrust of the Convention's provisions is towards comprehensive co-operation in legal as in other aspects.

This co-operation is set firmly within the established principles of inter-national law by the provisions of Article 2, which asserts the principle of non-intervention in the domestic affairs of other States,[18] and continues by prohibiting any State Party from undertaking:

in the territory of another Party the exercise of jurisdiction and performance of functions which are exclusively reserved for the authorities of that other Party by its domestic law.[19]

This outlaws the assertion and exercise of extra-territorial jurisdiction, and provides a secure base upon which to erect the structure of mutual assistance.

OFFENCES

Article 3 contains an elaborate set of provisions requiring Parties to estab-lish a range of criminal offences under domestic law. These include not only offences of production, cultivation and possession of drugs but also the manufacture, transport or distribution of equipment, materials, or specified substances knowing that they are to be used for their illicit cultivation, pro-duction or manufacture.[20] Organised drug-trafficking is directly attacked by the creation of the offence of organising, managing or financing drugs offences,[21] and of a series of offences of participation in 'laundering' the proceeds of such offences.[22] These offences may be committed by the drug-trafficker himself when he tries to launder his own profits; in United Kingdom law the money-laundering provisions of the Drug Trafficking Offences Act 1986[23] caught only other persons, and a more extensive

---

[14] Vienna, 20 Dec. 1988. For a detailed commentary, see W. C. Gilmore, *The United Nations Convention against Illicit Traffic in Narcotic Drugs and Psychotropic Substances* (Commonwealth Secretariat, 1991).   [15] Convention, Art. 29(1).
[16] Art. 2(1).   [17] Art. 7.
[18] Art. 2(2).   [19] Art. 2(3).
[20] Art. 3(1)(*a*)(iv) and Tables I and II.   [21] Art. 3(1)(*a*)(v).
[22] Conversion or transfer of property for the purpose of concealing or disguising its illicit origin (Art. 3(1)(*b*)(i)); concealing or disguising the true nature, source, location, disposition, movement, rights with respect to, or ownership of the proceeds of drugs offences (Art. 3(1)(*b*)(ii)); and, so far as the principles of the national legal system permit, the acquisition, possession or use of such proceeds (Art. 3(1)(*c*)(i)).   [23] s. 24.

provision meeting the requirements of the Vienna Convention was created by the Criminal Justice (International Co-operation) Act 1990.[24] The Convention goes into considerable detail as to such matters as the need for heavy penalties and a long limitations period.[25]

EXTRADITION AND JURISDICTION TO PROSECUTE

The implementation of all these provisions will improve the quality of national drugs legislation, but has a further significance in the context of extradition. Any problem of double criminality will be avoided as between States each of which has enacted offences in terms of Article 3, and it is further provided that such offences are not to be regarded for the purposes of extradition or mutual assistance as fiscal offences, political offences or as politically motivated.[26]

Extradition is dealt with in Article 6 which deems all offences established in accordance with Article 3(1) to be extraditable offences in relation to any pre-existing extradition treaties between Parties; the offences are to be included in any future extradition treaties between Parties.[27] If a Party needs to have an extradition treaty in place before it can act, and it receives a request from a State with whom it has no such treaty, it may consider the Vienna Convention itself as providing the necessary legal basis for extradition.[28] Article 6 contains the provision commonly found in modern extradition treaties that extradition may be refused where there are substantial grounds leading the authorities of the requested State to believe that compliance would facilitate the prosecution or punishment of any person[29] on account of his race, religion, nationality or political opinions, or would cause prejudice for any of those reasons to any person affected by the extradition request.[30] Parties also undertake to 'seek to conclude bilateral and multilateral agreements to carry out or to enhance the effectiveness of extradition';[31] such a positive requirement is unusual, and clearly unenforceable, but is an expression of the seriousness of purpose with which the matter of co-operation was addressed.

Article 4 specifies circumstances in which a State should itself exercise jurisdiction over Convention offences; these include cases where the offence, is committed, anywhere, by a national or habitual resident of the State[32] or was committed on board a vessel intercepted in accordance with the procedures established under the Convention.[33]

In some cases, several States will be entitled to exercise jurisdiction though one State might prove a more convenient forum from the prosecution's point of view, for example where that State alone has jurisdiction over other per-

---

[24] s. 14.
[25] Art. 3(4) (sanctions reflecting 'the grave nature of these offences') and 3(8).
[26] Art. 3(10).   [27] Art. 6(1)(2).   [28] Art. 6(3).
[29] Not necessarily the person whose extradition is sought.
[30] Art. 6(6).   [31] Art. 6(11).
[32] Art. 4(1)(*b*)(i).   [33] See Art. 17 and p. 180, below.

sons involved in the same series of offences. It was with these considerations in mind that the authors of the Convention included a provision requiring Parties to give consideration to the possibility of transferring to one another proceedings for criminal prosecution of offences established under the Convention 'in cases where such transfer is considered to be in the interests of a proper administration of criminal justice'.[34]

MUTUAL ASSISTANCE

The main provisions as to mutual assistance are to be found in Article 7, which provides that 'the Parties shall afford one another, pursuant to this article, the widest measure of mutual legal assistance in investigations, prosecutions and judicial proceedings in relation to criminal offences established in accordance with Article 3(1)'.[35] A list of purposes for which mutual legal assistance may be granted is found in Article 7(2), but although the list is a full one it is not intended to be exhaustive and any other forms of assistance permitted by the domestic law of the requested Party may also be given.[36]

In general, a request is to be executed in accordance with the domestic law of the requested country,[37] but in one respect the Convention clearly overrides domestic law. It is provided that a Party may not decline to render mutual legal assistance under Article 7 on the ground of bank secrecy.[38] This is of great importance in the drugs context where the identification and location of the proceeds of crime is such a prominent feature of the necessary international co-operation.[39]

Those who drafted the Vienna Convention were well aware of the growing volume of multilateral and bilateral arrangements for mutual assistance in criminal matters, and this is reflected in a number of ways in the Convention's text. The Parties are exhorted (that seeming to be the effect of the obligation to 'consider, as may be necessary, the possibility') to conclude bilateral or multilateral agreements or arrangements that would serve the purposes of, give practical effect to, or enhance the provisions of, Article 7.[40] It is further declared that the provisions of Article 7 do not affect the obligations under any other treaty, bilateral or multilateral, which governs or will in future govern, in whole or part, mutual legal assistance in criminal matters.[41] Although the drafting is not as clear as one might have wished, the effect appears to be that the Convention can extend but not diminish the scope of those obligations; so, for example, Article 7(4) prohibiting reliance on bank secrecy in the context of the Convention would seem to prevail over a general

---

[34] Art. 8. [35] Art. 7(1).

[36] Art. 7(3). See also Art. 7(4) which deals with assisting witnesses to travel to the requesting country, including the transfer in custody of willing witnesses; this assistance is to be given 'to the extent consistent with [the requested country's] domestic law and practice'.

[37] Art. 7(12). [38] Art. 7(5).

[39] The actual confiscation of proceeds is dealt with in Art. 5; see below. For bank secrecy generally, see pp. 271–86.

[40] Art. 7(20). [41] Art. 7(6).

mutual assistance treaty which did permit such reliance. A more extensive interpretation of the provision that the Convention is not to 'affect' the obligations under other treaties could rob it of all significance where the countries concerned were parties to a general mutual assistance treaty.

Where no such treaty relationship exists between the requesting and requested countries, Article 7(8)–(19) apply; they set out in effect a short form of mutual assistance treaty to operate in the Convention's sphere. Provision is made for designated authorities to transmit and receive requests for assistance,[42] the form and language of the request,[43] the provision of supplementary information to assist in the execution of the request,[44] the use of information obtained and confidentiality,[45] immunities of witnesses,[46] and the grounds upon which a request may be refused. These are quite limited: apart from non-compliance with the provisions of the Convention,[47] which, it is to be hoped, will not be invoked on mere technicalities, they are likely prejudice to the sovereignty, security, *ordre public* or other essential interests of the requested Party,[48] or impossibility of compliance having regard to prohibitions in the domestic law of the requested Party or the nature of its legal system.[49] Although these provisions are in the spirit of many mutual assistance arrangements, which seek to make available to foreign authorities the facilities available to the corresponding bodies within the requested country, the danger is that sufficient weight will not be given to the intention to make a real advance in the level of co-operation in the drugs field, and that pre-existing practices and attitudes will be relied upon unthinkingly: 'It is something we have never done'.

In addition, the giving of assistance may be postponed if it would interfere with an ongoing investigation, prosecution, or proceeding in the requested country;[50] in practice good communication between the relevant authorities should ensure that this happens rarely, for the strategy for handling the case will be an agreed one.

CONFISCATION

The confiscation of illicit profits is widely recognized as of great importance as part of any effective strategy to deal with drug trafficking. Article 5(1) requires each Party to adopt measures enabling it to confiscate both the drugs and instrumentalities used in or intended for use in the crime and also the proceeds of the offence or property the value of which corresponds to that of

---

[42] Art. 7(8).
[43] Art. 7(9)(10). The United Kingdom only accepts requests in English.
[44] Art. 7(11).   [45] Art. 7(13)(14).
[46] Art. 7(18). The United Kingdom will only consider granting immunity where this is specifically requested, and will not grant it if it considers that such a grant would be contrary to the public interest.
[47] Art. 7(15)(a).   [48] Art. 7(15)(b).
[49] Art. 7(15)(c)(d). In all cases, reasons for refusal must be given: Art. 7(16).
[50] Art. 7(17).

such proceeds. This provision has a dual advantage: it ensures that the greatest number of States possible can act against the trafficker in this way, and it also removes a possible impediment to the recognition of the confiscation orders of other States by ensuring that every Party has such a mechanism within its own legal system.

Each Party must also adopt such measures as may be necessary to enable its competent authorities to identify, trace, and freeze or seize proceeds and instrumentalities for the purposes of eventual confiscation.[51] In relation to the tracing and confiscation of property, each Party must ensure that its courts or other competent authorities may order the inspection or seizure of bank, financial or commercial records and may not decline to do so on the ground of bank secrecy.[52] This overcomes the reluctance of some States to waive the economic advantages of bank secrecy laws[53] and provides a basis for the provision of information to other States who make a request for assistance in tracing property.[54]

In addition to the tracing of property, other Parties may request that the property be frozen or seized and an order for confiscation be sought and enforced, or that a pre-existing order be submitted for enforcement.[55] The decisions or actions taken with regard to such requests for assistance are to be taken in accordance with the domestic law and procedural rules of the requested Party[56] and subject to any bilateral or multilateral treaty, agreement or arrangement to which it is bound in relation to the requesting Party.[57]

Despite the emphasis on the definition and implementation of the measures to be taken under Article 5 by the domestic law of the requested Party, the Article does go into considerable detail about the scope of the measures. So, if proceeds have been transformed or converted into other property, the 'new' property must be liable to seizure and confiscation; and where proceeds have been mixed with property acquired from legitimate sources, the intermingled property is liable to confiscation up to the value of the proceeds.[58] Income or other benefits derived from proceeds, from property into which proceeds have been transformed or converted, and from property with which proceeds have been intermingled must also be made liable to seizure and confiscation.[59] The Convention permits, but does not require, the reversal of the burden of proof regarding the lawful origin of alleged proceeds,[60] and saves (without detailed provisions) the rights of bona fide third parties.

OTHER FORMS OF ASSISTANCE

Although much of the Convention can be regarded as concerned with administrative rather than legal matters, some important improvements are

---

[51] Art. 5(2).
[53] See pp. 271–86.
[55] Art. 5(4)(a)(b).
[57] Art. 5(4)(c).
[59] Art. 5(6)(c).

[52] Art. 5(3).
[54] i.e. under Art. 5(4)(b).
[56] See the reiteration of this principle in Art. 5(9).
[58] Art. 5(6)(a)(b).
[60] Art. 5(7).

made in respect of practical co-operation between investigation agencies. For example, controlled delivery of drugs[61] can be of great assistance in tracing the network involved in their movement and distribution. States have sometimes been unwilling to co-operate, perhaps because of ethical concerns about allowing drug trafficking to continue when it can be prevented. Article 11 requires Parties, if permitted by the basic principles of their domestic legal systems, to take the necessary measures 'within their possibilities' to allow for controlled delivery at the international level. Arrangements, including financial arrangements, are to be made on a case-by-case basis, and it is specifically noted that these may include the interception of consignments and their being allowed to continue with the drugs intact or removed or replaced in whole or in part.

The problem of illicit traffic by sea is dealt with in some detail in Article 17.[62] The jurisdiction of the flag State may be ineffective, in the sense that the ship may be far away from its port of registry; the Convention encourages procedures under which the flag State authorizes another State Party to the Convention to take appropriate measures in regard to vessels suspected of being engaged in illicit traffic. These measures may include boarding and searching the vessel; if illicit traffic is found appropriate action may then be taken with respect to the vessel and persons and cargo on board.[63] A number of safeguards are built in: the rights of coastal States are protected;[64] intervention must be carried out by a warship or military aircraft, or by a ship or aircraft clearly identifiable as being on government service;[65] and due account must be taken of the need not to endanger life at sea, the security of the vessel and the cargo, or to prejudice the commercial and legal interests of the flag State or any other interested State.[66]

(C) European Community Action

The European Community might appear to have no obvious standing in the matter of drug-trafficking, there being at least as yet no European criminal law. In fact concern about the illicit trade in drugs has been expressed within the institutions of the Community for some time, and it is recognized that the completion of the Community's internal market and the possible emergence of a single European currency give greater relevance to the problem. The removal of barriers on the movement of goods and of money between Member States can be seen as facilitating money-laundering, with possible adverse effects on the developing financial system of the Community.

Concerted action within the Community was stimulated by a most

---

[61] See above, p. 174.
[62] See W. Gilmore, 'Narcotics Interdiction at Sea; U.K.–U.S. Co-operation' (1989) 13 Marine Policy 218.
[63] Art. 17(4).   [64] Art. 17(11).
[65] Art. 17(10).   [66] Art. 17(5).

influential report of a European Parliament Committee of Enquiry into the Drugs Problem in the Member States of the Community, for which Sir Jack Stewart-Clark acted as Rapporteur.[67] It emphasized that measures to combat an international network of criminal organizations had themselves to be taken at international level, with a common strategy, and rigorously co-ordinated legal measures. As part of a general interest in drug trafficking, the Community became involved in the negotiations leading up to the Vienna Convention and signed the resulting Convention on 8 June 1989.[68] This action was later approved by a Council Decision[69] and although it is not within the competence of the Community institutions to force criminal measures upon Member States, the Community has undertaken in a declaration in accordance with Article 27 of the Convention to do whatever it can to comply with its Convention obligations. This was reiterated in a Statement of June 1991, setting a target date of 31 December 1992.[70] Action by the Community has included a Directive on Money-Laundering,[71] and a Regulation dealing specifically with a drugs issue.

REGULATION ON TRADE IN 'PRECURSORS'

This Council Regulation aims to 'discourage the diversion of certain substances to the illicit manufacture of narcotic drugs and psychotropic substances'.[72] In seeking to comply with its obligations under the Vienna Convention the Community recognized that it should take action against the trade in 'precursors', the convenient term used to refer to the substances frequently used in the manufacture of drugs and psychotropic substances. So far as administrative co-operation was required between Member States, a basis for action was found in a 1981 Regulation on mutual assistance in ensuring the correct application of the law on customs and agricultural matters.[73]

The scheme of the Regulation on 'precursors' is based partly on that of the 1981 Regulation and partly on the requirements of Article 12 of the Vienna Convention which contains a minimum set of standards to help prevent otherwise licit substances being used to create illicit narcotic drugs and psychotropic substances. Article 12 contains various measures to deal with this problem, including the very general requirement that Parties take such measures as they deem appropriate to prevent the diversion of substances to illicit purposes.[74] The Parties are also required to take action that they deem appropriate to monitor the manufacture and distribution of certain

---

[67] The report is published as doc A2-114 in the *Working Documents of the European Parliament*, 1986–7.   [68] See Bull. EC 6-1989, point 2.2.50.

[69] Council Decision of 22 Oct. 1990, No.90/611/EC, OJ L326, 24 Nov. 1990.

[70] OJ L166/82, 28 June 1991.

[71] See pp. 189–91.

[72] Council Regulation (EC) No. 3677/90, OJ L357/1, 20 Dec. 1990.

[73] Council Regulation (EC) No. 1468/81, OJ L144/1, 2 June 1981; as amended by Council Regulation (EC) No. 945/87, OJ L90/3, 2 Apr. 1981.   [74] Art. 12(1).

substances,[75] but as the EC has not chosen any of the options permitted, such as introducing a system of licensing, it must be assumed that the action taken in accordance with Article 12(9) is deemed to be sufficient.

The Regulation is divided into three main areas, monitoring of trade, control measures and administrative co-operation, those provisions relating to the monitoring of trade being required by Article 12(9) of the Vienna Convention. The Convention demands that the Parties introduce measures to meet five objectives:

(a) Establish and maintain a system to monitor international trade in certain substances in order to facilitate the identification of suspicious transactions;
(b) Provide for the seizure of those substances if there is sufficient evidence that they are for use in the illicit manufacture of a narcotic drug or psychotropic substance;
(c) Notify the competent authorities and services of the Parties concerned if there is reason to believe that the import, export or transit of a substance is destined for the illicit manufacture of narcotic drugs or psychotropic substances;
(d) Require proper labelling and documentation of imports and exports;
(e) Ensure that the documents are maintained for not less than two years and are available for inspection by the competent authorities.

Article 1 of the Regulation provides the definitions of the principal terms used and more than meets the requirements of the Convention in that 'operator' includes not only 'any natural or legal person engaged in the manufacture, production, trade or distribution of scheduled substances' but also those involved in 'other related activities such as import, export, transit, broking and processing of scheduled substances', including 'in particular, persons pursuing the activity of making customs declarations on a self-employed basis'.[76] The list of scheduled substances is identical to that annexed to the Vienna Convention.

Article 2 deals with documentation, records and labelling as demanded by Article 12(9)(d) and (e) of the Convention and also exceeds its requirements in that the records are to be kept for the slightly longer period of not less than two years from the end of the calendar year in which the operation took place.[77] A duty of notification is placed on the operators by Article 3 which fulfils Article 12(9)(c) of the Convention, but the main provision is that in Article 4 which deals with pre-export notification. This places a positive duty on the operators to supply full details of exports to the competent authorities of the State where the customs export formalities are to be completed. The operators must ensure that the particulars have actually been received at least 15 working days before any customs export declaration is lodged.[78] The competent authorities must then decide whether or not the export should be permitted.

The competent authorities are required by Article 4(4) to make a decision

---

[75] Art. 12(8).   [76] Art. 1(2)(e).
[77] Art. 2(4).   [78] Art. 4(1).

with regard to the particulars within the fifteen working days prior to the lodging of the customs export declaration. Where there are reasonable grounds for suspecting that the substances are intended for the illicit manufacture of narcotic drugs or psychotropic substances the export must be forbidden by a written order from the competent authorities,[79] but where there are no such grounds and there has been no request for further information or a decision to extend the fifteen day period, an export permit must be issued. Article 4(5) deals with requests for information made by countries outside the Community in accordance with the Vienna Convention,[80] and provision is made in Article 5 for extending the notification requirements of Article 4 to any country which has informed the Commission that it wishes to be notified in advance of any shipment to it of the scheduled substances.

In order to enable the competent authorities of the Member States to have equal powers to enforce these requirements the Regulation also requires that certain measures be adopted.[81] Competent authorities must be able to obtain information on any orders for or operations involving scheduled substances, and they must also be able to enter operators' business premises to obtain evidence of irregularities. While these powers are a basic minimum for monitoring of the movement of these substances, they do not themselves meet the requirements of the Vienna Convention,[82] which requires that the competent authorities be given the power to seize any scheduled substance if there is sufficient evidence that it is intended for the illicit manufacture of narcotic drugs or psychotropic substances. The Regulation does not extend this far, no doubt because of sensitivities over Community action in the criminal law field.

In addition to these powers the customs authorities or other competent authorities of each Member State may prohibit the introduction into or removal from Community territory of scheduled substances if there are reasonable grounds for suspecting that the substances are intended for the illicit manufacture of narcotic drugs or psychotropic substances.[83] This provision is important as it allows use to be made of any information which comes to light after the decision is made in the country of export.

The Regulation is of limited scope in one very important respect. It is concerned only with the import of substances to the customs territory of the Community, their export from that territory, and the transit of substances between third countries through that territory.[84] In other words it does not address the movement of substances where the points of departure and of destination are both within the Community. The Community has however also established a permanent anti-drugs committee (CECAD)[85] which is to consider measures to produce more effective co-operation and to advise on priorities for EC action.

[79] Art. 4(3).   [80] Art. 12(10).   [81] Art. 6.
[82] Art. 12(9)(*b*).   [83] Art. 6(2).   [84] Art. 1(2).
[85] See Bull. EC 1/2–1990, point 1-3-16.

8

Money-Laundering

FROM the point of view of the criminal, it is no use making a large profit out of criminal activity if that profit cannot be put to use. Hence the strategy, reviewed below,[1] of legislating and devising means of international co-operation for the effective confiscation of the proceeds in an attempt to undermine the motivation behind much criminal activity.

Putting the proceeds to use is not as simple as it may sound. Although a proportion of the proceeds of crime will be kept as capital for further criminal ventures, the sophisticated offender will wish to use the rest for other purposes. In particular, he may wish to establish commercial enterprises or invest in existing enterprises, a process which may add to his power or influence and can be expected to generate for himself or his family a continuing and legitimate income. If this is to be done without running an unacceptable risk of detection, the money which represents the proceeds of the original crime must be 'laundered', put into a state in which it appears to have an entirely respectable provenance.

Money-laundering can present considerable problems to the criminal and correspondingly important opportunities for law enforcement agencies. Money-laundering devices have become increasingly sophisticated and have called for a major international effort by the law enforcement community.

The actual business of money-laundering has a number of stages.[2] The first is the *placement* of the 'dirty' money into a national financial system; the simplest example is the paying in to a bank account of the proceeds of the sale of drugs to the ultimate consumer, proceeds in the form of numerous and surprisingly bulky used bank-notes. It is at this point that money-laundering makes its contribution to the vocabulary of the English language in the form of the inelegant expression 'smurfing'. To smurf is to divide a large sum into small amounts and to make a series of small payments into bank accounts, perhaps using a number of different bank branches, so as to avoid drawing attention to the individual payments and keeping below the minimum amount attracting some requirement that the transaction be reported to a monitoring body.

Although that example refers to banks, it may well be that some other

---

[1] See pp. 199–238.

[2] See M. Trigg, 'Money-Laundering and Confiscation: an Enforcement Perspective', a paper at the Oxford Conference on International and White Collar Crime 1991; C. A. Intriago, *International Money-laundering*.

money-handling institution is preferred, on the grounds that it is likely to be less well regulated, and its staff less well trained. Bureaux de change and gambling casinos may provide convenient alternatives.

The second phase is that of *distancing* or *layering*, some transaction or series of transactions designed to make it difficult or impossible to trace the movement of the funds; an example might be the sale and re-sale of assets of high value but subject to no system of registration of title. At this stage there is likely to be an international dimension, funds being transferred to 'regulatory havens', countries in which the identity of those controlling bank-accounts or corporations is readily concealed. Bearer shares, nominee hold-ings, and other forms of anonymous control of assets are favoured; wherever possible funds will be deliberately mixed, so that at least a part can be shown to have a legitimate source.

The final stage is the *re-integration* of the money, now appearing to have an entirely legitimate source, into the economy in which it is intended for use, a process which may well again include its international transfer. Frequently bogus invoices and documents of carriage are employed, creating evidence of non-existent or grossly over-valued imports and exports. There can be com-plex loan arrangements, secured on valuable assets; borrower, lender, and guarantor are all in fact the same person, but the arrangement is resolved in a way which leaves the money where it is needed as the result of what seems a standard commercial transaction.

FINANCIAL ACTION TASK FORCE

The 'Group of Seven' economic summit, that is the leaders of the major industrial nations,[3] held in Paris in July 1989 found that the drug problem had reached 'devastating proportions'.[4] It urged the development of further bilateral and multilateral agreements, including measures to facilitate the identification, tracing, freezing, seizure, and forfeiture of the proceeds of drugs crimes. It also established a Financial Action Task Force to address the problem of money-laundering and the scope for enhanced multilateral judicial assistance in that field.

The Task Force (known by the rather unfortunate acronym FATF) proved to be a major venture, involving some 130 experts from fifteen countries, Australia, Austria, Belgium, Luxemburg, The Netherlands, Spain, Sweden, and Switzerland joining the original Group of Seven countries. It examined the scale of money-laundering, estimating the sums available from the sale of cocaine heroin and cannabis at $85 billion a year, and its methodology and addressed issues of legal and administrative counter-measures. A first report, with forty recommendations, was prepared in February 1990. At the next Economic Summit, in Houston in July 1990, FATF was continued for a second

---

[3] Canada, France, Germany, Italy, Japan, the United Kingdom, and the United States (plus the European Commission). [4] Economic Declaration, para. 51.

year and again enlarged.[5] The second report reviewed the progress made in implementing the earlier recommendations, especially through work at regional level, and set out guide-lines for future work including the continuance of FATF as an *ad hoc* body for at least three years.

In its 1990 analysis, the Financial Action Task Force wrote:

All these techniques . . . involve going through stages where detection is possible. Either cash has to be exported over a territorial frontier and then deposited in a foreign financial institution, or it requires the knowing or unknowing complicity of someone at home not connected with the drugs trade, or it requires convincing a domestic financial institution that a large cash deposit or purchase of a cashier's cheque is legitimate. Once these hurdles have been overcome, the way is much easier inside the legitimate financial system. *Hence, key stages for the detection of money-laundering operations are those where cash enters into the domestic financial system, either formally or informally, where it is sent abroad to be integrated into the financial systems of regulatory havens, and when it is repatriated in the form of transfers of legitimate appearance.*[6]

THE ROLE OF BANKS AND OTHER FINANCIAL INSTITUTIONS

At some stage in the process, money-launderers must make use of the facilities of banks or similar institutions. As a result much attention has been paid to finding ways of improving banking procedures, either by self-regulation or by legal requirements, so as to combat money-laundering. This involves in particular customer identification, the retention of transaction records, and the reporting to a specified authority of transactions which either meet certain pre-determined criteria or are for some other reason seen as suspicious. There is growing recognition that the aim of discovering the proceeds of crime (at least in the case of serious crime, including drug trafficking, and organized crime) is an appropriate justification for an exception to bank secrecy laws. The Swiss Confederation accepted this in its negotiations with the United States towards what became the first of the series of bilateral mutual assistance treaties negotiated by the United States Government. It is notable that a provision in the Drug Trafficking Offences Act 1986 of the United Kingdom that a production order[7] 'shall have effect notwithstanding any obligation as to secrecy or other restriction upon the disclosure of information imposed by statute or otherwise',[8] has been reproduced unchanged, despite the very different approach to bank secrecy, in the corresponding legislation of the Bahamas.[9] In the drugs context, the Vienna Convention of 1988[10] expressly provides that, in carrying out its Convention obligation to legislate for the identification, tracing and seizure of proceeds of drugs offences, a Party shall enable its authorities to obtain bank, financial

---

[5] Denmark, Finland, Greece, Hong Kong, Ireland, New Zealand, Norway, Portugal, and Turkey were the additional participants; 160 experts made contributions.
[6] Emphasis in original.
[7] See p. 192.   [8] s. 27(9)(b).
[9] Tracing and Forfeiture of Proceeds of Drug Trafficking Act 1986, s. 22(8)(b) (Bahamas).
[10] Art. 5(3). For the Convention, see pp. 174–80.

and commercial records and that a Party may not decline to act in that respect on the ground of bank secrecy.

The importance of customer identification was stressed in a Recommendation of the Committee of Ministers of the Council of Europe of 27 June 1980[11] and in the Statement of Principles of the Basel Committee on Banking Regulations and Supervisory Practices adopted on 12 December 1988;[12] the Statement of Principles is being adopted in many countries as the basis on which banks should operate, including the United Kingdom and the United States of America,[13] and indeed the Bank of England has threatened to remove the licences of those who fail to comply with the principles contained in it.[14] In the terms of one of the FATF recommendations, banks and similar institutions should not keep anonymous accounts or accounts in obviously fictitious names, and should establish and record the identity of their customers (on the basis of an official or other reliable identifying document) when establishing business relations or conducting transactions. The latter was particularly important when accounts were opened, pass-books issued, safe-deposit boxes rented, or fiduciary or large cast transactions carried out.[15]

Closely related to this is the retention of transaction records for a number of years (the FATF recommendation was 5 years)[16] in a form which enables the nature of the transaction, and the customer or customers involved, to be available to law enforcement agencies engaged in a criminal investigation. Modern data storage and retrieval systems make all this feasible, though not without considerable expense, but it is obvious that disclosure is incompatible with any absolute principle of bank secrecy or confidentiality.

MONEY-LAUNDERING OFFENCES

A first and obvious step in combating money-laundering is to ensure that it is within the reach of the criminal law. Offences of handling stolen goods, such as that created by section 22 of the Theft Act 1968 cover a small part of the ground, but are wholly inadequate in the face of sophisticated devices.

There is an emerging international consensus as to the scope of the concept of money-laundering and therefore of the definition of the necessary new offences. A most influential formulation is that in Article 3 of the United Nations Convention against Illicit Traffic in Narcotic Drugs and Psychotropic Substances (the Vienna Convention) of 1988.[17] The Article is concerned with

---

[11] Recommendation No. R(80)10, based on work done under the aegis of the European Committee on Crime Problems.

[12] Just 8 days before the signature of the Vienna Convention. For a discussion of the work of the Basel Supervisors Committee see P. C. Hayward, 'Prospects for International Co-operation by Bank Supervisors' (1990) 24 Int. L. 787.

[13] Bureau of National Affairs, BNA Banking Report, 30 Jan. 1989.

[14] *Financial Times*, 14 Nov. 1989.

[15] See FATF 1990 Report, Recommendation 12.

[16] Ibid., Recommendation 14.

[17] See generally, pp. 175–6.

offences which each Party must establish in its domestic law 'when committed intentionally'.[18]

In addition to offences concerning operations involving the production of drugs, these include:

the conversion or transfer of property, knowing that such property is derived from [one or more of the production-related offences], or from an act of participation in such offence or offences, for the purpose of concealing or disguising the illicit origin of the property or of assisting any person who is involved in the commission of such an offence or offences to evade the legal consequences of his actions;[19]

the concealment or disguise of the true nature, source, location, disposition, movement, rights with respect to, or ownership of property, knowing that such property is derived from [one or more production-related offences] or from an act of participation in such an offence or offences;[20]

and 'subject to [the Party's] constitutional principles and the basic concepts of its legal system':

the acquisition, possession or use of property, knowing at the time of receipt, that such property was derived from [one or more of the production-related offences] or from an act of participation in such offence or offences;[21]

publicly inciting or inducing others, by any means, to commit any of [these] offences;[22] and

participation in, association or conspiracy to commit, attempts to commit and aiding, abetting, facilitating and counselling the commission of any of [these] offences.[23]

The Financial Action Task Force in its 1990 Report adopted as a working definition a description of money-laundering virtually identical, though not linked to specifically drugs-related offences, to the first three paragraphs set out above.

Council of Europe Convention

In the Council of Europe Convention on Laundering, Search, Seizure and Confiscation of the Proceeds from Crime 1990,[24] the offences which Parties must establish in their domestic law follow a pattern which is again largely identical. Article 6(1) of that Convention contains provisions corresponding to the first, second, third, and fifth paragraphs quoted above from the Vienna

---

[18] Vienna Convention, Art. 3(1).

[19] Ibid., Art. 3(1)(*b*)(i). It has been suggested that this wording could even cover the position of a lawyer receiving fees from 'laundered' funds; the experts who adopted similar language in the European Convention (considered below) rejected that interpretation: *Explanatory Memorandum*, para. 33.

[20] Vienna Convention, Art. 3(1)(*b*)(ii).   [21] Ibid., Art. 3(1)(*c*)(i).

[22] Ibid., Art. 3(1)(*c*)(iii).   [23] Ibid., Art. 3(1)(*c*)(iv).

[24] Opened for signature on 8 Nov. 1990 and then signed by 12 States. For the confiscation aspects, see pp. 235–8. The title '*European* Convention' is not used as non-European States (Australia, Canada, and the USA) took part in its elaboration and can become Parties. For the text of the Convention, see the Appendix of Selected Documents, below.

text, the knowledge required in each case being that the property concerned was 'proceeds'.[25] In the first three contexts, the Convention omits the reference to an 'act of participation' as being, as a matter of drafting, redundant;[26] the issue of incitement or inducing a person to act, treated separately in the Vienna text, seems to be adequately covered by the reference to 'counselling'. The Convention provides additionally that a Party may establish as offences acts meeting the description drawn from the Vienna text but where the offender (*a*) did not know, but ought to have assumed, that the property was proceeds; or (*b*) acted for the purpose of making profit; or (*c*) acted for the purpose of promoting the carrying on of further criminal activity.[27] The Convention also applies where the 'predicate offence', that is the offence as a result of which proceeds were generated,[28] was committed outside the jurisdiction of the State in which the money-laundering offence is being tried;[29] this is not explicit in the Vienna text which is however certainly capable of bearing the same meaning.

European Community Directive

A European Community Directive on money laundering, the Council Directive of 10 June 1991 on prevention of the use of the financial system for money-laundering,[30] takes further the approaches of both the Vienna Convention and the European Convention; both are referred to in its preamble. It also reflects the view of the European Commission that the Community had a duty to protect its financial system.[31] The Commission recognized that money laundering must mainly be combated through criminal legislation and international co-operation between law enforcement agencies and judicial authorities, but argued that it could also be tackled by impeding the launderers from taking advantage of the single financial market. It was also necessary to ensure that Member States did not act unilaterally, as they might introduce measures incompatible with the completion of the single market. While the Directive requires that Member States ensure that the laundering of the proceeds of any serious crime is treated as a criminal offence[32] its main purpose is to ensure that credit and financial institutions adopt a system which allows effective supervision of their customers.

In the Directive, the definition of money-laundering is taken almost verbatim from Article 3(1)(*b*) of the Vienna Convention, but with a more general reference to 'criminal activity' substituted for that to drug offences. This led to some difficulty in the discussion of earlier drafts of the Directive. The Directive is intended to enable the Community to comply with its

---

[25] This is defined to include any economic advantage from criminal offences: European Convention, Art. 1(*a*).

[26] *Explanatory Memorandum*, para. 32.   [27] European Convention, Art. 6(3).

[28] Ibid., Art. 1(*e*).   [29] Ibid., Art. 6(2)(*a*).

[30] 91/308/EEC, OJ L166/77. For earlier published versions, see First Draft, OJ C106/6, 28 Apr. 1990; Second Draft, OJ C319/9 19 Dec. 1990.

[31] See the proposal contained in Com. (90) 106 final.   [32] Art. 2.

obligations under the Vienna Convention, and the definition of criminal activity includes crimes specified in Article 3(1)(*a*) of the Convention.[33] Earlier drafts also referred to 'terrorism and any other serious criminal offence (including in particular organized crime), whether or not connected with drugs, as defined by the Member States', but this was seen by some Member States as an intrusion into their exclusive jurisdiction over criminal law. The final text speaks more blandly of 'any other criminal activity designated as such for the purposes of this Directive by each Member State'.[34]

Under the Directive, which is to be complied with before 1 January 1993,[35] Member States are to ensure that credit and financial institutions,[36] and related professions and undertakings particularly susceptible of being used for money laundering,[37] require identification of their customers when entering into business relations, particularly when opening an account or arranging safe custody facilities.[38] The identification requirement also applies to transactions involving more than ECU15,000, and where an institution suspects that a person is acting on behalf of someone else it must take reasonable measures to discover the real identity of the customer.[39]

The Directive is so drafted as to ensure that all financial and credit institutions which operate within the Community are subject to its provisions, and not solely those institutions which have their head office within its borders. Records of the identity documents required are to be kept for at least five years after the relations with that client have ended, and the institutions must also keep records of transactions, in a form admissible in court proceedings under the applicable national legislation, for a minimum of five years from the time the transaction is completed.[40]

Member States are to ensure that institutions examine with especial attention any transaction which they regard as particularly likely, by its nature, to be related to money-laundering.[41] The institutions are expected to co-operate with the authorities responsible for combating money-laundering by volunteering information which they discover which could be related to a money laundering offence and by providing the agencies with all the information which is requested in relation to investigations of money laundering.[42] Transactions which are known or suspected of being related to money laundering are not to be entered into until the relevant authorities have been notified; if the delay would frustrate efforts to pursue the beneficiaries of a suspected money-laundering operation (by making them aware that they might have been detected, for example), the transaction may proceed, the authorities being notified immediately afterwards.[43] Member States must also ensure

---

[33] Art. 1.   [34] Ibid.
[35] Art. 16(1).   [36] As defined by Art. 1.
[37] Art. 8.   [38] Art. 3(1).
[39] Art. 3(2)(5). There are exemptions in the case of insurance policies (Art. 3(3)(4)) and in the case of certain dealings between credit and financial institutions covered by the Directive (Art. 3(7)).   [40] Art. 4.
[41] Art. 5.   [42] Art. 5(1).   [43] Art. 7.

that if inspections are carried out of the institutions by the competent authorities[44] and facts are discovered which could constitute evidence of money laundering, the authorities responsible for combating money-laundering are informed.[45]

Protection is afforded for those involved in that disclosure under the terms of the Directive and made in good faith by any employee or director of an institution is not to constitute a breach of any restriction on disclosure, whether imposed by contract or by a legislative, regulatory, or administrative provision; and the Directive prevents any civil or penal responsibility of any kind attaching either to the employee or director or to the institution itself.[46]

Member States are also to ensure that the credit and financial institutions establish adequate procedures of internal control and communication in order to forestall and prevent operations related to money-laundering, and also to establish suitable training and awareness programmes for their employees.[47] The extension of the provisions of the Directive to other professions and undertakings[48] is designed to ensure that other businesses which handle large amounts of money, e.g. casinos, would not escape the net.

The Member States are also required to take appropriate measures to ensure the application of the provisions of the Directive and in particular are to determine the penalties for infringements;[49] whether these penalties should be civil or criminal or both is not specified.

The Directive establishes what is to be known as the 'contact committee', composed of representatives of the Member States and the Commission. It is to facilitate the implementation of the Directive by regular consultation on practical problems; to arrange consultation on the possibility of more stringent or additional conditions and obligations which may be laid down at national level; to examine the professions or categories of undertaking to which the Directive may be extended; and to advise the Commission on possible supplements or amendments to the Directive.[50]

As the preamble to the Directive notes, it mirrors in many ways the Basel Statement of Principles and the earlier Recommendation of the Council of Europe.[51] Because of the Community's limited jurisdiction in criminal law, the Directive is not concerned with the enforcement phases addressed in the other international instruments. So, the Directive was accompanied by a Statement by the representatives of Governments of Member States meeting within the Council.[52] This recalls that Member States had signed the Vienna Convention and that most had also signed the European Convention; it contains an undertaking to enact criminal legislation complying with these obligations of these treaties by 31 December 1992.

---

[44] Defined in Art. 1 as those national authorities empowered by law or regulation to supervise credit or financial institutions.
[45] Art. 10.
[46] Art. 9.
[47] Art. 11.
[48] Art. 12.
[49] Art. 14.
[50] Art. 13.
[51] See above, p. 187.
[52] Printed at OJ l166/83.

TRACING THE PROCEEDS OF CRIME

A necessary first step in the forfeiture of the proceeds of crime, or indeed of the prosecution of a money-laundering offence, is to trace the whereabouts of the proceeds. The Commonwealth Scheme for Mutual Assistance in Criminal Matters provides for the giving of assistance in response to a request under the Scheme:

in identifying, locating, and assessing the value of, property believed to have been derived or obtained, directly or indirectly, from, or to have been used in, or in connection with, the commission of an offence and believed to be in the requested country.[53]

More recently the Council of Europe Convention of 1990 requires Parties to afford each other 'the widest possible measure of assistance in the identification and tracing of instrumentalities, proceeds and other property liable to confiscation';[54] this is to include measures providing and securing evidence as to the existence, location or movement, nature, legal status, or value of the property.

Domestic legislation to serve these ends will take a variety of forms depending on the procedures and traditions of individual States.

Production orders under the Drug Trafficking Offences Act (UK)

So far as drug trafficking offences are concerned, an important innovation in the Drug Trafficking Offences Act 1986 was the introduction of production orders. Under the Police and Criminal Evidence Act 1984 police access to certain types of material, including otherwise confidential material held by third parties, can in certain cases be ordered by a Circuit Judge.[55] New but related provisions were made in the Drug Trafficking Offences Act 1986. Production orders, 'orders to make material available', can be obtained under the 1986 Act by making an application to a Circuit Judge or sheriff under section 27.[56] If there are reasonable grounds for suspecting that a specified person has carried on or has benefited from drug trafficking, any person may be ordered to produce (or allow the inspection of) material likely to be of substantial value to the investigation.[57] These powers override any obligation as to secrecy imposed by statute or otherwise;[58] for example by the middle of 1989, over 2,250 production orders had been made in respect of bank accounts,[59] notwithstanding the general, though not unlimited, duty of a bank to preserve confidentiality.

---

[53] Commonwealth Scheme, para. 26(1).

[54] Convention, Art. 8, forming part of Chapter III, Section 2 ('Investigative Assistance').

[55] Police and Criminal Evidence Act 1984, (PACE), s. 9 and Sched. 1.

[56] For another power to obtain disclosure (in connection with a restraint order), see p. 212.

[57] Drug Trafficking Offences Act 1986 (DTOA), s. 27(2), (4)(a)(b).

[58] DTOA, s. 27(b).

[59] *Drug Trafficking and Related Serious Crime* (7th Report of Home Affairs Committee, Session 1989–9, H.C. 370), vol. 2, p. 104.

There are some safeguards. The judge is required to be satisfied that production would be in the public interest,[60] and 'items subject to legal privilege' and 'excluded material' (both as defined in the Police and Criminal Evidence Act 1984)[61] are immune from production or inspection[62] (although it remains possible to obtain access to 'excluded material' by an application under the 1984 Act). Despite this, the decision *R* v. *Central Criminal Court, ex p. Francis & Francis*[63] shows the potentially far-reaching effect of the Act on lawyers and their clients. The applicant solicitors had been served with an order to produce papers relating to one of their clients. The lawyers claimed that the papers were subject to legal privilege. However the Act excludes from the scope of legal privilege 'items held with the intention of furthering a criminal purpose'.[64] The House of Lords held it immaterial whether the intention was that of the person holding the documents or of any other person.[65]

These production orders may also be sought to obtain material which relates to a foreign investigation.[66] In so holding, Watkins LJ emphasized that when drafting the Misuse of Drugs Act 1971 and the Drug Trafficking Offences Act 1986 the international obligations of the United Kingdom under the Single Convention on Narcotics Drugs 1961[67] were kept in mind. However, when an application for a production order is made solely or partly in order to assist an investigation by a foreign law enforcement agency, this has to be made clear to the court and evidence should be adduced to show that the investigation is into possible breaches of a 'corresponding law' within the meaning of section 36(1) of the 1971 Act.

The Divisional Court in the same case also had to decide whether when exercising their power[68] of 'retaining' material obtained as a result of a production order for use at trial customs officers could make it available to foreign investigatory authorities. The court held that this could be done; if it were not possible the supposed purpose of the legislation would be completely frustrated. There was no need for the customs officers to lose possession of the material as copies could be supplied to the foreign investigatory authorities.

Production orders can, it seems, only relate to material which already exists; they cannot be made prospectively, to include material which may become available. That would require something along the lines of the 'monitoring order' available in some Australian jurisdictions.[69]

---

[60] DTOA, s. 27(4)(*c*).   [61] See ss. 10, 11 of the 1984 Act and DTOA, s. 29(2).
[62] DTOA, s. 27(4)(*b*)(ii), (9)(*a*).   [63] [1989] A.C. 346 (H.L.)
[64] DTOA, s. 29(2) applying Police and Criminal Evidence Act 1984, s. 10(2).
[65] *R* v. *Crown Court at Snaresbrook, ex p DPP* [1988] Q.B. 532, so far as it suggests the contrary, seems no longer good law.
[66] *R* v. *Crown Court at Southwark, ex p. Customs and Excise* [1990] Q.B. 650 (D.C.).
[67] See p. 173.
[68] Under section 22 of Police and Criminal Evidence Act 1984 as applied by DTOA, s. 29(1).
[69] See p. 194.

Australian developments

A considerable body of legislation resulted from a major political initiative in Australia in the late 1980s, including the Proceeds of Crime Act 1987, the Cash Transactions Reports Act 1988 and the Mutual Assistance in Criminal Matters Act 1988, accompanied by an intensive programme for the negotiation of extradition and mutual assistance treaties. Legislation on the proceeds of crime has been enacted in the majority of Australian jurisdictions.

Although there is a strong family resemblance between the legislation of the various Australian States and the Commonwealth (i.e. Federal) Parliament, there are significant differences and it is clear that a number of different models have been used. The earliest text was that of the Crimes (Confiscation of Profits) Act 1985 of New South Wales. This has now been replaced,[70] but was influential in the drafting of the Northern Territory legislation, the Crimes (Forfeiture of Proceeds) Act 1988 (N.T.). A rather different model is that of the Victorian draftsman in the Crimes (Confiscation of Profits) Act 1986 (Vic.) on which the Western Australian legislation, the Crimes (Confiscation of Profits) Act 1988 (W.A.) is modelled. The Commonwealth Parliament enacted very elaborate provisions in the Proceeds of Crime Act 1987 (Cwlth.), which in turn influenced the revised New South Wales legislation, the Confiscation of Proceeds of Crime Act 1989 (N.S.W.). The Queensland Act, the Crimes (Confiscation of Profits) Act 1989 (Qd.) draws on the Commonwealth and the Victorian models.[71]

Various 'information gathering powers' are created by the Proceeds of Crime Act 1987 of Australia. A judge may grant a production order where a person has been convicted of, or there are reasonable grounds for suspecting that he has committed, an indictable offence, and there are similar grounds for suspecting that a person (not necessarily the defendant) has possession or control of a 'property-tracking document' relating to the offence.[72] A property-tracking document is one relevant to identifying, locating or quantifying property of the defendant or other 'tainted property',[73] or identifying or locating a document necessary for the transfer of such property.[74] The document must be disclosed in accordance with the terms of the order. A judge may also make a 'monitoring order' directing a financial institution (a bank, building society, or credit union) to give information to a law enforcement authority; the information which may be obtained relates to transactions conducted through an account held by a specified person.[75] Related provisions require financial institutions to retain for a seven-year period certain classes of document of value in tracing the movement of funds, for exam-

---

[70] It is repealed by the Confiscation of Proceeds of Crime Act 1989 (N.S.W.).

[71] Following Australian practice, reference will be made to the current legislation as identified in the text by citing the jurisdiction and section number only.

[72] Cwlth., s. 66. For foreign offences, see s. 69.   [73] For this term, see below, p. 231.

[74] Ibid., s. 4(1).   [75] Ibid., s. 73. For foreign offences, see s. 75.

ple opening and closing accounts, transmitting funds abroad, and opening or using a deposit box.[76] Similar provisions are found in the legislation of a number of the Australian States and Territories.[77]

Reporting obligations

Even closer co-operation between banking institutions and law enforcement agencies is created when there is a legal duty on the banks not merely to respond to requests for information in aid of investigations, but to take active steps by reporting transactions as they occur.

In modern legislation, there is a growing practice of imposing upon banks and similar financial institutions an obligation to report certain types of financial transaction (chosen because of their potential relevance in money laundering) or more generally to report transactions creating a suspicion of money-laundering activities. Examples are to be found in the United States, where the Bank Secrecy Act of 1982 and the Money Laundering Control Act of 1986 contain detailed provisions as to the reporting of both domestic and foreign monetary transactions,[78] and in Australia.

Under the Cash Transaction Reports Act 1988 of Australia, which came into force in July 1990, a 'cash dealer' is under an obligation to report 'significant cash transactions' to the Director of the Cash Transaction Reports Agency.[79] The Agency analyses and disseminates reported information to the Australian tax authorities and to other law enforcement agencies for investigation and prosecution as appropriate; for example, tax and social security frauds have been uncovered. The term 'cash dealer' is given a very wide interpretation, including for example securities dealers, unit trust managers, bullion dealers, casino operators and bookmakers.[80] A 'significant cash transaction' is one involving the transfer of currency of not less that $Australian 10,000;[81] the movement of $5,000 in cash into or out of Australia must be reported, and it is understood that the legislation is to be amended to include electronic funds transfers. If foreign currency is involved the report is required within a day of the transaction; fifteen days is allowed in other cases.[82] The Act also requires cash dealers to verify the identity of those seeking to open accounts, and makes it an offence to open or operate an account under a false name.

---

[76] Ibid., ss. 76–80.

[77] Qd., Part V; N.S.W., Part 4 (production and monitoring orders); W.A., Part 6 (production and monitoring orders); N.T., Part VII, Division 1 (production orders).

[78] See 31 USC. ss. 5311–22; C. T. Plambeck, 'Confidentiality and disclosure: The Money Laundering Control Act of 1986 and bank secrecy' (1988) 22 Int. L. 69; S. N. Welling, 'Smurfs, money laundering and the federal common law' (1989) 41 Fla. L.R. 287.

[79] Cash Transaction Reports Act 1988, s. 7.

[80] Ibid., s. 3(1).   [81] Ibid.

[82] Ibid. (definition of 'reporting period'). In the first twelve months, the Agency received and processed 430,000 cash transaction reports, and 9,000 reports of the import or export of currency totalling $255 million in value.

United Kingdom approaches

A different technique was originally favoured in the United Kingdom. The Drug Trafficking Offences Act 1986 created the offence of assisting another to retain the benefit of drug trafficking. This is committed:

if a person enters into or is otherwise concerned in an arrangement whereby—
  (*a*) the retention or control by or on behalf of another (call him 'A') of A's proceeds of drug trafficking is facilitated (whether by concealment, removal from the jurisdiction, transfer to nominees or otherwise), or
  (*b*) A's proceeds of drug trafficking—
      (i) are used to secure that funds are placed at A's disposal, or
      (ii) are used for A's benefit to acquire property by way of investment, knowing or suspecting that A is a person who carries on or has carried on drug trafficking or has benefited from drug trafficking.[83]

However, where a person discloses to a constable a suspicion or belief that any funds or investments are derived from or used in connection with drug trafficking, or any matter on which such a suspicion or belief is based, such disclosure if timely will provide a defence to a charge which might otherwise be successfully brought for assisting another to retain the benefit of drug trafficking.[84] The disclosure will not be treated as a breach of any contractual restriction upon the disclosure of information;[85] a similar provision is to be found in the Criminal Justice Act 1988,[86] applying to offences other than drug trafficking offences, but there is no offence of assisting money-laundering in that Act.

The effect is to make it necessary in the drug trafficking context for a bank or other institution or individual concerned, although subject to no formal legal duty, to make disclosure once suspicions are aroused; and facilitate such disclosure in other contexts. The House of Commons Home Affairs Committee, reporting in 1989, supported this approach (despite some concerns as to its observance by the smaller banks, including overseas banks with branches in London, perhaps as a result of ignorance of the relevant provisions) in preference to the Australian approach of mandatory reporting of all transactions over a certain value. The Bank of England has issued *Guidance Notes* to banks on the types of activity which should give rise to suspicion, and similar advice to building societies and other financial institutions. The United Kingdom has established no new Agency such as that in Australia; reports of suspicious transactions are handled by the financial section of the National Drugs Intelligence Unit which co-ordinates police and customs activity in combating drugs-related crime.[87]

---

[83] DTOA, s. 24(1).   [84] Ibid., s. 24(3)(*b*).
[85] Ibid., s. 24(3)(*a*).   [86] s. 98.
[87] There are plans to incorporate the Unit in a broader National Criminal Intelligence Service, which would also include the UK National Central Bureau of Interpol.

To ratify the Vienna Convention 1988 the United Kingdom had to legislate to implement Article 3 as to the creation of money-laundering offences in the drugs field. Section 24 of the Drug Trafficking Offences Act 1986, quoted above, was inadequate for this purpose; it penalizes conduct by a person who assists the money-launderer, the one who is called 'A', but not that of A himself. The gap was filled by section 14 of the Criminal Justice (International Co-operation) Act 1990. A person is guilty of an offence under that section if he conceals or disguises any property which is, or in whole or part directly or indirectly represents, his proceeds of drug trafficking, or converts or transfers that property or removes it from the jurisdiction.[88] To ensure full compliance with the Convention, it is also made an offence for another person, knowing or having reasonable grounds to suspect that property is or represents such proceeds, to act in those ways for the purpose of assisting any person to avoid prosecution for a drug trafficking offence or the making of a confiscation order.[89]

CROSS-BORDER TRANSFER OF CASH

It will have been noted that the Australian provisions as to the reporting obligation deal expressly with the transmission of funds overseas. This is of obvious importance, for it is an obvious step in a money-laundering scheme. Practical difficulties have been experienced, or are feared, where States have dismantled exchange controls or are entering into regional arrangements which reduce border controls. This has become a matter of some controversy in the European Community in the context of the Schengen treaty discussions and the post-1992 Single Market.[90] This lies behind section 25 of the Criminal Justice (International Co-operation) Act 1990. This empowers a customs officer[91] or constable to seize and detain any cash (coins or notes in any currency) being imported into or exported[92] from the United Kingdom[93] if its amount is not less than a sum to be prescribed by order of the Secretary of State[94] and the customs officer or constable has reasonable grounds for suspecting that it directly or indirectly represents any persons proceeds of, or is intended by any person for use in, drug trafficking.

Cash seized under section 25 can be detained for 48 hours. A justice of the peace may authorize further detention for three months if he is satisfied that there are reasonable grounds for the suspicion and that continued detention is justified while further investigations are made or the institution of criminal proceedings is considered; a magistrates' court may make order further

---

[88] Criminal Justice (International Co-operation) Act 1990, s. 14(1).

[89] Ibid., s. 14(2). For confiscation orders, see pp. 216–24.

[90] See p. 129.

[91] Defined, as are other relevant terms, in s. 29(1).

[92] Including where it is being brought to any place in the United Kingdom for the purpose of being exported: s. 29(1).

[93] Including movements to or from the Isle of Man: s. 29(3).

[94] See s. 29(2).

extensions of three months at a time up to a total of two years from the date
of the first order by the single justice.[95] If the court is satisfied that detained
cash does directly or indirectly represent the proceeds of, or is intended for
use in, drug trafficking, it may order the cash to be forfeited.[96]

---

[95] Criminal Justice (International Co-operation) Act 1990, s. 25(2)(3). For procedure and the
placing of the cash in an interest-bearing account, see ss. 27–8.

[96] Ibid., s. 26.

9

The Proceeds of Crime

(A) Introduction

EVERY legal system would accept as axiomatic that an offender should not enjoy the profits of his criminal activities. In earlier centuries the rule of the common law was that the entire estate of a felon was forfeit to the Crown;[1] in modern times the imposition of fines and the making of orders in favour of the victims of crime (for example a restitution order on a conviction for theft, or a compensation order in a case of criminal damage to property) goes some way towards the same objective. There are, however, many highly profitable types of criminal activity—drug trafficking being a prime example—to which notions of restitution or compensation scarcely apply, because there is no readily identifiable 'victim'. A specific concept of forfeiture is clearly needed.

Its application is made more difficult by practical developments. The proceeds of crime were perhaps once typically pieces of personal property, for example stolen chattels, which could be seized or restored to their owner. Today they are more commonly represented by cash or choses in action, and subject to sophisticated 'money-laundering' techniques. In large-scale criminal conspiracies, where many more offences will be committed than can lead to convictions being obtained, the notion of 'forfeiting the property derived by the offender from the crime for which he has been convicted' is demonstrably inadequate.

In recent years, governments in many States have addressed this matter, and a growing body of legislation bears witness to the seriousness with which the problem is being tackled. That approaches should vary is not at all surprising, given the relative newness as well as the complexity of the issues; but the adoption of differing approaches can hinder international legal co-operation. Fortunately, this is an area in which formal devices such as the reciprocal enforcement of court orders are not essential; practical assistance, supported by legal rules and procedures allowing for a very rapid response to requests, is of the first importance.

Before there can be successful international co-operation, there has to be in place adequate domestic legislation; in many countries this requirement is still unmet, and the subject has proved a difficult and complex one for the legislator. This chapter examines earlier approaches to forfeiture and traces

---

[1] The history of this and related rules is examined in the argument of counsel for the appellant (L. Blom-Cooper QC) in *R. v. Cuthbertson* [1981] A.C. 470 (H.L.).

the more recent attempts, especially in England and in the various Australian jurisdictions, to secure a satisfactory legislative treatment.

English Experience with Forfeiture Provisions

The narrowest type of forfeiture provision concerns specific categories of forbidden articles. Where it is the policy of the law to prohibit the possession or exposure to view or offering for sale, of certain types of article, forfeiture (and sometimes destruction) will commonly be found as a method of enforcement. Typical examples are those of obscene publications,[2] firearms,[3] and offensive weapons.[4] A more general power was given to the courts by the Criminal Justice Act 1988 in substituting a new section 43(1) of the Powers of the Criminal Courts Act 1973.[5] This enables the court to make an order depriving the offender of any rights he might have in property where the relevant offence 'consists of unlawful possession of property'; the precise scope of this has not yet been tested.

Forfeiture of property related to a specific offence

Wider language may be used where the offence may not involve simple possession but the conduct of some transaction. In the drugs area, for example, articles such as scales and syringes may be part of the paraphernalia of the dealer. The language of section 27(1) of the Misuse of Drugs Act 1971 catches such articles and in some cases the monetary proceeds of a drugs offence. It provides that, subject to safeguards for third-party rights:

the court by or before which a person is convicted of an offence under this Act [or a drug trafficking offence as defined in section 38(1) of the Drug Trafficking Offences Act 1986][6] may order anything shown to the satisfaction of the court to relate to the offence to be forfeited and either destroyed or dealt with in such other manner as the court may order.[7]

This has been described, by way of illustration, as covering 'the drugs involved, apparatus for making them, vehicles used for transporting them, or cash ready to be, or having just been, handed over for them'.[8]

Section 27 does not authorize the forfeiture of property which cannot be shown to be related to the particular offence of which the offender has been convicted. It follows that money in the possession of the offender which clearly represents the proceeds of a series of drugs offences cannot be made the subject of a forfeiture order under this section unless it can be linked to the particular offences for which a conviction was obtained.[9] *A fortiori*, it is

---

[2] See e.g. Obscene Publications Act 1964, s. 1(4) (obscene articles kept for publication for gain); Protection of Children Act 1978, s. 5 (indecent photographs of children).
[3] Firearms Act 1968, s. 52.
[4] Prevention of Crime Act 1953, s. 1.　　　　　[5] Criminal Justice Act 1988, s. 69.
[6] The words in square brackets were inserted by Criminal Justice Act 1988, s. 70.
[7] s. 27(1).　　　　　[8] *R.* v. *Cuthbertson* [1981] A.C. 470, at 484 *per* Lord Diplock.
[9] *R.* v. *Morgan* [1977] Crim.L.R. 488, C.A.; *R.* v. *Llewellyn* (1985) 7 Cr. App. R. (S.) 225; *R.* v. *Cox* (1986) 8 Cr. App. R. (S.) 384; *R.* v. *Boothe* (1987) 9 Cr. App. R. (S.) 8.

not possible to 'follow the assets' in seeking to forfeit property which indirectly represents the proceeds of a drugs offence. As Lord Diplock pointed out in *R. v. Cuthbertson*,[10] no machinery is provided by the 1971 Act for effecting the assignment of choses in action or for creating and realising charges on real and personal property; so, 'orders of forfeiture under section 27 can never have been intended by Parliament to serve as a means of stripping the drug traffickers of the total profits of their unlawful enterprises'.[11]

In that case, popularly known as the 'Operation Julie' case, three men had been convicted of conspiracy to manufacture and supply LSD under section 4 of the Misuse of Drugs Act 1971. Their activities had produced considerable profits of approximately £750,000 and a forfeiture order was made under section 27(1) of the 1971 Act to deprive them of these profits. The House of Lords 'with considerable regret' had to allow an appeal against the forfeiture order on two grounds. First, the House of Lords was compelled to hold that conspiracy to commit an offence was not an offence within the meaning of the Act as was necessary to permit forfeiture under section 27. Secondly, even if conspiracy fell within the scope of the Act, forfeiture was only possible in relation to property which was connected to the offence, and money could not be said to relate to the offence of conspiracy which is only an unfulfilled agreement to do something.

Forfeiture of 'instrumentalities'

In some contexts there are powers to confiscate property used in the commission of offences, known by the convenient if ugly phrase 'the instrumentalities of the crime'. These forfeiture powers are sometimes developed in relation to particular types of crime, an early and notable example being that of smuggling. So the Customs and Excise Management Act 1979, having provided[12] for the forfeiture of goods improperly imported, goes on to permit the forfeiture of any

ship, aircraft, vehicle, animal, container (including any article of passengers' baggage) or other thing whatsoever which has been used for the carriage, handling, deposit or concealment of the thing so liable for forfeiture, either at a time when it is so liable or for the purpose of the commission of the offence for which it later became so liable,

and also of 'any other thing mixed, packed or found with the thing so liable'.[13] A similar United States provision expressly mentions things used to obtain information so as to facilitate an offence.[14]

---

[10] [1981] A.C. 470.
[11] Ibid., pp. 484–5.
[12] s. 49.
[13] Customs and Excise Management Act 1979, s. 14(1). See G. McFarlane, 'Customs and Excise Law: Seizure, Forfeiture and Condemnation' (1987) 137 N.LJ 683.
[14] 19 USC. 1595a.

A general forfeiture power

A more general power of forfeiture was created by section 43 of the Powers of Criminal Courts Act 1973 which followed a recommendation by the Advisory Council on the Penal System that post-conviction forfeiture powers should be generalised. This enables a court to make a deprivation order:

where a person is convicted of an offence and the court by or before which he is convicted is satisfied that any property which has been lawfully seized from him or which was in his possession or under his control at the time when he was apprehended for the offence or when a summons in respect of it was issued:
  (i) has been used for the purpose of committing, or facilitating the commission of, any offence; or
  (ii) was intended by him to be used for that purpose.[15]

The property must have served (or been intended to serve) the purpose of at least facilitating an offence, though not necessarily the offence of which the offender stands convicted. A car used to transport prohibited drugs will fall within this provision,[16] but a car which provides the setting for an indecent assault may not.[17] The section does not apply to the proceeds of past offences such as money gained in drug trafficking,[18] unless the court is persuaded that it was intended for use for the purpose of committing or facilitating further offences.[19]

Section 43(1A), inserted into the 1973 Act by section 69 of the Criminal Justice Act 1988, requires the court when considering whether to make a forfeiture order to have regard to the value of the property and to the likely financial and other effects on the offender, combined with the effects of any other order that the court contemplates making. The intention was to codify the principles which had already been established by case law to guide the courts when making forfeiture orders,[20] but according to one commentator, this may have produced a result which makes the section 43 power virtually impossible to use.[21] In *R* v. *Highbury Corner Stipendiary Magistrates' Court, ex p. Di Matteo*[22] an order for the forfeiture of a car was quashed as the defendant's solicitor was not asked to address the magistrate on the matter of the order and the likely effect on the defendant; the order had been made without sufficient information about the defendant's circumstances. The requirement

[15] The text is the amended version substituted by Criminal Justice Act 1988, s. 69.

[16] *R.* v. *Boothe* (1987) 9 Cr. App. R. (S.) 8 (C.A.).

[17] *R.* v. *Lucas* [1976] Crim.L.R. 79 (C.A.).

[18] *R.* v. *Slater* [1986] 1 W.L.R. 1340 (C.A.); *R.* v. *Neville* (1987) 9 Cr. App. R. (S.) 222 (C.A.).

[19] i.e. applying s. 43(1)(*a*)(ii). See *R.* v. *O'Farrell* [1988] Crim.L.R. 387 (C.A.), where *Slater* and *Neville* not cited.

[20] *Scully* (1985) 7 Cr. App. R. (S) 119; *Joyce and others* (1989) 11 Cr. App. R. (S) 253; *Taverner* (5 Apr. 1974), *Current Sentencing Practice* J4.4(*b*); *Bucholz* (10 May 1974), ibid.

[21] See D. A. Thomas [1991] Crim. L.R. 307 at p. 308 and 'The Criminal Justice Act 1988—The Sentencing Provisions', [1989] Crim. L.R. 43 at p. 51.

[22] [1991] Crim. L.R. 307.

to consider information on the value of the property and the likely effects on the offender is onerous but there is no guidance as to where this information should come from or how precise it should be. It does not appear to be sufficient for the court simply to invite the defence to make submissions or to object to the making of the order, as the obligation to have regard to the value of the property is positive and unqualified.

DEVELOPMENTS IN THE 1980s

The Hodgson Committee

The continued inadequacy of the law, especially as exposed in the *Cuthbertson* case,[23] caused much public concern. The Howard League for Penal Reform established a Committee under the chairmanship of Mr Justice Hodgson to examine the law on forfeiture of property associated with crime, to assess how far the powers of the criminal courts met the need to strip offenders of their ill-gotten gains and to determine whether the courts needed greater powers to make this possible. The Committee reported in 1984, and despite its unofficial status was to have a marked influence on subsequent legislation.[24]

The Committee examined questions of restitution, of 'forfeiture' (of property immediately connected with the offence) and of 'confiscation' (of the profit or proceeds of the offence), as well as the issue of pre-trial seizure.

So far as forfeiture was concerned, an amended version of section 43 of the Powers of the Criminal Courts Act 1973 was seen a providing an adequate basis for a general forfeiture power.[25] The legitimacy of using forfeiture either as a means of taking out of circulation goods that are inherently dangerous or contrary to the public interest or as a means of imposing an additional penalty was accepted, provided in the latter case that the cumulative effect of the penalties which were imposed was kept in mind.[26] The provision of a power of forfeiture in cases where there was no conviction was also considered but was not favoured as the Committee feared that this could too easily be used as a way of penalising criminal conduct without the safeguards of the ordinary criminal process.[27]

Probably the most important recommendation made by the Committee was that relating to the introduction of a new power to confiscate the profits of crime.[28] Where a person was convicted of an offence (or asked for an offence to be taken into consideration, or the relevant conduct was included in a defined course of illegal dealing covered by sample counts)[29] the Crown

---

[23] *R. v. Cuthbertson* [1981] A.C. 470 (H.L.); see above, p. 201.

[24] For the report of the committee (cited hereafter as Hodgson Committee Report) see *The Profits of Crime and Their Recovery* (Heinemann, 1984).

[25] Hodgson Committee Report, p. 95

[26] Ibid., pp. 97–100.

[27] Ibid., at p. 96.

[28] Ibid., at p. 70 *et seq.*

[29] For a full discussion of the problem of sample counts, see the Hodgson Committee report, pp. 75–81.

was to have the burden of demonstrating the gross value of the defendant's proceeds in relation to it. However, the defendant would be able to present evidence of his expenses (for example, the amounts he had had to pay to purchase drugs intended for resale) in order to reduce the amount to be specified in the confiscation order. Only the net profits of the crime were to be confiscated as this satisfied the perceived justification for confiscation orders: the restoration of the status quo prior to the commission of the crime.

A majority of the Committee considered that trafficking in drugs warranted the introduction of specific, more stringent, powers similar to those which had already been adopted in other countries such as the United States. They suggested that confiscation of all proceeds of drug trafficking should be possible, even in relation to actions that were not the basis of any specific charges. The prosecution would only have to prove when the first offence of drug trafficking took place and any increase in the value of the defendant's property after that date would be deemed to be the result of drug trafficking unless he could show otherwise. A minority disagreed with these proposals as they felt that even drug traffickers were entitled to the protection of the principle that the burden of proof rests upon the prosecution.[30]

Legislative action

The Drug Trafficking Offences Act 1986 introduced a comprehensive scheme giving powers in relation to the proceeds of drug trafficking offences extending from the initial stage of investigation to the making of a confiscation order after a conviction has been obtained. The Act implements many of the recommendations of the majority of the Hodgson Committee, and incorporates and develops many elements found in previous law, including the Police and Criminal Evidence Act 1984. Similar principles, but with some important variations, were applied outside the drug trafficking field by the Criminal Justice Act 1988 and the Prevention of Terrorism (Temporary Provisions) Act 1989.[31]

(B) Interim Seizure

Once relevant property has been identified it is clearly of the greatest importance that it be made subject to some procedure by which its further removal or dissipation is restrained. Many States have introduced legislation to allow for the making of some kind of 'restraining orders'. In most, such orders are to be sought *ex parte*; speed and confidentiality are of the essence. It is usually necessary to provide for a limited period of validity, so that either the order expires unless confiscation proceedings are commenced within a prescribed number of days or it has to be renewed (or is open to challenge) in subsequent inter partes proceedings. If the whole of an individual's property is restrained, there must be some provision enabling him to obtain sufficient

---

[30] See the Hodgson Committee report, pp. 82–4.   [31] See pp. 224–8.

funds for reasonable living expenses and legal costs. Some States have also found it desirable to make fairly full provision to safeguard the interests of third parties; others leave such protection to the confiscation stage.

THE POSITION AT COMMON LAW

Intervention to prevent the dissipation of property while civil legal proceedings are being taken has become familiar in English practice, and in many Commonwealth countries, in the form of the *Mareva* injunction.[32] Some attempts were made in England to persuade the courts, ahead of legislative developments, to exercise a similar power in the criminal context to supplement the existing powers of the police; they met with limited success.

The common law afforded the police certain powers in relation to the property of a suspect. It was originally held in *Dillon* v. *O'Brien and Davis*[33] that the police were entitled on a lawful arrest to take and detain property found in the possession of the suspect if it would form material evidence on his prosecution for that crime. That decision was limited to charges of treason or felony, but when considered by the court in *Chic Fashions (West Wales) Ltd* v. *Jones*[34] the power was extended to cover cases where the police entered premises with a search warrant or with the occupier's consent. Seizure of property was permitted where the police reasonably believed that the goods in question had been stolen or obtained fraudulently by deception, and this included property outwith the scope of a search warrant. There were now included as legitimate purposes of seizure the preservation of evidence for production at trial and the restoration of the property to its rightful owner.

The question of the seizure of intangible assets such as a credit balance in a bank account was first raised in *West Mercia Constabulary* v. *Wagener*.[35] Here the police sought an injunction to freeze a bank account which had been credited with large sums of cash suspected of being the proceeds of a crime with which the defendants had been charged. Forbes J. was initially very doubtful as to whether the West Mercia Constabulary had any *locus standi* on this issue but he was persuaded to make the order requested by the fact that if he could grant no order in this case there would be a lacuna in the law. Forbes J. was struck by the fact that were a bank to be robbed of £1,000,000 in cash and the robber to place the stolen money in the strong room of another bank, a search warrant could be granted. If the High Court had no power to make the injunction sought, then were the stolen money to be paid into the robber's bank account nothing could be done to reach it.

This new power was exercised again in *Chief Constable of Kent* v. *V.*[36] where freezing of a bank account was sought when the account was suspected of having been credited with the proceeds of an alleged forgery, but the judgments of the Court of Appeal provide no clear guidance as to the basis for its

---

[32] See pp. 65–72.
[33] (1887) 16 Cox C.C. 245.
[34] [1968] 1 All E.R. 229.
[35] [1981] 3 All E.R. 378.
[36] [1983] Q.B. 34 (C.A.).

exercise. Slade LJ dissented as he regarded the Chief Constable as unable to show any legal or equitable right sufficient to justify the grant of an injunction; he would not follow *West Mercia Constabulary* v. *Wagener.*[37] Of the majority, Lord Denning MR felt that the court was justified in granting the injunction under section 37(1) of the Supreme Court Act 1981; this he regarded as having 'circumvented' the limitations on the injunction relied on by more 'timorous souls'. It was now enough for the applicant to show a sufficient interest to apply for an injunction; here the Chief Constable had a duty to the public to apprehend the criminal and recover the proceeds, and that sufficed. Lord Denning also commented that he would make the same decision if a thief stole goods, sold them and then deposited the proceeds of the sale in his bank account.

The ratio is perhaps to be found in the judgment of Donaldson LJ whose approach was accepted by Slade LJ although he dissented on its application to the facts. An injunction would not be granted unless it were for the enforcement or protection of a legal or equitable right or interest. Donaldson LJ found that the Chief Constable did have such a right; the *Chic Fashions* case[38] had given the police a right to seize goods, and that right Donaldson LJ was prepared to extend to moneys standing to the credit of a bank account if and to the extent that they could be shown to have been obtained from another in breach of the criminal law.[39]

Limitations on the exercise of this new power emerged in the decisions in *Chief Constable of Hampshire* v. *A*[40] and *Chief Constable of Leicestershire* v. *M.*[41] These cases both involved a request for freezing money which could not be clearly identified as being directly obtained from a criminal act. In the *Hampshire* case two garage owners had been accused of dishonestly selling cars with the milometers wound back and of drawing up false financial documents. It was suspected that the proceeds from these crimes had been used to pay off the mortgages on two garage properties which had subsequently been sold. The injunction sought was one freezing the proceeds of the sale of the two garages. The court accepted that it did have jurisdiction to grant an injunction, but held that this was only possible where the proceeds could be identified; in the words of Donaldson LJ in the *Kent* case, freezing of credit balances was possible only 'if and to the extent that they can be shown' to have been obtained as a result of crime. Here the funds used were in part honestly obtained, and identification was not possible. Similar reasoning was adopted in the *Leicestershire* case. M was accused of having obtained mortgage advances by means of deception. By selling the relevant property in a rising housing market, he was able to pay off the loans and make a profit for himself. An injunction was refused as the property sought to be frozen could

---

[37] [1981] 3 All E.R. 378.   [38] [1968] 1 All E.R. 229.

[39] Donaldson LJ reserved the case in which stolen goods had been sold and the proceeds deposited in the account.

[40] [1985] Q.B. 132 (C.A.).   [41] [1988] 3 All E.R. 1014.

not be identified as money obtained by alleged fraud; it was rather profit obtained by the use of money obtained by alleged fraud.

One point which has been made very clear is that the court will not make orders of this type to preserve assets for the sole purpose of satisfying any compensation, forfeiture or restitution order which might be made. This was established in *Malone* v. *Commissioner of Police of the Metropolis*[42] when an order was sought by the police to allow them to retain money which they had seized during a search. The retention of the money was authorized, but only because it was material evidence for the case against Malone. The court emphasized that its retention for any other reason was impermissible. Counsel for Malone had suggested that the common law should be extended to supplement the statutory powers of the police, but this suggestion was firmly rejected. A similar result followed attempts to invoke the powers of the courts where the ultimate remedy sought was a declaration that the offender held the property as a constructive trustee.[43]

Since the enactment of the Drug Trafficking Offences Act 1986 and the Criminal Justice Act 1988, these powers have been largely superseded by the statutory powers considered below. The injunction power may, however, remain useful in relation to summary offences not covered by the statutory provisions.

RESTRAINT ORDERS

The Hodgson Committee noted the limitations on the availability of the criminal version of the *Mareva* injunction, and the impossibility of using in a criminal context other remedies such as the *Anton Piller* order or orders under the Bankers Books Evidence Act 1879. The Committee's recommendation was that a High Court judge should be given power to grant an injunction freezing the assets of a person against whom there existed a prima facie case and against whom a fine or a compensation order totalling at least £10,000 seemed likely. Once an injunction had been granted, third parties could be required to disclose information about the relevant assets.[44] The Drug Trafficking Offences Act 1986 contains provisions based on these recommendations.[45]

Where a person has been charged or is likely to be charged with a drug trafficking offence the prosecutor may make an *ex-parte* application to a judge in chambers for a restraint order to prohibit any person from dealing with any 'realisable property', subject to such conditions and exceptions as may be specified in the order.[46] Section 8 is seen as creating a criminal equivalent of

---

[42] [1980] Q.B. 49 (C.A.).
[43] *Chief Constable of Surrey* v. *Abbott*, unreported, Ognall J, 24 Oct. 1988; *R* v. *Robson* [1991] Crim L.R. 222 (C.A.).
[44] See Hodgson Committee Report, p. 108 *et seq*.
[45] Disclosure aspects are addressed via production orders, already examined.
[46] DTOA, s. 8(1).

the *Mareva* injunction to preserve the suspect's assets;[47] there is, however, no provision such as exists in civil *Mareva* cases for cross-undertakings to indemnify innocent parties against any misuse or abuse of the proceedings.

The restraint order was created to help the Act fulfil the aim of denying those involved in drug trafficking the benefits of their criminal acts and is designed solely to prevent the proceeds of crime being dissipated before a confiscation order can be made. The power of restraint does not permit the preservation of assets to satisfy a fine as was suggested by the Hodgson Committee.

A restraint order is a serious interference with the normal rights of a person holding property, and it is provided that the order (and any charging order) must be discharged if the proposed proceedings are not instituted within such time as the court considers reasonable.[48]

The application for a restraint order must contain[49] the grounds for believing that the defendant has benefited from drug trafficking and a statement that either proceedings for a drug trafficking offence have been or will be instituted against the defendant[50] and as far as possible particulars of the realisable property in respect of which the order is sought, and the person or persons holding such property. These requirements give some protection against 'fishing' applications. When examining the practical operation of the Act, the Home Affairs Committee found that the necessity of obtaining restraint orders from the High Court was possibly giving defendants time to transfer cash out of their bank accounts, and it was recommended that responsibility for issuing restraint orders could be devolved to District Registries of the High Court.[51] Although this recommendation was accepted by the Government[52] it has not been acted upon.

Property caught by a restraint order

The reach of a restraint order is defined in section 8 which provides that it shall apply to all 'realisable property' held by a specified person, whether the property is described in the order or not,[53] and all realisable property transferred to a specified person after the making of the order.[54] 'Realisable property' is defined[55] as any property held by the defendant and any property held by a person to whom the defendant had directly or indirectly made a gift

---

[47] The analogy with the Mareva injunction was accepted in *Re the Drug Trafficking Offences Act 1986* (unreported, Webster J., Mar. 1987); *Re Peters* [1988] Q.B. 871 (C.A.) and *Re I.* (unreported, MacPherson J., July 1988) but its limitations were noted in *Re R.* [1990] 2 Q.B. 307.

[48] DTOA, s. 7(4), as amended by Criminal Justice Act 1988, Sch. 5, paras. 1, 2.

[49] R.S.C. Ord. 115, r. 3.

[50] See ibid., r. 3(2)(*b*) (as amended by SI 1989 No. 386).

[51] *Drug Trafficking and Related Serious Crime*, Seventh Report, Session 1988–9, HC 370,, at para 73.

[52] *Government Response to the Seventh Report from the Home Affairs Committee*, Cm: 1164, Recommendation 16.   [53] DTOA, s. 8(2)(*a*).

[54] Ibid., s. 8(2)(*b*).   [55] Ibid., s. 5(1).

caught by the Act.[56] When these definitions are deciphered it can be seen that the consequences of a restraint order are far-reaching and that persons other than the defendant may be adversely, and quite unfairly, affected.

For example, if A (suspected of being involved in drug trafficking) has given a car to his wife B, not only the car but all of B's other property, from whatever source it came, can be restrained. The policy of the Act is to catch a large category of property pending detailed investigation as to exactly what may properly be subject to confiscation. The value of property held by persons other than the defendant may be included in the amount to be recovered from the defendant under the resulting confiscation order, and where a receiver is appointed under powers considered below,[57] those persons may be required to hand over some such property.

It is not just the recipients of gifts from the defendant who may be affected. It seems clear from the rather awkward drafting of section 5(4) that a person may 'hold' property in which he has only a limited interest, and almost inevitably an order will in practice catch all property in the possession of the named person, even that belonging to innocent third parties. Other third parties may supply goods or services to the person concerned, unaware of the fact that his assets are frozen and their bills will not be paid. A restraint order prohibits any 'dealing' with the relevant property.[58]

There are two provisions which may ease the position of third parties. The first is the provision in the Rules of the Supreme Court[59] that the order may be made subject to conditions and exceptions including but not limited to indemnifying third parties against expenses incurred in complying with the order and to providing for living and legal expenses of the defendant. The second is the possibility that the order may be discharged or varied in relation to any property[60] on the application of any person affected by the order.[61]

The courts are given no real guidance as to how they should exercise these powers. In *Re Watson*[62] it was observed that the purpose of a restraint order was to prevent the dissipation of assets, not to put the defendant in shackles. In that spirit, Hutchison J. suggested, obiter, that expenditure necessary to preserve and protect a legitimate business from collapse could probably be allowed. The courts have considered the question of legal expenses on a number of occasions.[63] The view has been taken that legal expenses include

---

[56] Defined in s. 5(9) as any gift made by the defendant within the six years before the institution of proceedings or a gift made at any time which was property received in connection with drug trafficking or which represented indirectly or directly property received in that connection.

[57] See p. 222.

[58] DTOA, s. 8(1). For a partial definition of 'dealing', of notable obscurity in its drafting, see s. 8(7).

[59] R.S.C. Ord. 115, r. 4.   [60] DTOA, s. 8(5).

[61] Ibid., s. 8(5A) added by Criminal Justice Act 1988, s.103(1) and Sched. 5, paras 1 and 3.

[62] Unreported, Hutchison J, 13 Feb. 1990.

[63] This topic has given rise to much difficulty and controversy in other jurisdictions, where a less generous stance has been adopted. See B. Fisse, 'Confiscation of Proceeds of Crime: Funny Money, Serious Legislation' (1989) 13 Crim. LJ 368, at 391–6.

whatever the defendant chooses to pay; there is no requirement that the expenses be 'reasonable',[64] nor any prohibition on the selection of 'Rolls-Royce' counsel.

The anxiety of the courts to protect lawyers' interests is clear in *Re Watson*.[65] The defendant was likely to incur very large legal costs due to the length of the trial. He had insufficient liquid assets to meet these expenses and in the event of a confiscation order being made counsel was going to be left out of pocket. Counsel therefore sought, by way of variation of the existing restraint order, to have a charge registered against the defendant's house so that in the event of such a confiscation order being made he would have a prior claim to the proceeds of any sale. This was allowed; it would be unfair to expect a lawyer to work when he might not be reimbursed for his time and effort.[66]

The courts have to balance the legitimate needs of those affected against the requirement that the assets are not dissipated. So, it was held in *Re Peters*[67] that variation would be allowed to provide £2,500 per term for the defendant's son's education, but would not extend to the release of a lump sum of £25,000 to set up a trust to provide for the boy's education.

There have been some cases where variations have been allowed where the apparent result is a diminishing of the assets, contrary to the whole purpose of the order. In *Re K*.[68] three bank accounts had been made the subject of a restraint order—two of the accounts had been credited with very large sums of money and on the security of these sums the bank had granted an overdraft facility in the third, coupled with a contractual right of combination of the accounts. At the time the restraint order was granted, the credit balance overall was some £700,000 and the bank sought a variation of the order to allow them to reduce that balance by combination to approximately £320,000. It was conceded by the bank that the money which had been used to credit the accounts (and so to obtain the overdraft) was the proceeds of drug trafficking. It is clear that the balances in the two accounts which were in credit, considered separately, were 'realisable property' quite properly the subject of a restraint order which directed that those assets be not diminished. Although for certain purposes the *value* of realisable property takes into account specified obligations having priority to the defendant's interest,[69] property subject to such an obligation is not removed from the category of 'realisable property'; and the bank's rights were in any case not within the class of prior obligations for this purpose. So far as the overdraft was concerned, the bank was in the position of a creditor with security which was likely to prove valueless given the operation of the Act; many other creditors

[64] *Re I.* (unreported, MacPherson J., 13 July 1988).
[65] Unreported, Hutchison J., 13 Feb. 1990.
[66] See further *D.P.P.* v. *P and W*, The Times, 11 Apr. 1990 (solicitor allowed to register a charge over a client's house, lest confiscation order be made).   [67] [1988] Q.B. 871 (C.A.).
[68] [1990] 2 Q.B. 298 (D.C.).   [69] See DTOA, s. 5 (3)(4)(7).

are in this position, and it is not obvious that a bank deserves special consideration. Otton J., however, not only varied the restraint order but indicated that, even without relying on any contractual terms, a bank could assert a common-law right of combination in respect of the accounts and could give effect to it without any application to the court, as the assets were not being 'diminished'. With respect, the judgment is far from convincing in its consideration of the Act and seems to give a priority to the claims of banks for which the Act provides no basis.

In *Re R.*[70] a restraint order was made as to all the defendant's property which included a lease of an industrial unit. The landlords sought a variation of the restraint order to allow them to forfeit the lease and sell the machinery that had been installed by the defendant. Otton J. pointed out that the right to be a tenant of property was an asset which was quite rightly covered by the order, but then decided that allowing the landlord to terminate the lease was not a diminishing of the assets and the order was varied accordingly.

These decisions show a willingness on the part of the courts to protect third parties to an extent seemingly not contemplated by the Act, so denying the Crown the right to restrain the dissipation of the proceeds of crime.

Finally, while it is competent for a third party to apply for variation of a restraint order to release his property, it is also permissible for the defendant to apply for variation to increase the amount of funds available to meet his living expenses and legal fees. This variation may also permit the release of money to finance an appeal, even where without the funds the defendant would be eligible for legal aid and in the event of the appeal failing, the funds available to satisfy a confiscation order would be substantially reduced.[71]

Compensation

Where proceedings are commenced against a person for a drug trafficking offence and no conviction results, or a conviction is obtained but later quashed or a royal pardon granted, the High Court may order the payment of compensation to any person who held realisable property and who suffered loss as a result of the making of a charging or restraint order.[72] Compensation can only be ordered if there is shown to have been some serious default on the part of someone concerned with the investigation or prosecution of the offence; but if the proceedings would have been instituted even if the serious default had not occurred, no compensation may be ordered.[73] Compensation is not available in cases where either a restraint or charging order was imposed but no proceedings were ever instituted.

[70] [1990] 2 Q.B. 307.
[71] *Commissioners of Customs and Excise* v. *Norris* [1991] 2 All E.R. 395 (C.A.).
[72] DTOA, s. 19(1)(2) as amended by Criminal Justice Act 1988, Sch. 5, paras 1, 12.
[73] DTOA, s. 19(2)(*a*), (2A) as amended and added by Criminal Justice Act 1988, Sch. 5, paras. 1, 12.

Similar provisions as to compensation are found in the Criminal Justice Act 1988, applying to offences outside the drug trafficking area.[74]

Disclosure orders

Just as a *Mareva* injunction may be accompanied by a disclosure order, so may a similar order be made in aid of a restraint order. That this jurisdiction existed was confirmed by the Court of Appeal in *Re O*.[75] This was a case under the provisions as to the proceeds of crime contained in the Criminal Justice Act 1988, which in many respects follow those of the Drug Trafficking Offences Act 1986 but contain no reference to production orders;[76] the Court of Appeal regarded its judgment as applying equally in the context of the 1986 Act. It also recognized that an order made in these circumstances could not deprive any person of the privilege against self-incrimination.[77] It was, however, proper to make a disclosure order if adequate protection were afforded, for example, if the prosecutor gave an undertaking not to use any of the information obtained under it for any purpose in the prosecution of an offence alleged to have been committed by the person making disclosure, or his or her spouse. Such a term is made a condition of the order.

In *Re Hosein*[78] it was held that a disclosure order could properly require information about property received during a period extending back from the date of the order; it need not be limited to a statement of presently held assets. The justification for this is that some of the previous history is needed to enable the prosecution to satisfy themselves that full disclosure of present assets is being made. Although a similar order will not be made in the context of a civil *Mareva* injunction,[79] that is because other methods of 'policing' obedience, including cross-examination of the person enjoined may be made available in that context but would be inappropriate here.

Criminal Justice Act 1988

The Criminal Justice Act 1988, which applies to offences outside the drug trafficking area,[80] contains provisions corresponding to those in the 1986 Act permitting the making of restraint or charging orders to preserve property until such time as a confiscation order may be made.[81] A disclosure order has been held to be implicit in section 77 as essential for the proper functioning of the restraint order.[82]

---

[74] Criminal Justice Act 1988, s. 89. For the Act generally, see pp. 224–7.

[75] [1991] 1 All E.R. 330 (C.A.).   [76] As to which see above, pp. 192–3.

[77] See, to the same effect, an earlier unreported decision, not cited to the Court of Appeal, *Re Drug Trafficking Offences Act 1986*, The Times, 7 Apr. 1987.

[78] Unreported, Kennedy J., 20 Mar. 1991.

[79] *Bekhor Ltd* v. *Bilton*, [1981] 2 All E.R. 565, (C.A.),

[80] See further pp. 224–7.   [81] Ibid., ss. 76–9.

[82] See above; thus where the restraint order is quashed, the discovery order must also fall: *Re K.* [1990] 2 Q.B. 298 (D.C.).

Similar Developments in Australia and Canada

There has been a parallel development of a restraint power in the various Australian jurisdictions and in Canada; the form of the legislation shows interesting variations.

For example, the South Australian legislation contains a relatively limited power, for the making of 'sequestration orders'. The court acts on an *ex-parte* application by the Attorney-General, and must be satisfied that there are reasonable grounds to suspect that certain property is liable to forfeiture under the South Australian legislation or the corresponding legislation of another Australian jurisdiction. The owner of the property may be heard on the question whether an order should continue in force. Its effect is to prohibit, subject to any express exceptions, any dealing with the property; the order may provide for the management and control of the property. The order lapses if no charge is laid within two months, and if the proceedings turn out to be unsuccessful.[83]

There is a more developed set of provisions as to 'restraining orders' in the New South Wales legislation.[84] Under these provisions, application may be made *ex-parte* by an 'appropriate officer', usually the Solicitor for Public Prosecutions, when a person has been, or is about to be, charged under the Act; the court must be satisfied that the person concerned is likely to be charged within 48 hours. The order applies to property of the person charged or about to be charged, either specified property or all his property; or in respect of specified property of a person other than the defendant, if it was the instrumentalities or proceeds of the offence. The court must be satisfied that there is a prospect of either a forfeiture or a pecuniary penalty order being made. The order may direct the Public Trustee to take control of all or part of the property, and may make provision for meeting the reasonable living and business expenses of the defendant out of the property. The State may be required to give undertakings as to damages or costs, or both. The Act provides in effect for forfeiture or pecuniary penalty orders to be discharged by the use of the restrained property. The order lapses after six months, but this period may be extended by the Supreme Court.

The legislation in other States is broadly similar, but has a number of differences from that in New South Wales:

(1) The court must be satisfied before making an order in any case that there is an unacceptable risk of the property being dealt with or disposed of so as to prevent a confiscation order being complied with.
(2) An ex parte order may be made only in an urgent case, and can have effect only for seven days.

---

[83] S.A., s. 6.

[84] N.S.W., Part 3 Division 2. The Northern Territory legislation is similar, being based on the earlier N.S.W. legislation, now repealed: N.T., Part. IV.

(3) The initial period of validity of a restraining order is twelve months, not six.

These same features, except for the last and with the substitution of fourteen for seven days in the second, are found in the Commonwealth legislation,[85] but there are some additional features including an express power to include in the order conditions as to meeting out of the property the person's reasonable expenses in defending a criminal charge, and specified debts incurred in good faith; and it is made clear that living expenses include those of dependants.

Restraint orders may be made under the Canadian legislation on an *ex-parte* application by the Attorney-General. The order, which prohibits 'any person from disposing of, or otherwise dealing with any interest in, the property specified in the order otherwise than in such manner as may be specified in the order'[86] and may also provide for the appointment of a person to manage the property, may be made if the judge is satisfied that there are reasonable grounds to believe that property exists in respect of which a forfeiture order may be made. The order expires after six months, unless the Attorney-General establishes that the property may still be required for forfeiture or as evidence or for the purposes of investigation.[87]

The novel feature of the Canadian legislation is the developed nature of the safeguards for those whose property may be affected by restraint orders, safeguards broadly comparable to those available once actual forfeiture has been ordered. Other legislative models proceed on the assumption that restraining orders are summary orders with no final effect on property rights; that is true, but the freezing of assets for six or more months may be a serious interference with an individual's rights and be highly detrimental to his economic interests. Under the Canadian provisions the judge may require notice to be given, before a restraint order is made, to persons appearing to have a valid interest in the property unless such notice 'would result in the disappearance, dissipation or reduction in value of the property so that all or a part thereof could not be subject to' forfeiture.[88] After a restraint order has been made, any person interested in the property can apply for leave to examine the property or for variation of the order; the latter procedure is available not only for the protection of innocent third parties but also in cases where some other adequate security is tendered, or to provide for reasonable living expenses (including those of dependants) and reasonable business and legal expenses.[89]

---

[85] Cwlth., Part 3, Division 2.
[86] Criminal Code, s. 420.13(3)(*a*), as added in 1988.
[87] Ibid., s. 420.15.   [88] Ibid., s. 420.13(5).
[89] Ibid., s. 420.14.

(C) Confiscation

An order for the confiscation of property, although an essential weapon in the armoury of law enforcement agencies in this field, does raise a number of legal issues of some complexity, and these may have constitutional implications. These arise out of the practical realities of the case. It is almost inevitable that funds illegally obtained will be mixed, perhaps inextricably mixed, with funds obtained by more orthodox means; it is most unlikely that clear and accurate accounts will be maintained, so that proof of the source of property will often be difficult and may need to be supported by statutory presumptions or reversal of the normal burden of proof;[90] an assortment of third parties will have interests in the funds, some of whom will be wholly innocent of complicity in the criminal enterprise. There will be a range of degrees of independence of the third parties: some will be associates of the criminals, some family members, some corporate bodies wholly or partly controlled (perhaps through a series of nominees and holding companies) by those involved in the offences.

Such an order can be framed in two different ways. It can be an order related primarily to a *person*, making him liable to pay over to the Crown or the State the value of the proceeds of his criminal activities; this type of order is commonly called a 'confiscation order' or, especially in Australian legislation, a 'pecuniary penalty order'. Its principal disadvantage is that it is often enforceable only against the offender's assets: property which belongs to, or is in the possession of, the offender. Unless an extended meaning is given to ownership or possession for this purpose, proceeds held by an associate or relative of the offender, by a 'shell' company, or otherwise removed from his formal entitlement, will escape confiscation. A variant is the provision found for example in New Zealand enabling increased fines to be imposed having regard to assets acquired by the offender as a result of drug dealing offences other than that for which he was convicted.[91]

A more powerful weapon is an order related primarily to *property*, identified as being or as representing the proceeds of crime and declared to be forfeited to the Crown or the State: a 'forfeiture order'. In this case the identity of the person in whose hands the property is found is either immaterial or material only if that person's innocence is established. The range of property subject to seizure is wider, and appropriately so, but there is a corresponding need to devise procedures for the protection of innocent third parties into whose hands the property has been transferred.

A practical consideration, of great importance in considering the relevant merits of these two approaches, is the need to secure international enforcement

---

[90] e.g. in the Guyana legislation in the drugs area (the Narcotics Drugs and Psychotropic Substances (Control) Act 1988), all the offender's property is liable to forfeiture unless he shows it to have been innocently acquired.

[91] Misuse of Drugs Amendment Act 1978 (N.Z.), s. 39.

of orders. The facility with which assets, particularly in the form of financial credits of some sort, can be passed across national boundaries means that an order enforceable only in the country of origin may be of limited value. It is undoubtedly the case that the 'confiscation order' approach, enforcing a pecuniary penalty against a convicted offender, presents fewer difficulties in this context than forfeiture.

This can be appreciated from the consideration of a case in which a forfeiture order made in State A purports to declare forfeit a corpus of property which includes property (and perhaps land) in State B. In State B legal title to the property is vested in X, a citizen of State B, who has not been the subject of any criminal proceedings. Quite apart from the entrenched approach giving primacy to the *lex situs* in matters of title to property, the attempt to enforce the order in State B and so to seize what is formally X's property will almost certainly raise constitutional arguments about the right to enjoy property, and also about due process. Even if these difficulties are absent, or can be overcome, it is not at all easy to graft procedures for the protection of innocent third parties appearing in State B on the enforcement of what purports to be a final order made in State A.

There is, however, another element in the total picture. Where a jurisdiction has created an offence of money-laundering, the effect is that the practical difference between the confiscation order and the forfeiture order approaches is much reduced. The latter approach seeks to reach property held by third parties, linked in some way to the primary offender but not themselves convicted of the primary offence. If, however, such a third party can himself be convicted of money-laundering, the confiscation order approach can be applied to him and to the property he controls. And if he can be convicted in State B of laundering the proceeds of a crime which took place in State A, some of the difficulties of international enforcement are circumvented.

CONFISCATION UNDER THE DRUG TRAFFICKING OFFENCES ACT

When a person has been convicted of one or more drug trafficking offences,[92] the Crown Court must determine whether he has benefited from drug trafficking.[93] The courts have made it clear that the use of the 1986 Act is now mandatory, in the sense that there is no choice between making a confiscation order under its provisions and a forfeiture order under section 43 of the Powers of Criminal Courts Act.[94]

Determining whether a defendant has benefited from drug trafficking involves a finding that he has[95] 'received any payment or other reward in

---

[92] Defined in DTOA, s. 38(1). A confiscation order cannot be made after a conviction for mere possession: *Blackford* (1989) 89 Cr. App. R. 239 (C.A.).

[93] DTOA, s. 1(1)(2).

[94] *R* v. *Stuart* (1989) 11 Cr. App. R. (S) 89 (cash found in the possession of the defendant).

[95] At any time, including a time before the coming into force of the Act: s. 1(3).

connection with drug trafficking'.[96] The courts have made it clear that 'payment' is not synonymous with 'profit'; the *gross* receipts are relevant, and not the net profit left in the defendant's hands after the transaction is complete.[97] However, the actual confication order is based on the amount which the court finds to be realisable at the time,[98] giving a result not dissimilar from the recommendation of the Hodgson Committee that the court make an allowance for expenses, whether legitimate or otherwise.[99]

A payment is relevant whenever it is 'in connection with' drug trafficking; the money does not have to be used directly in drug transactions or be a payment for services rendered. An example is *Osei*[100] where the money was provided, apparently by way of loan, so that a courier could satisfy the immigration officers that she had adequate means of support. A 'reward' need not be in monetary form.[101]

The Act contains elaborate procedures for assessing the proceeds of drug trafficking including provision for the court to make certain assumptions. Where there is prima facie evidence[102] that property has been held by the defendant at any time since his conviction or has been transferred to him within the previous six years, it is assumed to have been received as a payment or reward for drug trafficking carried on by him.[103] It was held in *Dickens* that the onus lies on the prosecution to prove that the defendant has benefited from drug trafficking and the amount of that benefit, the standard of proof being the criminal standard but subject to the assumptions that can be made under section 2.[104]

Any expenditure during the six year period is assumed to have been made out of payments received in connection with drug trafficking.[105] Of course the defendant may seek to show that the assumptions are incorrect (in effect, to rebut the presumption) but the assumptions amount to a partial reversal of the burden of proof otherwise resting on the prosecution. Where the ownership of certain property is disputed, the matter should be decided by the Crown Court when determining to what extent the defendant benefited from drug trafficking rather than through an application for variation of a restraint order.[106]

When assessing the defendant's benefit, evidence of an expensive life-style,

---

[96] Ibid. Where co-defendants share payments or rewards the court should still make individual orders against each defendant: *R. v. Porter* [1990] 1 W.L.R. 1260 (C.A.).

[97] *R. v. Smith (Ian)* [1989] 1 W.L.R. 765 (C.A.).   [98] DTOA, ss. 4, 5.

[99] See *R. v. Comiskey* (1991) 93 Cr.App.R.227 (where however the court seems to have applied an arbitrary deduction in a way difficult to justify by reference to the language of the Act).   [100] (1988) 10 Cr. App. R. (S) 289 (C.A.).

[101] Ibid., giving the example of a free air ticket.

[102] *Dickens* [1990] 2 All E.R. 626, 629 (C.A.).

[103] DTOA, s. 2(3)(*a*). See generally ss. 2 and 3.

[104] *Dickens* [1990] 2 All E.R. 626, 629 (C.A.); *R v. Enwezor* [1991] Crim. L.R. 483 (C.A.). For the right of the defendant to give evidence during the enquiry into the alleged benefit, see *R. v. Jenkins* [1991] Crim.L.R. 481 (C.A.).

[105] DTOA, s.2(3)(*b*).   [106] *Re Rose*, unreported, 6 Dec. 1989.

suggesting a high level of expenditure, will be very relevant. The courts recognize that drug traffickers do not keep audited accounts[107] and informed guesses by the trial judge have to be made; the evidence of the proceeds must be admissible,[108] and the notebook jottings of drug sales by a third party do not meet this requirement.[109] The Court of Appeal will not disturb an informed guess by a judge, where, as is usually the case, the defendant's failure to give detailed information created the difficulty.[110]

Once the assessment process is complete, the court must make a confiscation order[111] and decide the amount to be recovered by way of the order. The drafting of the Act seems almost calculated to obscure the important fact that the scope of a confiscation order is not the same as that of 'realisable property'. Instead, the maximum amount of the confiscation order is 'the amount that might be realised' at the time the order is made.[112] The two phrases have different meanings, the former being directly relevant only in the restraint order context; both are contained in section 5 of the Act. 'The amount that might be realised' is defined as the total of the values at the date of the order of all realisable property held by the defendant (less amounts payable in respect of a few prior obligations)[113] together with the total of the values at that time of all gifts caught by the Act.[114]

In some cases the court will find that nothing could be realised, in which case the mandatory assessment procedure achieves nothing.[115] In other cases, despite the fact that 'payments' are taken at the gross figure the amount that can be realised will be much less. A trafficker with a 'turnover' of £1 million may show a profit of, say, £300,000. The amount that can be realised may well be less than the £1 million; but if the defendant has assets of that value they may be confiscated, as it is immaterial that some of them were obtained quite legitimately.[116]

The Court of Appeal has now held that the burden of proving that the amount that might be realised is less than the value of the proceeds lies with the defendant; if he does not make any attempt to show that a lesser amount is applicable, the court does not have to undertake this assessment itself, and

---

[107] See *Fagher* (1989) 16 N.S.W.L.R. 67.   [108] *Dickens*, above.

[109] *R* v. *Chrastny (No 1)*, The Times, 14 Mar. 1991.

[110] *Small* (1989) 88 Cr. App. R. 184; *Dickens*, above. See also *Hopes* (1989) 11 Cr. App. R. (S) 38 (property in Australia and Wales; defence declined to produce evidence to prove that purchased from lawful earnings; order upheld).

[111] Compare Criminal Justice Act 1988 where the making of the order is discretionary and there are no provisions corresponding to ss. 2 and 3 of the 1986 Act. Under the Criminal Justice (Scotland) Act 1987, confiscation orders are also discretionary.

[112] DTOA, s. 4(3).   [113] See s. 5(7).

[114] Ibid., s. 5(3). For the gifts, see s. 5(9) and above, p. 000, n. 00. It is important that the value of assets be identified as at the time of the order: *R.* v. *Lemmon* [1991] Crim. L.R. 791 (C.A.) (house wrongly valued, trial judge having accepted out-of-date valuation).

[115] e.g. *Bragason* (1988) 10 Cr. App. R. (S) 258; but as the commentator at [1988] Crim. L.R. 778 rightly observes, property outside the jurisdiction should be taken into account, as international enforcement procedures are becoming available. Boats in Spain were treated as relevant in *Dickens* [1990] 2 All E.R. 626 (C.A.).   [116] See *R.* v. *Chrastny* [1991] Crim.L.R. 721 (C.A.).

can assume that the two sums are the same.[117] This contrasts with the way that the courts had previously been dealing with this, as in most cases the court took it upon itself to determine whether the amount that might be realised was less than the total of the defendant's benefit from drug trafficking.

Property held by third parties

There are further complexities as regards assets given to others. Lord Lane CJ examined aspects of these issues in *Dickens*.[118] There a Range Rover had been bought by the appellant within the relevant period, given by him to his wife, and (it seems) sold by her for value to a solicitor acting in good faith. The Range Rover was clearly not 'realisable property' within section 5(1), because it was no longer 'property held by a person to whom the defendant has . . . made a gift'. If the wife still retained the sale proceeds, they would be 'realisable property'; but those facts did not appear. As Lord Lane CJ rightly held, the relevant phrase in section 4(3) is 'the amount that might be realised'. This includes[119] the value as at the time of the order of all relevant gifts. This meant that the current value of the Range Rover (which might, of course, be less than, or more than, the actual sale proceeds) was to be included in the amount specified in the confiscation order.

One odd result is this: if the appellant had himself sold the car and had spent the proceeds on an expensive foreign holiday, its value would be ignored;[120] but if the wife had sold the car, and spent the proceeds in exactly the same way, the current market value of the car would be taken into account.[121] There is an element of rough justice in all this, but the courts have no discretion. Unlike some comparable legislation in other jurisdictions, possible hardship to the offender or his family is irrelevant; *Preston*[122] is misleading in so far as it suggests that it might be relevant that the sole realisable asset was the matrimonial home still occupied by the wife and children.[123]

A further example of the problems faced by third parties is found in the case of *R. v. Robson*[124] where a confiscation order was made on the basis that the defendant had an interest in a house which was in his mother's name. The court held that, although sums had been paid to her by the defendant which had been used to pay the mortgage and although the payments by the defendant could be assumed to be the proceeds of drug trafficking, there was no intent such as was required to create an interest in the house. If the order

---

[117] *R. v. Isemann* (1990) 12 Cr.App.R.(S) 398; *R. v. Comiskey* (1990) 12 Cr.App.R.(S) 562; *R. v. Carroll* [1991] Crim.L.R. 720 (C.A.).

[118] [1990] 2 All E.R. 626 (C.A.). [119] DTOA, s. 5(3).

[120] Because it would not be within the 'value of all the realisable property held by' him: s. 5(3)(*a*).

[121] DTOA, ss. 5(3) *in fine*, (4)(*b*). [122] [1990] Crim. L.R. 528 (C.A.).

[123] The appellant did not ultimately press for a reduction in the order; a reduction might have been justified under s. 5(4) to take account of the mortgagee's interest.

[124] (1991) 92 Cr. App. R. 1 (C.A.)

had been allowed to stand, the effects for the mother would have been quite severe; Rose J. commented on the extraordinary consequence of an Act which allowed the court such draconian powers as could deprive the owner of property of some or all of his beneficial interest without allowing him any opportunity to be heard.

Confiscation orders and sentencing

A confiscation order must be made before the court passes sentence;[125] however, except in the context of a fine[126] and certain other orders involving payments by the offender or forfeiture of his property, the court is directed to leave the order out of account in fixing the sentence.[127] The trial judge may receive, before he passes sentence, a great deal of material as to the defendant's financial circumstances over the previous six years; and make certain assumptions as to receipts being derived from drug trafficking; as part of the assessment procedure the defendant may have accepted that certain payments were so derived (though this acceptance will not be admissible evidence in any proceedings for an offence[128]). Much of this material will relate to matters not within the indictment, and will be governed by rules which place a heavy evidential burden on the defendant.

The Court of Appeal has emphasized in this context the principle that the actual sentence must relate only to matters covered in the indictment[129] but has also approved serious inroads into that principle. According to the Court of Appeal it is permissible to take note of the material gathered at the assessment stage as a basis for sentencing the defendant as a 'professional' criminal; this on the basis of a fragile distinction between sentencing for offences of which he had not been convicted, which was prohibited, and taking into account 'the degree of criminality' involved.

In R. v. Saunders[130] it was held that this should be subject to the provisos that the information used was proved to the criminal standard, and that the judge should ensure that he was not influenced by the adverse assumptions that he is entitled to make under the Act. A similar approach was taken in Harper,[131] where material relating to a house and a car purchased almost a year before the date of the offences of which Harper stood convicted was taken into account not so as to increase the sentence which would otherwise have been imposed but to prevent it being reduced (i.e. by relying on the material to negative a suggestion in mitigation that Harper was not a regular offender).

---

[125] Cf. the procedure under the Criminal Justice (Scotland) Act 1987, where the prosecutor's application for a (discretionary) confiscation order must be made before the sentencing, but provision is made (s. 2) for a postponed confiscation order.

[126] See e.g. Hedley (1990) 90 Cr. App. R. 70.

[127] DTOA, s. 1(5). For appeal purposes, the order is part of the sentence: R v. Johnson [1991] 2 Q.B.249 (C.A.).

[128] DTOA, s. 3(6).

[129] Bragason (1988) 10 Cr. App. R. (S) 258.

[130] (1991) 92 Cr. App. R. 6.

[131] (1989) 11 Cr. App. R. (S) 240.

It must be admitted that the present procedure makes the task of the sentencer peculiarly difficult, but given the admittedly Draconian nature of confiscation orders and the quite exceptional evidential rules affecting them, it is submitted that the courts must be particularly scrupulous in observing the normal principles governing sentencing.

Possible reforms

The operation of these provisions was examined in a report published in 1991 of a Home Office Working Group on Confiscation.[132] This group was established to review the operation of the restraint, confiscation and money laundering provisions and to identify areas where changes were needed as a matter of priority, bearing in mind the needs of practitioners and the key role of the confiscation powers in the fight against drug trafficking and other serious crime. The Working Group's first report concentrated on the Drug Trafficking Offences Act 1986 where problems requiring urgent attention mainly concerned the assessment of benefit and making of confiscation orders.

The first matter concerned the absence of guidance in the Act as to when the assumptions in section 2 should be used. The section merely says that

the Court *may*, for the purpose of determining whether the defendant has benefited from drug trafficking and, if he has, of assesssing the value of his proceeds of drug trafficking, make the following assumptions. . .[133]

It was recommended that the assumptions should be made in all cases unless the court was satisfied by the defendant or on the basis of any other information made available to it, either during the trial or otherwise, that it would be inappropriate to do so. Where the court did not apply the assumptions, it would be required to state its reasons so that these could be subject to challenge in a higher court. The assumptions would, of course, not be applied where it was obvious that they were incorrect.[134]

Secondly, the Working Group noted concern that often the information necessary for considering a confiscation order was not available immediately after conviction. As the Act requires the decisions as to confiscation to be taken before the convicted person is sentenced or otherwise dealt with,[135] this created delays in sentencing.[136] Under the Act, the prosecution tenders statements giving its view of the facts relevant to the assessment of the benefits received; delays may be caused by a need to amend this statement as a result of evidence presented at the trial or by the unwillingness or inability of the defence to respond to the statement until after conviction. The Working Group recommended that courts should be able to defer decisions on

---

[132] *Home Office Working Group on Confiscation, Report on the Drug Trafficking Offences Act 1986*, May 1991. [133] DTOA, s. 2(2) (emphasis added).
[134] *Home Office Working Group Report*, at para 2.6 *et seq.* [135] DTOA, s. 1(4).
[136] *Home Office Working Group Report*, above, at para 2.3.

confiscation for up to 6 months and in the meantime require the defence to respond to the prosecution statement; if the defendant failed to do so the court would be able to draw adverse inferences from his silence. Sentencing the defendant would be permitted, but the courts would not be allowed to make any order, such as a fine, which would have to take into account any sum made payable under a confiscation order.[137]

The Working Group also examined the uncertainties and difficulties that had been experienced as to the onus and standard of proof at various stages in the process. *Dickens*[138] held that the criminal standard of proof applied to the assessment of the benefits obtained by drug-trafficking, but the position at later stages remained unclear. The Working Group while noting that the criminal standard of proof was also required in the similar but not identical context of the Criminal Justice (Scotland) Act 1987,[139] recommended that once the conviction had been obtained the civil standard of proof should be applied, in determining whether the defendant had benefited from drug trafficking, in the assessment of those benefits, and in assessing the amount that might be realised for the purposes of the confiscation order.[140]

Enforcement of confiscation orders

The Drug Trafficking Offences Act 1986 contains a number of provisions relevant to the enforcement of orders. Section 9 enables the High Court to make a charging order on certain types of realisable property, essentially land and certain types of securities,[141] for securing the payment to the Crown an amount not exceeding the amount payable under the confiscation order.[142] A charging order can also be made at an earlier stage, that is before the making of the confiscation order, and is then to the full value of the affected property.[143] Notice of the making of the charging order must be given to persons affected by it, who may apply for its variation or discharge.[144]

Where a confiscation order has been made and is not subject to appeal, the High Court may exercise further powers, in particular that of appointing a receiver. The receiver may be authorized to take a variety of steps: to enforce a charging order; to take pos%esion of other realisable property; and to realise such property.[145] Third parties in whose hands realisable property is to be found may be ordered to give possession of it to the receiver.[146] Where third parties are to be affected by these provisions, the court may not exercise its powers without giving them the opportunity to make representations.[147]

---

[137] *Home Office Working Group Report*, para. 2.11.
[138] [1990] 2 All E.R. 626 (C.A.). See also *Enwezor* [1991] Crim. L.R. 483 (C.A.).
[139] The Scottish rules are under review: see Scottish Law Commission: *Forfeiture and Confiscation*. Discussion Paper No. 82, June 1989.
[140] *Home Office Working Group Report*, paras 2.5–2.10.   [141] DTOA, s. 9(5).
[142] Ibid., s. 9(1).   [143] Ibid., s. 9(1)(*a*).
[144] Ibid., s. 9(3)(8) as substituted and added by Criminal Justice Act 1988, s. 103(1) and Sch. 5, paras 1, 4.   [145] DTOA, s. 11.
[146] Ibid., s. 11(4); and see s. 11(6) for additional powers.   [147] Ibid., s. 11(8).

Where the powers just described are not exercised, compensation orders fall to be enforced much as if they were fines imposed by the Crown Court.[148] As the Home Office Working Group on Confiscation noted, the end result was a disappointing level of recovery, of only £1.1 m in 1989/90 compared to £7.9 m in confiscation orders in 1989.[149] Some of the difficulties were due to the role of magistrates' courts in the enforcement process; those courts and their staff found it difficult to locate and take action against an offender's assets.[150] The Group recommended an enlarged role for the Crown Court, armed with three new weapons: an order similar to a garnishee order nisi, to become absolute after a set period unless an application was made by the person to whom it was addressed; a distress warrant, issued by the Crown Court but with the magistrates' court responsible for enforcement; and the immediate appointment of a receiver by the Crown Court.[151]

The Working Group also looked at the anomalous position which virtually allows the defendant the choice of paying the sum due under the confiscation order or spending longer in prison. It was felt that service of a longer sentence should no longer eradicate the duty to pay, and while service of an additional period could count as settlement of the penalty for non-payment it should not eradicate the debt itself.[152] There is some evidence that magistrates' courts were too ready to make orders for imprisonment in default, so relieving the offender from the need to comply with at least some part of the confiscation order; as the Divisional Court observed, 'This we would hold to be in total contradiction to the plain purpose and effect of the Drug Trafficking Offences Act 1986, which is that a person convicted of a drugs trafficking offence should be deprived of the proceeds of such offence to the extent that the same are realisable'.[153] Urging compliance with the Home Office Circulars[154] designed to ease the relationship of the Crown Prosecution Service and the enforcing court in such cases, the court held that the court should always hear the prosecutor before issuing a warrant of commitment, and should consider all other methods of enforcement before issuing such a warrant.

Variation of confiscation orders

There are a number of powers under which a confiscation order can be varied, notably that in section 14 of the 1986 Act which is only available on the application of the defendant who demonstrates that his realisable

---

[148] See ibid., s. 6 as amended by Criminal Justice Act 1988, s 170(2) and Sch. 16.
[149] *Home Office Working Group Report*, para. 3.2.
[150] In R v. *Harrow Justices, ex p. D.P.P.* [1991] 1 W.L.R. 395 it was noted that typically justices were being left to enforce confiscation orders, their standard practice being to make orders for committal in default of payment without necessarily considering all the options.
[151] *Home Office Working Group Report on Confiscation*, para 3.3.
[152] Ibid., para. 3.11.
[153] R. v. *Harrow Justices, ex parte D.P.P.* [1991] 3 All E.R. 873 (Q.B.D.).
[154] Circulars 98/1986 and 10/1988.

property is inadequate to make payment of any amount remaining to be recovered under the confiscation order.

There was no provision in the 1986 Act enabling the amount payable under the order to be *increased* to take account of assets which come to light after the order has been made, or of interest which may be earned on those assets. The Criminal Justice (International Co-operation) Act 1990 enables upward revision to take place only to the ceiling of the value of the proceeds as originally assessed by the Crown Court.[155] It was noted by the House of Commons Home Affairs Committee that the 1986 Act was deficient in this respect,[156]and that amendment was likely to be necessary to allow the United Kingdom to meet its obligations under the United Nations Vienna Convention.[157] The Home Office Working Group recommended in 1991 that any benefits which might come to light up to six years from the start of the original proceedings should be capable of confiscation.[158] This would extend to property which had, unknown to the prosecution, been in the defendant's possession at the time of conviction, and to any benefits accruing after that time which were derived from drug trafficking.

CONFISCATION UNDER THE CRIMINAL JUSTICE ACT 1988

The Hodgson Committee wanted to see a new general power of confiscation applying to all criminal offences. Once new powers had been introduced in relation to drug trafficking offences similar legislation of more general application followed. Part VI of the Criminal Justice Act 1988 extended the power of confiscation to certain serious non-drug-related offences. The scheme of the new Act was similar to that of the 1986 Act (to which it made a number of amendments, improving the 1986 model in a number of respects) but there are important differences. Despite these differences, the courts feel that cases on the interpretation of the 1986 Act apply equally to the interpretation of the Criminal Justice Act provisions and *vice versa*.[159]

Confiscation orders

The extension of the power of confiscation to offences other than drug trafficking offences is carried out by Part VI of the Act. The Act permits either the Crown Court or a magistrates' court to make a confiscation order[160] requiring a convicted person to pay such sum as the court thinks fit in addition to dealing with him in any other way.

The Crown Court's power to make such an order exists where a person is found guilty of any offence to which Part VI of the Act applies and the court is

---

[155] Criminal Justice (International Co-operation) Act, s. 16.
[156] *Drug Trafficking and Related Serious Crime* (7th Report of Home Affairs Committee, Session 1989–9, H.C. 370), para. 77.
[157] i.e. the Convention against Illicit Traffic in Narcotic Drugs and Psychotropic Substances 1988; see p. 000.   [158] *Home Office Working Group Report*, para. 4.2.
[159] e.g. *Re O* [1991] 1 All E.R. 330, per Lord Donaldson MR at p. 334.
[160] Criminal Justice Act 1988 (CJA), s. 71(1).

satisfied that that person has benefited from that offence or from that offence taken together with some other offence of which he is convicted in the same proceedings, or which was taken into consideration in determining his sentence.[161] Offences which come within the scope of Part VI of the Act are indictable offences other than drug trafficking offences, plus a few miscellaneous offences listed in Schedule 4 to the Act,[162] and, since the Prevention of Terrorism (Temporary Provisions) Act 1989, offences under Part III of that Act.[163] The court must also be satisfied that the defendant benefited to at least a prescribed minimum amount which at present stands at £10,000,[164] although this figure may be altered by the Secretary of State by statutory instrument.[165] This can be contrasted with the rules under the Drug Trafficking Offences Act 1986 where there is no minimum amount.

The powers of magistrates' courts to make confiscation orders are limited to cases where the offender is convicted of an offence listed in Schedule 4 to the Act. The offender must also satisfy the requirement of having benefited to at least the minimum amount.[166]

A person is considered to have benefited from an offence if he obtains property[167] *as a result of or*[168] in connection with its commission; his benefit is the value of the property so obtained.[169] Property 'derived in connection with the offence' has been held to include proceeds from a book which the applicants had written about their part in the release of the Soviet double agent George Blake.[170]

It should be noted that, the authorities on the Drug Trafficking Offences Act 1986 applying equally in this context,[171] the gross proceeds of crime are liable to confiscation with no permitted deduction for expenses.

The confiscation order must be made for at least the minimum amount, but may not exceed the lesser of either the benefit in respect of which it is made or the amount appearing to the court to be the amount that might be realised.[172] The amount that might be realised at the time a confiscation order

---

[161] Ibid., s. 71(2).

[162] These are offences relating to sex establishments, supplying video recordings of unclassified work, certain offences against the Video Recordings Act 1984, and the offence under the Cinemas Act 1985 of using unlicensed premises for an exhibition which requires a licence. This list may be amended by the Secretary of State by statutory instrument by either adding or deleting offences.

[163] CJA s.71(9)(c) as amended by the Prevention of Terrorism (Temporary Provisions) Act 1989, Sched 8, para. 10.   [164] Ibid., s. 71(2).

[165] Ibid., s. 71(9).   [166] Ibid., s. 71(3).

[167] Compare the equivalent s. 1(3) of DTOA ('payment or other reward'). Property is defined in CJA, s. 102 as including money and all other property, real or personal, heritable or movable, including things in action and other intangible or incorporeal property. Where a person derives a pecuniary advantage as a result of or in connection with the commission of an offence, he is to be treated as if he had obtained a sum of money equal to the value of the pecuniary advantage (s. 71(5)).

[168] The words italicized do not appear in the corresponding provision in DTOA (s. 1(3)).

[169] CJA, s. 71(4).   [170] *Re Randle and Pottle, The Independent*, 26 Mar. 1991.

[171] *Re O* [1991] 1 All E.R. 330, per Lord Donaldson MR at p. 334.   [172] CJA, s. 71(6).

is made is the total of the values at that time of all the realisable property[173] held by the defendant, less, where there are obligations having priority at that time,[174] the total of the amounts due under those obligations, together with the total of the values at that time of all gifts[175] caught by Part VI of the Act. 'Realisable property' means any property held by the defendant and also any property held by a person to whom the defendant has directly or indirectly made such a gift.[176] A major differences in approach as compared with the Drug Trafficking Offences Act 1986 is that the court cannot rely on any assumptions regarding the origin of the relevant moneys.

A gift is caught by the Act if two criteria are fulfilled.[177] First, it must have been made by the defendant at any time after the commission of the offence or the earliest of the offences to which the proceedings relate. Secondly, the court must consider it appropriate in all the circumstances to take it into account. This is another significant change to the basic scheme which was introduced under the 1986 Act, as by permitting the court a discretion there is greater scope for property not to be confiscated.

In the drug trafficking context, the court must embark upon the confication process. Under the Criminal Justice Act 1988, confiscation orders may only be made on the written application of the prosecutor. Notice is given by the prosecutor when it seems that the court would be able to make an order against the defendant for at least the minimum amount.[178] An order can only be made in respect of offences of which the defendant was convicted (or which were taken into account) in the same proceedings.

When deciding whether or not to exercise its discretion to make a confiscation order the court is entitled to take into account any information which shows that a victim of an offence to which the proceedings relate has instituted or intends to institute civil proceedings against the defendant in respect of loss, injury or damage sustained in connection with the offence.[179] Once the decision to make an order has been taken, the court determines the amount to be recovered and makes an order for that amount. This has to be done before sentencing or otherwise dealing with the offender.[180]

As in the Drug Trafficking Offences Act 1986, the prosecutor may make a statement relating to possible benefit that the defendant may have received or an assessment of the value of such benefit. Where this is accepted to any extent by the defendant, the court may treat this acceptance as conclusive of the matters to which it relates. Provided that the court is satisfied that a copy of such a statement has been served on the defendant, it may require him to indicate to what extent he accepts each allegation, and to the extent that he

[173] CJA, s. 74(4)–(6).
[174] Defined, ibid., s. 74(9).   [175] Defined, ibid, s. 74(7)–(8).
[176] Ibid., s. 74(1). Property is not realisable if it is affected by certain prior forfeiture orders (s. 74(2)), as amended by Sched. 8, para 10, of the Prevention of Terrorism (Temporary Provisions) Act 1989.
[177] CJA, s. 74(10), (12).   [178] CJA, s. 72.
[179] Ibid., s. 72(3).   [180] Ibid., s. 72(4).

does not, what he proposes to rely on. If the defendant does not comply he may be treated as accepting every allegation except (*a*) any one in respect of which he complied with the requirement; and (*b*) any allegation that he has benefited from an offence or that any property was obtained by him as a result of or in connection with the commission of an offence.[181]

PREVENTION OF TERRORISM (TEMPORARY PROVISIONS) ACT 1989

Following the introduction of the powers of restraint and confiscation under the 1986 and 1988 Acts, similar provision has been made in relation to offences connected with terrorism by the Prevention of Terrorism (Temporary Provisions) Act 1989. In order to catch a wider scope of activity, the 1989 Act also creates new offences of funding terrorism and proscribed organizations. Unlike the other Acts dealing with confiscation, this Act extends to England and Wales, Northern Ireland and Scotland.

Part III of the 1989 Act creates three new offences in relation to terrorism. First, it is an offence to seek or accept money or other property from third persons with the intention that it be applied or used in connection with acts of terrorism,[182] or with reasonable cause to suspect that it may be so used. The person who provides this money or other property is also guilty of an offence if he knows or has reasonable cause to suspect that it will be so used or applied.[183] It is also an offence to seek or accept money or other property for the benefit of a proscribed organization, to make such money or other property available, or to enter into or otherwise be concerned in an arrangement whereby money or other property is or is to be made available for the benefit of such an organization. It is a defence to prove in relation to the latter two offences that the defendant did not know and had no reasonable cause to suspect that the money was for a proscribed organization.[184]

Confiscation powers

The confication powers under the 1989 Act are found in section 13 and Schedule 4. Section 13 gives the court a series of powers to order forfeiture of money or other property relating to an offence under Part III of the Act when a person is convicted of that offence. The powers are not available unless the court considers that the money or property will otherwise be applied or used in connection with acts of terrorism,[185] but in the absence of evidence to the contrary, there is a presumption that it will be so used.[186] In proceedings in

---

[181] Ibid., s. 73.

[182] i.e. acts of terrorism connected with the affairs of Northern Ireland and acts of terrorism of any other description, done or to be done outside the United Kingdom, where it constitutes or would constitute an offence triable in the United Kingdom; but not acts connected solely with the affairs of the United Kingdom or any part of the United Kingdom other than Northern Ireland: s. 9(3)(4).

[183] 1989 Act, s. 9.

[184] 1989 Act, s. 10.

[185] As defined in s. 9; see above.

[186] 1989 Act, s. 13(5).

Scotland the court may not act except upon the application of the prosecutor.[187] Where someone other than the convicted person claims to be interested in anything which can be forfeited by an order the court must give him an opportunity to be heard before forfeiture is ordered.[188]

The procedural provisions dealing with the making of forfeiture and ancillary orders are contained in Schedule 4. They allow the court to direct that certain money or property be handed over, to give directions that certain property be sold, to appoint a receiver and to make any other provision that appears to be necessary.[189] Other ancillary powers correspond closely to provisions in the Criminal Justice Act 1988. The Act provides for the making of restraint orders in the same circumstances as under the 1988 Act, but they are narrower in scope than those under both that Act and the Drug Trafficking Offences Act 1986 as they apply only to dealings with the property which is liable to forfeiture.[190]

Other provisions

There is also provision for compensation in cases which do not result in a conviction,[191] for affording protection to persons disclosing to a constable a suspicion or belief or any matter on which it is based,[192] for the enforcement of orders made elsewhere in the British Isles and for the enforcement of orders made in designated countries.[193] An order for production of related material may be made under wide powers set out in Schedule 7 to the Act.

PARALLEL DEVELOPMENTS IN OTHER COMMONWEALTH COUNTRIES

Confiscation or pecuniary penalty orders

Confiscation orders are found in almost all the Australian jurisdictions which have enacted provisions on the proceeds of crime,[194] but in the guise of 'pecuniary penalty orders' a designation adopted to avoid possible constitutional difficulties.

Power to make a pecuniary penalty order for an amount equal to the assessed value of the benefits derived by the defendant because of having committed the offence is given by most of the Australian Acts,[195] but the provisions as to the method of assessing the value of those benefits vary slightly.

The Victorian legislation, after providing that in fixing the amount to be paid the court must subtract from the value of the benefits the value of any

---

[187] 1989 Act, s. 13(7).
[188] Ibid., s. 13(6).   [189] 1989 Act, Sched. 4, para 1.
[190] See Sch. 4, para. 3.   [191] Ibid., para. 27.
[192] 1989 Act, s. 12.   [193] Ibid., Sch. 4, paras. 8–10.
[194] South Australia exceptionally provides a forfeiture power only.
[195] Cwlth, s. 26; N.S.W., s. 24; Vic., s. 12; W.A., s. 15, Qd., s. 13; N.T., s. 10.

property made subject to a forfeiture order and any amount payable by way of restitution or compensation[196] provides that in assessing benefits the court:

may treat as benefits such things as it thinks fit, including:

(a) any property (whether situated within or outside Victoria) that was derived or realised, directly or indirectly, by that person or another person, at the request or by the direction of the first-mentioned person, as the result of the commission of the offence;

(b) any benefit, service or financial advantage provided (whether within or outside Victoria) for that person or another person, at the request or by the direction of the first-mentioned person, as the result of the commission of the offence;

(c) any increase in the total value of that person's property (whether situated within or outside Victoria) in the period beginning immediately before the commission of the offence and ending at some time after the commission of the offence that the court is not satisfied was due to causes unrelated to the commission of the offence.[197]

The provisions in the Commonwealth of Australia legislation and New South Wales as to pecuniary penalty orders are rather more elaborate. It is expressly provided that the place of the receipt of property or benefits is immaterial, as is the fact that it may have preceded the Act.[198] In assessing the amount of the pecuniary penalty the court is to have regard to evidence as to a range of matters:

(1) the value of money and other property which came into the possession or under the control of the defendant (or of any other person at the defendant's request) by reason of any of the offences of which the defendant was convicted;

(2) the value of any other benefit provided for the defendant (or such other person) in these circumstances;

(3) if the offence is one relating to narcotics, the market value of similar substances or the amount ordinarily paid for doing the act in question;

(4) the value of the defendant's property before and after the relevant offence or offences; and

(5) the defendant's income and expenditure at those times.[199]

An increase in the value of the defendant's property raises a rebuttable presumption that the increase comprised benefits of the crime.

For the purposes of assessing the value of benefits, the court may treat as the property of a person anything which is subject to his effective control even if he has no interest, right, etc. in or in connection with the property. This relates in particular to corporate situations (as to share or debenture holders and directors; the court may 'lift the corporate veil'), trusts, and other family, domestic and business relationships.[200]

In most Australian legislation it is provided that any expenses or outgoings

---

[196] Vic., s. 12(1)(b).
[197] Vic., s. 13.
[198] Cwlth., s. 24; N.S.W., s. 23.
[199] Cwlth., s. 27; N.S.W., s. 25. Compare the similar Qd., s. 14.
[200] Cwlth., s. 28; N.S.W., s. 27. See to similar effect W.A., s. 17; Qd., s. 3(7)(8); N.T., s. 12.

in connection with the commission of the offence must be disregarded;[201] that is, the gross value of the benefits will be assessed. Queensland goes even further, providing that the value may be that as at the time of valuation; in other words, the court may take into account the effects of inflation since the benefit was first derived.[202] Queensland has another unusual provision designed to prevent notorious offenders making a profit by selling their stories to the media: 'special forfeiture orders' may lead to the seizure of the proceeds of the depiction of the offence in a 'movie, book, newspaper, magazine, radio or television production or live entertainment of any kind' or of the expression of the offender's 'thoughts, opinions or emotions' regarding the offence.[203]

Provisions reversing to some degree the burden of proof regarding the source of property alleged to be the proceeds of crime (and so corresponding to the United Kingdom provisions in the Drug Trafficking Offences Act 1986)[204] are found in some of the Australian legislation. New South Wales makes provision for 'drugs proceeds orders', the relevant provisions closely following the United Kingdom model.[205] The Commonwealth and Western Australian Acts create a presumption that property held by the defendant at the time of the application for a pecuniary penalty order in a drug offences case[206] or at any time within the previous 5 years was derived from the commission of the offence.[207] An identical Queensland provision applies to all indictable offences.[208]

There is no question in the various Australian Acts of the 'pecuniary penalty' process being a mandatory one in the sense in which the confiscation process is mandatory in the Drug Trafficking Offences Act 1986 of the United Kingdom. The power (and that of making forfeiture orders, considered below) is a matter of discretion.

Forfeiture of property

So far as the forfeiture order approach is concerned, the South Australian legislation enables property to be forfeited (subject to the provisions as to the protection of innocent third parties, considered below) if:

(1) it falls into the category of 'instrumentalities', that is, it is acquired for the purposes of committing or is used in connection with the commission of the relevant offence; or

(2) it is the proceeds of such an offence, meaning 'property derived directly or indirectly from the commission of the offence'; or

(3) it is property acquired with the proceeds of such an offence, or into which the proceeds of an offence have, in some other manner, been converted.[209]

---

[201] Cwlth., s. 27(8) (but see the allowance for tax paid on the proceeds: s. 26(4)); N.S.W., s. 25(5); Qd., s. 14(8); N.T., s. 11(5). [202] Qd., s. 14(3).
[203] Qd., s. 60.   [204] See pp. 000–000.
[205] N.S.W., ss. 28–44.   [206] Or an organized fraud offence in the Cwlth. Act.
[207] Cwlth., s. 27(6); W.A., s. 16(4).   [208] Qd., s. 14(6).
[209] S.A., ss. 3, 4.

This last case is a limited 'tracing' provision. It is supplemented by what can be described as the 'accretion provision' of section 4(2). This provides that where in consequence of a relevant offence there has been an accretion to the property of any person (the offender or any other), but for any reason specific property liable to forfeiture under the above rules cannot be identified, the whole of that person's property is liable to forfeiture to the extent necessary to realise a sum equal in value to the accretion.

In other Australian legislation, a similar result is achieved by different language. In some cases use is made of a concept of 'tainted property';[210] in all the effect is to render liable to forfeiture property that:

(*a*) was used in, or in connection with, the commission of a serious offence;[211] or
(*b*) was derived or realised, directly or indirectly, by any person, as a result of the commission of a serious offence.[212]

The inclusion of the word 'realised' may be sufficient to attract the third element of the South Australian definition, allowing an element of tracing. The New South Wales Act includes in the concept of 'tainted property' property that was 'derived or realised, directly or indirectly, by any person, from property used in, or in connection with' the commission of the offence, extending a similar notion to instrumentalities.[213]

In deciding whether to make a forfeiture order, the court must take into consideration available information on a number of matters. These include the use ordinarily made (or intended to be made) of the property and any hardship that might reasonably be likely to arise (whether on the part of the defendant or of any other person) following the making of the order.[214] The New South Wales legislation directs the court, when considering the 'hardship' factor, not to take into account the sentence imposed in respect of the offence.[215] Two Acts, probably unnecessarily, invite the court to weigh the gravity of the offence.[216]

Canada also has legislation enabling forfeiture orders to be made in respect of the proceeds of crime, meaning:

any property, benefit or advantage, within or outside Canada, obtained or derived directly or indirectly as a result of

(*a*) the commission in Canada of an enterprise crime offence or a designated drug offence, or
(*b*) an act or omission anywhere that, if it had occurred in Canada, would have constituted an enterprise crime offence or a designated drug offence.[217]

---

[210] So the Cwlth., N.S.W., Qd., and N.T. Acts.
[211] Extended in Queensland to property 'intended for' such use: Qd., s. 3(1).
[212] To this effect Cwlth., s. 4(1); Vic., s. 7(1); W.A., s. 10(1); N.T., s. 3(1).
[213] N.S.W., s. 4(1).
[214] Cwlth., s. 19(1); N.S.W., s. 18(1); Vic., s. 7(2); W.A., s. 10(2); Qd., s. 8(2); N.T., s. 5(1).
[215] N.S.W., s. 18(2). [216] Cwlth., s. 19(4); Qd., s. 8(2).
[217] Criminal Code, s. 420.1, as added in 1988.

The court may order the forfeiture of any property which it is satisfied, on a balance of probabilities, to be proceeds of crime and that the offence of which the offender stands convicted was committed 'in relation to' that property. If that relationship cannot be established, forfeiture may still be ordered if the court is satisfied, in this case beyond a reasonable doubt, that the property is proceeds of crime.[218] It is provided that the court may infer that property was obtained or derived as a result of the commission of a relevant offence when the value of the alleged offender's property after the commission of the offence is shown to exceed the value of all his property before that time, and the court is satisfied that his income from sources unrelated to relevant offences committed by him cannot reasonably account for the increase in value.[219]

Although this legislation adopts the forfeiture order approach, the scope for evasion by the offender is limited by further provisions: there are circumstances in which a confiscation order approach is available, the offender paying a fine equal to the value of property, or of an interest in property, which for some reason cannot be forfeited. This applies where property:

(*a*) cannot, on the exercise of due diligence, be located,
(*b*) has been transferred to a third party,
(*c*) is located outside Canada [so avoiding some of the problems of international enforcement to which reference has already been made],
(*d*) has been substantially diminished in value or rendered worthless, or
(*e*) has been commingled with other property that cannot be divided without difficulty.[220]

Forfeiture orders and third parties

To be effective, a forfeiture order must reach property held by persons other than one convicted of a specific offence. On the other hand, care must be taken not to prejudice innocent third parties. Both aspects need to be examined.

So, for example, the Malaysian Dangerous Drugs (Forfeiture of Property) Act 1988 contains a clear presentation of the types of relationships which may exist between a convicted offender and others who may have custody of relevant property. It contains[221] an elaborate definition of 'relative', and a detailed listing of those within the meaning of 'associate'. In short, this includes those sharing accommodation with the defendant, his agents, nominees, managers, accountants, or partners, any corporation in which he has a 10 per cent interest, or a director or manager of such a corporation, the trustee of any trust created by him, 'any person who has in his possession any property belonging to such person' and any debtor of his. The scheme of the

---

[218] Criminal Code, s. 420.17(1), (2). The provisions also apply to cases under the Foods and Drugs Act and the Narcotics Control Act.
[219] Criminal Code, s. 420.19.   [220] Ibid., s. 420.17(3).
[221] Dangerous Drugs (Forfeiture of Property) Act 1988, s. 3(2).

Malaysian Act is that all such 'liable persons' may be proceeded against for the forfeiture of any property which they hold and which the public prosecutor believes to be 'illegal property', essentially the proceeds or instrumentalities of defined prohibited activities.[222] The 'liable person' must show cause why the property should not be forfeited, and—though the matter is not expressly dealt with—appears to have the burden of proof.[223] There is also provision for the forfeiture of *other* property, where the property liable to forfeiture has, for example, lost value or is outside Malaysia.[224] All this operates, of course, only in the drugs context, but similar issues have to be addressed by all legislation adopting the forfeiture order approach.

The various Australian Acts contain provisions providing some protection for third parties. In South Australia it is provided that the property of 'a person who is innocent of any complicity in the commission of the offence' shall not be forfeited unless *either* he gave no valuable consideration for it *or* received it in circumstances such as to arouse a reasonable suspicion as to its origin.[225] The entirely innocent recipient of a gift derived from criminal activities will be at risk of the property being forfeited.

Similarly in New South Wales and the Northern Territory, any person, other than the offender, who claims an interest in respect of the property may apply to the court within six months of the making of a forfeiture order for the property to be transferred to him, or for an order that he is entitled to a sum representing the value of his interest, but the order can be made only if the court is satisfied on the balance of probabilities that the appellant 'was not in any way involved in the commission' of the relevant offence.[226] It is also provided that the order takes effect subject to existing charges, encumbrances, mortgages, leases, and registered interests in land.[227]

In the other States the effect of a forfeiture order is to vest the property absolutely in the Crown; there is no saving for existing charges, etc.[228] A third party may apply for an order requiring the transfer to him of the property or the value of his interest but the court must first be satisfied:

(1) that he was not in any way involved in the commission of the offence; and

(2) acquired the interest in good faith and for value; and

(3) did so in circumstances such as not to arouse a reasonable suspicion that the property was the proceeds or instrumentalities of a serious offence.[229]

The Commonwealth legislation follows the Victorian model in the standard case.[230] There are separate provisions in respect of the special class of 'serious offences', the proceeds of which are automatically forfeited if they

---

[222] Ibid., ss. 3(2).7.8.
[223] Ibid., ss. 9.10.
[224] Ibid., s. 11.
[225] S.A., s. 5(2).
[226] N.S.W., s. 20; N.T., s. 7.
[227] N.S.W., s. 19(1)(*b*); N.T., s. 6(1)(*b*).
[228] Vic., s. 8; W.A., s. 11; Qd., s. 9.
[229] Vic., s. 9(4); W.A., s. 12(4); Qd., s. 10(4).
[230] See Cwlth., s. 21 in particular.

remain six months after the date of the relevant conviction subject to a restraining order.[231] In such a case a third party may still apply for relief but that is subject to additional requirements: the court must be satisfied that the applicant's interest is not subject to the effective control of the defendant,[232] and that the interest was lawfully acquired, and that the property was not the instrumentalities or the proceeds of 'any unlawful activity'.[233]

Under the Canadian legislation, before making a forfeiture order, a court may require that notice be given to any person appearing to have a valid interest in the property concerned. The court may order the return of property or exclude certain interests from the scope of a forfeiture order already made, in favour of persons who meet certain criteria. These can be summarized as being:

(1) that the person was not charged with a relevant offence;
(2) that he did not receive title to or a right to possession of the property in circumstances giving rise to a reasonable inference that the transfer was for the purpose of avoiding forfeiture; and
(3) that he appears innocent of any complicity in, or collusion in relation to, the relevant offence.[234]

(D) International Action

Provision is made in a number of instruments to which the United Kingdom is, or may be expected to become, a party. These are examined in the material which follows.[235]

PROVISIONS IN THE COMMONWEALTH SCHEME

The Commonwealth Scheme for Mutual Assistance in Criminal Matters, as it emerged in draft form from a meeting of Senior Officials in January 1986 contained no provisions dealing with the proceeds of crime. Some provisions were prepared in time for their inclusion in the text as adopted by Law Ministers at Harare later in the year, but they were revised, and extended to instrumentalities, in 1990.

The current text of the Scheme refers to the two approaches which may be adopted, that of recognizing and enforcing an order relating to the proceeds or instrumentalities of crime made in the requesting country, and that of responding to a request by taking steps to secure the making in the requested country of such an order. The laconic text of paragraph 27 of the Scheme

---

[231] Cwlth., s. 30.

[232] Ibid., s. 31(6)(*a*)(ia) inserted by the Crimes Legislation Amendment Act 1987, s. 37.

[233] Ibid., s. 31(6)(*b*) substituted by the 1987 Act, s. 37.

[234] Criminal Code, ss. 420.21 and 420.22 as added in 1988. What appears in the text is a brief account of complex provisions; the requirements vary with the stage the forfeiture proceedings have reached.

[235] For UK legislation, see pp. 245–7; for the Vienna Convention, see pp. 174–80.

implies that each country may decide for itself whether it will adopt one or other, or both, of these approaches. If the requested country cannot enforce an order made in the requesting country (which is likely to be the first preference of the latter country), the requesting country may instead ask that the other approach be taken and a fresh order obtained in and under the law of the requested country.[236]

These provisions apply to three different types of order: those restraining dealings in property (i.e. by way of interim seizure); those confiscating property; and those imposing a penalty calculated by reference to the value of the illicitly-obtained property.[237] Where property is forfeited or obtained as a result of the enforcement of a pecuniary penalty order, the law of the requested country is to govern the disposal of the property.[238]

United Kingdom reservations

The United Kingdom has indicated that it may only provide assistance under paragraph 27 of the Scheme to countries designated under the relevant United Kingdom domestic legislation;[239] and may only provide assistance in the restraint of property where criminal proceedings have been or are to be instituted.

COUNCIL OF EUROPE CONVENTION OF 1990

Much more elaborate provisions are found in the Council of Europe's Convention on Laundering, Search, Seizure, and Confiscation of Proceeds from Crime of 1990.[240] They oblige Parties to take certain measures affecting the content of their domestic law as well as providing for international cooperation.

Domestic measures

At the national level, each Party must adopt legislative or other measures enabling it to confiscate instrumentalities or proceeds or property the value of which corresponds to such proceeds; the measures may be limited to offences or categories of offences identified in a declaration made by the Party concerned;[241] in the *Explanatory Memorandum* to the Convention, examples given include drug trafficking offences, organized crime, offences involving the sexual exploitation of children, economic fraud, and insider dealing.[242] These 'confiscation measures' must be supported by 'investigative and provisional measures', enabling a Party to identify, trace and restrain dealings in, relevant property.[243] The official *Explanatory Memorandum* observes[244] that as

---

[236] Scheme, para. 27(3); see para. 27(5) emphasizing the applicability of the law of the requested country to determine the circumstances and manner in which an order may be made, recognized or enforced in response to a request.   [237] Ibid., para. 27(2).
[238] Ibid., para. 28(1).   [239] See pp. 246–7.
[240] For the text see the Appendix of Selected Documents, below.
[241] Convention, Art. 2.   [242] *Explanatory Memorandum*, para. 27.
[243] Convention, Art. 3.   [244] Para. 28.

no declarations are provided for in Article 3 dealing with these measures, they must be available for *all* offences; as Article 3 refers only to property liable to confiscation under Article 2 (in which the reference to declarations appears) this observation appears to be incorrect.

A very significant provision is that national legislation must empower courts or other competent authorities to order that bank, financial or commercial records be made available or be seized to support those measures; bank secrecy may not be relied upon in this context.[245] Parties are not obliged to adopt, but are to consider the use of, special investigative techniques including monitoring orders, the interception of telecommunications, and access to computer systems.[246]

International co-operation

Chapter III of the Convention, comprising Articles 7–35, contains detailed provisions as to international co-operation. This takes the form of 'investigative assistance', provisional measures, and actual confiscation. The effect of these Articles is very similar to that in the much briefer text of the Commonwealth Scheme, but there are some novel features.

Article 13, dealing with confiscation, is very carefully drafted to reflect the distinction emphasized in the *Explanatory Memorandum* between what is called 'property confiscation' and 'value confiscation'. If a Party requests confiscation of specific property, the requested Party must provide assistance (either by enforcing a confiscation order or by obtaining a fresh confiscation order in its own courts); the same applies to a request expressed in terms of value; and if the initial request refers to specific property, the Parties may agree that confiscation of property of equivalent value may be substituted.

Although in general the law of the requested Party applies to the confiscation of property, in the context of enforcing a confiscation order that Party will be bound by findings of fact expressly stated or implicit in the conviction or other judicial decision of the requesting Party.[247] To avoid due process problems, a Party may subject this provision to its constitutional principles and the basic concepts of its legal system.[248]

There are two novelties in respect of the enforcement process. It is provided[249] that nothing in the Convention is to be interpreted as permitting the total value of the confiscation to exceed the amount of the sum of money specified in the confiscation order; if this becomes a possibility, the Parties concerned are to consult to avoid such a result. A power is given to the requesting Party to deny to the requested Party the possibility of imposing imprisonment (or other detention) in default of compliance;[250] this provision

---

[245] Convention, Art. 4(1).

[246] Ibid., Art. 4(2). For a Council of Europe Recommendation on the interception of telecommunications, see pp. 144–6.

[247] Convention, Art. 14(1).   [248] Ibid., Art. 14(2).

[249] Ibid., Art. 16(2).   [250] Ibid., Art. 17.

appears to have been included because in some States imprisonment in default is unconstitutional.[251]

Grounds for refusing assistance

There are elaborate provisions as to the grounds on which co-operation may be refused, provisions which distinguish between different types of assistance. Six of the grounds apply to any form of assistance:

(*a*) the action sought would be contrary to the fundamental principles of the legal system of the requested Party;[252]

(*b*) the execution of the request is likely to prejudice the sovereignty, security, *ordre public* or other essential interests of the requested Party;

(*c*) in the opinion of the requested Party, the importance of the case to which the request relates does not justify the taking of the action sought;

(*d*) the offence to which the request relates is a political or fiscal offence;

(*e*) the requested Party considers that compliance with the action sought would be contrary to the principle of *ne bis in idem*;

(*f*) the offence to which the request relates would not be an offence under the law of the requested Party if committed within its jurisdiction. However, this ground applies to co-operation under Section 2 [investigative assistance] only in so far as the assistance sought involves coercive action.[253]

In the case of investigative assistance involving coercive measures, and of provisional measures, assistance may also be refused if the measures sought are unavailable in those contexts in the law of the requested Party, or if the request is not authorized within the requesting Party by a judge or authority acting in its criminal, as opposed to civil, jurisdiction.[254]

In respect of actual confiscation, the drafting is yet more complex. In effect, assistance may be refused if confiscation is not available under the law of the requested Party because of the nature of the offence, its definition of 'proceeds' or 'instrumentalities', or its statute of limitations; in cases where confiscation has been ordered without a prior criminal conviction; where the confiscation order was not enforceable in the requesting Party or was subject to ordinary means of appeal; and where the order was made in default of appearance and without the grant of 'the minimum rights of defence recognized as due to everyone against whom a criminal charge is made'.[255]

Although earlier international texts have recognized the need to protect third parties' rights, the Convention is the first to make provision for international co-operation to this end. Article 21 provides for mutual assistance in the service of documents on third parties, those affected by provisional

---

[251] See *Explanatory Memorandum*, para. 57.

[252] Examples discussed during the negotiation of the Convention included contravention of the European Convention on Human Rights, and cases of exorbitant jurisdiction: ibid., para. 60.

[253] Convention, Art. 18(1).

[254] The text is an attempt to state the effect of the tortuously drafted Art. 18(2)(3) of the Convention.   [255] Ibid., Art. 18(4)(5)(6); *Explanatory Memorandum*, paras. 70–6.

measures or confiscation. Article 22 provides for the recognition by a Party requested to give assistance in respect of provisional measures or confiscation of judicial decisions in the requesting Party regarding rights claimed by third parties. If a third party (or indeed a defendant) brings a successful claim for compensation in respect of an act or omission relating to co-operation, the Parties concerned are to consult as to the apportionment of the sum due (i.e. as to the contribution each should make).[256]

---

[256] Convention, Art. 35.

10

United Kingdom Legislation and Treaties

MUTUAL ASSISTANCE LEGISLATION

IN 1990 the United Kingdom enacted for the first time comprehensive legislation on mutual assistance in criminal matters. The Criminal Justice (International Co-operation) Act 1990 enables the United Kingdom to comply with its moral obligations in respect of the Commonwealth Scheme and to ratify the European Convention on Mutual Assistance in Criminal Matters of 1957 and the United Nations Convention against Illicit Traffic in Narcotic Drugs and Psychotropic Substances 1988.

Requests to the United Kingdom

Provision is made under the Act for assistance to be given within the United Kingdom in response to a request received by the Secretary of State from the government or other authority in a country or territory outside the United Kingdom.[1] In some cases the Secretary of State will receive the request in his capacity as a 'central authority', for example in relation to a request under the Commonwealth scheme; but this is not required by the Act, which enables assistance to be given to any country which requests it, with no requirement of reciprocity. The United Kingdom will however normally require a multilateral or bilateral agreement to be in place before granting assistance in relation to the confiscation of the proceeds or instrumentalities of crime.

The Act contains no specific provisions as to the form and contents of requests, but the Home Office published in August 1991 a set of Guidelines[2] containing information on these and other practical matters. In general requests must be in writing and addressed 'To the Competent United Kingdom Authority'. Action may be taken on advance faxed copies of urgent requests (or if necessary telexed or radioed requests via Interpol), with an undertaking to send the formal request to arrive within seven days.[3]

So far as the contents of requests are concerned, these obviously vary with

---

[1] Criminal Justice (International Co-operation) Act 1990, s. 1(1).
[2] *International mutual legal assistance in criminal matters: United Kingdom guidelines.*
[3] *Guidelines*, paras. 14–15.

the nature of the assistance which is sought. The *Guidelines* indicate[4] that the following should be provided:

(*a*) details of the authority making the request;

(*b*) details of the purpose of the request and a summary of the reason for it;

(*c*) details of persons named in the request (full names, places and dates of birth, known addresses, nationality, etc.);

(*d*) a description of the offences or suspected offences charged or likely to be charged or under investigation;

(*e*) any relevant dates (e.g. date of trial) or cause for special urgency (e.g. where the accused is in detention pending the investigation of his or her case);

(*f*) in the case of a request for search and seizure, full details of the property to be seized, and other information specified in the *Guidelines*;

(*g*) in the case of a request for the freezing or confiscation of criminal assets, the information and documents indicated in the applicable bilateral confiscation agreement or side letter;

(*h*) in the case of a request for the attendance of a witness abroad, details of allowances and travelling and subsistence expenses payable by the requesting State;

(*i*) details of any rules on privilege which a witness or suspect may be entitled to claim, and any caution which should if possible be given under the law of the requesting State;

(*j*) where evidence is to be taken from a witness or suspect, details of whether the evidence is to be taken before a court, and whether it should be taken on oath or affirmation; alternatively, confirmation that a less formal interview not on oath, for example by the police, will suffice. (In the absence of such indication or confirmation the Central Authority may use its discretion.);

(*k*) a description of the evidence sought, and a list of any specific questions to be asked;

(*l*) where the evidence is to be taken before a court, certification should be provided by the authority forwarding the request to the Central Authority to the effect that there are reasonable grounds for suspecting that an offence has been committed, and either that proceedings in respect of the offence have been instituted or that an investigation is being carried out within its jurisdiction;

(*m*) whether it is desired that any persons from the requesting State should be present during the taking of evidence, and whether the request is for such persons to be permitted to participate in the questioning;

(*n*) in the case of a prisoner witness required abroad, information will be needed to enable the prisoner's informed consent to be sought and to satisfy the United Kingdom prison authorities that arrangements will be made to ensure his or her secure custody. This information will need to include details of proposed arrangements for collecting the prisoner from the United Kingdom; details of the type of secure accommodation in which he or she will be held in the requesting State; the type of escort available to and from his or her accommodation; the period during which attendance in the requesting State is required; the date on which the court or other proceedings for which the prisoner is required will commence, and are likely to be concluded; the privileges (letters, visits, etc.) to which the prisoner will be entitled during his

---

[4] *Guidelines*, para. 16.

or her attendance in the requesting State, and whether he or she will be accorded immunity in respect of previous offences.

If the request is in a language other than English, a translation must be provided.[5]

Service of process

The 1990 Act contains provisions enabling the United Kingdom to respond to a request for the service of 'overseas process'.

There are two types of 'overseas process' covered by the Act. The first comprises summonses or other process requiring a person to appear as defendant or attend as a witness in criminal proceedings in the overseas country.[6] There is no question of measures of compulsion being used: the Act provides that service shall not impose any obligation under the law of any part of the United Kingdom to comply with the summons, and when the documents are served they must be accompanied by a notice to that effect which will also suggest that the person served might seek advice on the effect of non-compliance under the law of the overseas country,[7] and pointing out that a witness attending in foreign proceedings may not enjoy the same rights and privileges as would be accorded by United Kingdom law.[8] The second type of document is one issued by a court exercising criminal jurisdiction in an overseas country and recording a decision of the court made in the exercise of that jurisdiction.[9] This service is solely for the information of the person affected; it does not involve the enforcement of the foreign decision, which could be, for example, the imposition of a fine or other penalty.

Service of process will normally be by post. If personal service is requested, this is arranged through the local police force.[10]

Service of process of a United Kingdom court summoning a person as a defendant or as a witness is also provided for in the Act. The Act merely enables such process to be issued; service outside the United Kingdom is to be 'in accordance with arrangements made by the Secretary of State'.[11] Non-compliance does not constitute contempt of court; though should it prove possible process can be served *within* the jurisdiction and the normal consequences of non-compliance will then follow.[12] The procedure for sending the documents to the Secretary of State, and for proving service outside the United Kingdom, is governed by rules of court.[13]

---

[5] Ibid., para. 18.   [6] Ibid., s. 1(1)(*a*).
[7] For example, if he has property there, it might be subject to seizure by way of sanction for non-appearance; or arrest for contempt of court might occur on a later visit to the country concerned.   [8] Criminal Justice (International Co-operation) Act 1990, s. 1(3)(4).
[9] Ibid., s. 1(1)(*b*).
[10] Ibid., s. 1(2). For completion of a certificate of service (or a research statement where service could not be effected) see s. 1(5).
[11] Ibid., s. 2(1).   [12] Ibid., s. 2(3)(4).
[13] See the Magistrates' Courts (Criminal Justice (International Co-operation)) Rules 1991, S.I. 1991 No. 1074, rr. 3, 4.

Evidence for use in the United Kingdom

Section 3 of the Act contains provisions enabling evidence to be obtained overseas for use in connection with criminal investigations or proceedings in the United Kingdom; 'evidence' in this context includes documents and other articles as well as testimony.[14]

Letters of request may be issued by a judge or justice of the peace on the application of either a prosecution authority or a defendant;[15] this recognition of the possibility that the defence may need help in obtaining evidence from overseas is a welcome one, for international agreements (negotiated by public officials concerned with effective law enforcement) are often drafted in terms which suggest or expressly provide that only the prosecution may seek assistance. The judge or justice must be satisfied that an offence has been committed, or that there are reasonable grounds for suspecting that an offence has been committed, and that proceedings in respect of the offence have been instituted or that the offence is being investigated;[16] presumably the mere assertion by the prosecuting authority that the offence is being investigated will be sufficient to satisfy the judge or justice of that fact.

It is not at all clear that the element of judicial oversight implied by these provisions will often be present. Section 3(3) of the Act enables designated prosecuting authorities themselves to issue letters of request in the same circumstances as a judge or justice. The authorities designated for this purpose include any Crown Prosecutor.[17] Although letters of request will normally be sent via the Secretary of State for onward transmission to the appropriate foreign court or central authority, in 'cases of urgency' a letter of request may be sent direct to a foreign court (but not to any other authority in the foreign country).[18]

Evidence obtained by virtue of a letter of request must not, without the consent of the appropriate overseas central authority, be used for any purpose other than that specified in the letter (which in practice will mean the proceedings or investigation so specified). Any document or article obtained and which is no longer required for the specified or another approved purpose must be returned to the relevant overseas authority unless that authority indicates that it need not be returned.[19]

The provisions of the Act are primarily concerned with a mechanism for

[14] Criminal Justice (International Co-operation) Act 1990, s. 3(6).
[15] Ibid., s. 3(2).   [16] Ibid., s. 3(1).
[17] Criminal Justice (International Co-operation) Act 1990 (Designation of Prosecuting Authorities) Order 1991, S.I. 1991 No. 1224, under which the following are designated: the Attorney-General, the Director of Public Prosecutions and any Crown Prosecutor, the Director of the Serious Fraud Office and any person designated under s. 1(7) of the Criminal Justice Act 1987, the Secretary of State for Trade and Industry, the Commissioners of Customs and Excise, and corresponding authorities in Scotland and Northern Ireland.
[18] Criminal Justice (International Co-operation) Act 1990, s. 3(4)(5). For procedural rules, see the Magistrates' Courts (Criminal Justice (International Co-operation)) Rules 1991, S.I. 1991 No. 1074, rr. 5–7.   [19] Criminal Justice (International Co-operation) Act 1990, s. 3(7).

obtaining evidential material; the use of the mechanism does not guarantee the admissibility of the material. This will be governed by the usual rules of evidence, including where statements are concerned, the provisions of the Criminal Justice Act 1988.[20] It is, however, provided that in exercising its discretion to exclude evidence which would otherwise be admissible (i.e. under section 25 of that Act), the court is to have regard to whether it was possible to challenge the statement contained in the evidence taken in response to a letter of request by questioning the person who made it; and, in cases where proceedings have been instituted,[21] whether the law of the overseas country allowed the parties to be legally represented when the evidence was being taken.[22]

Evidence for use abroad

Provision is also made for the taking in the United Kingdom of evidence for use overseas. The consultation process which preceded the enactment of the 1990 Act showed that this was a sensitive area; the sensitivities raised issues of double criminality and concerns about fiscal offences.

The powers can be exercised in the usual case if the Secretary of State is satisfied that an offence under the law of the overseas country has been committed or that there are reasonable grounds for suspecting that such an offence has been committed, and that proceedings have been instituted in the overseas country or that an investigation is being carried on there. A certificate as to these matters from the appropriate central authority of the overseas country will be regarded as conclusive.[23] In the case of a 'fiscal offence' (which is not defined in the Act), assistance may be given at the investigatory stage only if the request is from a Commonwealth country, or is made pursuant to a treaty binding on the United Kingdom, or if the relevant conduct would constitute an offence 'of the same or a similar nature'[24] if it had occurred in the United Kingdom.[25] These provisions enable the United Kingdom to ratify the Additional Protocol to the European Convention.[26]

Where a request is received from an overseas court, prosecuting authority or appropriate central authority, and the above requirements are satisfied, the Secretary of State 'may, if he thinks fit' take action to have the evidence taken;[27] the language emphasizes that his response is discretionary, but treaty obligations will exist in many cases.

If the evidence is to be taken, the Secretary of State issues a notice nominating a court to receive such of the evidence to which the request relates as may appear to the court to be appropriate to give effect to the

---

[20] See p. 123.
[21] In the context, this must mean that the proceedings had been instituted when the statement was taken. [22] Criminal Justice (International Co-operation) Act 1990, s. 3(8).
[23] Ibid., s. 4(2)(4). [24] The precise force of these words is very obscure.
[25] Criminal Justice (International Co-operation) Act 1990, s. 4(3).
[26] See pp. 142–3.
[27] Criminal Justice (International Co-operation) Act 1990, s. 4(2).

request.[28] The nominated court has the same powers for securing the attendance of a witness as it would have for the purpose of other proceedings before the court.[29] A witness may rely on any privilege available in criminal proceedings in England or (to the extent that the claim to privilege is conceded by the overseas court or authority) in the overseas country.[30] The powers of the English courts under the Bankers Books' Evidence Act 1879 are available in proceedings in response to letters of request.[31] The Secretary of State may, however, issue a certificate that it would be prejudicial to the security of the United Kingdom for evidence to be given, and in such a case the witness must not be compelled to give the evidence; similarly, no witness may be compelled to give evidence in his capacity as an officer or servant of the Crown.[32]

Transfer of persons in custody

The Act enables a person in custody in the United Kingdom to be transferred to a requesting country for the purpose of giving evidence in criminal proceedings there, or of being identified in, or otherwise by his presence assisting,[33] such proceedings or the investigation of an offence.[34] The section applies not only to persons serving a sentence of imprisonment but also those in custody awaiting trial or sentence and persons committed to prison in default of paying a fine.[35] The consent of the person in custody is an essential pre-requisite, but a consent once given cannot be withdrawn once the Secretary of State's warrant has been issued.[36] A rather surprising provision enables the consent of a person whose physical or mental condition or youth makes it inappropriate for him to act for himself to be given by some appropriate person on his behalf.[37]

There are detailed provisions giving the necessary authority to the person's custodians during transit, ensuring that he remains in legal custody, and for his arrest should he escape.[38] There is no formal provision that periods of absence from the United Kingdom will count in calculating the service of a sentence; this is certainly intended, and may be handled administratively.

Corresponding provisions are made to enable persons in custody in other countries to be transferred to the United Kingdom.[39] The Act is silent on the question of the grant of immunity from prosecution in respect of acts taking place before the transfer. The position of the United Kingdom is that its government will consider a grant of immunity where this is specifically requested and on a case-by-case basis; it will not grant it where to do so is judged not to be in the public interest. As a result formal reservations or

---

[28] Criminal Justice (International Co-operation) Act 1990, s. 4(2).
[29] Ibid., Sch. 1, para. 1.   [30] Ibid., Sch. 1, para 4.
[31] Ibid., Sch. 1, para. 6.   [32] Ibid., Sch. 1, paras. 4, 5.
[33] An example might be participation in a reconstruction of the events surrounding an alleged offence.   [34] Criminal Justice (International Co-operation) Act 1990, s. 5(1).
[35] Ibid., s. 5(9).   [36] Ibid., s. 5(2).   [37] Ibid.
[38] Ibid., s. 5(3)–(8).   [39] Ibid., s. 6.

declarations have been made in respect of the immunity provisions in the European Convention,[40] the Commonwealth Scheme,[41] and the Vienna Convention.[42] The United Kingdom will not agree to the transfer through its territory of persons in custody and in transit from one State to another;[43] whether the fact that one of the States involved would inevitably be the Irish Republic was determinative is a matter of speculation.

Search and seizure

In drafting the provisions dealing with requests from overseas courts or authorities for search and seizure, the draftsman had to reconcile the existing procedures of English domestic law with the expectations created under the various international arrangements. A two-track approach was adopted as a result.

The first was to apply Part II of the Police and Criminal Evidence Act 1984, and especially section 8 of that Act, to conduct occurring overseas. References to 'serious arrestable offences' in Part II include such conduct as would constitute a serious arrestable offence if it had occurred in any part of the United Kingdom.[44] If a search warrant is to be obtained by this route, the request must contain the information necessary to meet the various requirements of the 1984 Act; for example, that issue of a warrant is necessary on one of the grounds specified in section 8(3) of that Act (such as that it is impracticable to communicate with any person entitled to grant entry to the premises).

The second is a new power created by the 1990 Act. On the application of a constable or an officer of customs and excise,[45] a justice of the peace may grant a search warrant if he is satisfied that criminal proceedings have been instituted against a person in the overseas country (or that a person has been arrested in the course of a criminal investigation there); that the relevant conduct would be an arrestable offence as defined by section 24(1) of the Police and Criminal Evidence Act 1984 if it had occurred in any part of the United Kingdom; and that there are reasonable grounds for suspecting that evidence relating to the offence and not subject to legal privilege is on premises in the United Kingdom occupied or controlled by the person proceeded against or arrested.[46] The Act provides for the transmission and authentication (if required) of evidence seized under these powers.[47]

RECOGNITION AND ENFORCEMENT OF FOREIGN ORDERS

Provision is made in a series of statutory provisions for the registration and enforcement of external confiscation orders relating to the proceeds of crime and of other property used in connection with criminal activity.

[40] Art. 12.
[41] Para. 25.
[42] Art. 7(18).
[43] Cf. European Convention, Art. 11(2).
[44] Criminal Justice (International Co-operation) Act 1990, s. 7(1).
[45] See the Criminal Justice (International Co-operation) Act 1990 (Exercise of Powers) Order 1991, S.I. 1991 No. 1297, Arts. 2–3.
[46] Criminal Justice (International Co-operation) Act 1990, s. 7(2).
[47] Ibid., s. 7(4)(5).

External confiscation orders

Section 24A of the Drug Trafficking Offences Act 1986[48] enables Orders in Council to be made providing for the registration and enforcement in England of orders made under Part I of the Criminal Justice (Sctland) Act 1987, and also for property in England which is realisable property for the purposes of that Part to be used or realised for the payment of sums due under a Scottish confication order.[49] Section 25 of the Drug Trafficking Offences Act 1986 and section 94 of the Criminal Justice Act 1988 enable Orders in Council to be made providing for the enforcement in England of orders made in Northern Ireland which correspond to confiscation orders under those Acts.

Provision is made as to other external orders, those made outside the United Kingdom, in sections 26 and 26A of the Drug Trafficking Offences Act 1986[50] and sections 96 and 97 of the Criminal Justice Act 1988 in respect of 'external confication orders'. Such an order is one made in a country designated for the purpose of the relevant Act; it must be made for the purpose, in the case of the Drug Trafficking Offences Act 1986, of recovering payments or other rewards received in connection with drug trafficking or their value,[51] and, in the case of the Criminal Justice Act 1988, of recovering property (or its value) or a pecuniary advantage obtained as a result of or in connection with an offence to which Part VI of the Act applies.[52]

In these cases, an Order in Council may apply the relevant provisions of the appropriate Act, with such modifications as may be specified, to the external confiscation orders, and may also provide for circumstances in which action taken in a designated country with a view to satisfying a confiscation order is to be treated as reducing the amount payable under the order.[53] On an application made by or on behalf of the government of a designated country, the High Court may register an external confiscation order made there if it is satisfied that the order is in force and not subject to appeal, and that, if made in default of appearance, the person against whom the order is made received notice of the procedings in sufficient time to enable him to defend them; the court must also be of opinion that enforcing the order in England would not be contrary to the interests of justice.[54]

These powers have been exercised in respect of external confiscation orders under the Drug Trafficking Offences Act 1986 in the Drug Trafficking

---

[48] Inserted by the Criminal Justice (Sctland) Act 1987, s. 31.

[49] See the Drug Trafficking Offences (Enforcement in England and Wales) Order 1988, S.I. 1988 No. 593. [50] As substituted by Criminal Justice Act 1988, s. 103 and Sch. 5, para. 15.

[51] Drug Trafficking Offences Act 1986, s. 26(2) as substituted in 1988.

[52] Criminal Justice Act 1988, s. 96(2).

[53] Drug Trafficking Offences Act 1986, s. 26(1) as substituted in 1988; Criminal Justice Act 1988, s. 96(1).

[54] Drug Trafficking Offences Act 1986, s. 26A as substituted in 1988; Criminal Justice Act 1988, s. 97.

Offences Act 1986 (Designated Countries and Territories) Order 1990.[55] Fifty-one countries are designated.[56] The Order enables restraint and charging orders to be made in England when proceedings have been instituted in a designated country, and steps to be taken, by appointing a receiver and in other ways, to enforce the external order.[57] It also provides for the purposes of sections 26 and 26A of the 1986 Act as to proof of orders and other matters, and as to the role of the Crown Prosecution Service or the Commissioners of Customs and Excise in acting on behalf of the relevant foreign government;[58] and for the conversion of currency where sums are expressed in a currency other than sterling.[59]

External forfeiture orders

Provision is made in the Criminal Justice (International Co-operation) Act 1990 for the enforcement in the United Kingdom of a slightly different category of order, 'external forfeiture orders'. These are orders made in a designated country for the forfeiture, and the destruction or other disposal, of anything in respect of which a certain type of offence has been committed or which was used in connection with the commission of such an offence.[60] An Order in Council may be made providing for the enforcement of such orders, and may require their registration in a court in the United Kingdom as a condition of that enforcement.[61]

An Order in Council has been made in the exercise of these powers. The Criminal Justice (International Co-operation) Act 1990 (Enforcement of Overseas Forfeiture Orders) Order 1991[62] designates the same fifty-one countries as are designated for the purposes of enforcing external confiscation orders under the Drug Trafficking Offences Act 1986[63] and enables restraint orders to be made, external forfeiture orders to be registered in the High Court, and the property affected to be forfeited and disposed of under the court's directions. An application for forfeiture is made by a Crown Prosecutor or by a person acting on behalf of the Commissioners of Customs and Excise.[64]

---

[55] S.I. 1990 No. 1199 as amended by S.I. 1991 No. 1465. See also S.I. 1991 No. 2873 (re Criminal Justice Act 1988).

[56] Anguilla, Australia, the Bahamas, Bahrain, Bangladesh, Barbados, Bermuda, Bhutan, Bolivia, Canada, Cayman Islands, Chile, China, Costa Rica, Cyprus, Ecuador, Egypt, France, Ghana, Gibraltar, Grenada, Guatemala, Guernsey, Guinea, Hong Kong, India, Isle of Man, Italy, Jersey, Jordan, Madagascar, Malaysia, Mexico, Montserrat, Nicaragua, Nigeria, Oman, Paraguay, Qatar, Saudi Arabia, Senegal, Spain, Sweden, Switzerland, Togo, Tunisia, Uganda, USSR, United Arab Emirates, United States of America, and Yugoslavia.

[57] See the modified the Drug Trafficking Offences Act 1986 as set out in Sch. 3 to the Order.
[58] Order, Arts. 4–7.   [59] Ibid., Art. 8.
[60] Criminal Justice (International Co-operation) Act 1990, s. 9(1). The relevant offences are those corresponding to or similar to offences under the Misuse of Drugs Act 1971, a drug trafficking offence as defined by the Drug Trafficking Offences Act 1986, s. 38(1) as amended, an offence to which the Criminal Justice (Scotland) Act 1987, s. 1 relates, or to which the Criminal Justice Act 1988, Part VI applies: 1990 Act, s. 9(6).

[61] Criminal Justice (International Co-operation) Act 1990, s. 9(1)(2).
[62] S.I. 1991 No. 1463.   [63] See above, n. 56.   [64] Order, Art. 7(1).

BILATERAL TREATIES AND AGREEMENTS

In addition to the multilateral instruments providing for mutual assistance in criminal matters, there is a growing network of bilateral treaties and agreements. The United States and Australia have each been notably active in this field, with the United Kingdom's programme developing rapidly in the most recent period.

United States experience

Although the involvement of the United States in the negotiation of mutual assistance arrangements came much later than the pioneering efforts within Europe, since 1977 when the first United States mutual legal assistance treaty (MLAT) entered into force, a large network of co-operation has been developed.[65] The United States now has great experience in negotiating such agreements, and as the focus of concern shifted from commercial crime to drugs-related offences (the two categories do of course overlap greatly) the development of bilateral agreements has become a major feature of United States policy. The United States has thus had a pioneering role in bilateral assistance,[66] and continues to be a leading force in the growth of the mutual assistance network.

The pressure for action by the United States government came partly as a result of a realization that the legal position as it had developed in the United States by the 1970s remained highly unsatisfactory from the point of view of anyone seeking to promote co-operation in criminal matters. It was not until 1975 that the courts finally accepted that the execution of criminal letters rogatory was permitted.[67] Relying solely on the execution of letters rogatory as a means of obtaining evidence both by and from the United States was problematic as there were often excessive bureaucratic delays in the receiving country due to a lack of understanding of the legal procedure and terminology of the requesting country and a lack of incentive to co-operate. For private individuals the use of letters rogatory necessitated the use of lawyers in the receiving state and therefore greatly increased costs.

A growing need for the kind of information that was only available through co-operation with foreign courts or authorities precipitated a change of attitude.[68] At that time United States law enforcement agencies had

---

[65] As at Mar. 1991, the United States had MLATs in force with the Bahamas, Canada, Italy, The Netherlands, Switzerland, Turkey and the United Kingdom; treaties had been signed but were not yet in force with Argentina, Belgium, Colombia, Jamaica, Mexico, Nigeria, Spain, and Thailand: 7 International Law Enforcement Reporter 91 (1991).

[66] For a full comparison of some of the earlier texts, see 'The United States Treaties on Mutual Assistance in Criminal Matters: A Comparative Analysis', A. Ellis and R. L. Pisani, 19 Int'l Lawyer 189 (1985).

[67] See A. Ellis and R. L. Pisani, 'The United States Treaties on Mutual Assistance in Criminal Matters: A Comparative Analysis', (1985) 19 Int. L. 189 at pp. 191–6.

[68] The need for better co-operation was highlighted by incidents such as the Lockheed saga, see *Transnational Aspects of Criminal Procedure*, (1983) Michigan Yearbook of International Legal Studies, p. 85.

become aware that many criminals were using Swiss banks to hide the proceeds of various types of criminal activity and that efforts to obtain information on which to base a prosecutions were being greatly hampered by the strict bank secrecy laws in force in Switzerland.[69] The first step into the field of international mutual assistance was to seek greater co-operation with the Swiss in order to reach some compromise over the lifting of the veil of bank secrecy.

As the Swiss were already party to the Council of Europe Convention they responded by suggesting the negotiation of a similar treaty on a bilateral basis. Negotiations began in 1969 but proved difficult largely as a result of the Swiss attachment both to strict rules on bank secrecy and (on the basis of sovereignty arguments) to restrictions on the supply of information to foreign investigators. Problems were also caused by the different attitudes of the two States to such matters as the prosecution of tax evasion. However, the Swiss also attach great importance to law enforcement and Swiss bank secrecy rules (unlike, for example, those in Panama) do contain exceptions permitting disclosure to domestic law enforcement agencies. The result was a very lengthy and complex Treaty, which has however proved highly successful in practice.[70]

The conclusion of that first MLAT was an important event as the resulting assistance showed United States law enforcement agencies what was possible and interest was generated in Ministries of Justice around the world.[71] This encouraged the United States to expand its mutual assistance network using a variety of tactics to encourage co-operation from its partners. For example, it has now become a policy of the United States when re-negotiating old extradition treaties to make it a requirement that negotiations on the subject of mutual assistance be included. This has resulted in MLATs with such countries as Belgium, The Netherlands and Turkey. Treaties are also negotiated with countries which are identified as being particularly connected with international crime, especially those on the routes used for smuggling drugs into the United States. Those MLATs concluded with Italy,[72] Morocco, the Cayman Islands, and the Bahamas are evidence of this. Where co-operation might not otherwise be forthcoming, it is possible to oil the diplomatic wheels by either offering financial benefits such as tax concessions,[73] or by making it financially difficult to refuse.[74] In the resulting process

---

[69] 'Negotiations in Criminal Law Assistance Treaties', E. A. Nadelmann, 33 Am. J. Comp. L. 467 (1985). [70] See further, pp. 278–9.

[71] 'Mutual Assistance in Criminal Matters: a Commonwealth Perspective', D.A. Chaikin, LMM(83)29, at p. 310.

[72] 'A View from Italy on Judicial Co-operation Between Italy and the United States: the 1982 Mutual Assistance Treaty and the 1983 Extradition Treaty', P. Mengozzi, 18 Int'l Law and Politics 813 (1986).

[73] See, for example, the Caribbean Basin Initiative, where the negotiation of agreements was linked to financial aid through tax benefits.

[74] For example, the United States became very heavy handed with the Swiss and their financial interests in the US in order to force some kind of co-operation.

of treaty negotiation, the standard text offered by United States negotiators is much shorter than the original US–Swiss model.

Australian experience

In 1987 the Australian Parliament enacted the Mutual Assistance in Criminal Matters Act, and the government embarked on a major programme of treaty negotiation with over two dozen States in Europe, Asia, the Pacific, and South America.[75]

Australia is able to apply its Act by Regulations to a particular country either with or without a prior bilateral treaty. In the case of Commonwealth member countries, which are gradually passing legislation to implement the Commonwealth Scheme, there will usually be no need for a bilateral treaty; in fact, however, both Canada and the United Kingdom prefer to use bilaterals at least for certain purposes[76] and Australia has negotiated on that basis. There will commonly be treaties with non-Commonwealth countries, but this will not be insisted on where the other country already has legislation in place under which it can afford reciprocal treatment to Australia. Because of the time taken to ratify treaties, the first extensions of the Act (to Switzerland in respect of the whole Act, and to Japan, the United States and Vanuatu in respect of specified Parts) were all examples of non-treaty based Regulations.

UNITED KINGDOM PRACTICE

In recent years, the United Kingdom has engaged in a major programme designed to increase the level of assistance in criminal matters which it can both obtain and provide. The position is a fast-developing one, but at the time of writing there were three full Mutual Legal Assistance Treaties (MLATs) with Australia,[77] Canada,[78] and the United States of America with respect to the Cayman Islands.[79] By a Protocol to the last-named Treaty, its terms may be made applicable in whole or in part to the other United Kingdom dependencies in the Caribbean (Anguilla, the British Virgin Islands, Montserrat or the Turks and Caicos Islands) by Exchange of Notes between the Governments of the United Kingdom and the United States, and this

---

[75] A most useful account of the problems encountered in these negotiations is found in the *Materials* on the Commonwealth Scheme, vol. 4, p. 99.

[76] In the UK case, in the context of the confiscation of the proceeds of crime.

[77] Treaty between the Government of the United Kingdom and the Government of Australia concerning the Investigation of Drug Trafficking and the Confiscation of the Proceeds of Drug Trafficking (Cm. 1342), Canberra, 3 Aug. 1988. The Treaty entered into force on 12 Sept. 1990.

[78] Treaty between the Government of the United Kingdom and the Government of Canada on Mutual Assistance in Criminal Matters (Drug Trafficking) (Cm. 1326), Ottawa, 22 June 1988. The Treaty entered into force on 4 Aug. 1990.

[79] Treaty between the United Kingdom and the United States of America concerning the Cayman Islands relating to Mutual Assistance in Criminal Matters (Cm. 1316), Grand Cayman, 3 July 1986. The Treaty entered into force on 19 Mar. 1990.

occurred in 1990 and 1991.[80] In addition there is a large and growing number of Agreements providing for limited mutual assistance.

THE CARIBBEAN DRUGS AGREEMENTS

The earliest international agreements entered into by the United Kingdom were Exchanges of Letters with the United States, providing for co-operation in narcotics matters. These Agreements related to British dependencies in the Caribbean which are of particular concern to the United States because of both their proximity to the coast of America which makes them ideal bases for smuggling operations and also because of their strong financial secrecy laws which may attract the proceeds of the trafficking.

The Agreements have now been replaced by a full Mutual Legal Assistance Treaty,[81] but are worthy of note, not only because of their priority in time but also because of their remarkably 'unequal' nature; in effect, they conferred benefits on the United States and imposed obligations on the United Kingdom and the authorities in the relevant dependency.

The first Agreement was that concluded in relation to the Cayman Islands,[82] produced as a result of United States attempts to obtain evidence despite the strong financial secrecy laws.[83] It has been a major success, not only in leading to the full mutual legal assistance treaty but also because of the results produced in terms of arrests and convictions.[84] The United Kingdom government had already expressed an interest in concluding further drug co-operation Agreements with respect to British dependencies in the Caribbean,[85] and following the success of that relating to the Cayman Islands, its provisions were applied to the other dependencies, so producing an identical system of access for the United States to information in all of those countries.[86]

The Agreements allowed the United States to obtain 'documentary

---

[80] Agreement extending application of the Treaty to Anguilla, the British Virgin Islands, and the Turks and Caicos Islands, effected by Exchange of Notes on 9 Nov. 1990; Agreement extending application of the Treaty to Montserrat, effected by Exchange of Notes on 26 Apr. 1991.

[81] See below, pp. 254–62.

[82] Exchange of Letters between the United Kingdom and the United States concerning the Cayman Islands and Matters connected with, arising from, related to, or resulting from, any narcotics activity referred to in the Single Convention on Narcotic Drugs 1961, as amended, 26 July 1984, Cmnd. 9344. This Agreement is now no longer in force since the conclusion of the Treaty; see below.

[83] For a full discussion of the attempts to avoid the effects of the Cayman Islands bank secrecy laws, see above at Chapter X, and also W. Gilmore, 'International Action Against Drug Trafficking: Trends in United Kingdom Law and Practice', (1990) 24 Int. L. 365, 376.

[84] It has been reported that the United States made extensive use of the Agreement and received information which assisted in the investigation of million-dollar drug deals: Gilmore, above, at p. 382.   [85] See Cm. 216 at p. 3.

[86] UK–US Exchange of Letters with respect to Turks and Caicos, 18 Sept. 1986, Cm. 136; UK–US Exchange of Letters with respect to Anguilla, 11 Mar. 1987, Cm. 169; UK–US Exchange of Letters with respect to British Virgin Islands, 14 Apr. 1987, Cm. 216; UK–US Exchange of Letters with respect to Montserrat, 14 May 1987, Cm. 426. The Agreements were extended from time to time until replaced by the full Treaty in 1990 or 1991.

information' from an 'Assistor' within the relevant British dependency when the Attorney-General of the United States had reason to believe that identified persons were involved in a matter falling with the scope of the Agreement and documentary information relevant to the resolution of that matter was located within the requested dependency.[87] The Assistor was defined as the person from whom the documentary information is sought[88] with no restriction on who may be asked to provide it. The definition of 'documentary information' was equally broad; it included but was not limited to 'any document, memorandum, report, record or data compilation in any form, and any plan, graph, drawing or photograph, and any disc, tape or other device for audio reproduction or computer use, and any film, negative, tape or other device for visual image reproduction',[89] but more significantly also implicitly included 'official records'. 'Official records' are the publicly available records of the government of the requested country and its department and agencies, and also any record or information in the possession of such bodies which is not publicly available which may be made available subject to such terms and conditions as may be specified.[90] As the Agreement also made provision for the authentication of such records[91] it effectively enabled the United States to request any information, no matter what the source, and any person might be required to produce that information. There was no element of reciprocity.

The Agreement applied to:

all offences or ancillary civil or administrative proceedings taken by the United States government or its agencies connected with, arising from, related to, or resulting from, any narcotics activity referred to in Article 36 of the [1961 Convention][92] and falling within the jurisdiction of the United States.[93]

This would include offences such as laundering the proceeds of drug trafficking. It is also significant that the information sought might be in connection with ancillary civil or administrative proceedings, often excluded from more formal Agreements such as Mutual Legal Assistance Treaties, thus allowing requested information to be obtained for use in proceedings such as civil forfeiture of the proceeds of crime. Finally, it should be noted that the Agreement did not specify that any particular stage should have been reached in relation to the offence or the ancillary proceedings, and it therefore appears that provided that persons have been identified[94] a request for information might be made.

The procedure was that when a certificate requesting information was issued by the Attorney-General of the United States, the Attorney-General of the requested country would issue the Assistor with a notice requiring pro-

---

[87] Para. 3.1.   [88] Para. 1.1.   [89] Para. 1.4.
[90] Para. 1.6.   [91] Para 4.A.1.
[92] Single Convention on Narcotic Drugs, as amended, Cmnd. 7466.
[93] Para 2.1.   [94] Para. 3.1.i.

duction of the information sought in his possession, custody or control within fourteen days of the date of the notice.[95] The notice had to contain a warning stating that if the Assistor did not comply he would be liable to a substantial fine or imprisonment, and the information would be seized without his permission.[96] In order to protect the investigations being carried out in the United States, the Assistor was not permitted to tell any third party about the certificate, the notice, the documentary information or any communications in connection with the inquiry for ninety days from the date of the certificate. This ninety-day period might be extended for a further ninety days on request and thereafter for such further period or periods as the two Attorneys-General might mutually agree upon.[97]

The Agreement was unusual in that it allowed no exceptions to compliance, either to the requested Attorney-General or the Assistor. The normal practice in international Agreements is that the requested country will have the option of refusing to provide information on such grounds as prejudice to national security, *ordre public* or sovereignty[98] or on other grounds such as the request not having established that the offence was committed.[99] It is most unusual to find included as a term of an international instrument a requirement that a private individual must comply with a request and references to coercive measures by way of the imposition of a substantial fine or imprisonment.

However, the Agreement did provide substantial protection to the Assistor. Whether the evidence was taken in the requested country or in the United States, the Assistor was given the protection of the law of the requested country as regards immunity, self-incrimination, privilege, and incapacity,[100] and was also to enjoy 'in accordance with and to the full extent allowed under United States law', the protection of United States law as regards immunity, self-incrimination, privilege and incapacity.[101] No attempt was made to avoid the limitations provided by rules such as those of bank secrecy.

A significant concession was also made in that the United States agreed not to enforce any Federal subpoena—including a Grand Jury subpoena—related to documentary information falling within the Agreement in the United States without the prior agreement of either the government of the country where the information is located or the United Kingdom government.[102] The significance of this lies in the large part played by the subpoena in United States law enforcement practice in the context of seeking evidence

---

[95] Para. 3.2.a. This period might be shortened with the concurrence of the Attorney-General of the requested country: ibid.

[96] Para. 3.2.b. [97] Para. 3.4.

[98] For example, see the UK–Canada Treaty on Mutual Assistance in Criminal Matters, 22 June 1988, Cm. 1326, Art. VIII(1).

[99] For example the UK–US Cayman Islands Treaty, Art. 3(2). [100] Para. 4.C.4.

[101] Para. 4.C.6. [102] Para. 6.1.

from abroad;[103] it was in fact the excessive use of this weapon which in part prompted the negotiation of the Agreement.[104]

THE FULL MUTUAL ASSISTANCE TREATIES

Scope

While all of these treaties were concluded to provide mutual assistance, the scope of the assistance which may be provided varies between them. The Treaty with the most limited scope is that concluded with Australia as it is operates solely in the field of drug trafficking. It provides that the Parties shall grant each other assistance in 'investigations and proceedings in respect of drug trafficking, including the tracing, restraining and confiscation of the proceeds of drug trafficking'.[105] A definition is provided of when proceedings are deemed to have been instituted and concluded,[106] and of 'drug trafficking' and its 'proceeds'.[107] 'Proceeds' are limited in relation to this Treaty to any property or its value which is derived or realised, directly or indirectly, by any person from drug trafficking.

The UK–Canadian Treaty was negotiated with a view to full mutual assistance in criminal matters, but at the time of entry into force[108] was to be restricted to 'matters relating to the investigation, prosecution and suppression of offences related to drug trafficking.'[109] The Parties are to consult each other 'as soon as practicable' about extending the application of the Treaty to other offences.[110] Although the tracing, restraining and confiscation of the proceeds of drug trafficking is not expressly mentioned as being within the scope of application of the Treaty as is the case with the UK–Australian Treaty, it is included as one of the types of assistance which may be sought.[111] A greater measure of assistance is permitted under this Treaty as it may also be invoked in relation to the suppression of offences; there is therefore no requirement that an offence have actually been committed.

The Cayman Islands Treaty permits the greatest range of assistance of all the Treaties as it is a full mutual legal assistance treaty, concluded after earlier co-operation through a Agreement limited to narcotics matters.[112] Mutual assistance is to be provided for the investigation, prosecution and suppression of offences within the scope of the Treaty, including certain civil and administrative proceedings.[113] The list of offences in relation to which assist-

---

[103] See, for example, G. Crinion, 'Information Gathering on Tax Evasion in Tax Haven Countries', (1986) 20 Int. L. 1209 (1986).

[104] See above at pp. 157–9 and pp. 281–3.   [105] UK–Australian Treaty, Art. 1(1).

[106] Ibid., Arts 2(*a*) and 14.   [107] Ibid., Art. 2(*b*),(*e*).

[108] 4 Aug. 1990.   [109] UK–Canadian Treaty, Art. II(2).

[110] Ibid., Art. III.   [111] Ibid., Art. II(3)(*g*).

[112] Agreement between the Governments of the United Kingdom and the United States of America with respect to the Cayman Islands concerning matters connected with, arising from, related to or resulting from any narcotics activity referred to in the Single Convention on Narcotic Drugs (as amended), 26 July 1984 (Cmnd. 9344); see above.

[113] Cayman Islands Treaty, Art. 1(1).

ance may be sought includes not only narcotics trafficking but also a wide range of others including racketeering, insider trading, and foreign corrupt practices.[114]

The categories of offence to which the Treaty applies are never closed as assistance may be provided in relation to any unspecified offence provided that the conduct is punishable by more than one year's imprisonment in each State.[115] Further offences may be incorporated through exchange of diplomatic notes.[116] It is also significant that the Treaty expressly includes offences of a financial nature such as wilfully or dishonestly making false statements to government tax authorities[117] and wilfully or dishonestly failing to make a currency transaction report in respect of financial transactions connected with, arising from or related to the unlawful proceeds of crime.[118] The significance of this is that in order to co-operate in relation to these offences bank secrecy laws may have to be set aside.

There are provisions which the Treaties have in common, for example, the UK–Canadian and Cayman Islands Treaties both provide that they are not intended to create rights on the part of any private person to obtain, suppress or exclude any evidence, or to impede the execution of a request.[119]

Contents of requests

Each of the Treaties adopts the now commonplace procedure of establishing central authorities through which requests are to be channelled.[120] In the UK–Canadian and Cayman Islands Treaties it is stipulated that requests are to be made in writing, although in urgent cases the UK–Canadian Treaty permits oral requests later confirmed in writing.[121]

Each Treaty prescribes the necessary contents of a request (such as the facts of the case, and the relevant legal provisions) together with other details which may be included, such as any particular procedure which the Requesting State wishes to be followed, any time-limit which needs to be observed or any special requirement of confidentiality.[122] The inclusion of these, and other relevant, details can only serve to benefit the Requesting State as it will tend to improve the quality and utility of the information received. Where the details included is insufficient, the Requested State may ask for such further information as is necessary.[123]

Grant or refusal of assistance

A requested central authority has three options once a request has been received: the request can either be executed immediately, refused outright, or

---

[114] Ibid., Art. 19(3). See *Eisenberg* v. *Malone* (P.C., 1991), noted 17 C.L.B. 1028.   [115] Ibid.
[116] Ibid., Art. 19(3)(*k*).   [117] Ibid., Art. 19(3)(*e*).   [118] Ibid., Art. 19(3)(*f*).
[119] UK–Canadian Treaty, Art. II(4); Cayman Islands Treaty, Art. 1(3).
[120] UK–Australian Treaty, Art. 3; UK–Canadian Treaty, Arts. V and VI; Cayman Islands Treaty, Art. 2.
[121] UK–Canadian Treaty, Art VI(2); Cayman Islands Treaty, Art. 4(1).
[122] UK–Australian Treaty, Art. 4; UK–Canadian Treaty, Art. VII; Cayman Islands Treaty, Art. 4.   [123] UK–Australian Treaty, Art. 4(3); UK–Canadian Treaty, Art. VII(3).

execution may be postponed until a later date. Under the UK–Australian Treaty postponement is only available in relation to delivery of material, and only on the grounds that it is required for proceedings in respect of civil or criminal matters in the Requested State.[124] Postponement is available to the central authorities under the UK–Canadian and Cayman Islands Treaties when execution would interfere with an ongoing investigation or proceeding in the Requested State.[125]

The grounds for refusal of assistance vary between the Treaties. Assistance may be refused by the Parties to the UK–Australian Treaty on four grounds:

   (i) The person concerned has already been finally acquitted or pardoned in relation to the offence; or

  (ii) The person concerned has already served any sentence imposed and any order made as a result of a conviction for the offence specified has been satisfied; or

  (iii) Execution would seriously impair the security, sovereignty, national interest or other essential interests of the Requested State; or

  (iv) Execution could prejudice an investigation or proceedings in the Requested State, prejudice the safety of any person or impose an excessive burden on the resources of that Party.[126]

Insofar as financial constraints are sufficient reason for denying assistance, this is a matter which could be resolved by the requirement of consultation prior to refusal which is imposed by Article 5(5).

Although the UK–Canadian Treaty permits only three grounds for refusal of assistance they are broadly drawn:

   (i) Execution of the request would seriously impair its sovereignty, national security or other essential public interests, or for any reason related to its domestic law; or

  (ii) The request relates to conduct which, if it had occurred in the Requested State, would not have constituted an offence; or

  (iii) Provision of the assistance could prejudice an investigation or proceeding in the Requested State, prejudice the safety of any person or impose an excessive burden on the resources of that State.[127]

The words of particular concern are 'for any reason related to its domestic law', which appears to have no limits whatsoever, and the requirement of double criminality, which is not a common one in a bilateral treaty. However, it should be noted that these grounds are purely discretionary; they do not prevent assistance being granted if the requested State so decides.

The Cayman Islands Treaty has a further set of grounds for refusal which

---

[124] UK–Australian Treaty, Art. 5(2).
[125] UK–Canadian Treaty, Art. VIII(3); Cayman Islands Treaty, Art. 5(4).
[126] UK–Australian Treaty, Art. 6.
[127] UK–Canadian Treaty, Art. VIII; UK–Canadian Treaty, Art. VIII.

are very different to those in the UK–Australian and UK–Canadian Treaties. The central authority may choose not to render that assistance if

(i) The request is not in conformity with the provisions of the Treaty;

(ii) The request relates to a political offence or to an offence under military law which would not be an offence under ordinary criminal law;

(iii) The request does not establish that there are reasonable grounds for believing

   (*a*) that the specified offence has been committed; and

   (*b*) that the information sought relates to the offence and is located in the territory of the Requested Party.[128]

In addition to this assistance must be refused where the Attorney General of the Requested Party has issued a certificate stating that the execution is contrary to the public interest of the Requested Party.[129] These grounds of refusal effectively permit a review of the facts of the case by the requested central authority (point (iii) above) and this is neither usual nor desirable.

All the Treaties provide that before refusing assistance the Parties should consult one another to see whether assistance could still be granted subject to such terms and conditions as are deemed to be necessary.[130]

Execution of Requests

Once it has been decided that assistance is to be granted, the central authorities are to execute the request promptly.[131] In the case of the Cayman Islands Treaty, it is expressly declared that the courts of the Requested Party are to have jurisdiction to issue subpoenas, search warrants and other orders necessary to execute the request.[132] In each Treaty, execution of the request is to be carried out in accordance with the laws of the Requested Party, although any procedural requirements of the Requesting Party are to be complied with in so far as they are not prohibited by those laws.[133]

Limitations on the use of information and evidence

It is possible under all three of the Treaties for either Party to place conditions on the execution of a request. The Requested Party may require that any information or evidence provided in pursuance of the request is not to be used other than for any purposes specified in the request without its consent.[134] It may also demand that the information or evidence provided be kept confidential except to the extent that it is needed for the investigations or

---

[128] Cayman Islands Treaty, Art. 3(2).   [129] Ibid., Art. 3(3).

[130] UK–Australian Treaty, Art. 6(3); UK–Canadian Treaty, Art. VIII(4); Cayman Islands Treaty, Art. 3(4).

[131] UK–Australian Treaty, Art. 5(1); UK–Canadian Treaty, Art. IX(1); Cayman Islands Treaty, Art. 5(1).

[132] Cayman Islands Treaty, Art. 5(1).

[133] UK–Australian Treaty, Art. 5(1); UK–Canadian Treaty, Art IX(2); Cayman Islands Treaty, Art. 5(3).

[134] UK–Australian Treaty, Art. 10(3); UK–Canadian Treaty, Art. X(4); Cayman Islands Treaty, Art. 7(1).

proceedings described in the request.[135] The Requesting Party may for its part demand that the making of the request, its contents and related documents, and the granting of assistance be kept confidential; if it is necessary to breach that requirement of confidentiality in order to execute the request, then the Requesting Party must be informed to allow it to determine whether it still wishes the request to be executed.[136] Where information has already been made public in proceedings taken for the purposes specified in the request, the UK–Canadian and Cayman Islands Treaties permit that the information may then be used for certain other purposes.[137]

Categories of Assistance

(*a*) *Service of documents.*   This is provided for by only the UK–Canadian and Cayman Islands Treaties: service may be effected of any document relating to or forming part of a Request, and a proof of service is to be returned in the manner specified by the Requesting State.[138]

This is limited in the case of the Cayman Islands Treaty by a special provision that the Requested Party shall not be obliged to serve any subpoena or other process requiring the attendance of any person before any authority or tribunal in the territory of the Requesting Party.[139]

(*b*) *Taking of evidence.*   Each of the Treaties permits the requesting of assistance in the form of the taking of evidence. Under the UK–Australian Treaty the Requested Party is to take the evidence of witnesses 'as appropriate and in so far as its laws permit'.[140] The UK–Canadian Treaty provides that the Requesting State may specify any particular questions to be put to a witness.[141]

The Cayman Islands Treaty alone deals with measures of compulsion—the person concerned may be compelled to testify and produce documentary information or articles in the territory of the Requested Party in accordance with the requirements of the law of that Party[142]—and with questions of privilege. Where the witness asserts a claim of immunity, incapacity, or privilege under the laws of the Requesting Party, the evidence is still to be taken and the claim decided by the courts of the Requesting Party.[143] The Cayman Islands Treaty also requires the Requested Party to furnish information in advance about the date and place of the taking of the evidence[144] and

---

[135] UK–Australian Treaty, Art. 10(2); UK–Canadian Treaty, Art. X(3); Cayman Islands Treaty, Art. 7(2).

[136] UK–Australian Treaty, Art. 10(1); UK–Canadian Treaty, Art. X(1); Cayman Islands Treaty, Art. 7(3).   [137] UK–Canadian Treaty, Art. X(5); Cayman Islands Treaty, Art. 7(4).

[138] UK–Canadian Treaty, Art. XIV; Cayman Islands Treaty, Art. 13. The document must be sent by the Requesting Party a reasonable time before the scheduled response or appearance.

[139] Cayman Islands Treaty, Art. 13(1). For the background to this provision, see pp. 157–9.

[140] UK–Australian Treaty, Art. 7(2)(*b*).   [141] UK–Canadian Treaty, Art. XI.

[142] Cayman Islands Treaty, Art. 8(1). This presumably includes privileges etc. provided for under that law.

[143] Ibid., Art. 8(2).   [144] Ibid., Art. 8(3).

to allow the presence of persons specified in the request during the taking of evidence. Persons designated in the request must be permitted to question the person whose testimony or evidence is being taken.[145]

So far as the production of documents and other material is concerned, this is to be provided under the UK–Australian Treaty as appropriate and in so far as the laws of the Requested State permit. The Requested Party is to:

(a) Provide information and documents or copies thereof for the purpose of an investigation or a proceeding in the territory of the Requesting Party; and

(b) Require witnesses to produce documents, records or other material for transmission to the Requesting Party.[146]

All three Treaties make provision for search and seizure. The UK–Canadian Treaty has the fullest provisions. A request for assistance may seek the search for and seizure of material in the Requested State, and that State is to provide such information as may be required concerning, but not limited to, the identity, condition, integrity, and continuity of possession of the documents, records, or things seized and the circumstances of the seizure. For its part, the Requesting State must observe any conditions agreed with the Requested State in relation to any seized documents, records or things which may be delivered to the Requesting State.[147] The UK–Australian Treaty has briefer provisions to the same general effect.[148]

Under the Cayman Islands Treaty a request for search and seizure may only be executed if it includes the information justifying such action under the laws of the Requested Party.[149] There are provisions similar to those in the UK–Canadian Treaty as to the certification of custody and so forth, but there is also an express requirement that the Requested Party shall not be obliged to transfer the object seized unless the Requesting Party has agreed to such terms and conditions as may be required by the Requested Party to protect third party interests in the item to be transferred.[150]

The UK–Canadian and Cayman Islands Treaties provide that the Requested State is to furnish copies of publicly available documents and records of government departments and agencies. When those records are not publicly available, copies may be provided to the same extent and under the same conditions they would be available to domestic law enforcement or judicial authorities.[151]

Under all the Treaties, when the Requested Party so stipulates the Requesting Party is to return all material provided when no longer needed for any

---

[145] Ibid., Art. 8(4).
[146] UK–Australian Treaty, Art. 7(2).
[147] UK–Canadian Treaty, Art. XIII.
[148] UK–Australian Treaty, Art. 7(2)(c).
[149] Cayman Islands Treaty, Art. 14(1).
[150] Ibid., Art. 14(3).
[151] UK–Canadian Treaty, Art. XV; Cayman Islands Treaty, Art. 9(3). No special provision is made as to the supply of government documents in UK–Australian Treaty.

investigation or proceeding; the Requested Party may waive the right to have the material returned. [152]

(c) *Location of persons.* This is not a feature of the UK–Australian or the UK–Canadian Treaty. The Cayman Islands Treaty provides that the Requested Party is to take all necessary measures to locate or identify persons who are believed to be in its territory and who are needed in connection with the investigation, prosecution or suppression of a criminal offence in the territory of the Requesting Party. The results of these enquiries are to be communicated promptly.[153]

(d) *Attendance in requesting country to testify or assist with investigations.* This is not provided for in the UK–Australian Treaty. Under the UK–Canadian Treaty a request may be made for assistance to facilitate the attendance in the Requesting State of a person, other than a person charged in the relevant proceedings, to assist in an investigation or to appear as a witness. The Requested State is notify the person concerned, informing him of any expenses and allowances available, and seek his consent.[154] There is no provision in the UK–Canadian Treaty as to the immunities of the person accepting an invitation (probably due to the difficulty of giving an effective immunity within the Canadian federal system). In the corresponding provisions of the Cayman Islands Treaty, immunity is provided; the person attending is not to be subject to service of process and may not be detained or subjected to any restriction of personal liberty by reason of any acts or convictions in either the territory of the Requesting or Requested Party preceding their departure from the Requested State. This immunity ceases ten days after the person has been notified in writing by the appropriate authorities that his presence is no longer required, or when the person leaves the territory of the Requesting Party and then voluntarily returns to it.[155]

Only the Cayman Islands Treaty makes provision for the transfer of persons in custody. The Treaty stipulates that a person in the custody of the Requested Party who is needed as a witness in connection with the execution of a request in the territory of the Requesting Party shall be transported to that Party if both the prisoner and the Requested Party consent.[156] The Treaty also takes the unusual step of providing for the transfer of a person in the custody of the Requesting Party to the Requested State where this is necessary for the execution of the request and both the prisoner and both Parties consent.[157]

---

[152] UK–Australian Treaty, Art. 7(3); UK–Canadian Treaty, Art. IX(4); Cayman Islands Treaty, Art. 15.   [153] Ibid., Art. 12.

[154] UK–Canadian Treaty, Art. XII, which deserves an award for the ugliness of its drafting.

[155] Cayman Islands Treaty, Art. 10.

[156] Ibid., Art. 11(1).   [157] Ibid., Art. 11(2).

(*e*) *Proceeds of crime.*   The Treaties contain provisions of varying levels of elaboration in respect of the proceeds of crime.

The Cayman Islands Treaty provides that the Central Authority of one Party may notify the Central Authority of the other Party when it has reason to believe that proceeds of a criminal offence are located in the territory of the other Party.[158] The Parties are to assist each other to the extent permitted by their respective laws in proceedings related to:

(*a*) the forfeiture of the proceeds of criminal offences;
(*b*) restitution to the victims of criminal offences; and
(*c*) the collection of fines imposed as a sentence for a criminal offence.

The second and third items cover types of assistance not found under the other two Treaties.

Requests may also be made for assistance in connection with recovery of the proceeds of crime under the UK–Canadian Treaty.[159] In particular, requests may be made for assistance in the restraint of property for the purpose of ensuring that it is available to satisfy an order of a court for the recovery of proceeds;[160] and in securing the confiscation of proceeds. This latter type of assistance is to be given in accordance with the laws of the Requested State, by whatever means are appropriate. This may include giving effect to an order made by a court in the Requesting State and initiating or assisting in proceedings in relation to the proceeds to which the request relates.[161] In both the UK–Australian and the UK–Canadian Treaties, proceeds confiscated pursuant to a request are to be retained by the Requested Party, unless otherwise agreed in a particular case,[162] and where there is a representation made by a person affected by the confiscation (for example, by an innocent third party claiming an interest exempt from confiscation), the Requesting Party is to be informed of the representation and the outcome as soon as possible.[163]

The UK–Australian Treaty has the most elaborate set of provisions, reflecting the developed state of the law in the two countries. Restraint of property may be requested where proceedings in the territory of a Party may result in the making of a confiscation order or where such an order has already been made.[164] This applies to an order made by a court of the Requesting Party as a result of a conviction for a drug trafficking offence and for the purpose of the confiscation of the proceeds of drug trafficking. This means in the case of the United Kingdom a confiscation order and in the case of Australia a forfeiture order or a pecuniary penalty order.

---

[158] Cayman Islands Treaty, Art. 16(1). Note that this article is merely permissive, and does not deal with the situation in which a central authority suspects the presence of proceeds within its own territory.   [159] UK–Canadian Treaty, Art. XVII(1).
[160] Ibid., Art. XVII(2).   [161] Ibid., Art. XVII(3).
[162] UK–Australian Treaty, Art. 9(4); UK–Canadian Treaty, Art. XVII(4).
[163] UK–Australian Treaty, Art. 9(5); UK–Canadian Treaty, Art. XVII(5).
[164] UK–Australian Treaty, Art. 9.

Costs

The allocation of the costs of executing a request for assistance is addressed in each of the Treaties. The UK–Australian Treaty merely provides that the Requested Party is to bear any costs arising in its territory in executing a request unless otherwise mutually agreed in a particular case.[165]

Under the UK–Canadian Treaty the Requested State is also to bear all the costs of fulfilling the request for assistance but the Requesting State is to bear the expenses associated with conveying any person to or from the Requested State, and any fees, allowances or expenses payable to that person while in the Requesting State pursuant to a request.[166] If, during the execution of the request, it becomes apparent that expenses of an extraordinary nature are required to fulfil a request, the Parties will consult to determine the terms and conditions under which execution may continue.[167]

The Cayman Islands Treaty sets out a list of types of expense which 'and none other' shall be borne by the Requesting Party.[168] These include the items mentioned in the UK–Canadian Treaty and also fees of expert witnesses and of counsel, the reasonable costs of locating, reproducing and transporting documents and records, the costs of stenographic reports other than those prepared by a salaried government employee, and the reasonable costs of interpreters and translators.

Exclusivity

Each of the Treaties states that the Parties are not prevented from providing assistance under any other international arrangements or agreements which may be applicable.[169] The UK–Canadian Treaty provides that neither Party is to request any measure for the production of documents or information located within the territory of the other Party otherwise than under the Treaty (including any extension of the scope of the Treaty as envisaged by Article IV).[170]

An important provision of the Cayman Islands Treaty is that which prevents either Party from enforcing any compulsory measure, including a grand jury subpoena, for the production of documents located in the territory of the other Party with respect to any criminal offence within the scope of the Treaty unless its obligations under the Treaty have first been fulfilled pursuant to Article 17(4).[171] Article 17(4) lays down minimum periods of notice to be given where the Requesting Party considers that the request is being processed too slowly and wishes to take other measures to obtain the information or evidence which are not provided for in the Treaty.

---

[165] UK–Australian Treaty, Art. 12.   [166] UK–Canadian Treaty, Art. XVIII(2).
[167] Ibid., Art. XVIII(3).   [168] Cayman Islands Treaty, Art. 6.
[169] UK–Australian Treaty, Art. 1(2); UK–Canadian Treaty, Art. IV; Cayman Islands Treaty, Art. 1(3).
[170] UK–Canadian Treaty, Art. XX(1).   [171] Cayman Islands Treaty, Art. 17(3).

AGREEMENTS GIVING LIMITED ASSISTANCE

In addition to the full Treaties, the United Kingdom has recently concluded a large number of Agreements with foreign governments which are designed to produce a limited amount of mutual assistance, usually in a specific area such as drug trafficking. The position changes almost monthly; what follows reviews the Agreements concluded with the Bahamas,[172] Bahrain,[173] Italy,[174] Malaysia,[175] Nigeria,[176] Saudi Arabia,[177] Spain,[178] Sweden,[179] and the United States of America.[180] As at October 1991, an Agreement was also in force with Switzerland and with two dependent territories, Gibraltar and Hong Kong; and other Agreements had been reached, but were not yet in force, with Anguilla, Argentina, Barbados, Bermuda, Cayman Islands, Germany, Guyana, and Montserrat. As so many Agreements have been concluded within a short space of time, many of the provisions are comparable and indeed often identical.[181]

Scope of Assistance

In general the Parties agree to afford each other assistance in investigations and proceedings in respect of drug trafficking, including the tracing, restraining, and confiscation of the proceeds of drug trafficking,[182] although, as their

---

[172] Agreement between the United Kingdom and The Bahamas concerning the Investigation of Drug Trafficking and Confiscation of the Proceeds of Drug Trafficking (Cm. 475). Signed 28 June 1988; not yet in force.

[173] Agreement between the United Kingdom and Bahrain concerning Mutual Assistance in Relation to Drug Trafficking (Cm. 1305). Signed 24 June 1990; not yet in force.

[174] Agreement between the United Kingdom and Italy concerning Mutual Assistance in Relation to Traffic in Narcotic Drugs or Psychotropic Substances and the Restraint and Confiscation of the Proceeds of Crime (Cm. 1395). Signed 16 May 1990; not yet in force.

[175] Agreement between the United Kingdom and Malaysia on Mutual Assistance in relation to Drug Trafficking (Cm. 1176). Signed 17 Oct. 1989; not yet in force.

[176] Agreement between the United Kingdom and Nigeria concerning the Investigation and Prosecution of Crime and the Confiscation of the Proceeds of Crime (Cm. 901). Signed 18 Sept. 1989; not yet in force.

[177] Agreement between the United Kingdom and Saudi Arabia concerning the Investigation Drug Trafficking and Confiscation of the Proceeds of Drug Trafficking (Cm. 1308). Signed 2 June 1990; not yet in force.

[178] Agreement between the United Kingdom and Spain concerning the Prevention and Suppression of Drug Trafficking and the Misuse of Drugs (Cm. 830). Signed 26 June 1989; not yet in force.

[179] Agreement between the United Kingdom and Sweden concerning the Restraint and Confiscation of the Proceeds of Crime (Cm. 1307). Signed 14 Dec. 1989; not yet in force.

[180] Agreement between the United Kingdom and the United States of America concerning the Investigation of Drug Trafficking Offences and the Seizure and Forfeiture of Proceeds and Instrumentalities of Drug Trafficking (Cm. 755). Concluded 9 Feb. 1988; entered into force on 11 Apr. 1989. The Parties undertook to enter into negotiations within nine months of the coming into force of the Agreement, with a view to concluding a Treaty as soon as is possible: Art. 13.

[181] For a related agreement with Mexico, see p. 270.

[182] BAHAMAS, Art. 1(1); BAHRAIN, Art. 1(1); ITALY, Art. 1(1); MALAYSIA, Art. 1(1)–(3); NIGERIA, Art. 1(1)(2); SAUDI ARABIA, Art. 1(1); SPAIN, Art. 1(1); SWEDEN, Art. 1(1); UNITED STATES, Art. 1(1)(3).

titles indicate, some Agreements are not wholly limited to drug trafficking.[183] In some cases the scope of assistance available is wider than in the basic text, with the assistance relating also to the instrumentalities of drug trafficking or to the encouragement of co-operation between the respective law enforcement agencies.[184] Some texts include a list of the categories of assistance which may be given, but this is largely superfluous as the lists are not intended to be exhaustive.[185]

Exclusivity

In all cases the Agreements clearly state that they are not to derogate from other obligations between the Parties, or to prejudice co-operation through international agencies or in accordance with accepted practice.[186] The UK–US Agreement also states that it is not intended to create any right on the part of any private person to obtain, suppress, or exclude any evidence, or to impede the execution of a request.

Definitions

All the Agreements provide definitions of the key terms used in the text, such as when proceedings are deemed to be instituted or concluded for the purposes of the Agreement.[187] Because of the varying scope of the Agreements, in some texts the definition of 'proceeds' refers to any property that is derived as a result of drug trafficking,[188] and in others to property derived from any criminal activity.[189] It should also be noted that the definition of 'drug trafficking offence' varies from text to text. It may be taken from Article 3 of the Vienna Convention,[190] but in other cases a simpler definition is given. Offences relating to the possession, retention, control or disposal of the proceeds of the offences are covered by the Agreements.[191]

Procedure for making requests

Each Agreement adopts the now standard practice of international mutual assistance agreements of requiring each Party to appoint a central authority through which requests are to be transmitted and received. The central

---

[183] See ITALY; NIGERIA; SWEDEN.

[184] See BAHRAIN, Art. 1(1); SPAIN, Art. 1(1); SWEDEN, Art. 1(1); UNITED STATES, Art. 1(1).

[185] MALAYSIA, Art. 1(2) and (3); NIGERIA, Art. 1(2); UNITED STATES, Art. 1(3).

[186] BAHAMAS, Art. 1(2); BAHRAIN, Art. 1(2); ITALY, Art. 1(2); MALAYSIA, Art. 1(4); NIGERIA, Art. 1(3) and (4); SAUDI ARABIA, Art. 1(2); SPAIN, Art. 1(2); SWEDEN, Art. 1(2); UNITED STATES, Arts. 1(4) and 11.

[187] BAHAMAS, Art. 2; BAHRAIN, Art. 2; ITALY, Art. 2; MALAYSIA, Art. 2; NIGERIA, Art. 2; SAUDI ARABIA, Art. 2; SPAIN, Art. 2; SWEDEN, Art. 2; UNITED STATES, Art. 2.

[188] See BAHAMAS; BAHRAIN; MALAYSIA; SAUDI ARABIA; SPAIN; UNITED STATES.

[189] See ITALY; NIGERIA; SWEDEN.

[190] UN Convention Against Illicit Traffic in Narcotic Drugs and Psychotropic Substances, Vienna, 20 Dec. 1988, Cm. 804.

[191] In some cases the precise scope of the Agreement is set by reference to the content of domestic law, and the extent to which particular types of money-laundering are covered is therefore not clear from the text of the Agreement itself. See NIGERIA, Art. 2(2); SWEDEN, Art. 2(b).

authority has a duty to take whatever steps it considers necessary to give effect to a request.[192]

Many of the Agreements also follow the same pattern when laying down the requirements as to form and content of requests. The information which is required from the Requesting Party is of a practical nature, including the relevant facts and law, any particular procedure or requirement that might need to be followed, or whether a need for confidentiality exists. Additional information may also be requested where it is necessary for the Requested Party to be able to process the request.[193] In some cases provision is made for urgent requests, which should be made orally and then confirmed in writing.[194] The Spanish Agreement demands a special form of request where the request for assistance relates to the enforcement of a confiscation order, and if such a request is made, the channels for urgent requests may not be used.[195]

A few Agreements stipulate that the requests should be made in the language of the Requesting Party with a translation of the request and accompanying documents into the language of the Requested Party.[196] All the Agreements require some degree of certification and authentication.[197]

Execution of requests

Assistance is to be provided by the Requested Party in accordance with the request to the extent that this is permitted by its law and as soon as is reasonably practicable. The UK–US Agreement expressly requires the central authority to take compulsory measures where appropriate.[198]

The Requested Party is required to keep confidential a request, its contents and any supporting documents, and the fact of granting assistance. If so requested the Requesting Party must keep confidential any evidence and information provided to it, except to the extent that disclosure is necessary for the investigation or proceeding described in the request. The information provided may not be used other than as specified in the request.[199] Under the UK–Italy Agreement where information is made public in the Requesting

---

[192] BAHAMAS, Art. 3; BAHRAIN, Art. 3; ITALY, Art. 3; MALAYSIA, Art. 3; NIGERIA, Art. 3; SAUDI ARABIA, Art. 3; SPAIN, Art. 6; SWEDEN, Art. 3; UNITED STATES, Art. 3.

[193] BAHAMAS, Art. 4; ITALY, Art. 4; MALAYSIA, Art. 4; NIGERIA, Art. 4; SAUDI ARABIA, Art. 4; SPAIN, Arts. 8 and 14; UNITED STATES, Art. 4.

[194] MALAYSIA, Art. 4(1); NIGERIA, Art. 4(3); SPAIN, Art. 6(3); UNITED STATES, Art. 4(1).

[195] SPAIN, Art. 14.

[196] BAHRAIN, Art. 9; SPAIN, Art. 8(3); SWEDEN, Art. 9.

[197] BAHAMAS, Art. 11; BAHRAIN, Art. 10; ITALY, Art. 12; MALAYSIA, Art. 11; NIGERIA, Art. 10; SAUDI ARABIA, Art. 11; SPAIN, Art. 20; SWEDEN, Art. 10; UNITED STATES, Arts. 7(3) and 8.

[198] BAHAMAS, Art. 5; BAHRAIN, Art. 4(1) and (5)–(8); ITALY, Art. 6; MALAYSIA, Art. 5; NIGERIA, Art. 5; SAUDI ARABIA, Art. 5; SPAIN, Art. 9; SWEDEN, Art. 4(1) and (5)–(8); UNITED STATES, Art. 5(1)–(3), (8)–(9).

[199] BAHAMAS, Art. 10; MALAYSIA, Art. 10; NIGERIA, Art. 9; SAUDI ARABIA, Art. 10; SPAIN, Art. 19; UNITED STATES, Art. 4(5). There is no equivalent provision in the Agreements with BAHRAIN or SWEDEN.

State in accordance with the procedures specified in the request, that information may then be used for any purpose.[200]

Refusal of assistance

The area in which the Agreements differ most greatly is in relation to the refusal of assistance.[201] There are, however, some common grounds for refusal. The majority of the Agreements follow the standard pattern of permitting the refusal of assistance on the double jeopardy ground (if the person concerned has been finally acquitted or pardoned or if he has served any sentence imposed and any order made as a result of the conviction has been satisfied).[202] Some Agreements make the refusal of assistance for this reason a matter of discretion, and in others it is a mandatory requirement. The Spanish Agreement also permits refusal if the penalty is time-barred.[203] Another common ground is that assistance may be refused if the request would seriously impair the sovereignty, security, national interest, or other essential interests of the Requested Party.[204]

Other grounds for refusing assistance appear in a number of the Agreements. For example, the request may be refused because execution is not permitted under the law of the Requested Party[205] or the request is not in compliance with the Agreement.[206] Assistance may also be refused in some cases if the offence concerned is not an offence in the Requested State[207] or, where enforcement of a confiscation order is sought, if a confiscation order could not have been made in respect of that offence in the Requested State.[208] Refusal is also permitted under certain Agreements where the offence concerned is of a purely political or military nature,[209] or where granting the request would facilitate the prosecution or punishment of any person on account of his race, origin, religion, nationality, or political opinions or would cause prejudice for any of these reasons to any person affected by the request.[210]

In the Spanish Agreement the grounds for refusal are more generous in the context of the enforcement of confiscation orders. Here the requirement of dual criminality applies and special requirements as to the form and contents of request.[211]

---

[200] ITALY, Arts. 8 and 9. For rules in the Nigerian Agreement as to the manner in which the information, evidence, documents and records are to be provided, see NIGERIA, Art. 7.

[201] BAHAMAS, Art. 6; BAHRAIN, Art. 4(2)–(4); ITALY, Art. 5; MALAYSIA, Art. 6; NIGERIA, Art. 6; SAUDI ARABIA, Art. 6; SPAIN, Art. 10; SWEDEN, Art. 4(2)–(4); UNITED STATES, Art. 5(4)–(7).

[202] BAHAMAS, Art. 6(1); ITALY, Art. 5(1)(c); NIGERIA, Art. 6(1)(e); SAUDI ARABIA, Art. 6(1); SPAIN, Art. 10(1).   [203] SPAIN, Art. 10(1)(a).

[204] BAHAMAS, Art. 6(2)(a); BAHRAIN, Art. 4(2)(b); ITALY, Art. 5(2)(a); MALAYSIA, Art. 6(a); NIGERIA, Art. 6(2)(a); SAUDI ARABIA, Art. 6(2)(a); SPAIN, Art. 10(2)(a); SWEDEN, Art. 4(2)(b); UNITED STATES, Art. 5(5).

[205] BAHRAIN, Art. 4(2)(a); ITALY, Art. 5(1)(a); MALAYSIA, Art. 6(b); SWEDEN, Art. 4(2)(a).

[206] NIGERIA, Art. 6(1)(b) and (d).   [207] ITALY, Art. 5(1)(b); NIGERIA, Art. 6(1)(c).

[208] ITALY, Art. 5(1)(b).   [209] NIGERIA, Art. 6(1)(a).

[210] NIGERIA, Art. 6(2)(b).   [211] SPAIN, Arts. 12–18.

Before refusing Assistance the Requested Party should consider whether assistance can be granted subject to such conditions as it deems necessary. If the Requesting Party accepts these conditions it is bound to comply with them.[212] Postponement of execution of a request is also permitted under all the Agreements where the material requested is required for civil or criminal proceedings in the Requested State or where execution could prejudice any other investigation or proceedings, prejudice the safety of any person, or impose a disproportionate burden on the resources of the Requested Party.[213]

Costs

Generally, the Requested Party is expected to bear any costs arising in its territory unless the Parties otherwise agree in a particular case.[214] Special provision may also be made for the expenses of conveying persons to and from the Requesting State to appear in proceedings or assist in investigations,[215] and for the fees of experts.[216]

Specific types of assistance

(*a*) *Information and evidence*. The Agreements provide specific rules on the provision of information and evidence for the purpose either of an investigation or proceedings in relation to a drug trafficking offence. When such a request is made the Requested Party is, so far as its laws permit, to:

(*a*) Provide information and documents or copies thereof for the purpose of an investigation or proceeding in the Requesting State;
(*b*) Take the evidence of witnesses and require them to produce documents, records or other material for transmission to the Requesting Party;
(*c*) Search for and seize and deliver to the Requesting Party any relevant material and provide such information as may be required concerning the place and circumstances of seizure, and the subsequent custody of the material.[217]

In most cases the Requesting Party is to return information which is no longer needed for any investigation or proceeding, although some Agreements permit that the Requesting Party may retain the information and evidence provided.[218]

---

[212] BAHAMAS, Art. 6(3); BAHRAIN, Art. 6(4); ITALY, Art. 5(3); MALAYSIA, Art. 6; NIGERIA, Art. 6(5); SAUDI ARABIA, Art. 6(3); SPAIN, Art. 10(3); SWEDEN, Art. 6(4); UNITED STATES, Art. 5(6) and (7).

[213] BAHAMAS, Arts. 5(2) and 6(2)(*b*); BAHRAIN, Art. 4(3); ITALY, Arts. 5(2)(*b*) and 7(4); MALAYSIA, Arts. 5(2) and 6(*c*); NIGERIA, Art. 6(2)(*c*); SAUDI ARABIA, Arts. 5(2) and 6(2)(*b*); SPAIN, Arts. 9(2) and 10(2)(*b*); SWEDEN, Art. 4(3); UNITED STATES, Art. 5(4).

[214] BAHAMAS, Art. 12; BAHRAIN, Art. 8; ITALY, Art. 13; MALAYSIA, Art. 12; NIGERIA, Art. 8; SAUDI ARABIA, Art. 12; SPAIN, Art. 21; SWEDEN, Art. 8; UNITED STATES, Art. 6.

[215] MALAYSIA, Art. 12(2)(*b*); UNITED STATES, Art. 6.

[216] SPAIN, Art. 21; UNITED STATES, Art. 6.

[217] BAHAMAS, Art. 7; BAHRAIN, Art. 5; ITALY, Art. 7; MALAYSIA, Art. 7; NIGERIA, Art. 12; SAUDI ARABIA, Art. 7; SPAIN, Art. 7; SWEDEN, Art. 5. [218] See BAHRAIN, SWEDEN.

The Spanish Agreement permits that the taking of evidence be attended by representatives of the Parties,[219] and also provides for the exchange of information relating to criminal records and sentences connected with drug trafficking offences with this information being exchanged at least once a year.[220]

The US Agreement has detailed provisions as to the taking of testimony. Voluntary testimony may be taken by affidavit, deposition in the Requested or Requesting State, by appearance at a proceeding in the Requested State or any other procedure agreed between the Parties and the witness. If a deposition is to be taken in the Requested State, the Requested Party must authorize the presence of persons named in the request and permit them to put questions to the witness. The execution of compulsory process is to be permitted subject to the law of the Requested Party. British anxieties on this point are reflected in a provision that a Requested Party may decline to apply compulsory measures until court proceedings have been commenced in the Requesting State; however, the definition of court proceedings for this purpose includes grand jury investigations.[221]

(*b*) *Records of government agencies*   Special provision is also made in the UK–US Agreement for the provision of copies of records belonging to government departments and agencies. Copies of such records which are publicly available are to be provided, and copies of material which is not available to the public is to be provided to the same extent and subject to the same conditions as it would be provided to the law enforcement agencies or judicial authorities of the Requested Party. Requests for material which is not available to the public may be refused entirely or in part at the discretion of the Requested Party.[222]

(*c*) *Identifying and locating persons*   The Nigerian Agreement requires that, when requested, assistance be rendered in identifying or locating specified persons believed to be in the Requested State.[223]

The proceeds of crime

(*a*) *Tracing proceeds*   Assistance in tracing the proceeds of crime is granted only under the Italian and Nigerian Agreements. Under the Nigerian Agreement assistance may be requested in identifying, locating and assessing the value of property believed to be in the Requested State, for the purpose of tracing and recovering the proceeds of criminal activities.[224] The Italian Agreement grants such assistance under the general heading of information and evidence.[225]

---

[219] SPAIN, Art. 7(4).   [220] SPAIN, Art. 7(5) and (6).
[221] UNITED STATES, Art. 9.   [222] UNITED STATES, Art. 7.
[223] NIGERIA, Art. 11.   [224] NIGERIA, Art. 13.   [225] ITALY, Art. 7.

(*b*) *Restraint of property.*   The restraint of property in the territory of the Requested Party may be sought under some of the Agreements when a confiscation order either has been made or is likely to be made, as a result of a conviction for a drug trafficking offence. Third parties affected by the order are entitled to make representations,[226] presumably governed by the law of the Requested State as that is the *situs* of the property. The duration of the restraint may be limited by the Requested Party under both the Bahraini and Swedish Agreements.[227]

(*c*) *Confiscation of proceeds*   The Requesting Party may seek assistance in the enforcement of confiscation orders made by its courts as a result of a conviction for a drug trafficking offence,[228] or, under the Swedish Agreement for any offence.[229] The information required to be included in the request is specified, and third parties affected by the order may make representations. Where the law of the Requested Party does not permit effect to be given to a request in full, it is to comply with the request as far as possible.[230] Providing assistance in this area may be of substantial benefit to the Requested Party as unless otherwise agreed in a particular case the proceeds which are obtained are to remain with the Requested Party. The UK–US Agreement, however, permits either Party to transfer the property to the other to the extent permitted by their laws.

Under the Bahraini and US Agreements assistance may also be granted in relation to orders made for the purpose of confiscating the instrumentalities of drug trafficking, and under the US Agreement for the enforcement of fines. Under the US Agreement the assistance may also extend to informing the opposite central authority of the fact that there are proceeds or instrumentalities located within its territory which may be liable to freezing, seizing or forfeiture under its laws.

Other forms of assistance

The Agreements also provide for other sorts of assistance not of a strictly legal nature. For example, the Spanish Agreement contains provisions relating to co-operation in the fields of preventive welfare and treatment and rehabilitation with a particular focus on the work being carried out by the Pompidou Group. Co-operation at the inter-agency level is also permitted, which enables law enforcement agencies to exchange information directly, so facilitating their work in the prevention of drug trafficking.[231]

The Nigerian Agreement also provides for the collection of information

---

[226] BAHAMAS, Art. 8; BAHRAIN, Art. 6; ITALY, Art. 10; MALAYSIA, Art. 8; NIGERIA, Art. 14; SAUDI ARABIA, Art. 8; SPAIN, Art. 11; SWEDEN, Art. 6.

[227] BAHRAIN, Art. 6(4); SWEDEN, Art. 6(4).

[228] BAHAMAS, Art. 9; BAHRAIN, Art. 7; ITALY, Art. 11; MALAYSIA, Art. 9; NIGERIA, Art. 15; SAUDI ARABIA, Art. 9; SPAIN, Art 12–18; SWEDEN, Art. 7; UNITED STATES, Art. 10.

[229] SWEDEN, Art. 7(1) and (3).   [230] BAHRAIN, Art. 7(1) and (3).

[231] SPAIN, Arts 3–5.

and the sharing of findings, but also for visits and information between personnel and officers connected with investigation, detection, prosecution and the arrest of criminals. This may include practical and technical assistance.[232]

United Kingdom—Mexico Agreement[233]

This Agreement is unique among the Agreements signed by the United Kingdom in that its text contains no specific provisions as to mutual legal assistance. The purpose of the Agreement is stated as being 'to promote co-operation between the Parties so as to be able to combat more efficiently, on a bilateral basis, illicit traffic in and abuse of narcotic drugs and psychotropic substances.' The Parties are required to adopt the measures necessary in order to comply with their obligations, including those of a legislative and administrative nature, subject to the fundamental provisions of their respective laws.[234] The Parties are also required to adopt the necessary co-operation measures to give full effect to the obligations assumed in accordance with the Vienna Convention,[235] which do of course include the provision of mutual legal assistance. The Parties are to establish a Co-operation Commission which is to supervise the implementation of the Agreement.

---

[232] NIGERIA, Art. 16.

[233] Agreement between the United Kingdom and Mexico on Bilateral Co-operation in the Fight Against Illicit Traffic in and Abuse of Narcotic Drugs and Psychotropic Substances (Cm. 1398). Signed 29 Jan. 1990; entered into force on 1 Oct. 1990.

[234] MEXICO, Art. 1.

[235] Ibid., Art. 2.

11

Two Special Problems: Bank Secrecy and Insider Dealing

A NUMBER of special problems present themselves in some cases, in both the civil and commercial and the criminal areas. Two concern the financial services industry, the issue of bank secrecy and the whole area of insider dealing and securities regulation generally. International co-operation issues loom large in these contexts, and they are examined in the material which follows.

(A) Bank Secrecy

A request for assistance in obtaining information may conflict with requirements of bank secrecy binding on the person or institution from whom the information is to be obtained.

The existence of a duty of confidentiality between banker and client is of fundamental importance not only to the client but also to the State, as the extent to which the confidence is protected may affect levels of investment in a country's financial institutions and thus the general stability of its economy. The obligation is therefore a feature of every legal system, but the extent of the duty varies from country to country in terms both of its scope and the methods by which it is enforced. In some countries, including the United Kingdom, the obligation is a private one which will be enforced by the courts in a civil action. In some other countries, however, the obligation may originally have been purely contractual but it is now protected by statute and enforced by both criminal and civil sanctions.

The Position in English Law

In England, and in common law jurisdictions whose approach follows that of English law in treating the duty of confidentiality as resting in contract, the classic authority is the Court of Appeal decision in *Tournier* v. *National Provincial and Union Bank of England*.[1] In a much-cited passage, Bankes L. J. examined the qualifications on the duty of confidentiality:

On principle I think that the qualifications can be classified under four heads: (*a*) where disclosure is under compulsion by law; (*b*) where there is a duty to the public to disclose;

---

[1] [1924] 1 K.B. 461 (C.A.).

(c) where the interests of the bank require disclosure; (d) where the disclosure is made by the express or implied consent of the customer.[2]

It seems likely that the *Tournier* judgments will continue to set the framework for decisions in this area. Doubt was expressed by the Government's Review Committee on Banking Services (the Jack Committee) as to their adequacy in modern conditions, and codification of the law, in a largely similar but slightly modified form, was recommended.[3] Concern has also been expressed, both by the Jack Committee and others,[4] at the considerable inroads being made into the extent of the duty by the imposition of statutory requirements of disclosure on banks.[5] The Government's response was that the statutory provisions affected only a small minority of a bank's customers, and that there was no need for the *Tournier* principles to be codified by statute.[6]

In the present context, the key issue concerns the application of the *Tournier* principles in cases where banks or their officials are called upon to give evidence. There is a wider background against which that issue presents itself. As Lord Reid put it in the context of Crown privilege,

There is the public interest that harm shall not be done to the nation or the public service by disclosure of certain documents, and there is the public interest that the administration of justice shall not be frustrated by the withholding of documents which must be produced if justice is to be done.[7]

Similarly, in the context of 'confidential' social work records, Lord Diplock said,

The private promise of confidentiality must yield to the general public interest that in the administration of justice truth will out, unless by reason of the character of the information . . . a more important public interest is served by protecting the information . . . from disclosure in a court of law.[8]

There is no suggestion that the banker's duty of confidentiality ever protected him absolutely from being required to give evidence and produce accounts or other documents relevant to an issue before the courts. Before 1876 a subpoena *duces tecum* could issue and the relevant records would then have to be produced at the trial; after that date legislation, now the Bankers' Books Evidence Act 1879, enabled the court to permit a party to inspect and take copies of relevant entries, which would be admissible in evidence.[9] In effect, the Act provided a special form of discovery, subject in general to the usual rules as

---

[2] At 473.   [3] See the Committee's *Report* (Cm. 622), chap. 5.

[4] e.g. J. Wadsley, 'Banks' Confidentiality: A Much Reduced Duty' (1990) 106 L.Q.R. 204.

[5] e.g. Drug Trafficking Offences Act 1986, s. 24 discussed at p. 196. For a list of such statutes, see Jack Committee *Report*, Appendix Q.

[6] See *Banking Services: Law and Practice* (Cm. 1026), Annex 2, para. 2.12 *et seq.*

[7] *Conway* v. *Rimmer* [1968] A.C. 910 at 940.

[8] *D.* v. *National Society for the Prevention of Cruelty to Children* [1978] A.C. 171 at 218.

[9] For the background to the Act, see *Arnott* v. *Hayes* (1887) 36 Ch.D. 731 (C.A.); *Emmott* v. *Star Newspaper Co. Ltd.* (1892) 67 L.T. 829 (Q.B.D.).

to discovery.[10] Where the bank is not itself a party to the proceedings, the limitations on the discovery powers of the court are those set in *Bankers Trust Co. v. Shapira;*[11] the court may act 'when there is a good ground for thinking the money in the bank is the plaintiff's money, as for instance when the customer has got the money by fraud, or other wrongdoing, and paid it into his account at the bank'.[12]

An order for inspection under the Bankers' Books Evidence Act 1879 is available in criminal proceedings,[13] where the analogy of discovery is not available. In that context, the courts (including justices of the peace who have the same power as a High Court judge in this matter) recognize that an order can be a very serious interference with the liberty of the subject and is not to be made without careful consideration; but a plea that disclosure might serve to incriminate the accused account-holder will not be allowed to stand in the way of the making of an order.[14]

Whatever the context, the courts have a balancing exercise to perform, weighing the public interest in preserving the confidentiality expected of bankers against the public interest either in securing a full disclosure of relevant evidence for the purposes of a trial in the English courts or, in an international context, in the English courts assisting a foreign court in obtaining evidence in England. This balancing exercise was recognized as essential by the House of Lords in *Re the State of Norway's Application (Nos. 1 and 2).*[15] In a different context it also received the blessing of the European Court of Justice in 1985. On a reference from the Hoge Raad der Nederlanden, the Court had to consider the relationship of an EC Directive concerning credit institutions[16] which required Member States to bind the relevant authorities by an obligation of professional secrecy 'except by virtue of provisions laid down by law'[17] and Article 1946 of The Netherlands Civil Code which imposes an obligation to give evidence in legal proceedings. In effect the Court held that the Code provision was not inconsistent with the Directive and that it was for the relevant national court to weigh up the conflicting interests before deciding in a particular case whether to require the witness to testify.[18]

TERRITORIAL REACH OF ENGLISH ORDERS

Under English practice an order for disclosure by a bank can take a number of forms. The old practice of issuing a subpoena *duces tecum* remains available, as do orders under the Bankers' Books Evidence Act 1879 and orders for discovery

---

[10] *Parnell* v. *Wood* [1892] P. 137 (C.A.); *South Staffordshire Tramways Co.* v. *Ebbsmith* [1895] 2 Q.B. 669 (C.A.); *Waterhouse* v. *Barker* [1924] 2 K.B. 759 (C.A.).
[11] [1980] 1 W.L.R. 1274 (C.A.).
[12] Ibid., at 1282; see *MacKinnon* v. *Donaldson Lufkin & Jenrette Securities Corpn.* [1986] Ch. 482.
[13] Bankers' Books Evidence Act 1897, ss. 7, 10.
[14] *Williams* v. *Summerfield* [1972] 2 Q.B. 512 (D.C.); *Owen* v. *Sambrook* [1981] Crim.L.R. 329 (D.C.).
[15] [1990] A.C. 723.
[16] Council Directive 77/780.
[17] Ibid., Art. 12(1).
[18] Case 110/84 *Municipality of Hillegom* v. *Hillenius* [1985] E.C.R. 3947.

under the principle of *Bankers Trust Co.* v. *Shapira*.[19] The international juris-dictional limits are the same, whichever procedural route is followed.[20] An order designed to have extra-territorial effect will be made only in the most exceptional circumstances.

One case in which such circumstances were held to exist is the decision of Templeman J. in *London and County Securities* v. *Caplan*,[21] where an English bank was ordered to obtain from its foreign subsidiaries documents relating to accounts connected with the defendant who was suspected of having embezzled £5 million from the plaintiffs. The evidence of criminal fraud, and the need for urgent and effective relief to prevent evidence and the fruits of crime disappearing, justified what the judge himself described as an 'onerous' order.

In *R*. v. *Grossman*,[22] however, despite the need for the evidence in the context of a tax evasion prosecution, the Court of Appeal held that an order should not be made requiring an English bank (Barclays) to allow inspection under the Bankers' Books Evidence Act 1879 of an account held at its subsidiary in the Isle of Man. It was not denied that an order could be made in 'unusual circum-stances' but they were not present; indeed the existence of orders of the Manx court prohibiting the disclosure of the material sought was a circumstance telling against the making of an order.

Finally, in *Mackinnon* v. *Donaldson, Lufkin & Jenrette Securities Corpn.*,[23] following the *Grossman* principles, Hoffman J. set aside orders under the 1879 Act and subpoenas addressed to a New York bank (Citibank) with a branch in London which related to accounts and other documents held in the New York offices of the bank. In all the circumstances, which included the possibility that access to the material might be obtained by seeking an order from a New York court, Hoffman J. refused to let stand the orders which he regarded as 'exorbit-ant' and an infringement of the sovereignty of the United States.

Because the English court needs to consider the circumstances with especial care before deciding to follow the unusual course of making an order with extra-territorial effect, notice of any application should be given to the bank; *ex parte* applications are inappropriate.[24]

ASSISTANCE TO FOREIGN COURTS

The English courts may be asked to take evidence from banks in this country for use in foreign proceedings, criminal or civil in nature.

Where the assistance is sought for the purposes of a foreign criminal pro-

---

[19] [1980] 1 W.L.R. 1274 (C.A.), *supra*.

[20] *MacKinnon* v. *Donaldson Lufkin and Jenrette Securities Corpn.* [1986] Ch. 482.

[21] (26 May 1978, unreported), cited without disapproval in *Bankers Trust* v. *Shapira* and *Mac-Kinnon* v. *Donaldson Lufkin & Jenrette Securities Corpn.*

[22] (1981) 73 Cr.App.R. 302 (C.A.). It is not recognized that the Court of Appeal had no juris-diction to entertain the appeal in *Grossman*, as it concerned a 'criminal cause or matter': *Bonalumi* v. *Secretary of State for the Home Dept.* [1985] Q.B. 675 (C.A.).   [23] [1986] Ch. 482.

[24] *MacKinnon* v. *Donaldson Lufkin & Jenrette Corpn.* [1986] Ch. 482.

secution, the English courts will readily comply; that is to say, the 'balancing act' usually performed will generally be resolved in favour of taking the requested evidence. This was the approach of Macpherson J. in *Bonalumi* v. *Secretary of State for the Home Department*;[25] 'justice and comity' required that evidence be taken from the London branch of Banco di Roma, the Swedish Government having approached the Secretary of State who made an order under section 5 of the Extradition Act 1873 for the taking of the evidence.[26]

When section 4 of the Criminal Justice (International Co-operation) Act 1990 is brought into force, a notice by the Secretary of State will specify a court to receive 'such of the evidence to which the request [from a foreign court or authority] relates as may appear to the court to be appropriate for the purpose of giving effect to the request.[27] It is not wholly clear whether the word 'appropriate' is limited by the words which follow it, so that any exercise of discretion in the matter of bank confidentiality is excluded. Certainly the procedure under the Bankers' Books Evidence Act 1879 is available.[28]

In the civil area, the leading case is *Re the State of Norway's Application (Nos. 1 and 2)*; the confidentiality issue was one of many matters to be considered. On the first application for assistance from the Norwegian authorities, the Court of Appeal carried out a balancing exercise and held that an order should not be made.[29] Kerr LJ recognized that the veil of confidentiality should 'certainly be pierced in cases of bona fide allegations of crime and fraud',[30] but in a tax context he would not make an order which might lead to the disclosure of the private financial affairs of many persons who had entrusted those affairs to a highly reputable London merchant bank. Glidewell LJ agreed, but Ralph Gibson LJ dissented. In response to a second letter of request, the trial judge ordered that the required evidence be given, despite the confidentiality factor, and neither the Court of Appeal nor the House of Lords disturbed this point. The correctness of the 'balancing exercise' approach was accepted in each court.[31]

CONFLICTING PRESSURES

The facts that different countries take different positions on the question of bank secrecy and that a request by one State for assistance in obtaining evidence from banks will not necessarily be acted upon in another State create real difficulties for banks which maintain branches in several different jurisdictions. The practical issues are very clearly illustrated in *X. A.G.* v. *A Bank*.[32]

The plaintiffs in that case were a group of associated companies marketing crude oil, mineral ores, fertilizers, and other products. Much of their business was with governments in politically sensitive areas of the world. Disclosure of

[25] (16 Nov. 1984, unreported); see [1985] Q.B. 675 (C.A.) where it was held that no avenue of appeal was open from such an order.
[26] See p. 123.
[27] s. 4(2).
[28] Criminal Justice (International Co-operation) Act 1990, s. 4(6) and Sched. 1, para. 6.
[29] [1987] Q.B. 433 (C.A.).
[30] At p. 487.
[31] See [1990] A.C. 723, at 782 (C.A.), at 810 (H.L.).
[32] [1983] 2 All E.R. 464.

these dealings would not only damage the company commercially, by revealing its operating methods and strategies and its profit margins, but would also
have serious repercussions for their customers. It might reveal stockpiling of
strategic goods by particular governments, dealings by governments which
were in breach either of the policies publicly declared by those same governments or of a boycott on dealing with a particular State to which they publicly
adhered, or (because oil sales were the principal export of the country concerned) reveal the extent of its foreign exchange revenue. The companies'
evidence was that they had made London the centre of their banking arrangements because of the stringent standards of confidentiality there prevailing.

The companies' business was carried out in United States' dollars and,
perhaps for that reason, their chosen bank was the London branch of a bank
with its head office in New York, and so subject to the jurisdiction of the State of
New York. A New York grand jury, investigating possible tax evasion in the
crude oil business, issued a subpoena requiring the production of all relevant
documents and correspondence relating to the companies' London bank
accounts for a given three-year period. This was subsequently confirmed by an
order of a United States District Court.

The plaintiffs obtained interim injunctions in the Queen's Bench Division of
the High Court restraining the bank from passing any of the relevant information or documents to its head office; in effect, the English court prohibited the
bank from complying with the order of the New York court. This is an illustration of the wider problems experienced when attempts to assert extra-
territorial jurisdiction meet with resistance from the governments or courts of
other States, other aspects of which are examined below.[33]

In the particular banking context, it was recognized in *X A.G.* v. *A Bank* that
the ultimate decision would involve the application of the balancing exercise
described in the English cases, English law being the proper law of the contract
between the bank and the plaintiff companies. All that was actually decided
was that the injunctions should be continued, the balance of convenience
applicable at the interlocutory stage clearly favouring the plaintiffs. The court
recognized the 'immediate, irreparable and incalculable' harm which disclosure would cause them, and the improbability of the banks actually facing
contempt sanctions in New York.[34] International judicial assistance must,
therefore, take account of the importance of bank secrecy and of the differing
approaches taken in different legal systems. The issues must, in particular, be
addressed in the negotiation of mutual assistance treaties; the binding international obligations created by such treaties must either override the bank
secrecy law of the requested country or preserve it in whole or in part by
express provision. In the following pages, after a brief note concerning United

[33] pp. 278–82.
[34] Considering *US* v. *First National City Bank* 396 F. 2d 897 (2nd Cir., 1968) and what was then
the draft of s. 442 of the Third Restatement of Foreign Relations Law of the United States.

States law, these issues are further examined by reference to experience in relation to particular countries.

A Note on the United States Position

It is not possible here to undertake a detailed examination of the banker's duty of confidentiality in United States jurisdiction; State statutes will be relevant in many cases. The position at common law would seem very similar to that prevailing in England. So the Supreme Court of Idaho held in *Peterson* v. *Idaho First National Bank*[35] that 'inviolated secrecy is one of the inherent and fundamental precepts of the relationship between the bank and its customers', but also recognized that the disclosure of information would not be a breach of the duty of confidentiality where it was 'authorized by law'.[36]

In the latter context, some reference should be made to the Right to Financial Privacy Act 1978.[37] This federal statute, and a number of comparable State statutes, clarified the extent of the customer's rights after earlier Acts requiring banks to report certain types of financial transactions had survived constitutional challenge.[38]

The Act provides that no financial institution may provide to any Government authority access to, or copies of, or the information contained in, the financial records of any customer except in certain prescribed cases.[39] These include cases where an administrative subpoena or summons or a judicial subpoena has been issued and there is reason to believe that the records sought are relevant to a legitimate law enforcement enquiry.[40]

Switzerland

It is impossible to consider bank secrecy provisions without examination of the position in Switzerland, the country which is traditionally associated with banking, in which the obligation of confidentiality was a matter of customary law as early as the sixteenth century. It has since developed into part of a general right to privacy. Under contract law it is an implied condition of the contract of deposit that the banks maintain the confidentiality of all information relating to the client's affairs; the obligation is also enforced through actions in tort and through the criminal law.[41] The unauthorized disclosure of information became a criminal offence by virtue of Art. 47(*b*) of the Law on Banks and Savings Associations of 8 November 1934, which was prompted by a need to defend the Swiss banking industry and Swiss sovereignty in general against

---

[35] 367 P. 2d 284 (1961).

[36] At 290.   [37] Pub.L. 95–630, codified at 12 USC. 3401 *et seq.*

[38] See *California Bankers Assn.* v. *Shultz* 416 U.S. 21 (1974); *U.S.* v. *Miller* 425 U.S. 435 (1976). For the legislation, the Bank Secrecy Act 1970, see also p. 195, *supra*.

[39] 12 USC. 3403(*a*).

[40] Ibid., ss. 3405(1), 3407(1). In each case the customer must be notified of his right to apply to a court in opposition: ss. 3405(2), 3407(2).

[41] For a very thorough discussion of Swiss domestic law see E. A. Stultz, 'Swiss Bank Secrecy and United States Efforts to Obtain Information from Swiss Banks' (1988) 21 Vand. J. Transnat'l L. 63.

attempts by agents of the Hitler régime in Germany to discover assets held in Switzerland by German Jews and other 'enemies of the State'. The deployment of criminal sanctions thus has a specific historical origin, unrelated to concerns about investment and the state of the economy.

The secrecy imposed by Swiss law is not absolute. Article 47 of the Law of 8 November 1934 provides for criminal sanctions for breach of what is a private duty, and as a private duty it can always be overridden by a duty under public law. The extent to which it can be overridden depends on the law of the particular canton, as the scope of the duty is defined by cantonal law, but the duty to testify (which is a public law matter) normally extends to bankers and only lawyers, doctors, and the clergy enjoy in every canton professional privilege entitling them to refuse to testify as to confidential matters. 'Numbered bank accounts', a well-known feature of the service provided by Swiss banks, are in no special legal category; the only added security they afford arises from the fact that only senior managers will have access to the identity of the account-holder.

The Nazi régime in Germany featured in the background not only of the 1934 Law but also of significant later developments, which culminated in the United States–Swiss Mutual Assistance Treaty of 1973, a treaty of very considerable importance. It heralded the major developments in mutual assistance in criminal matters seen in the following decades, and was an especially notable achievement as crossing the common law–civil law divide.[42] During the Second World War United States displeasure at the refusal of the Swiss authorities to disclose banking information which might assist efforts to cripple German financial movements led to the freezing of Swiss assets in the United States.[43] There were further difficulties as a result of the *Interhandel* case.[44] The United States Alien Property Custodian had seized assets owned by a German company, and the plaintiffs (also known as Interhandel) claimed the release of those assets. In order to support its assertion that the plaintiffs were an 'enemy' within the meaning of the Trading with the Enemy Act, the United States Government obtained court orders for the disclosure by the plaintiffs of banking records held by a Swiss bank. The Supreme Court upheld these orders despite the fact that disclosure would be a criminal offence under Swiss law. A compromise was eventually reached, after diplomatic protests by Switzerland.

After these difficulties, and the identification by a Congressional committee of Switzerland as a country whose tax and bank secrecy laws were harmful to United States interests,[45] extended negotiations led to the signature of the

---

[42] See further, pp. 248–9, *supra*.

[43] For a history of Swiss–US relations, see E. A. Stultz, loc. cit.

[44] *Société Internationale pour Participations Industrielles et Commerciales S.A.* v. *Rogers* 357 US 197 (1958).

[45] *Legal and Economic Impact of Foreign Banking Procedures on the United States*, Hearings before the House Committee on Banking and Currency, 90th Congress, 2nd Sess. (1968).

Treaty on 25 May 1973. It came into effect on 23 January 1977.[46] Bank secrecy is specifically dealt with in Article 10(2):

The Swiss Central Authority shall, to the extent that a right to refuse to give testimony or produce evidence is not established, provide evidence or information which would disclose facts which a bank is required to keep secret or are manufacturing or business secrets, and which affect a person who, according to the request, appears not to be connected in any way with the offence which is the basis of the request, only under the following conditions:

(a) the request concerns the investigation or prosecution of a serious offence;[47]

(b) the disclosure is of importance for obtaining or proving facts which are of substantial significance for the investigation or proceedings; and

(c) reasonable but unsuccessful efforts have been made in the United States to obtain the evidence or information in other ways.

Evidence or information disclosed by Switzerland under this provision is given special protection by Article 15. If the Swiss authorities consider that the importance of the material so requires and makes application to the United States authorities accordingly, the material must be kept from public disclosure to the fullest extent compatible with United States constitutional requirements.

Although other Articles of the Treaty might be thought relevant, for example, the right to refuse assistance on the ground of prejudice to the sovereignty, security, or similar essential interests of the Requested State,[48] an Exchange of Notes on the signing of the Treaty recorded the understanding that Article 273 of the Swiss Penal Code and the Law of 1934 on Banks and Savings Associations would not limit the applicability of the Treaty except as provided by Article 10(2).

The experience of operating the Treaty has generally been very satisfactory, though there were difficulties over the *Marc Rich* case.[49] In 1982 the Swiss Bankers' Association, with the approval of the Swiss Government, entered into a private Agreement to provide certain information voluntarily in aid of insider dealing investigations by the United States Securities and Exchange Commission, and this was the subject of a Memorandum of Understanding between the two Governments, signed on 31 August 1982. More recently the Swiss authorities showed themselves ready to freeze bank accounts belonging to President Marcos of the Phillipines and President Ceaucescu of Romania, and to provide bank records in respect of the Iran–Contra investigation.[50]

---

[46] For the Treaty, see further pp. 248–9, *supra*.

[47] No definition of a 'serious' offence is given.　　　　[48] Art. 3(1)(a).

[49] For the subsequent Memorandum of Understanding, see pp. 287–9, *supra*.

[50] New York Times, 4 Nov. 1987: 'Swiss Bank Records in Iran–Contra Case are Released to United States'.

CAYMAN ISLANDS

Although they do not have the long-standing tradition of confidentiality that attaches to the Swiss banking community, the Cayman Islands have managed to attract the attentions of those who seek the protection of a country with strong financial secrecy rules, particularly since the inroads made into Swiss secrecy. The protection is provided in the Cayman Islands by the Banks and Trust Companies Regulation Law of 1966, which prohibits disclosure of information concerning the business affairs of any person making an application or holding a licence under the law, and also by the Confidential Relationships (Preservation) Law of 1976 as amended which prevents disclosure of information relating to customers and their accounts without full and free consent of the person affected or without an order of the Grand Court of the Cayman Islands. There are further attractions for prospective customers in that the Cayman Islands are an established financial centre close to the United States, with a great number of financial advisers offering their services and advantageous tax law. The political climate is also relatively stable given the Caymans' status as a dependent territory of the United Kingdom.

The confidentiality provided by the Caymans legislation has never been absolute. The Caymans Court of Appeal held in *US* v. *Carver (No. 5)*[51] that:

the policy of the legislature is that the confidentiality laws of the Cayman Islands should not be used as a blanket device to encourage or fester criminal activities. There is nothing in the statute to suggest it is the public policy of the Cayman Islands to permit a person to launder the proceeds of crime in the Cayman Islands, secure from detection and punishment.

However, any disclosure of information is permitted only in limited circumstances and subject to cumbersome procedures. Where a bank receives a request for disclosure of information for use in foreign proceedings, the Attorney-General must be notified of the fact and then directions are sought from the Grand Court of the Islands. Disclosure is not permitted in cases of tax evasion as it does not constitute a crime under the law of the Cayman Islands, though disclosure is possible in cases of fraud.

Before the international arrangements described below were negotiated, attempts by United States prosecutors to obtain information through criminal letters rogatory had met with limited success. The Cayman courts insisted on a two-stage procedure: they had to be satisfied first that the person concerned could properly be required to give evidence as to confidential information in his possession, and a judge would then determine whether, to what extent, and subject to what conditions he could testify.[52]

The procedure using criminal letters rogatory was notoriously slow. A good example of this is the *Interconex* case: the use of this procedure produced the

---

[51] Cayman Islands Civil Appeals 1982, unpublished.
[52] *U.S.* v. *Carver (No.5), supra.*

required evidence but took four years and was exceedingly expensive.[53] With the increased use of the Cayman Islands as a financial centre and the United States concern to close off as many exits as possible for criminally tainted money, it was inevitable that clashes would occur. The first of the clashes which led eventually to the United States–Cayman Islands Mutual Assistance Treaty was in the *Field* case[54] where the grand jury was investigating possible criminal violations of the tax laws and the use of foreign banks to evade enforcement of these laws. Field was a Canadian citizen and the managing director of Castle Bank and Trust Company (Cayman) Ltd. who was subpoenaed while temporarily in the United States on business. He objected to testifying before the grand jury as any testimony he might give could have made him liable to criminal prosecution on his return to the Cayman Islands. The court rejected the argument that requiring Field to testify violated his Fifth Amendment right not to incriminate himself,[55] and applied section 40 of the Restatement (2nd) of Foreign Relations Law to balance the possible prosecution against the importance of providing grand juries with the optimum amount of evidence. Not surprisingly the United States court felt that the interests of the grand jury were more important, but a significant factor in the judgment was the fact that a Cayman Island court could have compelled Field to reveal the information for internal investigation purposes.

After the problems were highlighted by the *Field* case the Caymans and United States governments entered into a 'gentleman's agreement' to lay down a procedure to be used when confidential information was sought. Unfortunately this agreement appeared to satisfy neither country as the Cayman Grand Court was still reluctant to allow disclosure and United States authorities continued to apply various types of pressure to obtain the quantity of information which they required. For example, any person resident in or a citizen of the United States who filed a motion in the Caymans' courts in opposition to a request for the disclosure of information, had to file a copy of the motion in the United States court, thus revealing an interest which might otherwise have been unknown or difficult to prove. It was also provided that the statute of limitation did not run when difficulties had arisen in relation to obtaining evidence from abroad.[56] The final straw which broke Cayman Islands' resistance to a weakening of bank secrecy was the approach of the United States courts in the *Bank of Nova Scotia* case.[57] In this case a grand jury was investigating possible tax violations by a customer of the Bahamian branch of the bank,

---

[53] For a full discussion of the case see Shire 'Transnational Litigation in Criminal Matters: A Case Study of the *Interconex* Prosecution', in Fedders, Herris, Olsen, and Ristow, *Transnational Litigation—Practical Approaches to Conflicts and Accommodations* (1984) at p. 533.

[54] *In re Grand Jury Proceedings, US* v. *Field* 532 F 2d 404 (5th Cir, 1976).

[55] The Court of Appeal distinguished between cases such as Field's in which the very action of giving evidence would expose the witness to penalties in the foreign jurisdiction, and those in which the *content* of his testimony could be used as evidence against him in foreign prosecutions; the Court ruled only on the former class of case. [56] 18 USC c 3506.

[57] *In re Grand Jury Proceedings, US* v. *Bank of Nova Scotia* 691 F. 2d 1384 (11th Cir. 1982), cert. den. 462 US 1119 (1983).

and sought documents and information about his affairs by a subpoena. This subpoena was later extended to the Cayman branch,[58] but the Grand Court of the Islands rule that the bank was not to make the disclosure. The United States courts were meanwhile fining the bank $25,000 per day for contempt of court. The district court[59] held that the existence of the gentleman's agreement was irrelevant to non-production and the bank was not acting in good faith. The bank reluctantly produced one document but before the case could run the full course through the courts the Governor of the Cayman Islands authorized the release of the information.[60]

Although the Cayman Islands, like other financial secrecy jurisdictions, were keen to keep a high level of confidentiality to prevent investors from taking their money elsewhere, the pressure applied by the United States, culminating in the *Bank of Nova Scotia* case, finally led to concessions, and on 26 July 1984 the governments of the United States, the United Kingdom and the Cayman Islands signed an Agreement on provision of information relating to matters covered by Article 36 of the 1961 Single Convention on Narcotic Drugs, which included an obligation to produce a full mutual legal assistance treaty within a short period of time. The Agreement only covered cases where a prosecution was under way and it provided protection under Caymans and United States law as far as immunity, self-incrimination, privilege, and incapacity were concerned. A major concession by the United States was a waiver of their prerogative to obtain a subpoena *duces tecum*[61] but the Agreement as a whole was very favourable to the United States as it produced a one-way flow of information with speedy processing of requests, as there was no requirement that the allegations be supported with documentation, merely a certificate from the United States Attorney-General that they were matters that fell within the scope of the Agreement and neither the Caymans' Attorney-General nor the person holding the information requested were permitted to reveal that a request for assistance had been made.

The full Treaty between the United Kingdom of Great Britain and Northern Ireland and the United States of America concerning the Cayman Islands relating to Mutual Legal Assistance in Criminal Matters was signed on 3 July 1985, the first mutual legal assistance treaty to be signed by the United Kingdom.[62] The Treaty is specifically designed to overrule bank secrecy laws and unlike the 1984 Agreement applies to investigations and proceedings in respect of all crimes punishable in both the Caymans and the United States by more than one year imprisonment[63] and also insider trading[64] and violations of the United

---

[58] 740 F. 2d 817 (11th Cir. 1984).   [59] Affirmed by the Eleventh Circuit, ibid., at 830.
[60] Pursuant to s. 3(2)(*b*)(iv) of the Confidential Relationships (Preservation) Law, Law 16 of 1976, as amended by the Confidential Relationships (Preservation) (Amendment) Law 1979 (Law 26 of 1979).   [61] See Nadelmann, above, at p. 56.
[62] The US Senate consented to the ratification of the Treaty only on 24 Oct. 1989. The 1984 Agreement had meanwhile been repeatedly extended by exchanges of diplomatic notes.
[63] Art. 19(3)(*a*). See *Eisenberg* v. *Malone* (P.C., 1991), noted 17 C.L.B. 1028.
[64] Art. 19(3)(*g*).

States Foreign Corrupt Practices Act 1977.[65] It also applies to all offences or ancillary civil or administrative proceedings related to narcotics activity[66] but does not extend to offences relating to tax laws except for tax matters arising from unlawful activities otherwise covered by the Treaty.[67] The procedure involves the requesting country presenting a request duly documented as per Article 4[68] to the designated Central Authority.[69] Limitations on the use of the information obtained are imposed by Article 7: the information cannot be used in relation to offences other than those stated in the request without the consent of the requested state, and the material must be kept confidential except to the extent necessary for investigations and proceedings or as permitted by the requested state.[70] The state can take compulsory measures to obtain documents located in the other's territory in respect of criminal offences within the scope of the Treaty provided the Treaty obligations have been fulfilled,[71] so subpoenas will not be enforced before the Treaty request has proved to be fruitless and notice has been given under Article 17(4).

It should also be noted that the Treaty does not extend to private parties[72] and this was reinforced by the decision in *United States of America* v. *Mann*[73] where the Court of Appeals pointed out that unless a treaty indicated the intention to 'establish direct affirmative and judicially enforceable rights' for individuals only a foreign sovereign could protest about the way it was being administered. Although this decision was based on an application for information made under the 1961 Single Convention[74] it is still of relevance to the present Treaty as it shows the United States courts' attitude towards the standing of private individuals, including financial institutions, who seek to become involved in the process.[75] A point which should also be noted about the *Mann* case is that it was decided that an individual has no Fourth Amendment right of privacy in a foreign bank account as the existence of exceptions to the foreign privacy statutes indicate that a bank customer does not have a reasonable expectation of privacy.

The Bahamas

The Commonwealth of the Bahamas is another 'bank secrecy' jurisdiction in that the obligation of confidentiality is protected by criminal sanctions. Section

---

[65] Art. 19(3)(*i*). The United Kingdom government were reluctant to extend the Treaty to cover foreign corrupt practices as the mutuality of offence element was not present.

[66] Art. 19(3)(*c*).   [67] Art. 19(3).

[68] Unlike procedure under the 1984 Agreement the Treaty requires that all requests for assistance contain documentation to support the alleged offence. This is obviously an inconvenience for the US

[70] Art. 7(3).   [69] Art. 2.

[72] Art. 1(3).   [71] Art. 17(3).

[74] Single Convention on Narcotic Drugs, 30 Mar. 1961, 18 UST. 1407.   [73] 829 F. 2d 849 (9th Cir. 1987).

[75] For a full discussion of the Mann case and the problems of the rights of private individuals under mutual legal assistance treaties see B. Zagaris, *Developments in International Judicial Assistance and Related Matters*, 18 Den. J. Int'l L. & Pol'y 339 (1990).

10 of the Banks and Trust Companies Regulation Act 1965[76] contains detailed provisions, the more important of which are as follows:

(1) No person who has acquired information in his capacity as

   (*a*)   director, officer, employee or agent of any licensees[77] or former licensee; . . .

. . .

shall without the express or implied consent of the customer concerned, disclose to any person any such information relating to the identity, assets, liabilities, transactions, accounts of a customer of a licensee . . . except—

. . .

   (iii)   when a licensee is lawfully required to make disclosure by any court of competent jurisdiction within The Bahamas, or under the provisions of any law of The Bahamas.

The penalty for breach of this prohibition is a fine of up to $15,000, imprisonment for up to two years, or both.[78]

The Supreme Court of The Bahamas has repeatedly held that, apart from the inclusion of criminal sanctions, these provisions preserve the common law principles governing confidentiality between bank and customer[79] and in considering those principles *Tournier* v. *National Provincial and Union Bank of England*[80] and other English cases are followed.

If letters of request are received from a foreign court, the court in The Bahamas will carry out the 'balancing exercise' identified in English case-law, and may order the disclosure of banking information under the procedure laid down in the Foreign Tribunals Evidence Act. This, and the Bankers' Books Evidence Act, follows the English model. Such an order was made in *Royal Bank of Canada* v. *Appollo Development Ltd*.[81] but the order made, although agreed by counsel for both parties, turned out to be defective; certain types of documents were omitted and it was held impossible to correct the error. This led the United States court concerned to issue a subpoena *duces tecum* addressed to the New York branch of the bank, requiring disclosure despite the prohibition in the law of The Bahamas. This produced a situation similar to that in the *Bank of Nova Scotia* case,[82] which was resolved when the Chief Justice of The Bahamas granted a declaration that the interests of the bank required that it produce the documents in obedience to the New York order. The strict legal effect of that declaration is far from clear, but Georges CJ regarded it as barring any claim by the bank's customer for breach of the contractual duty of confidentiality.

Relations between the United States and The Bahamas in terms of mutual

---

[76] As substituted by the Banks and Trust Companies Regulation (Amendment) Act 1980.

[77] A licensee is a person authorized under the 1965 Act to carry on a banking business or to operate a trust company: 1965 Act, ss. 1, 2.   [78] Ibid., s. 10(3).

[79] *Re Maynard and Double A Consultants Ltd.'s Application* (Georges CJ, Apr. 11, 1984); *Royal Bank of Canada* v. *Appollo Development Ltd.* (Georges CJ, 30 Apr. 1985).

[80] [1924] 1 K.B. 461 (C.A.); see pp. 271–2, *supra*.

[81] *Supra*.   [82] See pp. 281–2, *supra*.

assistance have had a chequered history. The Bahamas were identified by the United States as being a prime haven for money both from drug trafficking and tax evasion, and the perceived reluctance of its government to co-operate with the relaxation of their bank secrecy laws led to United States law enforcement agents taking unilateral steps to obtain the information required such as stealing a bank official's brief-case to gain access to details of accounts which would otherwise have been unavailable.[83] A low point in relations came after the *Bank of Nova Scotia* case, with the expulsion from The Bahamas of United States Drug Enforcement Agency and FBI personnel, allegations in United States television programmes of bribery of Bahamian government officials by drug traffickers, and the resulting establishment in The Bahamas of an official Commission of Inquiry, to inquire into 'the extent of, and the methods employed in, the illegal use of The Bahamas for the transhipment of drugs'. Ironically, bank secrecy and its possible abuse was both a subject of concern to the Commission and an obstacle to its work, summonses issued by the President of the Commission to the Bank of Montreal International Ltd. being set aside by the Supreme Court.[84]

When the Commission of Inquiry produced its report,[85] among its recommendations was one that a mutual assistance treaty be negotiated with the United States to put future relations on a firm footing. A treaty was duly concluded and signed on 12 June 1987; bank confidentiality questions were an important issue during the treaty negotiations.

The subject is not addressed directly in the text of the Treaty, although great care was taken to exclude tax matters from its scope except in so far as they concerned moneys derived from offences otherwise within the Treaty.[86] However, Article 1(4) contains the general principle that 'All requests under this Treaty shall be executed in accordance with *and subject to the limitations imposed by* the laws of the Requested State'; the words italicized were added at the suggestion of the Bahamas negotiators with bank secrecy considerations in mind. For similar reasons, the Mutual Legal Assistance (Criminal Matters) Act 1988 which enabled The Bahamas to ratify the Treaty provides that the Act shall prevail over any other written law 'other than the provisions of an Act prohibiting the disclosure of information or prohibiting its disclosure except under certain circumstances'.[87]

Article 9 of the Treaty deals with the giving of testimony in the requested State, and provides that any compulsion shall be in accordance with the law of that State.[88] The 1988 Act contains elaborate provisions which indicate what is

---

[83] For a full discussion of Project Haven and other unilateral Internal Revenue Service measures see G. Crinion, 'Information Gathering on the Tax Evasion in Tax Haven Countries', (1986) 20 Int'l Law 1209.

[84] *Re Maynard and Double A Consultants Ltd.'s Application* (Georges CJ, 11 Apr. 1984), applying the test indicated in *Williams* v. *Summerfield* (1972) 56 Cr.App.R. 597 (D.C.) as appropriate to an application under the Bankers' Books Evidence Act 1879 in a criminal context.

[85] *Report of the Commission of Inquiry (Appointed to Inquire into the Illegal Use of the Bahamas for the Transhipment of Dangerous Drugs Destined for the United States of America, Nov. 1983–Dec. 1984), Bahamas (Dec. 1984).*

[86] Art. 2(2).

[87] s. 3(1).

[88] Art. 9(1).

to happen if the witness refuses to answer one or more questions and bases the refusal on a law in force in The Bahamas. If the examiner is not himself a judge, the witness must provide the examiner within five days with a detailed statement in writing of all the reasons on which he bases his refusal. This statement is reported by the examiner to the Registrar of the Supreme Court and referred to a judge who determines whether the grounds are well-founded.[89] In the case of bank information, the effect is that the judge is able to exercise his discretion, performing the 'balancing exercise' indicated in the case-law.

In effect, The Bahamas was able to negotiate a Treaty with its powerful neighbour which covered satisfactorily the range of matters appropriate to a mutual assistance treaty, and yet left its bank confidentiality law intact. The success of the Treaty in that area must depend on the way in which judicial discretion is exercised.

(2) Insider Dealing and Other Securities Matters

The international enforcement of insider dealing laws has developed in very recent years.[90] This is a reflection partly of the general growth in the international character of crimes, partly of the computerization of the international stock exchanges which makes investigation and enforcement easier and partly of the simple fact that until recently insider dealing was not a criminal offence in many countries. For example in the United Kingdom it was a topic covered by the internal regulation of the Stock Exchange until first criminalized by the Companies Act 1980,[91] and it only became a criminal offence in Switzerland as recently as 1988.[92] There is therefore now an increased willingness to co-operate in the enforcement of such laws, and this is evidenced by the growing number of informal agreements and bilateral and multilateral treaties.

The difficulty of this area, apart from the very specialized nature of its subject-matter, is that it is difficult to bring within the more general international arrangements. So in many countries, securities regulation will be seen as of such a 'public law' nature as to fall outside the scope of 'civil and commercial matters' and so as outside, for example, the various civil procedure conventions negotiated at The Hague.[93] But other factors, including the late criminalization of insider dealing, may prevent requests for assistance from falling within general arrangements for mutual assistance in criminal matters.[94]

---

[89] Mutual Legal Assistance (Criminal Matters) Act 1988, s. 7.

[90] For a recent survey, see M. D. Mann and J. G. Mari, *Developments in International Securities Law Enforcement* (International Securities Markets Practising Law Institute, New York 1990). See also K. Hopt and E. Wymeerson, *European Insider Dealing*.

[91] The subject is now regulated by the Company Securities (Insider Dealing) Act 1985 as amended.   [92] Art. 161 of the Schweizerische Strafgesetzbuch.

[93] See pp. 18–19 and 87–9. See also case-law in the securities context (often in the form of unreported judgments) summarized in M. D. Mann and J. G. Mari, *Developments in International Securities Law Enforcement* at pp. 82–5.

[94] See the experience under the US–Swiss Treaty, noted below p. 287.

As in the general field of mutual assistance in criminal matters, early bilateral arrangements, pioneered by the United States and Switzerland, have led to a patchwork of bilateral, regional and multilateral agreements, supplemented by a good deal of informal co-operation between the relevant agencies. Initially, arrangements about insider dealing tended to be seen either as supplementary to mutual assistance treaties which failed to make satisfactory provision for this special subject-matter or as having an interim nature pending the negotiation of a comprehensive mutual assistance treaty. More recently co-operation in the field of insider dealing has emerged as a topic standing on its own, with multilateral agreements specifically designed to address this one area. Over the same period there has been some movement towards greater formality; the device of the Memorandum of Understanding,[95] for all its advantages of flexibility and relative ease of negotiation, is giving way in some areas to formally concluded Conventions.

In the following pages an account will be given first of the developing international practice and then of the United Kingdom statutory provisions enabling assistance to be given to regulatory agencies in other countries.

(1) DEVELOPING INTERNATIONAL PRACTICE

THE UNITED STATES AND SWITZERLAND

Background

The United States has been the most active in seeking extra-territorial enforcement of its insider dealing laws. Insider trading has been the subject of legislation there much longer than anywhere else[96] and the legislation is enforced by a permanent independent body which oversees the securities markets—the Securities and Exchange Commission (SEC).[97]

The first informal agreement concluded in relation to insider dealing was that in 1982 to deal with the lacuna in the Swiss-United States Treaty for Mutual Assistance in Criminal Matters.[98] The Treaty was of limited value to the United States in the enforcement of insider dealing laws because of the Treaty requirement that the matter complained of must amount to a crime in each State[99] and at the time Swiss law did not prohibit insider dealing as such. The United States government sought to obtain information by persuading the Swiss that insider trading fell within one of the special scheduled offences in the Treaty or was criminal under the Swiss Penal Code by virtue of the facts of the particular case; these efforts were often successful, but there were many challenges in the Swiss courts which led to delays in obtaining the information

---

[95] See generally, A. Aust, 'The Theory and Practice of Informal International Instruments' (1986) 35 I.C.L.Q. 787.   [96] Securities Exchange Act 1934, 15 USC s. 78a.
[97] This was established by the 1934 Act, 15 USC s. 78(*d*).
[98] *Treaty between the United States of America and the Swiss Confederation on Mutual Assistance in Criminal Matters*, entered into force 23 Jan. 1977, reproduced in (1973) 12 ILM 916.
[99] Art. 4(2).

sought.[100] A further difficulty was that the Treaty provided mutual assistance in relation to investigations or court proceedings in respect of offences which lay within the jurisdiction of the judicial authorities of the requesting State,[101] and most contraventions of the Securities Act were dealt with by the SEC through administrative proceedings.

The SEC sought to overcome these difficulties by obtaining the required information through the extensive powers available under the Federal Rules of Civil Procedure, which meant that those concerned were compelled to produce the material to a United States court under threat of heavy civil sanctions.[102] The use of these powers was controversial but did, however, lead to a sharpened awareness of the problems felt by the United States government.

The 1982 MOU

The 1982 Memorandum of Understanding (MOU) was produced to deal exclusively with assistance in relation to cases of alleged insider dealing.[103] It recorded two understandings as to practice under the Mutual Assistance Treaty. SEC investigations were to be considered investigations eligible for Treaty assistance so long as they related to conduct which might be dealt with by the criminal courts (even if in practice administrative proceedings were the more likely outcome). It was also noted that the Treaty would allow for disclosure of information where the facts alleged constituted fraud, unfaithful management or violation of business secrets under the Swiss Penal Code.[104] The Swiss Federal Council announced its intention to submit a bill to Parliament on the misuse of inside information to cover other cases.[105] In the meantime the situation was to be eased by a private agreement under the aegis of the Swiss Bankers' Association which would permit disclosure of normally confidential material in response to a request from the United States Department of Justice on behalf of the SEC in connection with a formal investigation into a violation of US insider trading laws. Breach of the normal duty of confidentiality was avoided by obtaining consent from the client either expressly or impliedly; implied consent was presumed in practice when there was a failure to respond to two successive requests for permission or where orders had been submitted for execution on the United States securities markets.[106]

The Bankers' Agreement contained a restricted definition of the insider dealing to which it applied. It applied only where a customer gave to a bank

---

[100] For an account of the leading cases, notably the *Santa Fe* litigation which went twice to the Swiss Federal Court, see M. D. Mann and J. G. Mari, *Developments in International Securities Law Enforcement*, pp. 51–6.   [101] Art. 1(1)(*a*).

[102] For a fuller note see E. Stultz, 'Swiss Bank Secrecy and United States Efforts to Obtain Information from Swiss Banks', (1988) 21 Vand J Transnat'l L 63 at p. 106.

[103] *Memorandum of Understanding to Establish Mutually Acceptable Means for Improving International Law Enforcement Cooperation in the Field of Insider Trading*, 31 Aug. 1982, reproduced in (1983) 22 ILM 1 .   [104] Ibid., Sect. II, para. 3.

[105] Ibid., Sect. III, para. 1.   [106] See E. Stultz, above, at p. 111.

an order to be executed in the US securities market for the purchase or sale of securities (or put or call options for securities), and the order was given within twenty-five trading days prior to the public announcement of a 'business combination' (typically a merger) or an 'acquisition' (the purchase of at least 10 *per cent* of a company's securities).[107] The Agreement provided for the appointment of a Commission of Inquiry which was to oversee the administration of the system in Switzerland.[108] The Commission was obliged under Article 3 to handle all enquiries provided the procedural requirements had been complied with. Once the Commission had been furnished with a report by a bank there were only two cases in which the information did not have to be passed on to the SEC: where either the bank's report or the customer established to the reasonable satisfaction of the Commission (*a*) that the person concerned was not an entity or individual which placed one of the specific purchases or sales mentioned in the SEC's inquiry or (*b*) that he was not an insider as defined in the Agreement.[109] The term 'insider' was wide enough to cover officers and agents of the company and their assistants, public servants and those who received information from such persons, but it did not extend to mere employees of the company.

A significant provision in the Bankers' Agreement was Article 9 which allowed the Commission to require a bank to block the account of the customer concerned to the extent of a sum equivalent to the profit gained or loss avoided. The amounts blocked were to be held by the bank pending disposition of the matter by SEC or the United States courts, but would be unblocked at the expiry of a limited period (in the usual case, thirty days) after the information sought in the inquiry had been sent to SEC.[110] This was of particular value, as no such interim measures were available under the US–Swiss Mutual Assistance Treaty.

Since insider dealing became a criminal offence in Switzerland in 1988, the Bankers' Agreement has been abrogated as specified by Article 11 and all requests must now be made under the Treaty, as was emphasized in a further Memorandum of Understanding agreed upon in 1987.[111]

THE UNITED STATES AND JAPAN

Since the experience with the Swiss in 1982, the United States has entered into various other informal agreements to assist in the enforcement of insider trading laws, and has adapted the 1982 model to fit new needs. An interesting example of the most informal type of agreement possible is that

---

[107] Art. 1. There are also criteria as to volume and price changes (see Art. 3(4)) but the Swiss banks indicated that they would consider enquiries in cases falling below these limits as a matter of discretion: MOU, Section III, para. 3.   [108] Art. 2.
[109] Art. 5.   [110] Art. 9(3).
[111] *Memorandum of Understanding Between the Government of Switzerland and the Government of the United States of America or Mutual Assistance in Criminal Matters and Ancillary Administrative Proceedings*, 10 Nov. 1987, reproduced in Stultz above. There were contemporaneous exchanges of Diplomatic Notes on related matters.

concluded between the regulatory organizations of the United States and Japan on 23 May 1986.[112] Securing an agreement with the Japanese over assistance in this area was more difficult than that with the Swiss for various reasons.

First, there was no history of mutual assistance in criminal matters generally in US–Japanese relations equivalent to that derived from the US–Swiss Treaty of 1977. Secondly, insider dealing was neither an offence under Japanese law nor regarded by most Japanese businessmen as unethical. Thirdly, there was a traditional reluctance in Japan to rely on formal mechanisms and procedures; there was a preference for the more subtle operation of peer group pressure and of public opinion to define the limits of acceptable conduct.[113] In terms of international co-operation, Japan had no specific secrecy laws or blocking statute but was anxious to retain the right to refuse requests for assistance on a case-to-case basis.[114] The difficulties were not all on the Japanese side; the SEC lacked until 1988 the ability to deploy its subpoena powers on behalf of foreign authorities, and so could offer only to use its 'best efforts' to respond to requests for assistance.

The conclusion of any agreement at all was therefore a major achievement, but the form of the United States–Japanese Agreement is highly unusual as it contains no definition of insider trading, no outline of any form of procedure, and not even any guidance as to the cases where assistance should be requested. The Agreement refers to the relative interests of the two States in co-operation and their reasons for agreeing to mutual assistance, but the only obligation which the agreement creates is to 'facilitate each agency's respective requests for surveillance and investigatory information on a case-by-case basis'. The success of this Agreement is therefore more dependent on the state of United States–Japanese relations than others in which a more defined procedure is laid down. Since the Agreement was signed the Japanese have legislated to make insider dealing a criminal offence, a development which may increase the effective use of the Agreement.

THE UNITED STATES AND THE UNITED KINGDOM

Since the completely informal agreement with the Japanese securities regulatory body, the form of Memoranda of Understanding has become much more procedure-based, and they are also taking a more standard form. For example, only four months after the conclusion of the United States–Japanese Agreement, agreement was reached between the SEC and the United Kingdom Department of Trade and Industry on a Memorandum of

---

[112] *Memorandum of the United States Securities and Exchange Commission and the Securities Bureau of the Japanese Ministry of Finance on the Sharing of Information*, reproduced in (1986) 25 ILM 1429.

[113] E. Barlow, 'Enforcing Securities Regulations through Bilateral Agreements with the United Kingdom and Japan: An Interim Measure or a Solution?' (1988) 23 Texas Int'l LJ 251 at p. 255.

[114] Ibid., at p. 257.

Understanding to facilitate the exchange of information between the regulatory agencies of the two countries.[115]

The MOU lays down a procedure to be followed when making requests for information with definite provisions as to cases when assistance should be provided and cases when there is a discretion to refuse the assistance. As it is an informal agreement there is no need to satisfy a requirement of dual criminality; it is sufficient that the requesting Authority suspects a breach of a relevant legal rule or requirement.[116] The relevant legal rules and requirements are defined in the MOU and include those relating to the prevention of insider dealing, misrepresentation in the course of dealing, and market manipulation, in each case in relation to securities or futures traded within the territory of the requesting Authority; or to the conduct of various types of securities or futures businesses.[117] The requested information must be reasonably relevant to securing compliance with that legal rule or requirement.[118]

The grounds for refusing to provide assistance are not extensive and are limited to public interest (determined so far as the United Kingdom is concerned by the Secretary of State)[119] and non-compliance with the requirements for requesting assistance in paragraph 7. In the latter case, where an Authority is not satisfied that a request fully meets the requirements of paragraph 7 it may require certification from the requesting Authority that the request does in fact fall within the terms of the Memorandum. Such a certification may not be challenged except on substantial grounds which are to be fully stated in writing.

The MOU goes considerably further than laying down procedures for requesting information. It also provides for the spontaneous provision of information by one agency to the other. Paragraph 11 recognizes that the regulatory bodies may gather material in the course of their own domestic investigations which point to a breach of a foreign law and it therefore provides that such bodies will, so far as its law allows, provide the information to the other Authority on the same terms as would have been applicable had a request been made. The MOU also allows an Authority to seek information from and pursue enquiries within the territory of the other Authority provided that it conducts itself 'with moderation and restraint'.[120] However, unless the information is sought from a person within the investigating Authority's own territory who has possession, custody or control of it, that Authority can only commence enquiries or seek information if it has made a

---

[115] *Memorandum of Understanding on Exchange of Information in Matters Relating to Securities and Futures*, 23 Sept. 1986, reproduced in (1986) 25 ILM 1431. On the United States side, the SEC was joined by the Commodity Futures Trading Commission; in the UK, the Department of Trade and Industry was responsible for both securities and futures matters. For a review of other aspects of US–UK dealings in this field (written before the Memorandum was agreed) see L. Collins, 'Problems of Enforcement in the Multinational Securities Market: A United Kingdom Perspective' (1967) 9 U.Pa.J. Int.Bus.L. 487.   [116] Para. 7(*b*)(iii).
[117] For the full definition, see para. 1 of the MOU.   [118] Para. 7(*d*).
[119] Para. 5.   [120] Para. 12(*a*).

request of the host Authority under the Memorandum and the host Authority has failed to satisfy the request after reasonable notice.[121] In urgent cases, these requirements need not be met, but the investigating Authority must notify and consult with the host Authority as fully as possible.[122] The investigating Authority must also enter into consultations with the host Authority about any activities within the latter's territory on request.[123]

There are stringent restrictions on the use to which that information may be put. Unless the requested Authority has been notified of the proposed use of information in other proceedings and has not objected, the information may only be used in procedures, including litigation and criminal prosecutions, relating to the legal rule or requirement specified in the request.[124] If the requested Authority has reason to believe that information is to be used for other purposes, it may demand the return of the relevant documents and material it supplied.[125] There are reciprocal obligations of confidentiality as to the use of the material and the fact that a request has been made.[126]

Paragraph 17 notes that this is to be an interim understanding with each Authority using its best efforts to ensure that within twelve months of the date of signature negotiations are entered into to conclude a treaty governing matters relating to the securities and futures laws of the United States and the United Kingdom. The date of signature was 23·September 1986 and that twelve-month period is now more than over with no sign of such a treaty as yet.

There have, however, been a number of cases in which the SEC has placed on public record the assistance it had received from the United Kingdom authorities under the MOU, one of which was of particular interest in that the actual trading had taken place on the London Stock Exchange.[127]

In August 1988 a further MOU was concluded between the SEC and other United States regulatory bodies and their United Kingdom counterparts (including the Securities and Investments Board and the Bank of England) concerning various aspects of financial regulation, notably the supply of information as to the capital position of certain dealers based in one country but conducting business in the other.

The United States and Canada

In 1988 the SEC concluded an MOU with some of the securities regulatory bodies in Canada.[128] It retains the same basic format as the MOU concluded

---

[121] Para. 12(*b*). [122] Ibid. [123] Para. 12(*c*).
[124] Para. 8. [125] Para. 10. [126] Paras. 9 and 15.
[127] This is the case of *SEC* v. *Collier* (see SEC Litigation Release 11817, 26 July 1988). See also the *Euramco* case in June 1989.
[128] *Memorandum of Understanding between SEC and Ontario Securities Commission, Commission des valeurs mobilières de Québec, and British Columbia Securities Commission,* 7 Jan. 1988, reproduced in (1988) 27 ILM 412. For the perceived need for enhanced powers to enable the Ontario Securities Commission fully to perform its part under the MOU, see 3 International Securities Regulation Report, p. 2 (14 Feb. 1990).

with the United Kingdom, and grounds for requesting and refusing assistance are the same as in the United Kingdom MOU.[129] There are provisions similar to those in the US–UK Memorandum as to the limitations on the use of the material once obtained[130] and in the fact that each Authority should provide information spontaneously when they suspect a breach of the other Authority's laws or regulations.[131] However, the US–Canada MOU incorporates many additional features designed to secure better enforcement of insider trading laws.

One change which has been made concerns the circumstances in which the requesting Authority may act itself or within the territory of the other State to obtain the relevant information, evidence or documents.[132] It is not necessary for a request for assistance to have been turned down, or not acted upon; it is enough that the request has been made. Also, where a person in the territory of the other State voluntarily agrees to provide information or documents to the Authority seeking them, there is no need for that Authority to make a request; an informal request will suffice where the material is available from a public source.

The principal difference between the Canadian and United Kingdom MOUs is that the Canadian MOU extends to regulating matters of procedure, which were not dealt with in the United Kingdom MOU. For example, Article 5 contains provisions, very similar to those commonly found in mutual assistance treaties, about the taking of testimony. So, there are detailed provisions as to the administration of the oath, transcripts, claims of privilege and the participation of representatives of the requesting Authority in the examination of witnesses.[133] The Canadian MOU also allows the requesting Authority access to information held in the files of the requested Authority.[134] Because of the existence of freedom of information legislation, the confidentiality provisions have additional features: a requesting Authority must notify the requested Authority of any legally enforceable demand for information prior to complying with the demand, and must assert appropriate legal exemptions from or privileges against disclosure where they are available.[135]

The reason that the Canadian MOU provides a much more complete scheme for assistance can be found in Article 11: when the United States–Canada Treaty on Mutual Legal Assistance in Criminal Matters comes into force,[136] the Canadian MOU is to continue in force and will be an additional method of obtaining assistance.

---

[129] Arts. 2, 3(4), and 4(3).   [130] Art. 6.

[131] Art. 9.   [132] Art. 3(2).

[133] There appear to be unresolved problems as to the admissibility in US proceedings of certain material obtained from interrogations in Canada where no equivalent of the Fifth Amendment privilege exists: see 2 International Securities Regulation Report, p. 6 (19 July 1989).

[134] Art. 5(4).   [135] Para. 7(4).

[136] *United States–Canada Treaty on Mutual Legal Assistance in Criminal Matters*, signed 18 Mar. 1985, to enter into force on the exchange of the instruments of ratification.

OTHER UNITED STATES INITIATIVES

The United States is continuing, through the SEC's Office of International Affairs, to negotiate MOUs with a view to enforcement of insider trading laws, the differing content of each Memorandum reflecting, amongst other factors, the state of the insider trading legislation in each partner country. So MOUs have been concluded with Brazil,[137] for mutual assistance between the SEC and the Brazilian *Comissao de Valores Mobiliarios*; with Mexico,[138] for similar co-operation with the equivalent Mexican body, the *Comision Nacional de Volores*. The agreement with the French *Commission des Opérations de Bourse*[139] contains provisions imposing an obligation on the requested authority to act; its implementation was delayed pending United States legislation (considered below) on aspects of confidentiality. The agreement was accompanied by an important Understanding providing for a wide measure of consultation to co-ordinate the oversight of the two markets. A few days earlier,[140] agreement had been reached with The Netherlands' Ministry of Finance for co-operation between the SEC, the Dutch Central Bank, and the Dutch Securities Board (*Stichting Toezicht Effectenverkeer*) which the SEC chairman described as 'the most comprehensive agreement on securities co-operation that the United States has ever entered into with a European nation'.[141] There is also an interim arrangement with the Italian *Commissione Nazionale per le Societa et la Borsa* providing for the exchange of information and contained in a Communiqué of 20 September 1989, and a Communiqué on Exchange of Information and the Establishment of a Framework of Co-operation between the SEC and the Swedish Bank Inspection Board, dated 27 June 1991; there have also been negotiations with Hungary, New Zealand, and Spain.

The conclusion of these MOUs has been made easier by the passing of two measures which give the SEC greater scope to act. The first of these is the Insider Trading and Securities Fraud Enforcement Act 1988[142] which formally allows the SEC to grant assistance on request to a foreign securities authority. The Act permits the SEC, in its discretion, to conduct such investigation as it deems necessary to collect information and evidence pertinent to the request, and assistance may be provided whether or not the facts stated constitute a violation of the laws of the United States. In deciding whether or not to provide the assistance, the SEC must consider whether:

(a) the requesting authority has agreed to provide reciprocal assistance in securities matters to the Commission; and

---

[137] Concluded 1 July 1988.   [138] Concluded 18 Oct. 1990.
[139] Concluded 14 Dec. 1989.   [140] 11 Dec. 1989.
[141] Signed at The Hague, 11 Dec. 1989, see The Bureau of National Affairs, Securities Regulation and Law Report, vol. 21, No. 49, p. 1820.
[142] Public Law 100–704, 19 Nov. 1988.

(*b*) compliance with the request would prejudice the public interest of the United States. [143]

While this Act made it easier for the SEC to respond to requests for assistance, the International Securities Enforcement Cooperation Act 1990[144] has provided some incentive for the foreign authorities to conclude MOUs. It has been reported that in the past the SEC has had difficulty in reaching agreement due to its inability to give assurances that confidential information would not be disclosed to third parties, for example under the Freedom of Information Act,[145] but this has been remedied by section 202 of the 1990 Act. Now where the SEC has received information under a MOU or an authorized procedure for the administration or enforcement of securities laws, and the foreign securities authority has in good faith determined and represented to the SEC that public disclosure of those records would violate its domestic law, disclosure of that material cannot be compelled.[146] This does not however extend to the withholding of information from Congress or prevent the SEC from complying with an order of a United States court in an action commenced by the SEC or the United States. It also does not affect the SEC's obligations under the Right to Financial Privacy Act.[147]

The 1990 Act also authorizes the disclosure of information by the SEC to such persons as it deems appropriate[148] and permits the SEC to take punitive measures against persons found guilty of certain activities under the laws of other countries.[149] These Acts should prove to be of great benefit to the SEC in future negotiations for the conclusion of MOUs as they have a defined procedure which allows them to guarantee the confidentiality of information and provision of assistance and also extended powers of investigation.

A DEVELOPING NETWORK

The work of the United States SEC in developing international co-operation is being copied in other countries, and a network of MOUs is gradually taking shape. For example the newly-established Securities and Futures Commission of Hong Kong signed an agreement with the United Kingdom SIB in November 1990. In Australia the Standing Committee on Legal and Constitutional Affairs of the House of Representatives in a report on insider trading[150] recommended that the Australian Government should pursue the development of Memoranda of Understanding with other countries with active securities markets. This implies that the National Companies and Securities Commission (or the Australian Securities Commission as its successor body) should be given the appropriate legal powers for it to be able to co-operate

---

[143] s. 6.
[144] Public Law 101–550, 15 Nov. 1990.
[145] See 2 International Securities Regulation Report, p. 2 (11 Oct. 1989).
[146] 1990 Act, s. 202(*a*).   [147] 12 USC. 3401 *et seq.*
[148] 1990 Act, s. 202(*a*).   [149] Ibid., ss. 203, 205.
[150] *Fair Shares for All: Insider Trading in Australia* (1989); see (1990) 16 C.L.B. 875.

effectively with overseas agencies in the detection and investigation of insider trading.[151]

(2) MULTILATERAL AGREEMENTS

While concluding an MOU with a foreign counterpart is obviously of great benefit to a regulatory agency, the negotiation of a multilateral agreement may in the end be less time-consuming and obtain a greater quantity of information. Also, more formal agreements would lead to a better degree of enforceability than MOUs which can only contain a statement of intent.[152] Two such multilateral agreements have recently come into existence. The more important of the two is probably the European Community's Council Directive on Insider Trading[153] as its provisions will have to be given legislative force by 1 June 1992[154] and compliance will be ensured by monitoring by the Commission.

THE EEC DIRECTIVE

The Directive provides a minimum definition of insider trading which prevents persons of a specified class possessing inside information from taking advantage of it by acquiring or disposing of transferable securities to which the information relates, either for their own benefit or that of a third party.[155] A minimum definition was necessary as certain Member States of the EEC do not yet consider insider trading an offence and others have varying degrees of regulation, so the aim of the EEC is to produce harmonization of laws by providing a basic standard which has to be adhered to throughout the Community. The definition is actually wider than that contained in the current United Kingdom legislation as under the Directive an insider includes anyone who possesses information by virtue of his holding in the capital of the issuer, and section 9 of the Company Securities (Insider Dealing) Act 1985 defines individuals connected with a company as those who are connected by virtue of being a director, officer or employee of the company or a related company or being in a professional or business relationship with that company. The implementation of this Directive will therefore require amendment of the present law to comply with the minimum standard prescribed by the EEC.

As well as prohibiting insider dealing the Directive also requires that a competent authority be established to ensure at a national level that the provisions are complied with, and requires these competent authorities to exchange information with each other to help carry out their duties.[156] The

---

[151] Ibid., recommendations 18 and 19.
[152] For example, see the Canada–United States MOU, Art. 3(1).
[153] Council Directive of 13 Nov. 1989 89/592/EEC, OJ/L334/30. See T. Tridimas, 'Insider trading: European Harmonisation and National Law Reform' (1991) 40 I.C.L.Q. 919.
[154] Art. 14(1).
[155] Art. 2. Art. 1 contains definitions of 'inside information' and 'transferable securities'.
[156] Arts. 8, 10.

employees of these competent authorities are to be bound by professional secrecy[157] which is also to extend to information provided to another Member State when requesting information. The exchange of information is mandatory except where excluded by Article 10(1) which allows two exceptions:

(*a*) where the communication of the information might adversely affect the sovereignty, security or public policy of the State addressed; or

(*b*) where judicial proceedings have already been initiated in respect of the same actions and against the same persons in the State addressed or where final judgment has already been passed on the same persons for the same actions by the State addressed.

The information is also limited to being used solely for the exercise of the functions as described in Article 8(1) and related judicial or administrative proceedings unless the Authority which provided the information consents to its use for other purposes or by other competent authorities.[158]

The importance of this Directive stems from the fact that it is to produce harmonized laws relating to insider dealing within the twelve Member States of the EEC with a virtually compulsory mutual assistance scheme attached. It contains a definition which is sufficiently wide to satisfy many States while not preventing the adoption of more stringent provisions.[159] Compliance with the terms of the Directive is to be ensured by the supervision of both the Commission and the competent authorities, who have the benefit of the co-operation required by the Directive to help fulfil their task. The terms of the Directive mean that it is not necessary that a breach of the rules be established before assistance is given and the assistance is available both for judicial or administrative proceedings. It is also significant that Article 11 permits the Community to conclude agreements with non-Member States on the matters governed by the Directive, thus leaving a door open for those outside the EEC to become party to the arrangement.

THE COUNCIL OF EUROPE CONVENTION

The second multilateral agreement which has recently been opened for signature is that produced under the auspices of the Council of Europe.[160] It was signed by the United Kingdom on 11 September 1989 and by the 30 January 1990 had been signed by Norway and Sweden, thus attaining the required number of signatures to bring it into force as specified in Article 14. The Convention is intended both to provide for mutual assistance in investigation of insider trading irregularities and also the surveillance of the stock markets to ensure honest dealing, although the latter is subject to reciprocity.[161]

The definition of insider trading given in Article 1 is not as wide as that

---

[157] Art. 9.
[158] Art. 10(3).   [159] Art. 6.
[160] Convention on Insider Trading, ETS No.130.
[161] Arts. 2–3.

contained in the EEC Directive as it extends only to those involved in the administration or supervision of the company and its employees and those obtaining information in the performance of their duties or the course of their occupations. It contains no equivalent to the category of person named in Article 2(1) of the EEC Directive as those holding capital in the issuer.

A further difference which could prove to be of importance is that while both agreements attempt to deal with the cases of those third parties who obtain insider information from persons directly connected with the company, the EEC Directive is so drafted as to catch a wider group. The Convention, by virtue of Article 1(1)(*c*), will apply to persons who knowingly use information communicated to them by those connected with the issuer of securities; the EEC Directive by virtue of Article 4 refers to those who possess inside information, the direct *or indirect* source of which could not be other than a person connected with the issuer as provided by Article 2(1). The Directive is therefore much wider as there is no requirement that the inside information has been communicated directly by the insider, and the burden of proof is less as the Authority need only show that the information must have come from an insider; there is no requirement to show which insider is involved.[162] There is no requirement that each State make insider trading an offence which limits the practical effect of the Convention as Article 7(2) permits a requested authority to refuse to supply the information unless certain conditions are fulfilled, including that the facts constitute in each State an irregularity as regards the rules of both States.

Article 6 of the Convention contains important practical provisions. The execution of requests is to be carried out in accordance with the rules and procedures of the law of the requested State, and the requested Authority may invoke the procedures of that law as to obtaining evidence on behalf of the requesting Authority.[163] The sanctions laid down in the governing legal rules for breach of professional secrecy do not apply in regard to the information provided compulsorily in the course of enquiries under the Convention.[164] A requirement of secrecy is imposed upon the requested Authority and on the persons seeking the information requested, applying to the request itself and the information gathered in response to it.[165] By way of exception to this requirement, States Parties to the Convention may declare the derogations from the principle of secrecy possibly imposed or permitted by national law:

(*a*) to guarantee free access of citizens to the files of the administration (i.e. freedom of information laws); or

(*b*) obliging the designated Authority to denounce to other administrative or

---

[162] The EEC Directive is also wider than the current United Kingdom legislation which also requires proof that the information came from a connected person (Company Securities (Insider Dealing) Act 1985, s. 1(3)(*a*)).   [163] Art. 6(1)(2).

[164] Art. 6(2).   [165] Art. 6(3).

judicial authorities information communicated or gathered within the framework of the request;[166] or

(*c*) provided that the requesting Authority has been informed, to investigate violations of the law of the requested country or secure compliance with that law.[167]

While it might initially appear beneficial that the Convention permits of so few reservations, the main reason for this is that the text contains so many exceptions to compliance with requests that a lengthy list of reservations is not necessary.

So, the requested Authority may refuse to supply the requested information (or supply it subject to conditions) in any case in which the request falls outside the scope of the Convention as stated in Article 1; or in which the purpose of the request (presumably as interpreted by the requested Authority) is not in conformity with the aims of the Convention stated in Article 2 (a distinctly puzzling provision, as Article 2 does not in terms state *any* aims);[168] or the facts do not constitute an 'irregularity' as regards the rules of both States.[169]

The Convention sets out no fewer than six further grounds upon which the requested Authority may refuse to give effect to a request for assistance or to supply the information obtained. These exist if:

(*a*) the request is not in conformity with this Convention;

(*b*) the communication of the information obtained might constitute an infringement of the sovereignty, security, essential interests or public policy (*ordre public*) of the requested Party;

(*c*) the irregularities to which the requested information relates or the sanctions provided for such irregularities are time-barred under the law of the requesting or of the requested Party;

(*d*) the requested information relates to matters which arose before the Convention entered into force for the requesting or the requested Party;

(*e*) proceedings have already been commenced before the authorities in the requested Party in respect of the same matters and against the same persons, or if they have been finally adjudicated upon in respect of the same matters by the competent authorities of the requested Party;

(*f*) the authorities of the requested Party have decided not to commence proceedings or to stop proceedings in respect of the same matters.[170]

---

[166] 'Denounce' is an unusual term in English. It is not clear what it adds to 'report'; in this and other respects the English text of the Convention reads very much as a literal translation from a foreign original, though both English and French texts are equally authentic.

[167] Art. 6(5).

[168] It provides: 'The Parties undertake, in accordance with the provisions of this chapter, to provide each other with the greatest possible measure of mutual assistance in the exchange of information relating to matters establishing or giving rise to the belief that irregular operations of insider trading have been carried out.'

[169] Art. 7(2).

[170] Art. 8. See also Art. 7(5) excluding the use of information for 'tax, customs or currency purposes' without the express consent of the requested Party.

Article 12 of the Convention is the sole Article of Chapter III of the text. Under it the States Parties 'undertake to afford each other the widest measure of mutual assistance in criminal matters relating to offences involving insider trading'.[171] This provision attracts, it seems, none of the grounds just referred to as grounds on which a request for assistance may be refused. Equally, there are no provisions as to when assistance of a particular kind will be given; yet Article 7(4) provides that information supplied will be used in a criminal court 'only in cases where it could have been obtained by application of Chapter III'. It seems that the intention is that mutual assistance not expressly covered by Chapter II (i.e. Articles 2–11) should be available only so far as other multilateral or bilateral arrangements allow, and that this is the meaning to be given to the language of Article 12(2) which declares that nothing in the Convention is to restrict or prejudice the application of such arrangements. Putting it bluntly, Chapter III merely points to the possibility that other mutual assistance arrangements exist without adding to or subtracting from them.

While the Convention permits for a substantial number of exceptions to co-operation and is subject to the EEC Directive for those Parties also members of the Community,[172] the Convention is none the less likely to be of benefit as, despite its flaws, it will produce more co-operation than would have arisen without it, and it provides a good foundation on which to base future agreement. With the growing concern for co-operation in the international enforcement of securities laws it is likely that further multilateral agreements will appear, though perhaps not on the scale of those produced by the EEC and the Council of Europe. The need for multilateral action has been recognized in papers considered by senior officials of Commonwealth Law Ministries and by Commonwealth Law Ministers, and it has been suggested that rather than informal bilateral Memoranda of Understanding the approach to be taken should follow the example of the United Kingdom's Securities Investment Board and other similar agencies throughout the Commonwealth which have mandatory powers to assist investigations by overseas agencies.[173] This need for co-operation has also been recognized by the International Organization of Securities Commissions (IOSCO)[174] which has passed a number of resolutions calling for the provision of information on a reciprocal basis to the extent permitted under existing law, and encouraging the negotiation of bilateral or multilateral understandings.

---

[171] Art. 12(1).

[172] Arts. 16 *bis* added by the Protocol of 11 Sept. 1989, ETS No.133.

[173] *Mutual Assistance in the Administration of Justice: Cooperating to Combat Fraud in the Financial Matters—A Memorandum Presented by the Commonwealth Secretariat* (Senior Officials' Meeting, 1989); *Mutual Assistance Between Business Regulatory Agencies*, A Paper by the Australian Attorney-General's Department, Meeting of Commonwealth Law Ministers, Christchurch, 1990.

[174] Originally an Inter-American body but now with a world-wide membership.

(3) UNITED KINGDOM LEGISLATION

During the 1980s the United Kingdom Parliament passed a series of Acts overhauling the system of controls on the work of financial institutions. The powers of investigation into the affairs of companies consolidated in Part XIV of the Companies Act 1985,[175] read with the Company Securities (Insider Dealing) Act 1985 and the Company Directors Disqualification Act 1986, were formidable in themselves. The Building Societies Act 1986 established the Building Societies Commission with its own investigative powers; the Banking Act 1987 strengthened the powers of the Bank of England over the banking sector; and the Financial Services Act 1986 overhauled the regulation of investment business and made specific provision for investigations into insider dealing.[176]

The need for statutory provisions covering international co-operation was recognized in the Companies Act 1989. Two types of provision were included: the first permitted the disclosure to 'overseas regulatory authorities' of information obtained under the existing investigative powers. So, where documents had been produced under section 447 of the Companies Act 1985, it was now provided that the information or the relevant document could be disclosed for the purpose of enabling or assisting an overseas regulatory authority to exercise its regulatory functions.[177] Similar changes were made in the Financial Services Act 1986,[178] the Building Societies Act 1986,[179] and the Banking Act 1987.[180]

The second type of provision in the Companies Act 1989 was a set of new powers exercisable to assist 'overseas regulatory authorities' and contained in sections 82–91 of Act. Here, as in the first type of provision, the definition of 'overseas regulatory authority' is of great importance. It includes[181] an authority which in a country or territory outside the United Kingdom exercises functions corresponding to those under certain pieces of domestic legislation: (i) a function under the Financial Services Act 1986 of a designated agency, transferee body or competent authority within the meaning of that Act;[182] (ii) a function of the Secretary of State under the Insurance Companies

---

[175] i.e. Companies Act 1985, ss. 431–53.   [176] Financial Services Act 1986, s. 177.

[177] Companies Act 1985, s. 449(1)(*m*) as substituted by Companies Act 1989, s. 65(2)(*i*) (in place of an earlier formulation introduced by the Financial Services Act 1986, Sch. 13, para. 9(1)(*c*)). See also Companies Act 1985, s. 449(1)(*c*), as substituted by Companies Act 1989, s. 65(2)(*d*), which authorizes disclosure for the purpose of assisting the Secretary of State to discharge his functions under, *inter alia*, Part III of the 1989 Act, which includes responding to assistance from overseas regulatory authorities.

[178] Financial Services Act 1986, s. 180(1)(*qq*) added by Companies Act 1989, s. 76(3)(*f*).

[179] Building Societies Act 1986, s. 53(7)(*b*)(iii), inserted by Companies Act 1989, s. 80 (reference to Part III of the 1989 Act).

[180] Banking Act 1987, s. 84(1) as amended by Companies Act 1989, s. 81(2) (again referring to Part III of the 1989 Act).   [181] Companies Act 1989, s. 82(2).

[182] i.e. bodies such as the Stock Exchange, the Securities and Investment Board and the Securities Association. For definitions see 1986 Act, ss. 114(3) ('designated agency') and 207(1) ('competent authority') and Sched. 11, para. 28(4) ('transferee body').

Act 1982, the Companies Act 1985, or the Financial Services Act 1986; or (iii) a function of the Bank of England under the Banking Act 1987. It also includes an authority similarly exercising a function in connection with the investigation of, or the enforcement of rules (whether or not having the force of law) relating to conduct of the kind prohibited by the Company Securities (Insider Dealing) Act 1985. It may also be extended by an order of the Secretary of State made as a statutory instrument to other bodies similarly exercising functions relating to companies or financial services.[183]

The Secretary of State is not to exercise any of the new powers conferred by section 83 of the 1989 Act unless he is satisfied that the assistance requested by the overseas regulatory authority is for the purposes of its regulatory functions.[184] In deciding whether or not to exercise these powers he may take into account, in particular,

(a) whether corresponding assistance would be given by that country to a United Kingdom regulatory body;
(b) whether the enquiries relate to the possible breach of a law or other requirement which has no close parallel in the United Kingdom or involves the assertion of a jurisdiction not recognized here;
(c) the seriousness of the matter, the importance to the enquiries of the information to be sought and whether the assistance could be obtained by other means; and
(d) whether it is otherwise in the public interest to grant the assistance.[185]

Where the overseas regulatory authority is a banking supervisor the Secretary of State must consult the Bank of England before making any decision.[186]

In the Committee stage of the Bill's passage through the House of Lords, Lord Young, then Secretary of State for Trade and Industry, stated that he would not exercise the powers unless he believed that the request had been made in good faith, and that, in order to protect confidentiality, information would only be released in two cases: (i) under arrangements such as bilateral MOUs which covered the exchange of regulatory information with provisions limiting disclosure and use by the requesting authority; and (ii) where such arrangements do not exist or are not applicable, subject to broadly similar conditions imposed on an *ad hoc* basis. If there was reason to suspect that these conditions would not be observed, the Secretary of State would have discretion on those grounds not to initiate an investigation or not to pass on some or all of the information obtained during the investigation.[187] The Secretary of State may also decline to exercise those powers unless the requesting authority agrees to make such contribution to the cost as he may deem appropriate.[188]

---

[183] Companies Act 1989, s. 82(2)(c); no such order has yet been made.
[184] s. 82(3).   [185] s. 82(4).   [186] s. 82(5).
[187] 504 *Parliamentary Debates (Lords)* 107.   [188] s. 82(6).

The powers of the Secretary of State are contained in section 83(2); he may exercise them if he considers that there is 'good reason' to do so.[189] He may require any person:

(*a*) to attend before him and answer questions or otherwise furnish information with respect to any matter relevant to the enquiries;
(*b*) to produce any specified documents which appear to him to relate to any matter relevant to the enquiries; and
(*c*) otherwise to give him such assistance in connection with the enquiries as they are reasonably able to give.

Persons required to appear may be examined on oath[190] and where documents are produced copies or extracts may be taken.[191] 'Documents' includes information recorded in any form; and where this recording is not in a legible form, the power to require production includes the power to require production in a legible form.[192] So, for example, a document may be held as a file in a computer system; a 'hard copy' print-out can be required. A statement made in compliance with a requirement under section 83 may be used in evidence against the person that made it.[193] Nothing requires a person to disclose information or produce a document which would be covered by legal professional privilege; however, a lawyer may be required to furnish the name and address of his client.[194]

The Secretary of State is entitled to delegate the exercise of any or all of the powers in section 83 to 'an officer of his or any other competent person'.[195] Such authority may only be granted for the purpose of investigating the affairs or any aspects of the affairs of a specified person or a specified subject-matter the subject of the enquiries being carried out by or on behalf of the overseas regulatory authority.[196] The authorized person (if not an officer of the Department of Trade and Industry) must report to the Secretary of State as required on the exercise of the powers and any results produced.[197] A person authorized to act in this way is not obliged to disclose any information or produce any documents in respect of which he owes his obligation of confidence by virtue of carrying on the business of banking unless (i) the imposing of a requirement of disclosure was specifically authorized by the Secretary of State; or (ii) the person to whom the obligation of confidence is owed consents.

While the 1989 Act gives the Secretary of State power to obtain information, it also imposes restrictions on the circumstances in which that information may be disclosed. The restrictions apply to information relating to the business or other affairs of a person which is either supplied by the overseas regulatory authority in connection with the request for assistance or which is obtained by virtue of the powers contained in section 83, whether in response

---

[189] s. 83(1).   [190] s. 83(3).   [191] s. 83(4).
[192] s. 83(8).   [193] s. 83(6).   [194] s. 83(5).
[195] s. 84(1).   [196] s. 84(2).   [197] s. 84(5).

to a requirement under that section or not;[198] except where permitted by section 87 the information is not to be disclosed by the 'primary recipient'[199] or by any person obtaining the information directly or indirectly from him without the consent of the person from whom the primary recipient obtained it. Where that is not the person to whom the information relates, his consent must also be obtained.[200] The use of information which is already public and was not disclosed in circumstances precluded by the section is not restricted.[201]

The exceptions to the restrictions on disclosure are contained in section 87 and are limited to six cases:

(*a*) with a view to the institution of, or otherwise for the purposes of, 'relevant proceedings'; 'relevant proceedings' are defined[202] as being any criminal proceedings, any civil proceedings under the Financial Services Act 1986, proceedings before the Financial Services Tribunal and disciplinary proceedings of solicitors, auditors, accountants, valuers, actuaries or public servants;

(*b*) to enable or assist a 'relevant authority' to discharge any relevant function, including functions in relation to proceedings; 'relevant authority' is defined[203] as including a large number of United Kingdom bodies from the Secretary of State to the Building Societies Commission and the Director General of Fair Trading[204] and, of particular importance in the present context, an overseas regulatory body in respect of its regulatory functions;

(*c*) to the Treasury, if made in the interests of investors or the public interest;

(*d*) if it has been available to the public from other sources;

(*e*) in a summary or collection of information framed in such a way that the identity of any person to whom it relates cannot be ascertained;

(*f*) in pursuance of any European Community obligation.

Failure to comply with a requirement to attend for questioning or to produce documents or give other assistance[205] is an offence carrying a maximum penalty of six months imprisonment, a fine not exceeding Level 5 on the standard scale, or both.[206] The provision of false information is also an offence, with a heavier penalty of up to two years imprisonment and a fine unlimited in amount.[207]

---

[198] s. 86(1).

[199] Defined in s. 86(3) to mean the Secretary of State, a person authorized to act for him under section 84, or an office or servant of any such person.   [200] s. 86(2).

[201] s. 86(4).   [202] s. 87(2).   [203] s. 87(4).

[204] The list of relevant authorities may be amended by the Secretary of State by order, s. 88(5).

[205] i.e. a requirement in pursuance of the powers given by s. 83.

[206] s. 85(1).

[207] s. 85(2). For the requirement of the consent of the Director of Public Prosecutions for a prosecution see s. 89; for offences by bodies corporate etc., see s. 90; for jurisdiction and procedure, see s. 91.

Appendix
of Selected Documents

(*a*) The Hague Service Convention

(*b*) The Hague Evidence Convention

(*c*) The Commonwealth Scheme for Mutual Assistance in Criminal Matters

(*d*) The Council of Europe Convention on Laundering, Search, Seizure and Confiscation of the Proceeds from Crime

(a) The Hague Service Convention

CONVENTION RELATIVE
A LA SIGNIFICATION ET LA NOTIFICATION
A L'ÉTRANGER DES ACTES JUDICIAIRES ET
EXTRAJUDICIAIRES EN MATIÈRE CIVILE OU
COMMERCIALE

CONVENTION ON THE SERVICE ABROAD OF
JUDICIAL AND EXTRAJUDICIAL DOCUMENTS
IN CIVIL OR COMMERCIAL MATTERS

Les Etats signataires de la présente Convention,

The States signatory to the present Convention,

Désirant créer les moyens appropriés pour que les actes judiciaires et extrajudiciaires qui doivent être signifiés ou notifiés à l'étranger soient connus de leurs destinataires en temps utile,

Desiring to create appropriate means to ensure that judicial and extrajudicial documents to be served abroad shall be brought to the notice of the addressee in sufficient time,

Soucieux d'améliorer a cette fin l'entraide judiciaire mutuelle en simplifiant et en accélérant la procédure,

Desiring to improve the organisation of mutual judicial assistance for that purpose by simplifying and expediting the procedure,

Ont résolu de conclure une Convention à ces effets et son convenus des dispositions ssuivantes:

Having resolved to conclude a Convention to this effect and have agreed upon the following provisions:

ARTICLE PREMIER

La présente Convention est applicable, en matière civile ou commerciale, dans tous les cas où un acte judiciaire ou extrajudiciaire doit être transmis à l'étranger pour y être signifié ou notifié.

La Convention ne s'applique pas lorsque l'adresse du destinataire de l'acte n'est pas connue.

ARTICLE 1

The present Convention shall apply in all cases, in civil or commercial matters, where there is occasion to transmit a judicial or extrajudicial document for service abroad.

This Convention shall not apply where the address of the person to be served with the document is not known.

CHAPITRE I—ACTES JUDICIAIRES

ARTICLE 2

Chaque Etat contractant désigne une Autorité centrale qui assume, conformément aux articles 3 à 6, la charge de recevoir les demandes de signification ou de notification en provenance d'un autre Etat contractant et d'y donner suite.

L'Autorité centrale est organisée selon les modalités prévues par l'Etat requis.

ARTICLE 3

L'autorité ou l'officier ministériel compétents selon les lois de l'Etat d'origine adresse à l'Autorité centrale de l'Etat requis une demande conforme à la formule modèle annexée à la présente Convention, sans qu'il soit besoin de la légalisation des pièces ni d'une autre formalité équivalente.

La demande doit être accompagnée de l'acte judiciaire ou de sa copie, le tout en double exemplaire.

ARTICLE 4

Si l'Autorité centrale estime que les dispositions de la Convention n'ont pas été respectées, elle en informe immédiatement le requérant en précisant les griefs articulés à l'encontre de la demande.

ARTICLE 5

L'Autorité centrale de l'Etat requis procède ou fait procéder à la signification ou à la notification de l'acte:

(a) soit selon les formes prescrites par la législation de l'Etat requis pour la signification ou la notification des actes dressés dans ce pays et qui sont destinés aux personnes se trouvant sur son territoire;

(b) soit selon la forme particulière demandée par le requérant, pourvu que celle-ci ne soit pas incompatible avec la loi de l'Etat requis.

Sauf le cas prévu à l'alinéa premier, lettre (b), l'acte peut toujours être remis au destinataire qui l'accepte volontairement.

Si l'acte doit être signifié ou notifié conformément à l'alinéa premier, l'Autorité centrale peut demander que l'acte soit rédigé ou traduit dans la langue ou une des langues officielles de son pays.

CHAPTER I—JUDICIAL DOCUMENTS

ARTICLE 2

Each contracting State shall designate a Central Authority which will undertake to receive requests for service coming from other contracting States and to proceed in conformity with the provisions of articles 3 to 6.

Each State shall organise the Central Authority in conformity with its own law.

ARTICLE 3

The authority or judicial officer competent under the law of the State in which the documents originate shall forward to the Central Authority of the State addressed a request conforming to the model annexed to the present Convention, without any requirement of legalisation or other equivalent formality.

The document to be served or a copy thereof shall be annexed to the request. The request and the document shall both be furnished in duplicate.

ARTICLE 4

If the Central Authority considers that the request does not comply with the provisions of the present Convention it shall promptly inform the applicant and specify its objections to the request.

ARTICLE 5

The Central Authority of the State addressed shall itself serve the document or shall arrange to have it served by an appropriate agency, either —

(a) by a method prescribed by its internal law for the service of documents in domestic actions upon persons who are within its territory, or

(b) by a particular method requested by the applicant, unless such a method is incompatible with the law of the State addressed.

Subject to sub-paragraph (b) of the first paragraph of this article, the document may always be served by delivery to an addressee who accepts it voluntarily.

If the document is to be served under the first paragraph above, the Central Authority may require the document to be written in, or translated into, the official language or one of the official languages of the State addressed.

La partie de la demande conforme à la formule modèle annexée à la présente Convention, qui contient les éléments essentiels de l'acte, est remise au destinataire.

That part of the request, in the form attached to the present Convention, which contains a summary of the document to be served, shall be served with the document.

ARTICLE 6

L'Autorité centrale de l'Etat requis ou toute autorité qu'il aura désignée à cette fin établit une attestation conforme à la formule modèle annexée à la présente Convention.

L'attestation relate l'exécution de la demande; elle indique la forme, le lieu et la date de l'exécution ainsi que la personne à laquelle l'acte a été remis. Le cas échéant, elle précise le fait qui aurait empêché l'exécution.

Le requérant peut demander que l'attestation qui n'est pas établie par l'Autorité centrale ou par une autorité judiciaire soit visée par l'une de ces autorités.

L'attestation est directement adressée au requérant.

ARTICLE 6

The Central Authority of the State addressed or any authority which it may have designated for that purpose, shall complete a certificate in the form of the model annexed to the present Convention.

The certificate shall state that the document has been served and shall include the method, the place and the date of service and the person to whom the document was delivered. If the document has not been served, the certificate shall set out the reasons which have prevented service.

The applicant may require that a certificate not completed by a Central Authority or by a judicial authority shall be countersigned by one of these authorities.

The certificate shall be forwarded directly to the applicant.

ARTICLE 7

Les mentions imprimées dans la formule modèle annexée à la présente Convention sont obligatoirement rédigées soit en langue française, soit en langue anglaise. Elles peuvent, en outre, être rédigées dans la langue ou une des langues officielles de l'Etat d'origine.

Les blancs correspondant à ces mentions sont remplis soit dans la langue de l'Etat requis, soit en langue française, soit en langue anglaise.

ARTICLE 7

The standard terms in the model annexed to the present Convention shall in all cases be written either in French or in English. They may also be written in the official language, or in one of the official languages, of the State in which the documents originate.

The corresponding blanks shall be completed either in the language of the State addressed or in French or in English.

ARTICLE 8

Chaque Etat contractant a la faculté de faire procéder directement, sans contrainte, par les soins de ses agents diplomatiques ou consulaires; aux significations ou notifications d'actes judiciaires aux personnes se trouvant à l'étranger.

Tout Etat peut déclarer s'opposer à l'usage de cette faculté sur son territoire, sauf si l'acte doit être signifié ou notifié à un ressortissant de l'Etat d'origine.

ARTICLE 8

Each contracting State shall be free to effect service of judicial documents upon persons abroad, without application of any compulsion, directly through its diplomatic or consular agents.

Any State may declare that it is opposed to such service within its territory, unless the document is to be served upon a national of the State in which the documents originate.

ARTICLE 9

Chaque Etat contractant a, de plus, la faculté d'utiliser la voie consulaire pour transmettre, aux fins de signification ou de notifica-

ARTICLE 9

Each contracting State shall be free, in addition, to use consular channels to forward documents, for the purpose of service, to those

tion, des actes judiciaires aux autorités d'un autre Etat contractant que celui-ci a désignées.

Si des circonstances exceptionnelles l'exigent, chaque Etat contractant a la faculté d'utiliser, aux mêmes fins, la voie diplomatique.

authorities of another contracting State which are designated by the latter for this purpose.

Each contracting State may, if exceptional circumstances so require, use diplomatic channels for the same purpose.

ARTICLE 10

La présente Convention ne fait pas obstacle, sauf si l'Etat de destination déclare s'y opposer:

(a) à la faculté d'adresser directement, par la voie de la poste, des actes judiciaires aux personnes se trouvant à l'étranger,

(b) à la faculté, pour les officiers ministériels, fonctionnaires ou autres personnes compétents de l'Etat d'origine, de faire procéder à des significations ou notifications d'actes judiciaires directement par les soins des officiers ministériels, fonctionnaires ou autres personnes compétents de l'Etat de destination,

(c) à la faculté, pour toute personne intéressée à une instance judiciaire, de faire procéder à des significations ou notifications d'actes judiciaires directement par les soins des officiers ministériels, fonctionnaires ou autres personnes compétents de l'Etat de destination.

ARTICLE 10

Provided the State of destination does not object, the present Convention shall not interfere with —

(a) the freedom to send judicial documents, by postal channels, directly to persons abroad,

(b) the freedom of judicial officers, officials or other competent persons of the State of origin to effect service of judicial documents directly through the judicial officers, officials or other competent persons of the State of destination,

(c) the freedom of any person interested in a judicial proceeding to effect service of judicial documents directly through the judicial officers, officials or other competent persons of the State of destination.

ARTICLE 11

La présente Convention ne s'oppose pas à ce que des Etats contractants s'entendent pour admettre, aux fins de signification ou de notification des actes judiciaires, d'autres voies de transmission que celles prévues par les articles qui précèdent et notamment la communication directe entre leurs autorités respectives.

ARTICLE 11

The present Convention shall not prevent two or more contracting States from agreeing to permit, for the purpose of service of judicial documents, channels of transmission other than those provided for in the preceding articles and, in particular, direct communication between their respective authorities.

ARTICLE 12

Les significations ou notifications d'actes judiciaires en provenance d'un Etat contractant ne peuvent donner lieu au paiement ou au remboursement de taxes ou de frais pour les services de l'Etat requis.

Le requérant est tenu de payer ou de rembourser les frais occasionnés par:

(a) l'intervention d'un officier ministériel ou d'une personne compétente selon la loi de l'Etat de destination,

(b) l'emploi d'une forme particulière.

ARTICLE 12

The service of judicial documents coming from a contracting State shall not give rise to any payment or reimbursement of taxes or costs for the services rendered by the State addressed.

The applicant shall pay or reimburse the costs occasioned by —

(a) the employment of a judicial officer or of a person competent under the law of the State of destination,

(b) the use of a particular method of service.

ARTICLE 13

L'exécution d'une demande de signification ou de notification conforme aux dispositions de la présente Convention ne peut être refusée que si l'Etat requis juge que cette exécution est de nature à porter atteinte à sa souveraineté ou à sa sécurité.

L'exécution ne peut être refusée pour le seul motif que la loi de l'Etat requis revendique la compétence judiciaire exclusive dans l'affaire en cause ou ne connaît pas de voie de droit répondant à l'objet de la demande.

En cas de refus, l'Autorité centrale en informe immédiatement le requérant et indique les motifs.

ARTICLE 14

Les difficultés qui s'élèveraient à l'occasion de la transmission, aux fins de signification ou de notification, d'actes judiciaires seront réglées par la voie diplomatique.

ARTICLE 15

Lorsqu'un acte introductif d'instance ou un acte équivalent a dû être transmis à l'étranger aux fins de signification ou de notification, selon les dispositions de la présente Convention, et que le défendeur ne comparait pas, le juge est tenu de surseoir à statuer aussi longtemps qu'il n'est pas établi:

(a) ou bien que l'acte a été signifié ou notifié selon les formes prescrites par la législation de l'Etat requis pour la signification ou la notification des actes dressés dans ce pays et qui sont destinés aux personnes se trouvant sur son territoire,

(b) ou bien que l'acte a été effectivement remis au défendeur ou à sa demeure selon un autre procédé prévu par la présente Convention,

et que, dans chacune de ces éventualités, soit la signification ou la notification, soit la remise a eu lieu en temps utile pour que le défendeur ait pu se défendre.

Chaque Etat contractant a la faculté de déclarer que ses juges, nonobstant les dispositions de l'alinéa premier, peuvent statuer si les conditions suivantes sont réunies, bien qu'aucune attestation constatant soit la signification ou la notification, soit la remise, n'ait été reçue:

(a) l'acte a été transmis selon un des modes prévus par la présente Convention,

ARTICLE 13

Where a request for service complies with the terms of the present Convention, the State addressed may refuse to comply therewith only if it deems that compliance would infringe its sovereignty or security.

It may not refuse to comply solely on the ground that, under its internal law, it claims exclusive jurisdiction over the subject-matter of the action or that its internal law would not permit the action upon which the application is based.

The Central Authority shall, in case of refusal, promptly inform the applicant and state the reasons for the refusal.

ARTICLE 14

Difficulties which may arise in connection with the transmission of judicial documents for service shall be settled through diplomatic channels.

ARTICLE 15

Where a writ of summons or an equivalent document had to be transmitted abroad for the purpose of service, under the provisions of the present Convention, and the defendant has not appeared, judgment shall not be given until it is established that —

(a) the document was served by a method prescribed by the internal law of the State addressed for the service of documents in domestic actions upon persons who are within its territory, or

(b) the document was actually delivered to the defendant or to his residence by another method provided for by this Convention,

and that in either of these cases the service or the delivery was effected in sufficient time to enable the defendant to defend.

Each contracting State shall be free to declare that the judge, notwithstanding the provisions of the first paragraph of this article, may give judgment even if no certificate of service or delivery has been received, if all the following conditions are fulfilled —

(a) the document was transmitted by one of the methods provided for in this Convention,

(*b*) un délai que le juge appréciera dans chaque cas particulier et qui sera d'au moins six mois, s'est écoulé depuis la date d'envoi de l'acte,

(*c*) nonobstant toutes diligences utiles auprès des autorités compétentes de l'Etat requis, aucune attestation n'a pu être obtenue.

Le présent article ne fait pas obstacle à ce qu'en cas d'urgence, le juge ordonne toutes mesures provisoires ou conservatoires.

(*b*) a period of time of not less than six months, considered adequate by the judge in the particular case, has elapsed since the date of the transmission of the document,

(*c*) no certificate of any kind has been received, even though every reasonable effort has been made to obtain it through the competent authorities of the State addressed.

Notwithstanding the provisions of the preceding paragraphs the judge may order, in case of urgency, any provisional or protective measures.

ARTICLE 16

Lorsqu'un acte introductif d'instance ou un acte équivalent a dû être transmis à l'étranger aux fins de signification ou de notification, selon les dispositions de la présente Convention, et qu'une décision a été rendue contre un défendeur qui n'a pas comparu, le juge a la faculté de relever ce défendeur de la forclusion résultant de l'expiration des délais de recours, si les conditions suivantes sont réunies:

(*a*) le défendeur, sans qu'il y ait eu faute de sa part, n'a pas eu connaissance en temps utile dudit acte pour se défendre et de la décision pour exercer un recours,

(*b*) les moyens du défendeur n'apparaissent pas dénués de tout fondement.

La demande tendant au relevé de la forclusion est irrecevable si elle n'est pas formée dans un délai raisonnable à partir du moment où le défendeur a eu connaissance de la décision.

Chaque Etat contractant a la faculté de déclarer que cette demande est irrecevable si elle est formée après l'expiration d'un délai qu'il précisera dans sa déclaration, pourvu que ce délai ne soit pas inférieur à un an à compter du prononcé de la décision.

Le présent article ne s'applique pas aux décisions concernant l'état des personnes.

ARTICLE 16

When a writ of summons or an equivalent document had to be transmitted abroad for the purpose of service, under the provisions of the present Convention, and a judgment has been entered against a defendant who has not appeared, the judge shall have the power to relieve the defendant from the effects of the expiration of the time for appeal from the judgment if the following conditions are fulfilled —

(*a*) the defendant, without any fault on his part, did not have knowledge of the document in sufficient time to defend, or knowledge of the judgment in sufficient time to appeal, and

(*b*) the defendant has disclosed a *prima facie* defence to the action on the merits.

An application for relief may be filed only within a reasonable time after the defendant has knowledge of the judgment.

Each contracting State may declare that the application will not be entertained if it is filed after the expiration of a time to be stated in the declaration, but which shall in no case be less than one year following the date of the judgment.

This article shall not apply to judgments concerning status or capacity of persons.

CHAPITRE II—ACTES EXTRAJUDICIAIRES

ARTICLE 17

Les actes extrajudiciaires émanant des autorités et officiers ministériels d'un Etat contractant peuvent être transmis aux fins de signification ou de notification dans un autre Etat contractant selon les modes et aux conditions prévus par la présente Convention.

CHAPTER II—EXTRAJUDICIAL DOCUMENTS

ARTICLE 17

Extrajudicial documents emanating from authorities and judicial officers of a contracting State may be transmitted for the purpose of service in another contracting State by the methods and under the provisions of the present Convention.

CHAPITRE III—DISPOSITIONS GÉNÉRALES

ARTICLE 18

Tout Etat contractant peut désigner, outre l'Autorité centrale, d'autres autorités dont il détermine les compétences.

Toutefois, le requérant a toujours le droit de s'adresser directement à l'Autorité centrale.

Les Etats fédéraux ont la faculté de désigner plusieurs Autorités centrales.

ARTICLE 19

La présente Convention ne s'oppose pas à ce que la loi interne d'un Etat contractant permette d'autres formes de transmission non prévues dans les articles précédents, aux fins de signification ou de notification, sur son territoire, des actes venant de l'étranger.

ARTICLE 20

La présente Convention ne s'oppose pas à ce que des Etats contractants s'entendent pour déroger:

(a) à l'article 3, alinéa 2, en ce qui concerne l'exigence du double exemplaire des pièces transmises,

(b) à l'article 5, alinéa 3, et à l'article 7, en ce qui concerne l'emploi des langues,

(c) à l'article 5, alinéa 4,

(d) à l'article 12, alinéa 2.

ARTICLE 21

Chaque Etat contractant notifiera au Ministère des Affaires Etrangères des Pays-Bas soit au moment du dépôt de son instrument de ratification ou d'adhésion, soit ultérieurement:

(a) la désignation des autorités prévues aux articles 2 et 18,

(b) la désignation de l'autorité compétente pour établir l'attestation prévue à l'article 6,

(c) la désignation de l'autorité compétente pour recevoir les actes transmis par la voie consulaire selon l'article 9.

Il notifiera, le cas échéant, dans les mêmes conditions:

CHAPTER III—GENERAL CLAUSES

ARTICLE 18

Each contracting State may designate other authorities in addition to the Central Authority and shall determine the extent of their competence.

The applicant shall, however, in all cases, have the right to address a request directly to the Central Authority.

Federal States shall be free to designate more than one Central Authority.

ARTICLE 19

To the extent that the internal law of a contracting State permits methods of transmission, other than those provided for in the preceding articles, of documents coming from abroad, for service within its territory, the present Convention shall not affect such provisions.

ARTICLE 20

The present Convention shall not prevent an agreement between any two or more contracting States to dispense with —

(a) the necessity for duplicate copies of transmitted documents as required by the second paragraph of article 3,

(b) the language requirements of the third paragraph of article 5 and article 7.

(c) the provisions of the fourth paragraph of article 5,

(d) the provisions of the second paragraph of article 12.

ARTICLE 21

Each contracting State shall, at the time of the deposit of its instrument of ratification or accession, or at a later date, inform the Ministry of Foreign Affairs of the Netherlands of the following —

(a) the designation of authorities, pursuant to articles 2 and 18,

(b) the designation of the authority competent to compete the certificate pursuant to article 6,

(c) the designation of the authority competent to receive documents transmitted by consular channels, pursuant to article 9.

Each contracting State shall similarly inform the Ministry, where appropriate, of —

(*a*) son opposition à l'usage des voies de transmission prévues aux articles 8 et 10,

(*b*) les déclarations prévues aux articles 15, alinéa 2, et 16, alinéa 3,

(*c*) toute modification des désignations, opposition et déclarations mentionnées ci-dessus.

(*a*) opposition to the use of methods of transmission pursuant to articles 8 and 10,

(*b*) declarations pursuant to the second paragraph of article 15 and the third paragraph of article 16,

(*c*) all modifications of the above designations, oppositions and declarations.

ARTICLE 22

La présente Convention remplacera dans les rapports entre les Etats qui l'auront ratifiée, les articles 1 à 7 des Conventions relatives à la procédure civile, respectivement signées à La Haye, le 17 juillet 1905 et le premier mars 1954, dans les mesure où lesdits Etats sont Parties à l'une ou à l'autre de ces Conventions.

ARTICLE 22

Where Parties to the present Conention are also Parties to one or both of the Conventions on civil procedure signed at The Hague on 17th July 1905, and on 1st March 1954, this Convention shall replace as between them articles 1 to 7 of the earlier Conventions.

ARTICLE 23

La présente Convention ne porte pas atteinte à l'application de l'article 23 de la Convention relative à la procédure civile, signée à La Haye, le 17 juillet 1905, ni de l'article 24 de celle signée à La Haye, le premier mars 1954.

Ces articles ne sont toutefois applicables que s'il fait usage de modes de communication identiques à ceux prévus par lesdites Conventions.

ARTICLE 23

The present Convention shall not affect the application of article 23 of the Convention on civil procedure signed at The Hague on 17th July 1905, or of article 24 of the Convention on civil procedure signed at The Hague on 1st March 1954.

These articles shall, however, apply only if methods of communication, identical to those provided for in these Conventions, are used.

ARTICLE 24

Les accords, additionnels auxdites Conventions de 1905 et de 1954, conclus par les Etats contractants, sont considérés comme également applicables à la présente Convention à moins que les Etats intéressés n'en conviennent autrement.

ARTICLE 24

Supplementary agreements between Parties to the Convention of 1905 and 1954 shall be considered as equally applicable to the present Convention, unless the Parties have otherwise agreed.

ARTICLE 25

Sans préjudice de l'application des articles 22 et 24, la présente Convention ne déroge pas aux Conventions auxquelles les Etats contractants sont ou seront Parties et qui contiennent des dispositions sur les matières réglées par la présente Convention.

ARTICLE 25

Without prejudice to the provisions of articles 22 and 24, the present Convention shall not derogate from Conventions containing provisions on the matters governed by this Convention to which the contracting States are, or shall become, Parties.

ARTICLE 16

La présente Convention est ouverte à la signature des Etats représentés à la Dixième session de la Conférence de La Haye de droit international privé.

Elle sera ratifiée et les instruments de ratification seront déposés auprès du Ministère des Affaires Etrangères des Pay-Bas.

ARTICLE 26

The present Convention shall be open for signature by the States represented at the Tenth Session of the Hague Conference on Private International Law.

It shall be ratified, and the instruments of ratification shall be deposited with the Ministry of Foreign Affairs of the Netherlands.

ARTICLE 27

La présente Convention entrera en vigueur le soixantième jour après le dépôt du troisième instrument de ratification prévu par l'article 26, alinéa 2.

La Convention entrera en vigueur, pour chaque Etat signataire ratifiant postérieurement, le soixantième jour après le dépôt de son instrument de ratification.

ARTICLE 28

Tout Etat non représenté à la Dixième session de la Conférence de La Haye de droit international privé pourra adhérer à la présente Convention après son entrée en vigueur en vertu de l'article 27, alinéa premier. L'instrument d'adhésion sera déposé auprès du Ministère des Affaires Etrangères des Pays-Bas.

La Convention n'entrera en vigueur pour un tel Etat qu'à défaut d'opposition de la part d'un Etat ayant ratifiée la Convention avant ce dépôt, notifiée au Ministère des Affaires Etrangères des Pays-Bas dans un délai de six mois à partir de la date à laquelle ce Ministère lui aura notifié cette adhésion.

A défaut d'opposition, la Convention entrera en vigueur pour l'Etat adhérant le premier jour du mois qui suit l'expiration du dernier des délais mentionnés à l'alinéa précédent.

ARTICLE 29

Tout Etat, au moment de la signature, de la ratification ou de l'adhésion, pourra déclarer que la présente Convention s'étendra à l'ensemble des territoires qu'il représente sur le plan international, ou à l'un ou plusieurs d'entre eux. Cette déclaration aura effet au moment de l'entrée en vigueur de la Convention pour ledit Etat.

Par la suite, toute extension de cette nature sera notifiée au Ministère des Affaires Etrangères des Pays-Bas.

La Convention entrera en vigueur, pour les territoires visés par l'extension, le soixantième jour après la notification mentionnée à l'alinéa précédent.

ARTICLE 30

La présente Convention aura une durée de cinq ans à partir de la date de son entrée en vigueur conformément à l'article 27, alinéa

ARTICLE 27

The present Convention shall enter into force on the sixtieth day after deposit of the third instrument of ratification referred to in the second paragraph of article 26.

The Convention shall enter into force for each signatory State which ratifies subsequently on the sixtieth day after the deposit of its instrument of ratification.

ARTICLE 28

Any State not represented at the Tenth Session of the Hague Conference on Private International Law may accede to the present Convention after it has entered into force in accordance with the first paragraph of article 27. The instrument of accession shall be deposited with the Ministry of Foreign Affairs of the Netherlands.

The Convention shall enter into force for such a State in the absence of any objection from a State, which has ratified the Convention before such deposit, notified to the Ministry of Foreign Affairs of the Netherlands within a period of six months after the date on which the said Ministry has notified it of such accession.

In the absence of any such objection, the Convention shall enter into force for the acceding State on the first day of the month following the expiration of the last of the periods referred to in the preceding paragraph.

ARTICLE 29

Any State may, at the time of signature, ratification or accession, declare that the present Convention shall extend to all the territories for the international relations of which it is responsible, or to one or more of them. Such a declaration shall take effect on the date of entry into force of the Convention for the State concerned.

At any time thereafter, such extensions shall be notified to the Ministry of Foreign Affairs of the Netherlands.

The Convention shall enter into force for the territories mentioned in such an extension on the sixtieth day after the notification referred to in the preceding paragraph.

ARTICLE 30

The present Convention shall remain in force for five years from the date of its entry into force in accordance with the first para-

premier, même pour les Etats qui l'auront ratifiée ou y auront adhéré postérieurement.

La Convention sera renouvelée tacitement de cinq en cinq ans, sauf dénonciation.

La dénonciation sera, au moins six mois avant l'expiration du délai de cinq ans, notifiée au Ministère des Affaires Etrangères des Pays-Bas.

Elle pourra se limiter à certains des territoires auxquels s'applique la Convention.

La dénonciation n'aura d'effet qu'à l'égard de l'Etat qui l'aura notifiée. La Convention restera en vigueur pour les autres Etats contractants.

graph of article 27, even for States which have ratified it or acceded to it subsequently.

If there has been no denunciation, it shall be renewed tacitly every five years.

Any denunciation shall be notified to the Minsitry of Foreign Affairs of the Netherlands at least six months before the end of the five year period.

It may be limited to certain of the territories to which the Convention applies.

The denunciation shall have effect only as regards the State which has notified it. The Convention shall remain in force for the other contracting States.

ARTICLE 31

Le Ministère des Affaires Etrangères des Pays-Bas notifiera aux Etats visés à l'article 26, ainsi qu'aux Etats qui auront adhéré conformément aux dispositions de l'article 28:

(a) les signatures et ratifications visées à l'article 26;

(b) la date à laquelle la présente Convention entrera en vigueur conformément aux dispositions de l'article 27, alinéa premier;

(c) les adhésions visées à l'article 28 et la date à laquelle elles auront effet;

(d) les extensions visées à l'article 29 et la date à laquelle elles auront effet;

(e) les désignations, opposition et déclarations mentionnées à l'article 21;

(f) les dénonciations visées à l'article 30, alinéa 3.

En foi de quoi, les soussignés, dûment autorisés, ont signé la présente Convention.

Fait à La Haye, le quinze novembre 1965, en français et en anglais, les deux textes faisant également foi, en un seul exemplaire, qui sera déposé dans les archives du Gouvernement des Pays-Bas et dont une copie certifiée conforme sera remise, par la voie diplomatique, à chacun des Etats représentés à la Dixième session de la Conférence de La Haye de droit international privé.

ARTICLE 31

The Ministry of Foreign Affairs of the Netherlands shall give notice to the States referred to in article 26, and to the States which have acceded in accordance with article 28, of the following —

(a) the signatures and ratifications referred to in article 26;

(b) the date on which the present Convention enters into force in accordance with the first paragraph of article 27;

(c) the accessions referred to in article 28 and the dates on which they take effect;

(d) the extensions referred to in article 29 and the dates on which they take effect;

(e) the designations, oppositions and declarations referred to in article 21;

(f) the denunciations referred to in the third paragraph of article 30.

In witness whereof the undersigned, being duly authorised thereto, have signed the present Convention.

Done at The Hague, on the fifteenth day of November, 1965, in the English and French languages, both texts being equally authentic, in a single copy which shall be deposited in the archives of the Government of the Netherlands, and of which a certified copy shall be sent, through the diplomatic channel, to each of the States represented at the Tenth Session of the Hague Conference on Private International Law.

Forms

REQUEST

FOR SERVICE ABROAD OF JUDICIAL OR EXTRAJUDICIAL DOCUMENTS

Convention on the service abroad of judicial and extrajudicial documents in civil or commercial matters, signed at The Hague, 15 November 1965.

Identity and address of the applicant	Address of receiving authority

The undersigned applicant has the honour to transmit—in duplicate—the documents listed below and, in conformity with article 5 of the above-mentioned Convention, requests prompt service of one copy thereof on the addressee, i.e.,

(identity and address) _____

(*a*) in accordance with the provisions of sub-paragraph (*a*) of the first paragraph of article 5 of the Convention*.

(*b*) in accordance with the following particular method (sub-paragraph (*b*) of the first paragraph of article 5)*:

_____

_____

_____

(*c*) by delivery to the addressee, if he accepts it voluntarily (second paragraph of article 5)*.

The authority is requested to return or to have returned to the applicant a copy of the documents—and of the annexes*—with a certificate as provided on the reverse side.

List of documents

_____

_____

_____

_____

_____

_____   Done at _____, the _____

_____

_____   Signature and/or stamp.

*Delete if inappropriate.

CERTIFICATE

The undersigned authority has the honour to certify, in conformity with article 6 of the Convention,

1) that the document has been served*
   —the (date) _____
   —at (place, street, number) _____
   _____

   —in one of the following methods authorised by article 5—
   (*a*) in accordance with the provisions of sub-paragraph (*a*) of the first paragraph of article 5 of the Convention*.
   (*b*) in accordance with the following particular method*: _____
   _____
   (*c*) by delivery to the addressee, who accepted it voluntarily*.

   The documents referred to in the request have been delivered to:
   —(identity and description of person) _____
   _____

   —relationship to the addressee (family, business or other): _____
   _____

2) that the document has not been served, by reason of the following facts*:
   _____
   _____
   _____

In conformity with the second paragraph of article 12 of the Convention, the applicant is requested to pay or reimburse the expenses detailed in the attached statement*.

Annexes
Documents returned:_____
_____
_____

Done at _____, the _____

In appropriate cases, documents establishing
the service:
_____   Signature and/or stamp.
_____
_____

*Delete if inappropriate

SUMMARY OF THE DOCUMENT TO BE SERVED

Convention on the service abroad of judicial and extrajudicial documents in civil or commercial matters, signed at The Hague, the 15 November 1965.

(article 5, fourth paragraph)

Name and address of the requesting authority: _____

_____

Particulars of the parties*: _____

_____

JUDICIAL DOCUMENT**

Nature and purpose of the document: _____

_____

Nature and purpose of the proceedings and, where appropriate, the amount in dispute: _____

_____

Date and place for entering appearance**: _____

Court which has given judgment**: _____

Date of judgment**: _____

Time limits stated in the document**: _____

EXTRAJUDICIAL DOCUMENT**

Nature and purpose of the document: _____

_____

Time limits stated in the document**: _____

_____

*If appropriate, identity and address of the person interested in the transmission of the document.
**Delete if inappropriate.

(b) The Hague Evidence Convention

CONVENTION SUR L'OBTENTION DES
PREUVES A L'ÉTRANGER EN MATIÈRE
CIVILE OU COMMERCIALE

CONVENTION ON THE TAKING OF
EVIDENCE ABROAD IN CIVIL OR
COMMERCIAL MATTERS

Les Etats signataires de la présente Convention,

The States signatory to the present Convention.

Désirant faciliter la transmission et l'exécution des commissions rogatoires et promouvoir le rapprochement des diverses méthodes qu'ils utilisent à ces fins,

Desiring to facilitate the transmission and execution of Letters of Request to further the accommodation of the different methods which they use for this purpose,

Soucieux d'accroître l'efficacité de la coopération judiciaire mutuelle en matière civile ou commerciale,

Desiring to improve mutual judicial cooperation in civil or commercial matters,

Ont résolu de conclure une Convention à ces effets et sont convenus des dispositions suivantes:

Have resolved to conclude a Convention to this effect and have agreed upon the following provisions —

CHAPITRE I—COMMISSIONS ROGATOIRES

CHAPTER I—LETTERS OF REQUEST

Article Premier

Article 1

En matière civile ou commerciale, l'autorité judiciaire d'un Etat contractant peut, conformément aux dispositions de sa législation, demander par commission rogatoire à l'autorité compétente d'un autre Etat contractant de faire tout acte d'instruction, ainsi que d'autres actes judiciaires.
Une acte d'instruction ne peut pas être demandé pour permettre aux parties d'obtenir des moyens de preuves qui ne soient pas destinés à être utilisés dans une procédure engagée ou future.
L'expression «autres actes judiciaires» ne vise ni la signification ou la notification d'actes judiciaires, ni les mesures conservatoires ou d'exécution.

In civil or commercial matters a judicial authority of a Contracting State may, in accordance with the provisions of the law of that State, request the competent authority of another Contracting State, by means of a Letter of Request, to obtain evidence, or to perform some other judicial act.
A Letter shall not be used to obtain evidence which is not intended for use in judicial proceedings, commenced or contemplated.

The expression 'other judicial act' does not cover the service of judicial documents or the issuance of any process by which judgments or orders are executed or enforced, or orders for provisional or protective measures.

Article 2

Article 2

Chaque Etat contractant désigne une Autorité centrale qui assume la charge de recevoir les commissions rogatoires émanant d'une autorité judiciaire d'un autre Etat contractant et de les transmettre à l'autorité compétente aux fins d'exécution. L'Autorité centrale est organisée selon les modalités prévues par l'Etat requis.
Les commissions rogatoires sont transmises à l'Autorité centrale de l'Etat requis sans intervention d'une autre autorité de cet Etat.

A Contracting State shall designate a Central Authority which will undertake to receive Letters of Request coming from a judicial authority of another Contracting State and to transmit them to the authority competent to execute them. Each State shall organize the Central Authority in accordance with its own law.
Letters shall be sent to the Central Authority of the State of execution without being transmitted through any other authority of that State.

Article 3

La commission rogatoire contient les indications suivantes:

(*a*) l'autorité requérante et, si possible, l'autorité requise;

(*b*) l'identité et l'adresse des parties et, le cas échéant, de leurs représentants;

(*c*) la nature et l'objet de l'instance et un exposé sommaire des faits;

(*d*) les actes d'instruction ou autres actes judiciaires à accomplir.

Le cas échéant, la commission rogatoire contient en outre:

(*e*) les nom et adresse des personnes à entendre:

(*f*) les questions à poser aux personnes à entendre ou les faits sur lesquels elles doivent être entendues;

(*g*) les documents ou autres à objets examiner;

(*h*) la demande de recevoir la déposition sous serment ou avec affirmation et, le cas échéant, l'indication de la formule à utiliser;

(*i*) les formes spéciales dont l'application est demandée conformément à l'article 9.

La commission rogatoire mentionne aussi, s'il y a lieu, les renseignements nécessaires à l'application de l'article 11.

Aucune légalisation ni formalité analogue ne peut être exigée.

Article 3

A Letter of Request shall specify —

(*a*) the authority requesting its execution and the authority requested to execute it, if known to the requesting authority;

(*b*) the names and addresses of the parties to the proceedings and their representatives, if any;

(*c*) the nature of the proceedings for which the evidence is required, giving all necessary information in regard thereto;

(*d*) the evidence to be obtained or other judicial act to be performed.

Where appropriate, the Letter shall specify, inter alia —

(*e*) the names and addresses of the persons to be examined;

(*f*) the questions to be put to the persons to be examined or a statement of the subject-matter about which they are to be examined;

(*g*) the documents or other property, real or personal, to be inspected;

(*h*) any requirement that the evidence is to be given on oath or affirmation, and any special form to be used;

(*i*) any special method or procedure to be followed under Article 9.

A Letter may also mention any information necessary for the application of Article 11.

No legalization or other like formality may be required.

Article 4

La commission rogatoire doit être rédigée dans la langue de l'autorité requise ou accompagnée d'une traduction faite dans cette langue.

Toutefois, chaque Etat contractant doit accepter la commission rogatoire rédigée en langue française ou anglaise, ou accompagnée d'une traduction dans l'une de ces langues, à moins qu'il ne s'y soit opposé en faisant la réserve prévue à l'article 33.

Tout Etat contractant qui a plusieurs langues officielles et ne peut, pour des raisons de droit interne, accepter les commissions rogatoires dans l'une de ces langues pour l'ensemble de son territoire, doit faire connaître, au moyen d'une déclaration, la langue dans laquelle la commission rogatoire doit être

Article 4

A Letter of Request shall be in the language of the authority requested to execute it or be accompanied by a translation into that language.

Nevertheless, a Contracting State shall accept a Letter in either English or French, or a translation into one of these languages, unless it has made the reservation authorized by Article 33.

A Contracting State which has more than one official language and cannot, for reasons of internal law, accept Letters in one of these languages for the whole of its territory, shall, by declaration, specify the language in which the Letter or translation thereof shall be expressed for execution in the specified parts

rédigée ou traduite en vue de son exécution dans les parties de son territoire qu'il a déterminées. En cas d'inobservation sans justes motifs de l'obligation découlant de cette déclaration, les frais de la traduction dans la langue exigée sont à la charge de l'Etat requérant.

Tout Etat contractant peut, au moyen d'une déclaration, faire connaître la ou les langues autres que celles prévues aux alinéas précédents dans lesquelles la commission rogatoire peut être adressée à son Autorité centrale.

Toute traduction annexée à une commission rogatoire doit être certifiée conforme, soit par un agent diplomatique ou consulaire, soit par un traducteur assermenté ou juré, soit par toute autre personne autorisée à cet effet dans l'un des deux Etats.

of its territory. In case of failure to comply with this declaration, without justifiable excuse, the costs of translation into the required language shall be borne by the State of origin.

A Contracting State may, by declaration, specify the language or languages other than those referred to in the preceding paragraphs, in which a Letter may be sent to its Central Authority.

Any translation accompanying a Letter shall be certified as correct, either by a diplomatic officer or consular agent or by a sworn translator or by any other person so authorized in either State.

Article 5

Si l'Autorité centrale estime que les dispositions de la Convention n'ont pas été respectées, elle en informe immédiatement l'autorité de l'Etat requérant qui lui a transmis la commission rogatoire, en précisant les griefs articulés à l'encontre de la demande.

Article 5

If the Central Authority considers that the request does not comply with the provisions of the present Convention, it shall promptly inform the authority of the State of origin which transmitted the Letter of Request, specifying the objections to the Letter.

Article 6

En cas d'incompétence de l'autorité requise, la commission rogatoire est transmise d'office et sans retard à l'autorité judiciaire compétente du même Etat suivant les règles établies par la législation de celui-ci.

Article 6

If the authority to whom a Letter of Request has been transmitted is not competent to execute it, the Letter shall be sent forthwith to the authority in the same State which is competent to execute it in accordance with the provisions of its own law.

Article 7

L'autorité requérante est, si elle le demande, informée de la date et du lieu où il sera procédé à la mesure sollicitée, afin que les parties intéressées et, le cas échéant, leurs représentants puissent y assister. Cette communication est adressée directement auxdites parties ou à leurs représentants, lorsque l'autorité requérante en a fait la demande.

Article 7

The requesting authority shall, if it so desires, be informed of the time when, and the place where, the proceedings will take place, in order that the parties concerned, and their representatives, if any, may be present. This information shall be sent directly to the parties or their representatives when the authority of the State of origin so requests.

Article 8

Tout Etat contractant peut déclarer que des magistrats de l'autorité requérante d'un autre Etat contractant peuvent assister à l'exécution d'un commission rogatoire. Cette mesure peut être soumise à l'autorisation préalable de l'autorité compétente désignée par l'Etat déclarant.

Article 8

A Contracting State may declare that members of the judicial personnel of the requesting authority of another Contracting State may be present at the execution of a Letter of Request. Prior authorization by the competent authority designated by the declaring State may be required.

Article 9

L'autorité judiciaire qui procède à l'exécution d'une commission rogatoire, applique les lois de son pays en ce qui concerne les formes à suivre.

Toutefois, il est déféré à la demande de l'autorité requérante tendant à ce qu'il soit procédé suivant une forme spéciale, à moins que celle-ci ne soit incompatible avec la loi de l'Etat requis, ou que son application ne soit pas possible, soit en raison des usages judiciaires de l'Etat requis, soit de difficultés pratiques.

La commission rogatoire doit être exécutée d'urgence.

Article 9

The judicial authority which executes a Letter of Request shall apply its own law as to the methods and procedures to be followed.

However, it will follow a request of the requesting authority that a special method or procedure be followed, unless this is incompatible with the internal law of the State of execution or is impossible of performance by reason of its internal practice and procedure or by reason of practical difficulties.

A Letter of Request shall be executed expeditiously.

Article 10

En exécutant la commission rogatoire, l'autorité requise applique les moyens de contrainte appropriés et prévus par sa loi interne dans les cas et dans la même mesure où elle y serait obligée pour l'exécution d'une commission des autorités de l'Etat requis ou d'une demande formulée à cet effet par une partie intéressée.

Article 10

In executing a Letter of Request the requested authority shall apply the appropriate measures of compulsion in the instances and to the same extent as are provided by its internal law for the execution of orders issued by the authorities of its own country or of requests made by parties in internal proceedings.

Article 11

La commission rogatoire n'est pas exécutée pour autant que la personne qu'elle vise invoque une dispense ou une interdiction de déposer, établies:

(a) soit par la loi de l'Etat requis;

(b) soit par la loi de l'Etat requérant et spécifiées dans la commission rogatoire ou, le cas échéant, attestées par l'autorité requérante à la demande de l'autorité requise.

En outre, tout Etat contractant peut déclarer qu'il reconnaît de telles dispenses et interdictions établies par la loi d'autre Etats que l'Etat requérant et l'Etat requis, dans la mesure spécifiée dans cette déclaration.

Article 11

In the execution of a Letter of Request the person concerned may refuse to give evidence in so far as he has a privilege or duty to refuse to give the evidence —

(a) under the law of the State of execution; or

(b) under the law of the State of origin, and the privilege or duty has been specified in the Letter, or, at the instance of the requested authority, has been otherwise confirmed to that authority by the requesting authority.

A Contracting State may declare that, in addition, it will respect privileges and duties existing under the law of States other than the State of origin and the State of execution, to the extent specified in that declaration.

Article 12

L'exécution de la commision rogatoire ne peut être refusée que dans la mesure où:

(a) l'exécution, dans l'Etat requis, ne rentre pas dans les attributions du pouvoir judiciaire; ou

(b) l'Etat requis la juge de nature à porter atteinte à sa souveraineté ou à sa sécurité.

Article 12

The execution of a Letter of Request may be refused only to the extent that —

(a) in the State of execution the execution of the Letter does not fall within the functions of the judiciary; or

(b) the State addressed considers that its sovereignty or security would be prejudiced thereby.

L'exécution ne peut être refusée pour le seul motif que la loi de l'Etat requis revendique une compétence judiciaire exclusive dans l'affaire en cause ou ne connaît pas de voies de droit répondant à l'objet de la demande portée devant l'autorité requérante.

Execution may not be refused solely on the ground that under its internal law the State of execution claims exclusive jurisdiction over the subject-matter of the action or that its internal law would not admit a right of action on it.

Article 13

Les pièces constatant l'exécution de la commission rogatoire sont transmises par l'autorité requise à l'autorité requérante par la même voie que celle utilisée par cette dernière.

Lorsque la commission rogatoire n'est pas exécutée en tout ou en partie, l'autorité requérante en est informée immédiatement par la même voie et les raisons lui en sont communiquées.

Article 13

The documents establishing the execution of the Letter of Request shall be sent by the requested authority to the requesting authority by the same channel which was used by the latter.

In every instance where the Letter is not executed in whole or in part, the requesting authority shall be informed immediately through the same channel and advised of the reasons.

Article 14

L'exécution de la commission rogatoire ne peut donner lieu au remboursement de taxes ou de frais, de quelque nature que ce soit.

Toutefois, l'Etat requis a le droit d'exiger de l'Etat requérant le remboursement des indemnités payées aux experts et interprètes et des frais résultant de l'application d'une forme spéciale demandée par l'Etat requérant, conformément à l'article 9, alinéa 2.

L'autorité requise, dont la loi laisse aux parties le soin de réunir les preuves et qui n'est pas en mesure d'exécuter elle-même la commission rogatoire, peut en charger une personne habilitée à cet effet, après avoir obtenu le consentement de l'autorité requérante. En demandant celui-ci, l'autorité requise indique le montant approximatif des frais qui résulteraient de cette intervention. Le consentement implique pour l'autorité requérante l'obligation de rembourser ces frais. A défaut de celui-ci, l'autorité requérante n'est pas redevable de ces frais.

Article 14

The execution of the Letter of Request shall not give rise to any reimbursement of taxes or costs of any nature.

Nevertheless, the State of execution has the right to require the State of origin to reimburse the fees paid to experts and interpreters and the costs occasioned by the use of a special procedure requested by the State of origin under Article 9, paragraph 2.

The requested authority whose law obliges the parties themselves to secure evidence, and which is not able itself to execute the Letter, may, after having obtained the consent of the requesting authority, appoint a suitable person to do so. When seeking this consent the requested authority shall indicate the approximate costs which would result from this procedure. If the requesting authority gives its consent it shall reimburse any costs incurred; without such consent the requesting authority shall not be liable for the costs.

CHAPITRE II—OBTENTION DES PREUVES PAR DES AGENTS DIPLOMATIQUES OU CONSULAIRES ET PAR DES COMMISSAIRES

CHAPTER II—TAKING OF EVIDENCE BY DIPLOMATIC OFFICERS, CONSULAR AGENTS AND COMMISSIONERS

Article 15

En matière civile ou commerciale, un agent diplomatique ou consulaire d'un Etat contractant peut procéder, sans contrainte, sur le territoire d'un autre Etat contractant et dans la circonscription où il exerce ses fonctions, à tout acte d'instruction ne visant que les ressortissants d'un Etat qu'il représente et concernant une procédure engagée devant un tribunal dudit Etat.

Article 15

In a civil or commercial matter, a diplomatic officer or consular agent of a Contracting State may, in the territory of another Contracting State and within the area where he exercises his functions, take the evidence without compulsion of nationals of a State which he represents in aid of proceedings commenced in the courts of a State which he represents.

Tout Etat contractant a la faculté de déclarer que cet acte ne peut être effectué que moyennant l'autorisation accordée sur demande faite par cet agent ou en son nom par l'autorité compétente désignée par l'Etat déclarant.

A Contracting State may declare that evidence may be taken by a diplomatic officer or consular agent only if permission to that effect is given upon application made by him or on his behalf to the appropriate authority designated by the declaring State.

Article 16

Un agent diplomatique ou consulaire d'un Etat contractant peut en outre procéder, sans contrainte, sur le territoire d'un autre Etat contractant et dans la circonscription où il exerce ses functions, à tout acte d'instruction visant les ressortissants de l'Etat de résidence ou d'un Etat tiers, et concernant une procédure engagée devant un tribunal d'un Etat qu'il représente:

(a) si une autorité compétente désignée par l'Etat de résidence a donné son autorisation, soit d'une manière générale, soit pour chaque cas particulier, et

(b) s'il respecte les conditions que l'autorité compétente a fixées dans l'autorisation.

Tout Etat contractant peut déclarer que les actes d'instruction prévus ci-dessus peuvent être accomplis sans son autorisation préalable.

Article 16

A diplomatic officer or consular agent of a Contracting State may, in the territory of another Contracting State and within the area where he exercises his functions, also take the evidence, without compulsion, of nationals of the State in which he exercises his functions or of a third State, in aid of proceedings commenced in the courts of a State which he represents, if —

(a) a competent authority designated by the State in which he exercises his functions has given its permission either generally or in the particular case, and

(b) he complies with the conditions which the competent authority has specified in the permission.

A Contracting State may declare that evidence may be taken under this Article without its prior permission.

Article 17

En matière civile ou commerciale, toute personne régulièrement désignée à cet effet comme commissaire, peut procéder, sans contrainte, sur le territoire d'un Etat contractant à tout acte d'instruction concernant une procédure engagée devant un tribunal d'un autre Etat contractant:

(a) si une autorité compétente désignée par l'Etat de l'exécution a donné son autorisation, soit d'une manière générale, soit pour chaque cas particulier; et

(b) si elle respecte les conditions que l'autorité compétente a fixées dans l'autorisation.

Tout Etat contractant peut déclarer que les actes d'instruction prévus ci-dessus peuvent être accomplis sans son autorisation préalable.

Article 17

In a civil or commercial matter, a person duly appointed as a commissioner for the purpose may, without compulsion, take evidence in the territory of a Contracting State in aid of proceedings commenced in the courts of another Contracting State, if —

(a) a competent authority designated by the State where the evidence is to be taken has given its permission either generally or in the particular case; and

(b) he complies with the conditions which the competent authority has specified in the permission.

A Contracting State may declare that evidence may be taken under this Article without its prior permission.

Article 18

Tout Etat contractant peut déclarer qu'un agent diplomatique ou consulaire ou un commissaire, autorisé à procéder à une acte d'instruction conformément aux articles 15, 16 et 17, a la faculté de s'adresser à l'autorité compétente désignée par ledit Etat, pour

Article 18

A Contracting State may declare that a diplomatic officer, consular agent or commissioner authorized to take evidence under Articles 15, 16 or 17, may apply to the competent authority designated by the declaring State for appropriate assistance to obtain the

obtenir l'assistance nécessaire à l'accomplissement de cet acte par voie de contrainte. La déclaration peut comporter toute condition que l'Etat déclarant juge convenable d'imposer.

Lorsque l'autorité compétente fait droit à la requête, elle applique les moyens de contrainte appropriés et prévus par sa loi interne.

evidence by compulsion. The declaration may contain such conditions as the declaring State may see fit to impose.

If the authority grants the application it shall apply any measures of compulsion which are appropriate and are prescribed by its law for use in internal proceedings.

Article 19

L'autorité compétente, en donnant l'autorisation prévue aux articles 15, 16 et 17 ou dans l'ordonnance prévue à l'article 18, peut déterminer les conditions qu'elle juge convenables, relatives notamment aux heure, date et lieu de l'acte d'instruction. Elle peut de même demander que ces heure, date et lieu lui soient notifiés au préalable et en temps utile; en ce cas, un représentant de ladite autorité peut être présent à l'acte d'instruction.

Article 19

The competent authority, in giving the permission referred to in Article 15, 16 or 17, or in granting the application referred to in Article 18, may lay down such conditions as it deems fit, *inter alia*, as to the time and place of the taking of the evidence. Similarly, it may require that it be given reasonable advance notice of the time, date and place of the taking of the evidence; in such a case a representative of the authority shall be entitled to be present at the taking of the evidence.

Article 20

Les personnes visées par un acte d'instruction prévu dans ce chapitre peuvent se faire assister par leur conseil.

Article 20

In the taking of evidence under any Article of this Chapter persons concerned may be legally represented.

Aricle 21

Lorsqu'un agent diplomatique ou consulaire ou un commissaire est autorisé à procéder à un acte d'instruction en vertu des articles 15, 16 et 17:

(a) il peut procéder à tout acte d'instruction qui n'est pas incompatible avec la loi de l'Etat de l'exécution ou contraire à l'autorisation accordée en vertu desdits articles et recevoir, dans les mêmes conditions, une déposition sous serment ou avec affirmation;

(b) à moins que la personne visée par l'acte d'instruction ne soit ressortissante de l'Etat dans lequel la procédure est engagée, toute convocation à comparaître ou à participer à un acte d'instruction est rédigée dans la langue du lieu où l'acte d'instruction doit être accompli, ou accompagnée d'une traduction dans cette langue;

(c) la convocation indique que la personne peut être assistée de son conseil, et, dans tout Etat qui n'a pas fait la déclaration prévue à l'article 18, qu'elle n'est pas tenue de comparaître ni de participer à l'acte d'instruction;

Article 21

Where a diplomatic officer, consular agent or commissioner is authorized under Articles 15, 16 or 17 to take evidence —

(a) he may take all kinds of evidence which are not incompatible with the law of the State where the evidence is taken or contrary to any permission granted pursuant to the above Articles, and shall have power within such limits to administer an oath or take an affirmation;

(b) a request to a person to appear or to give evidence shall, unless the recipient is a national of the State where the action is pending, be drawn up in the language of the place where the evidence is taken or be accompanied by a translation into such language;

(c) the request shall inform the person that he may be legally represented and, in any State that has not filed a declaration under Article 18, shall also inform him that he is not compelled to appear or to give evidence;

(*d*) l'acte d'instruction peut être accompli suivant les formes prévues par la loi du tribunal devant lequel la procédure est engagée, à condition qu'elles ne soient pas interdites par la loi de l'Etat de l'exécution;

(*e*) la personne visée par l'acte d'instruction peut invoquer les dispenses et interdictions prévues à l'article 11.

(*d*) the evidence may be taken in the manner provided by the law applicable to the court in which the action is pending provided that such manner is not forbidden by the law of the State where the evidence is taken;

(*e*) a person requested to give evidence may invoke the privileges and duties to refuse to give the evidence contained in Article 11.

Article 22

Le fait qu'un acte d'instruction n'ait pu être accompli conformément aux dispositions du présent chapitre en raison du refus d'une personne d'y participer, n'empêche pas qu'une commission rogatoire soit adressée ultérieurement pour le même acte, conformément aux dispositions du chapitre premier.

Article 22

The fact that an attempt to take evidence under the procedure laid down in this Chapter has failed, owing to the refusal of a person to give evidence, shall not prevent an application being subsequently made to take the evidence in accordance with Chapter I.

CHAPITRE III—DISPOSITIONS GÉNÉRALES

Article 23

Tout Etat contractant peut, au moment de la signature, de la ratification ou de l'adhésion, déclarer qu'il n'exécute pas les commissions rogatoires qui ont pour objet une procédure connue dans les Etats du *Common Law* sous le nom de «pre-trial discovery of documents».

CHAPTER III—GENERAL CLAUSES

Article 23

A Contracting State may at the time of signature, ratification or accession, declare that it will not execute Letters of Request issued for the purpose of obtaining pre-trial discovery of documents as known in Common Law countries.

Article 24

Tout Etat contractant peut désigner, outre l'Autorité centrale, d'autres autorités dont il détermine les compétences. Toutefois, les commissions rogatoires peuvent toujours être transmises à l'Autorité centrale.

Les Etats fédéraux ont la faculté de désigner plusieurs Autorités centrales.

Article 24

A Contracting State may designate other authorities in addition to the Central Authority and shall determine the extent of their competence. However, Letters of Request may in all cases be sent to the Central Authority.

Federal States shall be free to designate more than one Central Authority.

Article 25

Tout Etat contractant, dans lequel plusieurs systèmes de droit sont en vigueur, peut désigner les autorités de l'un de ces systèmes, qui auront compétence exclusive pour l'exécution des commissions rogatoires en application de la présente Convention.

Article 25

A Contracting State which has more than one legal system may designate the authorities of one of such systems, which shall have exclusive competence to execute Letters of Request pursuant to this Convention.

Article 26

Tout Etat contractant, s'il y est tenu pour des raisons de droit constitutionnel, peut inviter l'Etat requérant à rembourser les frais d'exécution de la commission rogatoire et concernant la signification ou la notification à comparaître, les indemnités dues à la personne

Article 26

A Contracting State, if required to do so because of constitutional limitations, may request the reimbursement by the State of origin of fees and costs, in connection with the execution of Letters of Request, for the service of process necessary to compel the appearance

qui fait la déposition et l'établissement du procès-verbal de l'acte d'instruction.

Lorsqu'un Etat a fait usage des dispositions de l'alinéa précédent, tout autre Etat contractant peut inviter cet Etat à rembourser les frais correspondants.

of a person to give evidence, the costs of attendance of such persons, and the cost of any transcript of the evidence.

Where a State has made a request pursuant to the above paragraph, any other Contracting State may request from that State the reimbursement of similar fees and costs.

Article 27

Les dispositions de la présente Convention ne font pas obstacle à ce qu'un Etat contractant:

(*a*) déclare que des commissions rogatoires peuvent être transmises à ses autorités judiciaires par d'autres voies que celles prévues à l'article 2.

(*b*) permette, aux termes de sa loi ou de sa coutume interne, d'exécuter les actes auxquels elle s'applique dans des conditions moins restrictives;

(*c*) permette, aux termes de sa loi ou de sa coutume interne, des méthodes d'obtention de preuves autres que celles prévues par la présente Convention.

Article 27

The provisions of the present Convention shall not prevent a Contacting State from —

(*a*) declaring that Letters of Request may be transmitted to its judicial authorities through channels other than those provided for in Article 2;

(*b*) permitting, by internal law or practice, any act provided for in this Convention to be performed upon less restrictive conditions;

(*c*) permitting, by internal law or practice, method of taking evidence other than those provided for in this Convention.

Article 28

La présente Convention ne s'oppose pas à ce que des Etats contractants s'entendent pour déroger:

(*a*) à l'article 2, en ce qui concerne la voie de transmission des commissions rogatoires;

(*b*) à l'article 4, en ce qui concerne l'emploi des langues;

(*c*) à l'article 8, en ce qui concerne la présence de magistrats à l'exécution des commissions rogatoires;

(*d*) à l'article 11, en ce qui concerne les dispenses et interdictions de déposer;

(*e*) à l'article 13, en ce qui concerne la transmission des pièces constatant l'exécution;

(*f*) à l'article 14, en ce qui concerne le règlement des frais;

(*g*) aux dispositions du chapitre II.

Article 28

The present Convention shall not prevent an agreement between any two or more Contracting States to derogate from —

(*a*) the provisions of Article 2 with respect to methods of transmitting Letters of Request;

(*b*) the provisions of Article 4 with respect to the languages which may be used;

(*c*) the provisions of Article 8 with respect to the presence of judicial personnel at the execution of Letters;

(*d*) the provisions of Article 11 with respect to the privileges and duties of witnesses to refuse to give evidence;

(*e*) the provisions of Article 13 with respect to the methods of returning executed Letters to the requesting authority;

(*f*) the provisions of Article 14 with respect to fees and costs;

(*g*) the provisions of Chapter II.

Article 29

La présente Convention remplacera, dans les rapports entre les Etats qui l'auront ratifiée, les articles 8 à 16 des Conventions relatives à la procédure civile, respectivement signées à La

Article 29

Between Parties to the present Convention who are also Parties to one or both of the Conventions on Civil Procedure signed at the Hague on the 17th of July 1905 and the 1st of

Haye le 17 juillet 1905 et le premier mars 1954, dans la mesure où lesdits Etats sont Parties à l'une ou l'autre de ces Conventions.

March 1954, this Convention shall replace Articles 8–16 of the earlier Conventions.

Article 30

La présente Convention ne porte pas atteinte à l'application de l'article 23 de la Convention de 1905, ni de l'article 24 de celle de 1954.

Article 30

The present Convention shall not affect the application of Article 23 of the Convention of 1905, or of Article 24 of the Convention of 1954.

Article 31

Les accords additionnels aux Conventions de 1905 et de 1954, conclus par les Etats contractants, sont considérés comme également applicables à la présente Convention, à moins que les Etats intéressés n'en conviennent autrement.

Article 31

Supplementary Agreements between Parties to the Conventions of 1905 and 1954 shall be considered as equally applicable to the present Convention unless the Parties have otherwise agreed.

Article 32

Sans préjudice de l'application des articles 29 et 31, la présente Convention ne déroge pas aux conventions auxquelles les Etats contractants sont ou seront Parties et qui contiennent des dispositions sur les matières réglées par la présente Convention.

Article 32

Without prejudice to the provisions of Articles 29 and 31, the present Convention shall not derogate from conventions containing provisions on the matters covered by this Convention to which the Contracting States are, or shall become Parties.

Article 33

Tout Etat, au moment de la signature, de la ratification ou de l'adhésion, a la faculté d'exclure en tout ou en partie l'application des dispositions de l'alinéa 2 de l'article 4, ainsi que du chapitre II. Aucune autre réserve ne sera admise.

Tout Etat contractant pourra, à tout moment, retirer une réserve qu'il aura faite; l'effet de la réserve cessera le soixantième jour après la notification du retrait.

Lorsqu'un Etat aura fait une réserve, tout autre Etat affecté par celle-ci peut appliquer la même règle à l'égard de l'Etat qui a fait la réserve.

Article 33

A State may, at the time of signature, ratification or accession exclude, in whole or in part, the application of the provisions of paragraph 2 of Article 4 and of Chapter II. No other reservation shall be permitted.

Each Contracting State may at any time withdraw a reservation it has made; the reservation shall cease to have effect on the sixtieth day after notification of the withdrawal.

When a State has made a reservation, any other State affected thereby may apply the same rule against the reserving State.

Article 34

Tout Etat peut à tout moment retirer ou modifier une déclaration.

Article 34

A State may at any time withdraw or modify a declaration.

Article 35

Tout Etat contractant indiquera au Ministère des Affaires Etrangères des Pays-Bas, soit au moment du dépôt de son instrument de ratification ou d'adhésion, soit ultérieurement, les autorités prévues aux articles 2, 8, 24 et 25.

Article 35

A Contracting State shall, at the time of the deposit of its instrument of ratification or accession, or at a later date, inform the Ministry of Foreign Affairs of the Netherlands of the designation of authorities, pursuant to Articles 2, 8, 24 and 25.

Il notifiera, le cas échéant, dans les mêmes conditions:

(*a*) la désignation des autorités auxquelles les agents diplomatiques ou consulaires doivent s'adresser en vertu de l'article 16 et des celles qui peuvent accorder l'autorisation ou l'assistance prévues aux articles 15, 16 et 18;

(*b*) la désignation des autorités qui peuvent accorder au commissaire l'autorisation prévue à l'article 17 ou l'assistance prévue à l'article 18;

(*c*) les déclarations visées aux articles 4, 8, 11, 15, 16, 17, 18, 23 et 27;

(*d*) tout retrait ou modificaton des désignations et déclarations mentionnées ci-dessus;

(*e*) tout retrait de réserves.

A Contracting State shall likewise inform the Ministry, where appropriate, of the following —

(*a*) the designation of the authorities to whom notice must be given, whose permission may be required, and whose assistance may be invoked in the taking of evidence by diplomatic officers and consular agents, pursuant to Articles 15, 16 and 18 respectively.

(*b*) the designation of the authorities whose permission may be required in the taking of evidence by commissioners pursuant to Article 17 and of those who may grant the assistance provided for in Article 18;

(*c*) declarations pursuant to Articles 4, 8, 11, 15, 16, 17, 18, 23 and 27;

(*d*) any withdrawal or modification of the above designations and declarations;

(*e*) the withdrawal of any reservation.

Article 36

Les difficultés qui s'élèveraient entre les Etats contractants à l'occasion de l'application de la présente Convention seront réglées par la voie diplomatique.

Article 36

Any difficulties which may arise between Contracting States in connection with the operation of this Convention shall be settled through diplomatic channels.

Article 37

La présente Convention est ouverte à la signature des Etats représentés à la Onzième session de la Conférence de La Haye de droit international privé.

Elle sera ratifiée et les instruments de ratification seront déposés auprès du Ministère des Affaires Etrangères des Pays-Bas.

Article 37

The present Convention shall be open for signature by the States represented at the Eleventh Session of the Hague Conference on Private International Law.

It shall be ratified, and the instruments of ratification shall be deposited with the Ministry of Foreign Affairs of the Netherlands.

Article 38

La présente Convention entrera en vigueur le soixantième jour après le dépôt du troisième instrument de ratification prévu par l'article 37, alinéa 2.

La Convention entrera en vigueur, pour chaque Etat signataire ratifiant postérieurement, le soixantième jour après le dépôt de son instrument de ratification.

Aricle 38

The present Convention shall enter into force on the sixtieth day after the deposit of the third instrument of ratification referred to in the second paragraph of Article 37.

The Convention shall enter into force for each signatory State which ratifies subsequently on the sixtieth day after the deposit of its instrument of ratification.

Article 39

Tout Etat non représenté à la Onzième session de la Conférence de La Haye de droit international privé qui est Membre de la Conférence ou de l'Organisation des Nations Unies ou d'une institution spécialisée de celle-

Article 39

Any State not represented at the Eleventh Session of the Hague Conference on Private International Law which is a Member of this Conference or of the United Nations or of a specialized agency of that Organization, or a

ci ou Partie au Statut de la Cour Internationale de Justice pourra adhérer à la présente Convention après son entrée en vigueur en vertu de l'article 38, alinéa premier.

L'instrument d'adhésion sera déposé auprès du Ministère des Affaires Etrangères des Pays-Bas.

La Convention entrera en vigueur, pour l'Etat adhérant, le soixantième jour après le dépôt de son instrument d'adhésion.

L'adhésion n'aura d'effet que dans les rapports entre l'Etat adhérant et les Etats contractants qui auront déclaré accepter cette adhésion. Cette déclaration sera déposée auprès du Ministère des Affaires Etrangères des Pays-Bas; celui-ci en enverra, par la voie diplomatique, une copie certifiée conforme, à chacun des Etats contractants.

La Convention entrera en vigueur entre l'Etat adhérant et l'Etat ayant déclaré accepter cette adhésion soixante jours après le dépôt de la déclaration d'acceptation.

Party to the Statute of the International Court of Justice may accede to the present Convention after it has entered into force in accordance with the first paragraph of Article 38.

The instrument of accession shall be deposited with the Ministry of Foreign Affairs of the Netherlands.

The Convention shall enter into force for a State acceding to it on the sixtieth day after the deposit of its instrument of accession.

The accession will have effect only as regards the relations between the acceding State and such Contracting States as will have declared their acceptance of the accession. Such declaration shall be deposited at the Ministry of Foreign Affairs of the Netherlands; this Ministry shall forward, through diplomatic channels, a certified copy to each of the Contracting States.

The Convention will enter into force as between the acceding State and the State that has declared its acceptance of the accession on the sixtieth day after the deposit of the declaration of acceptance.

Article 40

Tout Etat, au moment de la signature, de la ratification ou de l'adhésion, pourra déclarer que la présente Convention s'étendra à l'ensemble des territoires qu'il représente sur le plan international, ou à l'un ou plusieurs d'entre eux. Cette déclaration aura effet au moment de l'entrée en vigueur de la Convention pour ledit Etat.

Par la suite, toute extension de cette nature sera notifiée au Ministère des Affaires Etrangères des Pays-Bas.

La Convention entrera en vigueur, pour les territoires visés par l'extension, le soixantième jour après la notification mentionnée à l'alinéa précédent.

Article 40

Any State may, at the time of signature, ratification or accession, declare that the present Convention shall extend to all the territories for the international relations of which it is responsible, or to one or more of them. Such a declaration shall take effect on the date of entry into force of the Convention for the State concerned.

At any time thereafter, such extensions shall be notified to the Ministry of Foreign Affairs of the Netherlands.

The Convention shall enter into force for the territories mentioned in such an extension on the sixtieth day after the notification indicated in the preceding paragraph.

Article 41

La présente Convention aura une durée de cinq ans à partir de la date de son entrée en vigueur, conforméement à l'article 38, alinéa premier, même pour les Etats qui l'auront ratifiée ou y auront adhéré postérieurement.

La Convention sera ronouvelée tacitement de cinq en cinq ans, sauf dénonciation.

La dénonciation sera, au moins six mois avant l'expiration du délai de cinq ans, notifiée au Ministère des Affaires Etrangères des Pays-Bas.

Elle pourra se limiter à certains des territoires auxquels s'applique la Convention.

Article 41

The present Convention shall remain in force for five years from the date of its entry into force in accordance with the first paragraph of Article 38, even for States which have ratified it or acceded to it subsequently.

If there has been no denunciation, it shall be renewed tacitly every five years.

Any denunciation shall be notified to the Ministry of Foreign Affairs of the Netherlands at least six months before the end of the five year period.

It may be limited to certain of the territories to which the Convention applies.

La dénonciation n'aura d'effet qu'à l'égard de l'Etat qui l'aura notifiée. La Convention restera en vigueur pour les autres Etats contractants.

The denunciation shall have effect only as regards the State which has notified it. The Convention shall remain in force for the other Contracting States.

Article 42

Le Ministère des Affaires Etrangères des Pays-Bas notifiera aux Etats visés à l'article 37, ainsi qu'aux Etats qui auront adhéré conformément aux dispositions de l'article 39:

(a) les signatures et ratifications visées à l'article 37;

(b) la date à laquelle la présente Convention entrera en vigueur conformément aux dispositions de l'article 38, alinéa premier;

(c) les adhésions visées à l'article 39 et la date a laquelles elles auront effet;

(d) les extensions visées à l'article 40 et la date à laquelle elles auront effet;

(e) les désignations, réserves et déclarations mentionnées aux articles 33 et 35;

(f) les dénonciations visées à l'article 41, alinéa 3.

En foi de quoi, les soussignés, dûment autorisés, ont signé la présente Convention.

Fait à La Haye, le premier mars 1970, en français et en anglais, les deux textes faisant également foi, en un seul exemplaire, qui sera déposé dans les archives du Gouvernement des Pays-Bas et dont une copie certifiée confome sera remise, par la voie diplomatique, à chacun des Etats représentés à la Onzième session de la Conférence de La Haye de droit international privé.

Article 42

The Ministry of Foreign Affairs of the Netherlands shall give notice to the States referred to in Article 37, and to the States which have acceded in accordance with Article 39, of the following —

(a) the signatures and ratifications referred to in Article 37;

(b) the date on which the present Convention enters into force in accordance with the first paragraph of Article 38;

(c) the accessions referred to in Article 39 and the dates on which they take effect;

(d) the extensions referred to in Article 40 and the dates on which they take effect;

(e) the designations, reservations and declarations referred to in Articles 33 and 35;

(f) the denunciations referred to in the third paragraph of Article 41.

In witness whereof the undersigned, being duly authorised thereto, have signed the present Convention.

Done at The Hague, on the first day of March 1970, in the English and French languages, both texts being equally authentic, in a single copy which shall be deposited in the archives of the Government of the Netherlands, and of which a certified copy shall be sent, through the diplomatic channel, to each of the States represented at the Eleventh Session of the Hague Conference on Private International Law.

(c) Scheme Relating to Mutual Assistance in Criminal Matters within the Commonwealth
including amendments made by Law Ministers in April 1990

PURPOSE AND SCOPE

1 (1) The purpose of this Scheme is to increase the level and scope of assistance rendered between Commonwealth Governments in criminal matters. It augments, and in no way derogates from existing forms of cooperation, both formal and informal; nor does it preclude the development of enhanced arrangements in other fora.

(2) This Scheme provides for the giving of assistance by the competent authorities of one country (the requested country) in respect of criminal matters arising in another country (the requesting country).

(3) Assistance in criminal matters under this Scheme includes assistance in

(*a*) identifying and locating persons;

(*b*) serving documents;

(*c*) examining witnesses;

(*d*) search and seizure;

(*e*) obtaining evidence;

(*f*) facilitating the personal appearance of witnesses;

(*g*) effecting a temporary transfer of persons in custody to appear as a witness;

(*h*) obtaining production of judicial or official records; and

(*i*) tracing, seizing and confiscating the proceeds or instrumentalities of crime.

MEANING OF COUNTRY

2 For the purposes of this Scheme, each of the following is a separate country, that is to say

(*a*) each sovereign and independent country within the Commonwealth together with any dependent territories which that country designates; and

(*b*) each country within the Commonwealth which, though not sovereign and independent, is not designated for the purposes of the preceding sub-paragraph.

CRIMINAL MATTER

3 (1) For the purposes of this Scheme, a criminal matter arises in a country if the Central Authority of that country certifies that criminal or forfeiture proceedings have been instituted in a court exercising jurisdiction in that country or that there is reasonable cause to believe that an offence has been committed in respect of which such proceedings could be so instituted.

(2) 'Offence', in the case of a federal country or a country having more than one legal system, includes an offence under the law of the country or any part thereof.

(3) 'Forfeiture proceedings' means proceedings, whether civil or criminal, for an order —

(*a*) restraining dealings with any property in respect of which there is reasonable cause to believe that it has been

  (i) derived or obtained, whether directly or indirectly, from; or

  (ii) used in, or in connection with,

  the commission of an offence;

(*b*) confiscating any property derived or obtained as provided in paragraph (*a*)(i) or used as provided in paragraph (*a*)(ii); or

(*c*) imposing a pecuniary penalty calculated by reference to the value of any property derived or obtained as provided in paragraph (*a*)(i) or used as provided in paragraph (*a*)(ii).

CENTRAL AUTHORITIES

4 Each country shall designate a Central Authority to transmit and to receive requests for assistance under this Scheme.

ACTION IN THE REQUESTING COUNTRY

5 (1) A request for assistance under this Scheme may be initiated by any law enforcement agency or public prosecution or judicial authority competent under the law of the requesting country.

(2) The Central Authority of the requesting country shall, if it is satisfied that the request can properly be made under this Scheme, transmit the request to the Central Authority of the requested country and shall ensure that the request contains all the information required by the provisions of this Scheme.

(3) The Central Authority of the requesting country shall provide as far as practicable additional information sought by the Central Authority of the requested country.

ACTION IN THE REQUESTED COUNTRY

6 (1) Subject to the provisions of this Scheme, the requested country shall grant the assistance requested as expeditiously as practicable.

(2) The Central Authority of the requested country shall, subject to the following provisions of this paragraph, take the necessary steps to ensure that the competent authorities of that country comply with the request.

(3) If the Central Authority of the requested country considers

(*a*) that the request does not comply with the provisions of this Scheme, or

(*b*) that in accordance with the provisions of this Scheme the request for assistance is to be refused in whole or in part, or (*c*) that the request cannot be complied with, in whole or in part, or

(*d*) that there are circumstances which are likely to cause a significant delay in complying with the request,

it shall promptly inform the Central Authority of the requesting country, giving reasons.

REFUSAL OF ASSISTANCE

7　(1) The requested country may refuse to comply in whole or in part with a request for assistance under this Scheme if the criminal matter appears to the Central Authority of that country to concern

(*a*) conduct which would not constitute an offence under the law of that country; or

(*b*) an offence or proceedings of a political character; or

(*c*) conduct which in the requesting country is an offence only under military law or a law relating to military obligations; or

(*d*) conduct in relation to which the person accused or suspected of having committed an offence has been acquitted or convicted by a court in the requested country.

(2) The requested country may refuse to comply in whole or in part with a request for assistance under this Scheme

(*a*) to the extent that it appears to the Central Authority of that country that compliance would be contrary to the Constitution of that country, or would prejudice the security, international relations or other essential public interests of that country; or

(*b*) where there are substantial grounds leading the Central Authority of that country to believe that compliance would facilitate the prosecution or punishment of any person on account of his race, religion, nationality or political opinions or would cause prejudice for any of these reasons to any person affected by the request.

(3) The requested country may refuse to comply in whole or in part with a request for assistance to the extent that the steps required to be taken in order to comply with the request cannot under the law of that country be taken in respect of criminal matters arising in that country.

(4) An offence shall not be an offence of a political character for the purposes of this paragraph if it is an offence within the scope of any international convention to which both the requesting and requested countries are parties and which imposes on the parties thereto an obligation either to extradite or prosecute a person accused of the commission of the offence.

MEASURES OF COMPULSION

8 (1) The competent authorities of the requested country shall in complying with a request under this Scheme use only such measures of compulsion as are available under the law of that country in respect of criminal matters arising in that country.

(2) Where under the law of the requested country measures of compulsion cannot be applied to any person to take the steps necessary to secure compliance with a request under this Scheme but the person concerned is willing to act voluntarily in compliance or partial compliance with the terms of the request, the competent authorities of the requested country shall make available the necessary facilities.

SCHEME NOT TO COVER ARREST OR EXTRADITION

9 Nothing in this Scheme is to be construed as authorising the extradition, or the arrest or detention with a view to extradition, of any person.

CONFIDENTIALITY

10 The Central Authorities and the competent authorities of the requesting and requested countries shall use their best efforts to keep confidential a request and its contents and the information and materials supplied in compliance with a request except for disclosure in criminal proceedings and where otherwise authorised by the Central Authority of the other country.

LIMITATION OF USE OF INFORMATION OR EVIDENCE

11 The requesting country shall not use any information or evidence obtained in response to a request for assistance under this Scheme in connection with any matter other than the criminal matter specified in the request without the prior consent of the Central Authority of the requested country.

EXPENSES OF COMPLIANCE

12 (1) Except as provided in the following provisions of this paragraph, compliance with a request under this Scheme shall not give rise to any claim against the requesting country for expenses incurred by the Central Authority or other competent authorities of the requested country.

(2) The requesting country shall be responsible for the travel and incidental expenses of witnesses travelling to the requesting country, including those of accompanying officials, for fees of experts, and for the costs of any translation required by the requesting country.

(3) If in the opinion of the requested country the expenses required in order to comply with the request are of an extraordinary nature, the Central Authority of the requested country shall consult with the Central Authority of the requesting country as to the terms and conditions under which compliance with the request may

continue, and in the absence of agreement the requested country may refuse to comply further with the request.

CONTENTS OF REQUEST FOR ASSISTANCE

13 (1) A request under the Scheme shall

(*a*) specify the nature of the assistance requested;

(*b*) contain the information appropriate to the assistance sought as specified in the following provisions of this Scheme;

(*c*) indicate any time-limit within which compliance with the request is desired, stating reasons;

(*d*) contain the following information:
  (i) the identity of the agency or authority initiating the request;
  (ii) the nature of the criminal matter; and
  (iii) whether or not criminal proceedings have been instituted;

(*e*) where criminal proceedings have been instituted, contain the following information:
  (i) the court exercising jurisdiction in the proceedings;
  (ii) the identity of the accused person;
  (iii) the offences of which he stands accused, and a summary of the facts;
  (iv) the stage reached in the proceedings; and
  (v) any date fixed for further stages in the proceedings;

(*f*) where criminal proceedings have not been instituted, state the offence which the Central Authority of the requesting country has reasonable cause to believe to have been committed, with a summary of the known facts.

(2) A request shall normally be in writing, and if made orally in case of urgency shall be confirmed in writing forthwith.

IDENTIFYING AND LOCATING PERSONS

14 (1) A request under this Scheme may seek assistance in identifying or locating persons believed to be within the requested country.

(2) The request shall indicate the purpose for which the information is requested and shall contain such information as is available to the Central Authority of the requesting country as to the whereabouts of the person concerned and such other information as it possesses as may facilitate the identification of that person.

SERVICE OF DOCUMENTS

15 (1) A request under this Scheme may seek assistance in the service of documents relevant to a criminal matter arising in the requesting country.

(2) The request shall be accompanied by the documents to be served and, where those documents relate to attendance in the requesting country, such notice as the Central Authority of that country is reasonably able to provide of outstanding warrants or other judicial orders in criminal matters against the person to be served.

(3) The Central Authority of the requested country shall endeavour to have the documents served.

(*a*) any particular method stated in the request, unless such method is incompatible with the law of that country; or

(*b*) by any method prescribed by the law of that country for the service of documents in criminal proceedings.

(4) The requested country shall transmit to the Central Authority of the requesting country a certificate as to the service of the documents or, if they have not been served, as to the reasons which have prevented service.

(5) A person served in compliance with a request with a summons to appear as a witness in the requesting country and who fails to comply with the summons shall not by reason thereof be liable to any penalty or measure of compulsion in either the requesting or the requested country notwithstanding any contrary statement in the summons.

EXAMINATION OF WITNESSES

16   (1) A request under this Scheme may seek assistance in the examination of witnesses in the requested country.

(2) The request shall specify, as appropriate and so far as the circumstances of the case permit:

(*a*) the names and addresses or the official designations of the witnesses to be examined;

(*b*) the questions to be put to the witnesses or the subject-matter about which they are to be examined;

(*c*) whether it is desired that the witnesses be examined orally or in writing;

(*d*) whether it is desired that the oath be administered to the witnesses (or, as the law of the requested country allows, that they be required to make their solemn affirmation);

(*e*) any provisions of the law of the requesting country as to privilege or exemption from giving evidence which appear especially relevant to the request; and

(*f*) any special requirements of the law of the requesting country as to the manner of taking evidence relevant to its admissibility in that country.

(3) The request may ask that, so far as the law of the requested country permits, the accused person or his legal representative may attend the examination of the witness and ask questions of the witness.

SEARCH AND SEIZURE

17   (1) A request under this Scheme may seek assistance in the search for and seizure of property in the requested country.

(2) The request shall specify the property to be searched for and seized and shall contain, so far as reasonably practicable, all information available to the Central

Authority of the requesting country which may be required to be adduced in an application under the law of the requested country for any necessary warrant or authorisation to effect the search and seizure.

(3) The requested country shall provide such certification as may be required by the requesting country concerning the result of any search, the place and circumstances of seizure, and the subsequent custody of the property seized.

OTHER ASSISTANCE IN OBTAINING EVIDENCE

18   (1) A request under this Scheme may seek other assistance in obtaining evidence.

(2) The request shall specify, as appropriate and so far as the circumstances of the case permit:

(*a*) the documents, records or property to be inspected, preserved, photo-graphed, copied or transmitted;

(*b*) the samples of property to be taken, examined or transmitted; and

(*c*) the site to be viewed or photographed.

PRIVILEGE

19   (1) No person shall be compelled in response to a request under this Scheme to give any evidence in the requested country which he could not be compelled to give

(*a*) in criminal proceedings in that country; or

(*b*) in criminal proceedings in the requesting country.

(2) For the purposes of this paragraph any reference to giving evidence includes references to answering any question and to producing any document.

PRODUCTION OF JUDICIAL OR OFFICIAL RECORDS

20   (1) A request under this Scheme may seek the production of judicial or official records relevant to a criminal matter arising in the requesting country.

(2) For the purposes of this paragraph 'judicial records' means judgments, orders and decisions of courts and other documents held by judicial authorities and 'official records' means documents held by government departments or agencies or prosecu-tion authorities.

(3) The requested country shall provide copies of judicial or official records which are publicly available.

(4) The requested country may provide copies of judicial or official records not publicly available, to the same extent and under the same conditions as apply to the provision of such records to its own law enforcement agencies or prosecution or judicial authorities.

TRANSMISSION AND RETURN OF MATERIAL

21 (1) Where compliance with a request under this Scheme would involve the transmission to the requesting country of any document, record or property, the requested country

(*a*) may postpone the transmission of the material if it is required in connection with proceedings in that country, and in such a case shall provide certified copies of a document or record pending transmission of the original;

(*b*) may require the requesting country to agree to terms and conditions to protect third party interests in the material to be transmitted and may refuse to effect such transmission pending such agreement.

(2) Where any document, record or property is transmitted to the requesting country in compliance with a request under this Scheme, it shall be returned to the requested country when it is no longer required in connection with the criminal matter specified in the request unless that country has indicated that its return is not desired.

(3) The requested country shall authenticate material that is to be transmitted by that country.

AUTHENTICATION

22 A document or other material transmitted for the purposes of or in response to a request under this Scheme shall be deemed to be duly authenticated if it:

(*a*) purports to be signed or certified by a judge or magistrate, or to bear the stamp or seal of a Minister, government department or Central Authority; or

(*b*) is verified by the oath of a witness or of a public officer of the Commonwealth country from which the document or material emanates.

PERSONAL APPEARANCE OF WITNESSES IN THE REQUESTING COUNTRY

23 (1) A request under this Scheme may seek assistance in facilitating the personal appearance of witnesses before a court exercising jurisdiction in the requesting country.

(2) The request shall specify

(*a*) the subject matter upon which it is desired to examine the witnesses;

(*b*) the reasons for which the personal appearance of the witnesses is required; and

(*c*) details of the travelling, subsistence and other expenses payable by the requesting country in respect of the personal appearance of the witnesses.

(3) The competent authorities of the requested country shall invite persons whose appearance as witnesses in the requesting country is desired; and

(*a*) ask whether they agree to appear;

(*b*) inform the Central Authority of the requesting country of their answer; and (*c*) if they are willing to appear, make appropriate arrangements to facilitate the personal appearance of the witnesses.

(4) A person whose appearance as a witness is the subject of a request and who does not agree to appear shall not by reason thereof be liable to any penalty or measure of compulsion in either the requesting or requested country.

PERSONAL APPEARANCE OF PERSONS IN CUSTODY

24 (1) A request under this Scheme may seek the temporary transfer of persons in custody in the requested country to appear as witnesses before a court exercising jurisdiction in the requesting country.

(2) The request shall specify

(*a*) the subject matter upon which it is desired to examine the witnesses;

(*b*) the reasons for which the personal appearance of the witnesses is required;

(3) The requested country shall refuse to comply with a request for transfer of persons in custody if the persons concerned do not consent to the transfer.

(4) The requested country may refuse to comply with a request for the transfer of persons in custody and shall be under no obligation to inform the requesting country of the reasons for such refusal.

(5) A person in custody whose transfer is the subject of a request and who does not consent to the transfer shall not by reason thereof be liable to any penalty or measure of compulsion in either the requesting or requested country.

(6) Where persons in custody are transferred, the requested country shall notify the requesting country of

(*a*) the dates upon which the persons are due under the law of the requested country to be released from custody and

(*b*) the dates by which the requested country requires the return of the persons and shall notify any variations in such dates.

(7) The requesting country shall keep the persons transferred in custody, and shall return the persons to the requested country when their presence as witnesses in the requesting country is no longer required, and in any case by the earlier of the dates notified under sub paragraph (6).

(8) The obligation to return the persons transferred shall subsist notwithstanding the fact that they are nationals of the requesting country.

(9) The period during which the persons transferred are in custody in the requesting country shall be deemed to be service in the requested country of an equivalent period of custody in that country for all purposes.

(10) Nothing in this paragraph shall preclude the release in the requesting country without return to the requested country of any person transferred where the two countries and the person concerned agreed.

IMMUNITY OF PERSONS APPEARING

25 (1) Subject to the provisions of paragraph 24, witnesses appearing in the requesting country in response to a request under paragraph 23 or persons transferred to that country in response to a request under paragraph 24 shall be immune in that country from prosecution, detention or any other restriction of personal liberty in respect of criminal acts, omissions or convictions before the time of their departure from the requested country.

(2) The immunity provided for in that paragraph shall cease

(*a*) in the case of witnesses appearing in response to a request under paragraph 23, when the witnesses having had, for a period of 15 consecutive days from the dates when they were notified by the competent authority of the requesting country that their presence was no longer required by the court exercising jurisdiction in the criminal matter, an opportunity of leaving have nevertheless remained in the requesting country, or having left that country have returned to it;

(*b*) in the case of persons transferred in response to a request under paragraph 24 and remaining in custody when they have been returned to the requested country.

TRACING THE PROCEEDS OR INSTRUMENTALITIES OF CRIME

26 (1) A request under this Scheme may seek assistance in identifying, locating, and assessing the value of, property believed to have been derived or obtained, directly or indirectly, from, or to have been used in, or in connection with, the commission of an offence and believed to be within the requested country.

(2) The request shall contain such information as is available to the Central Authority of the requesting country as to the nature and location of the property and as to any person in whose possession or control the property is believed to be.

SEIZING AND CONFISCATING THE PROCEEDS OR INSTRUMENTALITIES OF CRIME

27 (1) A request under this Scheme may seek assistance in securing

(*a*) the making in the requested country of an order relating to the proceeds or instrumentalities of crime; or

(*b*) the recognition or enforcement in that country of such an order made in the requesting country.

(2) For the purpose of this paragraph, 'an order relating to the proceeds or instrumentalities of crime' means

(*a*) an order restraining dealings with any property in respect of which there is reasonable cause to believe that it has been derived or obtained, directly or indirectly, from, or used in, or in connection with, the commission of an offence;

(*b*) an order confiscating property derived or obtained, directly or indirectly, from, or used in or in connection with, the commission of an offence; and

(*c*) an order imposing a pecuniary penalty calculated by reference to the value of any property so derived, obtained or used.

(3) Where the requested country cannot enforce an order made in the requesting country, the requesting country may request the making of any similar order available under the law of the requested country.

(4) The request shall be accompanied by a copy of any order made in the requesting country and shall contain, so far as reasonably practicable, all information available to the Central Authority of the requesting country which may be required in connection with the procedures to be followed in the requested country.

(5) The law of the requested country shall apply to determine the circumstances and manner in which an order may be made, recognised or enforced in response to the request.

DISPOSAL OR RELEASE OF PROPERTY

28 (1) The law of the requested country shall apply to determine the disposal of any property

(*a*) forfeited; or

(*b*) obtained as a result of the enforcement of a pecuniary penalty order

as a result of a request under this Scheme.

(2) The law of the requested country shall apply to determine the circumstances in which property made the subject of interim seizure as a result of a request under this Scheme may be released from the effects of such seizure.

CONSULTATION

29 The Central Authorities of the requested and requesting countries shall consult promptly, at the request of either, concerning matters arising under this Scheme.

OTHER ASSISTANCE

30 After consultation between the requesting and the requested countries assistance not within the scope of this Scheme may be given in respect of a criminal matter on such terms and conditions as may be agreed by those countries.

NOTIFICATION OF DESIGNATIONS

31 Designations of dependent territories under paragraph 2 and of Central Authorities under paragraph 4 shall be notified to the Commonwealth Secretary-General.

(d) Council of Europe Convention on Laundering, Serach, Seizure and Confiscation of the Proceeds from Crime

PREAMBLE

The member States of the Council of Europe and the other States signatory hereto,

Considering that the aim of the Council of Europe is to achieve a greater unity between its members;

Convinced of the need to pursue a common criminal policy aimed at the protection of society;

Considering that the fight against serious crime, which has become an increasingly international problem, calls for the use of modern and effective methods on an international scale;

Believing that one of these methods consists in depriving criminals of the proceeds from crime;

Considering that for the attainment of this aim a well-functioning system of international cooperation also must be established,

Have agreed as follows:

CHAPTER I

USE OF TERMS

ARTICLE 1

Use of terms

For the purposes of this Convention:

a. 'proceeds' means any economic advantage from criminal offences. It may consist of any property as defined in sub-paragraph *b* of this article;

b. 'property' includes property of any description, whether corporeal or incorporeal, movable or immovable, and legal documents or instruments evidencing title to, or interest in such property;

c. 'instrumentalities' means any property used or intended to be used, in any manner, wholly or in part, to commit a criminal offence or criminal offences;

d. 'confiscation' means a penalty or a measure, ordered by a court following proceedings in relation to a criminal offence or criminal offences resulting in the final deprivation of property;

e. 'predicate offence' means any criminal offence as a result of which proceeds were generated that may become the subject of an offence as defined in Article 6 of this Convention.

CHAPTER II

MEASURES TO BE TAKEN AT NATIONAL LEVEL

ARTICLE 2

Confiscation measures

1. Each Party shall adopt such legislative and other measures as may be necessary to enable it to confiscate instrumentalities and proceeds or property the value of which corresponds to such proceeds.

2. Each Party may, at the time of signature or when depositing its instrument of ratification, acceptance, approval or accession, by a declaration addressed to the Secretary General of the Council of Europe, declare that paragraph 1 of this article applies only to offences or categories of offences specified in such declaration.

ARTICLE 3

Investigative and provisional measures

Each Party shall adopt such legislative and other measures as may be necessary to enable it to identify and trace property which is liable to confiscation pursuant to Article 2, paragraph 1, and to prevent any dealing in, transfer or disposal of such property.

ARTICLE 4

Special investigative powers and techniques

1. Each Party shall adopt such legislative and other measures as may be necessary to empower its courts or other competent authorities to order that bank, financial or commercial records be made available or be seized in order to carry out the actions referred to in Articles 2 and 3. A Party shall not decline to act under the provisions of this article on grounds of bank secrecy.

2. Each Party shall consider adopting such legislative and other measures as may be necessary to enable it to use special investigative techniques facilitating the identification and tracing of proceeds and the gathering of evidence related thereto. Such techniques may include monitoring orders, observation, interception of telecommunications, access to computer systems and orders to produce specific documents.

ARTICLE 5

Legal remedies

Each Party shall adopt such legislative and other measures as may be necessary to ensure that interested parties affected by measures under Articles 2 and 3 shall have effective legal remedies in order to preserve their rights.

ARTICLE 6

Laundering offences

1.   Each Party shall adopt such legislative and other measures as may be necessary to establish as offences under its domestic law, when committed intentionally:

a. the conversion or transfer of property, knowing that such property is proceeds, for the purpose of concealing or disguising the illicit origin of the property or of assisting any person who is involved in the commission of the predicate offence to evade the legal consequences of his actions;

b. the concealment or disguise of the true nature, source, location, disposition, movement, rights with respect to, or ownership of, property, knowing that such property is proceeds;

and, subject to its constitutional principles and the basic concepts of its legal system:

c. the acquisition, possession or use of property, knowing, at the time of receipt, that such property was proceeds;

d. participation in, association or conspiracy to commit, attempts to commit and aiding, abetting, facilitating and counselling the commission of any of the offences established in accordance with this article.

2.   For the purposes of implementing or applying paragraph 1 of this article:

a. it shall not matter whether the predicate offence was subject to the criminal jurisdiction of the Party:

b. it may be provided that the offences set forth in that paragraph do not apply to the persons who committed the predicate offence;

c. knowledge, intent or purpose required as an element of an offence set forth in that paragraph may be inferred from objective, factual circumstances.

3.   Each Party may adopt such measures as it considers necessary to establish also as offences under its domestic law all or some of the acts referred to in paragraph 1 of this article, in any or all of the following cases where the offender:

a. ought to have assumed that the property was proceeds;

b. acted for the purpose of making profit;

c. acted for the purpose of promoting the carrying on of further criminal activity.

4.   Each Party may, at the time of signature or when depositing its instrument of ratification, acceptance, approval or accession, by declaration addressed to the

Secretary General of the Council of Europe declare that paragraph 1 of this article applies only to predicate offences or categories of such offences specified in such declaration.

CHAPTER III

INTERNATIONAL CO-OPERATION

Section 1

Principles of international co-operation

ARTICLE 7

General principles and measures for international co-operation

1.   The Parties shall co-operate with each other to the widest extent possible for the purposes of investigations and proceedings aiming at the confiscation of instrumentalities and proceeds.

2.   Each Party shall adopt such legislative or other measures as may be necessary to enable it to comply, under the conditions provided for in this chapter, with requests:

   a. for confiscation of specific items of property representing proceeds or instrumentalities, as well as for confiscation of proceeds consisting in a requirement to pay a sum of money corresponding to the value of proceeds;

   b. for investigative assistance and provisional measures with a view to either form of confiscation referred to under *a* above.

Section 2

Investigative assistance

ARTICLE 8

Obligation to assist

The Parties shall afford each other, upon request, the widest possible measure of assistance in the identification and tracing of instrumentalities, proceeds and other property liable to confiscation. Such assistance shall include any measure providing and securing evidence as to the existence, location or movement, nature, legal status or value of the aforementioned property.

ARTICLE 9

Execution of assistance

The assistance pursuant to Article 8 shall be carried out as permitted by and in accordance with the domestic law of the requested Party and, to the extent not incompatible with such law, in accordance with the procedures specified in the request.

ARTICLE 10

Spontaneous information

Without prejudice to its own investigations or proceedings, a Party may without prior request forward to another Party information on instrumentalities and proceeds, when it considers that the disclosure of such information might assist the receiving Party in initiating or carrying out investigations or proceedings or might lead to a request by that Party under this chapter.

Section 3

Provisional measures

ARTICLE 11

Obligation to take provisional measures

1.   At the request of another Party which has instituted criminal proceedings or proceedings for the purpose of confiscation, a Party shall take the necessary provisional measures, such as freezing or seizing, to prevent any dealing in, transfer or disposal of property which, at a later stage, may be the subject of a request for confiscation or which might be such as to satisfy the request.

2.   A Party which has received a request for confiscation pursuant to Article 13 shall, if so requested, take the measures mentioned in paragraph 1 of this article in respect of any property which is the subject of the request or which might be such as to satisfy the request.

ARTICLE 12

Execution of provisional measures

1.   The provisional measures mentioned in Article 11 shall be carried out as permitted by and in accordance with the domestic law of the requested Party and, to the extent not incompatible with such law, in accordance with the procedures specified in the request.

2.   Before lifting any provisional measure taken pursuant to this article, the requested Party shall wherever possible, give the requesting Party an opportunity to present its reasons in favour of continuing the measure.

Section 4

Confiscation

ARTICLE 13

Obligation to confiscate

1. A Party, which has received a request made by another Party for confiscation concerning instrumentalities or proceeds, situated in its territory, shall:

 a. enforce a confiscation order made by a court of a requesting Party in relation to such instrumentalities or proceeds; or

 b. submit the request to its competent authorities for the purpose of obtaining an order of confiscation and, if such order is granted, enforce it.

2. For the purposes of applying paragraph 1.*b* of this article, any Party shall whenever necessary have competence to institute confiscation proceedings under its own law.

3. The provisions of paragraph 1 of this article shall also apply to confiscation consisting in a requirement to pay a sum of money corresponding to the value of proceeds, if property on which the confiscation can be enforced is located in the requested Party. In such cases, when enforcing confiscation pursuant to paragraph 1, the requested Party shall, if payment is not obtained, realise the claim on any property available for that purpose.

4. If a request for confiscation concerns a specific item of property, the Parties may agree that the requested Party may enforce the confiscation in the form of a requirement to pay a sum of money corresponding to the value of the property.

ARTICLE 14

Execution of confiscation

1. The procedures for obtaining and enforcing the confiscation under Article 13 shall be governed by the law of the requested Party.

2. The requested Party shall be bound by the findings as to the facts in so far as they are stated in a conviction or judicial decision of the requesting Party or in so far as such conviction or judicial decision is implicitly based on them.

3. Each Party may, at the time of signature or when depositing its instrument of ratification, acceptance, approval or accession, by a declaration addressed to the Secretary General of the Council of Europe, declare that paragraph 2 of this article applies only subject to its constitutional principles and the basic concepts of its legal system.

4. If the confiscation consists in the requirement to pay a sum of money, the competent authority of the requested Party shall convert the amount thereof into the

currency of that Party at the rate of exchange ruling at the time when the decision to enforce the confiscation is taken.

5.   In the case of Article 13, paragraph 1.*a*, the requesting Party alone shall have the right to decide on any application for review of the confiscation order.

ARTICLE 15

Confiscated property

Any property confiscated by the requested Party shall be disposed of by that Party in accordance with its domestic law, unless otherwise agreed by the Parties concerned.

ARTICLE 16

Right of enforcement and maximum amount of confiscation

1.   A request for confiscation made under Article 13 does not affect the right of the requesting Party to enforce itself the confiscation order.

2.   Nothing in this Convention shall be so interpreted as to permit the total value of the confiscation to exceed the amount of the sum of money specified in the confiscation order. If a Party finds that this might occur, the Parties concerned shall enter into consultations to avoid such an effect.

ARTICLE 17

Imprisonment in default

The requested Party shall not impose imprisonment in default or any other measure restricting the liberty of a person as a result of a request under Article 13, if the requesting Party has so specified in the request.

Section 5

Refusal and postponement of co-operation

ARTICLE 18

Grounds for refusal

1.   Co-operation under this chapter may be refused if:

a. the action sought would be contrary to the fundamental principles of the legal system of the requested Party; or

b. the execution of the request is likely to prejudice the sovereignty, security, *ordre public* or other essential interests of the requested Party; or

c. in the opinion of the requested Party, the importance of the case to which the request relates does not justify the taking of the action sought; or *d.* the offence to which the request relates is a political or fiscal offence; or

e. the requested Party considers that compliance with the action sought would be contrary to the principle of *ne bis in idem*; or

f. the offence to which the request relates would not be an offence under the law of the requested Party if committed within its jurisdication. However, this ground for refusal applies to co-operation under Section 2 only in so far as the assistance sought involves coercive action.

2. Co-operation under Section 2, in so far as the assistance sought involves coercive action, and under Section 3 of this chapter, may also be refused if the measures sought could not be taken under the domestic law of the requested Party for the purposes of investigations or proceedings, had it been a similar domestic case.

3. Where the law of the requested Party so requires, co-operation under Section 2, in so far as the assistance sought involves coercive action, and under Section 3 of this chapter may also be refused if the measures sought or any other measures having similar effects would not be permitted under the law of the requesting Party, or, as regards the competent authorities of the requesting Party, if the request is not authorised by either a judge or another judicial authority, including public prosecutors, any of these authorities acting in relation to criminal offences.

4. Co-operation under Section 4 of this chapter may also be refused if:

a. under the law of the requested Party confiscation is not provided for in respect of the type of offence to which the request relates; or

b. without prejudice to the obligation pursuant to Article 13, paragraph 3, it would be contrary to the principles of the domestic laws of the requested Party concerning the limits of confiscation in respect of the relationship between an offence and:
i. an economic advantage that might be qualified as its proceeds; or
ii. property that might be qualified as its instrumentalities; or

c. under the law of the requested Party confiscation may no longer be imposed or enforced because of the lapse of time; or

d. the request does not relate to a previous conviction, or a decision of a judicial nature or a statement in such a decision that an offence or several offences have been committed, on the basis of which the confiscation has been ordered or is sought; or

e. confiscation is either not enforceable in the requesting Party, or it is still subject to ordinary means of appeal; or

f. the request relates to a confiscation order resulting from a decision rendered *in absentia* of the person against whom the order was issued and, in the opinion of the requested Party, the proceedings conducted by the requesting Party leading to such decisions did not satisfy the minimum rights of defence recognised as due to everyone against whom a criminal charge is made.

5. For the purposes of paragraph 4.*f* of this article a decision is not considered to have been rendered *in absentia* if:

a. it has been confirmed or pronounced after opposition by the person concerned; or

b. it has been rendered on appeal, provided that the appeal was lodged by the person concerned.

6. When considering, for the purposes of paragraph 4.*f* of this article, if the minimum rights of defence have been satisfied, the requested Party shall take into account the fact that the person concerned has deliberately sought to evade justice or the fact that that person, having had the possibility of lodging a legal remedy against the decision made *in absentia*, elected not to do so. The same will apply when the person concerned, having been duly served with the summons to appear, elected not to do so nor to ask for adjournment.

7. A Party shall not invoke bank secrecy as a ground to refuse any co-operation under this chapter. Where its domestic law so requires, a Party may require that a request for co-operation which would involve the lifting of bank secrecy be authorised by either a judge or another judicial authority, including public prosecutors, any of these authorities acting in relation to criminal offences.

8. Without prejudice to the ground for refusal provided for in paragraph 1.*a* of this article:

a. the fact that the person under investigation or subjected to a confiscation order by the authorities of the requesting Party is a legal person shall not be invoked by the requested Party as an obstacle to affording any co-operation under this chapter;

b. the fact that the natural person against whom an order of confiscation of proceeds has been issued has subsequently died or the fact that a legal person against whom an order of confiscation of proceeds has been issued has subsequently been dissolved shall not be invoked as an obstacle to render assistance in accordance with Article 13, paragraph 1.*a*.

Article 19

Postponement

The requested Party may postpone action on a request if such action would prejudice investigations or proceedings by its authorities.

Article 20

Partial or conditional granting of a request

Before refusing or postponing co-operation under this chapter, the requested Party shall, where appropriate after having consulted the requesting Party, consider whether the request may be granted partially or subject to such conditions as it deems necessary.

Section 6

Notification and protection of third parties' rights

ARTICLE 21

Notification of documents

1. The Parties shall afford each other the widest measure of mutual assistance in the serving of judicial documents to persons affected by provisional measures and confiscation.

2. Nothing in this article is intended to interfere with:

a. the possibility of sending judicial documents, by postal channels, directly to persons abroad;

b. the possibility for judicial officers, officials or other competent authorities of the Party of origin to effect service of judicial documents directly through the consular authorities of that Party or through judicial officers, officials or other competent authorities of the Party of destination,

unless the Party of destination makes a declaration to the contrary to the Secretary General of the Council of Europe at the time of signature or when depositing its instrument of ratification, acceptance, approval or accession.

3. When serving judicial documents to persons abroad affected by provisional measures or confiscation orders issued in the sending Party, this Party shall indicate what legal remedies are available under its law to such persons.

ARTICLE 22

Recognition of foreign decisions

1. When dealing with a request for co-operation under Sections 3 and 4, the requested Party shall recognise any judicial decision taken in the requesting Party regarding rights claimed by third parties.

2. Recognition may be refused if:

a. third parties did not have adequate opportunity to assert their rights; or

b. the decision is incompatible with a decision already taken in the requested Party on the same matter; or

c. it is incompatible with the *ordre public* of the requested Party; or

d. the decision was taken contrary to provisions on exclusive jurisdiction provided for by the law of the requested Party.

Section 7

Procedural and other general rules

ARTICLE 23

Central authority

1.   The Parties shall designate a central authority or, if necessary, authorities, which shall be responsible for sending and answering requests made under this chapter, the execution of such requests or the transmission of them to the authorities competent for their execution.

2.   Each Party shall, at the time of signature or when depositing its instrument of ratification, acceptance, approval or accession, communicate to the Secretary General of the Council of Europe the names and addresses of the authorities designated in pursuance of paragraph 1 of this article.

ARTICLE 24

Direct communication

1.   The central authorities shall communicate directly with one another.

2.   In the event of urgency, requests or communications under this chapter may be sent directly by the judicial authorities, including public prosecutors, of the requesting Party to such authorities of the requested Party. In such cases a copy shall be sent at the same time to the central authority of the requested Party through the central authority of the requesting Party.

3.   Any request or communication under paragraphs 1 and 2 of this article may be made through the International Criminal Police Organisation (Interpol).

4.   Where a request is made pursuant to paragraph 2 of this article and the authority is not competent to deal with the request, it shall refer to the competent national authority and inform directly the requesting Party that it has done so.

5.   Requests or communications under Section 2 of this chapter, which do not involve coercive action, may be directly transmitted by the competent authorities of the requesting Party to the competent authorities of the requested Party.

ARTICLE 25

Form of request and languages

1.   All requests under this chapter shall be made in writing. Modern means of telecommunications, such as telefax, may be used.

2.   Subject to the provisions of paragraph 3 of this article, translations of the requests or supporting documents shall not be required.

3.   At the time of signature or when depositing its instrument of ratification, acceptance, approval or accession, any Party may communicate to the Secretary General of the Council of Europe a declaration that it reserves the right to require that requests made to it and documents supporting such requests be accompanied by a translation into its own language or into one of the official languages of the Council of Europe or into such one of these languages as it shall indicate. It may on that occasion declare its readiness to accept translations in any other language as it may specify. The other Parties may apply the reciprocity rule.

ARTICLE 26

Legalisation

Documents transmitted in application of this chapter shall be exempt from all legalisation formalities.

ARTICLE 27

Content of request

1.   Any request for co-operation under this chapter shall specify:

a. the authority making the request and the authority carrying out the investigations or proceedings;

b. the object of and the reason for the request;

c. the matters, including the relevant facts (such as date, place and circumstances of the offence) to which the investigations or proceedings relate, except in the case of a request for notification;

d. in so far as the co-operation involves coercive action:

i.   the text of the statutory provisions or, where this is not possible, a statement of the relevant law applicable; and

ii.   an indication that the measure sought or any other measures having similar effects could be taken in the territory of the requesting Party under its own law;

e. where necessary and in so far as possible:

i.   details of the person or persons concerned, including name, date and place of birth, nationality and location, and, in the case of a legal person, its seat; and

ii.   the property in relation to which co-operation is sought, its location, its connection with the person or persons concerned, any connection with the offence, as well as any available information about other persons' interests in the property; and

f. any particular procedure the requesting Party wishes to be followed.

2.   A request for provisional measures under Section 3 in relation to seizure of property on which a confiscation order consisting in the requirement to pay a sum of money may be realised shall also indicate a maximum amount for which recovery is sought in that property.

3. In addition to the indications mentioned in paragraph 1, any request under Section 4 shall contain:

   a. in the case of Article 13, paragraph 1.*a*:
   i. a certified true copy of the confiscation order made by the court in the requesting Party and a statement of the grounds on the basis of which the order was made, if they are not indicated in the order itself;
   ii. an attestation by the competent authority of the requesting Party that the confiscation order is enforceable and not subject to ordinary means of appeal;
   iii. information as to the extent to which the enforcement of the order is requested; and
   iv. information as to the necessity of taking any provisional measures;

   b. in the case of Article 13, paragraph 1.*b,* a statement of the facts relied upon by the requesting Party sufficient to enable the requested Party to seek the order under its domestic law;

   c. when third parties have had the opportunity to claim rights, documents demonstrating that this has been the case.

ARTICLE 28

Defective requests

1. If a request does not comply with the provisions of this chapter or the information supplied is not sufficient to enable the requested Party to deal with the request, that Party may ask the requesting Party to amend the request or to complete it with additional information.

2. The requested Party may set a time-limit for the receipt of such amendments or information.

3. Pending receipt of the requested amendments or information in relation to a request under Section 4 of this chapter, the requested Party may take any of the measures referred to in Sections 2 or 3 of this chapter.

ARTICLE 29

Plurality of requests

1. Where the requested Party receives more than one request under Sections 3 or 4 of this chapter in respect to the same person or property, the plurality of requests shall not prevent that Party from dealing with the requests involving the taking of provisional measures.

2. In the case of plurality of requests under Section 4 of this chapter, the requested Party shall consider consulting the requesting Parties.

ARTICLE 30

Obligation to give reasons

The requested Party shall give reasons for any decision to refuse, postpone or make conditional any co-operation under this chapter.

ARTICLE 31

Information

1. The requested Party shall promptly inform the requesting Party of:

   a. the action initiated on a request under this chapter;

   b. the final result of the action carried out on the basis of the request;

   c. a decision to refuse, postpone or make conditional, in whole or in part, any co-operation under this chapter;

   d. any circumstances which render impossible the carrying out of the action sought or are likely to delay it significantly; and

   e. in the event of provisional measures taken pursuant to a request under Sections 2 or 3 of this chapter, such provisions of its domestic law as would automatically lead to the lifting of the provisional measure.

2. The requesting Party shall promptly inform the requested Party of:

   a. any review, decision or any other fact by reason of which the confiscation order ceases to be wholly or partially enforceable; and

   b. any development, factual or legal, by reason of which any action under this chapter is no longer justified.

3. Where a Party, on the basis of the same confiscation order, requests confiscation in more than one Party, it shall inform all Parties which are affected by an enforcement of the order about the request.

ARTICLE 32

Restriction of use

1. The requested Party may make the execution of a request dependent on the condition that the information or evidence obtained will not, without its prior consent, be used or transmitted by the authorities of the requesting Party for investigations or proceedings other than those specified in the request.

2. Each Party may, at the time of signature or when depositing its instrument of ratification, acceptance, approval or accession, by declaration addressed to the Secretary General of the Council of Europe, declare that, without its prior consent, information or evidence provided by it under this chapter may not be used or transmitted by the authorities of the requesting Party in investigations or proceedings other than those specified in the request.

ARTICLE 33

Confidentiality

1. The requesting Party may require that the requested Party keep confidential the facts and substance of the request, except to the extent necessary to execute the request. If the requested Party cannot comply with the requirement of confidentiality, it shall promptly inform the requesting Party.

2. The requesting Party shall, if not contrary to basic principles of its national law and if so requested, keep confidential any evidence and information provided by the requested Party, except to the extent that its disclosure is necessary for the investigations or proceedings described in the request.

3. Subject to the provisions of its domestic law, a Party which has received spontaneous information under Article 10 shall comply with any requirement of confidentiality as required by the Party which supplies the information. If the other Party cannot comply with such requirement, it shall promptly inform the transmitting Party.

ARTICLE 34

Costs

The ordinary costs of complying with a request shall be borne by the requested Party. Where costs of a substantial or extraordinary nature are necessary to comply with a request, the Parties shall consult in order to agree the conditions on which the request is to be executed and how the costs shall be borne.

ARTICLE 35

Damages

1. Where legal action on liability for damages resulting from an act or omission in relation to co-operation under this chapter has been initiated by a person, the Parties concerned shall consider consulting each other, where appropriate, to determine how to apportion any sum of damages due.

2. A Party which has become subject of a litigation for damages shall endeavour to inform the other Party of such litigation if that Party might have an interest in the case.

CHAPTER IV

FINAL PROVISIONS

ARTICLE 36

Signature and entry into force

1. This Convention shall be open for signature by the member States of the Council of Europe and non-member States which have participated in its elaboration. Such States may express their consent to be bound by:

   a. signature without reservation as to ratification, acceptance or approval; or

   b. signature subject to ratification, acceptance or approval, followed by ratification, acceptance or approval.

2. Instruments of ratification, acceptance or approval shall be deposited with the Secretary General of the Council of Europe.

3. This Convention shall enter into force on the first day of the month following the expiration of a period of three months after the date on which three States, of which at least two are member States of the Council of Europe, have expressed their consent to be bound by the Convention in accordance with the provisions of paragraph 1.

4. In respect of any signatory State which subsequently expresses its consent to be bound by it, the Convention shall enter into force on the first day of the month following the expiration of a period of three months after the date of the expression of its consent to be bound by the Convention in accordance with the provisions of paragraph 1.

ARTICLE 37

Accession to the Convention

1. After the entry into force of this Convention, the Committee of Ministers of the Council of Europe, after consulting the Contracting States to the Convention, may invite any State not a member of the Council and not having participated in its elaboration to accede to this Convention, by a decision taken by the majority provided for in Article 20.*d* of the Statute of the Council of Europe and by the unanimous vote of the representatives of the Contracting States entitled to sit on the Committee.

2. In respect of any acceding State the Convention shall enter into force on the first day of the month following the expiration of a period of three months after the date of deposit of the instrument of accession with the Secretary General of the Council of Europe.

ARTICLE 38

Territorial application

1.   Any State may, at the time of signature or when depositing its instrument of ratification, acceptance, approval or accession, specify the territory or territories to which this Convention shall apply.

2.   Any State may, at any later date, by a declaration addressed to the Secretary General of the Council of Europe, extend the application of this Convention to any other territory specified in the declaration. In respect of such territory the Convention shall enter into force on the first day of the month following the expiration of a period of three months after the date of receipt of such declaration by the Secretary General.

3.   Any declaration made under the two preceding paragraphs may, in respect of any territory specified in such declaration, be withdrawn by a notification addressed to the Secretary General. The withdrawal shall become effective on the first day of the month following the expiration of a period of three months after the date of receipt of such notification by the Secretary General.

ARTICLE 39

Relationship to other conventions and agreements

1.   This Convention does not affect the rights and undertakings derived from international multilateral conventions concerning special matters.

2.   The Parties to the Convention may conclude bilateral or multilateral agreements with one another on the matters dealt with in this Convention, for purposes of supplementing or strengthening its provisions or facilitating the application of the principles embodied in it.

3.   If two or more Parties have already concluded an agreement or treaty in respect of a subject which is dealt with in this Convention or otherwise have established their relations in respect of that subject, they shall be entitled to apply that agreement or treaty or to regulate those relations accordingly, in lieu of the present Convention, if it facilitates international co-operation.

ARTICLE 40

Reservations

1.   Any State may, at the time of signature or when depositing its instrument of ratification, acceptance, approval or accession, declare that it avails itself of one or more of the reservations provided for in Article 2, paragraph 2, Article 6, paragraph 4, Article 14, paragraph 3, Article 21, paragraph 2, Article 25, paragraph 3 and Article 32, paragraph 2. No other reservation may be made.

2.   Any State which has made a reservation under the preceding paragraph may wholly or partly withdraw it by means of a notification addressed to the Secretary

General of the Council of Europe. The withdrawal shall take effect on the date of receipt of such notification by the Secretary General.

3.   A Party which has made a reservation in respect of a provision of this Convention may not claim the application of that provision by any other Party; it may, however, if its reservation is partial or conditional, claim the application of that provision in so far as it has itself accepted it.

ARTICLE 41

Amendments

1.   Amendments to this Convention may be proposed by any Party, and shall be communicated by the Secretary General of the Council of Europe to the member States of the Council of Europe and to every non-member State which has acceded to or has been invited to accede to this Convention in accordance with the provisions of Article 37.

2.   Any amendment proposed by a Party shall be communicated to the European Committee on Crime Problems which shall submit to the Committee of Ministers its opinion on that proposed amendment.

3.   The Committee of Ministers shall consider the proposed amendment and the opinion submitted by the European Committee on Crime Problems and may adopt the amendment.

4.   The text of any amendment adopted by the Committee of Ministers in accordance with paragraph 3 of this article shall be forwarded to the Parties for acceptance.

5.   Any amendment adopted in accordance with paragraph 3 of this article shall come into force on the thirtieth day after all Parties have informed the Secretary General of their acceptance thereof.

ARTICLE 42

Settlement of disputes

1.   The European Committee on Crime Problems of the Council of Europe shall be kept informed regarding the interpretation and application of this Convention.

2.   In case of a dispute between Parties as to the interpretation or application of this Convention, they shall seek a settlement of the dispute through negotiation or any other peaceful means of their choice, including submission of the dispute to the European Committee on Crime Problems, to an arbitral tribunal whose decisions shall be binding upon the Parties, or to the International Court of Justice, as agreed upon by the Parties concerned.

ARTICLE 43

Denunciation

1.   Any Party may, at any time, denounce this Convention by means of a notification addressed to the Secretary General of the Council of Europe.

2.   Such denunciation shall become effective on the first day of the month following the expiration of a period of three months after the date of receipt of the notification by the Secretary General.

3.   The present Convention shall, however, continue to apply to the enforcement under Article 14 of confiscation for which a request has been made in conformity with the provisions of this Convention before the date on which such a denunciation takes effect.

ARTICLE 44

Notifications

The Secretary General of the Council of Europe shall notify the member States of the Council and any State which has acceded to this Convention of:

   a. any signature;

   b. the deposit of any instrument of ratification, acceptance, approval or accession;

   c. any date of entry into force of this Convention in accordance with Articles 36 and 37;

   d. any reservation made under Article 40, paragraph 1;

   e. any other act, notification or communication relating to this Convention.

In witness whereof the undersigned, being duly authorised thereto, have signed this Convention.

Done at Strasbourg, this 8th day of November 1990, in English and in French, both texts being equally authentic, in a single copy which shall be deposited in the archives of the Council of Europe. The Secretary General of the Council of Europe shall transmit certified copies to each member State of the Council of Europe, to the non-member States which have participated in the elaboration of this Convention, and to any State invited to accede to it.

Index

Additional Protocol of 1978 to European
    Convention for Mutual Assistance in
    Criminal Matters 142–4, 243
affidavit evidence in English practice 73
Akrotiri and Dhekelia, party to Hague
    Evidence Convention 86
Andean Common Market 48
Anguilla:
    enforcement of confiscation and forfeiture
        orders in UK 247
    mutual assistance Agreement with UK 263
    mutual assistance with USA 250–4
Anton Piller orders 63–6, 207
Arab League Agreement relating to Writs and
    Letters of Request 1952 51
Argentina:
    MLAT with USA 248
    mutual assistance Agreement with UK 263
    party to Inter-American Protocol (1979)
        45
Asian–African Legal Consultative Committee
    18, 51, 155
    Model Bilateral Agreement for the Service
        of Process and the Taking of Evidence
        Abroad (1986) 18, 51–2, 104–5
assessing proceeds of crime 217–18, 221–2
Australia:
    approach to taking evidence abroad 76–80
    backing of summonses 158
    and Commonwealth Scheme 150, 154, 161,
        163
    enforcement of confiscation and forfeiture
        orders in UK 247
    extension of United Kingdom bilateral
        Conventions 14
    and Financial Action Task Force 185
    and Hague Conference 3
    insider dealing 295–6
    legislation on proceeds of crime 213–14,
        228–31, 233–4
    MLAT with Canada 250
    MLAT with UK 250, 254–62
    Mutual Assistance Treaties 250
    mutual assistance with Japan 250
    mutual assistance with Switzerland 250
    mutual assistance with USA 250
    mutual assistance with Vanuatu 250
Austria:
    bilateral Civil Procedure Convention with
        UK 15, 84
    bilateral Convention with France (1954) 14

practice under Hague Evidence
    Convention 93
and Financial Action Task Force 185
aviation crimes, mutual assistance 129

backing of summonses 158
Bahamas:
    bank secrecy 186–7, 283–6
    enforcement of confiscation and forfeiture
        orders in UK 247
    MLAT with USA 157, 159, 248–9, 285–6
    Mutual Assistance Agreement with UK
        263–70
Bahrain:
    enforcement of confiscation and forfeiture
        orders in UK 247
    mutual assistance Agreement with UK
        263–70
Bangladesh, enforcement of confiscation and
    forfeiture orders in UK 247
bank account, injunction to freeze 205–7
Bank of England 187, 196, 292, 301–2
bank secrecy 10, 96, 186–7, 249, 271–86
    in Bahamas 186–7, 283–6
    in Cayman Islands 280–3
    and Council of Europe Convention on
        Insider Trading 298
    and Council of Europe Convention on
        Laundering etc. 236
    in England 271–7
    in Switzerland 277–9
    and UN Model Treaty on Mutual
        Assistance in Criminal Matters 165
    in United States 277
    and Vienna Convention 177–9
Bankers' Books Evidence Act procedures 61–
    2, 207, 244, 273–5
banks and money-laundering 186–7, 196–7
Barbados:
    enforcement of confiscation and forfeiture
        orders in UK 247
    and Hague Evidence Convention 86, 91
    mutual assistance Agreement with UK 263
Basel Committee on Banking Regulations
    187, 191
Bavaria, service of process in exemplary
    damage cases 18–19
Belgium:
    bilateral Civil Procedure Convention with
        UK (1922) 15, 84
    and Financial Action Task Force 185

Belgium (*cont.*)
  and Hague Service Convention 25, 30–1
  MLAT with USA 248–9
  party to Schengen agreements 129
  use of *notification au parquet* 16
Bermuda:
  enforcement of confiscation and forfeiture
    orders in UK 247
  mutual assistance Agreement with UK 263
Bhutan, enforcement of confiscation and
  forfeiture orders in UK 247
blocking statutes 93, 101, 107
Bolivia, enforcement of confiscation and
  forfeiture orders in UK 247
bookmakers, and money-laundering 195
Botswana, and Hague Service Convention
  24, 30
Brazil, MOU with USA 294
British Columbia, MOU with USA 292–3
British Virgin Islands, mutual assistance with
  USA 250–4
Brunei, backing of summonses 158
Brussels Convention on jurisdiction and the
  enforcement of judgments in civil and
  commercial matters (1968) 28, 33–4, 65
business names, service of process when
  used 37
Bustamente Code (1928) 42

California, case-law on Hague Evidence
  Convention 108–10
Canada:
  approach to taking evidence abroad 76–80
  and Commonwealth Scheme 163
  enforcement of confiscation and forfeiture
    orders in UK 247
  extension of United Kingdom bilateral
    Conventions 14
  and Financial Action Task Force 185
  and Hague Conference 3
  legislation on proceeds of crime 214, 231–4
  MLAT with Australia 250
  MLAT with UK 254–62
  MLAT with USA 150, 162, 248, 253, 293
  MOU with USA 292–3
Caribbean Basin Initiative 249
Caribbean drugs agreements 251–4
cash transactions:
  cross-border transfers 195, 197
  monitoring 184, 193–6
casinos, and money-laundering 185, 191, 195
Cayman Islands:
  bank secrecy 280–3
  enforcement of confiscation and forfeiture
    orders in UK 247
  MLAT with USA 157, 250–62, 282–3
  Mutual Assistance Agreement with UK
    263
  party to Hague Evidence Convention 86

Central Authority:
  under Commonwealth Scheme 153, 239
  under Hague Evidence Convention 91
  under Hague Service Convention 17,
    20–1
  under Inter-American Convention on
    Letters Rogatory 46–7
  under Inter-American Protocol of 1979 49
Channel Islands, service of English process
  in 54
charging order, under Drug Trafficking
  Offences Act (1986) 208–11
Child Abduction, Hague Convention on Civil
  Aspects of 3
Chile:
  enforcement of confiscation and forfeiture
    orders in UK 247
  party to Inter-American Convention on
    Letters Rogatory (1975) 45
China:
  enforcement of confiscation and forfeiture
    orders in UK 247
  and Hague Conference 3
civil and commercial matters:
  in Brussels Convention (1968) 18
  in English law 88–9
  in Hague Evidence Convention 19, 87–9,
    286
  in Hague Service Convention 18–19, 286
  in Inter-American Convention on Letters
    Rogatory 46
Civil Procedure, Hague Conventions on, *see*
  Hague Conventions on Civil Procedure
Colombia, MLAT with USA 248
comity, and Hague Evidence Convention in
  US practice 114–18
Commonwealth Commercial Crime Unit 128,
  153
Commonwealth Extradition Scheme 150–1,
  161
Commonwealth Scheme for Mutual
  Assistance in Criminal Matters 128, 137,
  140, 149–64, 166, 168
  appearance in requesting country of
    persons in custody 161
  appearance of witness in requesting
    country 161
  criminal matter 153–4
  expenses 161–2
  immunity of witnesses 161
  implementation 162–4
  instrumentalities of crime 234–5
  location of persons 157
  obtaining evidence 160
  proceeds of crime 162, 192, 234–5
  refusal of assistance 154–6
  scope 152–3
  search and seizure 160
  service of process 157–60

text 331–41
United Kingdom adaptations 163–4, 235
Commonwealth Schemes 150–2
Commonwealth Secretariat 14, 51, 127–8,
  150, 157
compensation:
  under Criminal Justice Act (1988) 212
  under Drug Trafficking Offences Act
    (1986) 211
  under Prevention of Terrorism Act (1989)
    228
Conferencia Especializada Inter-Americana sobre
  DIP (CIDIP) 45–50
confiscation of proceeds of crime 215–34
confiscation orders 215–16
  comparable powers in terrorism cases
    227–8
  under Criminal Justice Act (1988) 224–7;
    assessment of proceeds 226–7; realisable
    property 225–6
  under Drug Trafficking Offences Act
    (1986) 216–24; and sentencing 220–1;
    assessing proceeds 217–18, 221–2;
    burden of proof 218–19, 222;
    enforcement 222–3; possible reforms
    in law 221–2; realisable property 218–
    20; third parties 219–20; variation 223–
    4
  under Scottish legislation 220
Confrontation Clause 121
Congreso Sudamericana de DIP 41
consular channel for service of process 10
  in Hague Convention on Civil Procedure
    (1896) 12
  in Hague Convention on Civil Procedure
    (1905) 13
  in Hague Service Convention 25
controlled delivery (of drugs) 174, 180
corporations, service of process on 35–41
corruption 120
Costa Rica:
  enforcement of confiscation and forfeiture
    orders in UK 247
  party to Inter-American Convention on
    Letters Rogatory (1975) 45
costs, *see* expenses
Council of Europe 16, 128, 130, 144, 146, 169,
  187–8, 191, 235, 297–300
Council of Europe Convention on Insider
  Trading 297–300
Council of Europe Convention on
  Laundering, Search, Seizure and
  Confiscation of Proceeds from Crime
  (1990) 188–9, 192, 235–8
  bank secrecy 236
  confiscation measures 235–8
  grounds for refusing assistance 237
  investigative assistance 236–8
  investigative measures 235–6

text 342–60
third parties' rights 237–8
credibility of witness 77–9
criminal proceedings, transfer of:
  under European Convention on the
    Transfer of Proceedings in Criminal
    Matters (1972) 146–9, 169
  under UN Model Treaty on the Transfer
    of Proceedings in Criminal Matters 169–
    71
Crown Agent for Scotland 21
Customs Co-operation Council 126–7
Cyprus:
  enforcement of confiscation and forfeiture
    orders in UK 247
  and Hague Evidence Convention 86, 91
Czechoslovakia:
  bilateral Civil Procedure Convention with
    UK (1924) 15, 84
  and Hague Evidence Convention 86
  and Hague Service Convention 21, 25–6,
    30
  position on taking of evidence by
    commissioners 103

defence, taking evidence abroad 123
Denmark:
  bilateral Civil Procedure Convention with
    UK (1932) 14–15, 84
  and Financial Action Task Force 186
  and Hague Evidence Convention 86, 93
  and Hague Service Convention 28, 30–1
depositions in English practice 73
detention, custody and preservation of
  property 62
diplomatic and consular officers taking
  evidence,
  English legal position 101–2
  French position 102–3
  under Hague Evidence Convention
    101–4
  United States position 102
diplomatic channel for service of process 9
  in Hague Convention on Civil Procedure
    (1896) 12, 82–3
disclosure orders:
  in criminal contexts 212
  in Mareva injunction context 71–2
discovery 58–62
  English practice 59–61
  and Hague Evidence Convention 97–101
  territorial reach of English discovery 59,
    61–2
  United States practice 98–101
double jeopardy:
  and Commonwealth Scheme for Mutual
    Assistance in Criminal Matters 156
  and Council of Europe Convention on
    Laundering, etc. 237

double jeopardy (*cont.*)
  and European Convention on the Transfer
    of Proceedings in Criminal Matters
    (1972) 148
  in UK–Australia MLAT 256
drug-trafficking 4, 172–83
dual criminality:
  and Commonwealth Scheme for Mutual
    Assistance in Criminal Matters 155
  and European Convention on the Transfer
    of Proceedings in Criminal Matters 1972
    148
  in UK–Canada MLAT 256
  and UN Model Treaty on the Transfer of
    Proceedings in Criminal Matters 169–70
  in United Kingdom legislation 243
due process, relevance to Hague Service
    Convention 37, 40

Ecuador:
  enforcement of confiscation and forfeiture
    orders in UK 247
  party to Inter-American Protocol of (1979)
    45
Egypt:
  enforcement of confiscation and forfeiture
    orders in UK 247
  and Hague Service Convention 25–6
  party to Agreement relating to Writs and
    Letters of Request (1952) 51
El Salvador, party to Inter-American
    Convention on Letters Rogatory (1975)
    45
election of domicile 35, 37
England:
  affidavit evidence 73
  assistance to foreign criminal courts 123–4
  depositions in criminal cases 122
  practice under Hague Evidence
    Convention 93, 95
  service of process in 7, 55
  service of English process abroad 52–4
  taking evidence abroad for the defence 123
  written statements in criminal cases 122–3
  see also United Kingdom
Estonia, bilateral Civil Procedure Convention
    with UK (1931) 14, 85
European Committee on Crime Problems 142
European Community 1, 125, 174, 180–3, 197
  Directive on Insider Trading 296–7
  Directive on Money-Laundering 181, 189–
    91
  and Financial Action Task Force 185
  Regulation on Trade in Precursors 181–3
  and Vienna Convention 181
European Convention on Mutual Assistance
    in Criminal Matters (1959) 125, 130–42,
    159, 161, 165, 168
  Additional Protocol to (1978) 142–4

appearance in requesting country of
    persons in custody 137–8
appearance of witnesses in requesting
    country 136–8
  'evidence' 134
  expenses 140
  immunity of witnesses 138
  information as to proceedings 141
  judicial records 138–9
  Letters Rogatory 133–5
  oaths 134
  refusal of assistance 132–3
  relation to other Conventions 141
  reservations 141–2
  scope 131–2
  search and seizure 135
  service of writs and verdicts 135–6
  subpoenas 159
  transit in custody 137–8
  translation requirements 140
European Convention on the Transfer of
    Proceedings in Criminal Matters 1972
    146–9, 169
European Parliament 181
evidence, common law and civil law
    approaches 56–9
evidence, English practice:
  evidence for use abroad 243–4
  under Hague Evidence Convention
    105–7
  taking evidence abroad 73–80, 242–3
  under UK MLATs 258–60
examiners 73, 75
expenses:
  under Hague Evidence Convention 96–7
  under Hague Service Convention 32
  under Inter-American Convention on
    Letters Rogatory 47–8
  under Inter-American Protocol (1979) 50–1
  of service of foreign process in the United
    Kingdom 55
  under UK Agreements 267
  under UK MLATs 262
external confiscation and forfeiture orders,
    enforcement in UK 246–7
extra-judicial documents 31–2

facsimile transmission 11
Falkland Islands, party to Hague Evidence
    Convention 86
Fiji:
  backing of summonses 158
  extension of United Kingdom bilateral
    Conventions on Civil Procedure 14
Financial Action Task Force 127, 185–7
fines, enforcement of, under Additional
    Protocol to European Convention for
    Mutual Assistance in Criminal Matters
    143–4

Finland:
  bilateral Civil Procedure Convention with
    UK (1933) 15, 84
  and Financial Action Task Force 186
  party to Hague Evidence Convention 86
fiscal offences 132
  under Additional Protocol to European
    Convention for Mutual Assistance in
    Criminal Matters 142–3, 243
  under UN Model Treaty on Mutual
    Assistance in Criminal Matters 165
fishing expeditions 106, 165, 208
foreign penal laws 119–21
forfeiture:
  at common law 199
  of forbidden articles 200
  of instrumentalities 20
  Powers of Criminal Courts Act powers
    202–3
  of property related to specific offences
    200–1
forfeiture orders 215–16, 231–4
  and third parties 232–4
  under Prevention of Terrorism Act (1989)
    227–8
France:
  attitude to Aérospatiale case 114
  bilateral Civil Procedure Convention with
    Luxembourg (1884) 29
  bilateral Civil Procedure Convention with
    UK (1922) 14–15, 84
  bilateral Convention with Austria (1954)
    14
  bilateral Convention with Italy (1955) 14
  enforcement of confiscation and forfeiture
    orders in UK 247
  and Financial Action Task Force 185
  and Hague Evidence Convention 86, 91,
    93–5
  and Hague Service Convention 20, 23–5,
    29–31
  MOU with USA 294
  party to Schengen agreements 129
  position on taking of evidence by
    commissioners 103
  position on taking of evidence by
    diplomats and consuls 102–3
  procedure for service of process abroad 9
  use of *notification au parquet* 16

Germany:
  attitude to Aérospatiale case 114
  attitude to Anschuetz case 113
  attitude to Schlunk case 38–41
  bilateral agreement with the Netherlands
    (1962) 83
  bilateral Civil Procedure Convention with
    UK (1928) 15, 84
  and Financial Action Task Force 185
  and Hague Evidence Convention 86, 95,
    102
  and Hague Service Convention 18–19, 21–
    6
  mutual assistance Agreement with UK 263
  party to Schengen agreements 129
Ghana, enforcement of confiscation and
    forfeiture orders in UK 247
Gibraltar:
  enforcement of confiscation and forfeiture
    orders in UK 247
  mutual assistance Agreement with UK 263
  party to Hague Evidence Convention 86
grand jury subpoenas 253–4
Greece:
  bilateral Civil Procedure Convention with
    UK (1936) 15, 84
  and Financial Action Task Force 186
  use of *notification au parquet* 16
Grenada:
  enforcement of confiscation and forfeiture
    orders in UK 247
  implementation of Commonwealth Scheme
    for Mutual Assistance in Criminal
    Matters 162
Group of Seven 127, 185
Guam, party to Hague Evidence Convention
    86
Guatemala:
  enforcement of confiscation and forfeiture
    orders in UK 247
  party to Inter-American Convention on
    Letters Rogatory (1975) 45
Guernsey, enforcement of confiscation and
    forfeiture orders in UK 247
Guinea, enforcement of confiscation and
    forfeiture orders in UK 247
Guyana:
  legislation on proceeds of crime 215
  mutual assistance Agreement with UK 263

Hague Conference on Private International
    Law 2–4, 12–13, 15–16 19, 44–5, 51, 82,
    85, 97, 105
Hague Convention Abolishing Requirement
    of Legalisation (1961) 2
Hague Convention for the Suppression of
    Unlawful Seizure of Aircraft (1970)
    118
Hague Convention on Civil Aspects of Child
    Abduction (1980) 3
Hague Convention on Civil Procedure (1896)
    12–13, 82–3
Hague Convention on Civil Procedure (1905)
    12–13, 82–4
Hague Convention on Civil Procedure (1954)
    15–16, 82, 85, 102
Hague Convention on International Access to
    Justice (1980) 2

Hague Convention on the Service of Abroad of Judicial and Extra-judicial Documents in Civil and Commercial Matters, *see* Hague Service Convention
Hague Convention on the Taking of Evidence Abroad, *see* Hague Evidence Convention
Hague Evidence Convention 75, 82, 85–104, 160
    Central Authorities 91
    'civil and commercial' 87–9
    commissioners 101, 103–4
    diplomatic and consular officers 101–4
    discovery 97–101
    'evidence' 90
    execution of letter of request 93–4
    expenses 96–7
    judicial authorities 89–90, 93–4
    legalization 92
    letters of request 91–2
    measures of compulsion 95, 103
    obligatory quality 112–15
    'other judicial act' 90–1
    privilege 95–6, 107
    rejection of letter of request 92–3
    scope 86
    text 318–30
    translation requirements 92
Hague Service Convention (1965) 8, 16–41, 53–5, 85, 157
    assessment 41
    and Brussels Convention 33–4
    Central Authorities 17, 20–1
    Certificate of Service 22–3, 49
    civil and commercial matters 18–19
    consular channel 25
    default judgments 31
    extra-judicial documents 31–2
    guarantees for defendants 17, 29–31
    huissiers 28
    indirect consular channel 25–6
    initiation of request 21–2
    and national law 34–41
    obligatory character 17, 37–41
    postal channel 26–9
    principal changes made by 17
    procedures for service 22–9
    Request for Service 22–3, 49
    Summary of Document to be Served 22–4, 49
    text 305–17
    time-limits for service 24–5
    translation requirements 22–5, 27–8
    unknown address of defendant 19–20
Harare Scheme, *see* Commonwealth Scheme for Mutual Assistance in Criminal Matters
Harvard Draft Convention (1939) 43–4, 125
Hodgson Committee 203–4, 207, 217, 224

Home Office Working Group on Confiscation 221–4
Honduras, party to Inter-American Convention on Letters Rogatory (1975) 45
Hong Kong:
    enforcement of confiscation and forfeiture orders in UK 247
    and Financial Action Task Force 186
    and Hague Evidence Convention 86, 91
    MOU with UK 295
    mutual assistance Agreement with UK 263
Howard League for Penal Reform 203
huissier de justice 7–8, 11, 16, 21, 28, 39
Hungary:
    bilateral Civil Procedure Convention with UK (1935) 14–15, 84
    negotiations on insider dealing with USA 294

identity, issues of 78–9
Illinois, involuntary agency in 37–40
illness of witness 76
India, enforcement of confiscation and forfeiture orders in UK 247
indirect consular channel, for service of process 10
    in Hague Convention on Civil Procedure (1905) 12
    in Hague Service Convention 25–6
insider dealing 286–304
    in Switzerland 286–7
instrumentalities of crime 201
    see also proceeds of crime
Inter-American Convention on Letters Rogatory (1975) 18, 45–8, 51–2
    civil and commercial matters 46
    documentation 47
    expenses 47–8
    modes of transmission 46–7
    and other international instruments 48
    procedures for execution 47
    protection for defendants 48
    scope 45–6
Inter-American Convention on the Taking of Evidence Abroad 1975 49, 100, 104
    Additional Protocol (1984) 100, 104
Inter-American Council of Jurists 44
Inter-American Judicial Commitee 44
Inter-American Protocol (1979) 48–51
    Central Authorities 49
    documentation 49–50
    expenses 50–1
    legalization 50
    modes of transmission 49
    scope 48–9
Inter-American Specialized Conferences on PIL 45–50
interdiction of illicit drugs traffic by sea 180

interim relief under Brussels Convention (1968) 65, 68
interim seizure of proceeds of crime 204–14
International Access to Justice, Hague Convention 2
International Criminal Police Organization (Interpol) 126, 131, 140, 148, 150
International Opium Conventions 173
International Organization of Securities Commissions 300
international subpoena 158
involuntary agency:
  in Illinois 37–40
  in New York 40–1
Iraq, bilateral Civil Procedure Convention with UK (1935) 15, 84
Ireland:
  and Council of Europe 16
  and Financial Action Task Force 186
  and Hague Conference 3
  service of English process in 54
Isle of Man:
  enforcement of confiscation and forfeiture orders in UK 247
  party to Hague Evidence Convention 86
  service of English process in 54
Israel:
  bilateral Civil Procedure Convention with UK (1966) 14–15, 84
  and Hague Service Convention 31
  party to Hague Evidence Convention 86
Italy:
  bilateral Civil Procedure Convention with UK (1930) 15, 84
  bilateral Convention with France (1955) 14
  enforcement of confiscation and forfeiture orders in UK 247
  and Financial Action Task Force 185
  and Hague Evidence Convention 86
  and Hague Service Convention 25
  MLAT with USA 158, 248–9
  MOU with USA 294
  mutual assistance Agreement with UK 263–70
  position on taking of evidence by commissioners 103
  service of process in 7
  use of *notification au parc* : 16

Jack Committee on Banking services 272
Jamaica:
  reservations to Commonwealth Scheme for Mutual Assistance in Criminal Matters 152, 159
  views on Commonwealth Schemes 152
Japan:
  and Financial Action Task Force 185
  and Hague Service Convention 24, 27–30

MOU with USA 289–90
  mutual assistance with Australia 250
Jersey, enforcement of confiscation and forfeiture orders in UK 247
Jordan:
  enforcement of confiscation and forfeiture orders in UK 247
  party to Agreement relating to Writs and Letters of Request (1952) 51

language requirements, *see* translation requirements
Latin America:
  attachment to Letters Rogatory system 8, 42, 45
  and Hague Conference 3, 44–5
Latin American Free Trade Association 48
Latvia, bilateral Civil Procedure Convention with UK (1939) 14, 85
League of Arab States 51
League of Nations Committee of Experts on Progressive Codification of International law 124–5
Lebanon, party to Agreement relating to Writs and Letters of Request (1952) 51
Legalisation:
  in Hague Evidence Convention 92
  Hague Convention Abolishing Requirement of (1961) 2
  under Inter-American Convention on Letters Rogatory 47
  under Inter-American Protocol (1979) 50
letters of request, in English practice 74–5, 242–3
letters rogatory:
  under European Convention for Mutual Assistance in Criminal Matters 133–5
  for the interception of telecommunications 144–6
  as mode of service of process abroad 8, 42
Lithuania, bilateral Civil Procedure Convention with UK (1934) 14, 85
London Scheme for Rendition of Fugitive Offenders 151–2, 161
Luxembourg:
  bilateral arrangement with France 29
  bilateral Civil Procedure Convention with France (1884) 29
  and Financial Action Task Force 185
  and Hague Evidence Convention 86
  and Hague Service Convention 24–6, 30–1
  party to Schengen agreements 129

Madagascar, enforcement of confiscation and forfeiture orders in UK 247
Malawi, and Hague Service Convention 30
Malaysia:
  backing of summonses 158

Malaysia (*cont.*):
   enforcement of confiscation and forfeiture
      orders in UK 247
   mutual assistance Agreement with UK
      263–70
Man, Isle of, *see* Isle of Man
Mareva injunctions 65–72, 205, 208, 211
   disclosure orders 71–2
   requirement of personal jurisdiction 65–9
   territorial reach 69–71
   world-wide injunction 70–1
   materiality of evidence 77
Mexico:
   enforcement of confiscation and forfeiture
      orders in UK 247
   MLAT with USA 248
   MOU with USA 294
   mutual assistance Agreement with UK 270
   party to Inter-American Protocol of 1979
      45
ministère public, see *parquet*
Ministries of Justice, role in service of process
      abroad 10–11
money-laundering 4, 175, 184–99, 216
   offences in UK 196–7
monitoring of cash transactions 184, 193–6
monitoring orders (in Australia) 193–5
Montevideo Convention on Civil Procedure
      (1889) 41
Montevideo Convention on International
      Procedural Law (1940) 40–1
Montreal Convention for the Suppression of
      Unlawful Acts against the Safety of Civil
      Aviation (1971) 118
Montserrat:
   enforcement of confiscation and forfeiture
      orders in UK 247
   mutual assistance Agreement with UK 263
   mutual assistance with USA 250–4
Morocco, MLAT with USA 249

Nairobi Convention on Mutual Assistance for
      the Prevention, Investigation and
      Repression of Customs Offences (1977)
      127
Naples Convention (1967) 128–9
ne bis in idem, see double jeopardy
Netherlands:
   bilateral agreement with Germany (1962)
      83
   bilateral Civil Procedure Convention with
      UK (1932) 15, 84
   and Council of Europe 16
   and Financial Action Task Force 185
   and Hague Evidence Convention 86, 95
   and Hague Service Convention 20, 30–1
   MLAT with USA 248–9
   MOU with USA 294

party to Schengen agreements 129
   use of *notification au parquet* 16
New South Wales, legislation on proceeds of
      crime 213, 229–31, 233
New Zealand:
   backing of summonses 158
   and Commonwealth Scheme for Mutual
      Assistance in Criminal Matters 153–4
   extension of United Kingdom bilateral
      Conventions on Civil Procedure 14
   and Financial Action Task Force 186
   freezing proceeds of crime 204–14
   and Hague Conventions 3
   legislation on proceeds of drugs crimes 215
   negotiations on insider dealing with USA
      294
Nicaragua, enforcement of confiscation and
      forfeiture orders in UK 247
Nigeria:
   enforcement of confiscation and forfeiture
      orders in UK 247
   mutual assistance Agreement with UK
      263–70
Northern Ireland, authority for Hague Service
      Convention 21
Northern Territory of Australia, legislation on
      proceeds of crime 213, 228–31, 233
Norway:
   bilateral Civil Procedure Convention with
      UK (1931) 15, 84
   and Council of Europe Convention on
      Insider Trading 297
   and Financial Action Task Force 186
   and Hague Evidence Convention 86, 93
   and Hague Service Convention 25–6, 28,
      31
notification au parquet 16–17, 30, 38–9

oath:
   under European Convention for Mutual
      Assistance in Criminal Matters 134
   not used in Switzerland 83
Oman, enforcement of confiscation and
      forfeiture orders in UK 247
Ontario, MOU with USA 292–3
Optional Protocol on Proceeds of Crime to
      UN Model Treaty on Mutual Assistance
      in Criminal Matters 168–9
Organization of American States 45, 47, 49–
      50

Panama:
   bank secrecy laws 249
   party to Inter-American Convention on
      Letters Rogatory (1975) 45
Paraguay, party to Inter-American Protocol
      (1979) 45

parquet 8–9
  in Hague Convention on Civil Procedure
    (1896) 12
  see also *notification au parquet*
partnerships, service of process on 37
pecuniary penalty orders, in Australian
    legislation 215, 228–30
penal laws, enforcement of 119–21
Peru, party to Inter-American Protocol (1979)
    45
Poland, bilateral Civil Procedure Convention
    with UK (1931) 15, 84
Portugal:
  bilateral Civil Procedure Convention with
    UK (1931) 15, 84
  and Financial Action Task Force 186
  and Hague Evidence Convention 86, 95
  and Hague Service Convention 25, 30–1
postal channel for service of process 9, 11–12
  in Hague Convention on Civil Procedure
    (1896) 12
  in Hague Convention on Civil Procedure
    (1905) 13
  in Hague Service Convention 26–8
pre-trial discovery, see discovery
Precursors, European Community Regulation
    on Trade in 181
private international law, excluding criminal
    matters 119–20
privilege:
  and disclosure orders in Mareva injunction
    context 71–2
  interception of telecommunications 146
  under Hague Evidence Convention 95–6,
    107
proceeds of crime 199–238
  Australian legislation 193–6, 213–14, 228–
    31, 233–4
  Canadian legislation 214, 231–4
  and Commonwealth Scheme for Mutual
    Assistance in Criminal Matters 162
  confiscation 215–38
  freezing 204–14
  interim seizure 204–14
  in UK Agreements 268–9
  in UK MLATs 261–2
  and UN Model Treaty on Mutual
    Assistance in Criminal Matters 168–9
  United Kingdom legislation 192–3, 207–12,
    216–28
production orders (in England) 192–3, 212
Psychotropic Substances Convention (1971)
    173
Puerto Rico, party to Hague Evidence
    Convention 86

Quebec, MOU with USA 292–3
Queensland, legislation on proceeds of crime
    228–31, 233–4

realisable property, under Drug Trafficking
    Offences Act (1986) 207–11, 218–20
regulatory havens 185
remise simple (simple delivery) 8
  under Hague Service Convention 23, 32
reporting cash transactions 184, 193–6
Restatement of Foreign Relations Law of
    United States 114–16
restraining orders 204
  in Australia 213–14
restraint order:
  in Canadian legislation 214; and third
    parties 214
  in enforcing foreign orders 247
  under Criminal Justice Act (1988) 228
  under Drug Trafficking Offences Act
    (1986) 207–11; and banks 210–11; and
    lawyers' interests 209–10; and third
    parties 209–10
  under Prevention of Terrorism Act (1989)
    228

Saudi Arabia:
  enforcement of confiscation and forfeiture
    orders in UK 247
  mutual assistance Agreement with UK
    263–70
  party to Agreement relating to Writs and
    Letters of Request (1952) 51
Schengen agreements 129
Scotland:
  and Hague Evidence Convention 95
  and Hague Service Convention 31
  see also United Kingdom
search and seizure:
  under Commonwealth Scheme for Mutual
    Assistance in Criminal Matters 160
  under European Convention for Mutual
    Assistance in Criminal Matters 135
  under UK MLATs 259
  under UN Model Treaty on Mutual
    Assistance in Criminal Matters 167
Secretary of State, service of process on 39
Securities and Exchange Commission 287–95
Securities and Investment Board 292, 301
Senegal, enforcement of confiscation and
    forfeiture orders in UK 247
Senior Master of the Supreme Court 21, 91
sequestration orders, in South Australia 213
service of process:
  common law and civil law approaches 7
  by consular channel 10, 25–6
  on corporations 35–41
  by court officer 7
  by diplomatic channel 9; in Hague
    Convention on Civil Procedure (1896)
    12; in Hague Convention on Civil
    Procedure (1905) 13
  in England 7

service of process (*cont.*)
  in France 23–4
  generally 5–9
  in Germany 22–4
  Hague Convention, *see* Hague Service
    Convention
  by *huissiers de justice* 11
  by indirect consular channel 10; in Hague
    Convention on Civil Procedure (1905)
    12; in Hague Service Convention 25–6
  in Italy 7
  by Letters Rogatory 8
  on partnerships 37
  personal service 7; under European
    Convention for Mutual Assistance in
    Criminal Matters 135–6
  by post 9, 11–12; in Hague Convention on
    Civil Procedure (1896) 12; in Hague
    Convention on Civil Procedure (1905)
    13; in Hague Service Convention 26–8
  on Secretary of State 39
  by simple delivery 8
  in Switzerland 7
  under UK MLATs 258; under UN Model
    Treaty on Mutual Assistance in Criminal
    Matters 166
  in the United Kingdom 241
  in the United States 7, 23
  via Ministries of Justice 10–11
Seychelles, and Hague Service Convention
  25, 30–1
simple delivery 8
Singapore:
  backing of summonses 158
  and Hague Evidence Convention 86, 91
Single Convention on Narcotic Drugs (1961)
  173, 252, 254
solicitors, as 'competent persons' under
  Hague service Convention 28
South Australia, legislation on proceeds of
  crime 213, 228, 231, 233
Spain:
  bilateral Civil Procedure Convention with
    UK (1929) 15, 84
  enforcement of confiscation and forfeiture
    orders in UK 247
  and Financial Action Task Force 185
  MLAT with USA 248
  mutual assistance Agreement with UK
    263–70
  negotiations on insider dealing with USA
    294
Sri Lanka, extension of United Kingdom
  bilateral Conventions on Civil Procedure
  14
Stewart–Clark Committee 181
subpoena:
  English practice 62, 73
  extra-territorial 81, 137, 157–60, 241, 253–4

subpoena *duces tecum*, territorial reach 273–4
Sumner Committee (on British and Foreign
  Legal Procedure) 13–14, 84–5
Sweden:
  bilateral Civil Procedure Convention with
    UK (1930) 15, 84
  and Council of Europe Convention on
    Insider Trading 297
  enforcement of confiscation and forfeiture
    orders in UK 247
  and Financial Action Task Force 185
  and Hague Evidence Convention 86, 93
  MOU with USA 294
  mutual assistance Agreement with UK
    263–70
Switzerland:
  bankers' agreement 288–9
  bank secrecy 96, 186, 248, 277–9
  enforcement of confiscation and forfeiture
    orders in UK 247
  and Financial Action Task Force 185
  fiscal offences and European Convention
    132
  and the Hague Conference 19
  insider dealing 286–7
  MLAT with USA 186, 248–9, 278–9, 287–9
  MOU with USA 279, 287–9
  mutual assistance Agreement with UK 263
  mutual assistance with Australia 250
  service of process in 7, 53
  use of oath 83
Syria, party to Agreement relating to Writs
  and Letters of Request (1952) 51

tainted property, in Australian legislation 231
taking of evidence, *see* evidence
telecommunications, interception of,
  Recommendation of Council of Europe
  144–6
telex 11
terminology:
  international judicial assistance 1–2
  mutual assistance 4
Thailand, MLAT with USA 248
Togo, enforcement of confiscation and
  forfeiture orders in UK 247
translation requirements:
  in European Convention for Mutual
    Assistance in Criminal Matters 140
  in Hague Evidence Convention 92
  in Hague Service Convention 22–5, 27–8
  of United Kingdom 241
Trevi 128–9
Trinidad and Tobago, extension of United
  Kingdom bilateral Conventions on Civil
  Procedure 14
Tunisia, enforcement of confiscation and
  forfeiture orders in UK 247

Turkey:
  bilateral Civil Procedure Convention with
    UK (1931) 15, 84
  and Financial Action Task Force 186
  and Hague Service Convention 25–6, 31
Turks and Caicos, mutual assistance with
  USA 250–4

ufficiale giudiziario 7
Uganda, enforcement of confiscation and
  forfeiture orders in UK 247
United States:
  assistance to litigants in foreign
    proceedings 72, 80
  bank secrecy 277
  and CIDIP 45, 48–9
  constitutional right to confrontation 121
  discovery practice 98–101, 107–15
  enforcement of confiscation and forfeiture
    orders in UK 247
  Federal Rules of Civil Procedure 26, 34, 98,
    107, 118, 121
  and Financial Action Task Force 185
  and Hague Conference 3, 85
  and Hague Evidence Convention 86, 94–5,
    107–18
  and Hague Service Convention 23, 26–7,
    30–2, 35–41
  MLAT with Argentina 248
  MLAT with Argentina 248
  MLAT with Bahamas 157, 159, 248–9, 285–
    6
  MLAT with Belgium 248–9
  MLAT with Canada 150, 162, 248, 253, 293
  MLAT with Cayman Islands 157, 250–4,
    282–3
  MLAT with Colombia 248
  MLAT with Italy 158, 248
  MLAT with Mexico 248
  MLAT with Morocco 249
  MLAT with Netherlands 248–9
  MLAT with Spain 248
  MLAT with Switzerland 186, 248–9, 278–
    9, 287–9
  MLAT with Thailand 248
  MLAT with Turkey 248–9
  MLAT with UK 248–9
  MOU with Brazil 294
  MOU with Canadian Provinces 292–3
  MOU with France 294
  MOU with Italy 294
  MOU with Japan 289–90
  MOU with Mexico 294
  MOU with Netherlands 294
  MOU with Sweden 294
  MOU with Switzerland 279, 287–9
  MOU with UK 290–2
  mutual assistance Agreement with UK
    263–70

Mutual Assistance Treaties 248–50
  mutual asistance with Anguilla 250–4
  mutual assistance with Australia 250
  mutual assistance with British Virgin
    Islands 250–4
  mutual assistance with Montserrat 250–4
  mutual assistance with Turks and Caicos
    Islands 250–4
  negotiations on insider dealing with
    Hungary 294
  negotiations on insider dealing with New
    Zealand 294
  negotiations on insider dealing with Spain
    294
  party to Inter-American Protocol of (1979)
    45
  position on taking of evidence by
    commissioners 103
  position on taking of evidence by
    diplomats and consuls 102–3
  quasi in rem jurisdiction 66
  service of process in 7, 23
Union Internationale des Huissiers de Justice 16
United Arab Emirates, enforcement of
  confiscation and forfeiture orders in UK
  247
United Kingdom:
  and Additional Protocol to European
    Convention for Mutual Assistance in
    Criminal Matters 144
  assistance to overseas regulatory
    authorities 301–4
  attitude to Aérospatiale case 114
  attitudes at the Hague Conference re
    discovery 97–100
  bilateral Convention on Civil Procedure
    14–15, 54–5, 84–5, 101–2
  and Council of Europe 16
  and Council of Europe Convention on
    Insider Trading 297
  and Commonwealth Scheme for Mutual
    Assistance in Criminal Matters 154,
    163–4
  and European Convention for Mutual
    Assistance in Criminal Matters 141–2
  and Financial Action Task Force 185
  and Hague Conference 3
  and Hague Evidence Convention 86, 91,
    97–100
  and Hague Service Convention 20–1, 24,
    26–8, 30–1
  MLAT with Australia 250, 254–62
  MLAT with Canada 254–62
  MOU with Hong Kong 295
  MOU with USA 290–2
  mutual assistance Agreements 262–70
  mutual assistance legislation 239–47;
    evidence for use abroad 243–4; evidence
    for use in UK 242–3; recognition and

United Kingdom:
  mutual assistance legislation (*cont.*)
    enforcement of foreign orders 245–7;
    requests for mutual assistance by UK
    239–41; search and seizure 245; service
    of process 241; transfer of persons in
    custody 244–5
  Mutual Assistance Treaties 254–62;
    attendance of witnesses 260; expenses
    262; exclusivity 262; proceeds of crime
    261; search and seizure 259; service of
    documents 258; taking evidence 258–9
  Mutual Assistance Agreements 251–4,
    263–70
  and Vienna Convention 175
United Nations 120, 127, 164, 173–4
UN Convention against Illicit Traffic in
  Narcotic Drugs and Psychotropic
  Substances 1988, *see* Vienna Convention
UN International Drug Control Programme
  127
UN Model Treaty on Mutual Assistance in
  Criminal Matters 164–9
  appearance of witnesses 167
  bank secrecy 165
  immunity of witnesses 167
  obtaining evidence 166
  Optional Protocol on Proceeds of Crime
    168–9
  refusal of assistance 165–6
  scope 165–8
  search and seizure 167
  service of process 166
UN Model Treaty on the Transfer of
  Proceedings in Criminal Matters 169–71
Uruguay, party to Inter-American Protocol
  (1979) 45

USSR, enforcement of confiscation and
  forfeiture orders in UK 247

Vanuatu:
  and Commonwealth Scheme for Mutual
    Assistance in Criminal Matters 162
  mutual assistance with Australia 250
Venezuela, party to Inter-American
  Convention on Letters Rogatory (1975)
  45
Victoria, legislation on proceeds of crime
  228–31, 233–4
Vienna Convention (1988) 158–9, 174–82,
  187–91
  bank secrecy 177–9
  controlled delivery 180
  extradition 176
  interdiction of illicit traffic by sea 180
  jurisdiction 176
  money-laundering 187–8
  mutual assistance 177–8
  offences 175–6
  proceeds of crime 178–9
Virgin Islands of USA, party to Hague
  Evidence Convention 86

Western Australia, legislation on proceeds of
  crime 228–31, 233–4

Yemen, party to Agreement relating to Writs
  and Letters of Request (1952) 51
Yugoslavia:
  bilateral Civil Procedure Convention with
    UK (1936) 15, 84
  enforcement of confiscation and forfeiture
    orders in UK 247